Catherine Mallette

Ironwork Today 4

INSIDE AND OUT

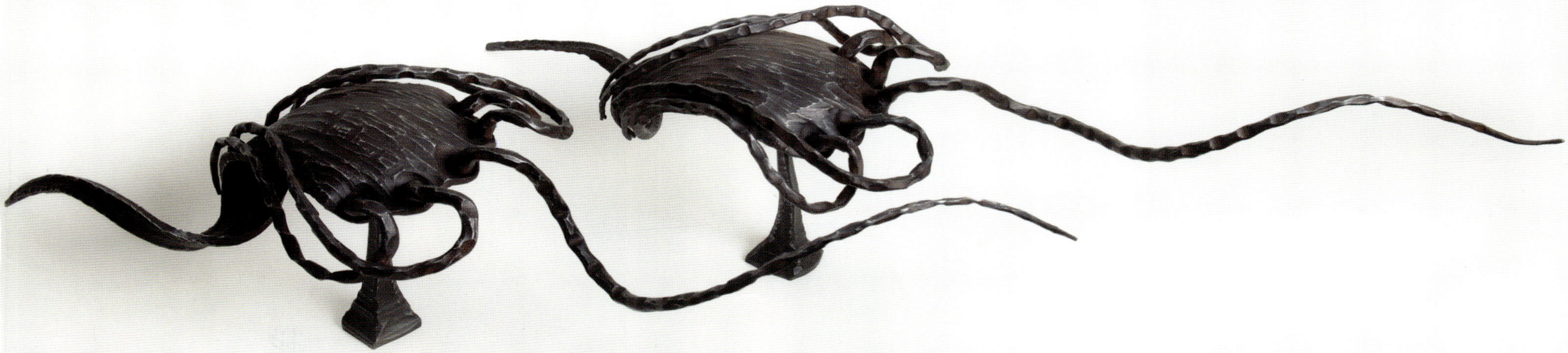

Schiffer Publishing Ltd

4880 Lower Valley Road • Atglen, PA 19310

Other Schiffer Books by the Author:

Art Jewelry Today: Europe. 978-0-7643-4678-1. $50.00

Other Schiffer Books on Related Subjects:

Ironwork Today: Inside & Out. Dona Z. Meilach. 978-0-7643-2390-4. $49.95

Ironwork Today 2: Inside & Out. Jeffrey B. Snyder. 978-07643-3064-3. $50.00

Ironwork Today 3: Inside & Out. Jeffrey B. Snyder. 978-0-7643-38762. $50.00

Architectural Ironwork. Dona Z. Meilach. 978-0-7643-1324-0. $49.95

Library of Congress Control Number: 2005028431

Designed by Brenda McCallum
Cover design by RoS

Type set in Futura Std/Agenda

ISBN: 978-0-7643-4673-6

Printed in China

Published by Schiffer Publishing, Ltd.

4880 Lower Valley Road | Atglen, PA 19310
Phone: (610) 593-1777; Fax: (610) 593-2002
E-mail: Info@schifferbooks.com

For our complete selection of fine books on this and related subjects, please visit our website at www.schifferbooks.com. You may also write for a free catalog.

This book may be purchased from the publisher. Please try your bookstore first.

We are always looking for people to write books on new and related subjects. If you have an idea for a book, please contact us at proposals@schifferbooks.com.

Schiffer Publishing's titles are available at special discounts for bulk purchases for sales promotions or premiums. Special editions, including personalized covers, corporate imprints, and excerpts can be created in large quantities for special needs. For more information, contact the publisher.

On the front cover: Clockwise from left: Margo and Dennis Proska, *Enfolded*; Lynda Metcalfe, log house railing; Richard Rozinski, *Nebula*; John Shearin, *Composite Wing—Maquette*; Danielle Miller, detail of *Ways of Eros* fireplace tools. Center: Mark Puigmarti, *WoodHaven*.

On the spine: Roberta Elliott, *Flamenco*

On the back cover: John Creed, *Crater*

On the title page: Nicholas Ireys, *Twin Erchant*

Contents

Acknowledgments

This book would not have been possible without the help and encouragement of all the art organizations and individuals who contributed information and images. They are gratefully credited in the text and caption lines. Special thanks go to The Artist Blacksmith's Association of North America and its chapters for supporting and encouraging this series.

Introduction

Welcome to the fourth volume in Schiffer Publishing's *Ironwork Today* series. Like the books that came before it, this one hopes to capture the wide range of creative work being done by artist-blacksmiths at a particular moment in time: The works shown here were primarily completed between 2010 and 2013, though occasionally an earlier piece has been included if it helped show a notable development in the artist's work.

These artist-blacksmiths use a variety of methods and equipment in their craft. We asked each to provide a statement giving readers a broad idea of their aesthetics and perspectives. We also asked them to share information on their techniques. By letting the artists speak for themselves, we hope readers will gain a unique insight into the passions that drive today's working artist-blacksmiths.

The works are arranged alphabetically by the artists' last names so you can see the scope of their work. Please note that while most of the artists are from the United States, we also included artists from Canada, Europe, Australia and other parts of the world. See page 255 for a list of artists by where they live.

You'll see a vast variety of projects, from jewelry, bowls, and boxes to wall art and large-scale public installations. For your convenience, our Index on page 256 lists the works by category of project, so whether you're interested in gazebos and gates, mirrors and mailboxes, porticos and pavilions, or indoor and outdoor sculpture, you'll be easily able to search for those particular items.

Sometimes these artful works serve a practical purpose; sometimes their purpose is simply to inspire.

Read and enjoy!

The Artists and Their Works

Sean Ahern

Ahern's Anvil Inc., Charleston, South Carolina
www.ahernsanvil.com

ARTIST'S STATEMENT

Growing up in Charleston, I've been surrounded my entire life by Lowcountry landscapes, like marsh grass, Spanish moss, and architecture steeped in hundreds of years of history. Iron work is an integral element in many of the historical homes here. I draw inspiration from my surroundings and enjoy working with clients who have a connection to the natural elements of the Lowcountry, like cattails, grasses, and palm fronds, and I want these things worked into their designs. I derive so much of my creative energy from organic landscapes of all kinds.

My designs are always based on a few things: first, what makes the client tick stylistically? Do they love architectural and modern, classic and traditional, or more of a nature-inspired look? Second, what is the surrounding environment, including both the existing architecture and landscape? Lastly, how can I merge their design sensibilities with my own, and create something truly unique?

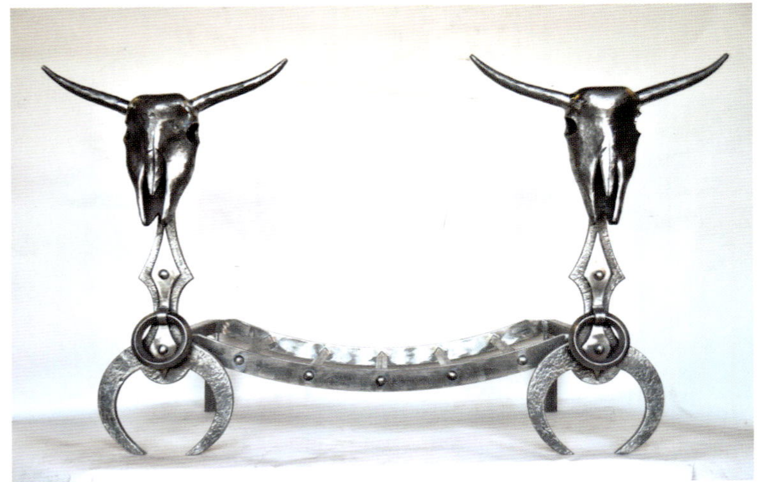

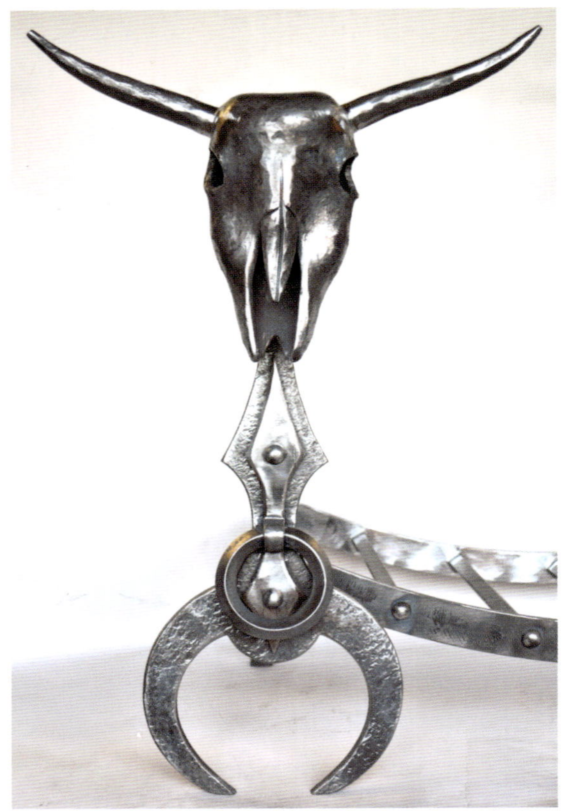

Forged Cow Skull Andirons

This piece was designed for a client who asked (with a smile) if I have ever made cow skulls before. I said, with a smile, "No, but I bet we can and I always like a good challenge."

Forged cow skull andirons. 2012. Forged steel.

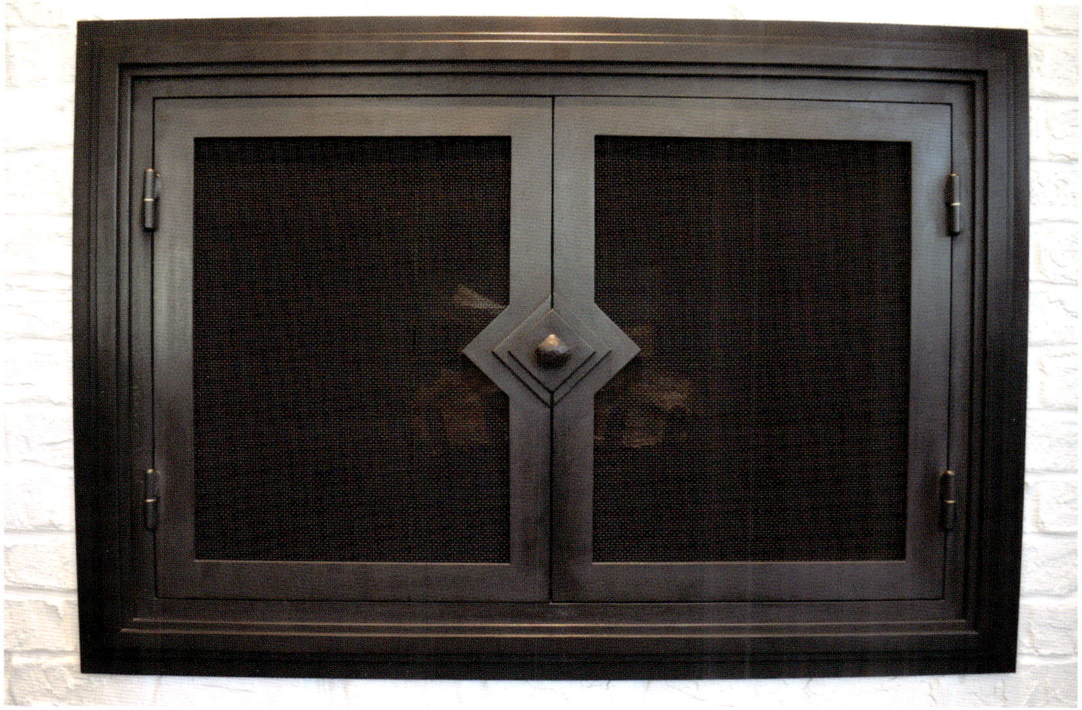

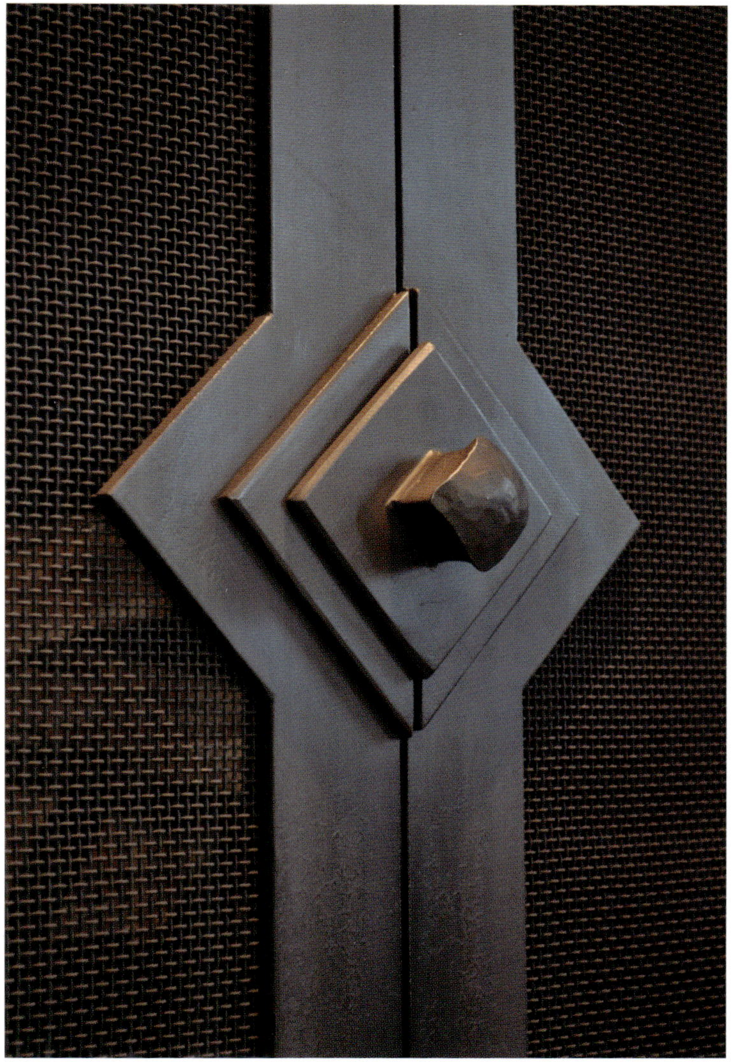

Fire screen

This fire screen was designed for a client who wanted minimal but clean, crisp lines that gave the piece a strong presence in the room.

Fire screen. 2013. Fabricated and forged steel.

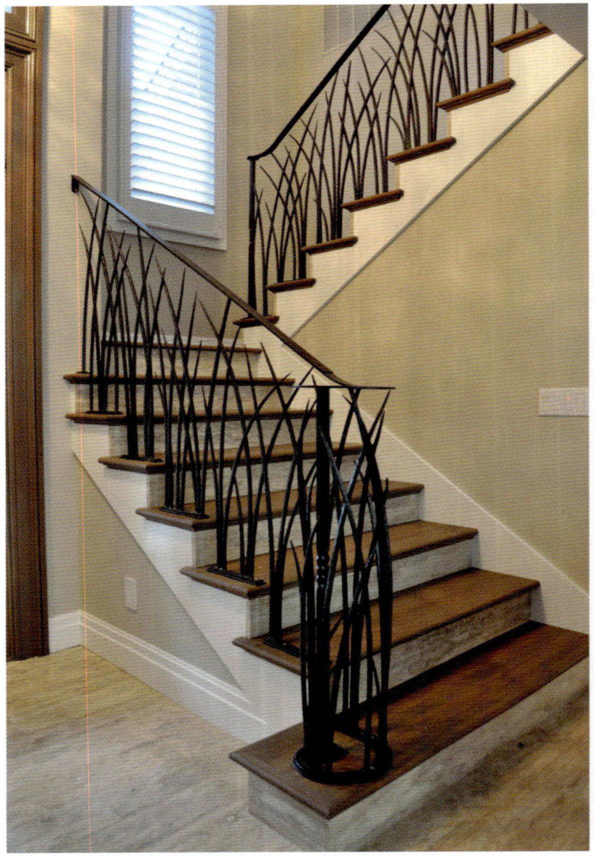

Forged Steel Grass Interior Handrail

This railing system was designed for a client who wanted to bring the image of surrounding marshlands of the Lowcountry into the interior of the home.

Forged grass interior handrail. 2012. Forged steel.

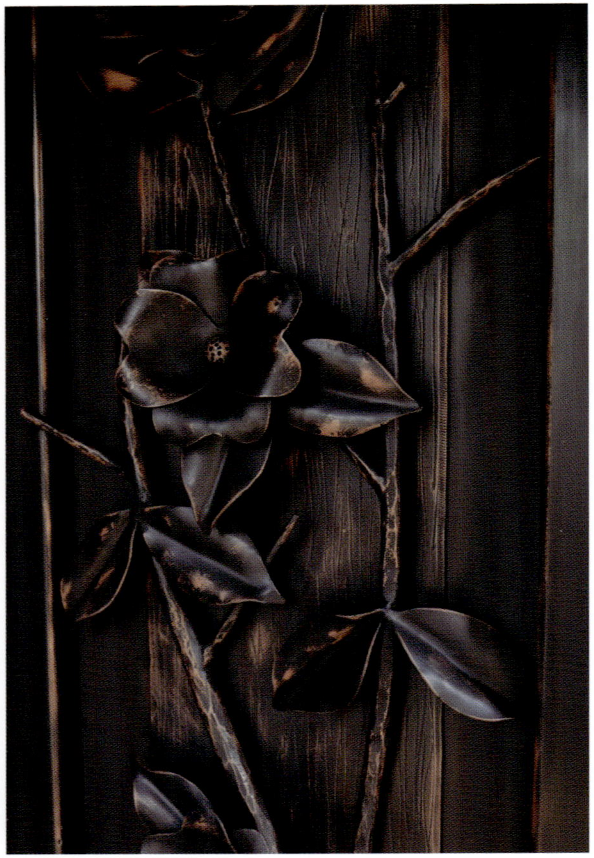

Dogwood Blossoms

For a top local restaurant in Charleston, we designed and built a log rack with cat tails and marsh grass. When they opened a new location in Nashville, I decided to go with a more local type of vegetation for our Tennessee friends.

Detail of panel with forged dogwood blossoms. 2013. Forged steel.

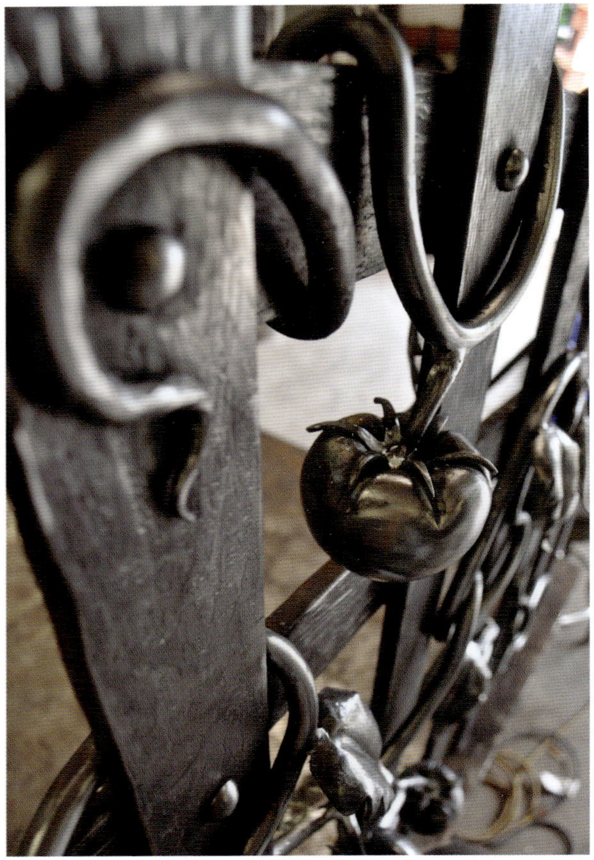

Tomatoes

This is a detail of one of four gates we built for the Medical University of South Carolina and their Urban Farm garden. Each gate was forged with wood grain texture and vined with its own forged local vegetable.

Detail of gate with forged tomatoes. 2013. Forged steel.

Frank Annighofer

Wood and Iron Works, Roscoe, Montana
www.woodandironworks.com

ARTIST'S STATEMENT

Growing up in a thousand-year-old town in Northern Germany, I always admired the ironwork that decorated old buildings and parks. I liked the old arrowhead pickets and the endless repetitive patterns of scrolls and flower motifs. A lot of my own architectural ironwork is inspired by these old designs. In my sculptural work I try to employ the same traditional blacksmithing techniques. There might be a lot of intricate detail work, but I try to keep it in the background. My focus typically is on the overall theme and aesthetics. I like to leave some room for the observer to come up with their own interpretation.

Indian Chief Sculpture

This forged sculpture was inspired by a photograph of Wild Horse taken by David F. Barry in the late 1800s. Sioux Chief Wild Horse was a brother of the better-known Chief Crazy Horse. He was with the Ogalala Lakota and fought in the battle of the Little Big Horn. My sculpture design evolved from this face profile, which I hammered out of a piece of copper. There is some more copper and brass in other parts but the main sculpture is made from unpolished stainless steel. It was assembled with copper and steel rivets, the face being brazed on.

Sioux Chief Wild Horse. Sculpture. 2012.
Forged stainless steel, copper and brass. Private residence, Roscoe, Montana. 44" x 30" x 16".

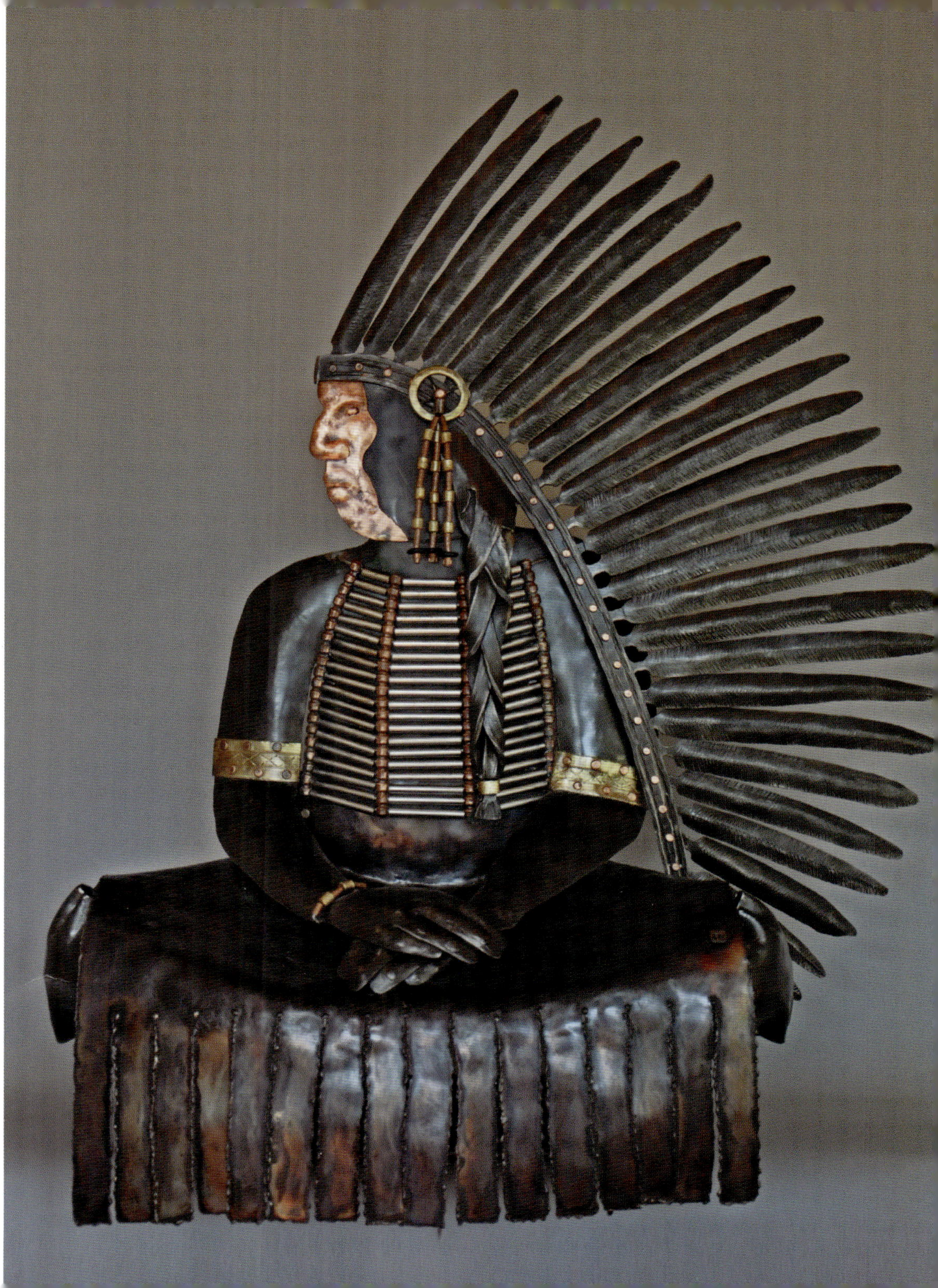

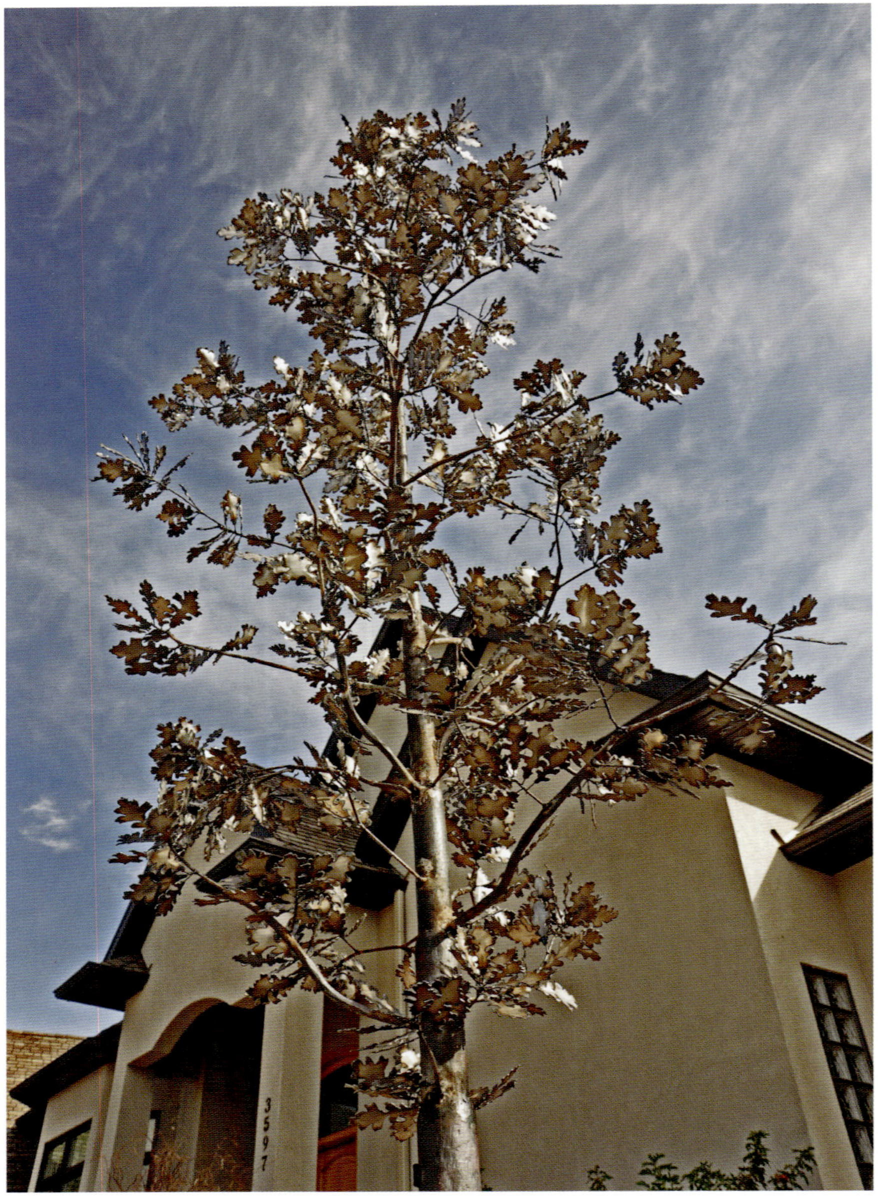

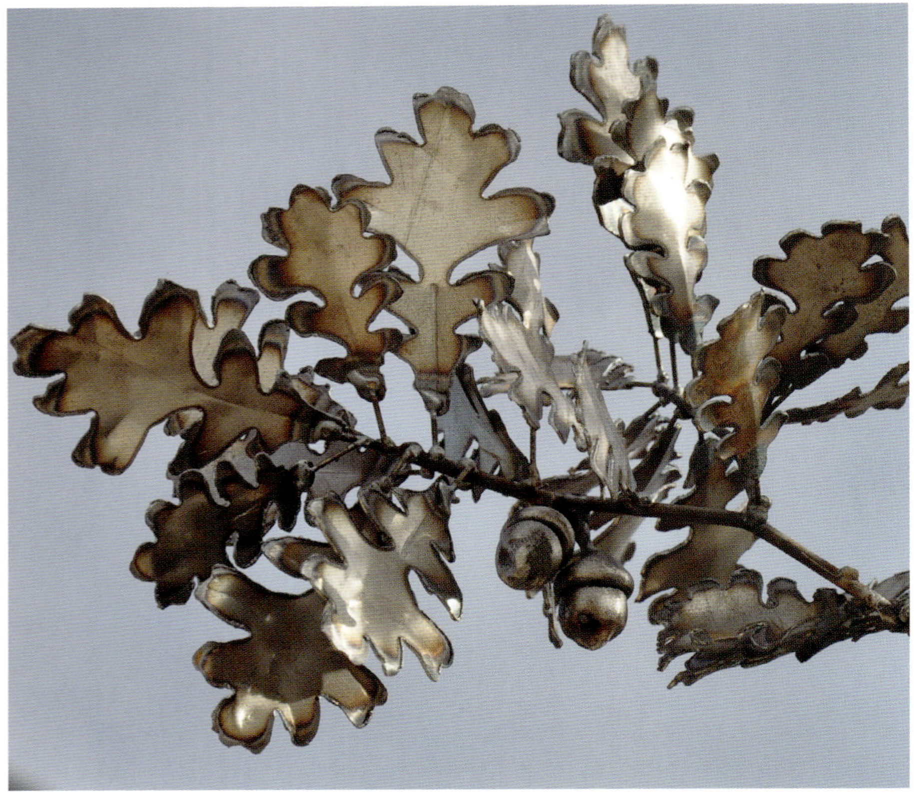

Oak Tree Sculpture

What do you do when you have a burr oak on your front lawn and want another one but without the need for sweeping leaves each fall? Well, you might call a metal artist and ask to have one built from steel. Leaves for this oak tree sculpture were cut out of sheet steel and shaped with hammer and chisel on a wooden block. It took 1,500 leaves to create enough volume for the 16-foot high tree.

Oak Tree. 2012. Sculpture. Forged and fabricated steel.
Yellowstone Country Club, Billings, Montana. 16′ x 4′ x 4′.

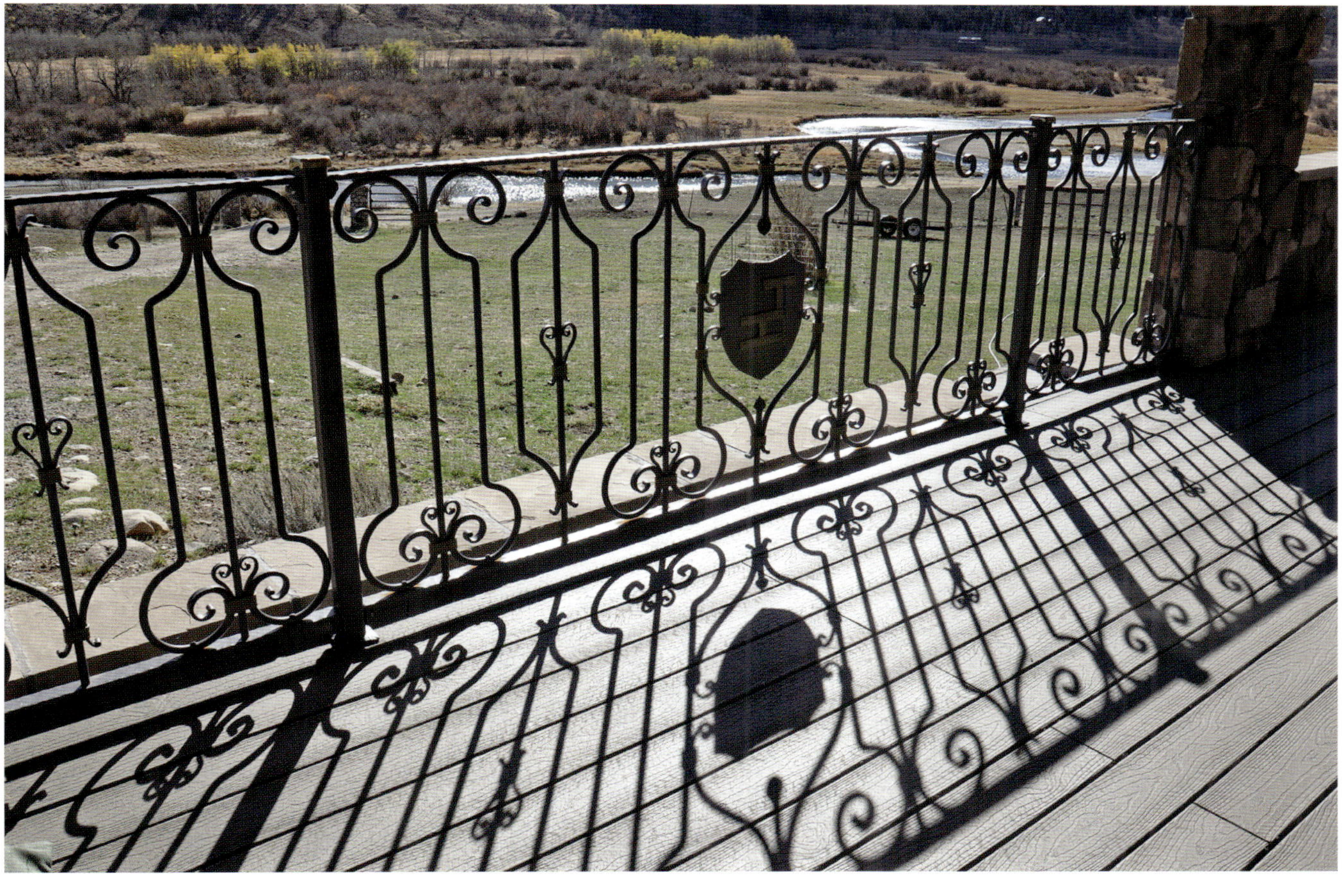

Deck Railing

A traditional European design for third-generation immigrants from Europe, this deck railing is traditionally forged. Rivets and brass collars are used for assembly. The ranch brand is incorporated in the style of a coat of arms, the lettering forged from brass. This project started with a stair railing made in the same style for the interior of the house.

Deck railing. 2011. Hand-forged steel with brass accents. All traditional joinery. Private residence, Roscoe, Montana. 12′ x 3′.

Brass and steel detail.

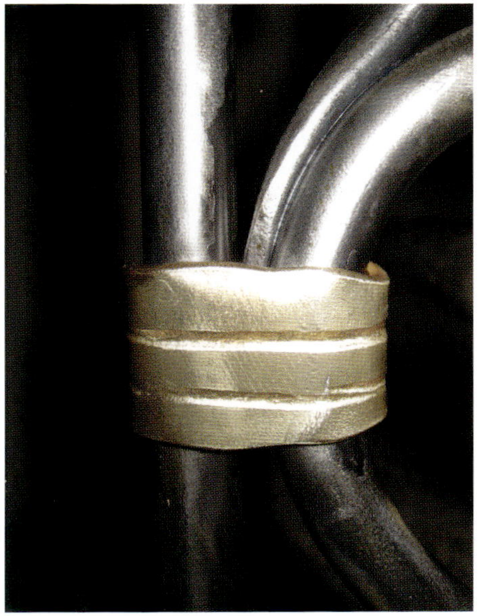

A.C. Tony Austin

Dragon's Rest Working Studios, Kimberley, British Columbia, Canada, tnt-austin@shaw.ca

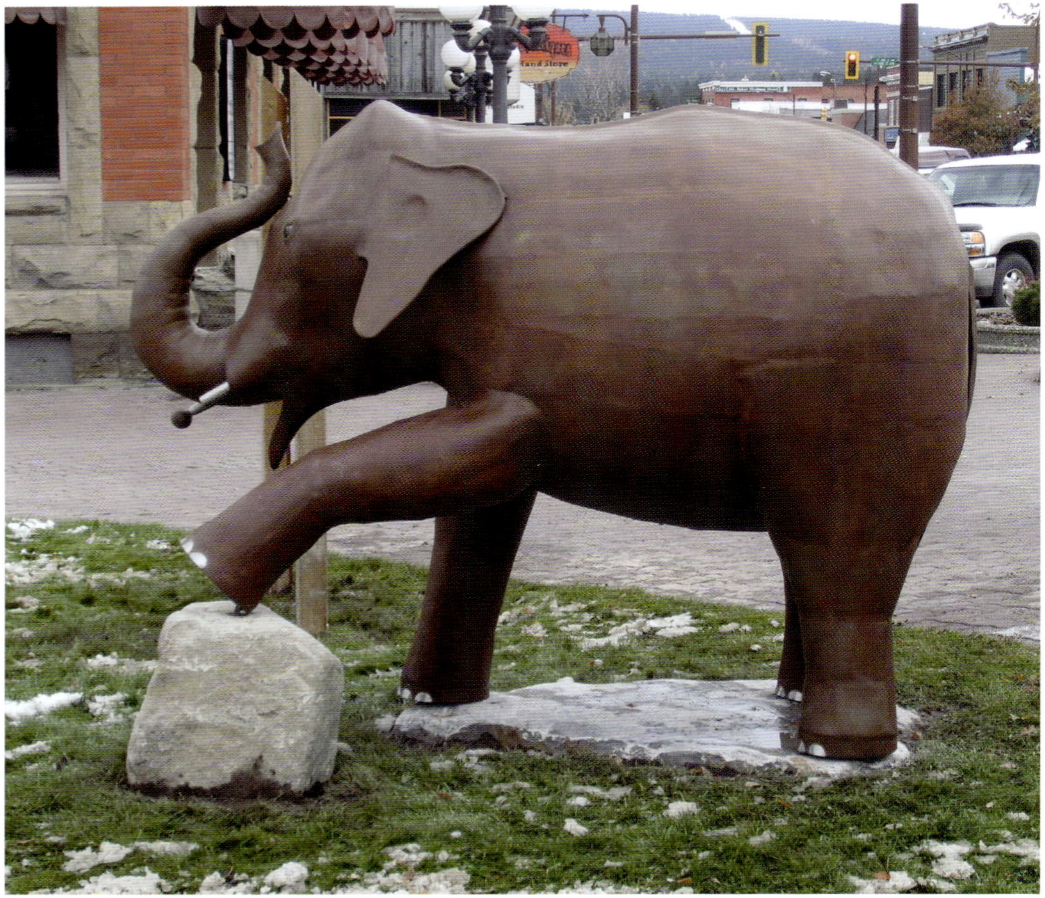

ARTIST'S STATEMENT

My art is about translating visions into visuals, telling stories with shapes and colors, creating works that can be seen, touched, and felt both physically and mentally. I have devoted the last ten years primarily to ironwork, hand forging and repoussé. There are three guiding elements in my work: line, color, and texture. Line and color draw the eye; texture draws the hand. I use both traditional and modern joinery, embellish many of my creations with repoussé, and color them with flame or patinas. My sculptures are interactive, on ground level, meant to be touched, climbed on, fed, and talked to, because, as a child, I was never able to touch those beautiful horses mounted on their six-foot high pedestals.

A.C. TONY AUSTIN

Cranbrook Ed

On the morning of August 6 , 1926, the Sills-Floto Circus train arrived in Cranbrook, B.C., with fourteen nervous Indian elephants on board. As they were being unloaded, something scared them, and they stampeded through the town and out into the bush. Thus began the Great Cranbrook Elephant Hunt. The majority of the animals were rounded up in a matter of days, but Charlie Ed, a four-year-old, eluded capture for thirty-nine days. Finally, on September 15, it snowed two inches, and the following day Charlie was recaptured. He was the star of the Cranbrook Fall Fair and was christened Cranbrook Ed, prior to being shipped back to the circus. Cranbrook Ed is a full-sized replica of the young elephant. His base frame is constructed of 1" tubing. The frame was fleshed out to size with ½" square bar, bent to fit using a fly press and bending forks, and MIG welded. The 14 gauge skin was hand formed over wood stakes and MIG welded in place.

Cranbrook Ed. Interactive public sculpture. 2009.
16 gauge mild steel repoussé, welded construction, ferric nitrate patina with Incralac lacquer finish.
Baker Street Park, Cranbrook, B.C., Canada.
7′ x 3′x 5′.

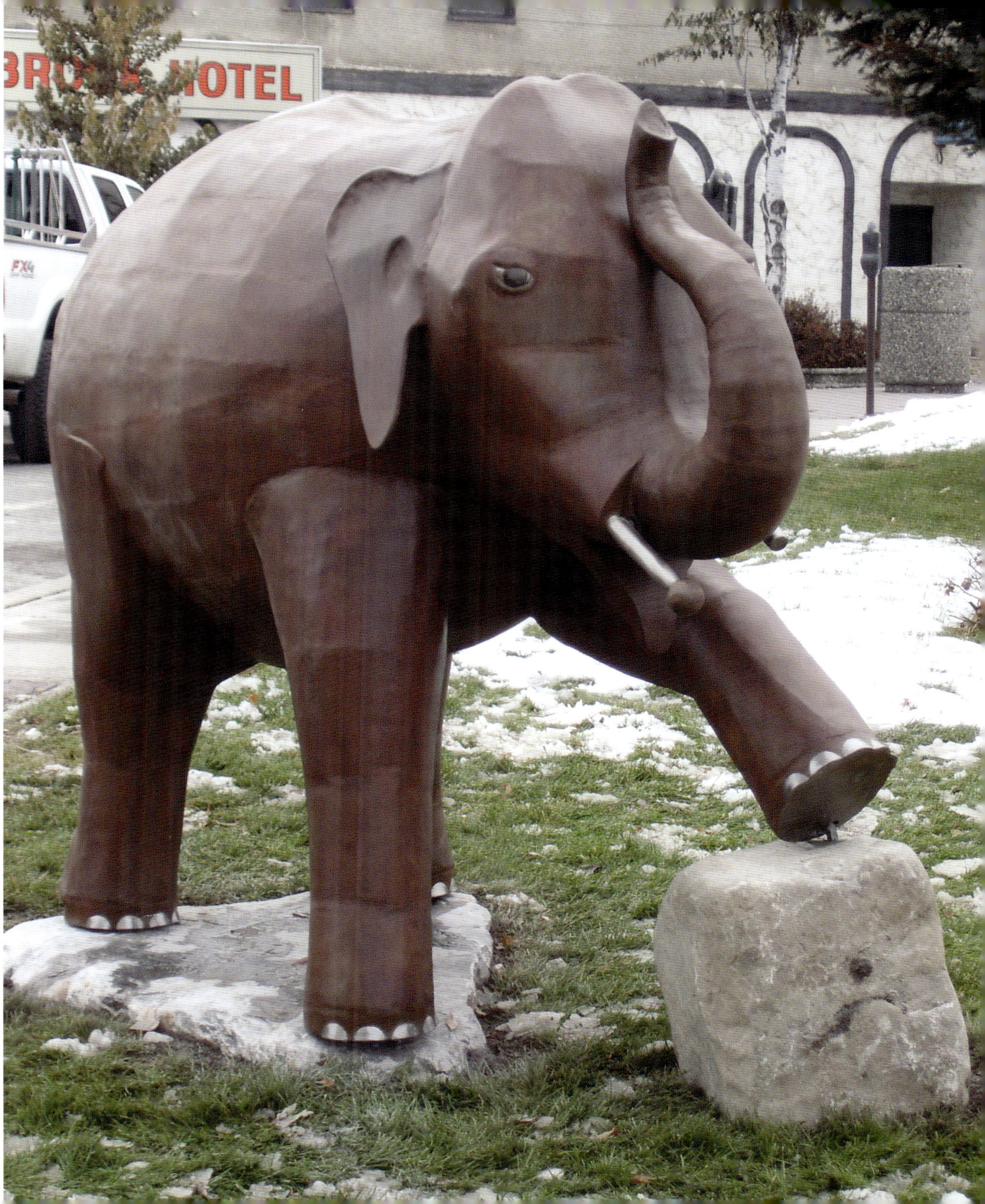

Lost Salmon of the Columbia

Invermere is situated on Windermere Lake, near the headwaters of the mighty Columbia River, the traditional salmon fishing grounds of the Ktunaxa People. For eons, before dams were built downstream, the annual Chinook salmon run sustained aboriginal peoples from the Pacific Northwest to deep within the interior of what is now the Kootenay Region of British Columbia. With the building of the Grand Coulee Dam in the 1940s, the mighty Chinook were seen no more. In the spring of 2009, I was approached by the Ktunaxa to design a monument to the Lost Salmon as a visual anchor for the continued efforts to return the salmon to the upper Columbia River. Lost Salmon of the Columbia is comprised of three 5′ Chinook salmon leaping up a steel waterfall. Each salmon has a 3⁄16″ plate core, which was bent to shape prior to cutting out the silhouette by plasma cutter. The 14 gauge sheet sides were then sunk hot through the silhouette, the features were done in repoussage cold, and the finished sides MIG welded to the core. The finished salmon were lightly sand blasted, colored with ferric nitrate, and painted with clear Incralac. The waterfall has a 3″ channel frame with 1″ x ¼″ flat bar to simulate the flowing water welded to the frame. The waterfall was sand blasted and powder coated with a metallic silver.

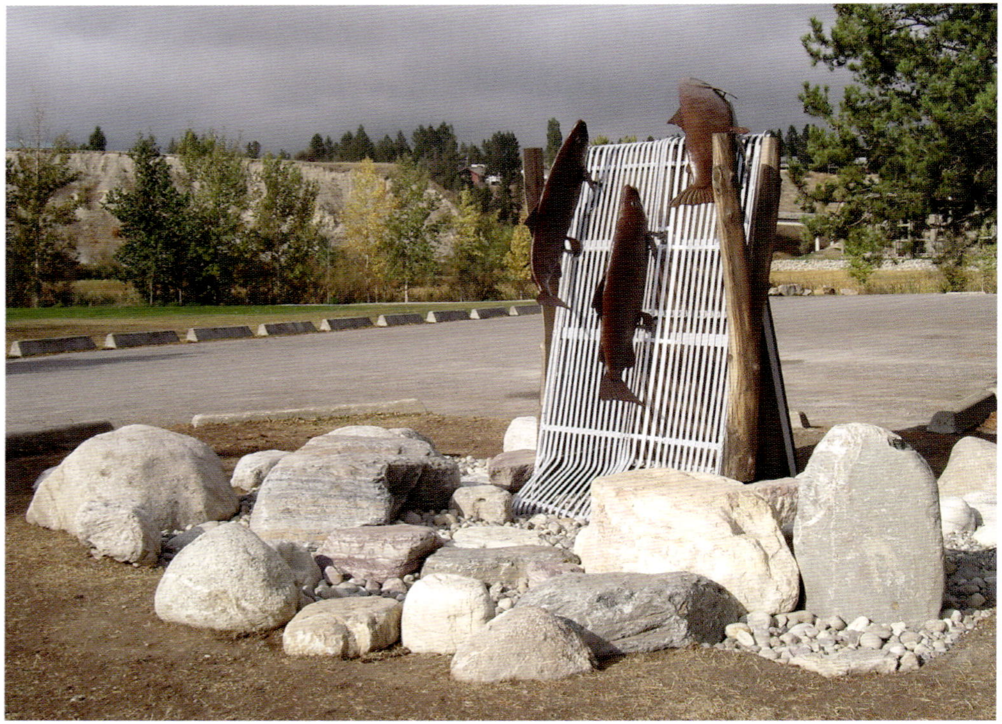

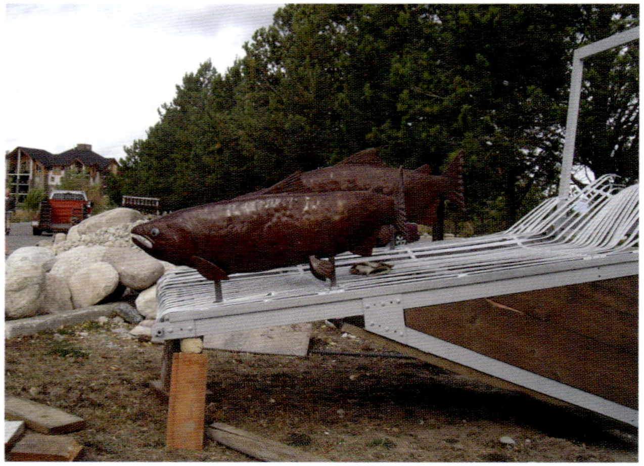

Lost Salmon of the Columbia. Public sculpture. 2011. 14 gauge mild steel repoussé, welded construction, ferric nitrate patina with Incralac lacquer finish on the fish and a silver powder coat on the waterfall. James Cabot Provincial Park, Invermere, BC, Canada. 8′ x 6′ x 12′.

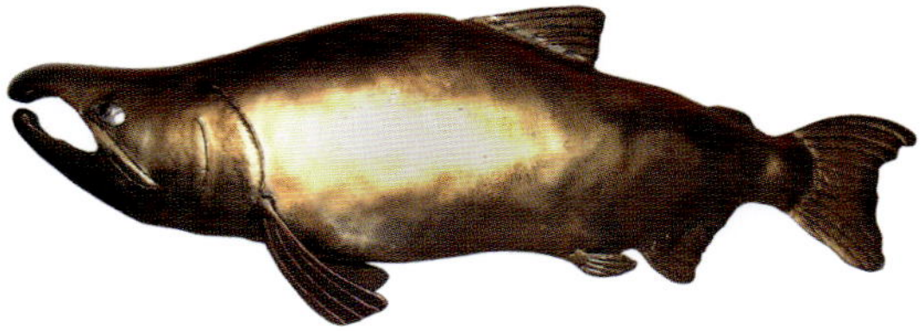

Chinook Salmon

Chinook Salmon. Sculpture. 2012. 16 gauge mild steel repoussé, welded construction, flame-colored with clear semi-gloss acrylic finish. B. Greene, Kimberley, B.C., Canada. 16″ x 2″ x 6″.

Lee W. Badger

Anvil Works, Hedgesville, West Virginia
anvilworks.net

ARTIST'S STATEMENT

A tale of two railings: The two railings on these three pages illustrate contrasts in the scope of architectural projects that are challenging the versatility of artist-blacksmiths today. The *'R' Monogram Railing* was commissioned by a jewelry designer for the front porch and entry stairs of her personally expressive, suburban family home. The budget was ample, the schedule and time-frame was generously flexible, and the elaborate design, inspired by art nouveau ironwork, was prescribed by the client's own drawings.

Great challenges lay in realizing the drawn design in three-dimensional forged steel, with complex twists and irregular compound curves in almost every piece. In addition, the client's design drawings had to be scaled and reproportioned to fit the measurements of the existing porch and stairs.

In contrast, the *Rustic Railing* (see page 17) came with an appeal for help with a new log house, built on speculation and finished quickly by the builder with an inexpensive wood deck railing system installed on 65 feet of interior stairs and balconies in the soaring great room. The clients who purchased this home hoped for a new ornamental iron railing that would accommodate their modest budget and restricted schedule, and also express qualities of hand-forged craftsmanship complementary to the hewn log construction.

"R" Monogram Railing. As designed by the client, the 'R' monogram railing required forging complex twists and irregular compound curves in almost every piece. In order to create perfectly symmetrical stair railings, each piece had to be reproduced in three-dimensional reversal. Specific drawings by the client were inspired by art nouveau ironwork in Paris during the 1890s.

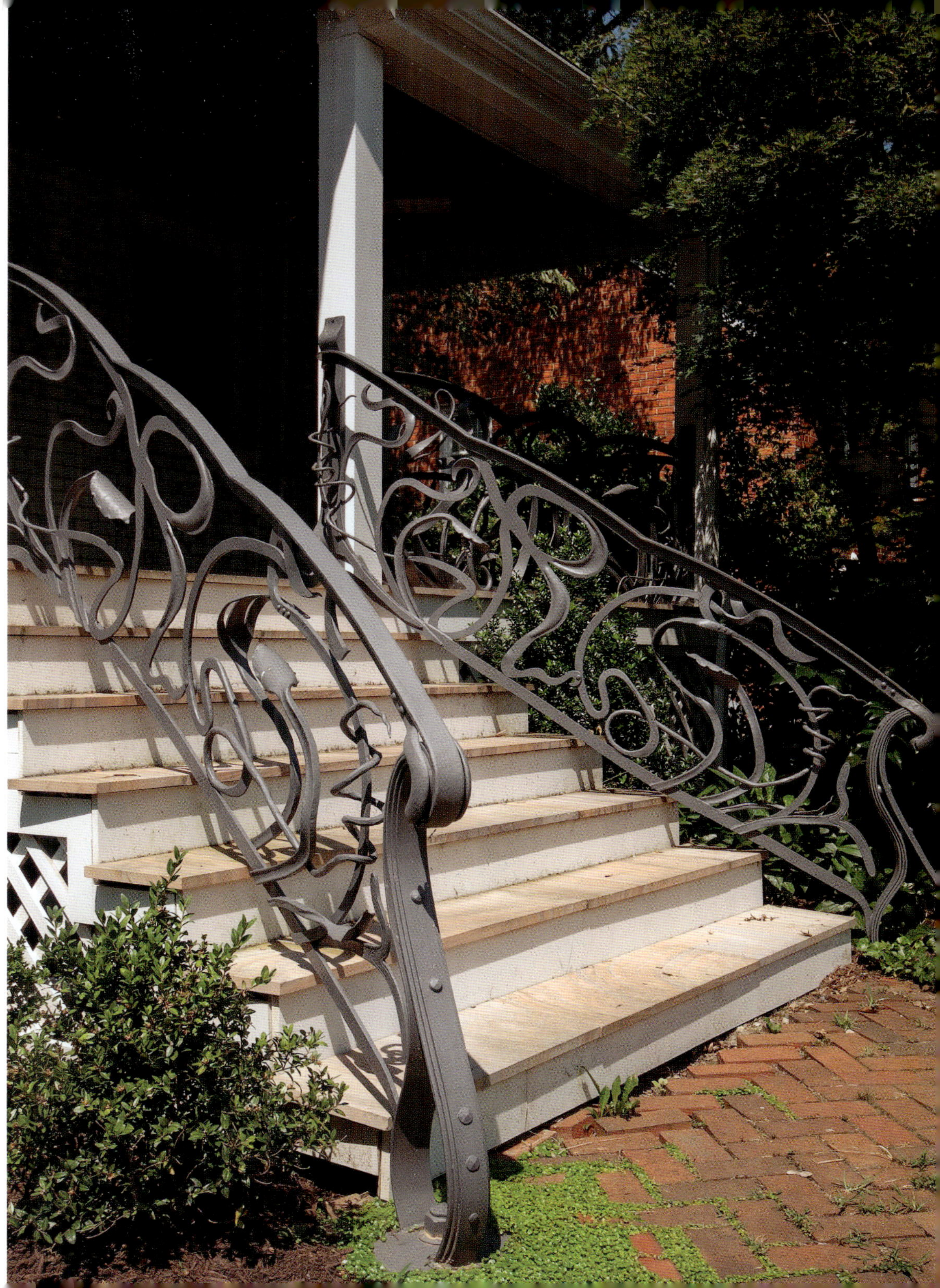

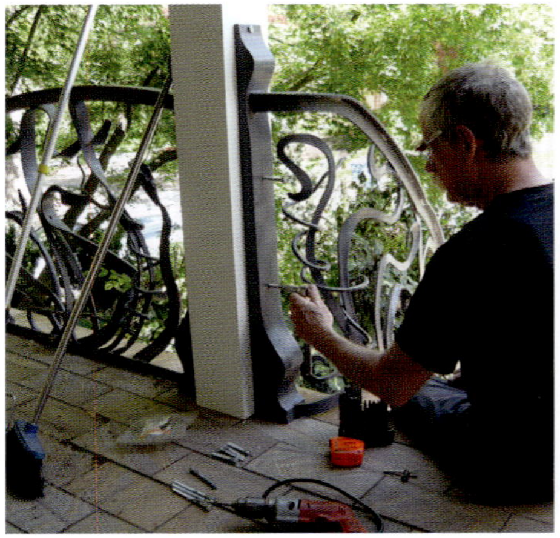

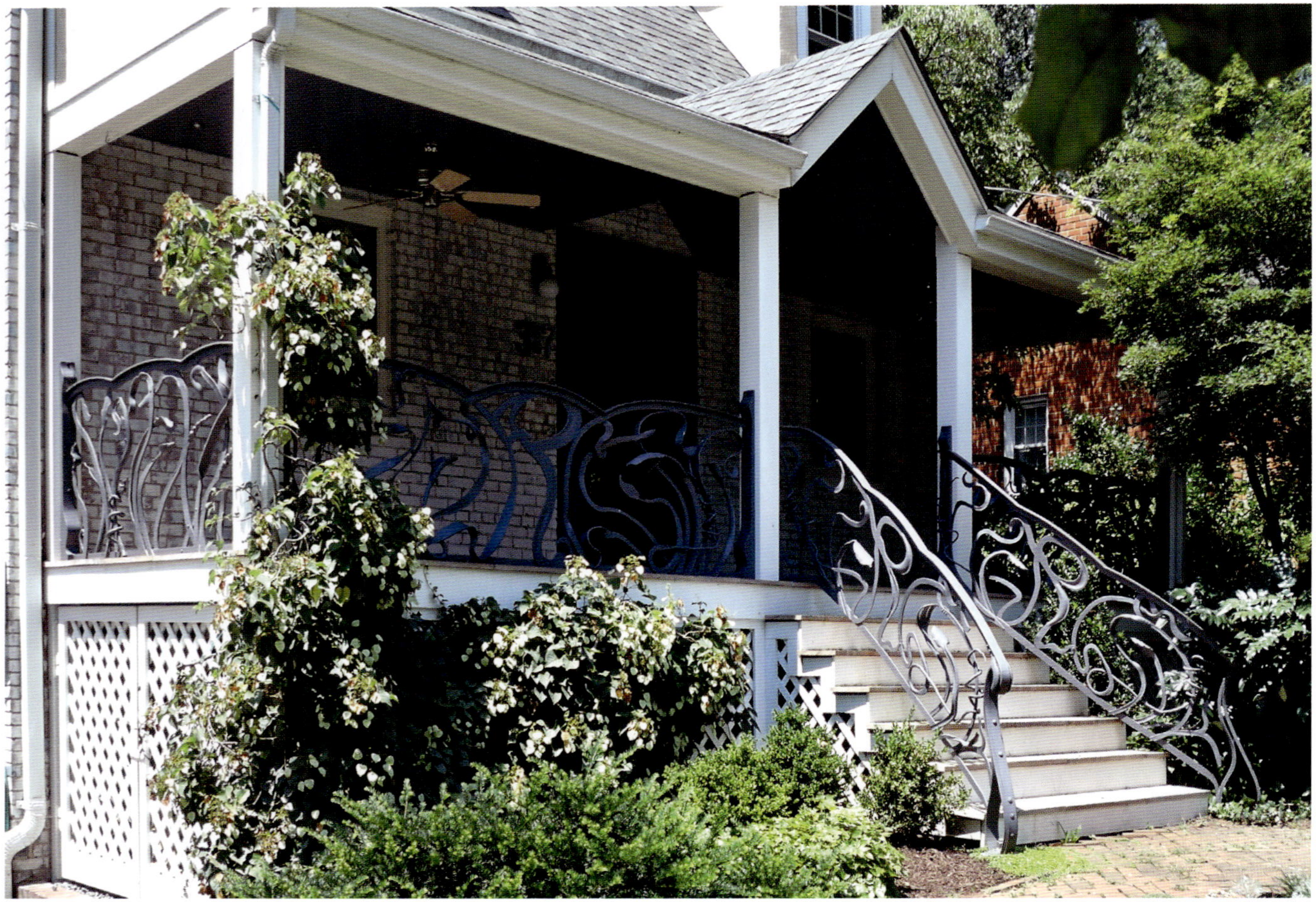

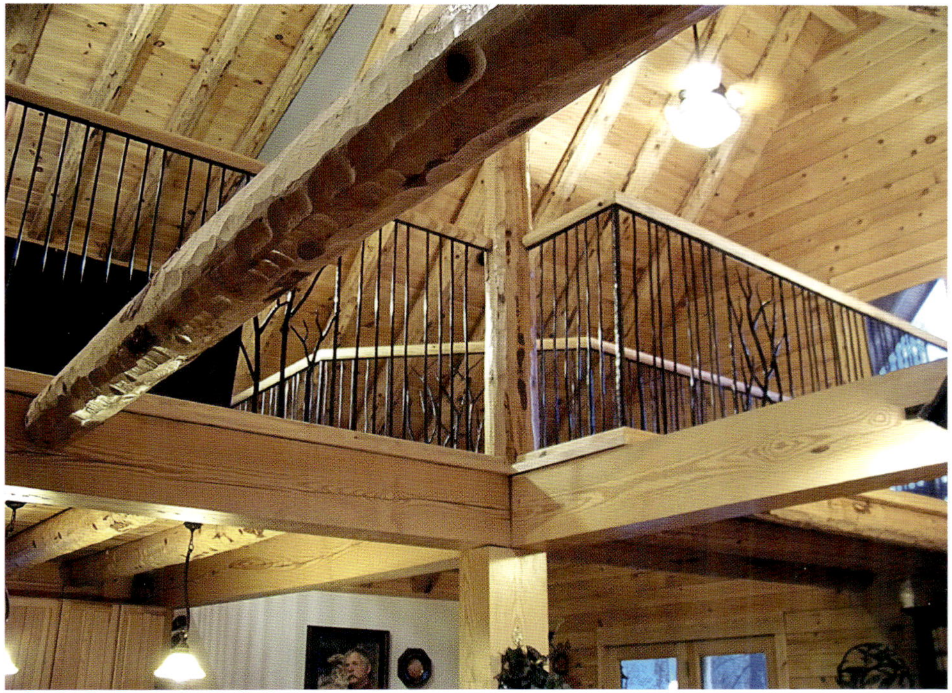

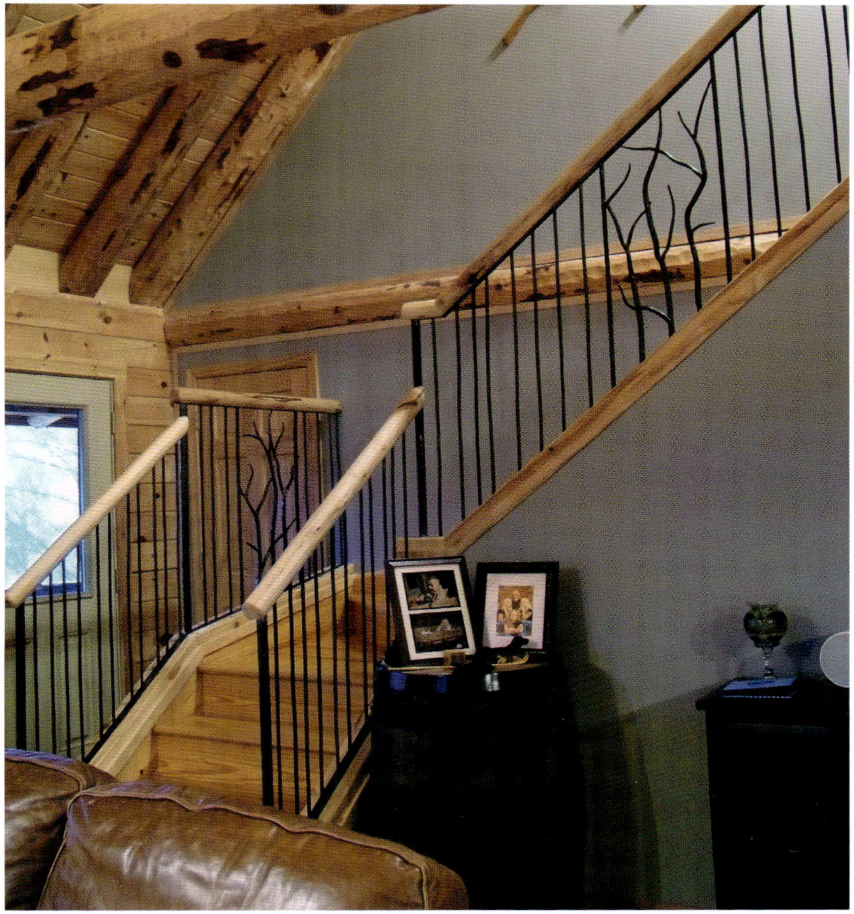

Rustic Railing. The new railing was designed to take advantage of existing carpentry, using the same wood curb rail to anchor the new steel balustrade.
A collaborating carpenter matched the log construction with a wood handrail fastened to a top channel, further simplifying construction and installation of the steel.

William J. Bastas

Austin, Texas
www.wbastas@gmail.com

ARTIST'S STATEMENT

After graduating from UT–Austin in 1989, I decided to learn blacksmithing. I then graduated from the Code welding program at Austin Community College in 1991, and I was invited to teach blacksmithing in the fledgling art metals program. I created the classes I always wanted to take. The program now offers its own metalsmithing AAS degree within the welding department. We offer college credit classes in traditional blacksmithing, power hammer, tool making, functional and sculptural forging, and hardware. I designed the pieces shown here as assignments for students and use the projects to demonstrate skills and processes. I am particularly drawn to lighting, as the pieces can encompass all of the skills expected of a journeyman smith, in an easily stored and useful format. As well, lighting allows twin characters, one based on the design of the iron and the other on the interplay of light. Additionally, lighting initiates the idea of applying how a learned skillset can be used to create marketable products.

Autumnal Glow

I designed this lamp to incorporate very few elements, as well to have clever transitions and to encourage the most light out of the lamp. As well, I am inspired by the arts and crafts tradition, and its philosophy of noncomplexity and serenity. Artists who inspired the design are: Edgar Brandt, for the stylized oval scrolls, and Dirk Van Erp, for the use of fine frame lines and mica. The legs represent journeyman sensitivity to the line test, fishtails forged at right angles to one another without a discernible transition. The bolt end rolled fishtails give students an opportunity to learn and enjoy the efficiency of forge welding.

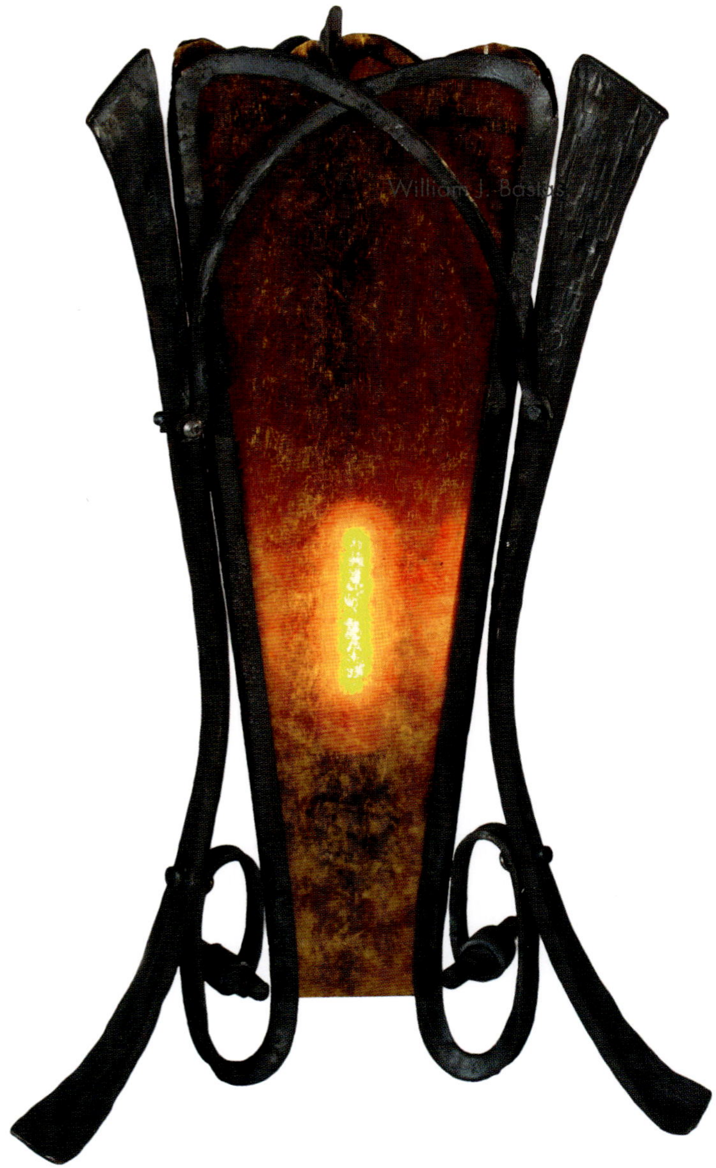

Autumnal Glow. Lamp. 2013.
Forged steel, amber mica. 16" w x 24" h. *Photo: Bill Bastas CPP*

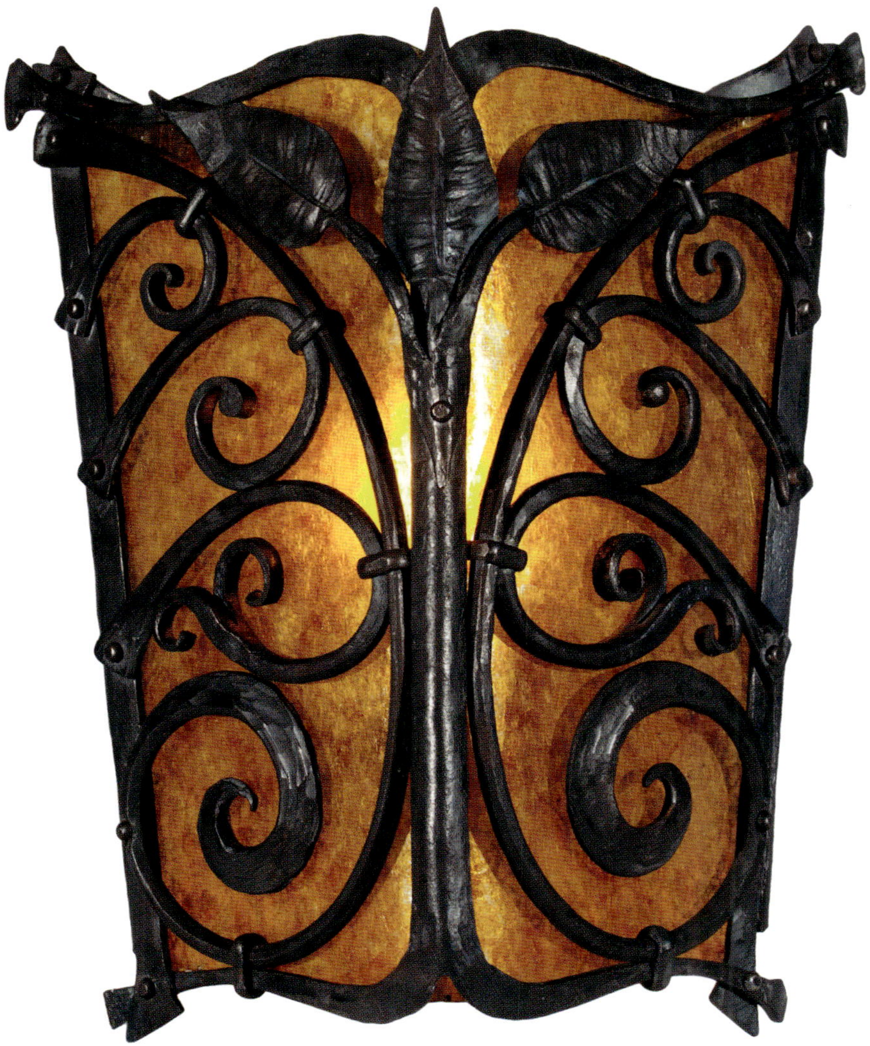

Tiger Sconce

I designed this sconce as a format for learning the different finials in scroll work and the skills in forging and fitting them. It was inspired by a bracket that I made that had scrolls within a larger scroll, like a sectioned nautilus. It has an art nouveau line, as well as a bilateral symmetry of golden proportion.

Tiger Sconce. Sconce. 2012.
Forged steel, amber mica. 16"w x 24"h. *Photo: Bill Bastas CPP*

Revival

This sconce draws its inspiration from the piece at the door to what was the upstairs office of Jim Wallace at the Metal Museum. It had a center laminate from which scrolls branched off. I was artist-in-residence there in 1997 and was inspired by the library within this office. The piece also has some influence of Mayan revival art deco. I decided that instead of leaves, the outlines would project more light and give us a fun way of using forge welding. The scrolls are fiddlehead ferns, the leaves inspired by dogwood.

Revival. Sconce. 2011. Forged steel, clear mica. 14"w x 24"h. *Photo: Bill Bastas CPP*

Paris

I designed this lamp to showcase not only the skills expected of a journeyman smith but also the importance of clever transitions. I was inspired some years ago upon viewing a Chris Winterstein chandelier at an ABANA conference, as well as the flying buttresses of Notre Dame.

Paris. Lamp. 2011. Forged steel, amber mica. 12"w x 30"h. *Photo: Bill Bastas CPP*

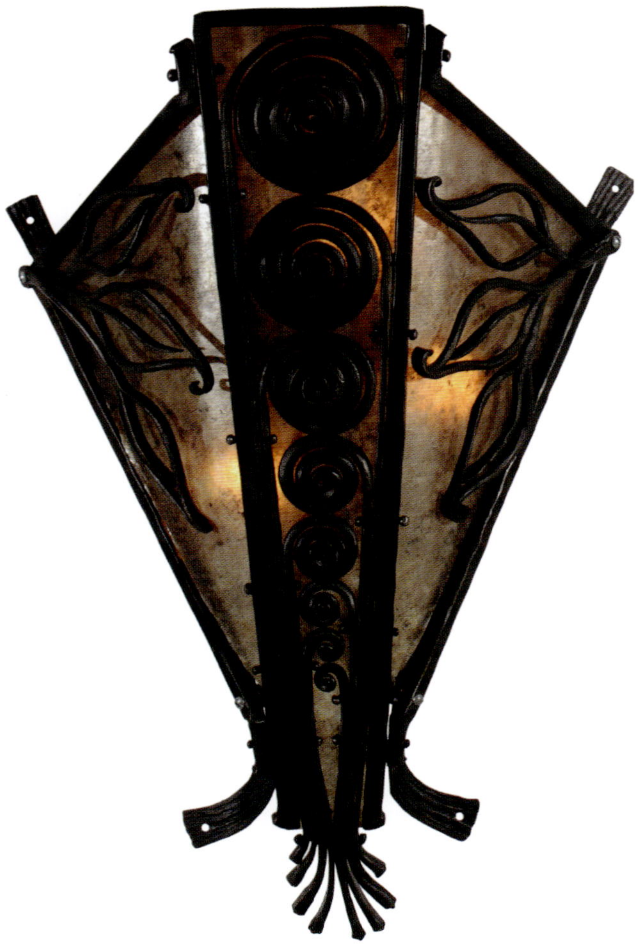

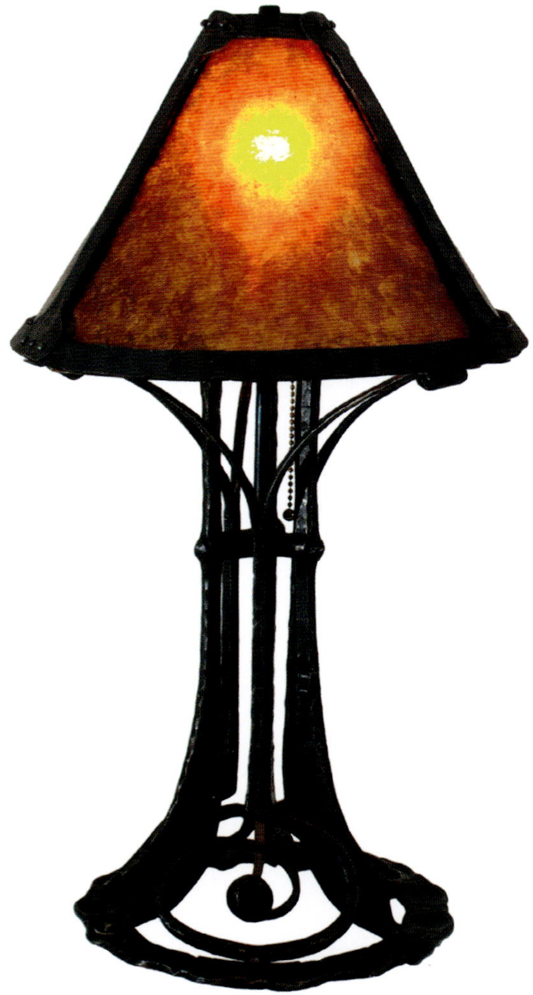

Nicole Beck

Chicago, Illinois
nicolebeck.com

ARTIST'S STATEMENT

The backbone of my work fuses rhythmic and poetic systems found in nature and the sciences. I find a harmonic balance between the perceived world and the theoretical, often incorporating concepts of physics and mathematics. Wholly unique sculptures pulse with paradigm shifts and hyper colors that are dynamic and quirky. I master a mixture of various materials and textures. Most recently these featured materials include the beauty, strength, and stability of stainless steel with the light and color of mosaic, dichroic glass, and programmable RGB LEDs. These materials allow me to explore a vast range of sculptural processes that invite collaborative input necessary for large, public artworks.

Prairie Town Dweller

A respectful and playful homage to Frank Lloyd Wright. A partition screen from Wright's famous Chicago Robie house has been referenced with pared-away elements that reveal a female figure, a "muse" for Wright. The extreme mitering was accomplished while in residence at The Anderson Ranch Arts Center in Snowmass, Colorado, then transported to my Chicago studio where stainless steel wire mesh was custom fitted to the open geometries so the mosaic could be epoxied into place on both sides.

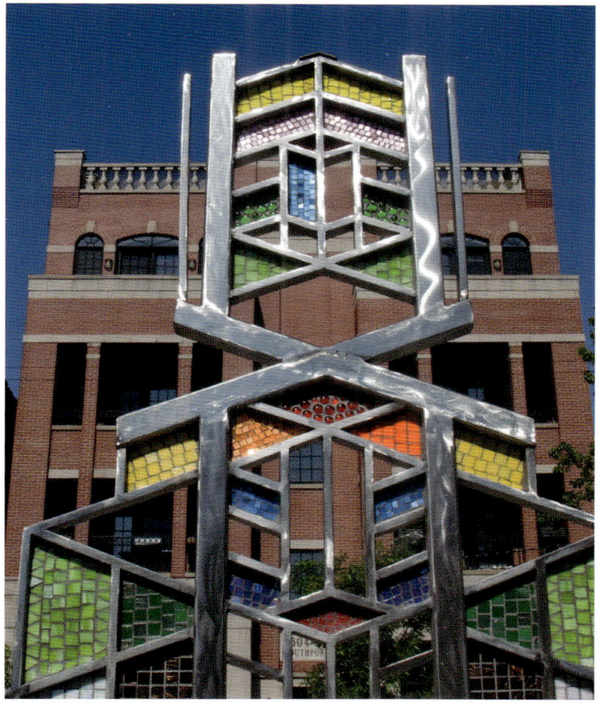

Prairie Town Dweller. Sculpture. 2011. Stainless steel and mosaic. Permanent collection, Lakeview Chamber of Commerce, Sheil Park, Chicago. 10′ x 4′ x 3′.

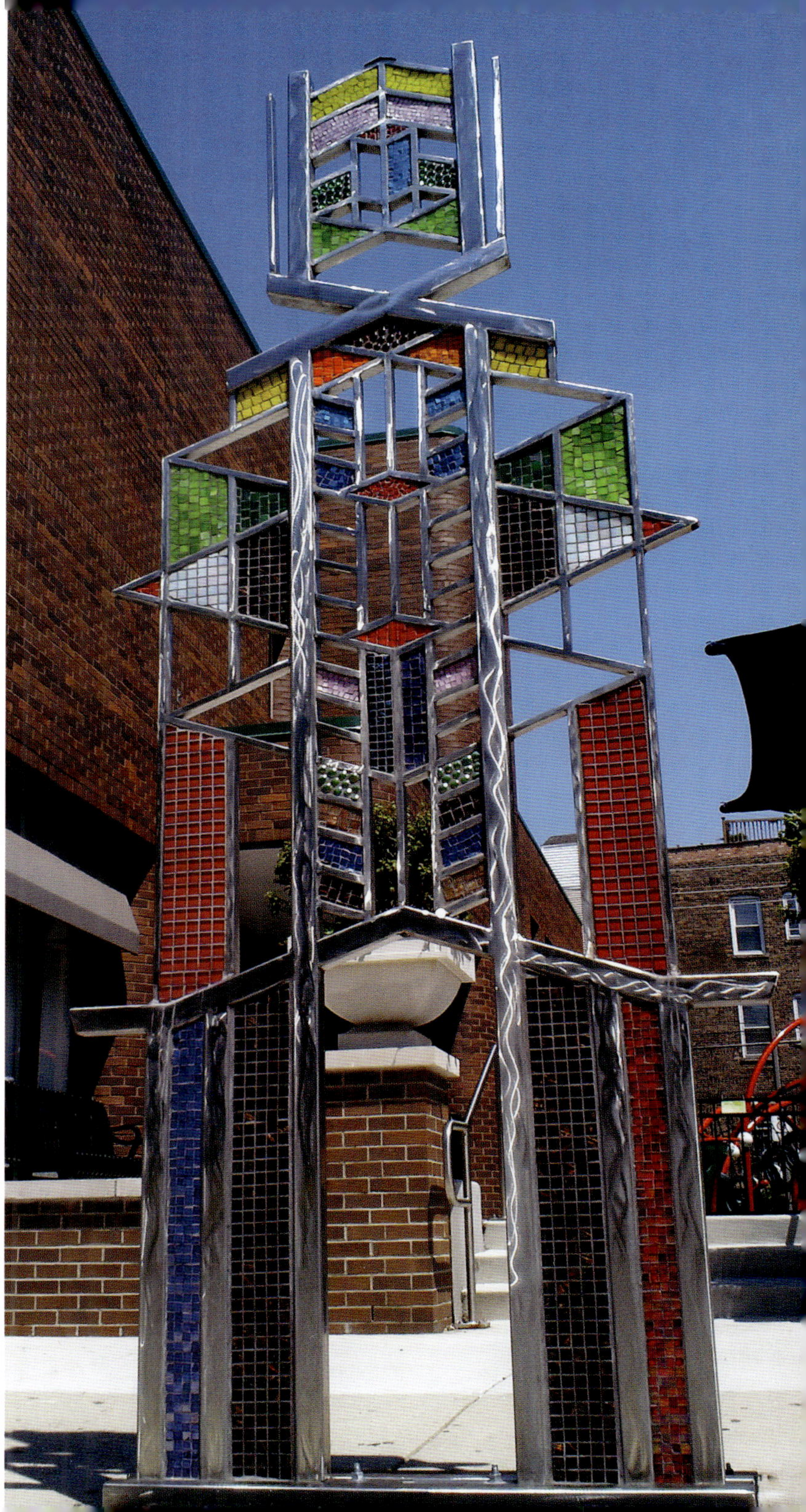

NICOLE BECK

Asteray

This work has both botanical and astronomical references as the Midwestern wildflower "Prairie Smoke," and as an asteroid just prior to Earthly impact carrying otherworldly miasma. The stainless steel "tail" or "filaments" were hand bent with a roller and welded together at random spots with customized stainless cuffing. The branch-like body was also hand rolled. Three industrial tank heads of various dimensions were welded successively to create a dynamic angle for the piece that simulates a comet's trajectory. All mosaic was epoxied in place and then epoxy-grouted for the best possible bond to the metal.

Asteray. Sculpture. 2012.
Stainless steel and mosaic. 18′ x 5′ x 4′.

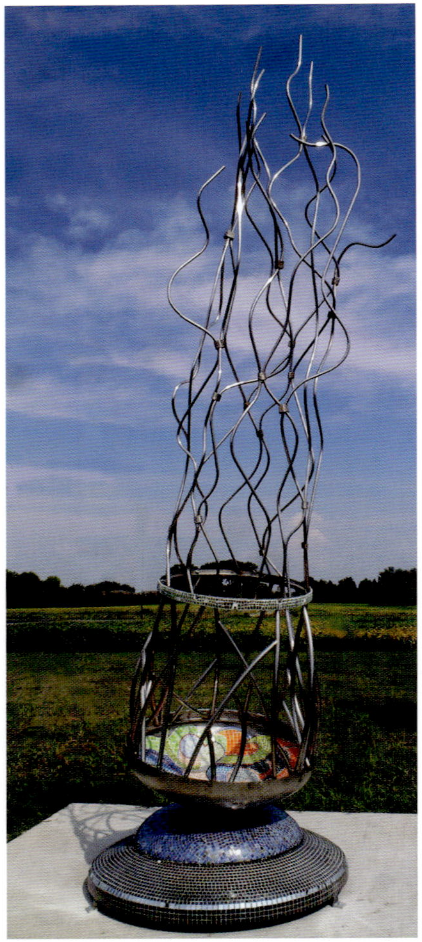

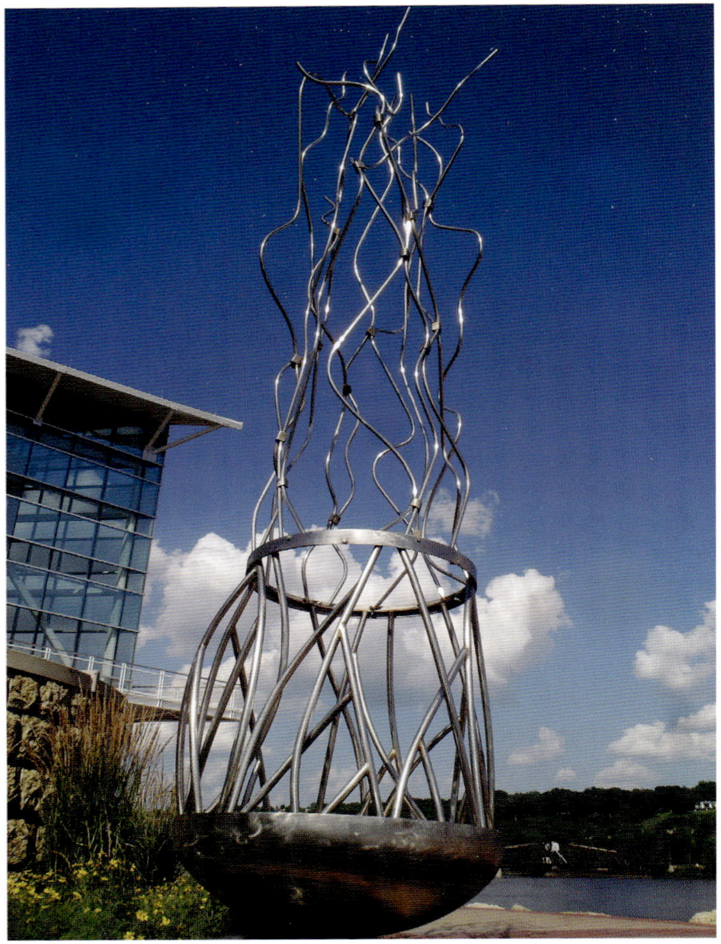

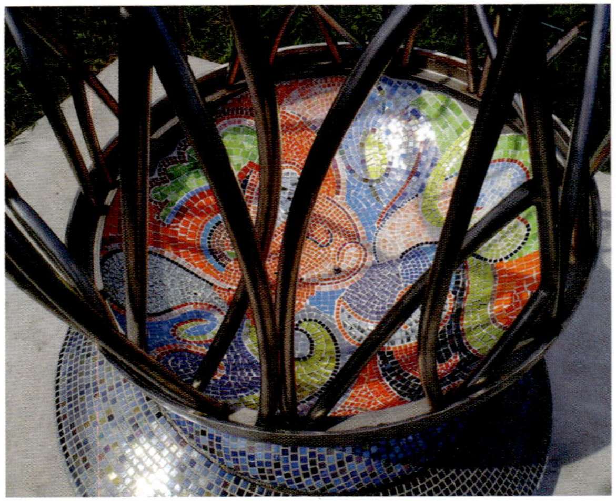

NICOLE BECK

Oscill8

Oscill8 *refers to an infinite wave of light oscillating between spectrums in equilibrium. It also refers to the phenomenon of many continuous systems naturally occurring. Several hundred stainless steel rings of various dimensions were production-cut and then de-burred. Using a template, I then welded each and every ring together with a spontaneous and random approach. The overall arc of the piece was created while fabricating the scale maquette.*

Oscill8. Sculpture. 2013. Stainless steel, concrete and mosaic. Lincoln Park, Chicago, at Clark St. and Racine. 8′ x 6′ x 4′.

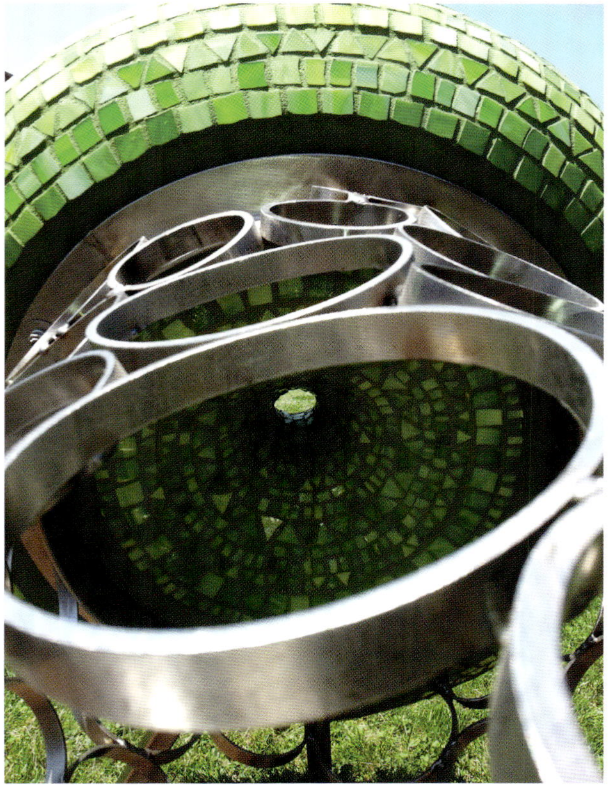

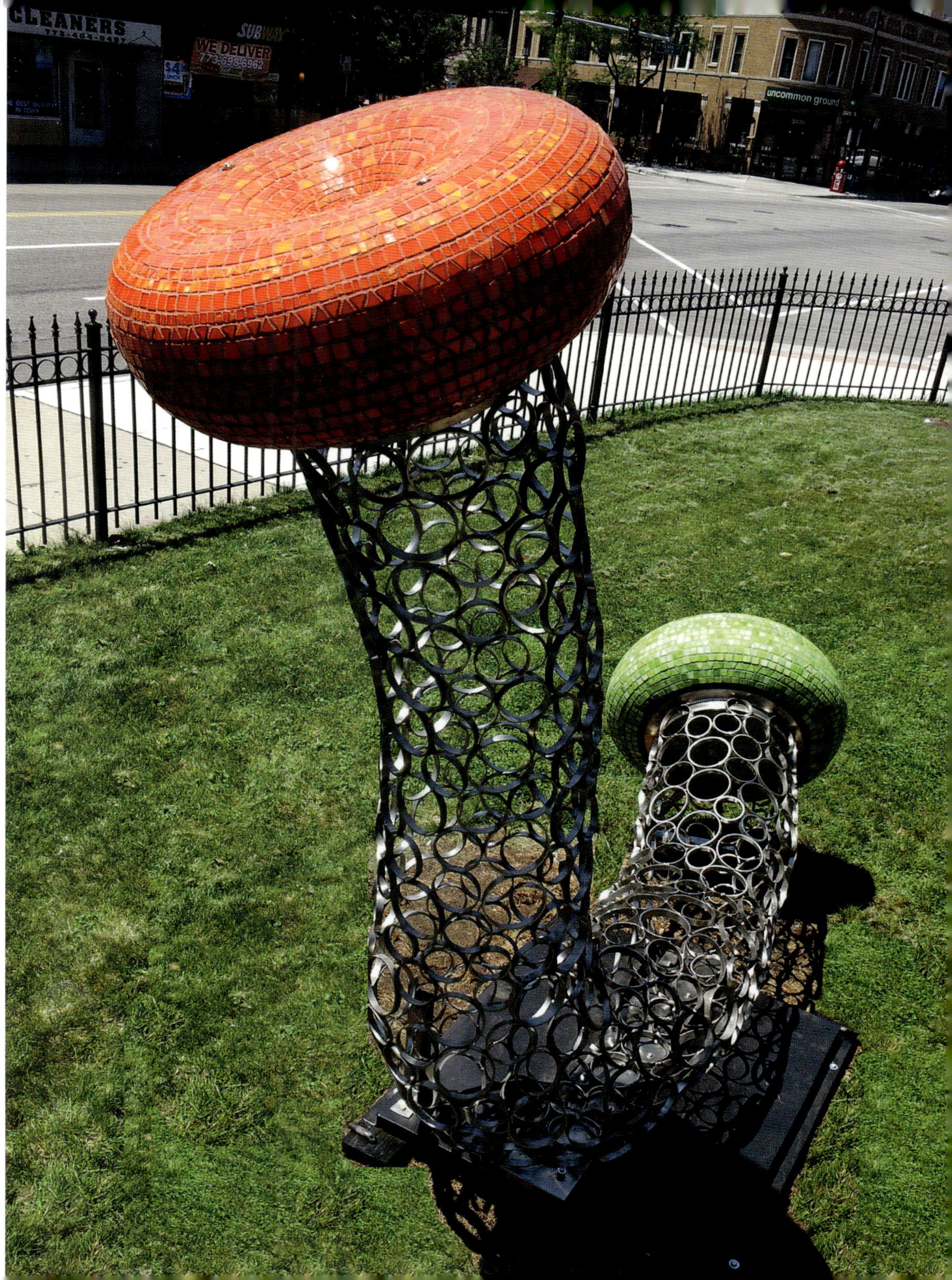

Jeff Benson

Benson Designs, Green Bay, Wisconsin
www.bensondesigns.com

ARTIST'S STATEMENT

I've been a creator all my life. Like most children, I loved to draw and paint, but I also wanted to make things with my hands, things that would last. Early on my father taught me how to use tools. As a furniture maker in the 1990s, I wanted to add woodcarving to my list of skills. A book about how to make woodcarving tools introduced me to blacksmithing. I soon found a forge and anvil and from the first hammer blow was hooked! The process of physically changing the shape of a piece of hot steel fascinated me. The versatility of steel and the broad range of methods used to shape and form it satisfy my need to explore and learn more. My ability to forge hot steel into graceful organic forms and then combine those elements into strong structural elements or sensuous sculptures fulfills my longing to create. For me, my work has purpose, function, and beauty.

Spiral Staircase for a North Woods Home

In late 2010, I was asked to create a spiral staircase for a new construction home in northern Wisconsin. My clients wanted a 14' spiral staircase from the main floor to the loft to be the architectural centerpiece of their new home. The clients gave me a list of 27 specific flora and fauna to include in the railing. They also had several small sentimental items that they wanted incorporated into the design. What resulted was a North Woods panorama that starts under the surface of the lake, proceeds up the hill, and ends in the night sky. Atop the central log column, a bald eagle sits overlooking the lake.

This project required many different techniques including fabrication, welding, and forging solid and hollow forms.

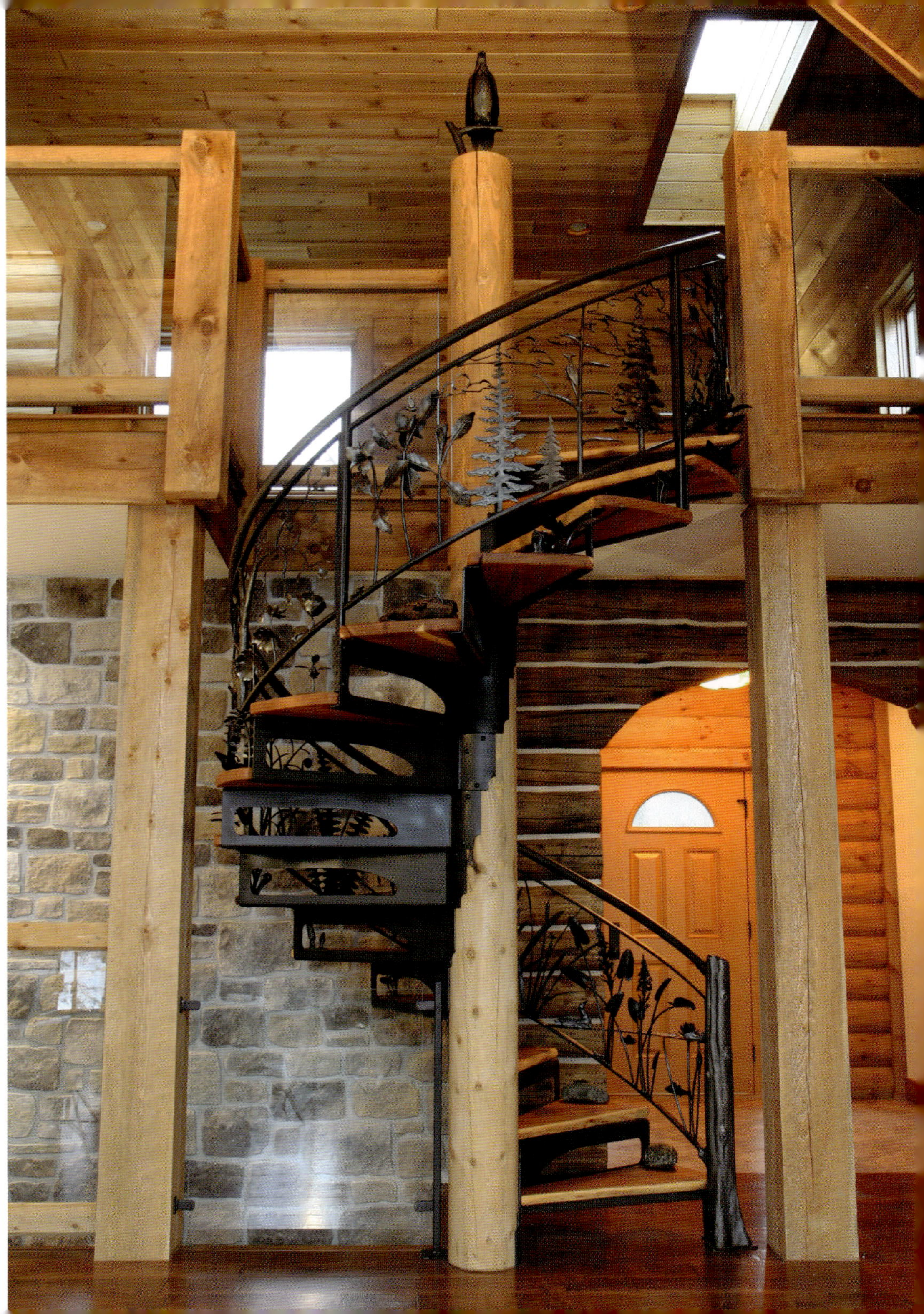

Spiral staircase for a North Woods home. Mild steel, Insta-Blak and clear lacquer finish. *Photos: Jane Benson*

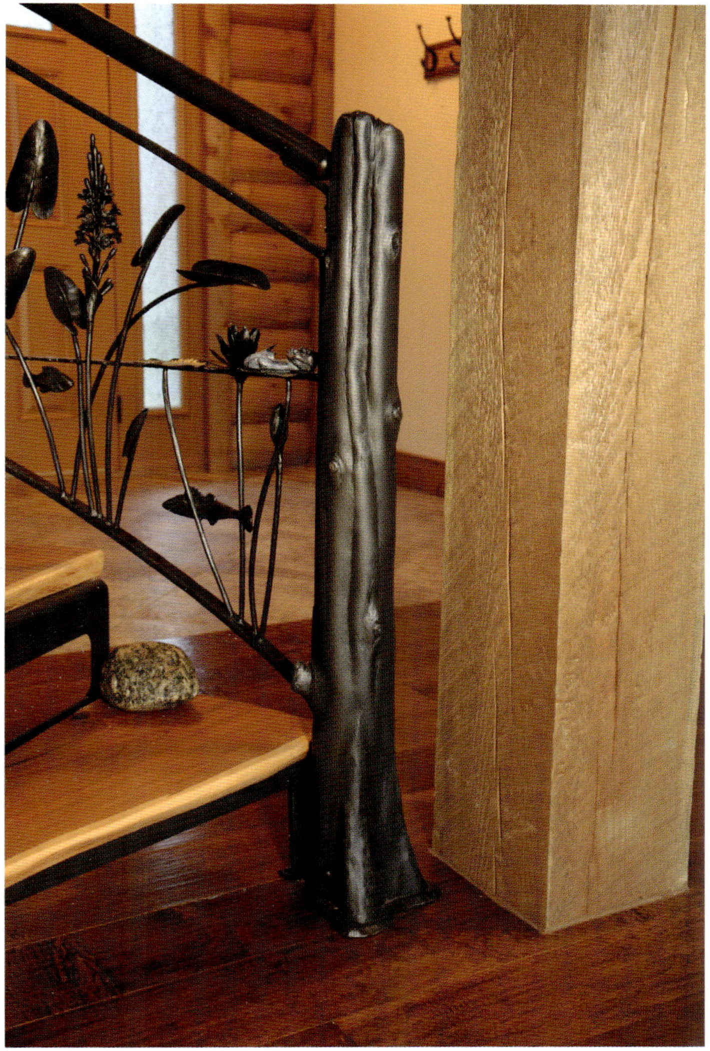

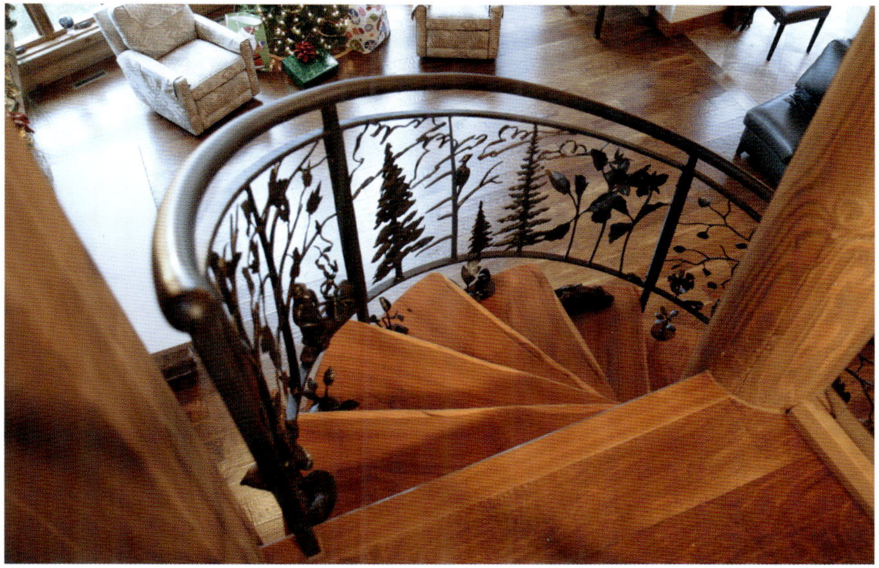

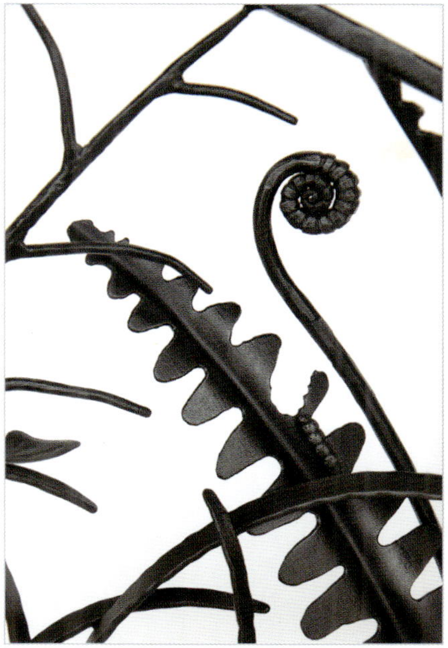

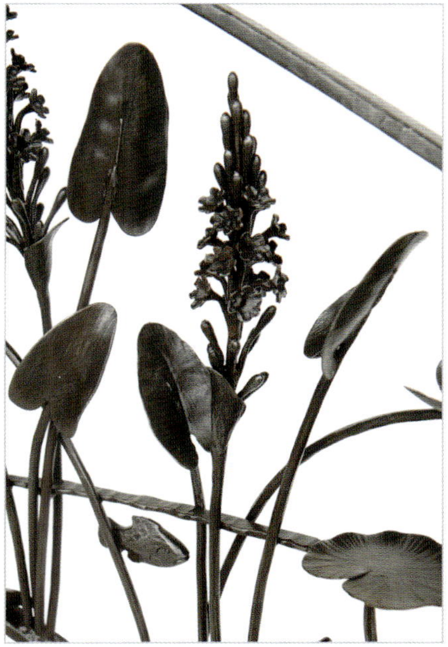

Bottom, near right: Plasma-torch-cut fern with forged fiddlehead. Notice caterpillar chewing the fern—a little surprise for the client! *Photo: Jane Benson*

Bottom, far right: Pickerelweed blossom made up of many hand-forged elements. *Photo: Jane Benson*

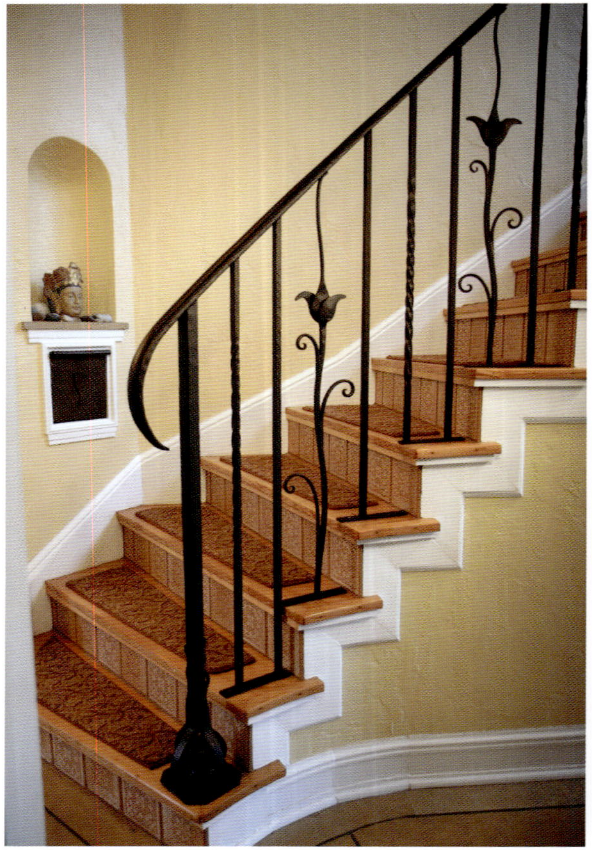

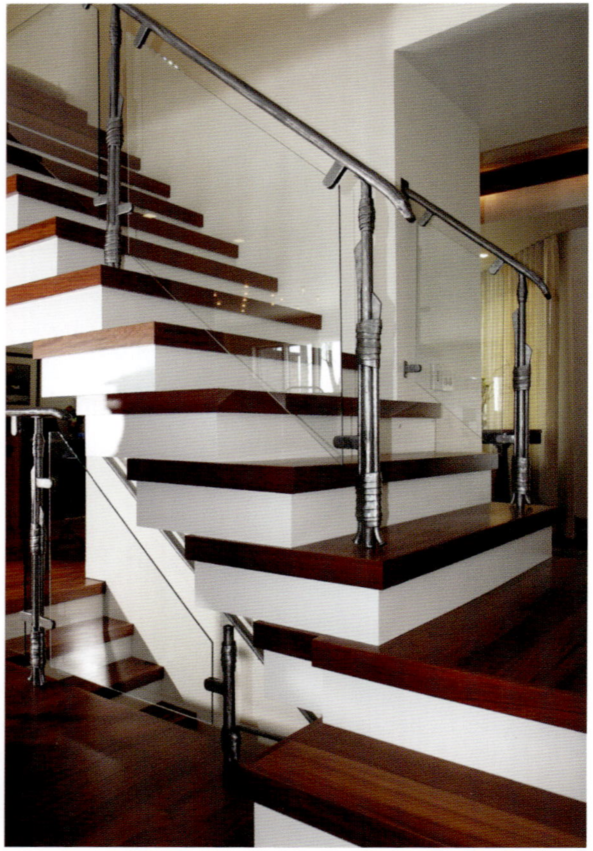

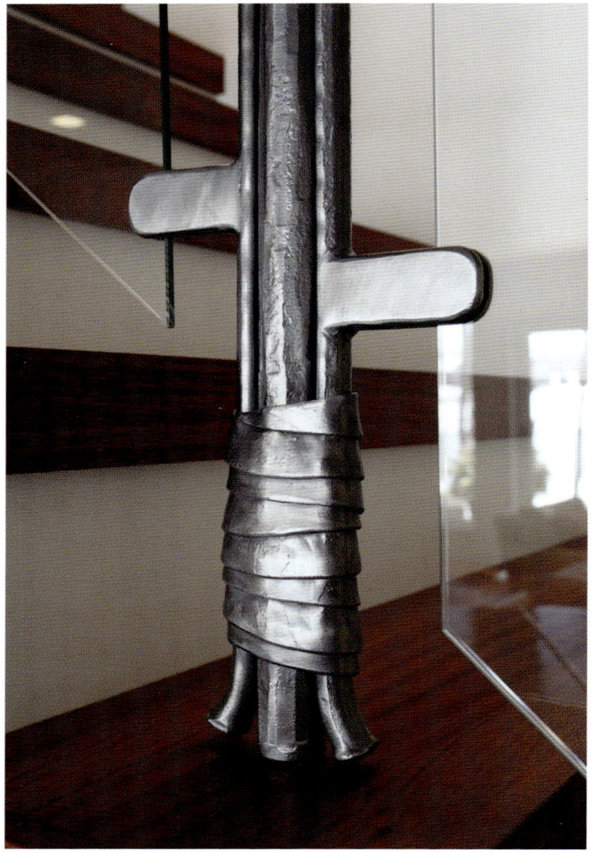

Tulip Railing

This curved railing design incorporates the tulip motif found throughout the Spanish revival home. Stones were incorporated into the newel posts.

Curved section of tulip railing on main floor landing. Mild steel, stone, antique bronze powder coat finish. *Photo: Jane Benson*

Rawhide Wraps Railing

This steel and glass balustrade expresses the homeowner's contemporary aesthetic. Upon entry to the home, the glass panels allow a view through to large windows and a beautiful riverfront outside.

"Rawhide wraps" railing. The railing incorporates forged mild steel newel posts and a handrail in a contemporary balustrade. Mild steel "rawhide wraps" bind three baluster elements. *Photos: Jane Benson*

Andrew Bibby

Black Knight Forge, Creston, British Columbia, Canada
blackknightforge.com

ARTIST'S STATEMENT

I am a journeyman welder by trade and got my start in the welding industry while still in high school. Since 2002, I've owned and operated Black Knight Welding & Fabrication in Creston, B.C., recently reorganized as Black Knight Forge. Shortly after starting my own business, I became intrigued by the opportunities to explore my artistic side and joined the local Kootenay Blacksmiths' Association. Since then I have drawn from the considerable resources and personal experiences of my fellow members in developing my own personal style. I have also been able to use my experience in the structural aspect of metal work to make pieces of art that are not only beautiful, but functional as well.

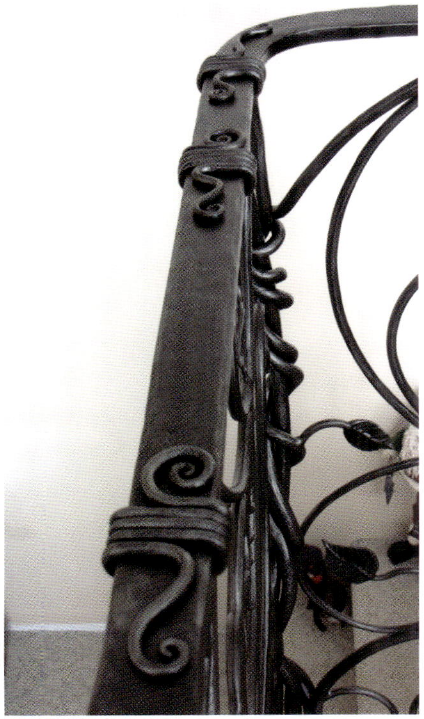

Vine Railing

The vines and leaves of this railing are made of solid ⅞" round bar. The railing is finished with a 50-50 mixture of linseed oil and a linseed-oil-based black paint, giving the railing a black look without diminishing the texture of the forged metal.

Vine railing. 2011. Round bar, linseed oil, linseed-oil-based black paint.

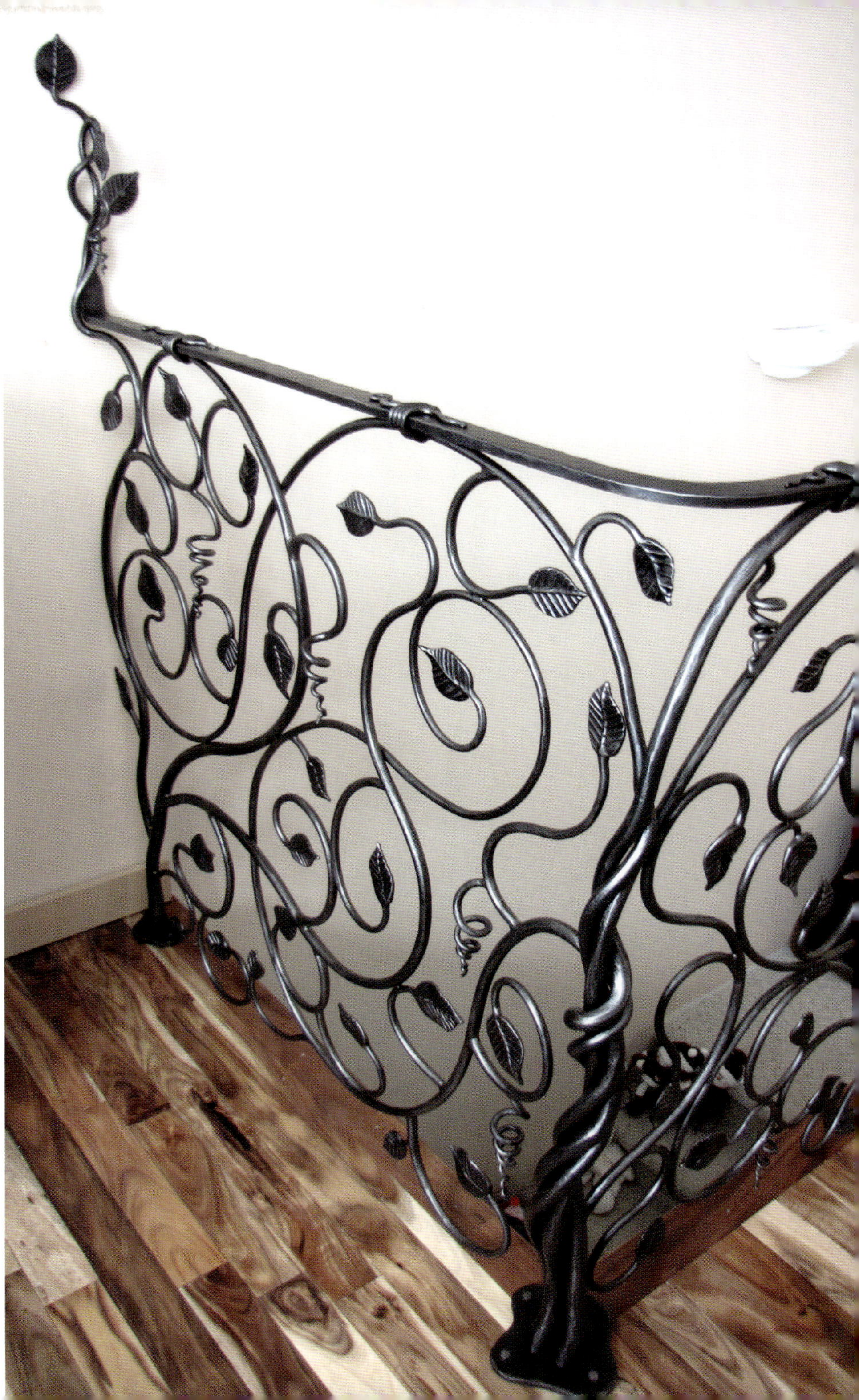

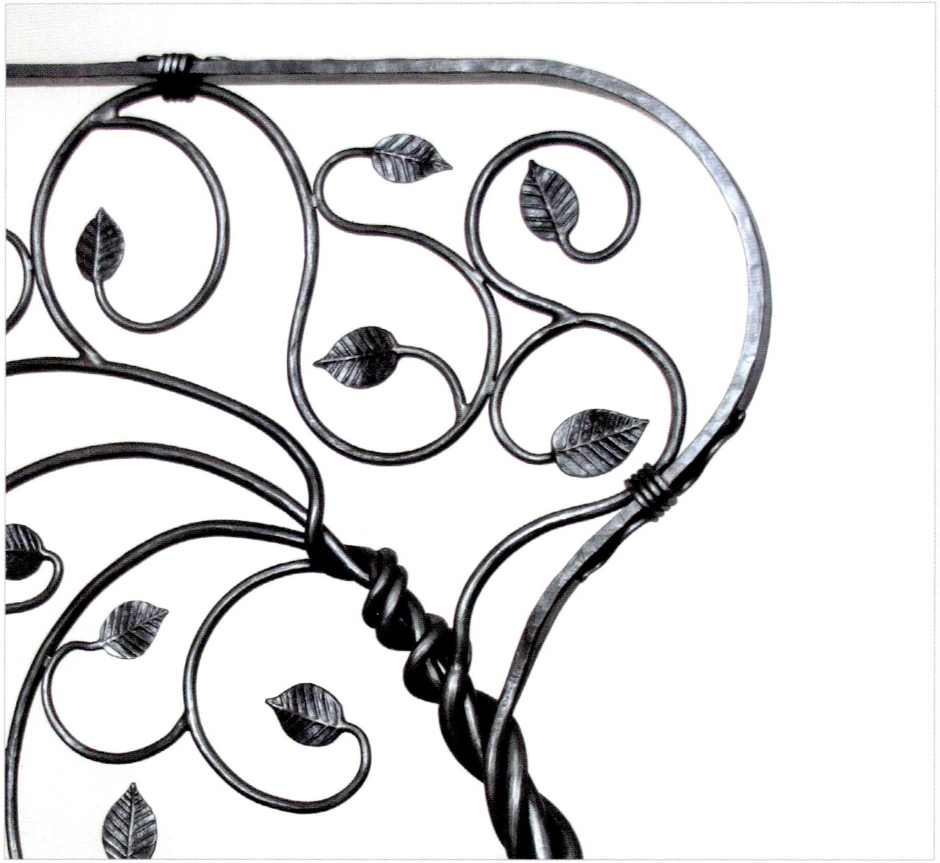

Detail: Vine railing. 2011.
Round bar, linseed oil, linseed-oil-based black paint.

Anchor Door Knocker

The anchor is heat-colored and brass-brushed with a clear lacquer top coat. The rope is also colored with brushed brass and tied with a bowline to complete the nautical feel.

Anchor door knocker. 2011. 16" h.

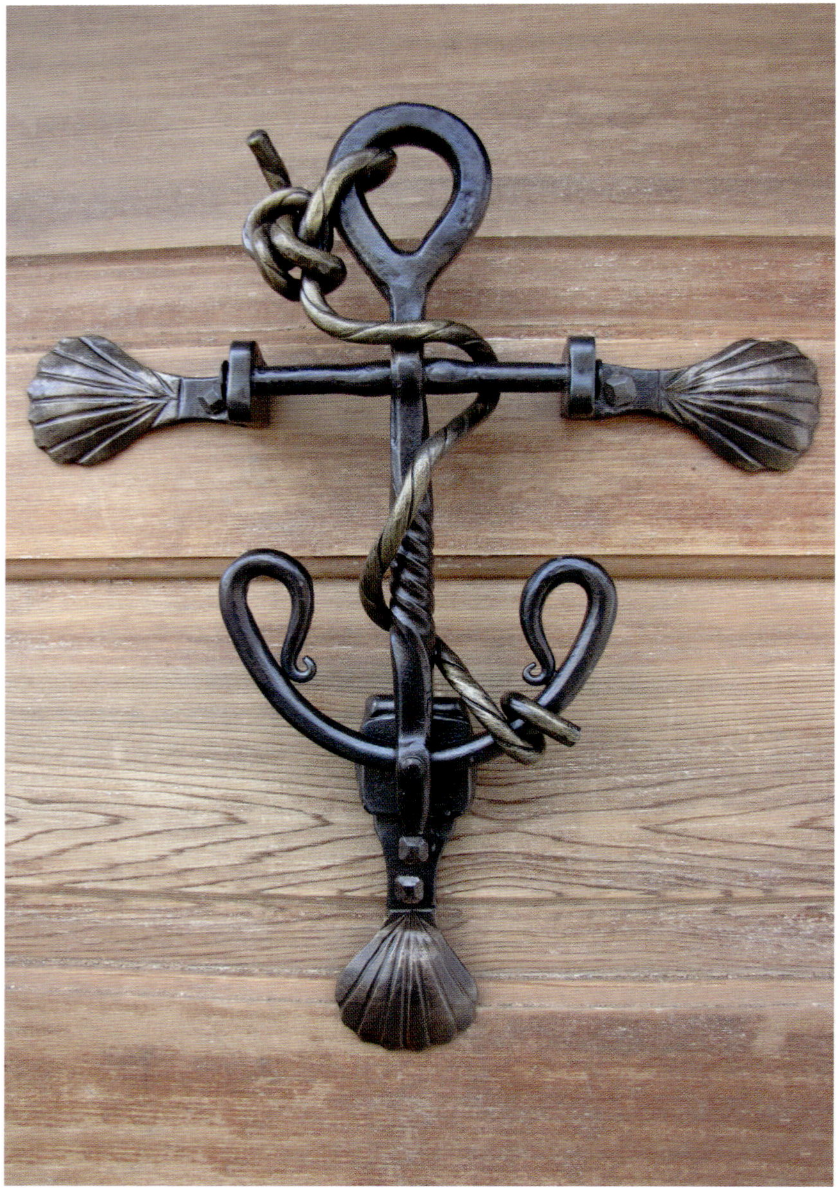

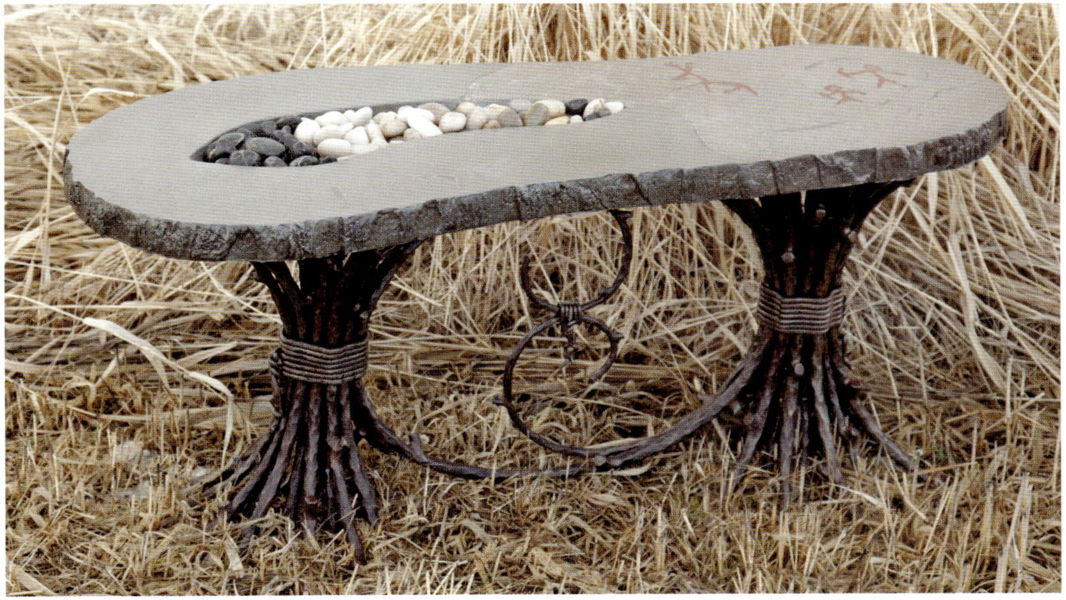

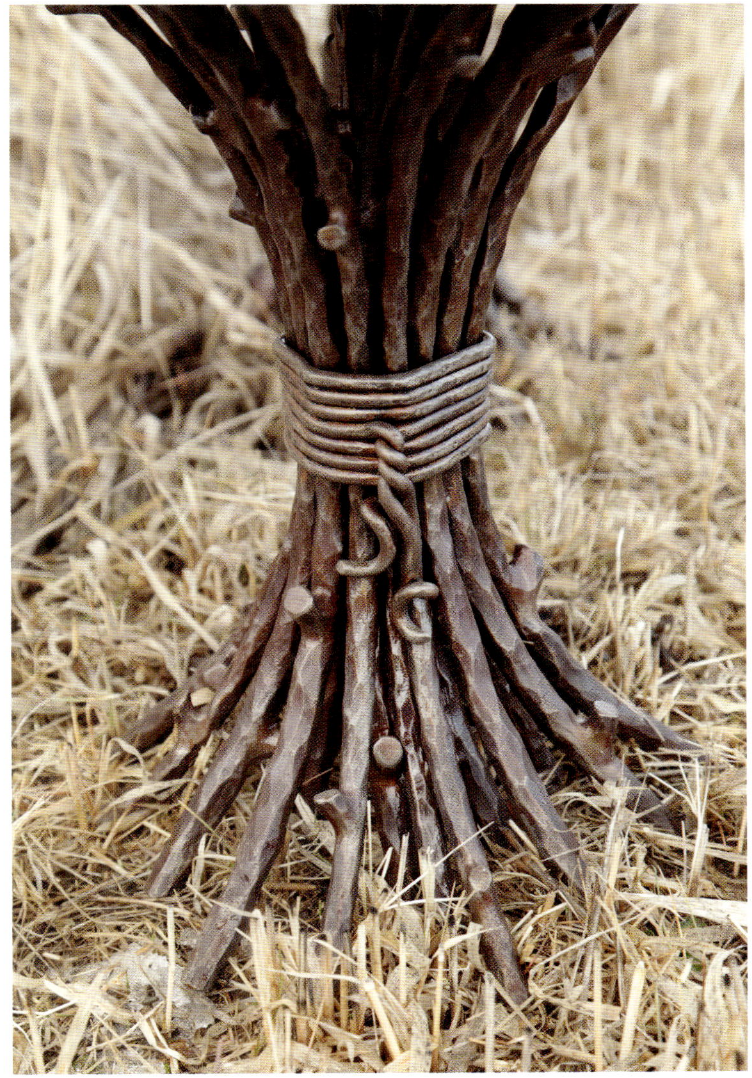

Vision Quest Fire Table

This table is made with a base of bunched twigs. The twigs are forged from ⅝" solid round bar and coated with a mixture of salt, vinegar, and hydrogen peroxide to give it a rust color, then finished with linseed oil to seal in the rust color and enhance the forged texture. The tabletop, made by Legend Rock Designer Concrete, is concrete with North American cave paintings and has a fire pit incorporated into the surface.

Vision quest fire table. 2011.

Margie Bivens

Austin, Texas
Margie.Bivens@gmail.com

ARTIST'S STATEMENT

This tree, *The Butterfly Effect*, was commissioned by a lovely daughter in memory of her mother who adored butterflies. It was installed in the butterfly garden of the Tye Preston Memorial Library in Canyon Lake, Texas. It was designed from five large panels of plate steel, which were then crafted to resemble a native Red Bud tree. As the piece evolves from left to right, the detail intensifies and the leaves eventually hint at becoming butterflies. At nearly 9′ tall and 13′ wide, the scale balances with the surrounding landscape, and the layering of the rust finish gives the illusion of texture, making the steel look right at home with nature. The five panels were staggered to lend a sense of depth and dimension, allowing the viewer a new incarnation of the tree from every vantage point.

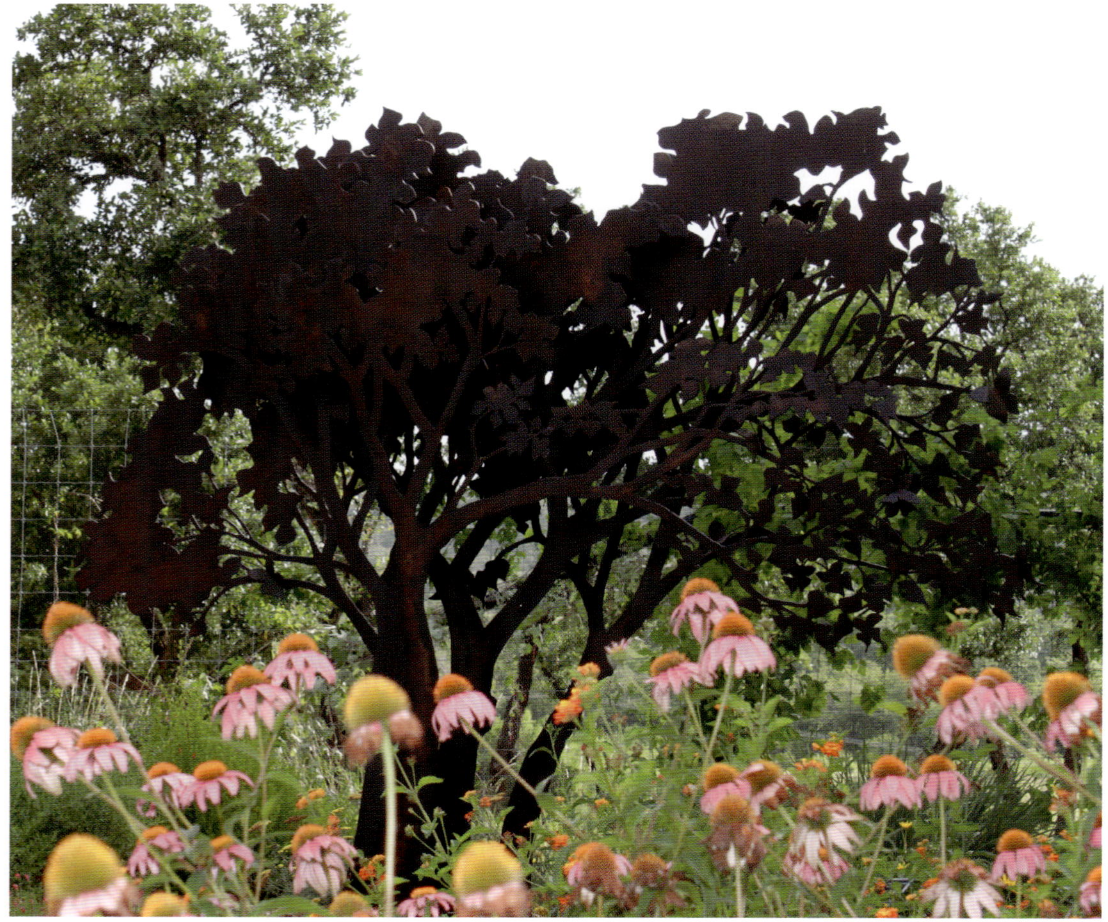

The Butterfly Effect. 2013. Sculpture. Steel. 108″ x 156″.
Photos: Jennifer Driskell

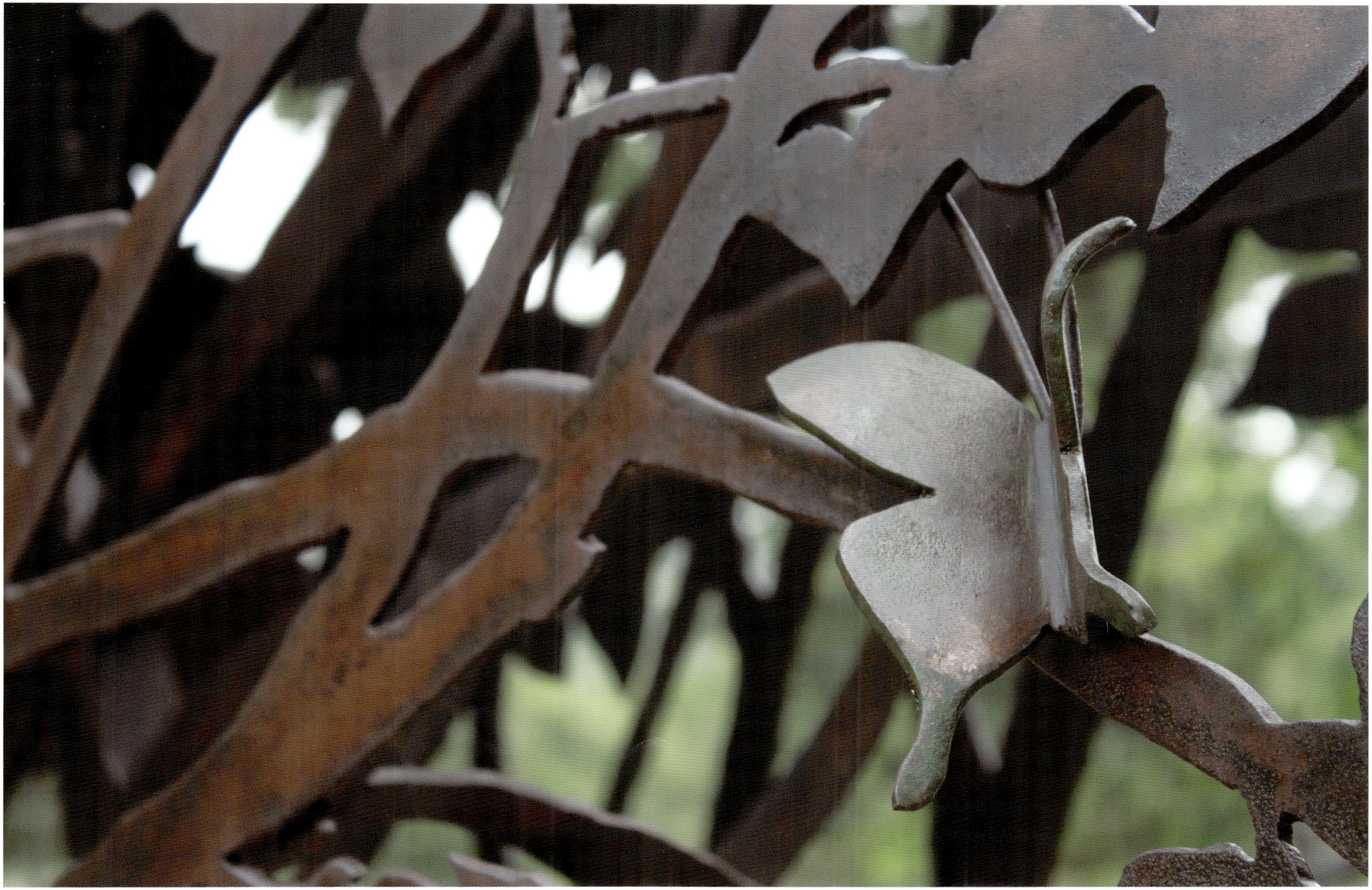

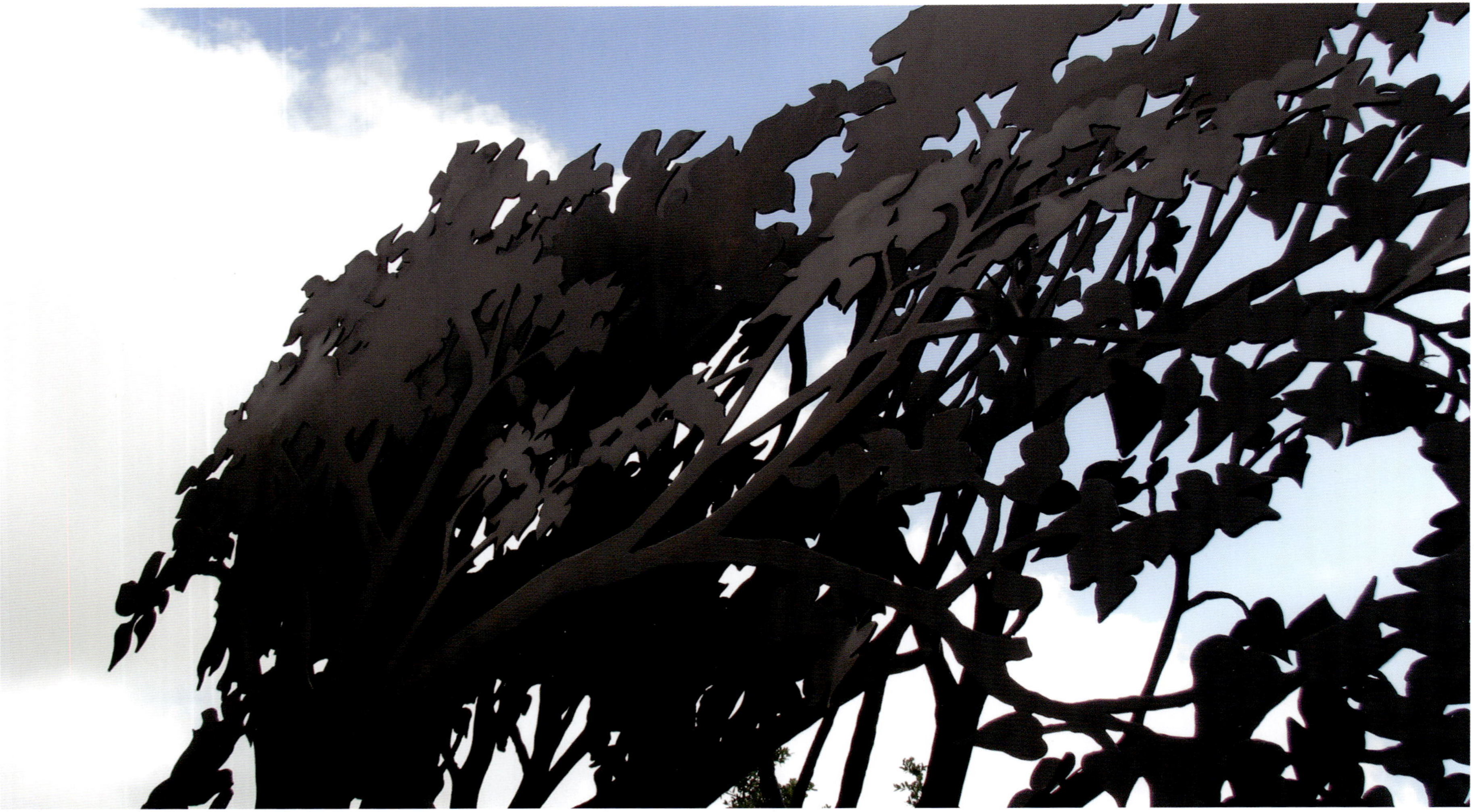

The Butterfly Effect. 2013. Sculpture. Steel. 108″ x 156″.

M. Craig Campbell

Saskatoon, Saskatchewan, Canada
http://m.craigcampbell.ca/

ARTIST'S STATEMENT

This is what my wife says about me: "You create because you have to create. You like the feel of metal, you like the potential in metal. You like simplicity in your designs because the metal itself has something to say. You like having a lot of tools and a studio to spend time in. You like the noise, the smells, the fire, and the weight of what you do. You like to open the doors and let people wander in. You like to talk about what you do. You never tire of telling people about the material, techniques, joinery, and finishes. You like to teach. You want to learn."

Creatures of the Night Herd

The inspiration for these "creatures" came during a group critique on a completely different project. Each one is forged from a single piece of pipe.

Creatures of the Night Herd. Sculpture. 2013. Forged and fabricated. Steel, copper, clear paint. 8"h, 9"h, and 21"h. *Photo: Trent Watts*

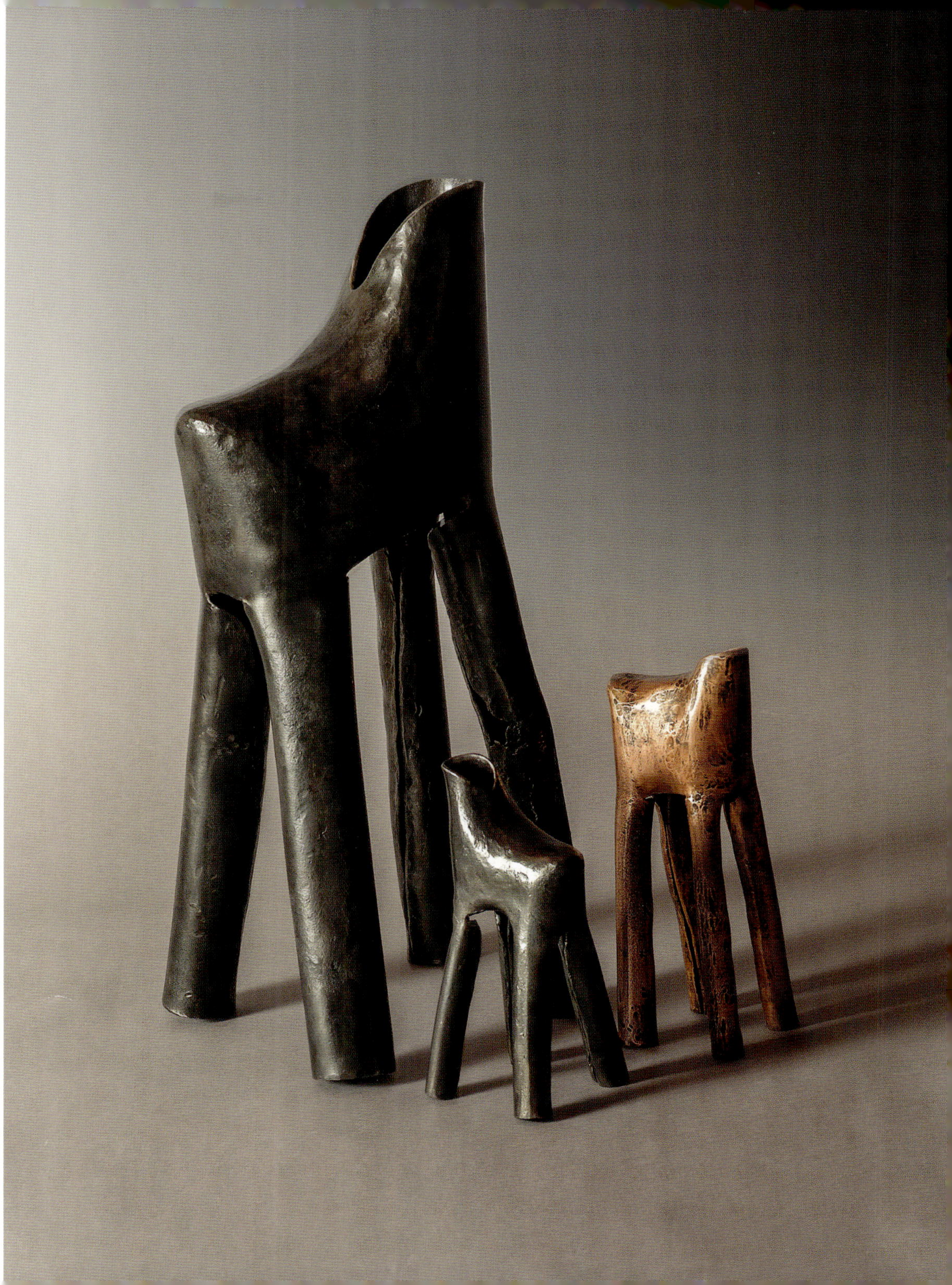

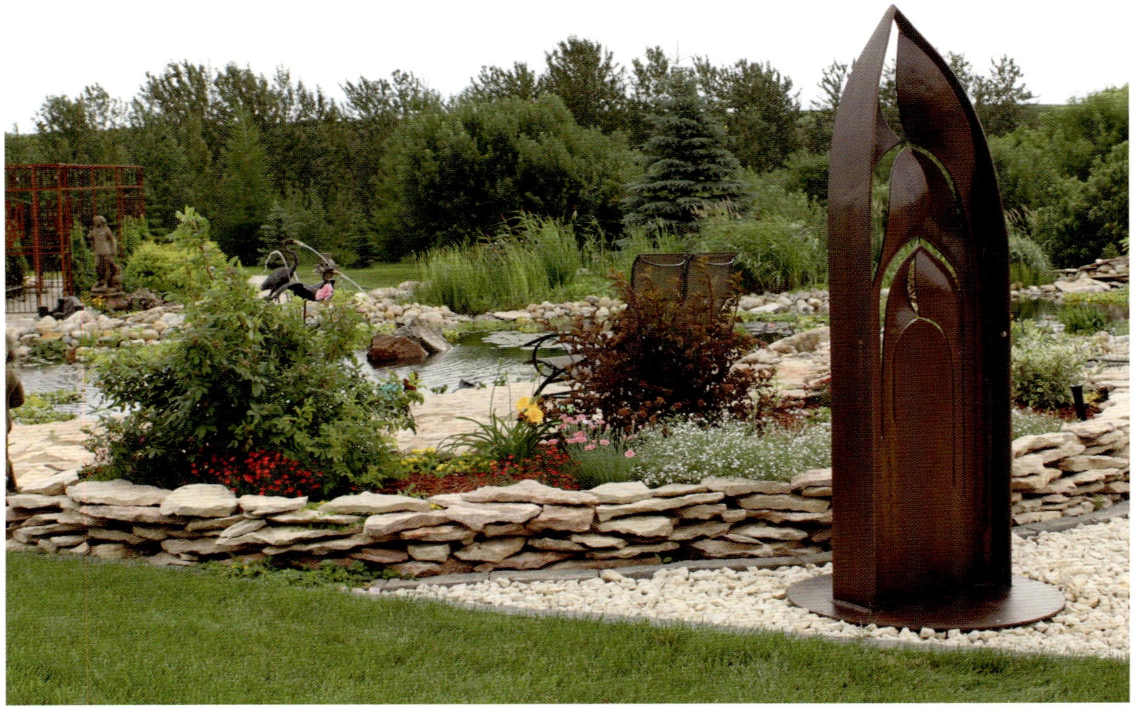

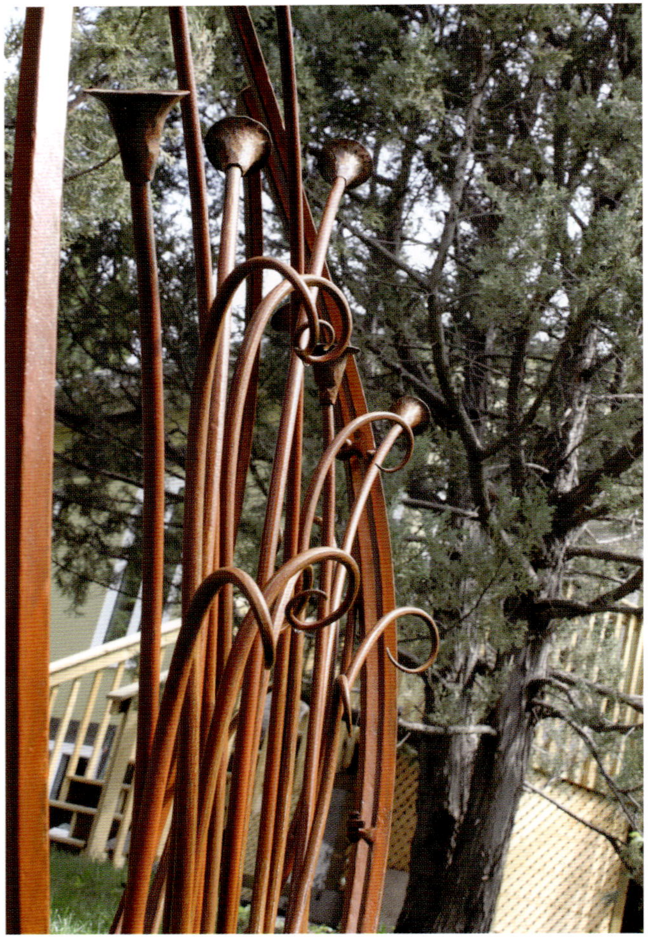

Cathedral

Stalled at a critical design point, I asked colleagues to visit my work studio for a consultation session. Their comments inspired this sculpture, a new direction for my work with structural I-beam.

Cathedral. Sculpture. 2011.
Forged and fabricated. Steel, natural rust patina, tung oil. 60" x 20" x 5" on a 30" diameter base.
Photo: M. Craig Campbell

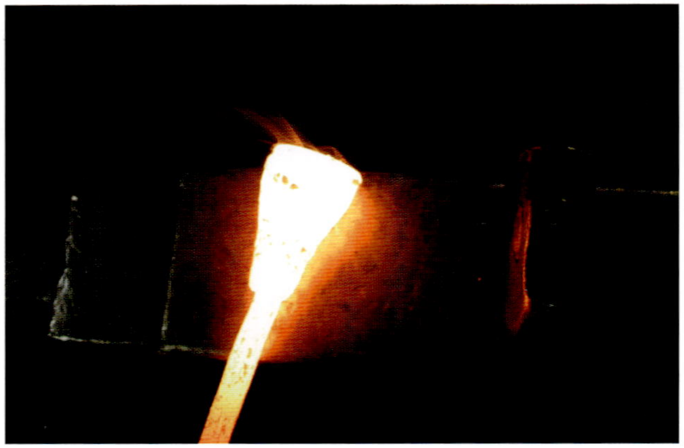

Garden Screen

A client's request for a "trumpet handrail" inspired this flower form and then this garden sculpture.

Garden screen. Forged and fabricated. Steel, natural rust patina. 47"h x 74"w x 22"d. *Photo: M. Craig Campbell*

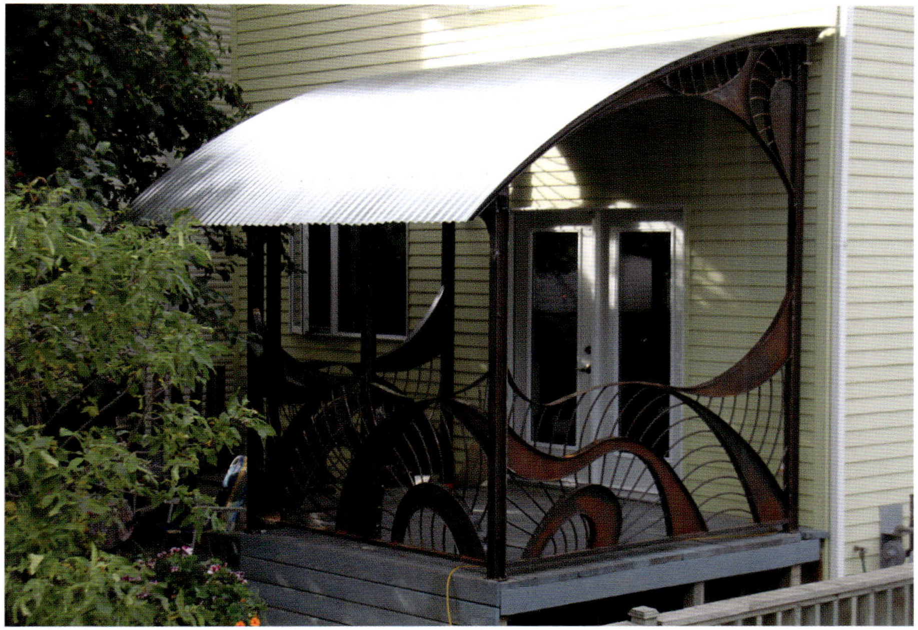

Gazebo

A good example of creative fabrication, this piece has very little forge work.

Gazebo. 2011. Fabricated and forged. Steel, galvanized steel. 125″ x 135″ x 110″. *Photo: M. Craig Campbell*

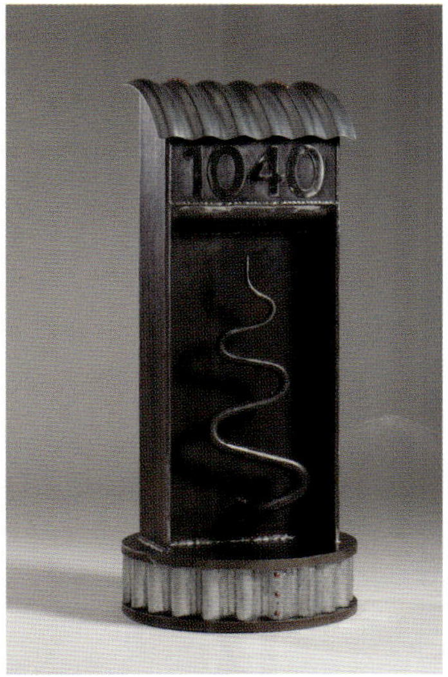

Mailbox

The fourth outdoor I-beam project for a favorite client.

Mailbox. Sculpture. 2013. Forged and fabricated. Steel, stainless steel, galvanized steel, copper. 46″h on a 19″diameter base. *Photo: Kevin Hogarth*

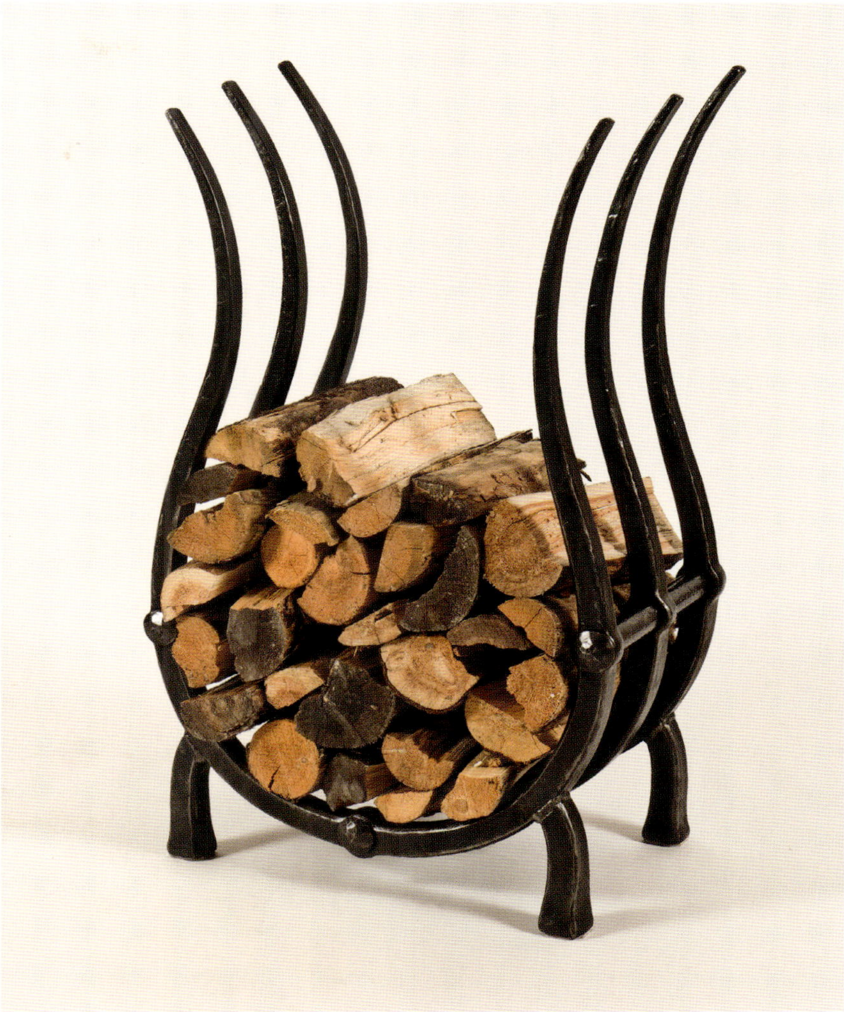

Wood basket

Forged 1 ½″ bar stock with 1″ rivets.

Wood basket. 2011. Forged and fabricated. Steel. 46″h x 15″d x 27″w. *Photo: Trent Watts*

Scott Cawood

Sharpsburg, MD
www.CawoodArt.com

ARTIST'S STATEMENT

Rise Up was commissioned for the Center for Joint Surgery & Sports Medicine in Hagerstown, Maryland.

Resurrection, Revival, and Reincarnation: My work centers around the concept that everything is in a constant state of transformation and that change is the natural state of the universe. Deterioration is simply the process of everything returning to dust.

I use steel, because its qualities speak to me, most especially scrap steel because I feel it has no equal in visually expressing my ideas on transformation. In *Rise Up,* I used derelict steel heating oil tanks to further the idea of overcoming challenges including deterioration, in order to move forward. To, in a sense, rise from the ashes, or the scrap pile, and tenaciously move forward past the obstacles we encounter in life. The piece attempts to express the energy and emotion of positive transformation.

I used mostly found auto parts to represent mechanical joint replacements. I had to be careful to walk the fine line between mechanically repaired human beings and cyborgs. It was imperative that I maintain the "human" aspect in the figures.

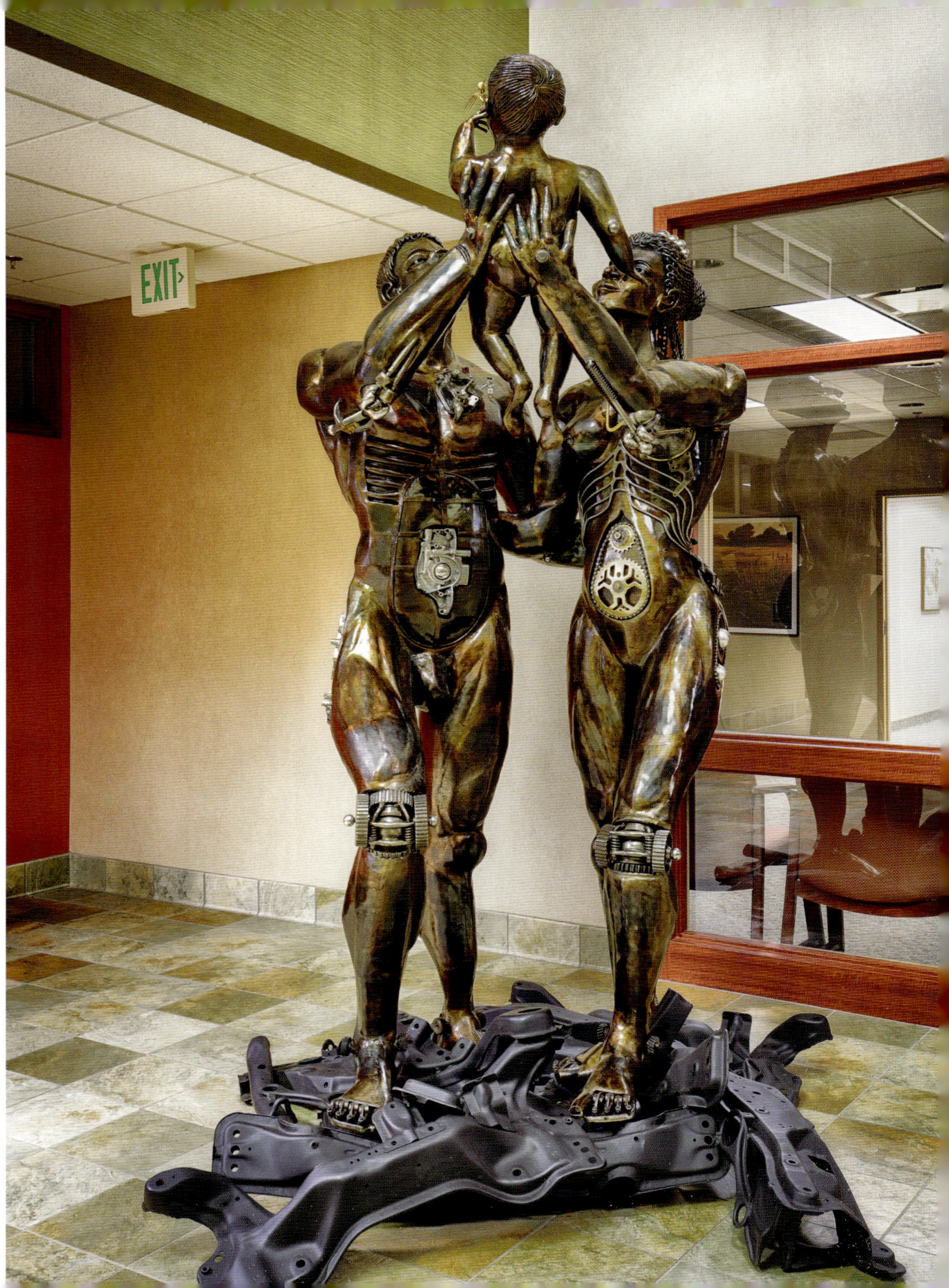

Rise Up. Sculpture. 2013. ¼" steel rod, sections of derelict steel heating oil tanks, found auto parts, medical prothesis. Burnt oil finish. 10'h. *Photos by C. Kurt Holter*

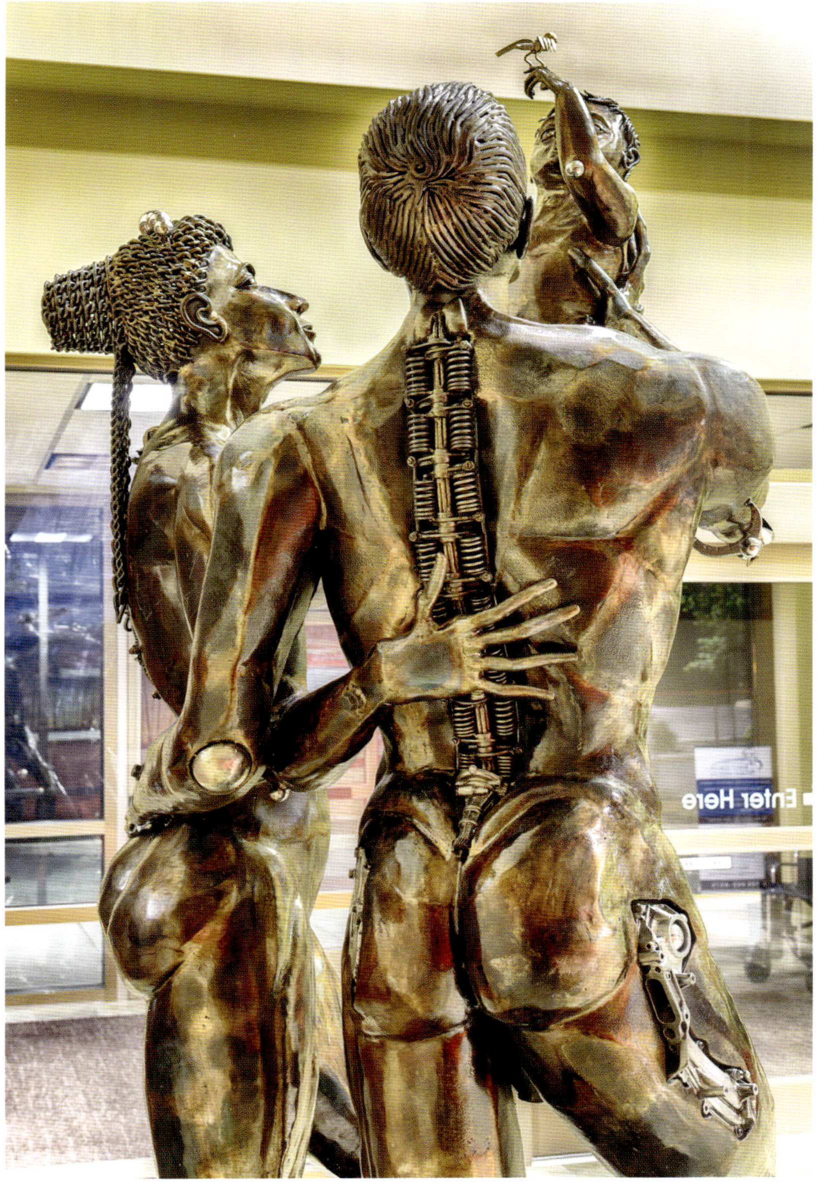
Enter Here

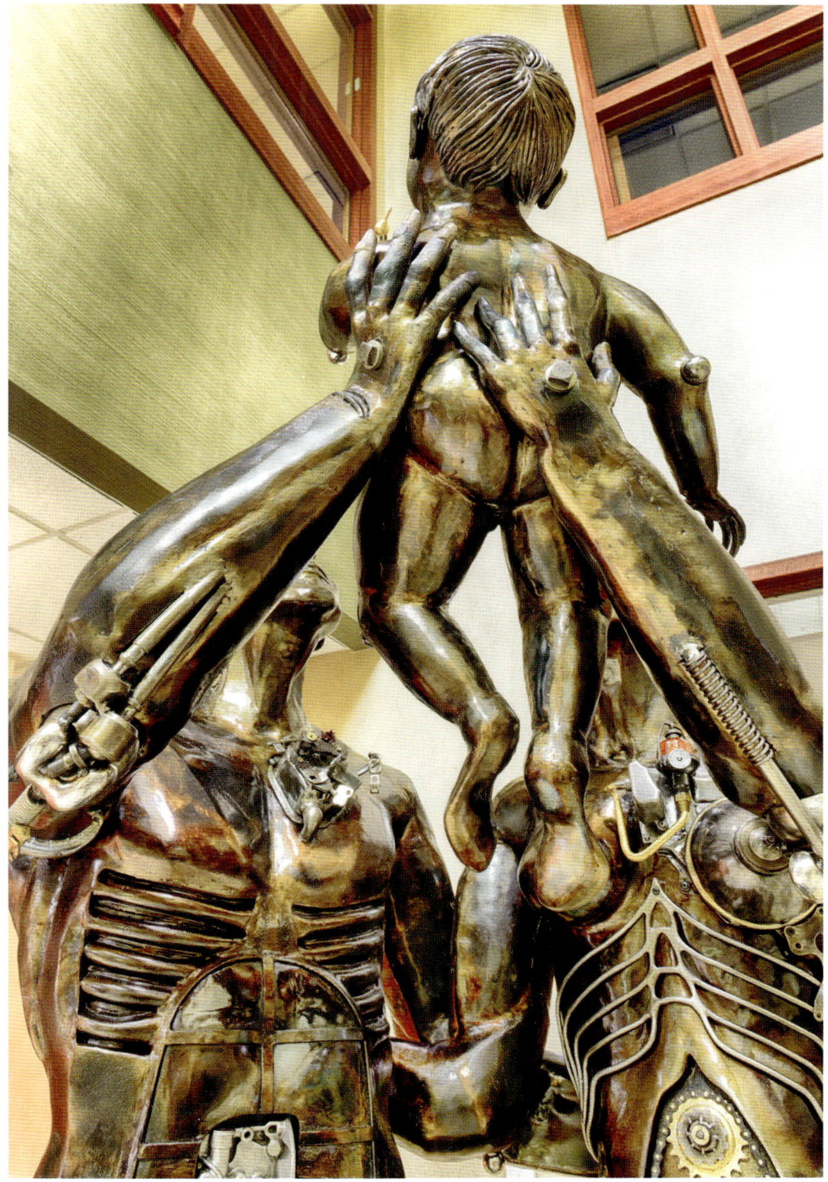

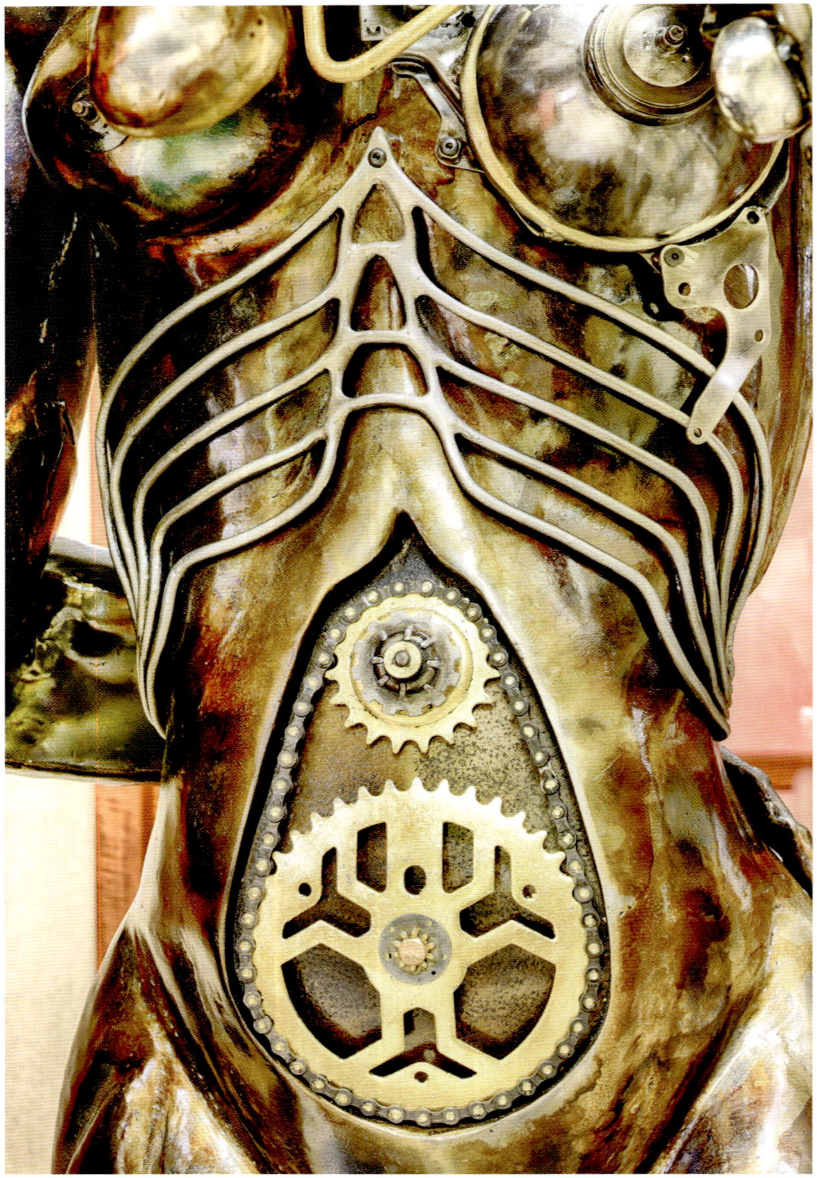

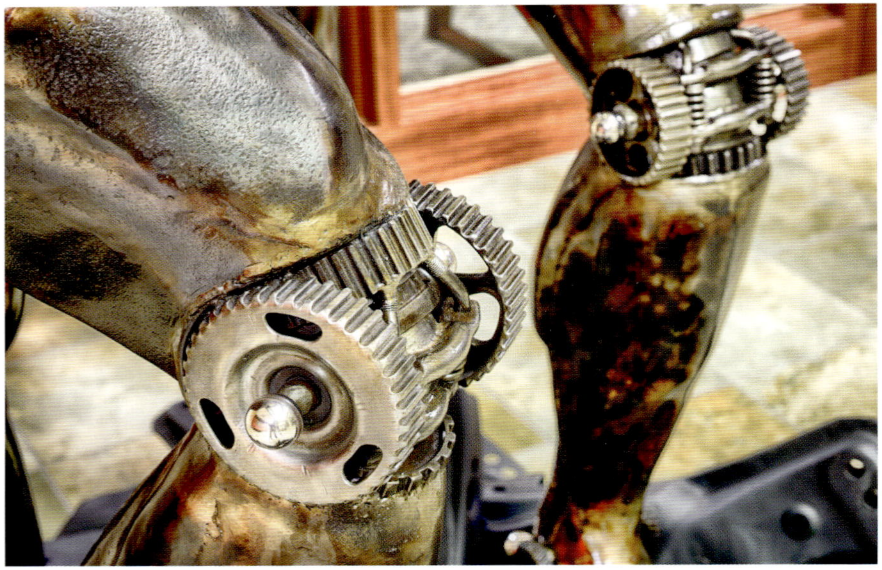

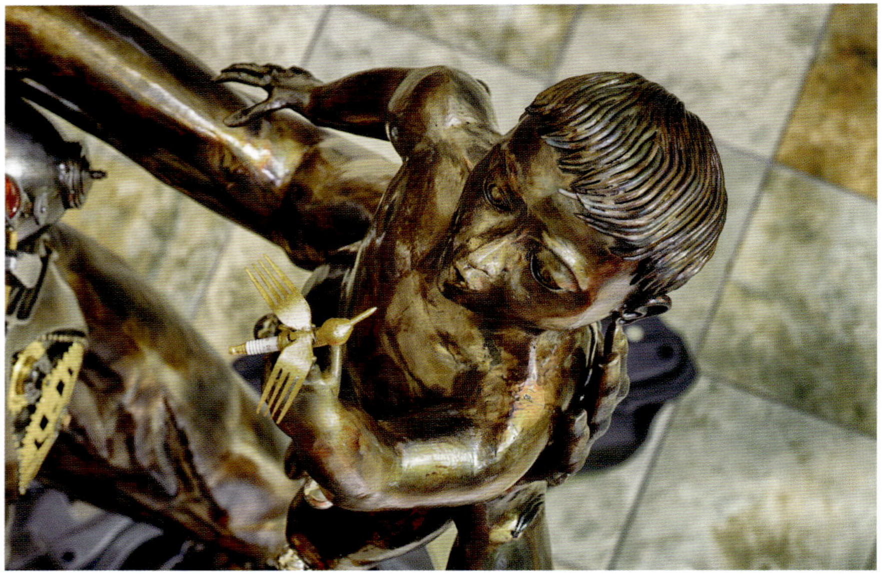

Andrew R. Chambers, Jr.

ARC Iron Creations, Buffalo, NY
www.arcironcreations.com

ARTIST'S STATEMENT

I forge for the love of forging: to create works, functional and non, that will become conversation pieces; to make items of high quality that easily separate themselves from the mass produced.

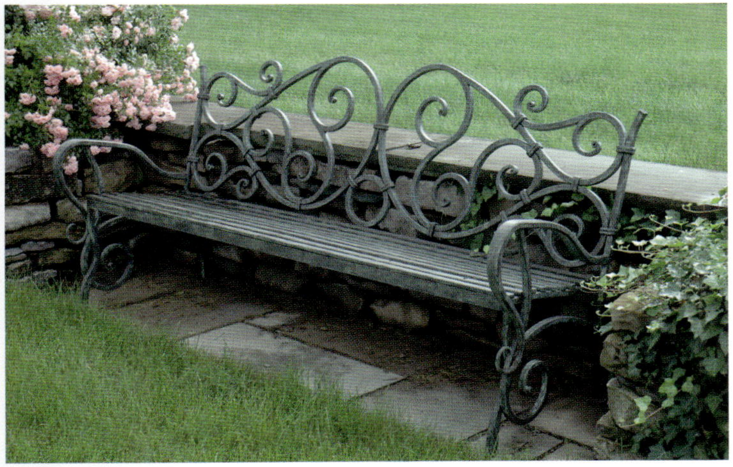

Iron Bench

This bench was built at a private residence for the Junior League of Buffalo, New York, designer show home.

Iron bench. 2009. Hand forged steel, painted patina finish. 6′.
Photo: Arc Iron Creations

Vortex

This sculpture was also built for the Junior League of Buffalo, New York, designer show home.

Vortex. Sculpture. 2009.

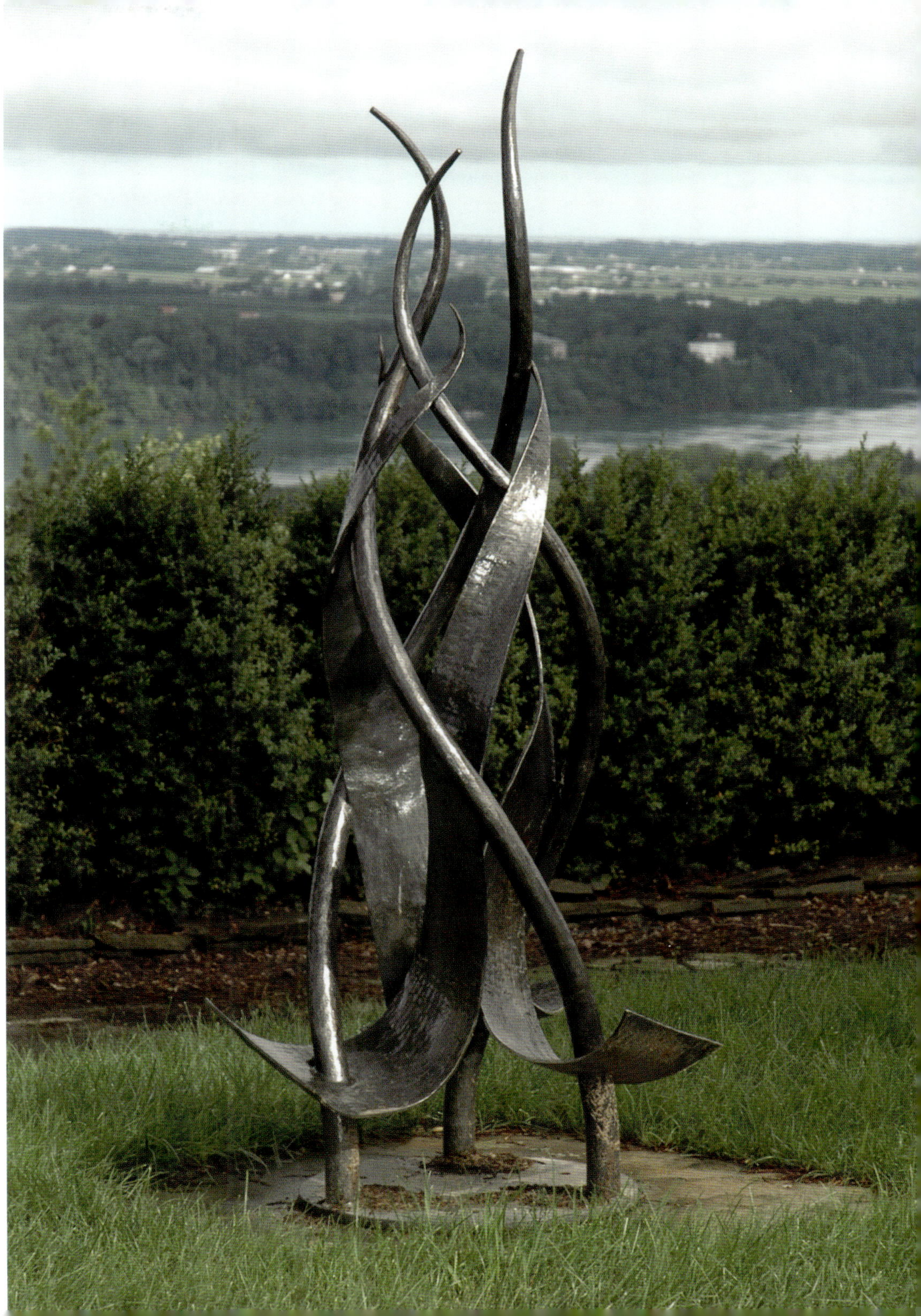

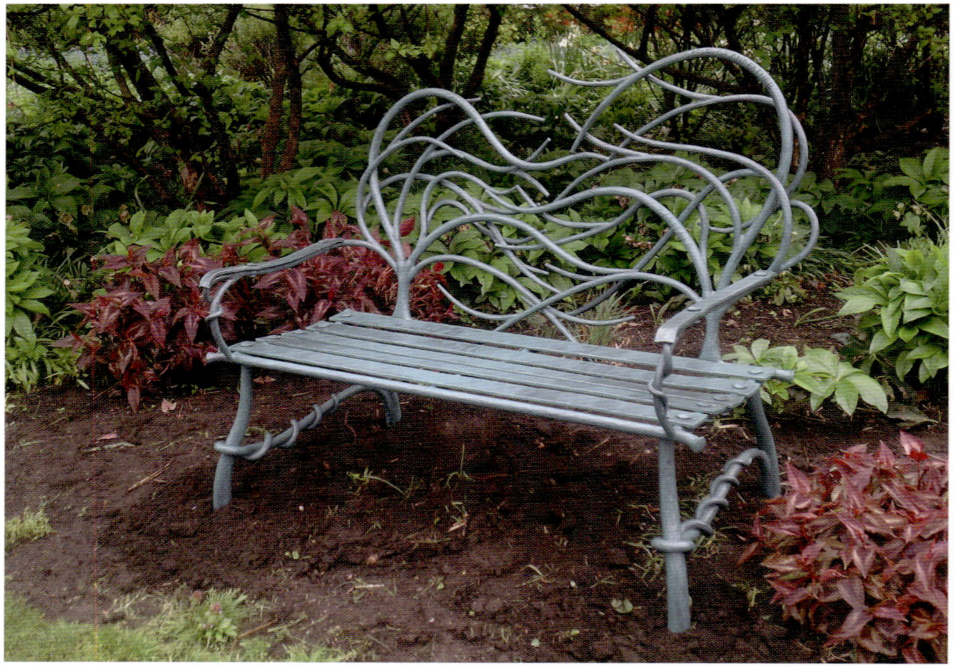

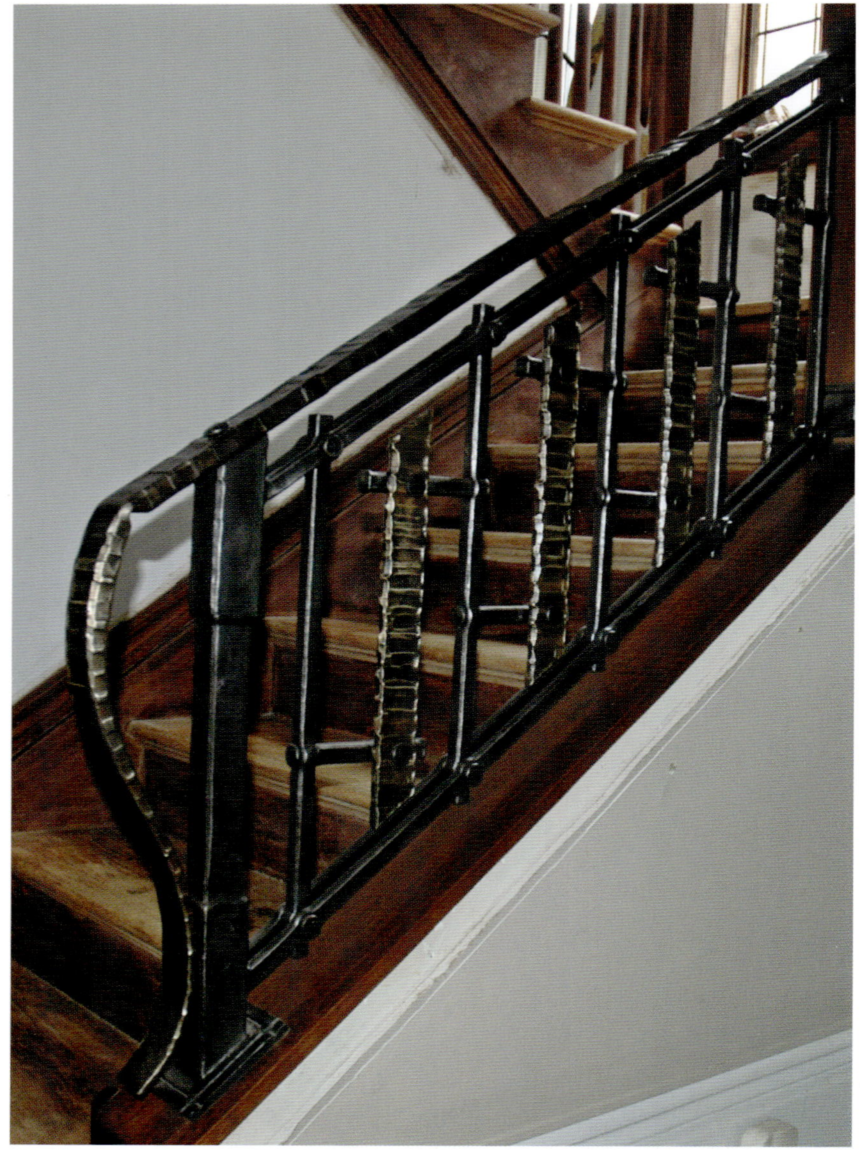

Memorial Bench

This bench in the Buffalo Botanical Gardens was a private commission.

Andrew R. Chambers, Jr. memorial bench. 2010. Hand-forged steel, painted verdigris patina. 4'l x 40"h. *Photo: Arc Iron Creations*

Arts & Crafts-style Railing

Created for a private residence, this railing features hand-forged steel and bronze with a natural finish.

Arts & Crafts-style railing. 2013. 50"l. Photo: Arc Iron Creations.

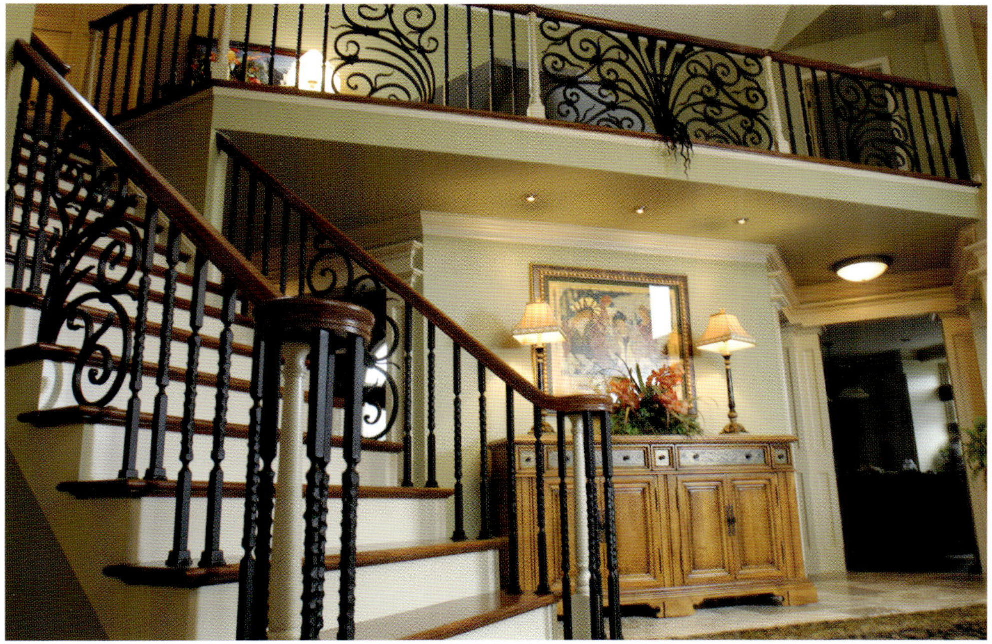

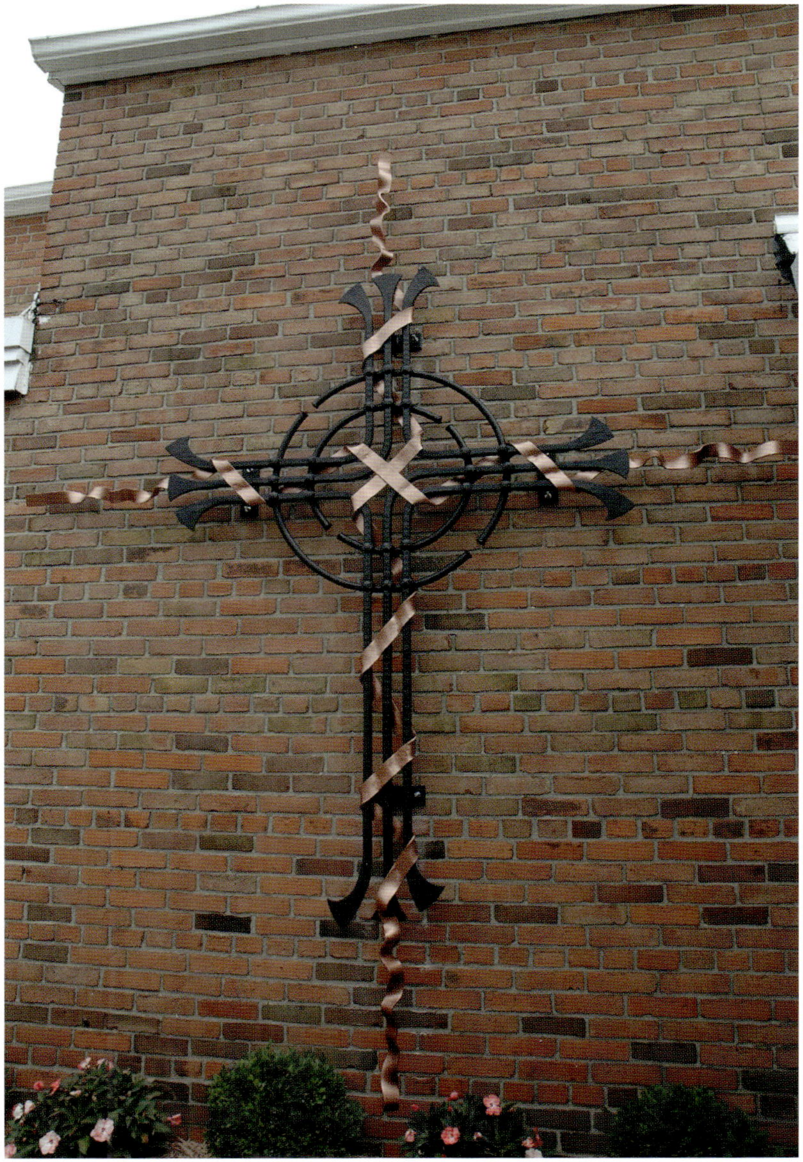

Calla Lily Railing

Created for a private residence, this railing features a hand-forged baluster with an accent scroll section with a black powder coat finish.

Calla lily railing. 2011. *Photo: Onion Studios*

Cross

This cross hangs at the Amherst Presbyterian Church in Amherst, New York.

Cross. 2012. Hand-forged, black finish and copper highlighted ribbon. 11'h x 9'w. *Photo: Arc Iron Creations*

Monica Coyne

Redway, California
www.monicacoyneartistblacksmith.com

ARTIST'S STATEMENT

The first time I put a simple bar of steel into the fire, watched it become yellow hot and changed it with my hammer, I was possessed. Part of myself flows through the hammer and into the steel. I hand forge many of the tools that I use to move the metal so every mark and form that is created has my accent. My favorite metal to work with is iron or mild steel. The beauty of steel emerges when you heat and move it by hand.

When I create a piece, my goal is to honor the art with clean, solid technique. Although my design is contemporary, I try to use traditional methods of shaping and joinery to create the structure and balance of a piece. The ferrous metal, after having been worked, when cold, still portrays the power that was needed to coax it into form. Yet, a finished piece also denies its hard, rigid origins by becoming something soft, fluid, and organic. I pull an idea from my experience, from stories, and from inanimate and living things. I have lived in rural Humboldt County for thirty years and I am heavily influenced by the natural world that surrounds me.

Diamond Point Chandelier

All of the parts of this chandelier are held together by gravity. The hook at the top runs down and becomes the point at the bottom. All of the other parts fit and rest on the shoulder of the diamond-shaped point and are banded tight.

Diamond point chandelier.

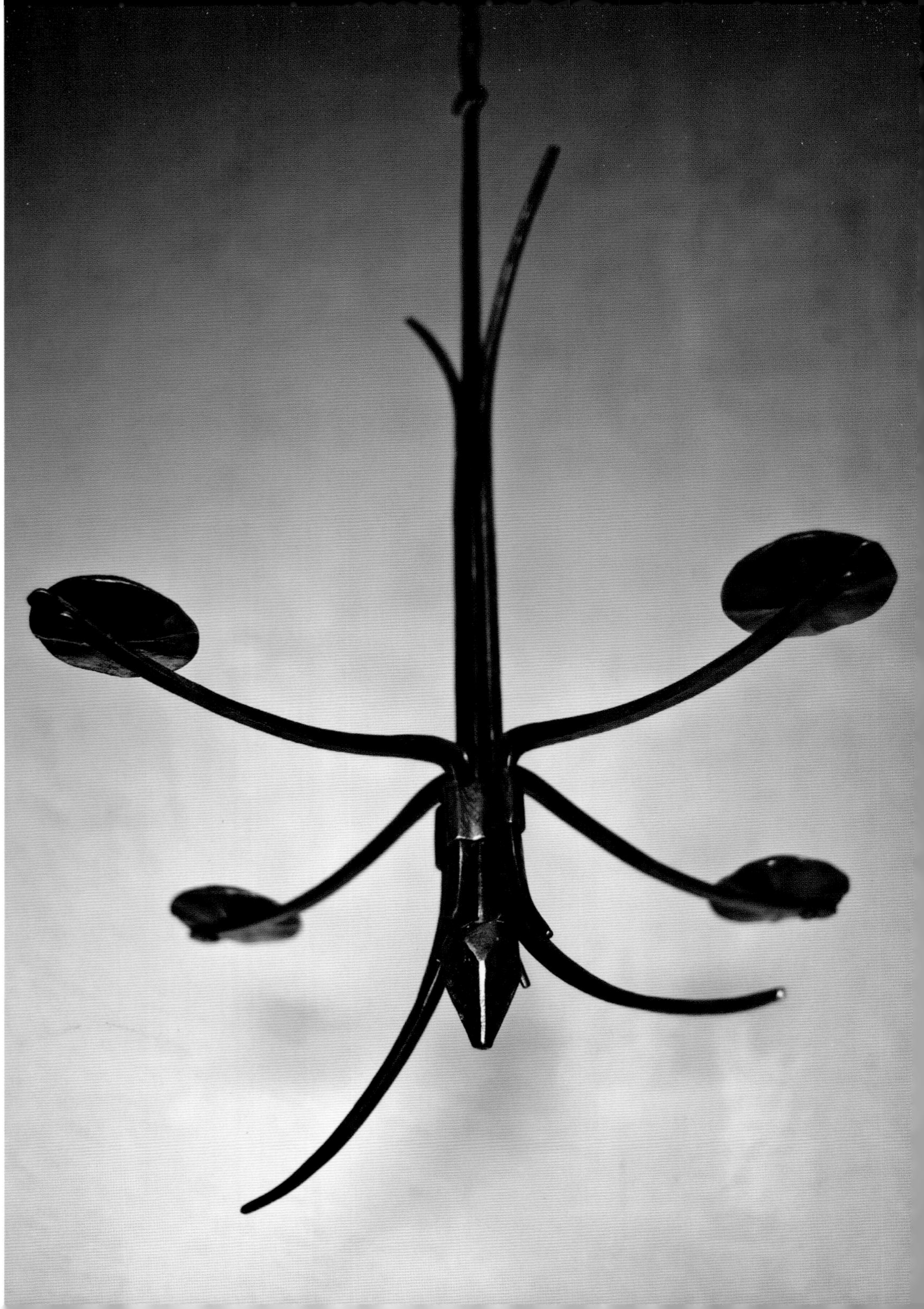

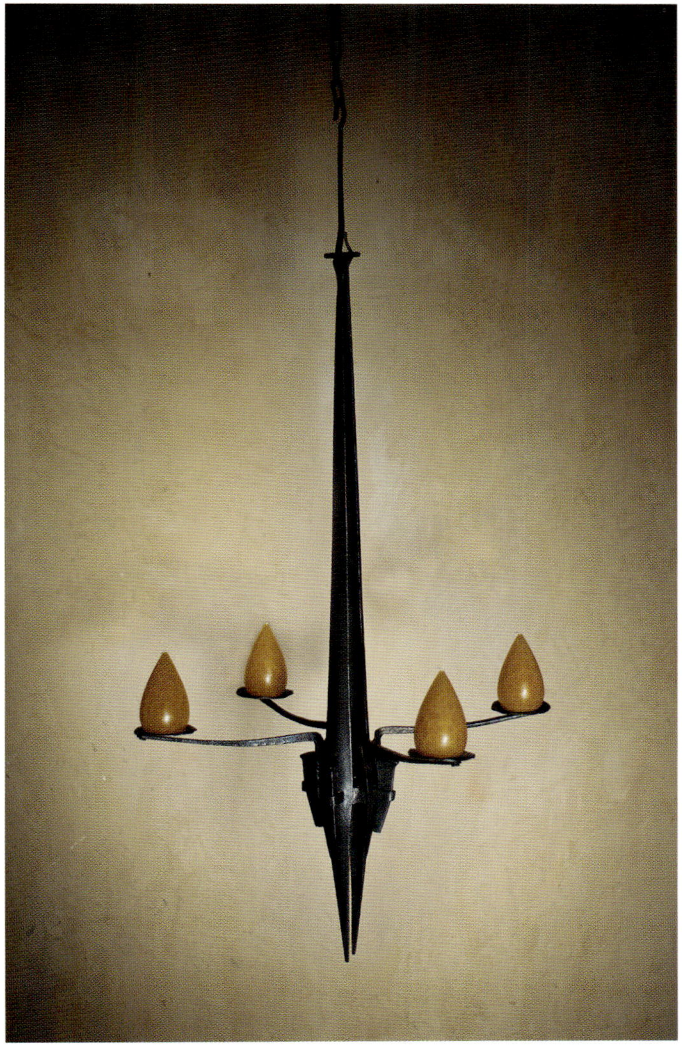

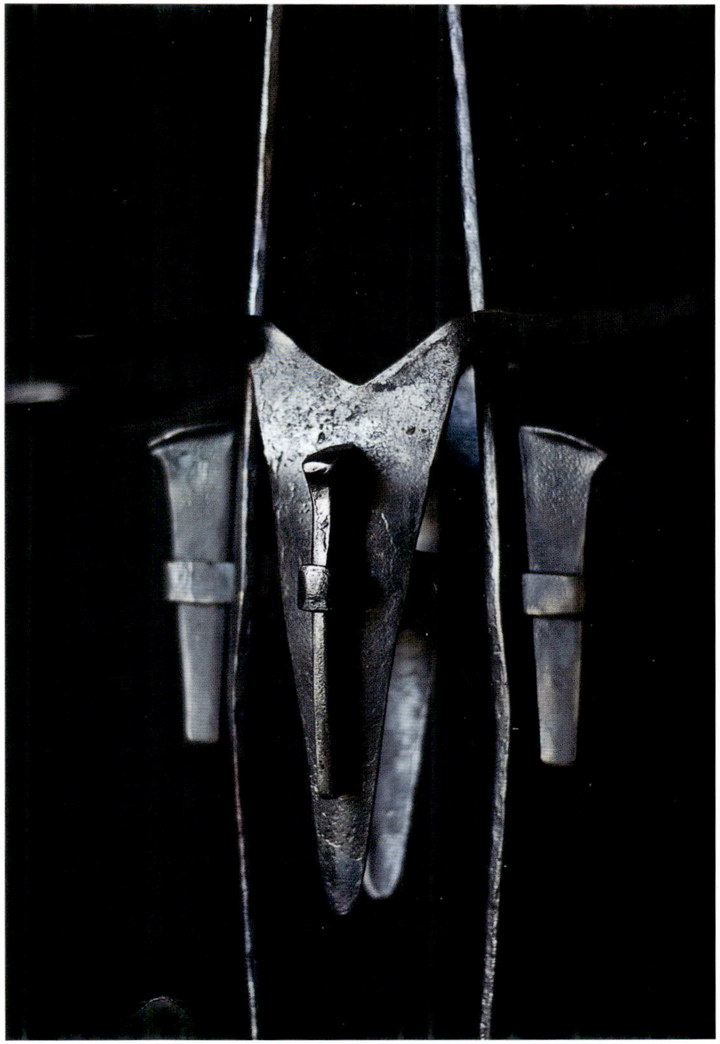

Wedge Chandelier

When making a chandelier, I know I have succeeded if the finished chandelier appears to be floating in the air. This chandelier is also held together by gravity and friction. The ring in the center is shaped so that four slots protrude from it. The candle arms and the hanging arms slide over the slots and are wedged tight. At the top of the hanging arms is a hinge. The piece can be completely taken apart.

Wedge chandelier.

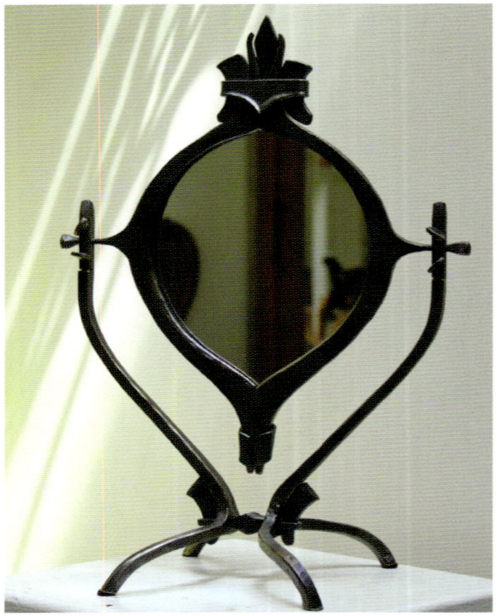

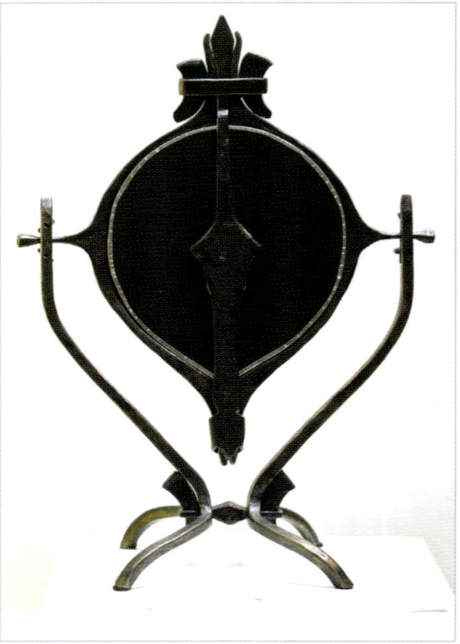

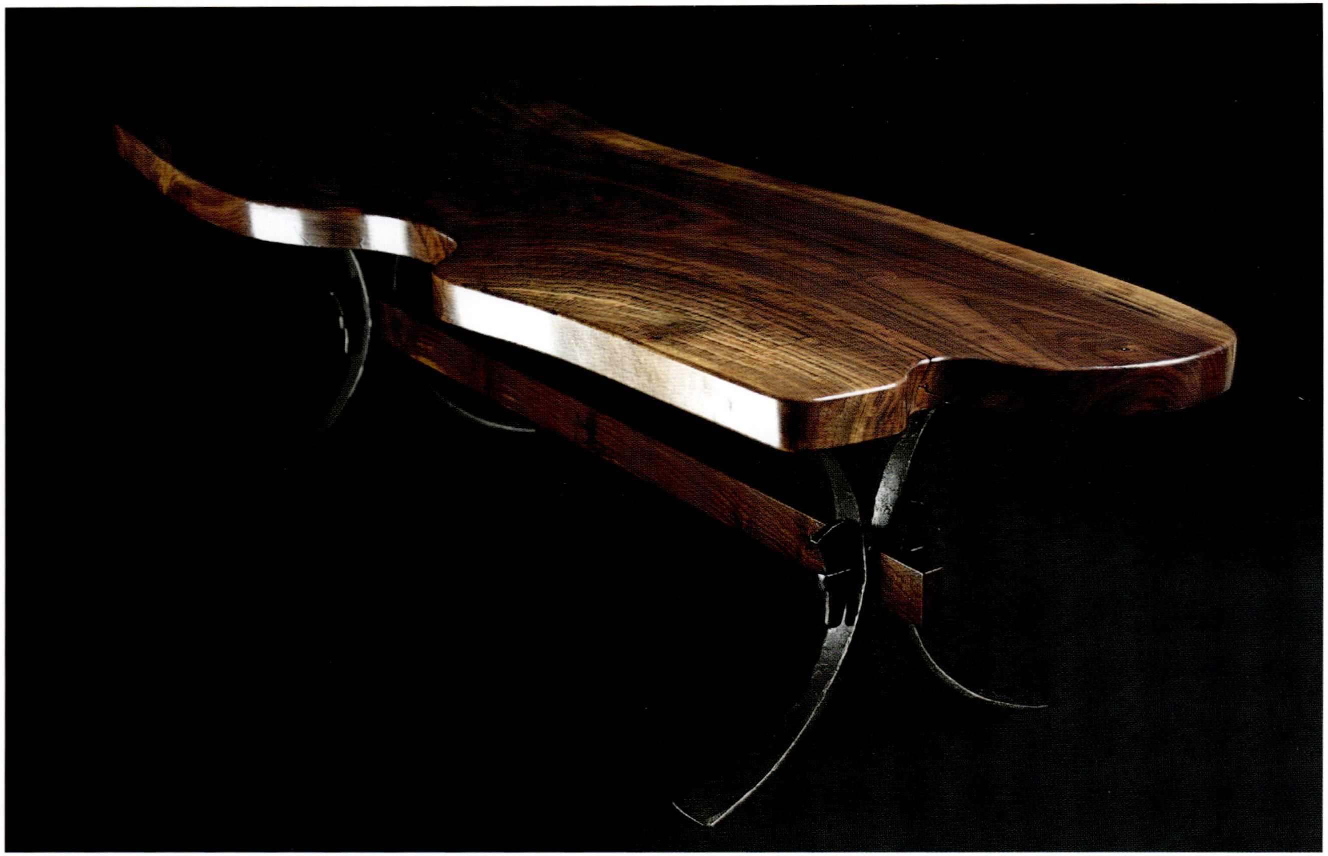

The Vanity Mirror

In making this vanity mirror, I wanted the owner to feel regal. The back side shows how the mirror is put together. To remove the glass, the top wedges are tapped out and the band is lifted off. This releases the two sides, which sit in the bottom of the middle piece. The mirror is held together entirely by friction. If you look at the front of the mirror, you can see the thumbscrews that hold the mirror in place and control the angle.

Vanity mirror, front and back.

Removable-Wedge Walnut Table

I work with a small local company, Whitethorn Hardwoods. They cut and dry beautiful slabs from local hardwoods. They work with the local community and collect all of their wood sustainably. Steel and wood are beautiful together. This table uses a rectangular band that slides through the steel legs and the walnut rail. Wedges hold it all together. Or you can take it apart.

Removable-wedge walnut table.

John Creed

Glasgow, Scotland
www.creedmetalwork.com

ARTIST'S STATEMENT

My work explores the special relationship between line and surface and the interplay of balance and gravity. Concept and ideas often pursue complementary and contrasting materials. The interaction of the viewer with the object and the place it occupies is embodied in a concept. Recent small works reference the fragility of the Earth.

Crater IV. Sculpture. 2013. Formed bronze, damascus steel, forged mild steel. About 15" x 6¾". *Photo: Tom Dobbie*

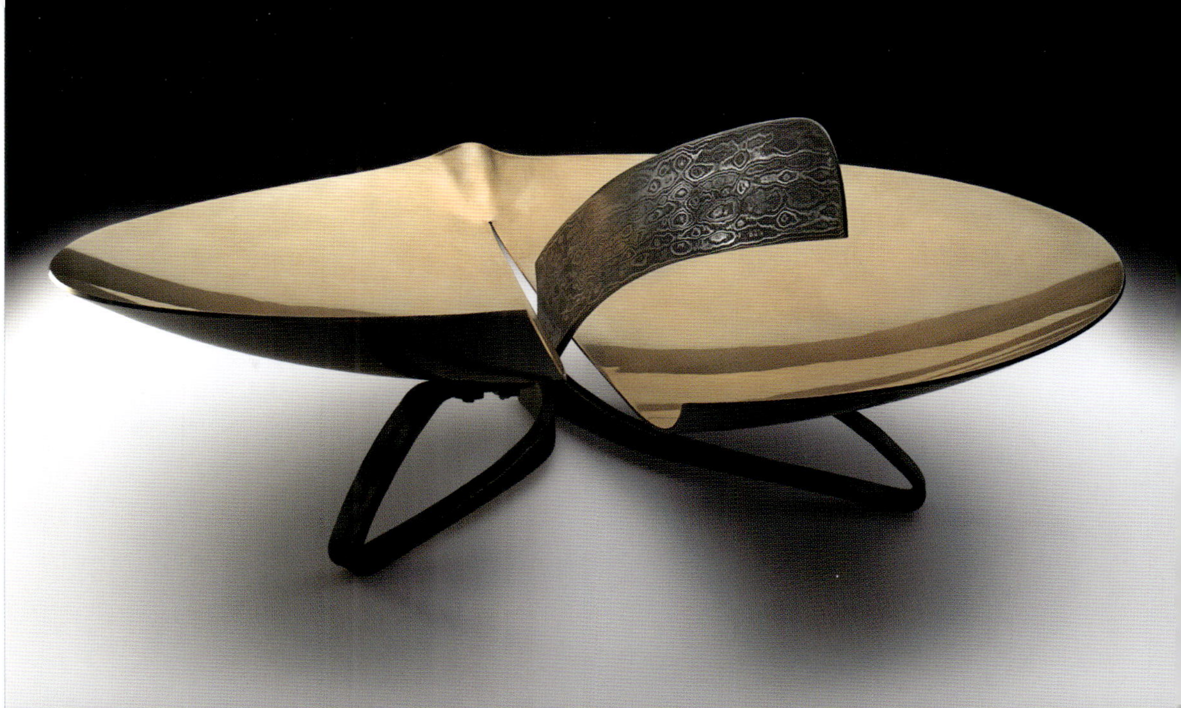

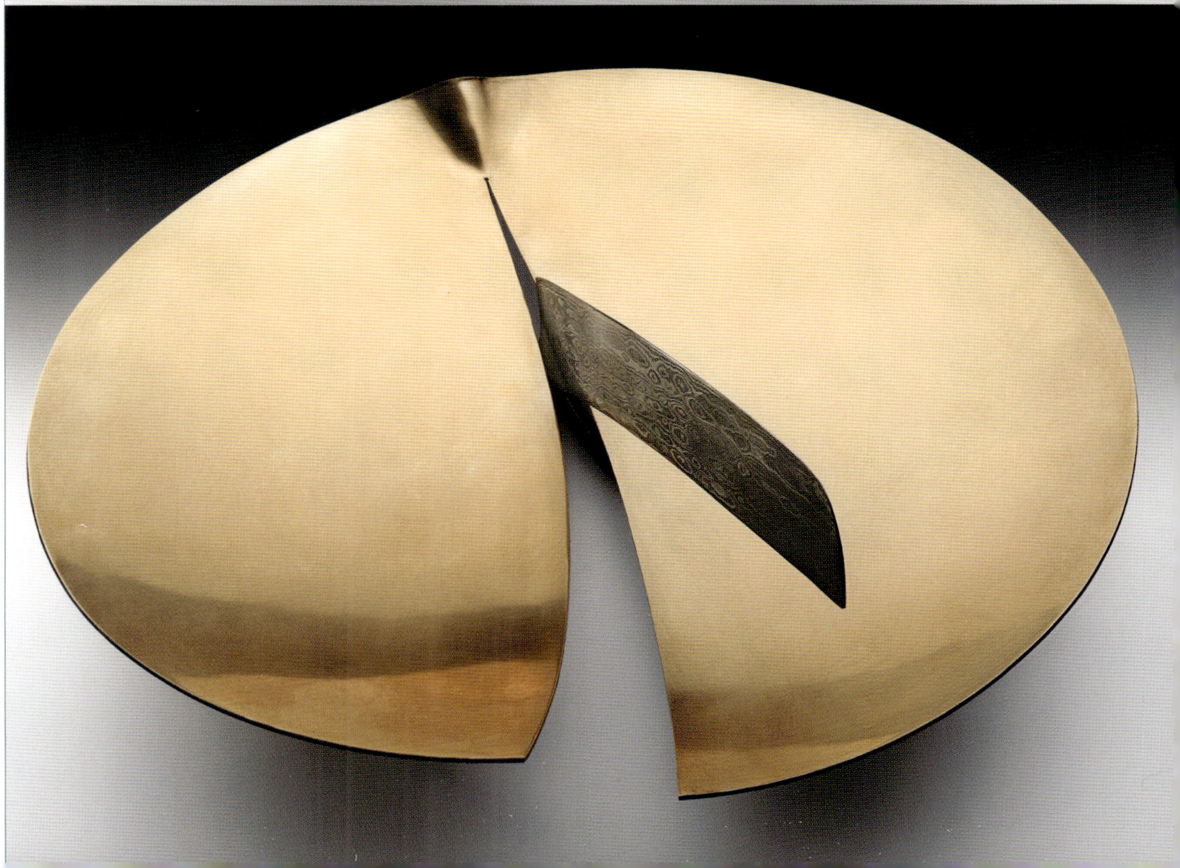

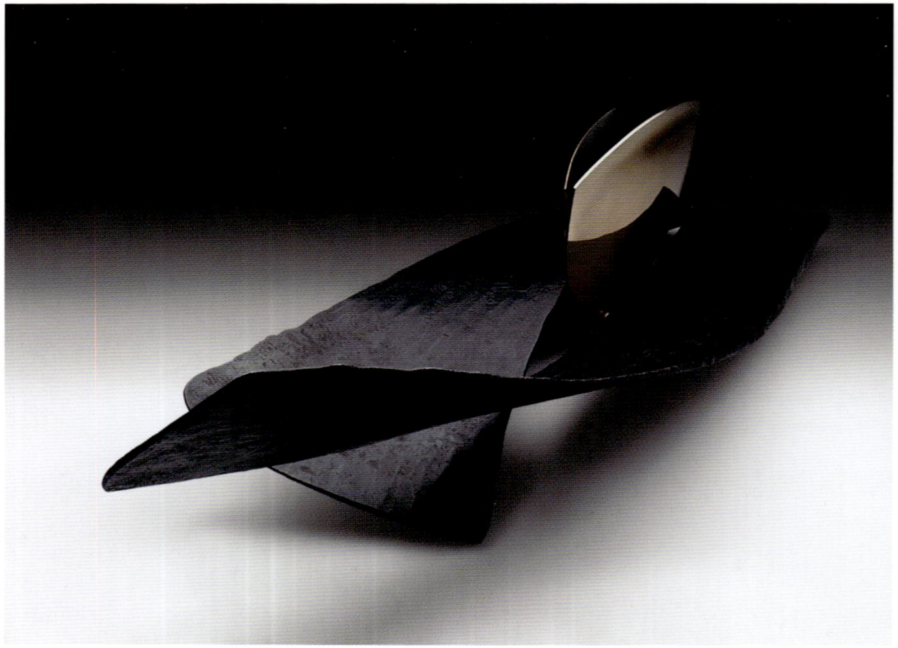

Wave I. Sculpture. 2013. Forged mild steel, formed bronze.
About 20" x 6½" x 4¼". *Photo: Tom Dobbie*

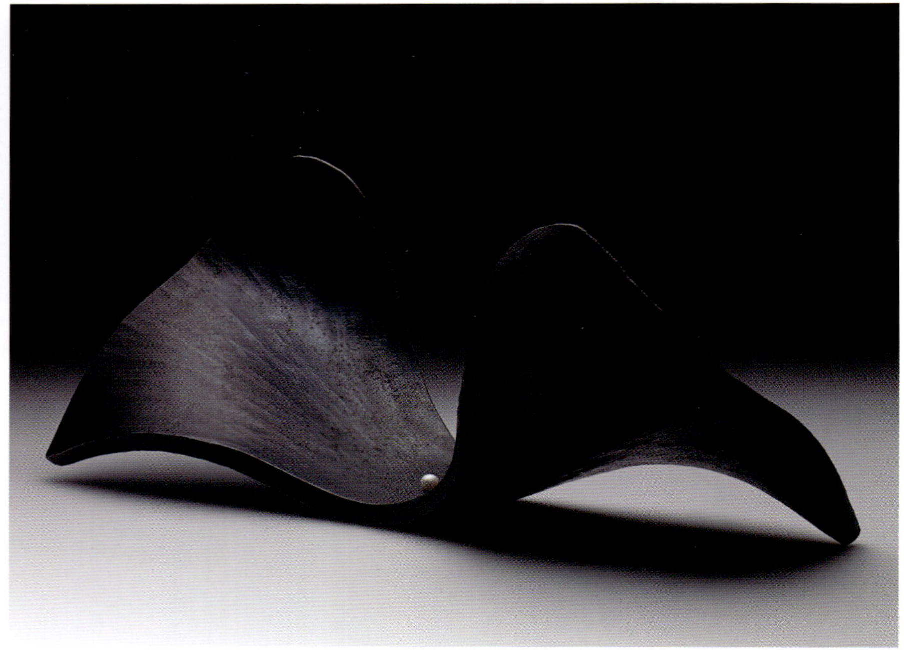

Wave II. Sculpture. 2013. Forged steel with baroque pearl.
About 14" x 4¼" x 5¾". *Photo: Tom Dobbie*

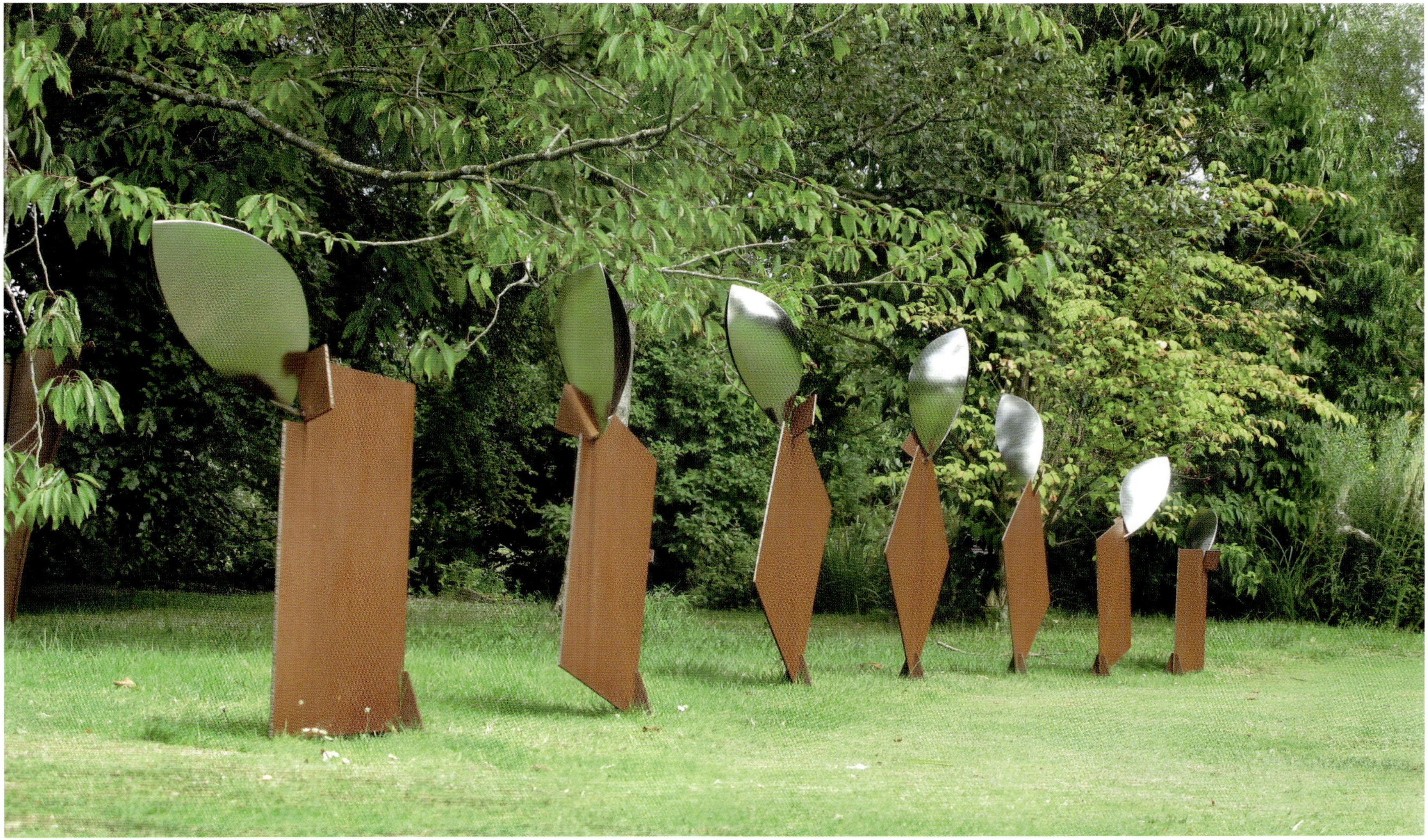

Roll Over. Sculpture. 2011. Weathering steel, stainless steel. *Photo: Tom Dobbie*

Rachel David

Red Metal, New Orleans, Louisiana
www.redmetal.net

ARTIST'S STATEMENT

I am an artist-blacksmith, mostly self-taught, with brief yet very influential teachers. I mix the ancient magical, alchemical traditions of the blacksmith with modern aesthetics and my needs as an artist to express myself. I make one-of-a-kind architectural elements, furniture, and sculptures. Each element in each piece is individually heated and hammered into shape. It is a time-consuming and exacting process, but the finished piece shows the labor and love of each hammer blow. I see my job as two sided. As a blacksmith, I follow a specific, logic and efficient order of operations, producing beautiful hand-wrought products. As an artist, I follow my guts, winding my way from an idea through trials and tribulations, decisions, and inspirations to the final product—one that is beautiful, thoughtfully created, and uniquely handmade.

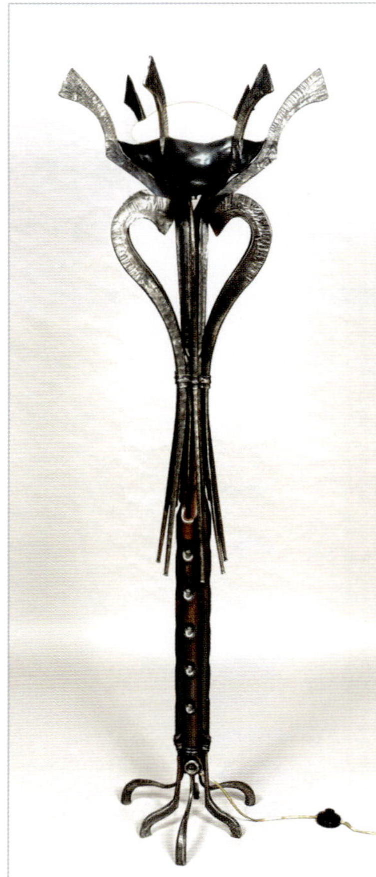

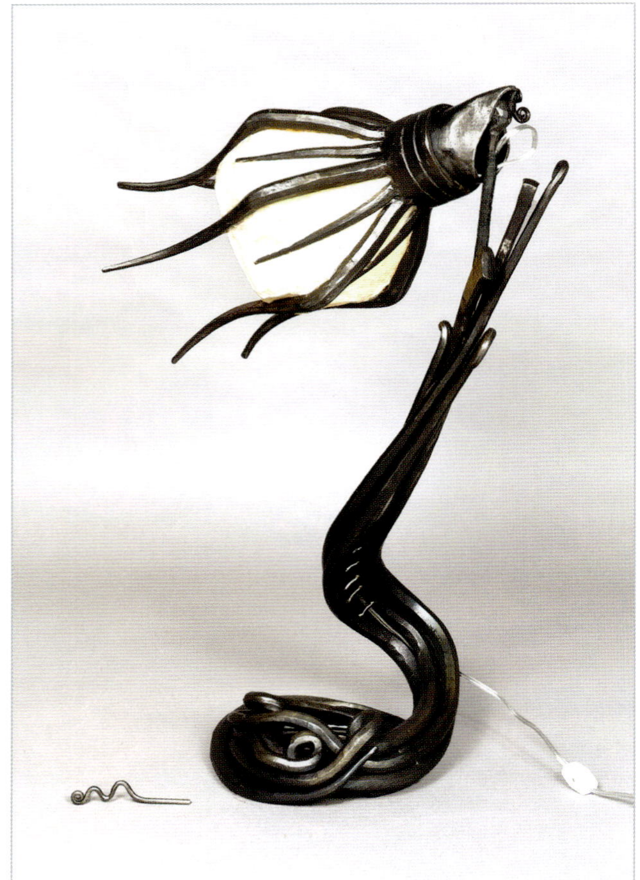

Floor lamp. 2013. Hand-forged steel, lamp wiring. 72″ x 20″ x 20″. *Photo: Krisztian Megyeri*

Floor lamp. 2013. Hand-forged steel, paper, wood glue, lamp wiring. 28″ x 16″ x 10″. *Photo: Krisztian Megyeri*

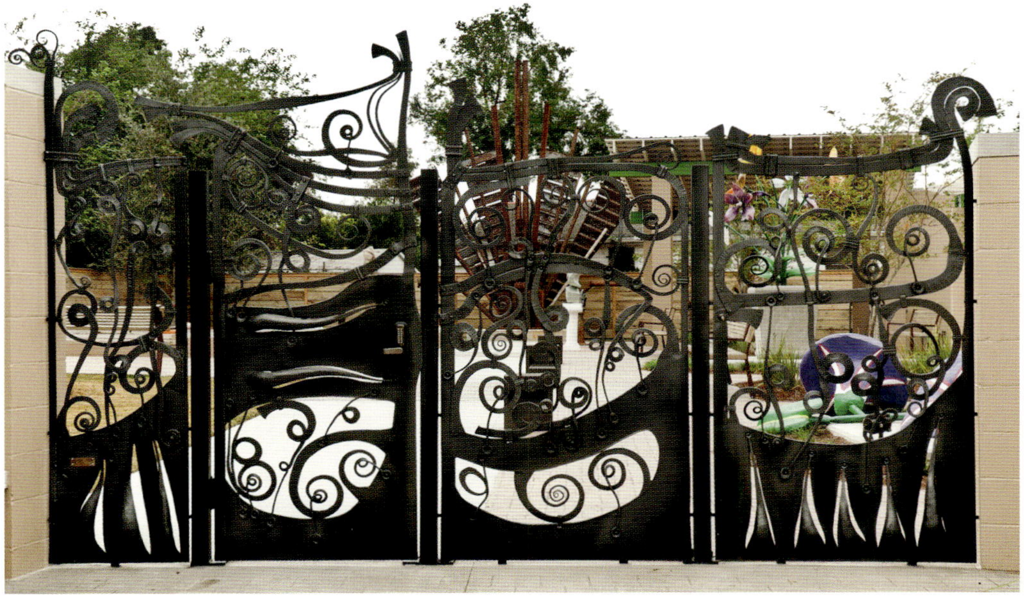

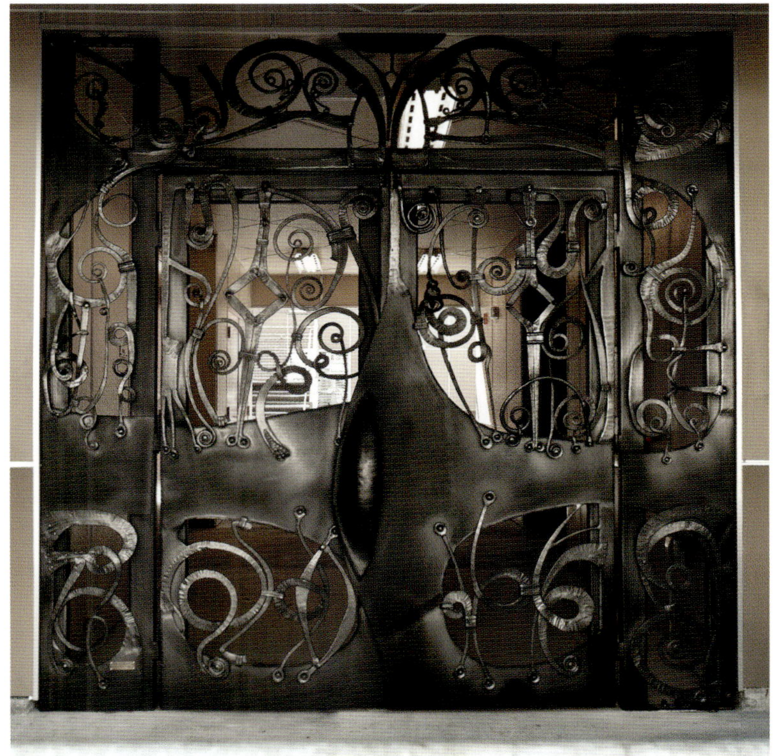

Bywater Art Lofts sculpture garden gate. 2012. Hand-forged steel, painted, with graphite rub, based on the Mississippi River's currents. 9'h x 26'w.
Photo: Krisztian Megyeri

Bywater Art Lofts main entrance gate. 2012. Hand-forged steel, painted with graphite rub. Based on the clothing factory that once inhabited this building. 9' x 9'.
Photo: Krisztian Megyeri

RACHEL DAVID

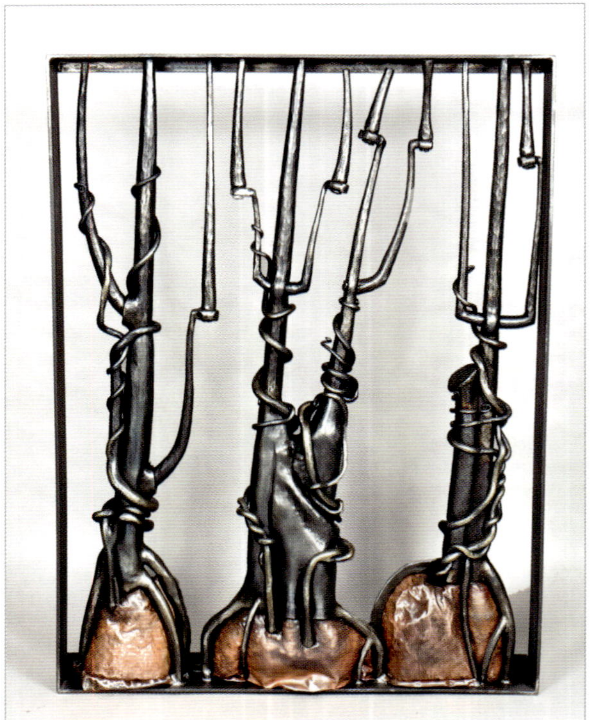

Freudenberger Trees. Sculpture. 2013. Hand-forged steel, copper. 48″ x 36″. *Photo: Krisztian Megyeri*

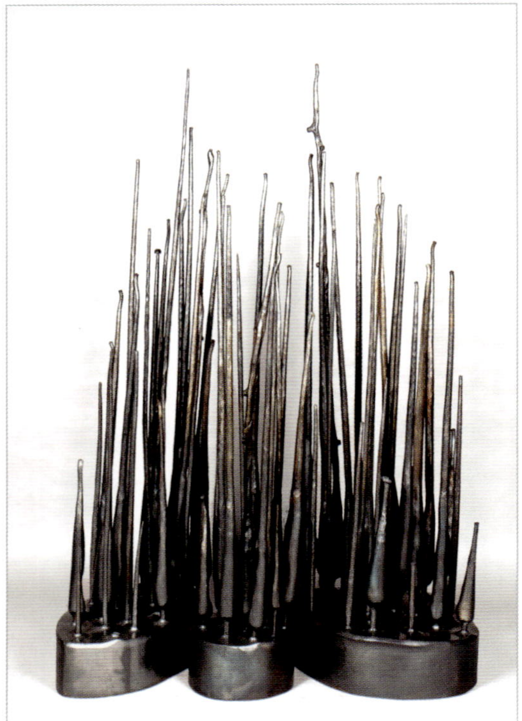

For Rest. Sculpture. 2012. Hand-forged steel, copper. Dimensions variable, 52″ h. *Photo: Krisztian Megyeri*

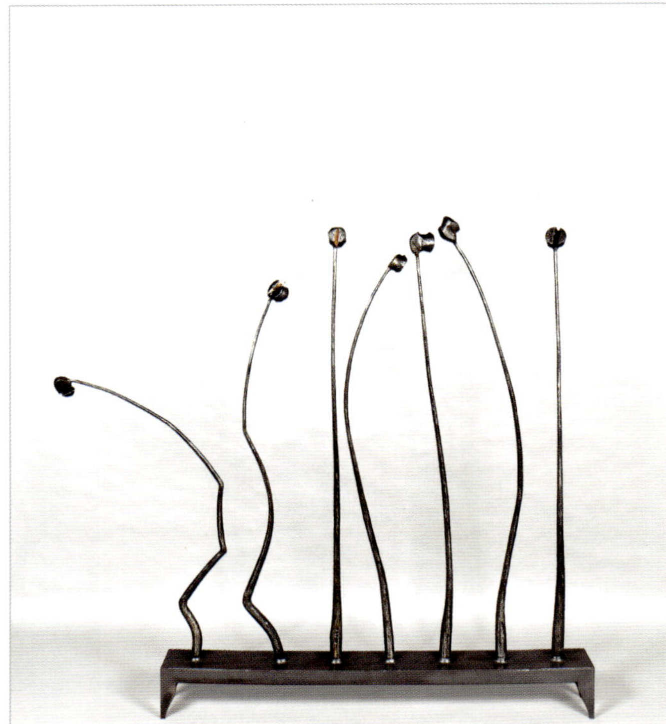

Out cast/progression. Sculpture. 2012. Hand-forged steel, silver, gold leaf, cubic zirconia. 53″ x 65″ x 6″. *Photo: Krisztian Megyeri*

Mike Edelman

Frostburg, Maryland
www.medelmanart.com

ARTIST'S STATEMENT

Experimentation and curiosity permeate my work. It is too caustic to have a speculative idea and not resolve it—so I bring sculptures into the world to find my own peace and resolve my curiosity about structure and form.

Clock. Steel, brass. 48″ x 18″ x 4″.

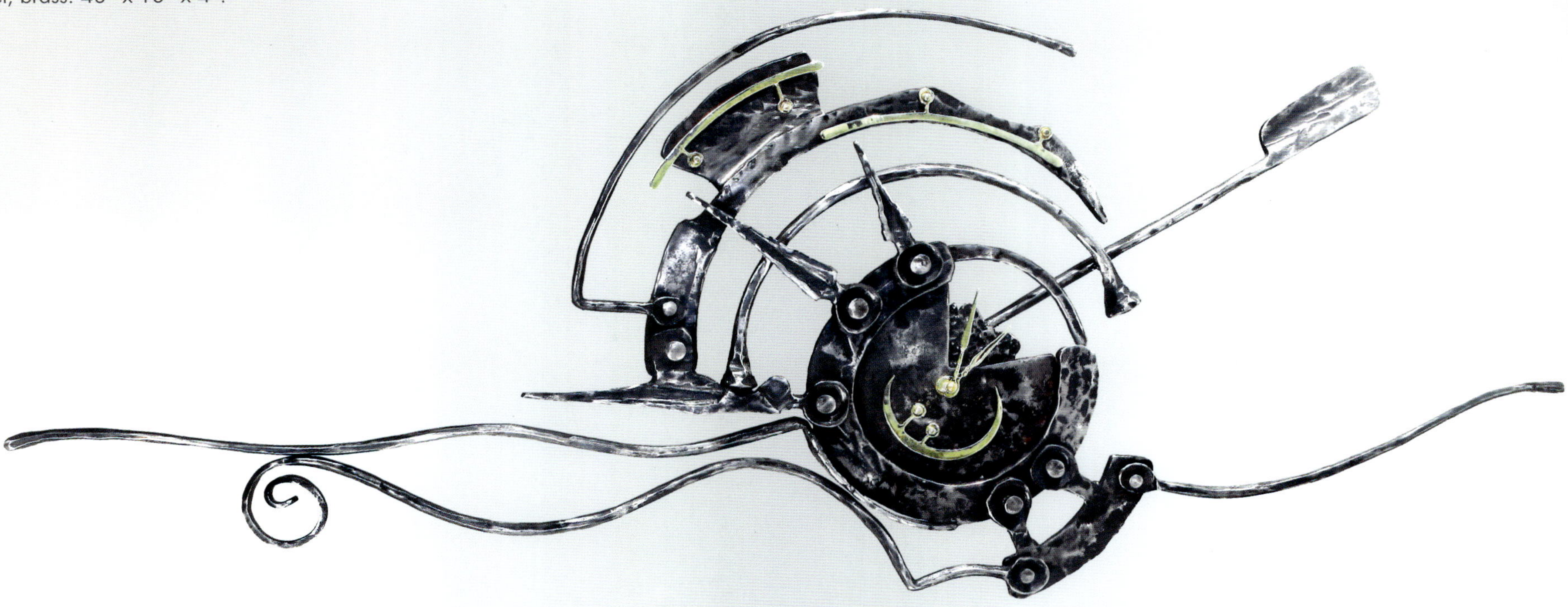

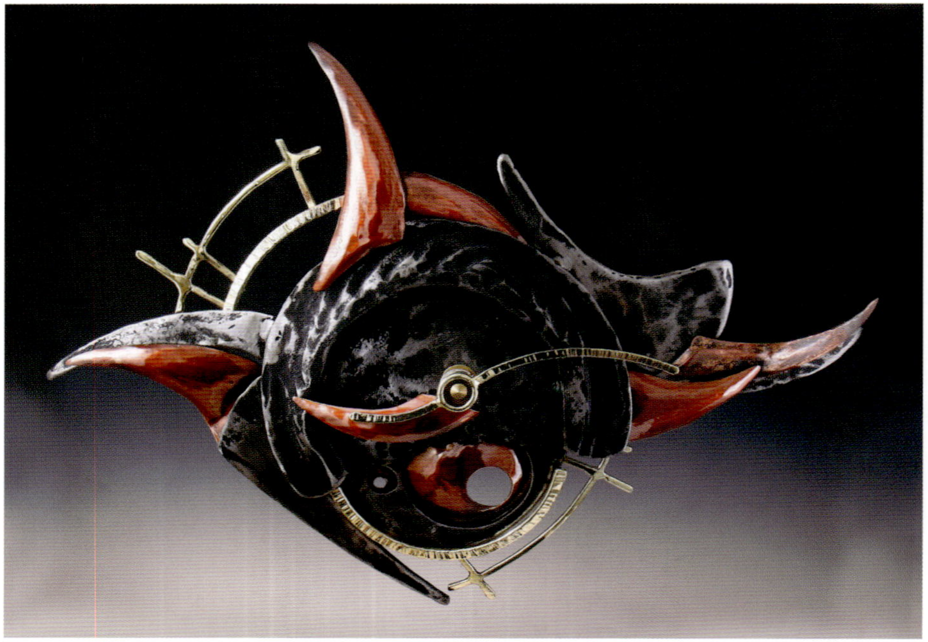

Clock #2. Steel, brass, copper. 14″ x 8″ x 2″.

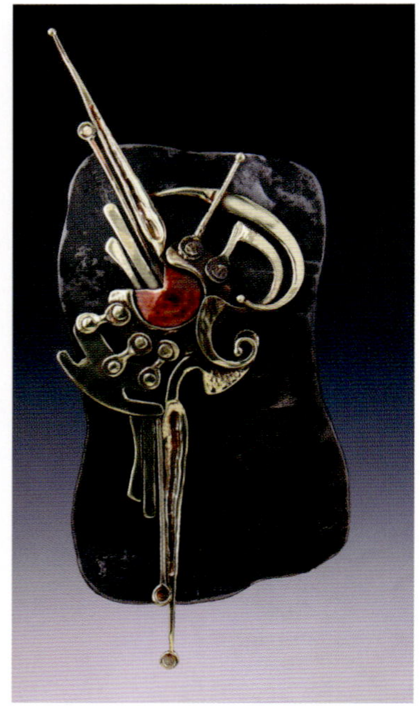

Experiments #17. Wall art.
Steel, brass, copper. 6″ x 3″ x 1″.

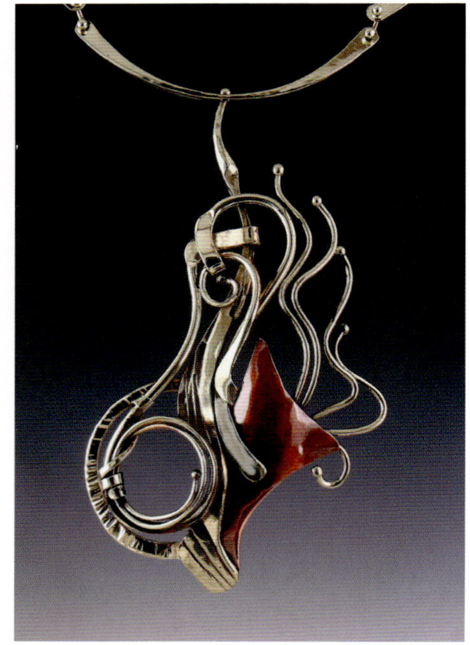

Experiments #44. Necklace.
Brass, copper. 3½″ x 2″ x 1″.

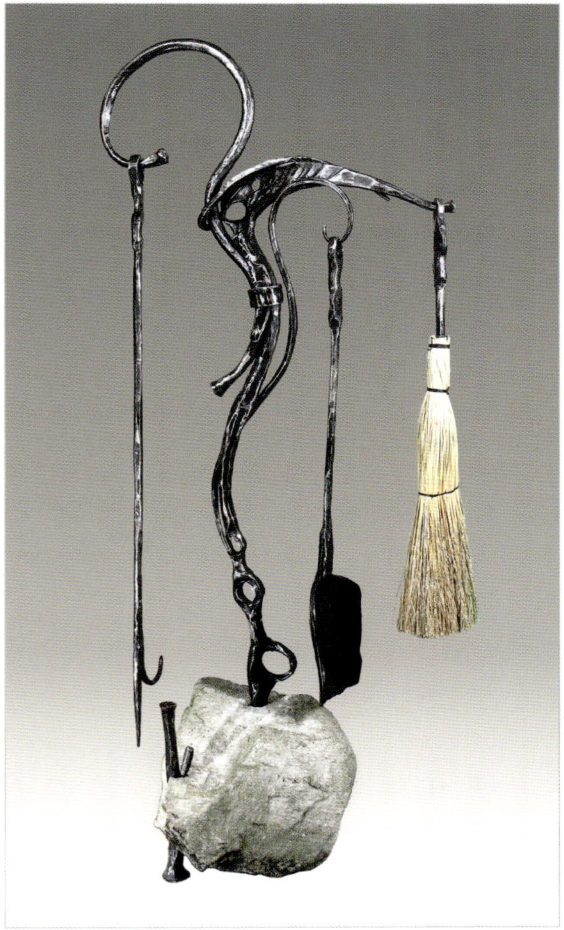

Fireplace set. Steel, limestone. 42" x 20" x 14".

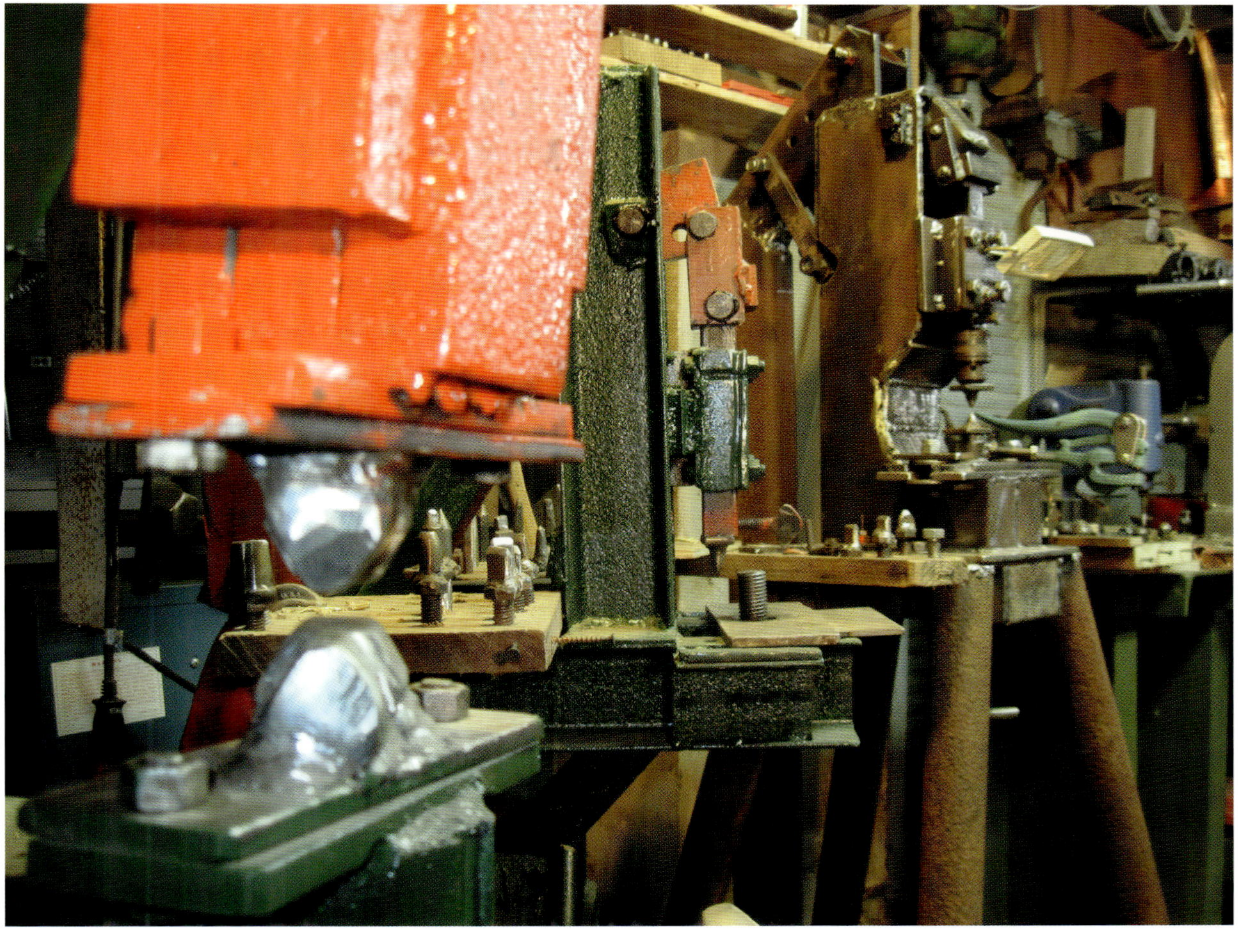

Edelman's custom-built machines are designed to help work small pieces of metal using the same "displacement" technique that is used for forging hot steel.

Lisa Elias

Elias Metal Studio, Minneapolis, Minnesota
www.eliasmetalstudio.com

ARTIST'S STATEMENT

I have almost twenty years of experience working with metal, creating elegant, functional sculptures inspired by traditional blacksmithing techniques. A linear, fluid touch allows me to create a diversity of sculptures, from fences to gates and lighting. I work with homeowners, designers, and architects on private commissions. Recently, my work includes a number of collaborations with landscape architects and people in other disciplines to create and enhance public spaces. My inspiration comes from simple lines, light, and organic forms.

I've been selected to incorporate public artwork into several neighborhoods for the city of St. Paul in Minnesota.

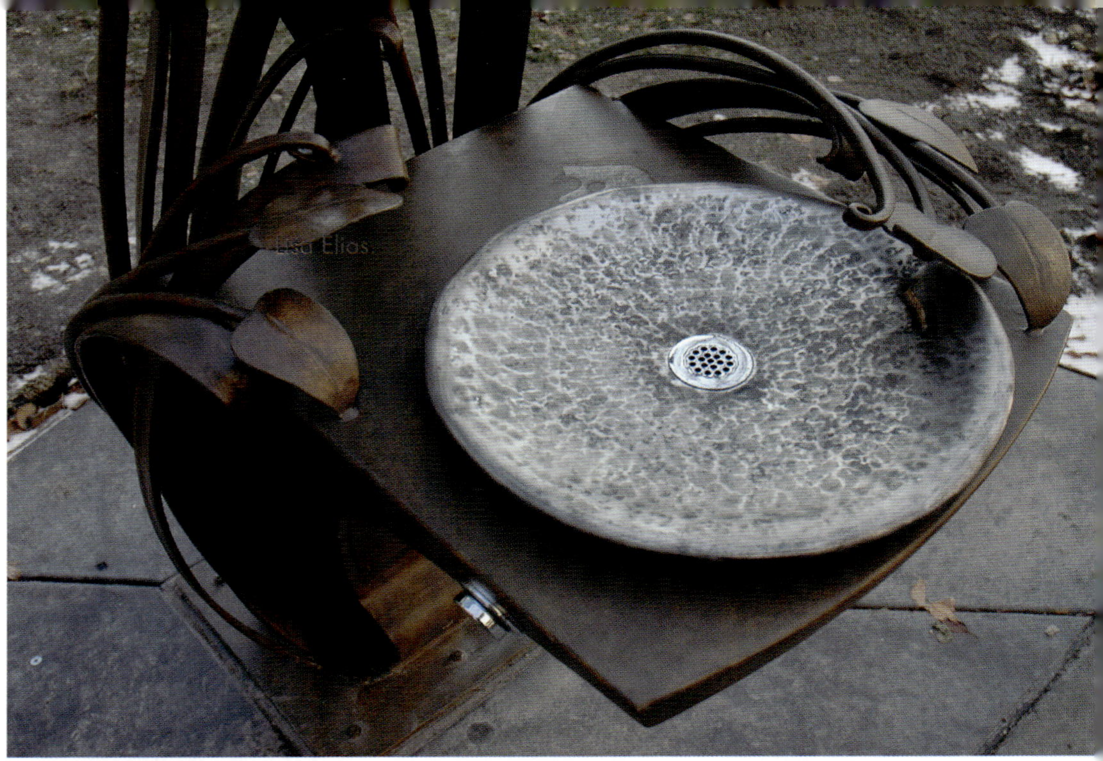

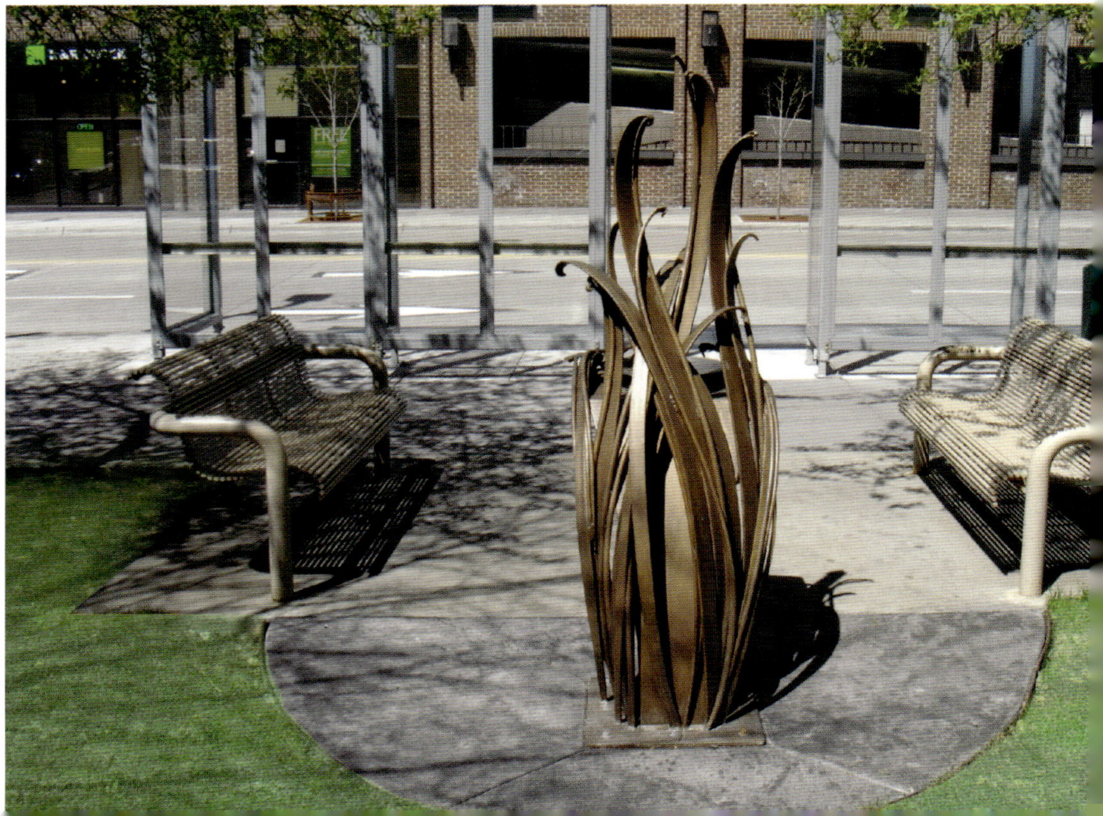

The Field Drinking Fountain

I was selected to design and build a drinking fountain in downtown Minneapolis in 2010. My fountain, called The Field, *stands within a pocket park off a busy street in the hear of the city. The fountain celebrates our city's great drinking water, which is filtrated through the Mississippi River just blocks away. My hope is that we can reduce the amount of plastic bottles and assure that we all have clean water to drink.*

The Field. Drinking fountain/sculpture. 2010. Galvanized and painted steel, hammered stainless steel basin and spout. 6½' x 3½'. *Photos: Lisa Elias*

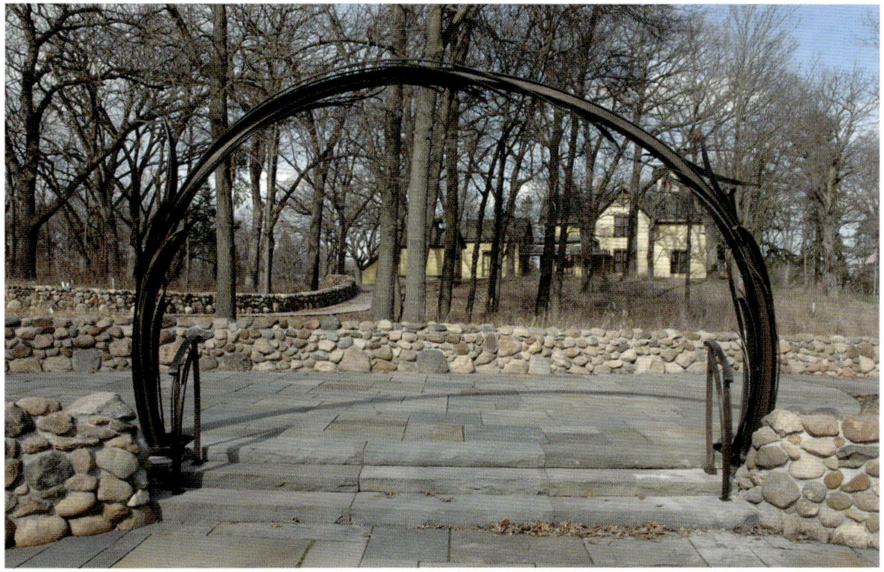

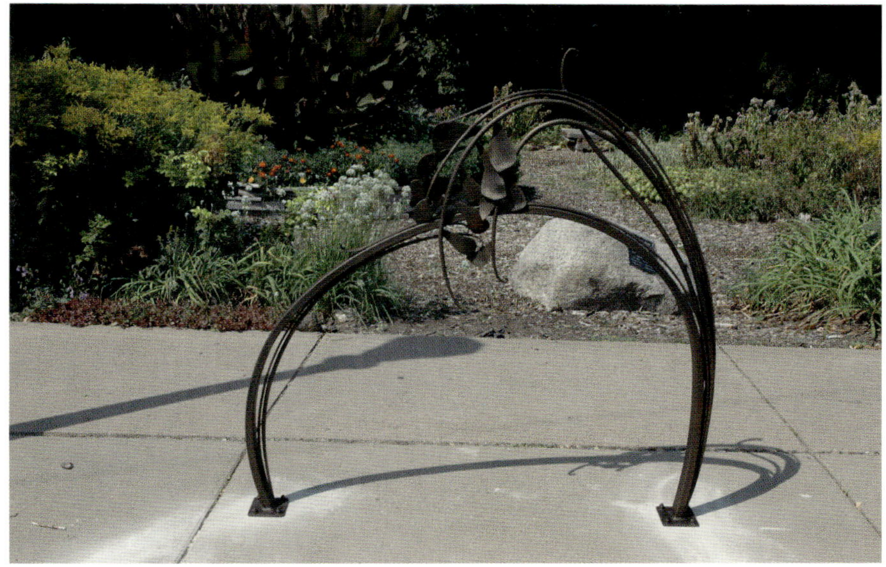

A Canopy of Grass

A Canopy of Grass *stands within the Minnetonka Mills Park in Minnesota. The Burwell House behind the canopy was built in 1883 and is a historical site off Minnehaha Creek. Because of the size of the sculpture, I had to make it in three parts and bolt it together on site.*

A Canopy of Grass. Sculpture. 2012. Forged steel, galvanized and painted. 10½' x 15'. *Photo: Lisa Elias*

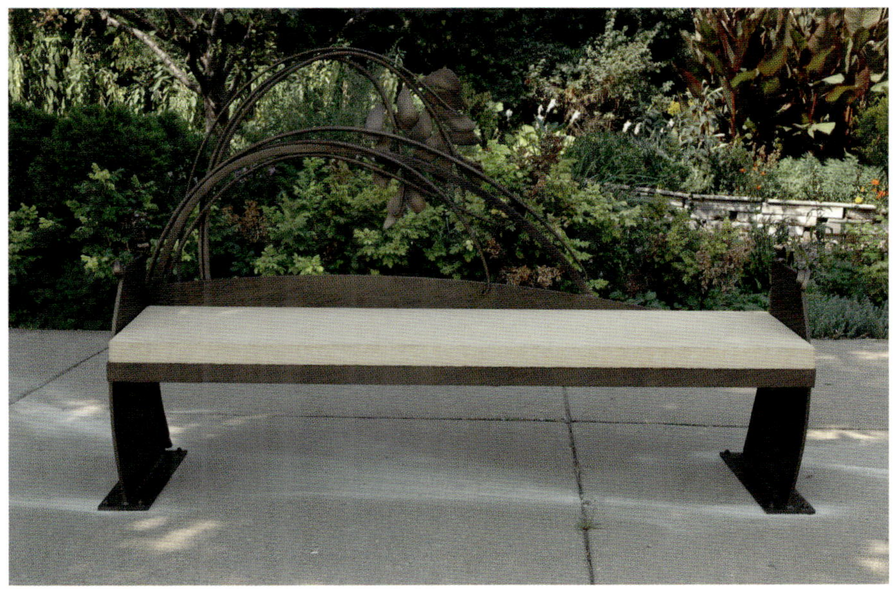

Wisteria Bench and Bike Rack

Wisteria bench and bike rack (rack, top right; bench, bottom right). 2012. Forged steel, galvanized and painted, Minnesota dolomite stone. Bench: 6½' x 4½'. Bike rack: 3½' x 4½'.
Photos: Lisa Elias

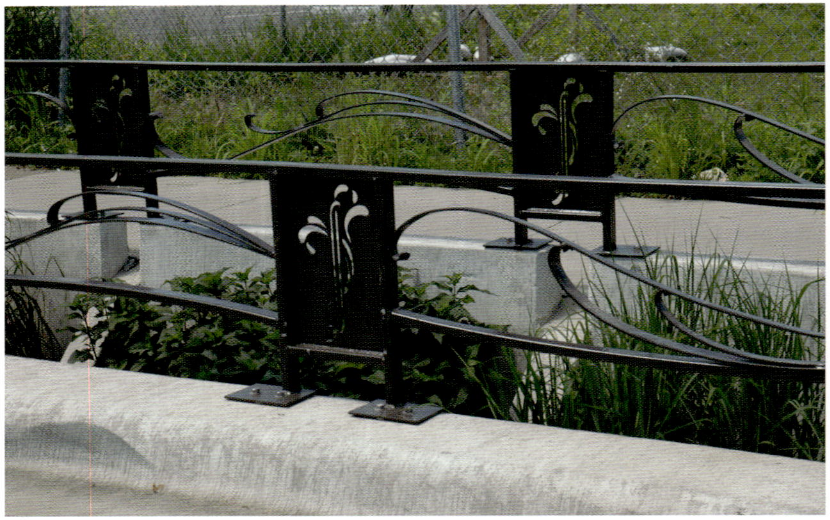

Storm Water Railings

Ten storm water planters were installed on the city's central corridor light rail transit system in St. Paul.

Storm water railings. 2012. Forged and fabricated steel, galvanized and painted. 24′ x 5′. *Photo: Lisa Elias*

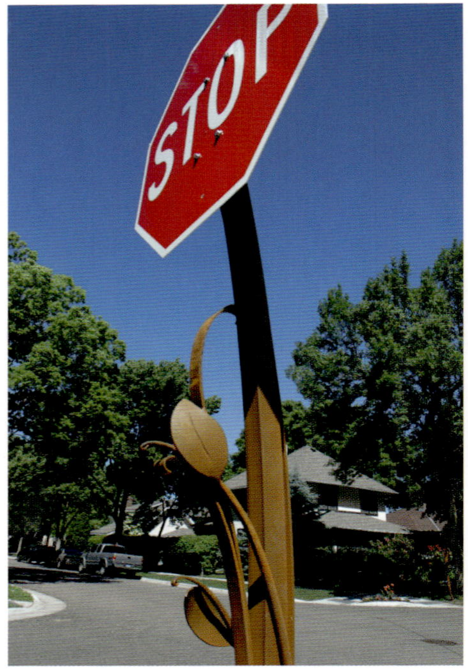

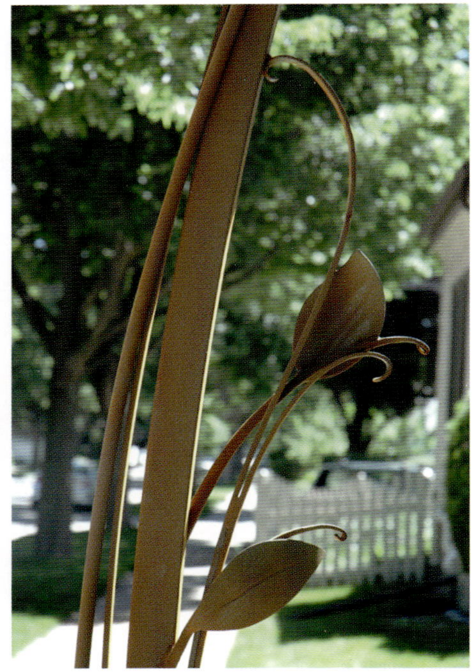

Stop Signs

I've designed a series of one hundred stop sign posts that, with time, will become a collection of sculptural elements that can be adapted to and added to the streetscapes throughout the city. I believe that public art strengthens public places and promotes identity as a livable and desirable place to visit. Why is it that we overlook aesthetics that have important functions, such as a stop sign post or a railing to a storm water planter when we can aesthetically enhance our surroundings in a sustainable way?

Stop sign. *Photos: Lisa Elias*

Roberta Elliott

Velvet Hammer Ltd., Cobden, Illinois
www.velvethammerltd.com

ARTIST'S STATEMENT

What do you get when you cross a tennis player with an artist? A blacksmith. Throw in a lifetime gardener and that blacksmith works in an organic style with a nature theme. The first time I struck iron, I was smitten. There is something wonderfully indescribable about the energy exchange that takes place while blacksmithing. The heat from the fire and the force of the hammer's blow feed and energize me. My primary material is mild steel. I particularly enjoy using pipe. This hollow material gives an impression of mass without the actual weight and provides an additional surface (the interior) with its own potential to be worked. It is a form that requires a gentle and patient hammer blow, so it doesn't collapse. Currently, I use only recycled pipe; the other ends are running around in John Deere tractors.

Sculptures from recycled pipes

In these sculptures, the central stem is forged from recycled steel pipe. The top is flared and the bottom is flattened then rippled. In between, the pipe is tapered to create an even flow. The legs are forged from ¼" x 1" steel strap. One end is rippled similar to making a fish tail. Then it is tapered into a long thin tendril. These legs are held in place with a 3/16" round steel wrap. Final shaping is done with a torch. The piece is finished with the abrasive brass brush technique and topped with a wax finish.

Carmen. From *Dancer* series. Sculpture. 2012. Forged steel. 13" x 22" x 8". *Photo: Shari Smiley*

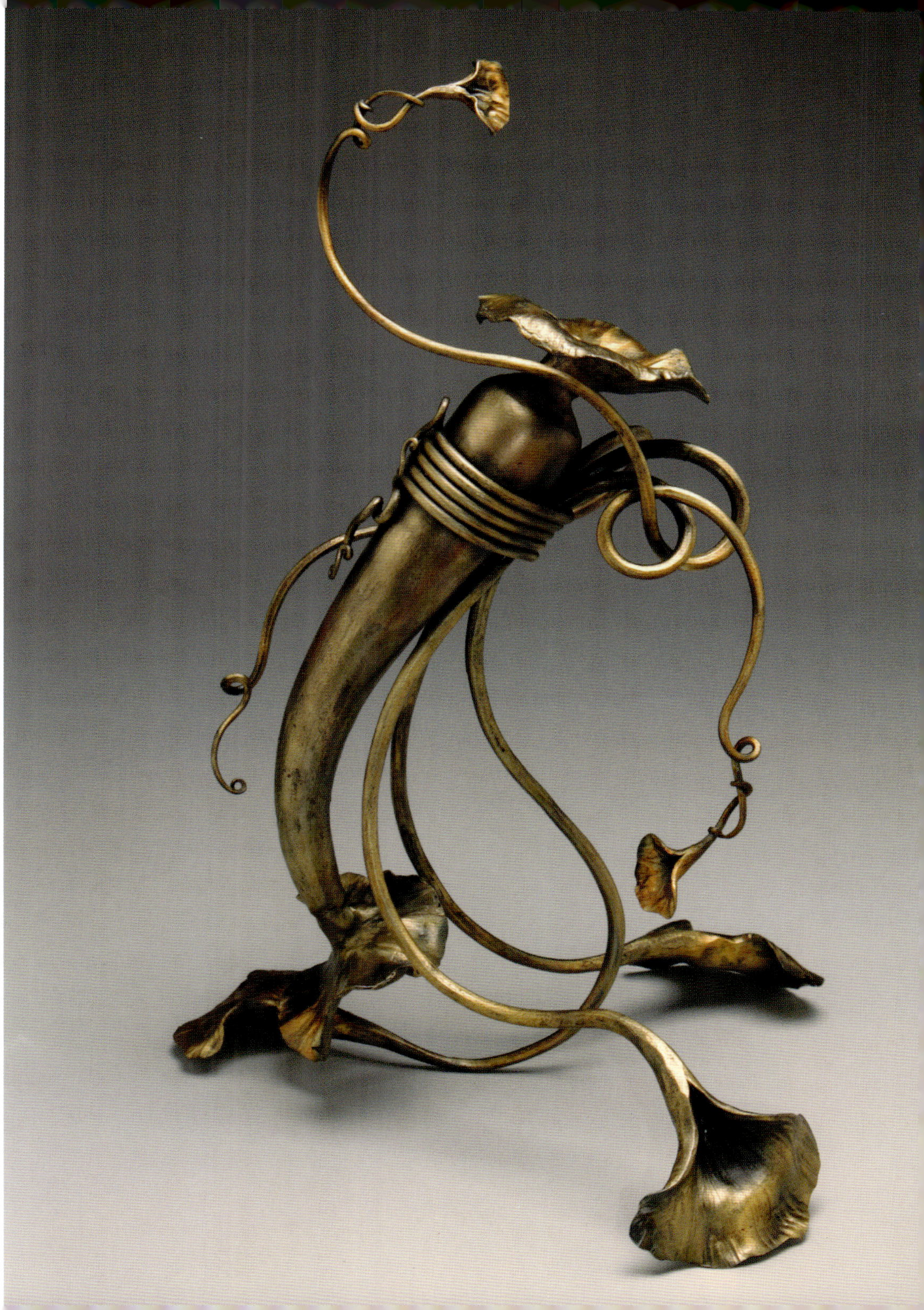

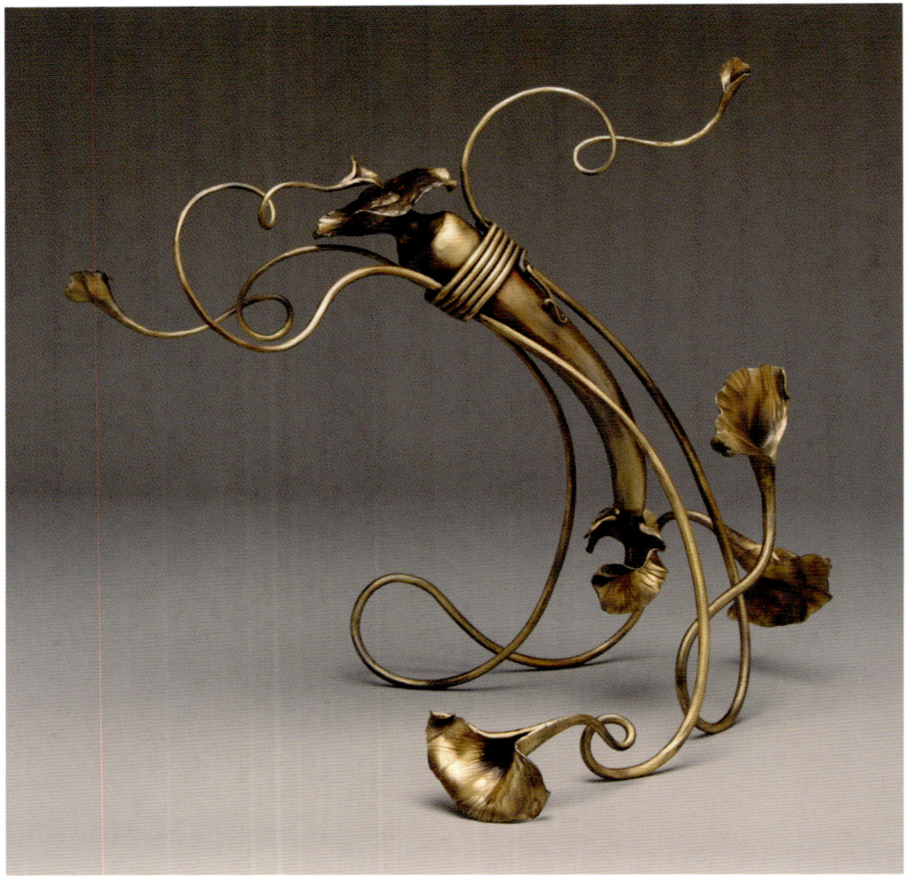

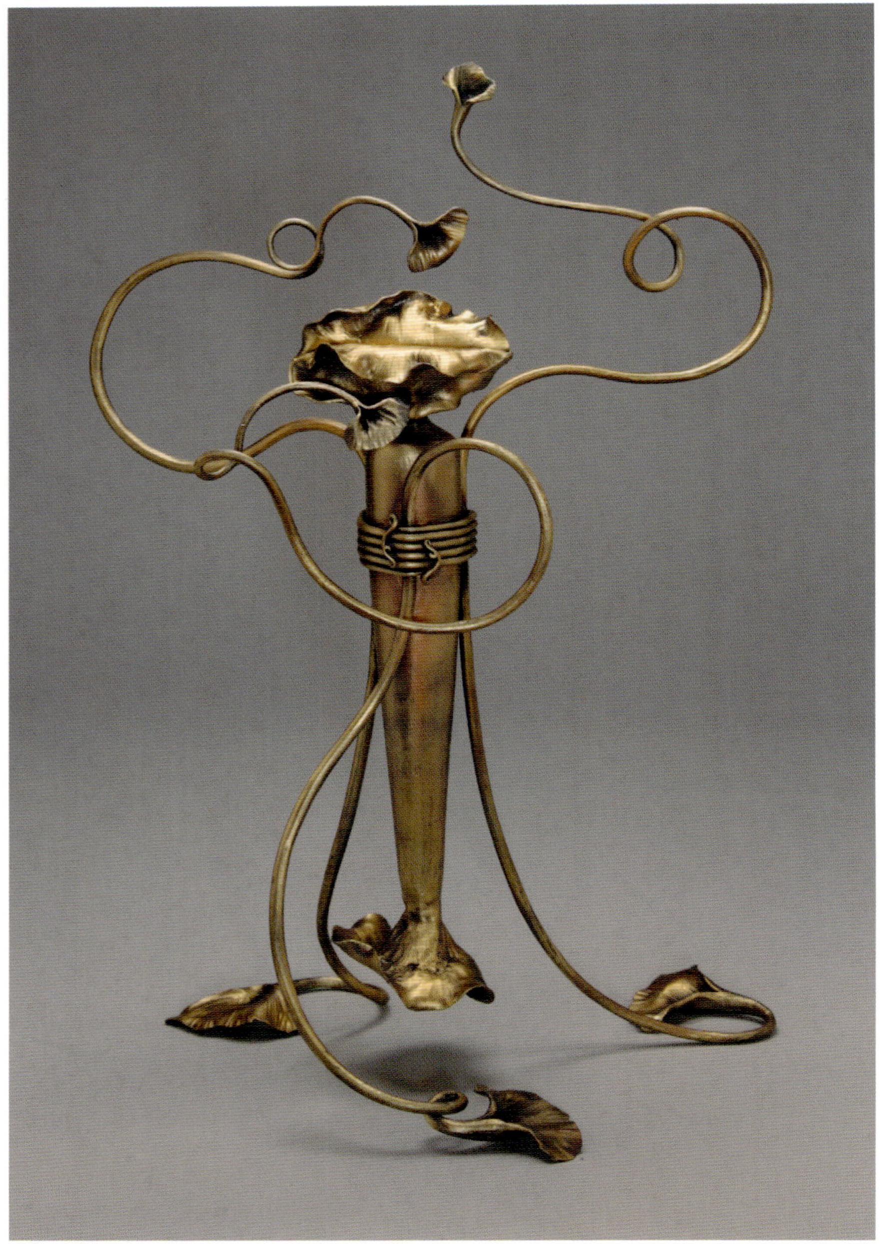

Flamenco. From *Dancer* series. Sculpture. 2012. Forged steel. 23″ x 25″ x 13″. *Photo: Shari Smiley*

Pygmalion. From *Dancer* series. Sculpture. 2012. Forged steel. 16″ x 26″ x 8″. Photo: Shari Smiley

Dysfunctional Spoons

For these pieces, the skeleton of the spoon is forged from recycled steel pipe. I split the handle end, ruffling one side then punching and drifting it to receive the other side, which has been folded and forge welded into a taper. I collapse and forge weld out the hole for the stem so I can draw it out into a thin section. I flatten the remaining 2" and punch a hole in it, drifting it until the rim is very thin. The face is comprised of individually forged gingko and apple leaves hammer welded together. The patina is achieved with an abrasive brass brush rubbing and baked vegetable oil.

Gingko Dude. Sculpture. 2011. Forged steel. 11" x 13" x 3". *Photo: Roberta Elliott*

Dream Girl. Sculpture. 2011. Forged steel. 9" x 16" x 3". *Photo: Roberta Elliott*

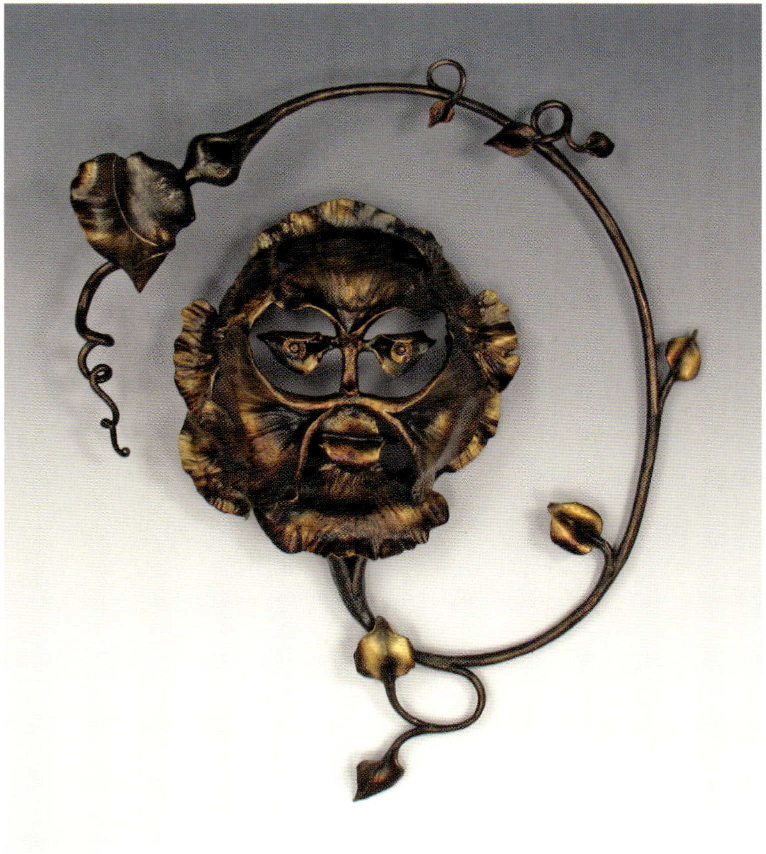

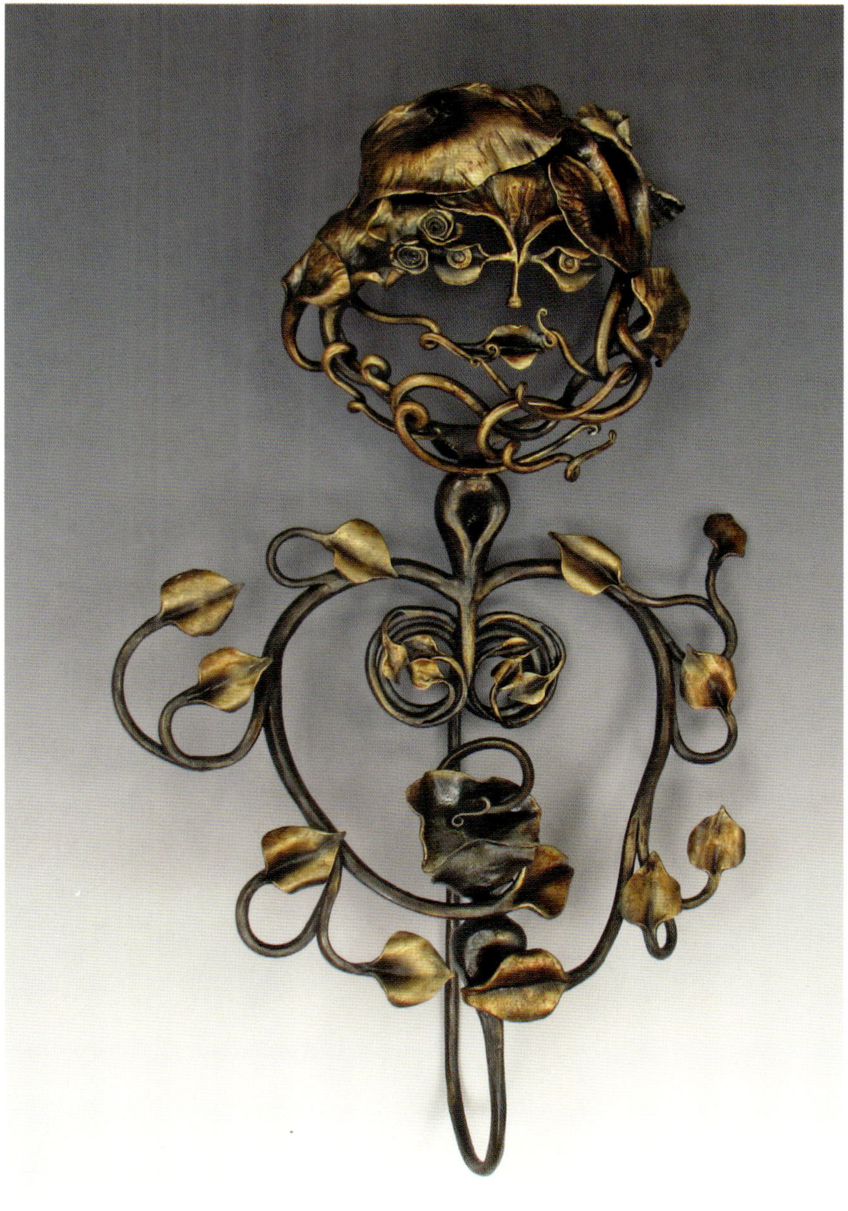

Peg Fetter

St. Louis, Missouri
pegfetter@yahoo.com

ARTIST'S STATEMENT

I work with found steel or ordinary items (such as steel coat hangers). I manipulate, forge, solder gold, and add a diamond or other lovely stone to make the rawness of the steel really a thing of beauty. My newest creations are neckpieces made from forged coat hangers, gold heat rivets, forged gold, and raw stones. Please notice the pieces are articulated, but not at regular intervals. A favorite piece is my bracelet *Mommy Dearest II*. The bracelet is forged from steel coat hangers. an homage to Joan Crawford, "No more wire hangers, ever!"

The combination of rough, fundamental steel against the elegance and richness of gold is just so wrong it is simply perfection. I have distilled my work down to the bare necessities, only what is imperative to convey my aesthetic. The devil is in the details, so pay attention or you will miss something beautiful!

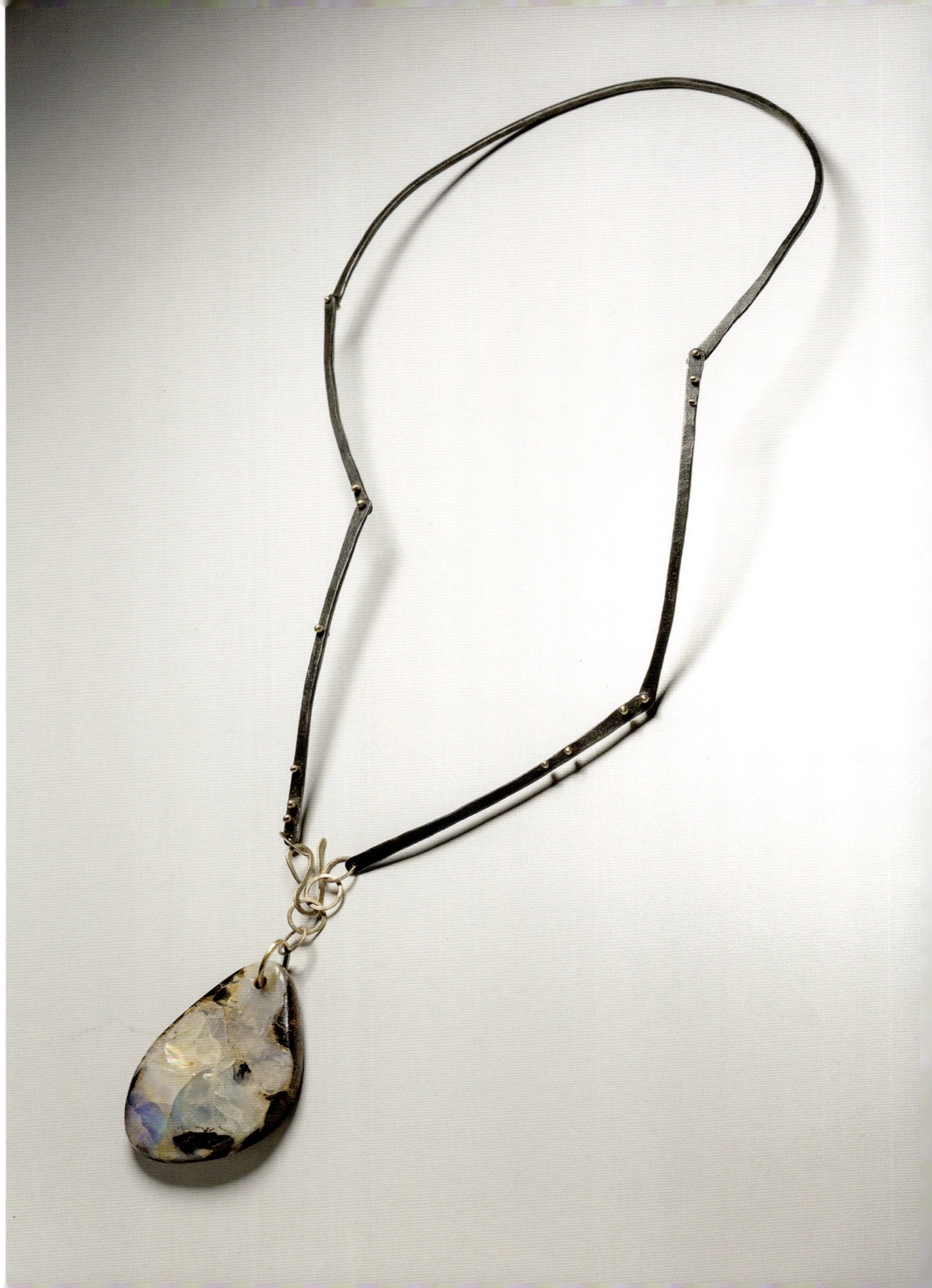

Sticks and Stones and 'Dem Bones series. Necklace. 2013. Forged, fabricated. Steel, 14k yellow gold, boulder opal. 22"l x 1"w x ¼"d. *Photo: Don Casper*

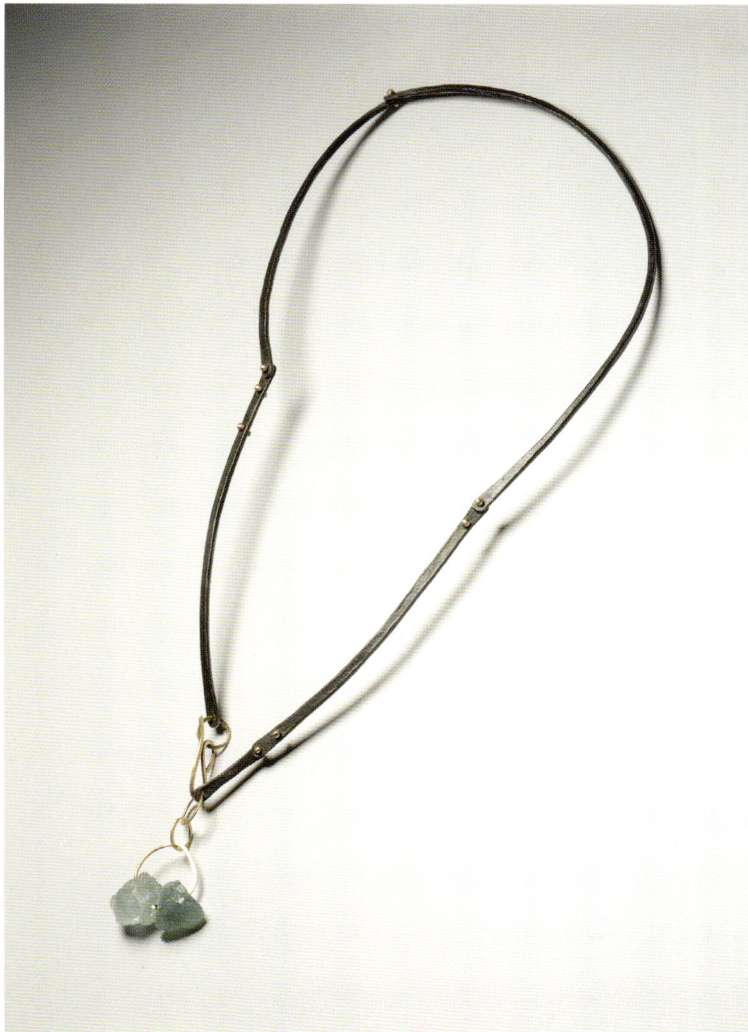

Sticks and Stones and 'Dem Bones series. Necklace. 2013. Forged, fabricated. Steel, 14k yellow gold, aquamarine. 20"l x 1"w x ¼"d. *Photo: Don Casper*

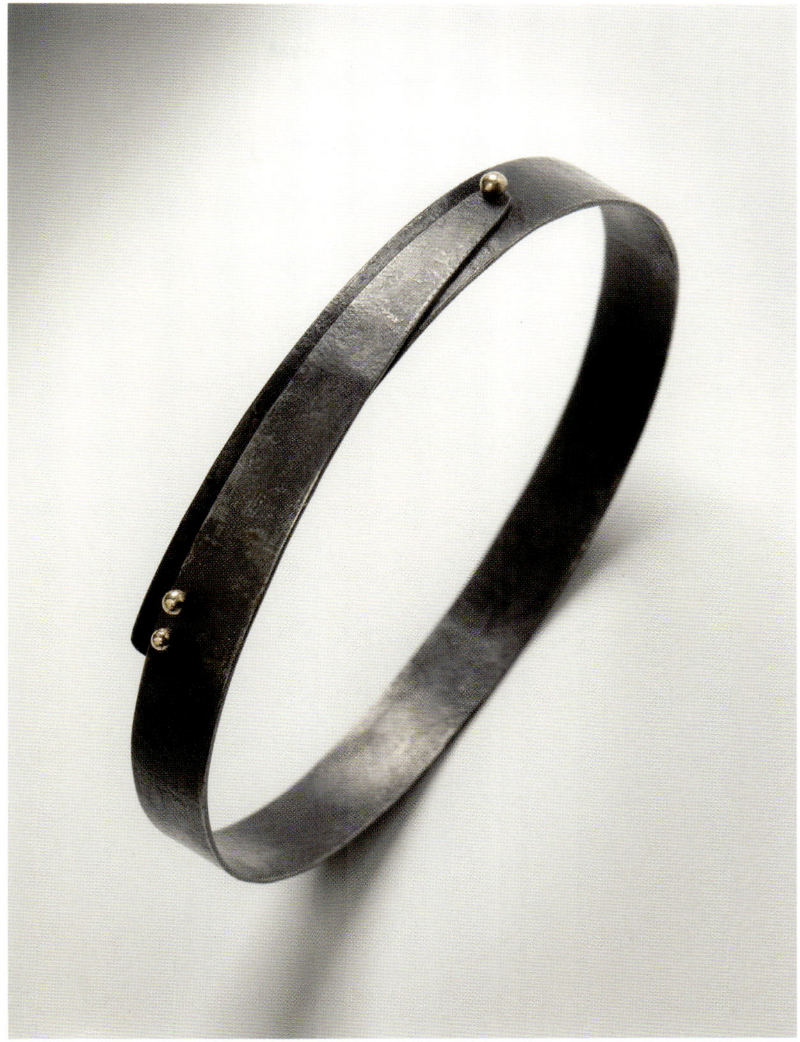

Rivet. Bracelet. 2013. Forged, fabricated. Steel, 14k yellow gold. 3 ½"l x ¾"w x 3"h. *Photo: Don Casper*

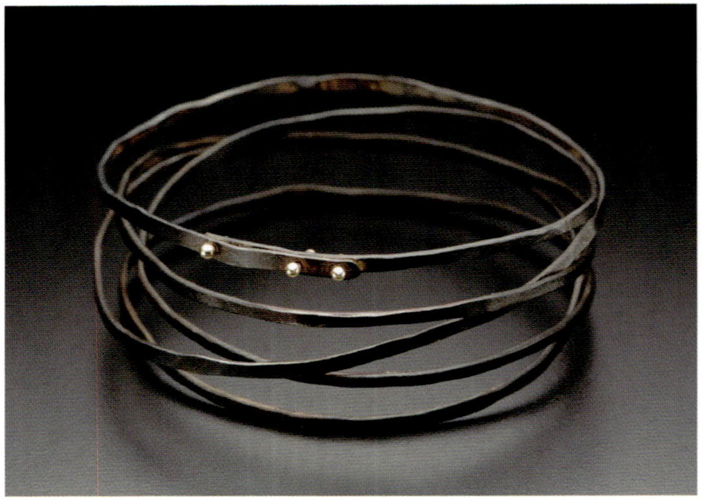

Mommy Dearest II. Bracelet. 2012. Forged, fabricated. Steel, 14k yellow gold. 3½" l x 2"w x 3"h. *Photo: Don Casper*

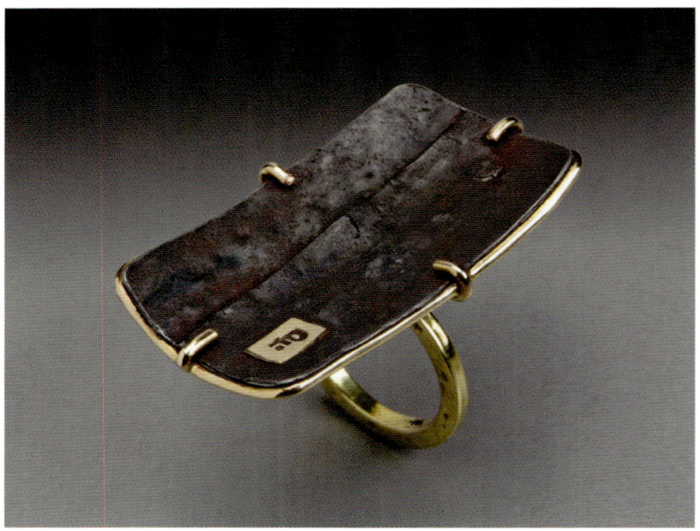

Acid Test. Ring. 2010. Forged, fabricated. Steel, 14k yellow gold. 1½" l x 1"w x 1⅛"h. *Photo: Don Casper*

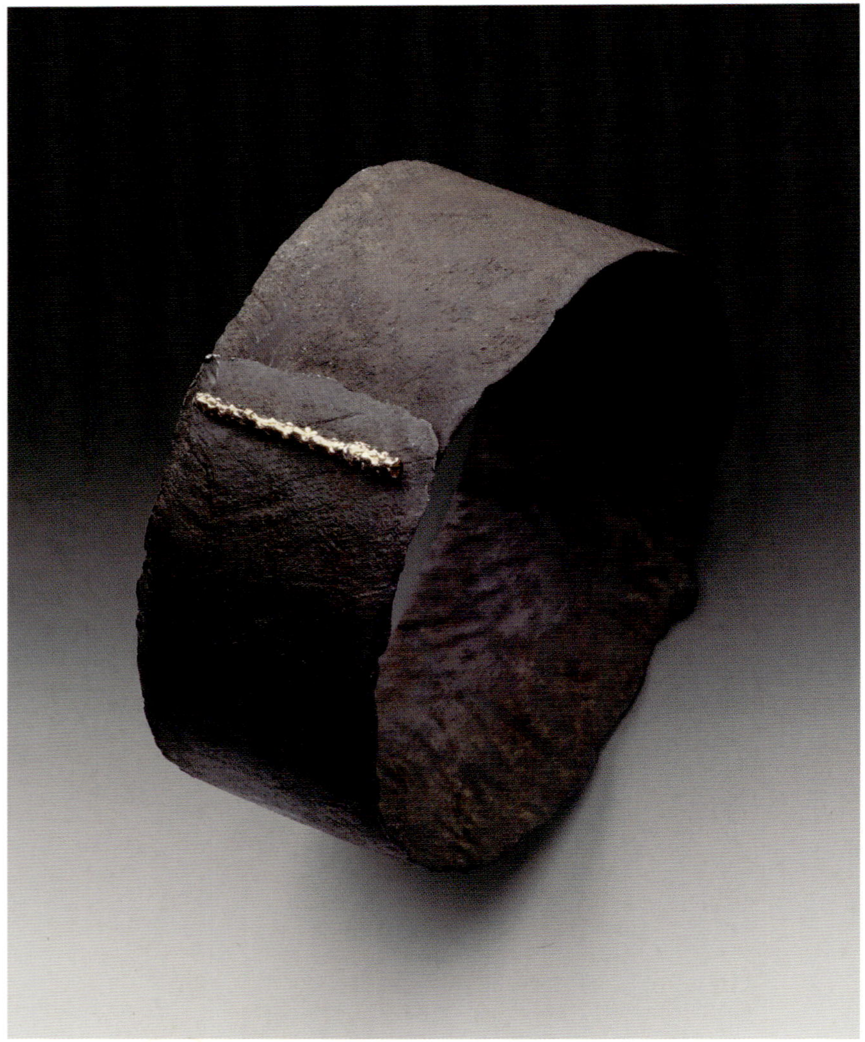

Branch. Bracelet. 2013. Forged, fabricated, cast. Steel, 14k yellow gold. 3½" x l ½"w x 3"h. *Photo: Don Casper*

Jeff Fetty

Jeff Fetty Designs, Spencer, West Virginia
www.jefffetty.com

ARTIST'S STATEMENT

The appeal of working with iron lies in the traditional role of blacksmiths and the permanence of their work. Historically, blacksmiths contributed to the well-being of their neighbors by creating the tools that sustained the community. Their implements and art served and gave pleasure to many generations. I am thankful that I am able to share my work with a broad range of viewers. I hope my art contributes to their well-being.

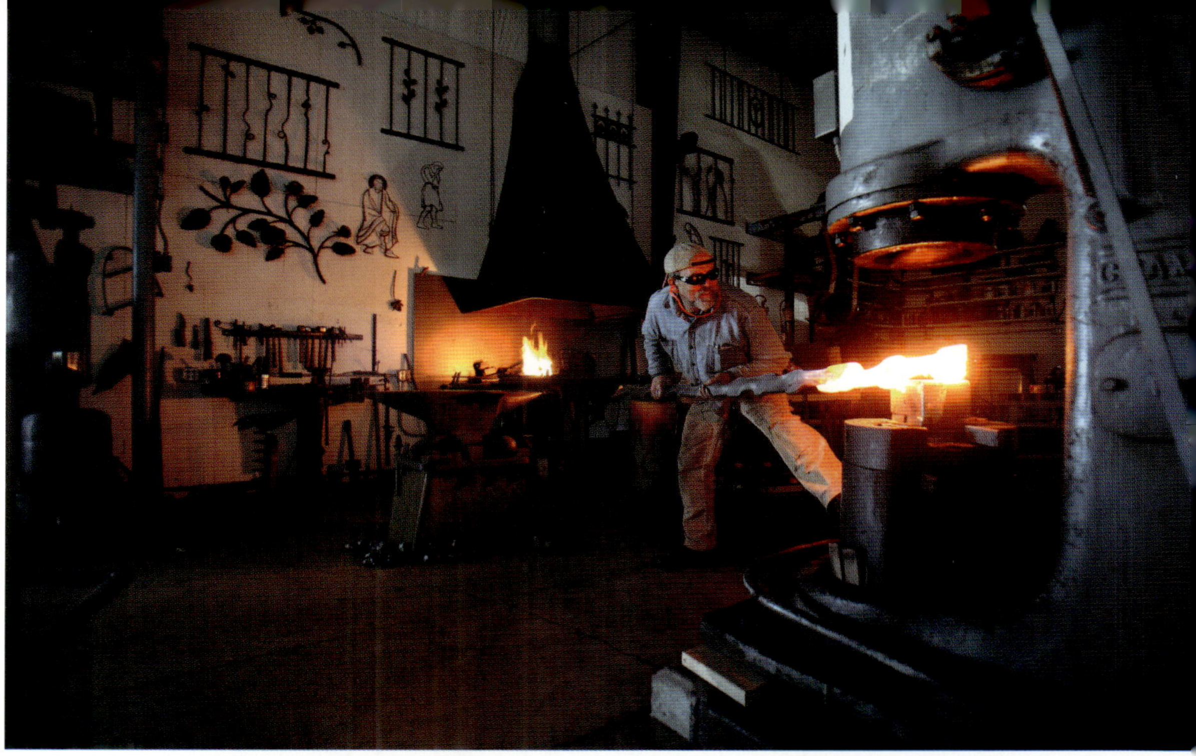

Top: Jeff Fetty at power hammer, forging.

Maple Hills Centre Entrance Project

This entrance was created as a commission in 2011 for a local oil and gas developer and utilizes recycled materials from that industry. The various patinas used are harmonized through the texture of this weathered steel. The elemental design captures the curve of the entrance portico and echoes it in the sign, lamp, and benches.

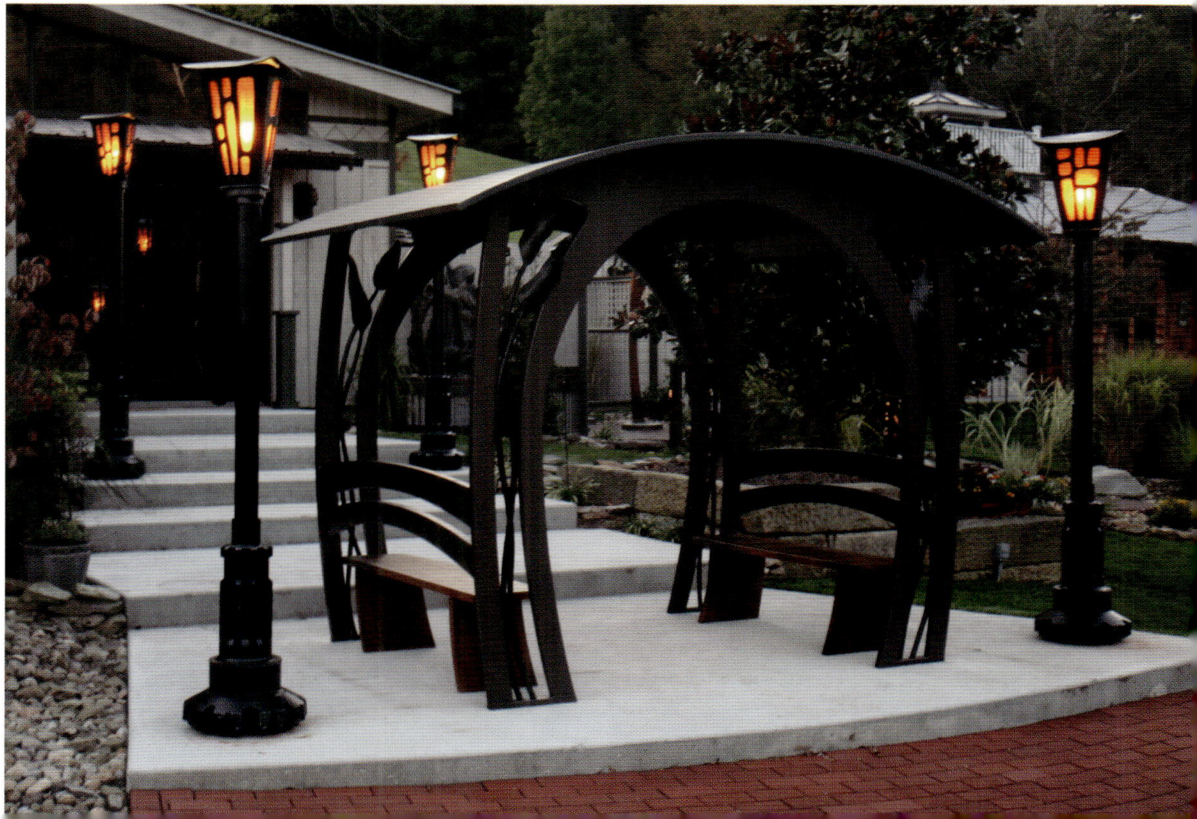

Maple Hills Centre portico. 2011.
Ends cut from single pieces of 1½″ plate-steel.
Roof is ¼″ curved plate-steel. The overall size of the portico is 97″h x 93″w x 72″d.

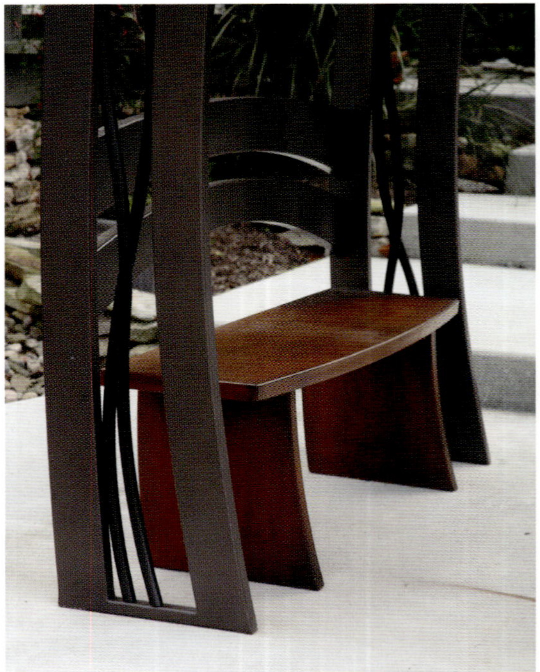

Maple Hills Centre bench. 2011.
Cut from inch-and-a-half plate steel and finished with copper patina.
18″h x 60″w x 20″d.

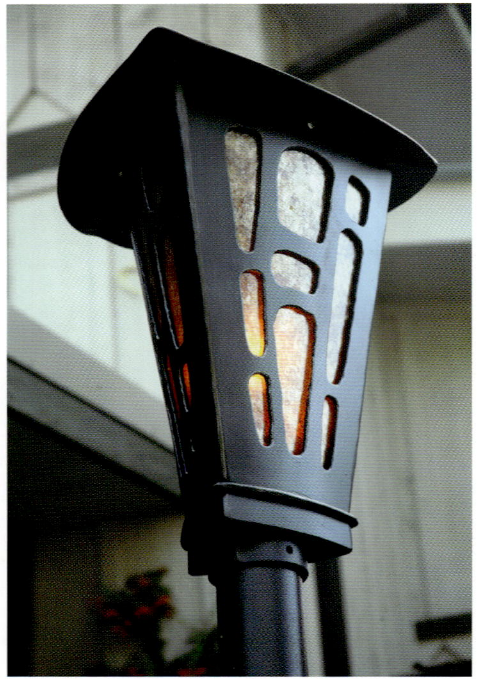

Maple Hills Centre lamp. 2011.
The base is a bit used to drill oil and gas wells throughout the Appalachian region. Sections of pipe, like those used in the lamps, are attached to the bit as the well deepens. Lined with a material from the earth—mica.
104″h x 18″d.

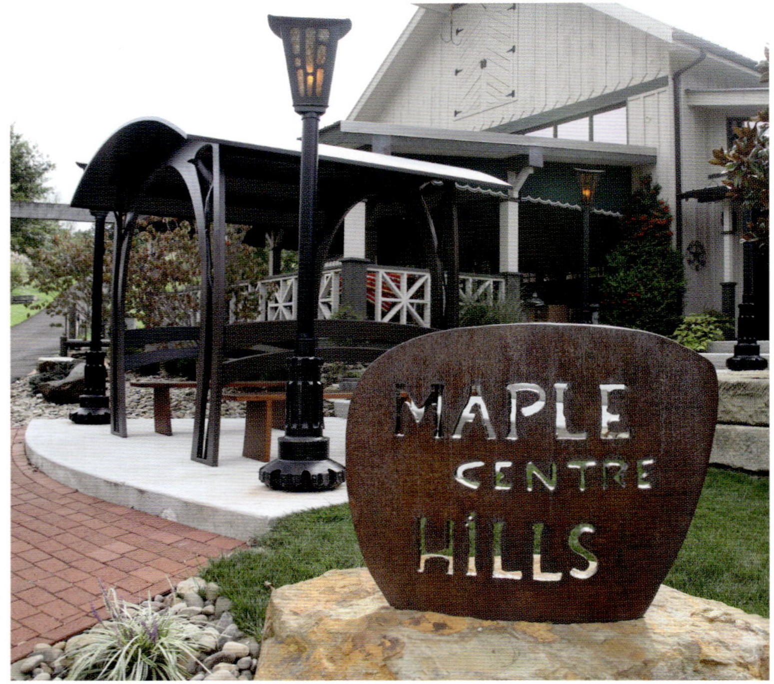

Maple Hills Centre sign. 2011.
Made of 1½″ road plate. The patina reflects the decades spent in the oil field before being formed and cut for its current use. The font was custom designed and hand cut. 40″h x 44″w x 6 ″d.

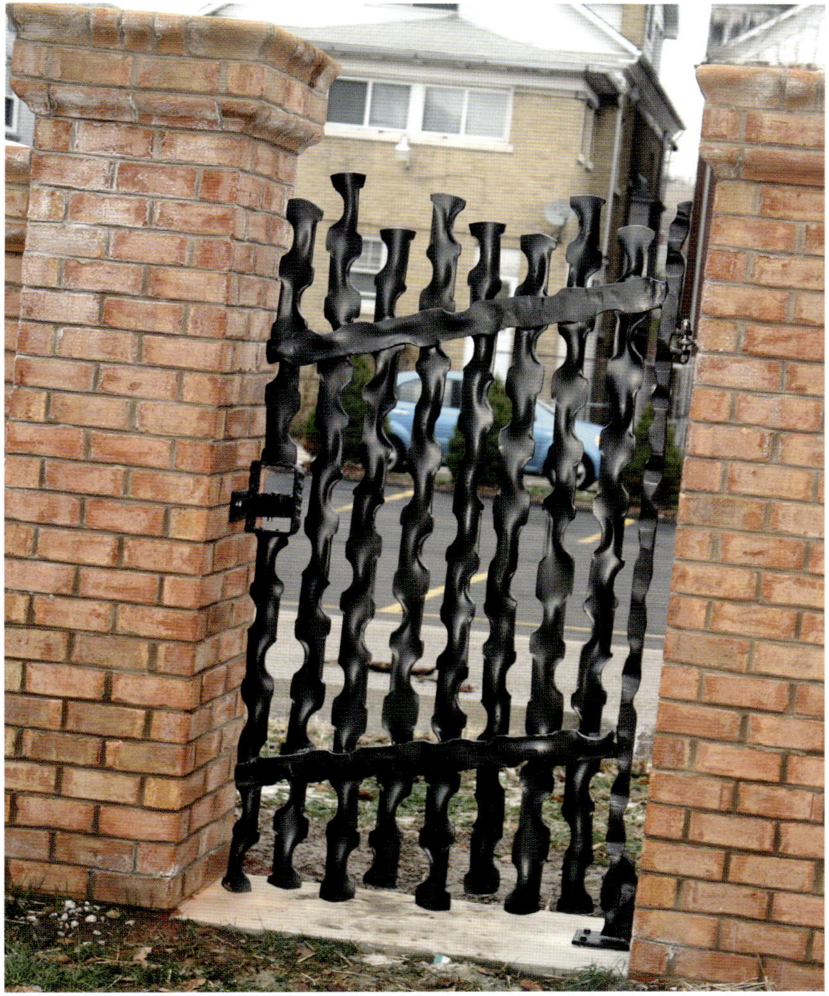

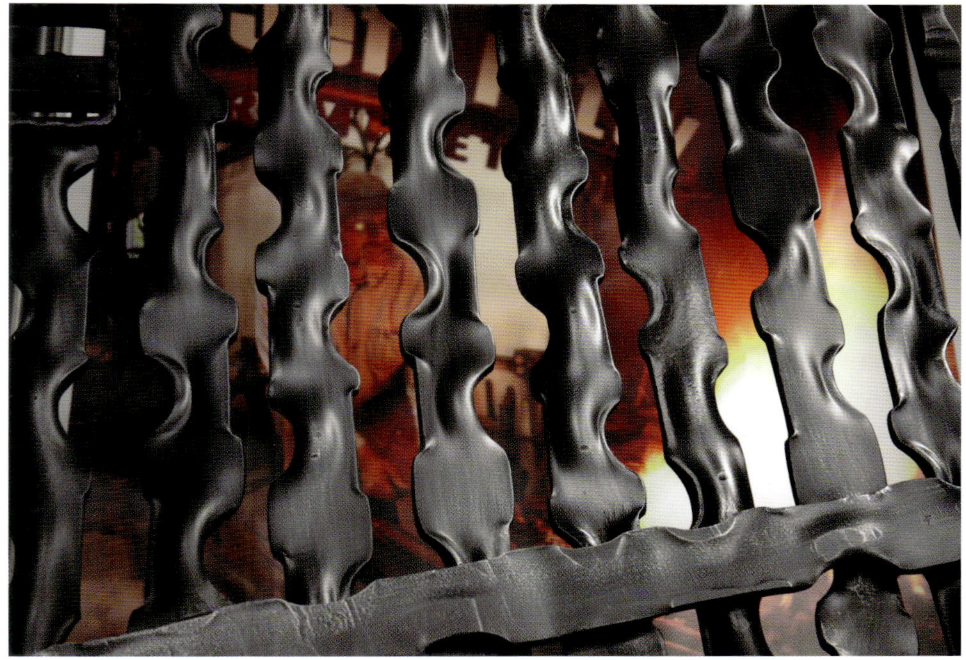

Pedestrian Gate

This heavily forged gate has a customized hinging system carefully designed to operate smoothly and effortlessly. The detail image (above) was taken at the forge before delivery. The gate is positioned in front of a promotional poster.

Pedestrian gate. Commission, 2010.
39″w x 63″h x 3″d.

Steve Fontanini

Jackson, Wyoming
http://fontaniniblacksmith.com

ARTIST'S STATEMENT

Since being introduced to metal work in high school, I have continued to learn more techniques to change metal into desired shapes. Forging is the technique that gives the widest range of possibilities, from daydreams to drawings to reality. Using blacksmithing techniques allows pencil drawings to become "hard" realities. Being able to build projects with unusual designs, using hot metal as my medium, is my goal.

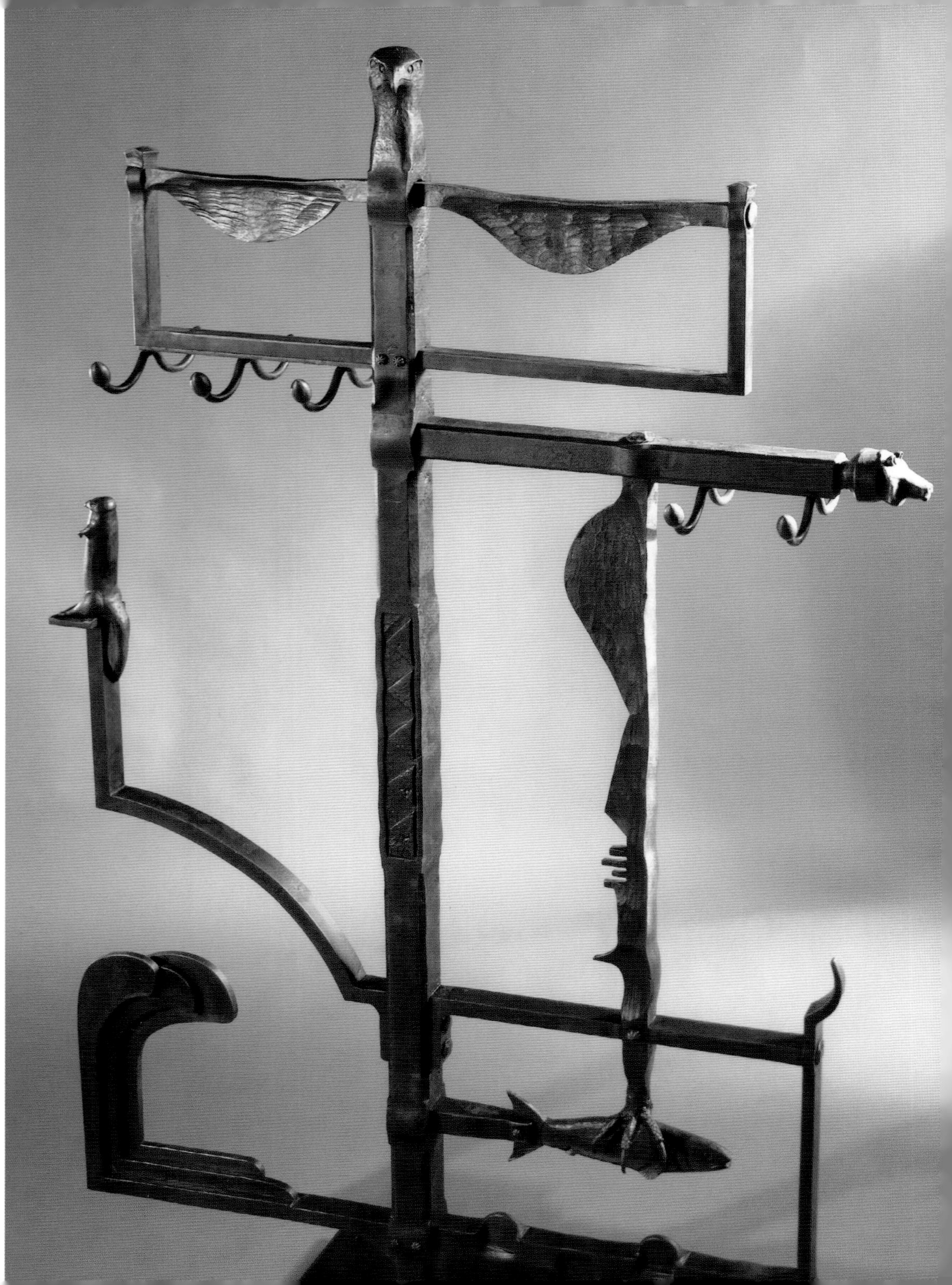

Totem sculpture, or hall tree, with eagle head, talon, fish, otter and bear head and hanging hooks. 2011. Forged. Mild steel. 84" w x 43" h x 6" d.

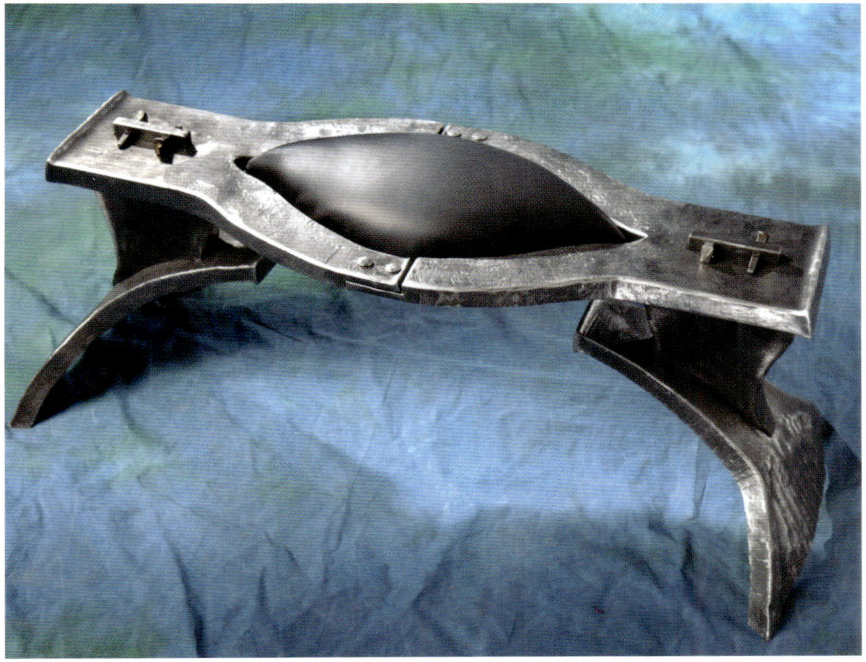

Fluke bench. Forged from 1¼" x 7" mild steel, tapered and split, and held together with wedges and rivets. Padded leather seat. 36"l x 15"h.

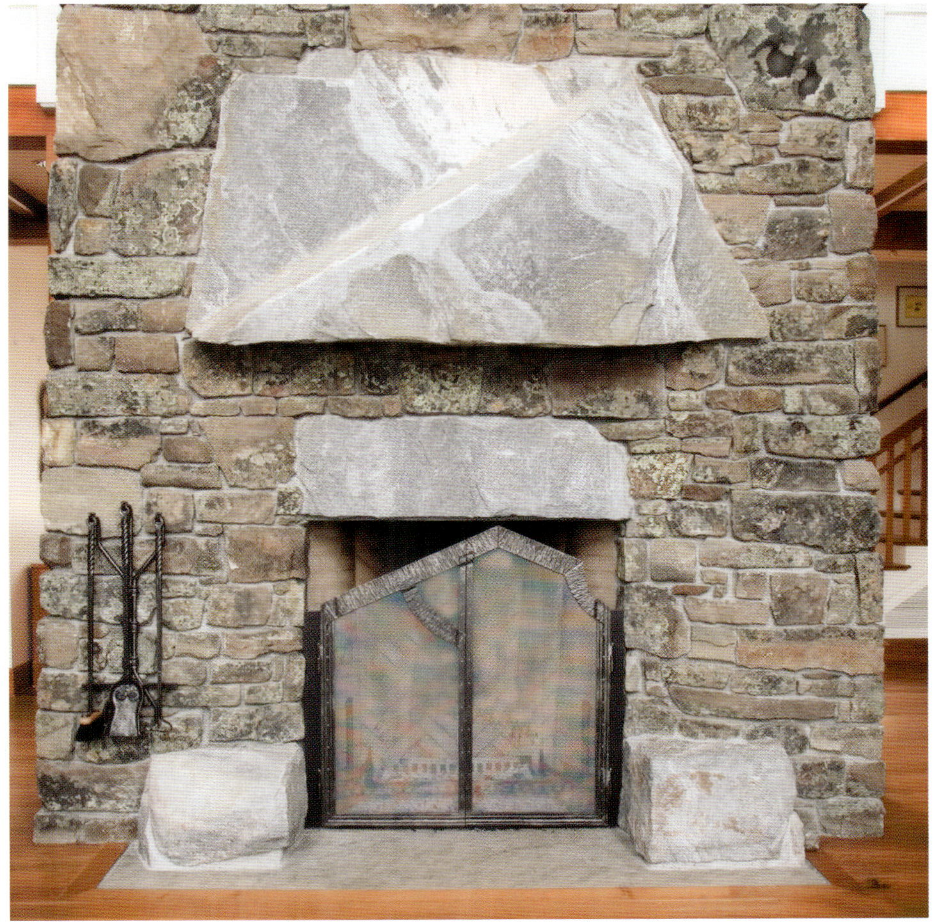

Hinged fire screen doors and tools. Mild steel. Custom designed to fit the rock fireplace.

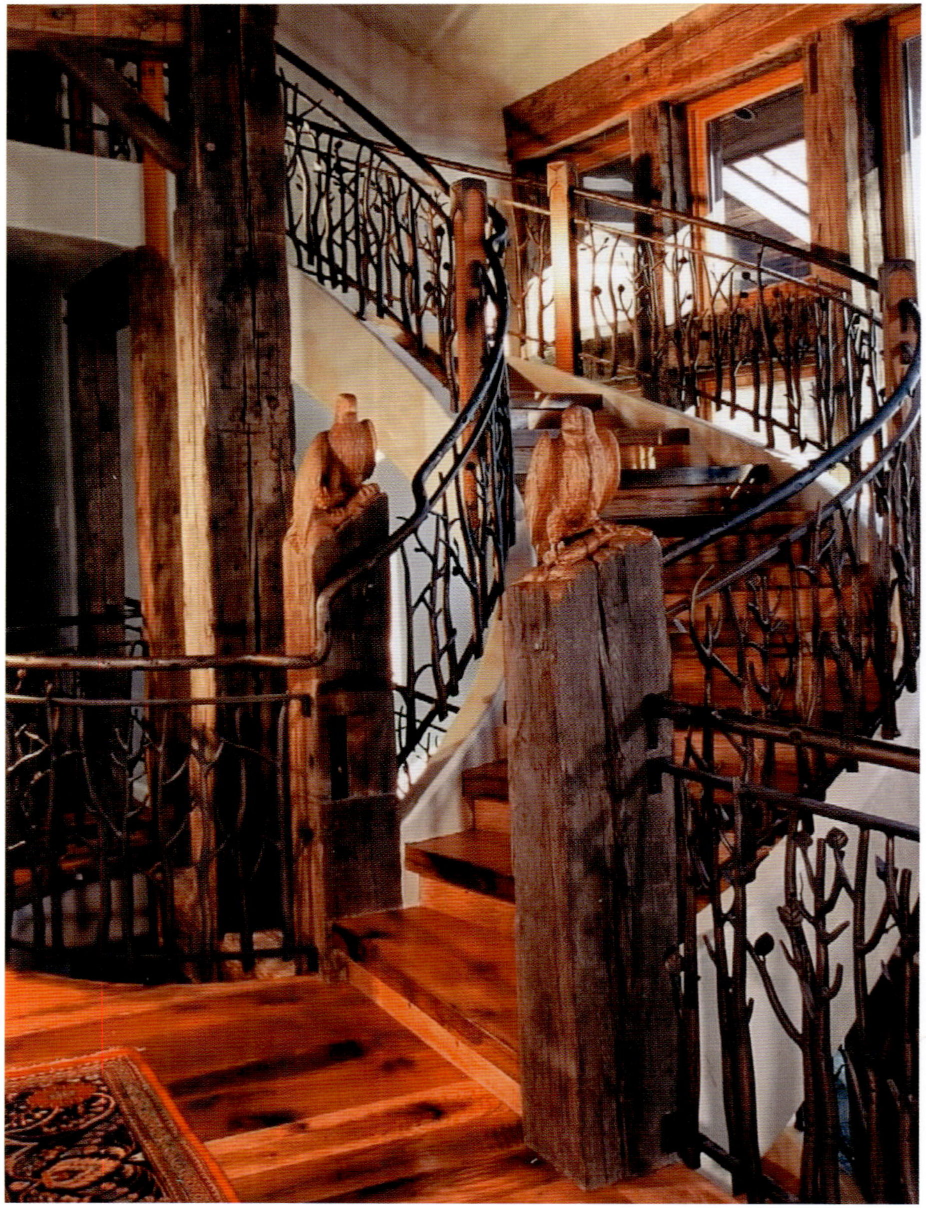

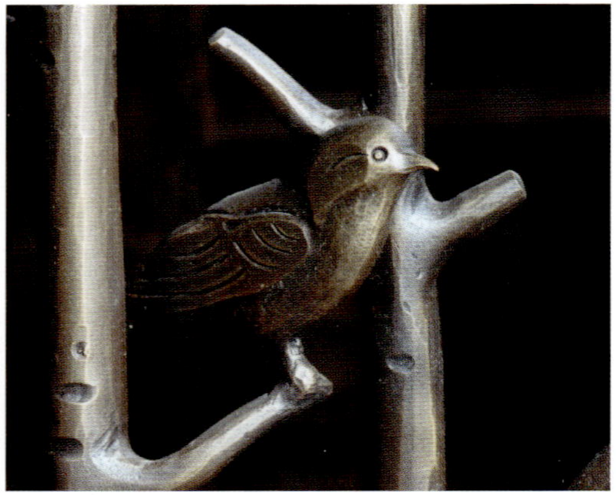

Railing featuring a grove of aspen trees with sixty-five birds representing five species. Bronze.

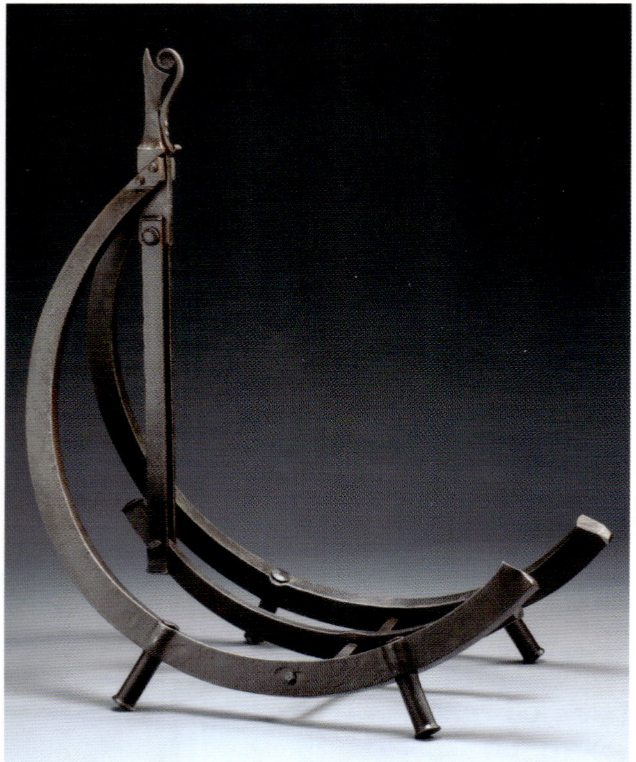

Curved log rack with finial. Mild steel. Hand curved, assembled with mortise and tenon joints and rivets.

Lorenzo Fortunato

Italian Iron Works, Kyle, Texas
Italianironworks.com

ARTIST'S STATEMENT

Life is art. Nature inspires me…the shapes of tree branches, the delicate silhouettes of leaves and flowers along with their infinite textures. I have been creating functional art in Austin, Texas, for over two decades. Inspired by an uncle in Italy during my boyhood, I spent much of my free time watching and learning this ancient craft.

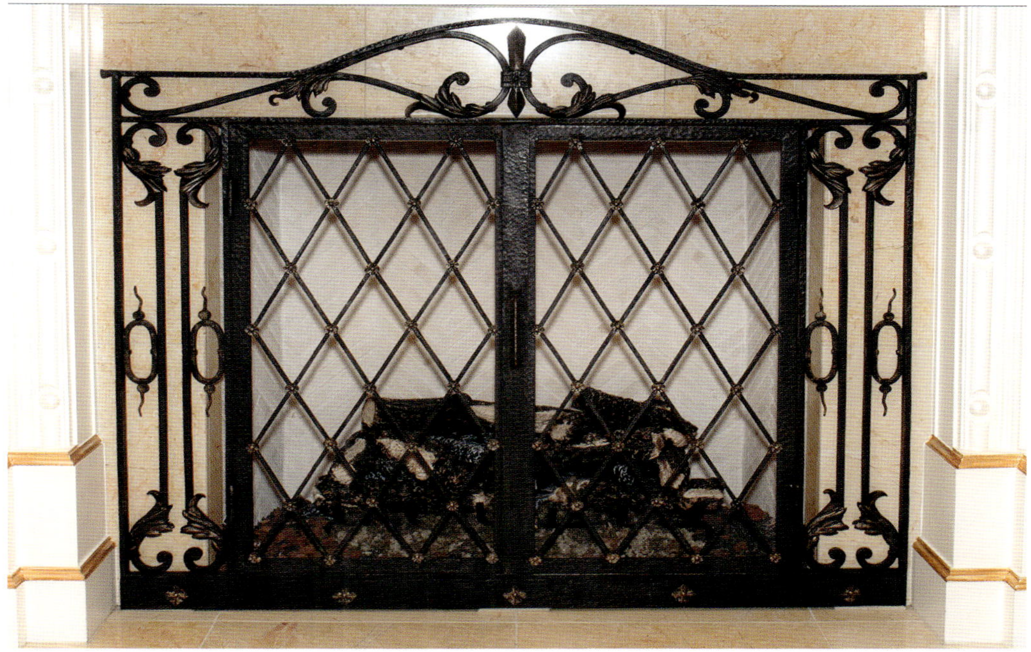

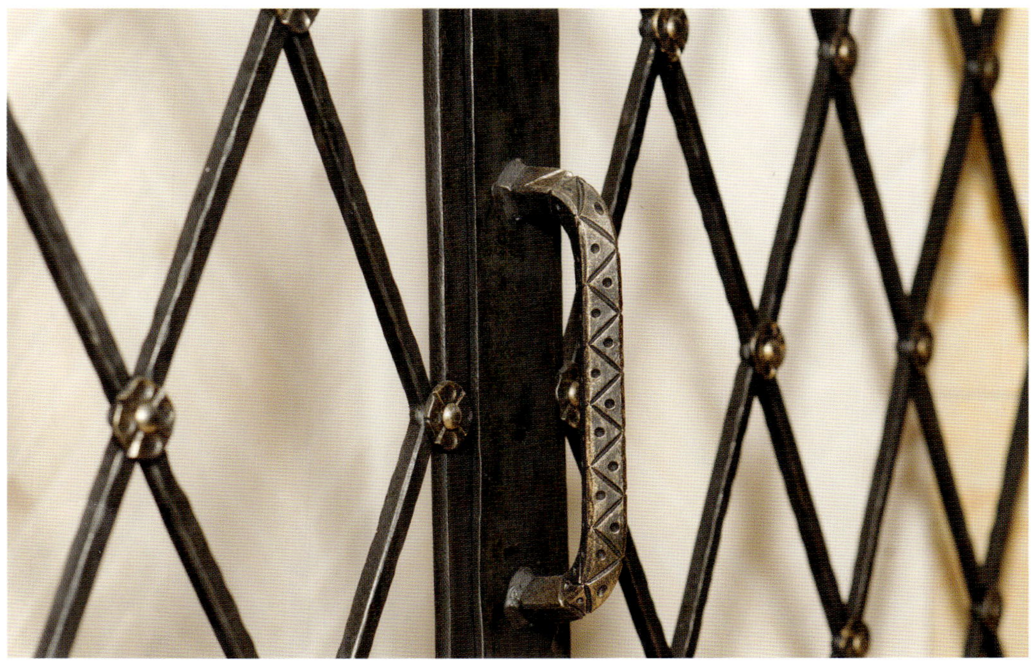

Fire screens

My client wanted two fire screens for her home. She asked that the shape of the mantle and fireplace be an influence in my design. I enjoy detailing my work and customizing each piece into a work of functional art.

Diamond screen. Hammer-textured flower and leaf accents attached with rivets. Traditional beeswax finish with antique gold patina. *Photos: Laurie Fryar Photography*

Door Handle

I enjoy doing oversized door pulls. My back appreciates it as well! I think door hardware definitely makes a door more interesting. Again, it's the detail.

Door handle. Random twist with a traditional beeswax finish. *Photo: Laurie Fryar Photography*

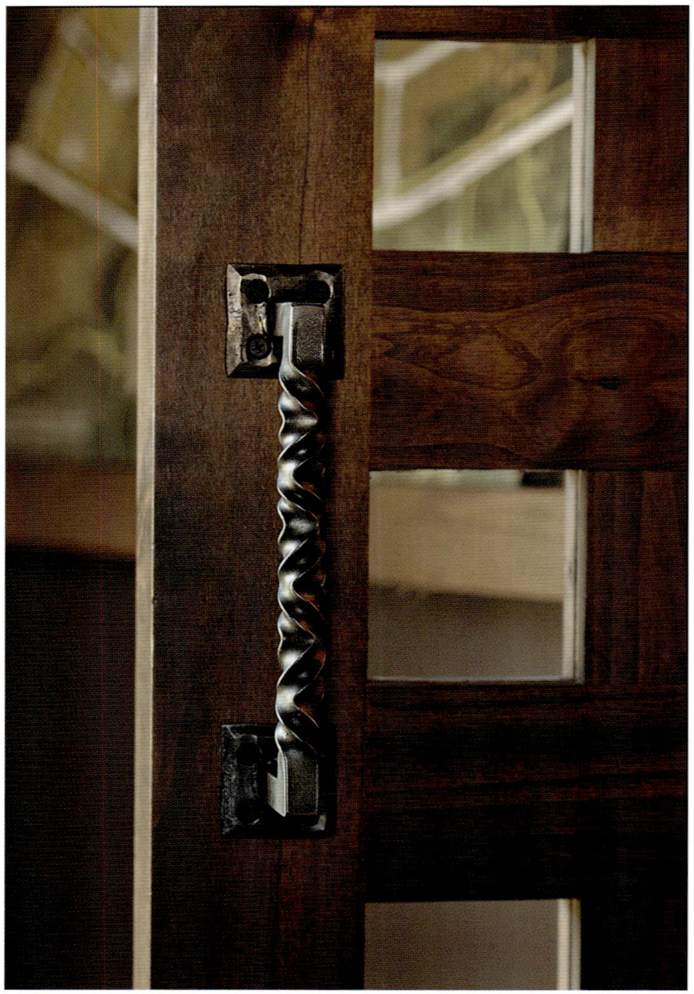

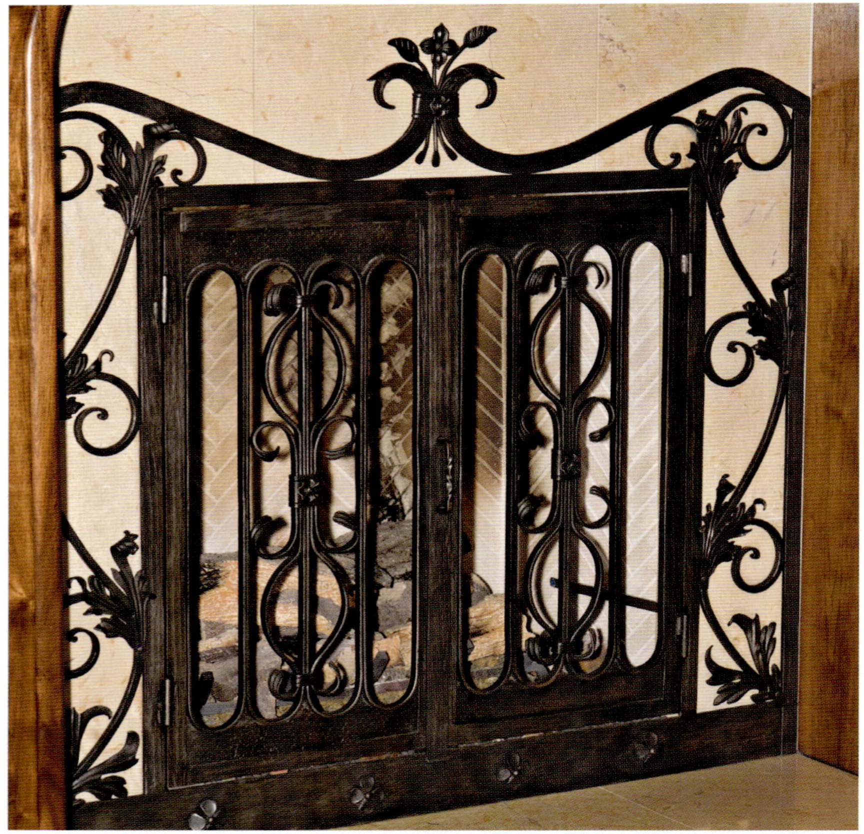

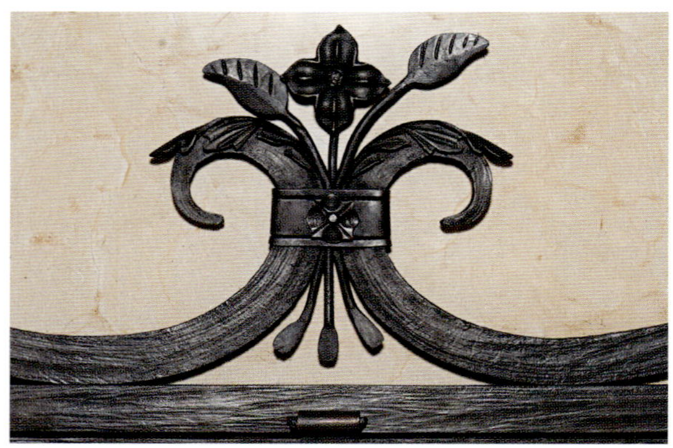

Old World-style screen.
Wood texture finish, center bouquet accent with collar and traditional beeswax. *Photos: Laurie Fryar Photography*

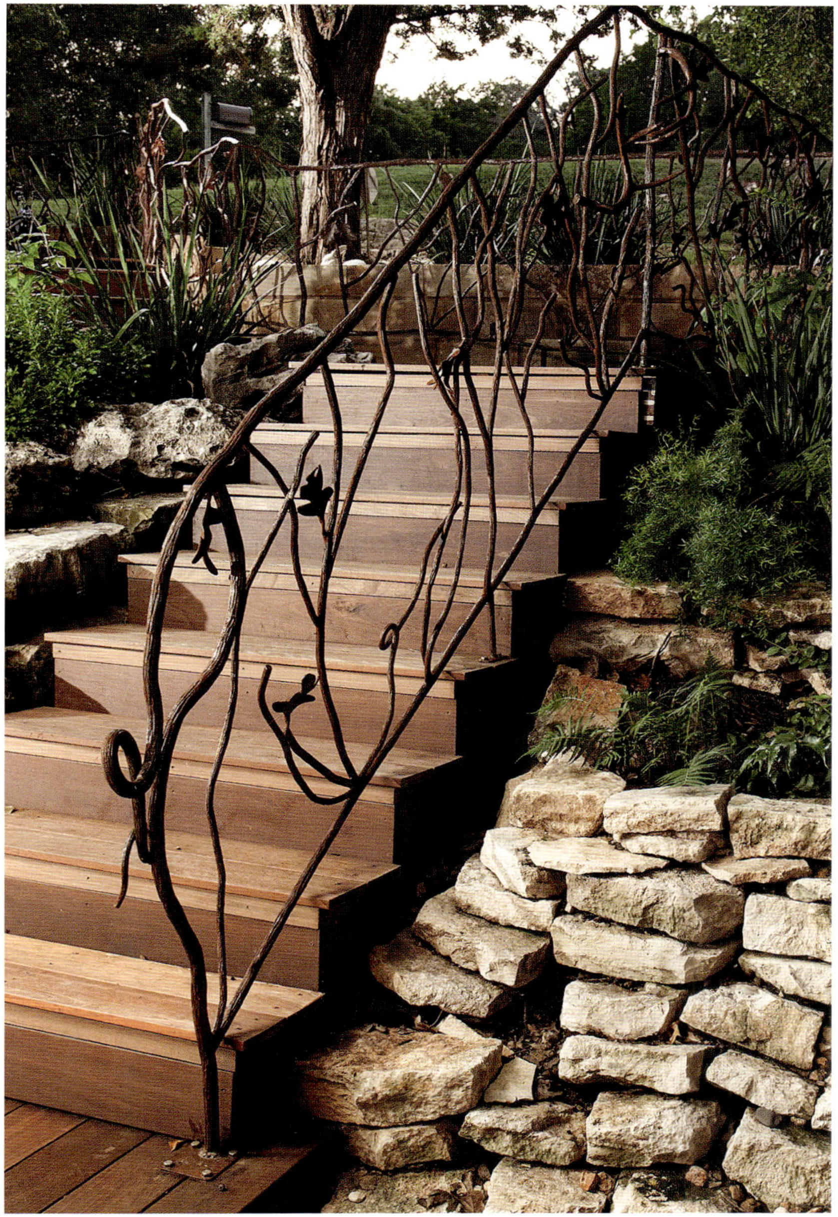

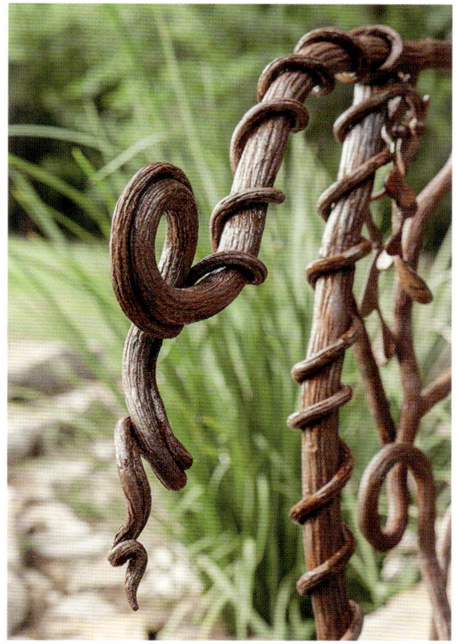

Railing

This was a fun project. My clients wanted a railing that blended into the natural environment of the landscape. They sent photos of deer antlers, trees, limbs, and vines for the feel they wanted and gave me carte blanche! I enjoyed the unstructured look of the railing complemented by intricate detail.

Railing. Natural wood texture, scattered acorns and oak leaves with vines wrapped organically throughout. Rust finish with clear coat seal. *Photos: Laurie Fryar Photography*

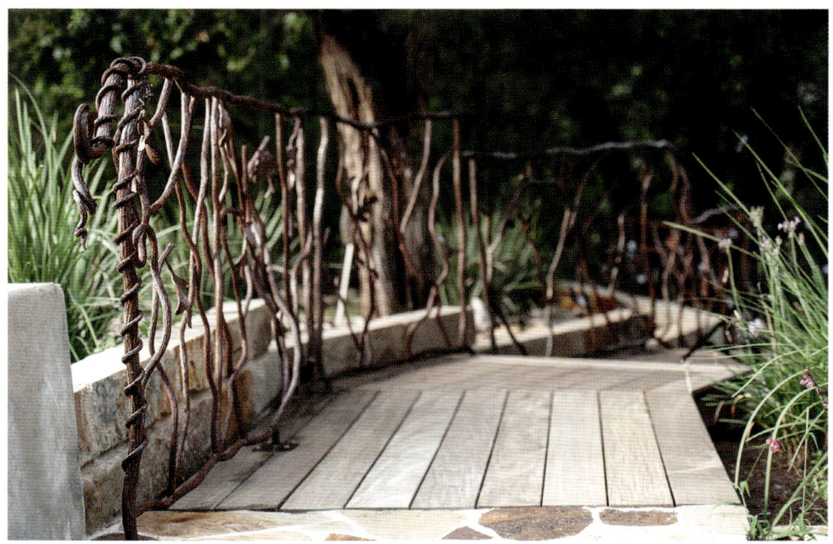

Brady Shea Foster

Metalshop Studio, Austin, Texas
bradyfoster.com

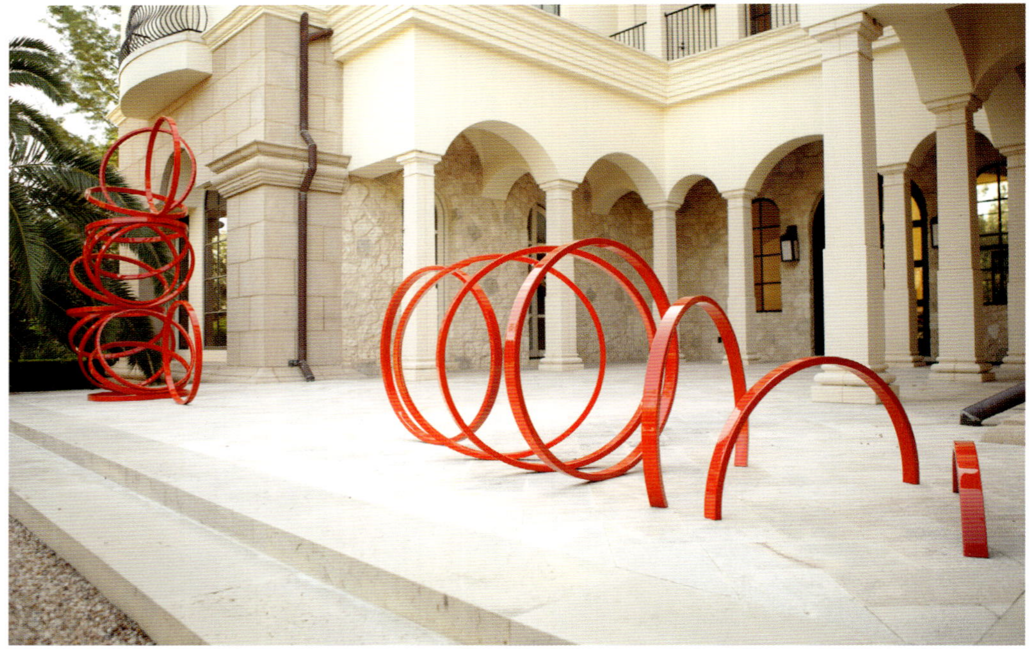

ARTIST'S STATEMENT

I produce as much interesting metalwork as I can, not only by facilitating my designs, but also by collaborating with many different types of clients. I am a husband and a father of two. I work in Austin, Texas, and do my best to handle long days in the heat. I love everything about metal.

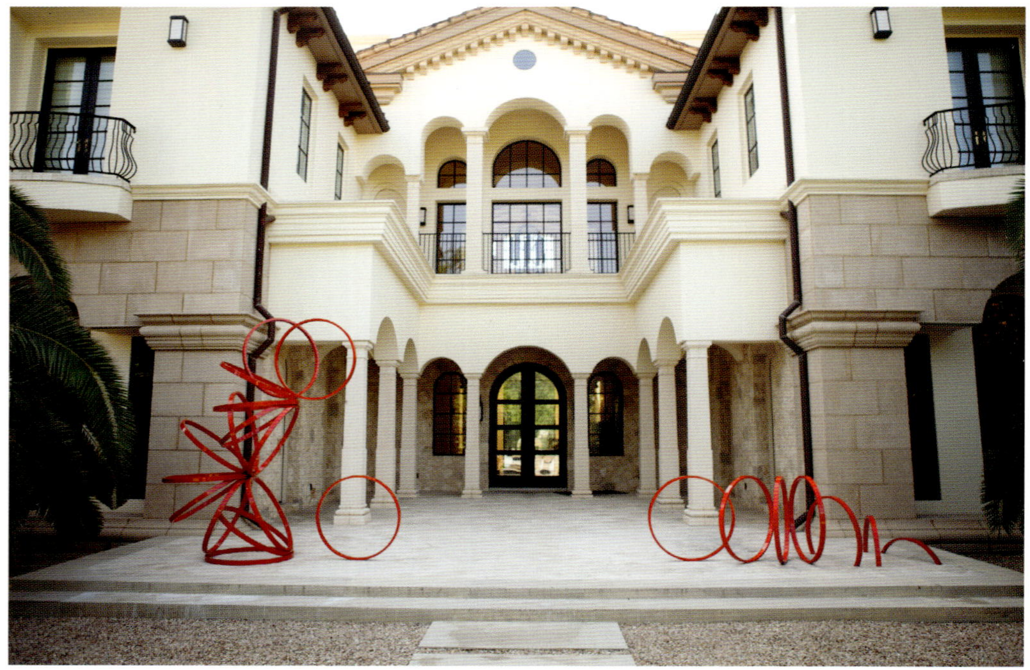

Abundance

This piece was commissioned by a private collector. They asked for a piece for a specific location at their residence. I studied their art collection to find out what their aesthetics in art were and developed a model. They loved it, and I got to produce this piece.

Abundance. Fabricated steel, paint.
108"x 36"x 28'.

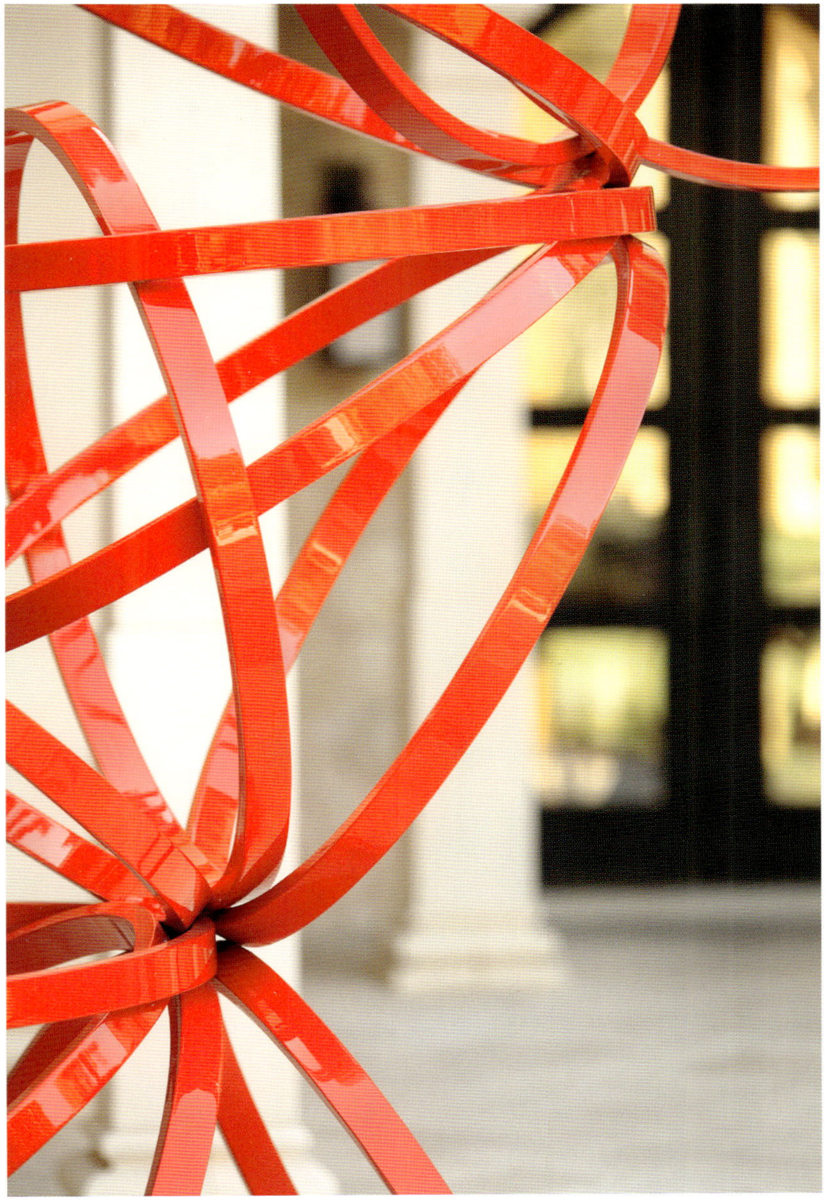

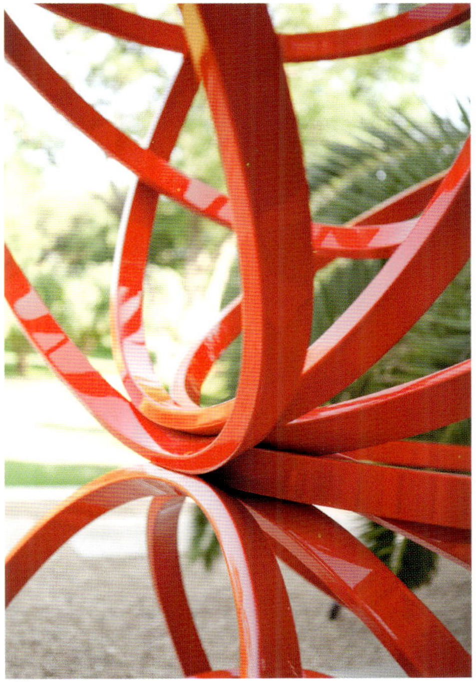

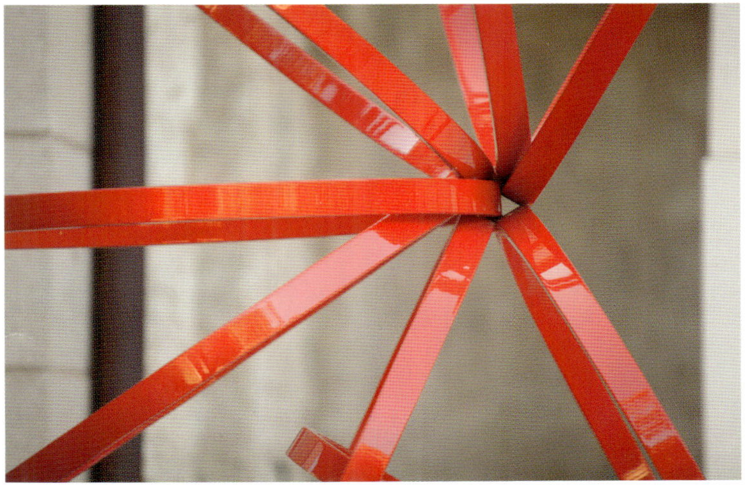

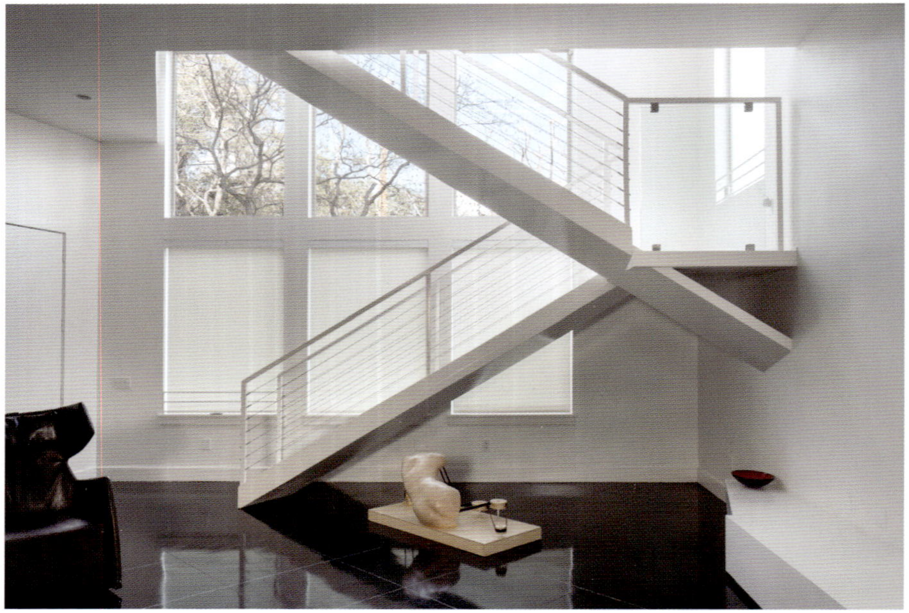

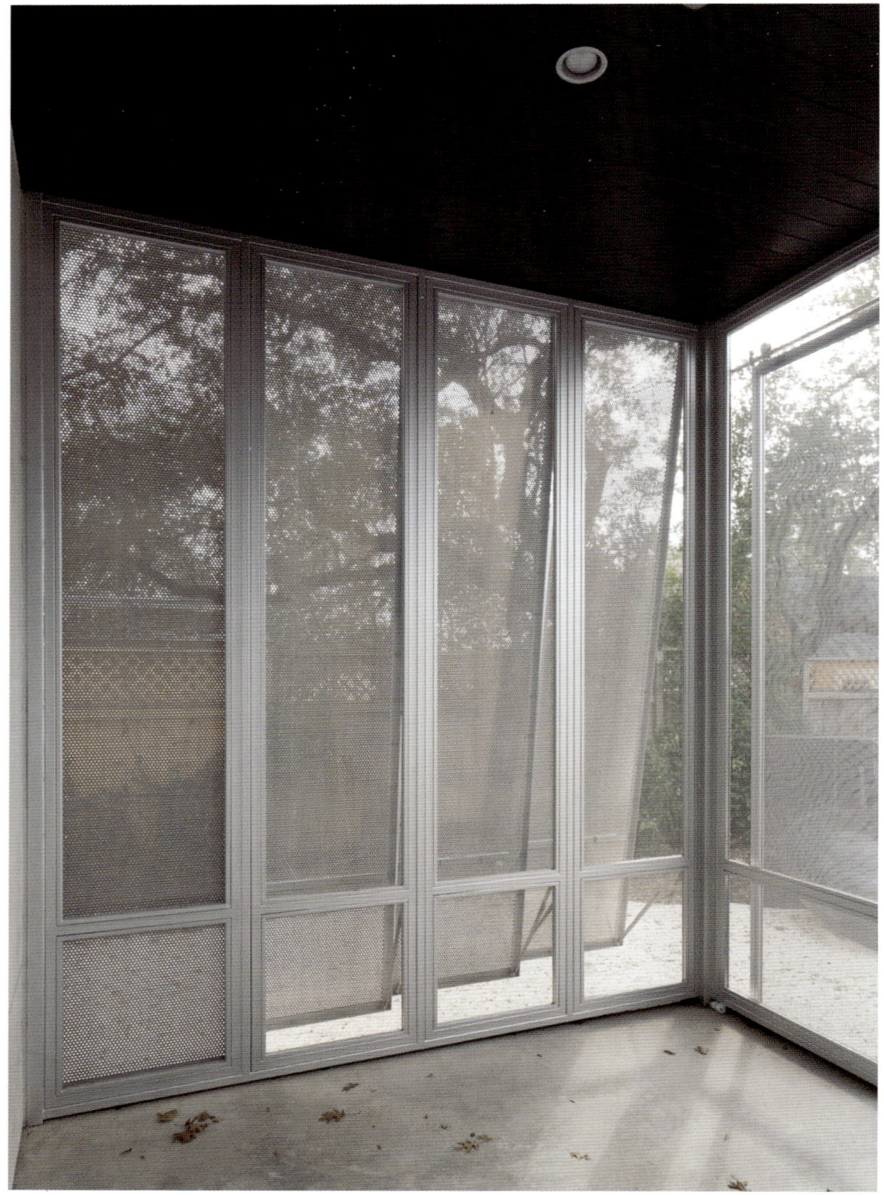

Cheesar Staircase and Shutter Porch

This staircase was a "remodel" of an existing stair. It was done collaboratively by Cass Cheesar, Cass Cheesar Architects, and his clients while I assisted on the technical side of the design to incorporate their aesthetics into a structural and beautiful stairwell. This also is true for the shutter porch on the same residence.

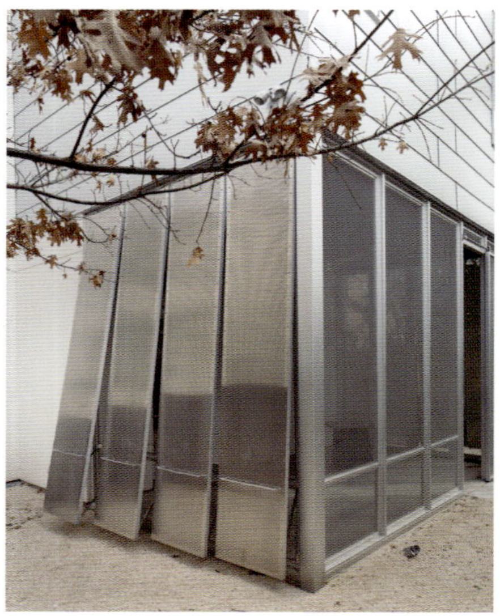

Cheesar staircase and shutter porch.
Private residence.

Rebekah Frank

San Francisco, California
www.rebekahfrank.com

ARTIST'S STATEMENT

Working with steel was my first love, a continual fascination. The way the material resists your efforts, the way it hits back, the way it absorbs the warmth of your skin while also being receptive to imprint, possessing a softness that belies the initial obstinacy. When I began making objects for the body, it was natural for me to continue to use steel. It is where my skills lie, where my knowledge has been focused, and the lack of preciousness makes experimentation possible. While it may not be a traditional material for creating jewelry, I have found it to be full of potential and a constant source of surprises.

Experimental Forms

I love this collection of twisted pieces: a piece of overworked steel, the heart of a chain sawed tree, and a pinecone. The steel was twisted past the acceptable working heat so there is a frayed quality to the material, which feels wonderful in the hand, as does the rest of the collection.

Experimental forms. Objects. 2010. Steel, wood, pine cone. Twisting. Each object approximately 7". *Photo: Rebekah Frank*

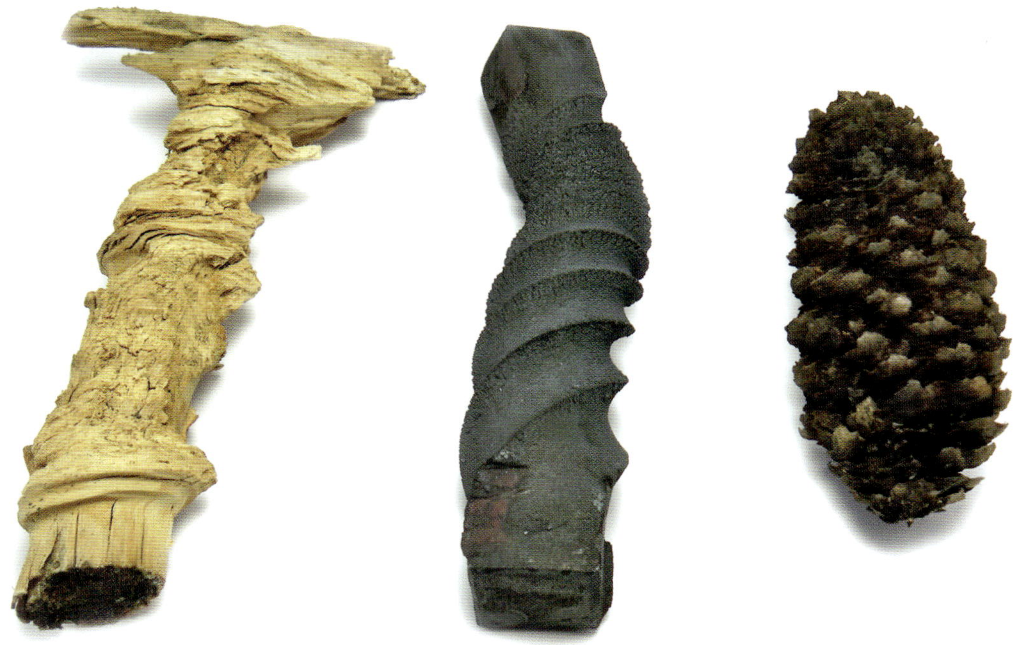

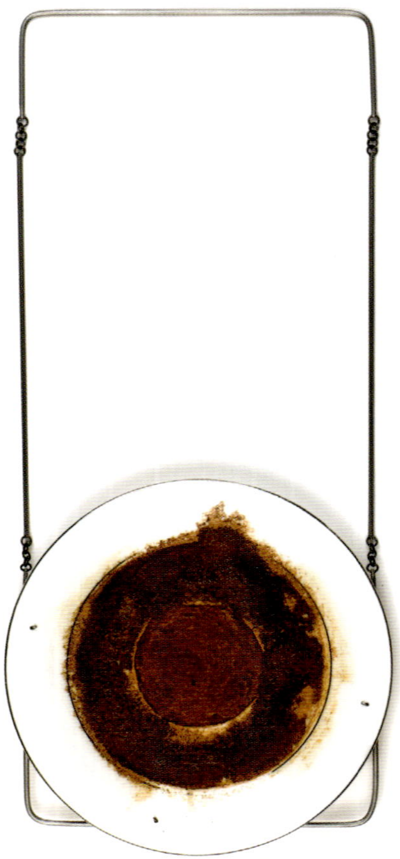

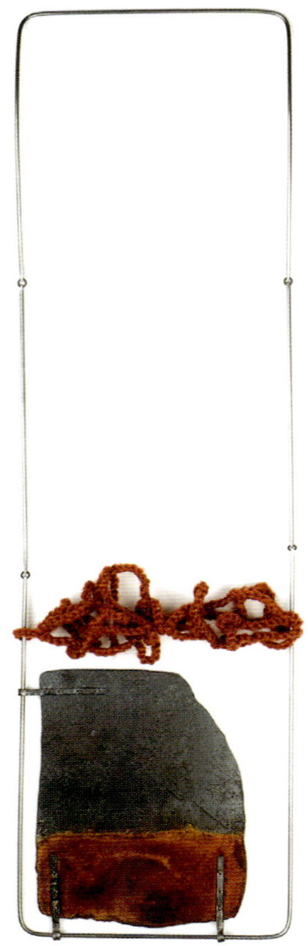

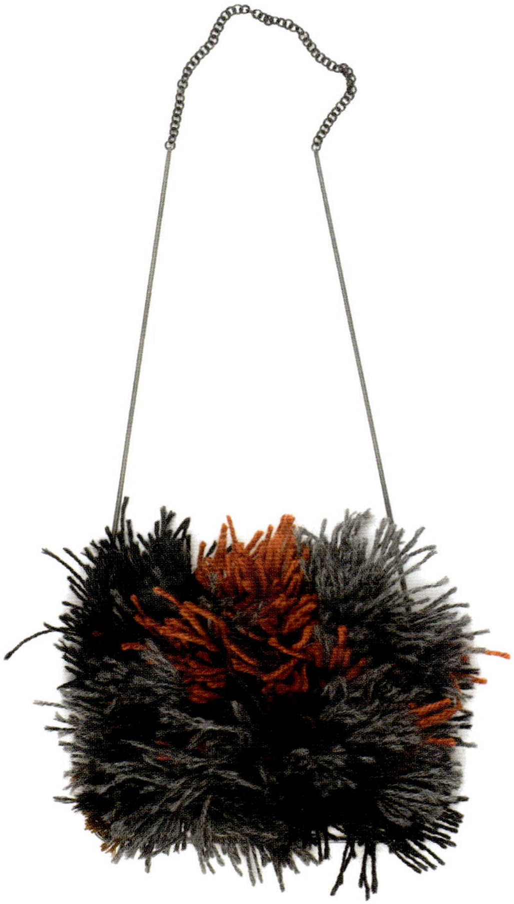

Rust Rhymes

This collection of necklaces was a collaborative experiment between Iris Eichenberg and myself. Starting with steel and rust, we played around with different ways of seeing the material. A patchwork of different colors of wool that brings to mind a rusty piece of steel, a porcelain plate stained with iron filings that were rusted a gorgeous red brown, a steel plate dipped in rusted iron filings held in place by tiny strap hinges, riveted in place. It was a fun project and the pieces were exhibited at Galerie Louise Smit (Amsterdam, the Netherlands) in 2012.

Rust Rhyme 1. Necklace. 2012.Steel, porcelain, rust. Drilling, chain making. 16″ x 6″ x ¼″. *Photo: Katie MacDonald*

Rust Rhyme 2. Necklace. 2012. Steel, rust, wool. Welding, drilling, knitting, riveting, chain making. 20″ x 6″ x ¼″. *Photo: Katie MacDonald*

Rust Rhyme 3. Necklace. 2012. Steel, wool. Latch hook, chain making. 15″ x 6″ x ¼″. *Photo: Katie MacDonald*

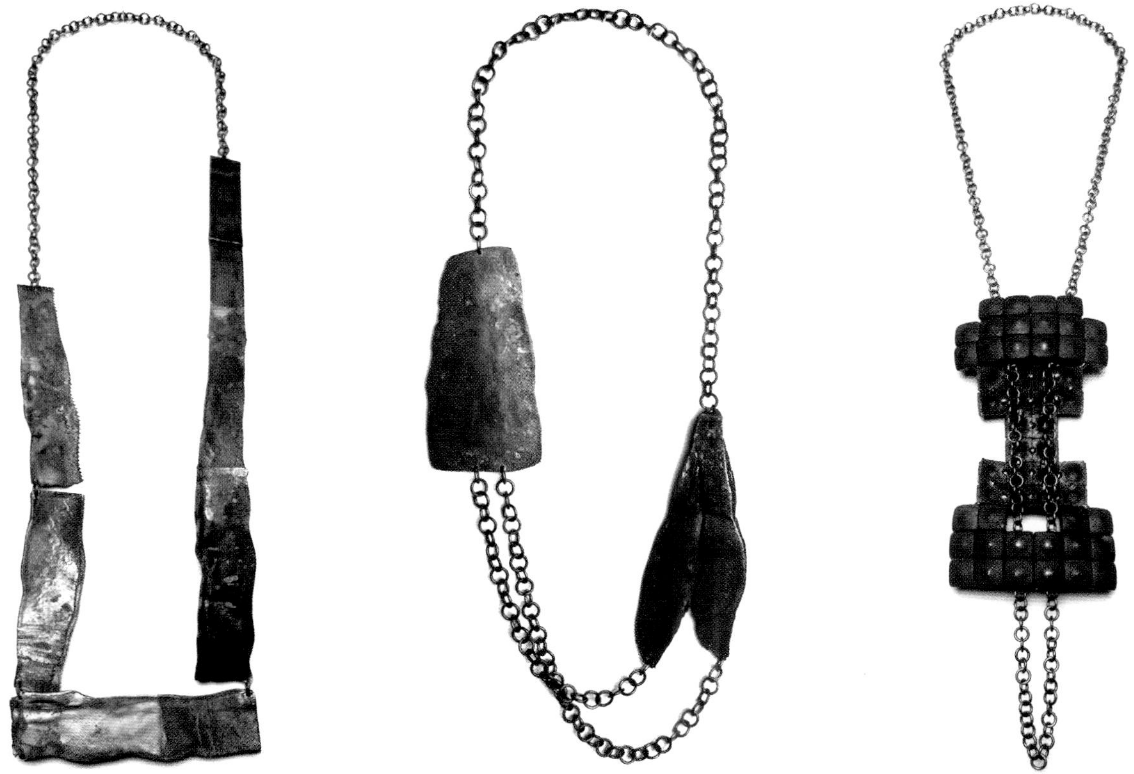

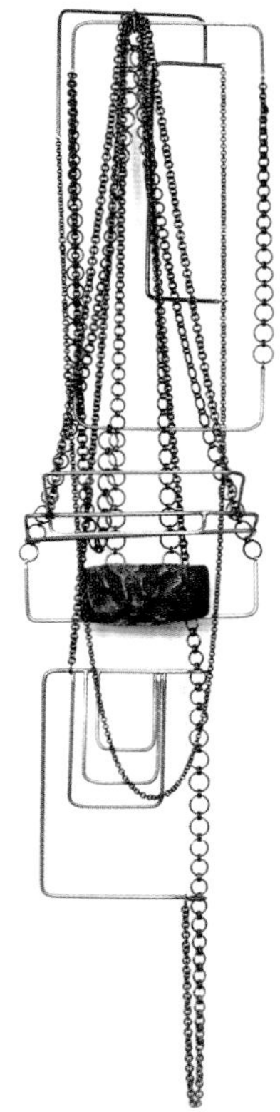

010 Trio

These three pieces were some of the first successful explorations of using steel components on the body. Figuring out the balance of the pieces so they sat well on the body was important, as well as making sure that the weight wasn't too heavy to be worn comfortably. Two of these three pieces are in private collections and are worn by their owners.

Untitled, Sawblades. Necklace. 2010. Steel, tool steel. Forge welding, drilling, chain making. 18" x 6" x ¼". *Photo: Rebekah Frank*

Untitled, Cloven. Necklace. 2010. Steel, iron. Welding, soldering, chain making. 16" x 4" x ¼". *Photo: Rebekah Frank*

Untitled, Shell. Necklace. 2010. Steel. Welding, chain making. 17" x 6" x ½". *Photo: Rebekah Frank*

Collection, Jumble

This image shows the current direction of my work with steel wire and chain, using some forged elements. Playing with the line weight of the chain and the way that the body interacts with the moving parts became a place that I could experiment.

Collection, Jumble. 15 necklaces. 2012. Steel. Soldering, drilling, chain making. Varying measurements. *Photo: Rebekah Frank*

Chuck Fraser

Fraser Ironworks LLC , Joseph, Oregon
www.fraserironworks.com

ARTIST'S STATEMENT

When I was ten years old, my cousins and I were playing at my grandparents' farm near Rockford, Washington, when we discovered what I was sure could only be a coal grinder. I had my cousin turn the crank while I fed lumps of coal into the fan blades. It made a loud enough noise to cause our grandfather to come out of the house and put a stop to all coal grinding. Later, he explained to me that what I thought was a coal grinder was really a forge and what I was feeding coal into was the blower. He then lit the forge, showed me how it worked, explained to me what a blacksmith did, the things that he made, and how he made them. I found blacksmithing fascinating then and, forty years later, I still do.

When it comes to my work, if you see something you like that came from my shop, give part of the credit to my grandfather; the people who work for me; and the people who have found, sold, or given me the old tools that make it possible for me to work. Also, credit my wife, Chris, who critiques my work and puts up with a lot of dirty hand prints on her clean house, and my daughters, Ginger and Jill, who put up with a soot-covered father who was always dragging home rusty, greasy tools.

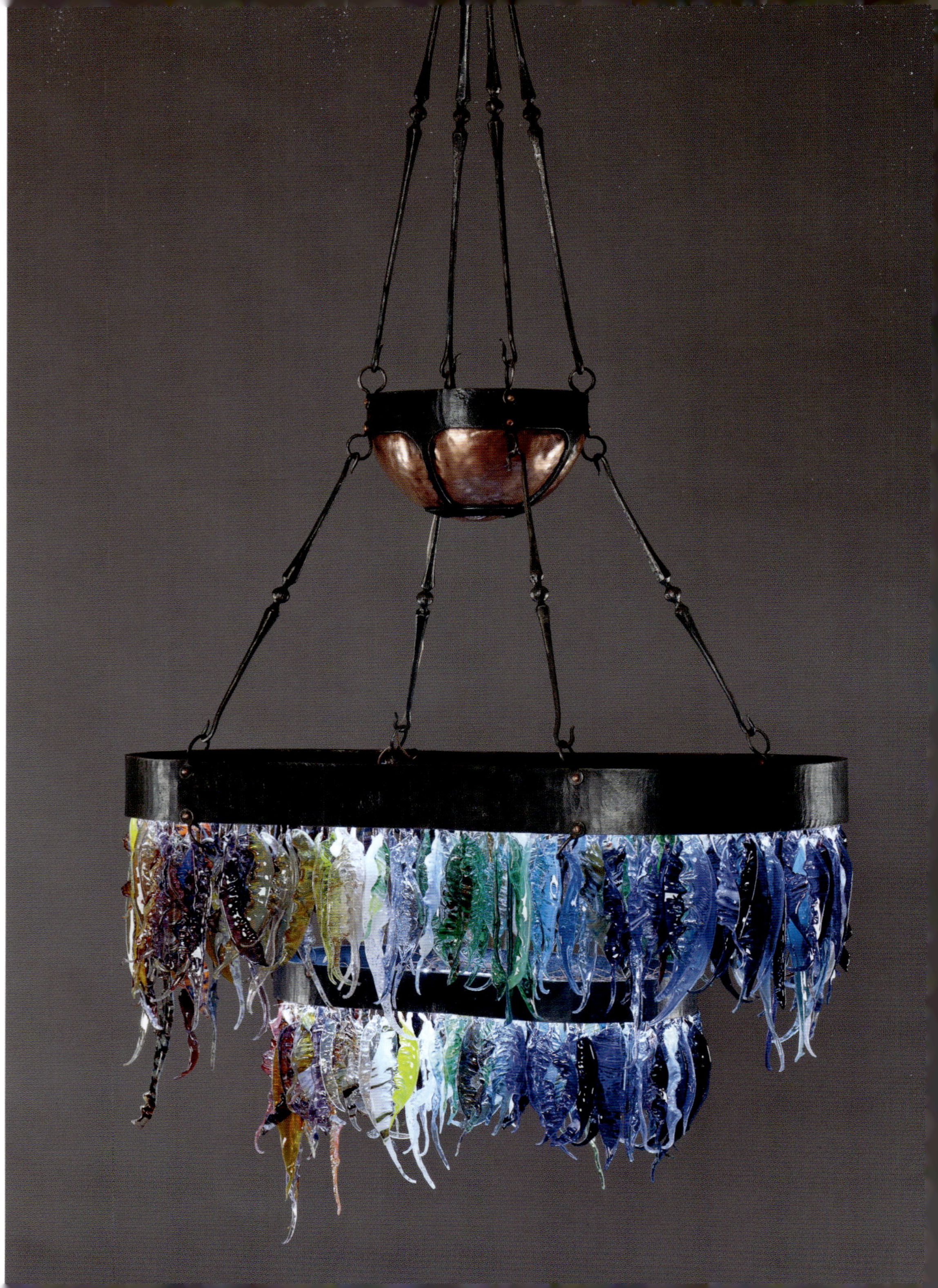

Chandelier. Bowl is made with a hammered copper inlay. All iron forged and textured with texturing tools under power hammer, with handmade colored glass strips from Moonshine Glass in Wallowa, Oregon. Dimmable LED strip lights. 32"l x 20"w x 60"h.
Photo: Kendrick Moholt Photography

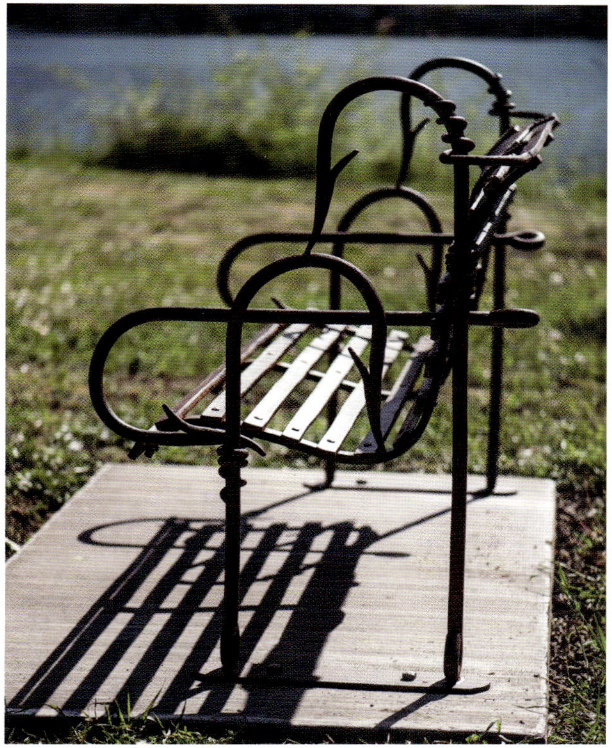

Mr. Bill Knox memorial bench. Wallowa Lake, Oregon. Forged giant iron fish hooks form the legs and arms of the bench; textured seat slats are riveted to the frame. Rust patina with wax finish. *Photo: Kendrick Moholt Photography*

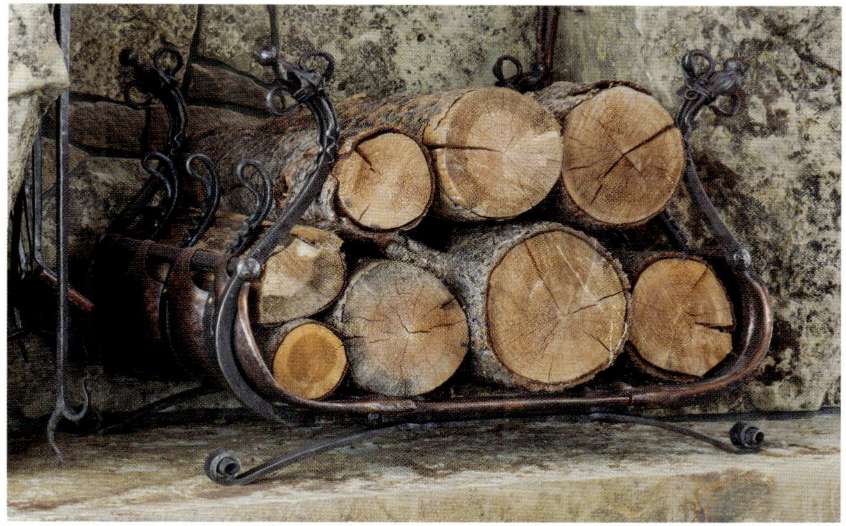

Firewood rack. Forged iron held together with hot punched mortise holes that receive swagged tenons that are hot riveted. A 1/8″ thick hammered copper liner, with brass rivets, lines the inside of the rack. 40″w x 36″d x 28″h. D. Holm collection. *Photo: Kendrick Moholt Photography*

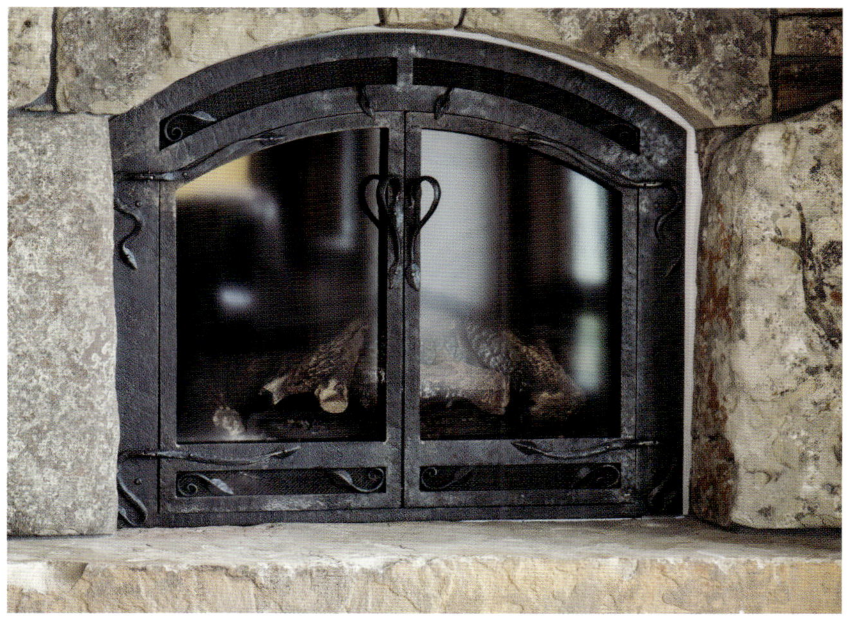

Custom fireplace doors. Forged textured iron, glass, and iron screen. D. Holm collection. *Photo: Kendrick Moholt Photography*

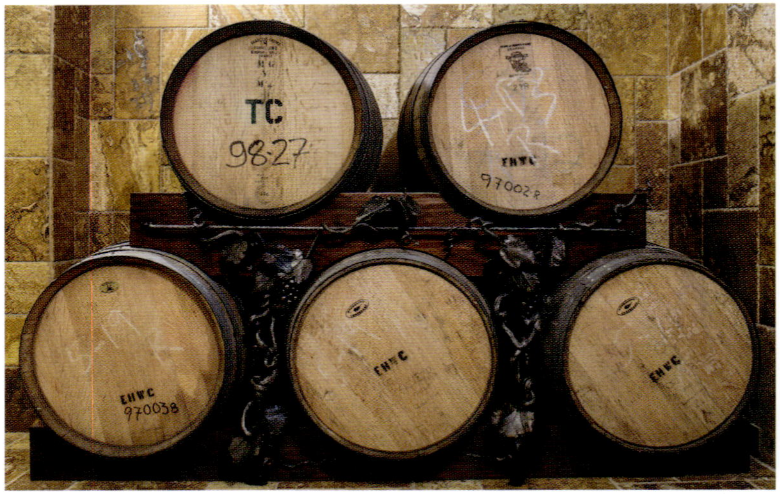

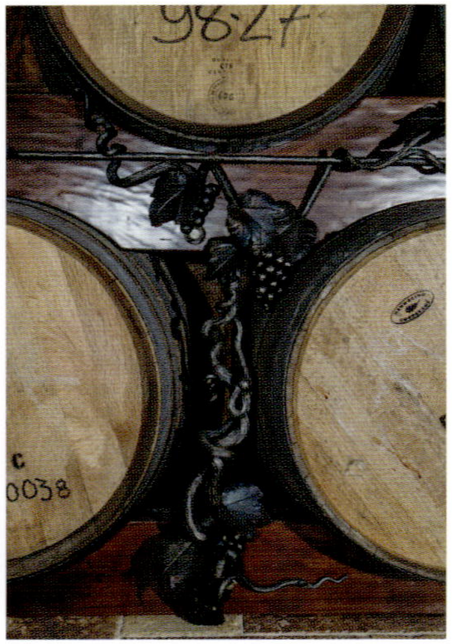

Ironwork on a wine barrel rack. Each grape is forged in my shop-made dies on the end of a yellow-hot iron bar, then is cut off the bar and welded into bunches. Vines have a bark texture done with my shop-made dies under the power hammer and leaves that have been textured, curved, and welded to the vines. Wire brushed and waxed finish. D. Holm collection. *Photo: Kendrick Moholt Photography*

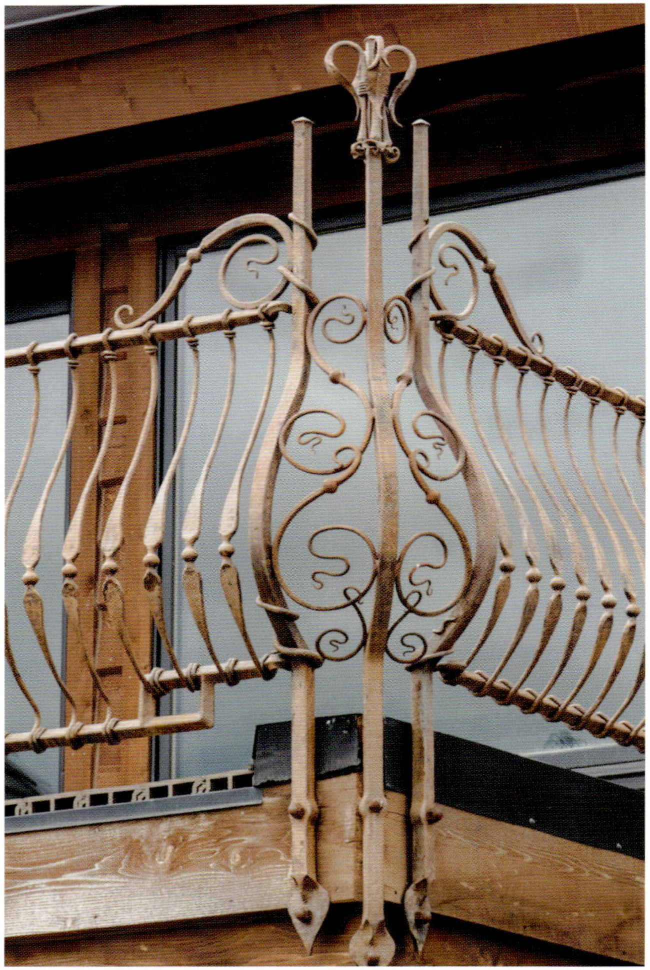

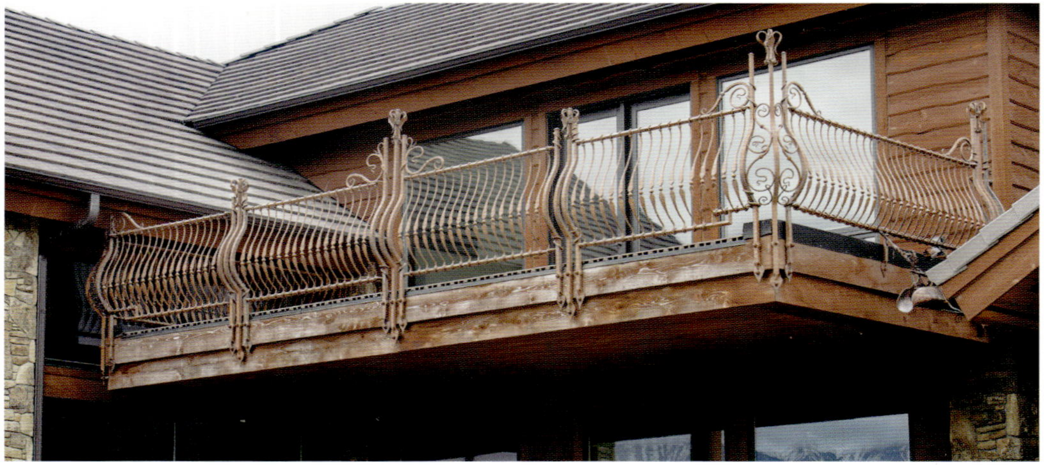

Deck railing. Forged iron posts are 1½'' square, tapered with hot punched mounting holes. Bowed balusters have a 1¼'' ball in the center. Each baluster has a long tail forged on the top and bottom that is wrapped on the horizontal bars of the railing. Rust finish. D. Holm collection. *Photo: Kendrick Moholt Photography*

Jim Gallucci

Jim Gallucci Sculptor, Ltd., Greensboro, North Carolina
www.jimgalluccisculptor.com

ARTIST'S STATEMENT

Art is a physical manifestation of an idea or event that calls forth an emotional response from the viewer. It speaks to us and evokes a chord deep within us. Good art challenges us, can make us feel righteous, moves us, soothes us, and can bring us peace.

Cotton Columns

We were selected to create sculpture for a Park and Ride in Goodyear, Arizona. After researching the area we discovered that the city of Goodyear was built for the company of Goodyear Tires as a farm for the cotton for their tires. I decided to incorporate the cotton bolls into the artwork and to use the cotton boll cutout design as a wrap around the light poles the city was adding.

Cotton Columns. Light towers. Sculpture. 2011. Welded stainless steel. 12'h x 7'w x 7'd.

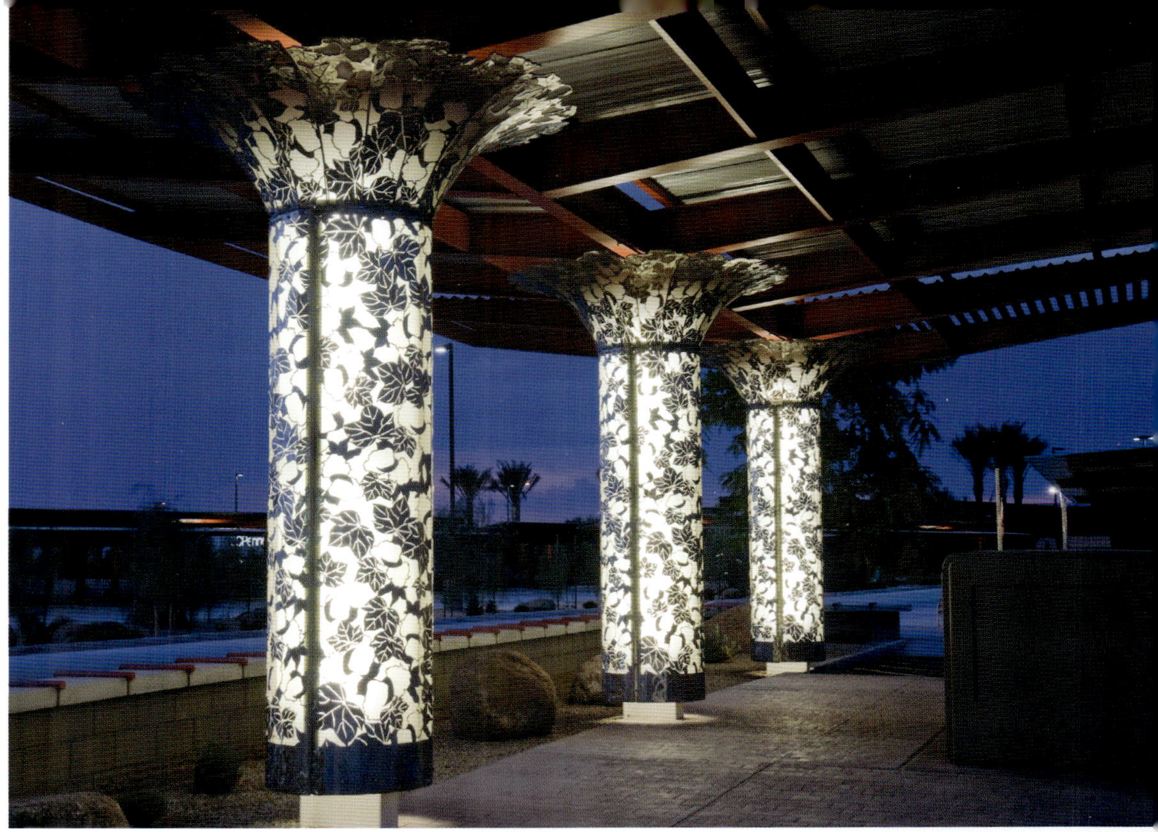

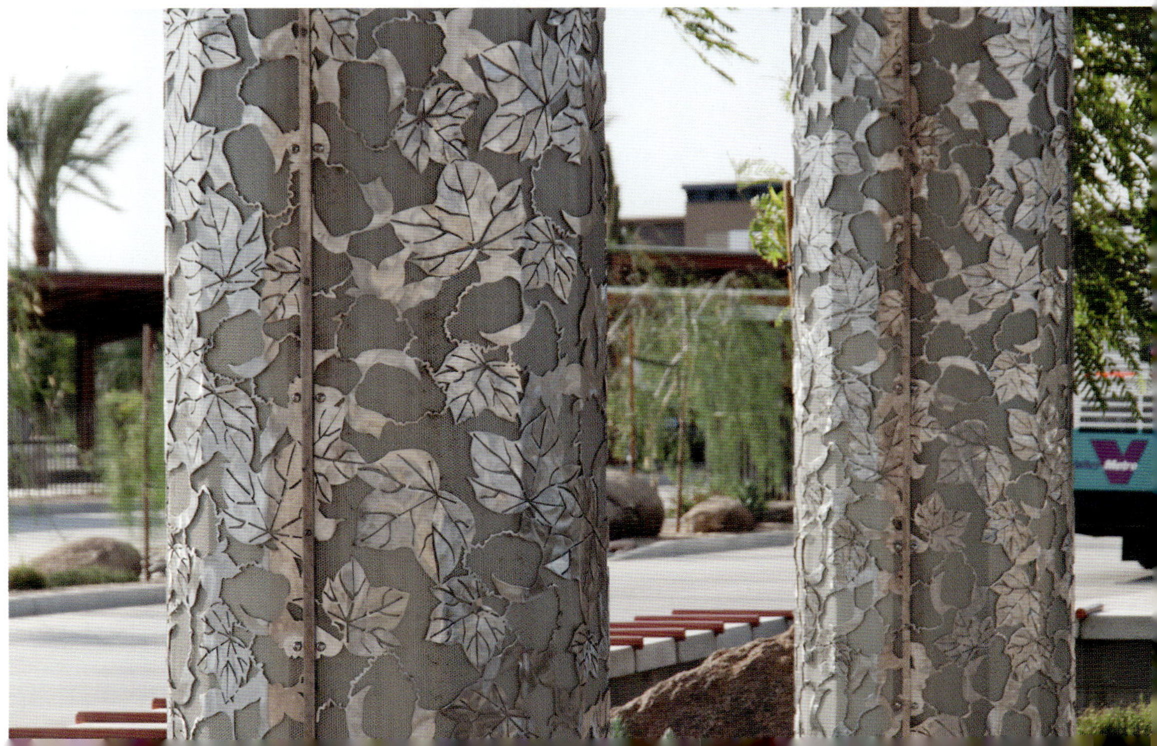

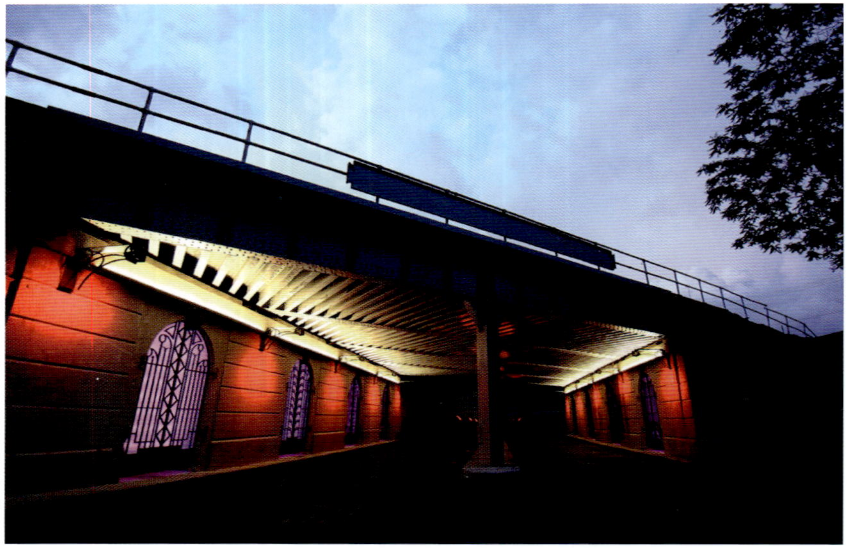

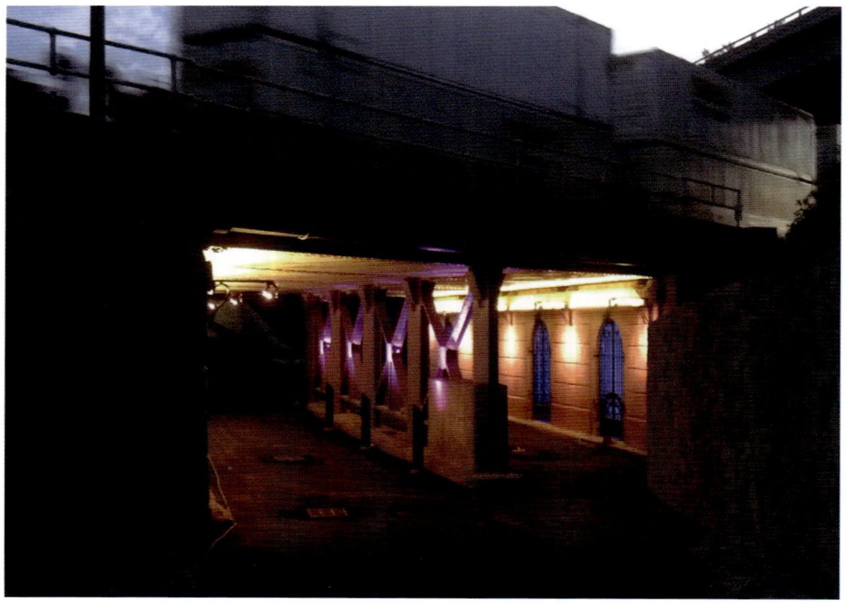

Greensboro Greenway Underpass

In July, 2010, the National Endowment for the Arts awarded the Greensboro, North Carolina, Downtown Greenway a grant of $100,000 as a part of its Mayor's Institute on City Design 25th Anniversary Initiative. From over 200 applicants from across the country, the Downtown Greenway project was selected as one of 21 grants totaling $3 million. The grant supported the restoration of an abandoned railroad underpass in a section of the Downtown Greenway to be known as Morehead Linear Park. The restoration project includes decorative iron gates designed and fabricated in my studio and placed in existing doorways along the underpass. LED lights provide backlight for the gates and create an interactive element to the underpass.

Downtown Greensboro Underpass Gateway. Light towers. Sculpture. 2012. Welded powder-coated steel. Each gate (of 11) is 9′ x 6′.

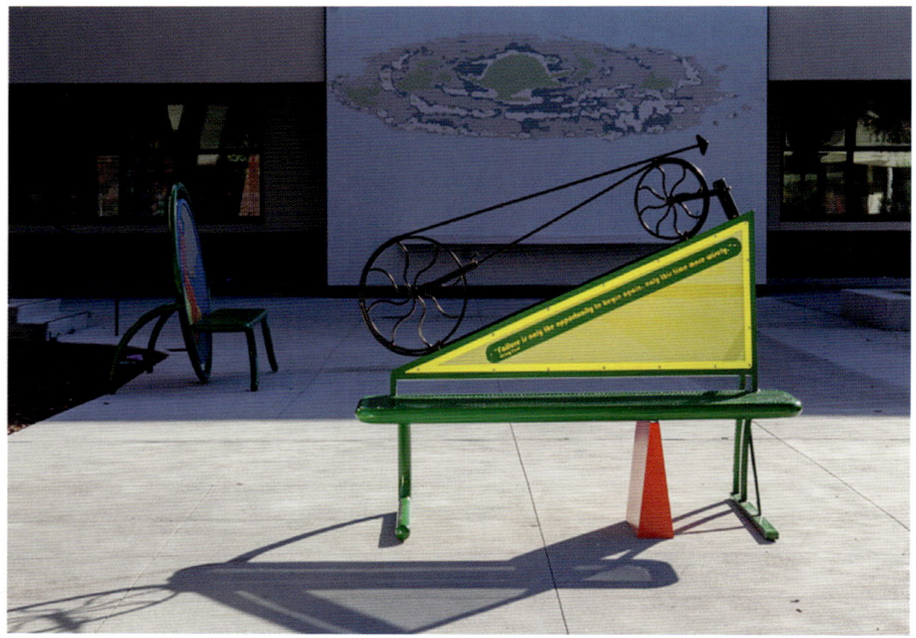

Engineer bench. Bench/Sculpture. Welded and powder-coated metal. 4′ x 6′ x 3′. *Photo: Joel Simon Images*

Sacred Heart School Benches

We were contacted in 2012 about creating benches for the Sacred Heart School in Atherton, California. They wanted benches that focused on learning and education and some to include quotes from inspirational people. We designed and fabricated ten colorful, unique benches, ranging from a physics bench with a quote from John Kennedy to a music bench with a quote from e.e. cummings. These benches were fun to design and fabricate, and receiving photos from the school with the benches in place was the icing on the cake.

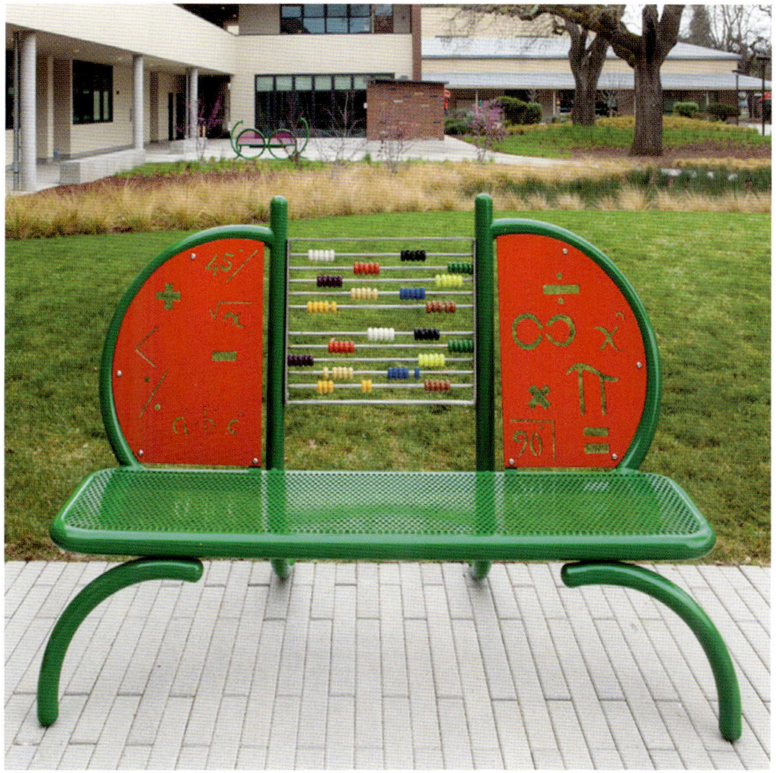

Math bench. Bench/Sculpture. Welded and powder-coated metal. 4′ x 6′ x 3′. *Photo: Joel Simon Images*

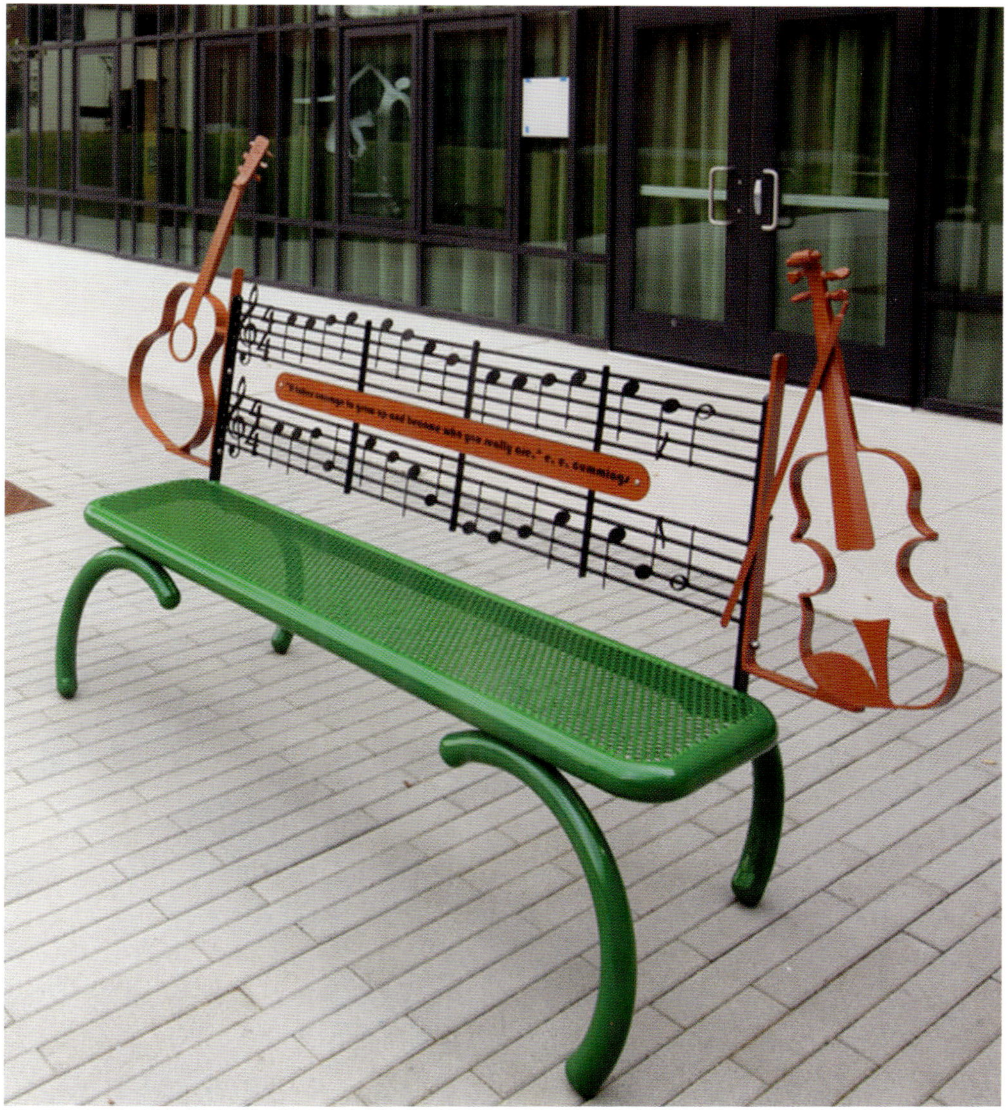

Music bench. Bench/Sculpture. Welded and powder-coated metal. 4′ x 6′ x 3′. *Photo: Joel Simon Images*

John Gehl

Manitowish Waters, Wisconsin, and Brookings, Oregon

ARTIST'S STATEMENT

Inspired primarily by nature, I have developed a style of sculpture that rarely repeats motifs. I work primarily with steel, both new and scrap. In addition to my own experimental projects, I accept private commissions. I avoid the harsh winter weather of Wisconsin by escaping to the West Coast each year. My Brookings, Oregon, shop, while less well equipped than my Manitowish Waters, Wisconsin, shop, is located in an area with an active artist community. Splitting the year between the North Woods and the Pacific Coast provides me with a spectacular array of the elements of nature that inspire my work.

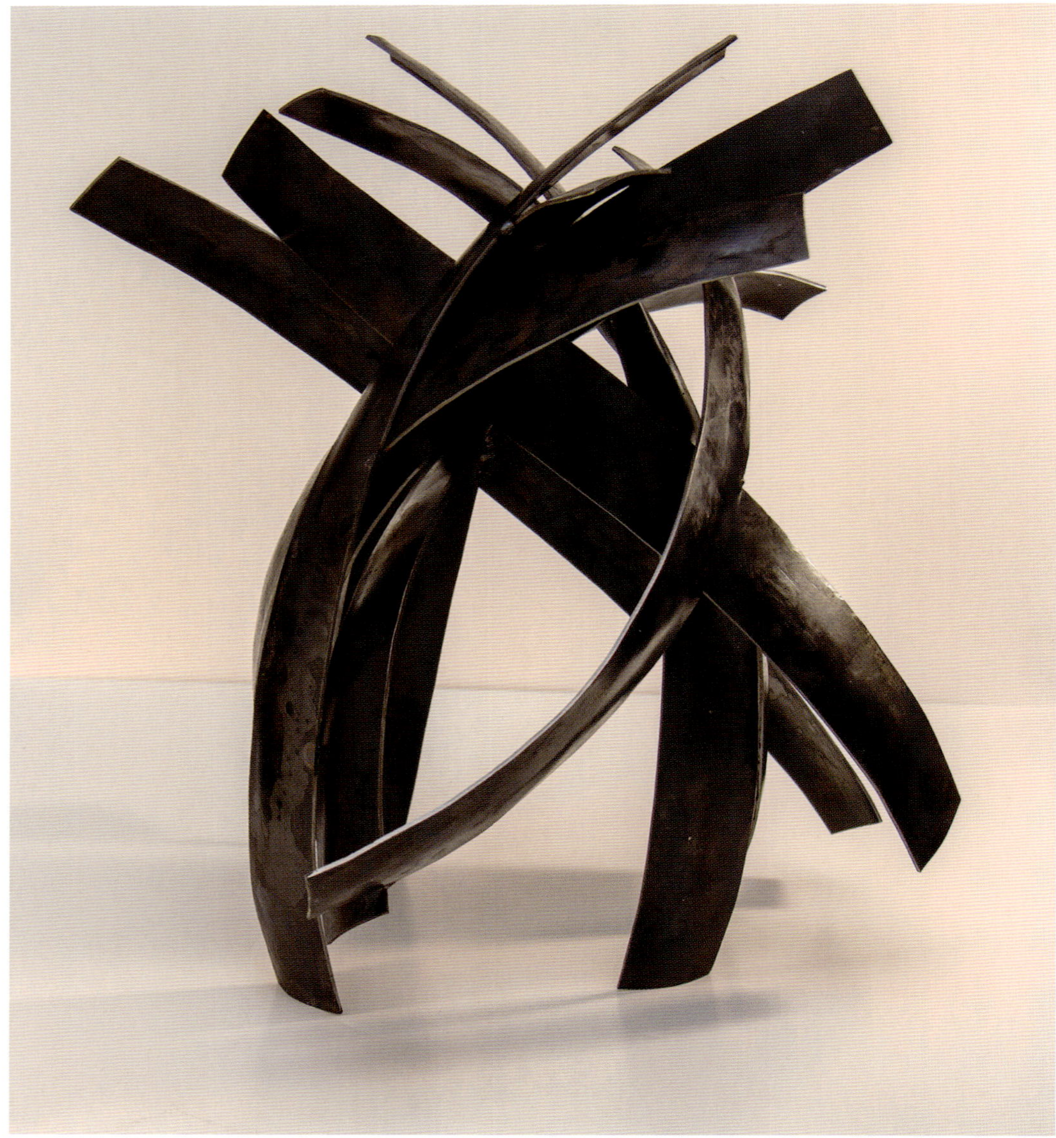

Curves. Sculpture. Formed from mild steel sheet and finished with gun bluing and polished edges. Protected with beeswax. 24"h x 18"l x 18"w.

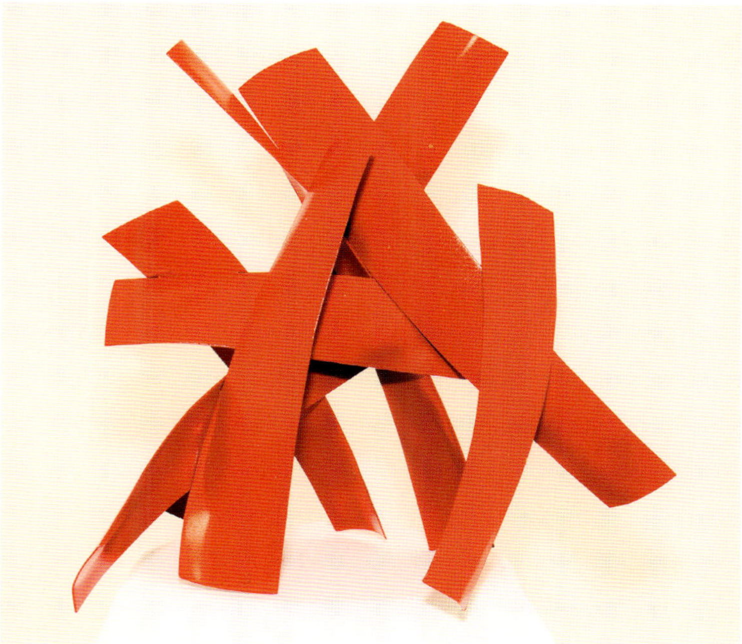

Curves II. Sculpture. Shaped, welded mild steel, automotive paint. 19″h x 18″l x 18″w.

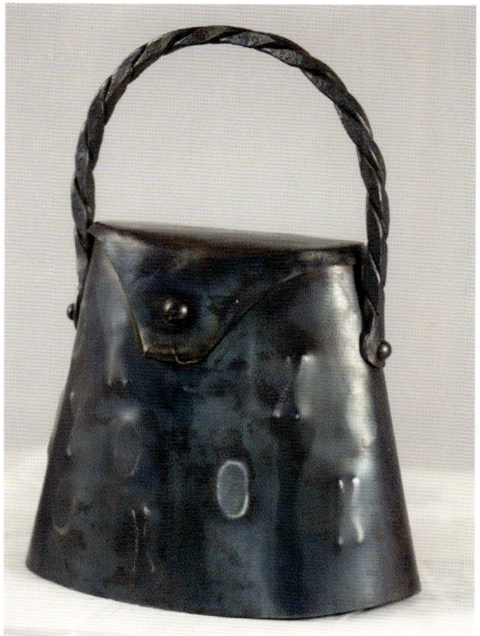

Old Purse of Lost Dreams. Sculpture. Mild steel sheet, embossed with Xs and Os, recalling kisses and hugs from long ago. Sealed with a rivet at top to lock in forgotten dreams that have fallen through its unsealed bottom—lost forever. Finished with a brass brush and gun bluing. Protected with beeswax. 11″h x 8″w x 4″d.

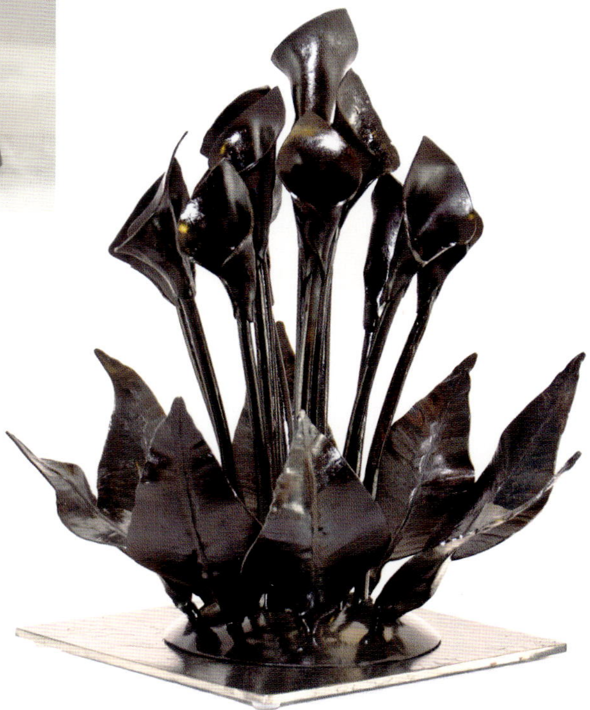

Flower Circle. Sculpture. Formed and welded mild steel. Flame-colored, finished with gun bluing and protected with lacquer. 14″h x 12″l x 12″w.

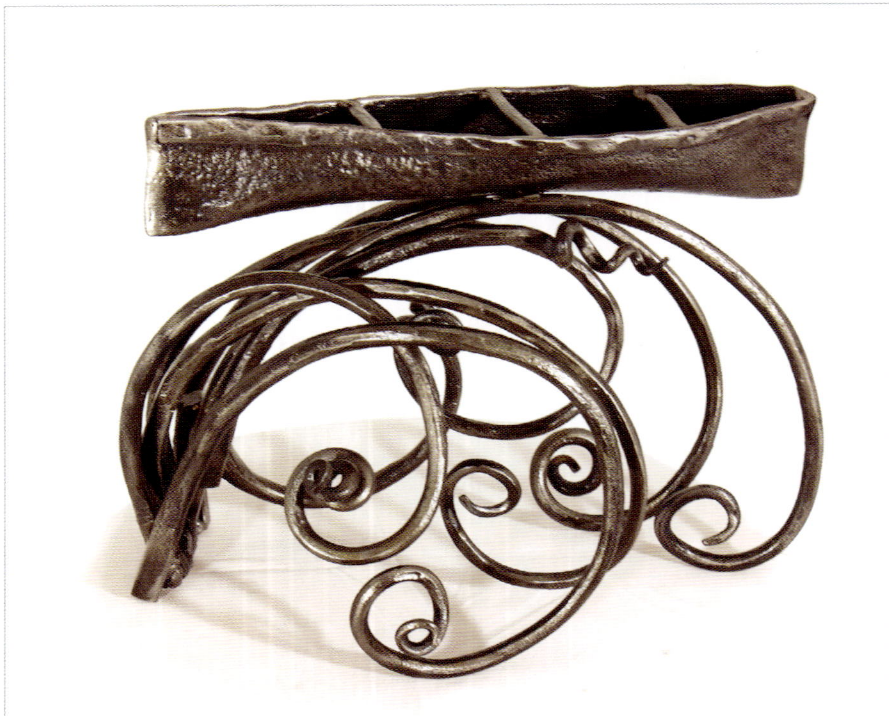

Wahoo Canoo. Sculpture. Flame-colored and lacquer-coated, the canoe is a heavily pitted and rusted steel plate, while the water is welded, tapered, steel rods. 10"h x 13"l x 9"w.

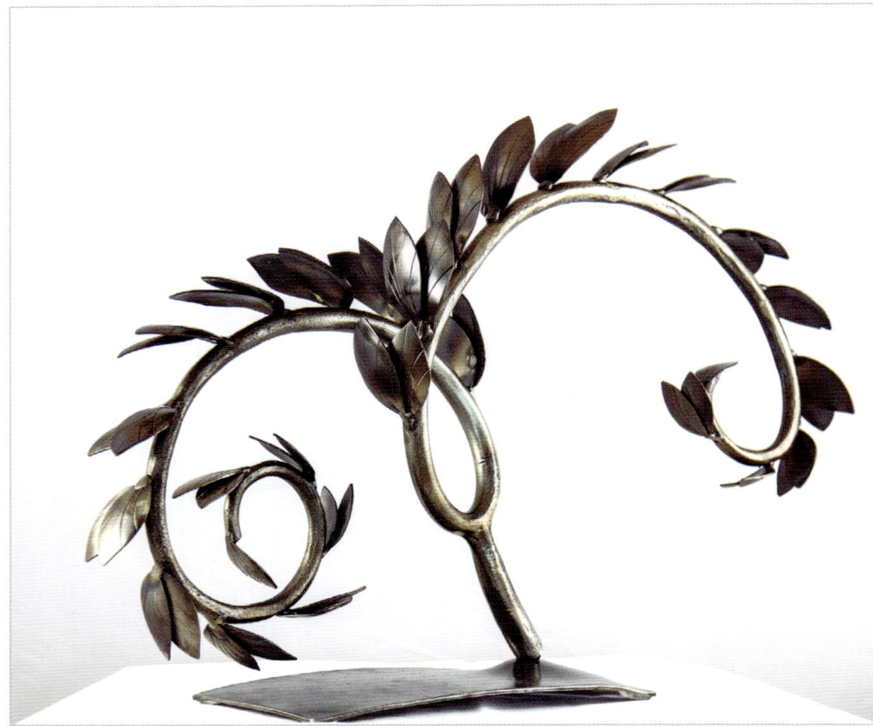

Laurel. Sculpture. Flame-colored, brass-brushed, lacquer-coated steel rods and embossed leaves. 12"h x 18"l x 4"w.

Glenn Gilmore

Hamilton, Montana
www.gilmoremetal.com

ARTIST'S STATEMENT

I have been very fortunate in being able to do my own design work, whether for commissions or myself. This has allowed me to create challenges in the work for my continual growth and self-expression. I enjoy using bold, clean lines in my designs, always striving for a balance between mass, form, and function. I want the piece to have enough body that it will stand on its own, yet not be lost or feel overwhelming.

I enjoy hot forging the metal because it is a very direct process. When I want a desired form, I have to know where and how to hit the metal, and with each hammer blow it moves in the desired direction. It is hard work and I put a great deal of attention into creating visually pleasing objects. Whether forging a set of large driveway gates or a small coat hook, all the elements need to be in balance with one another.

One of the important design concepts in my work is the method I use to join different elements together. I often use traditional methods of joinery, rivets, collars, mortise, and tenon. Though these are traditional methods, I create contemporary pieces using them. These methods not only provide an important part of the overall design, but add structural integrity to the work.

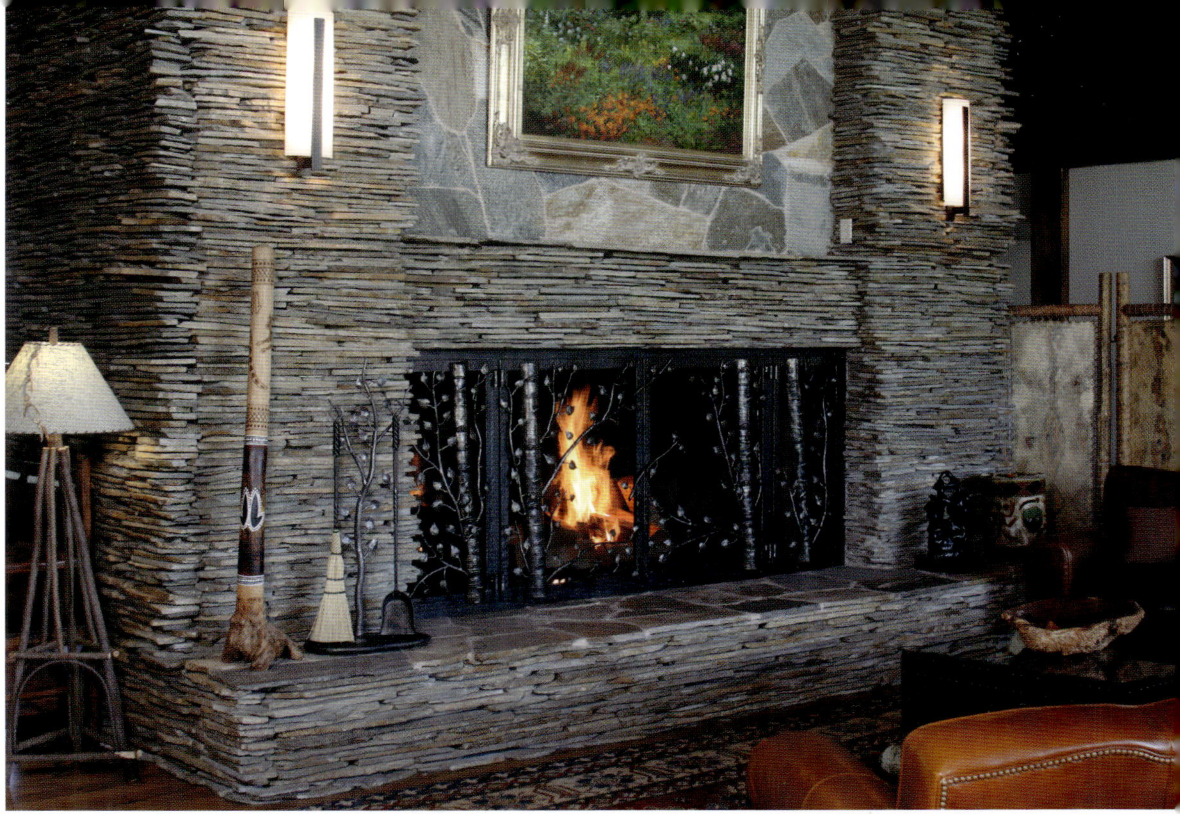

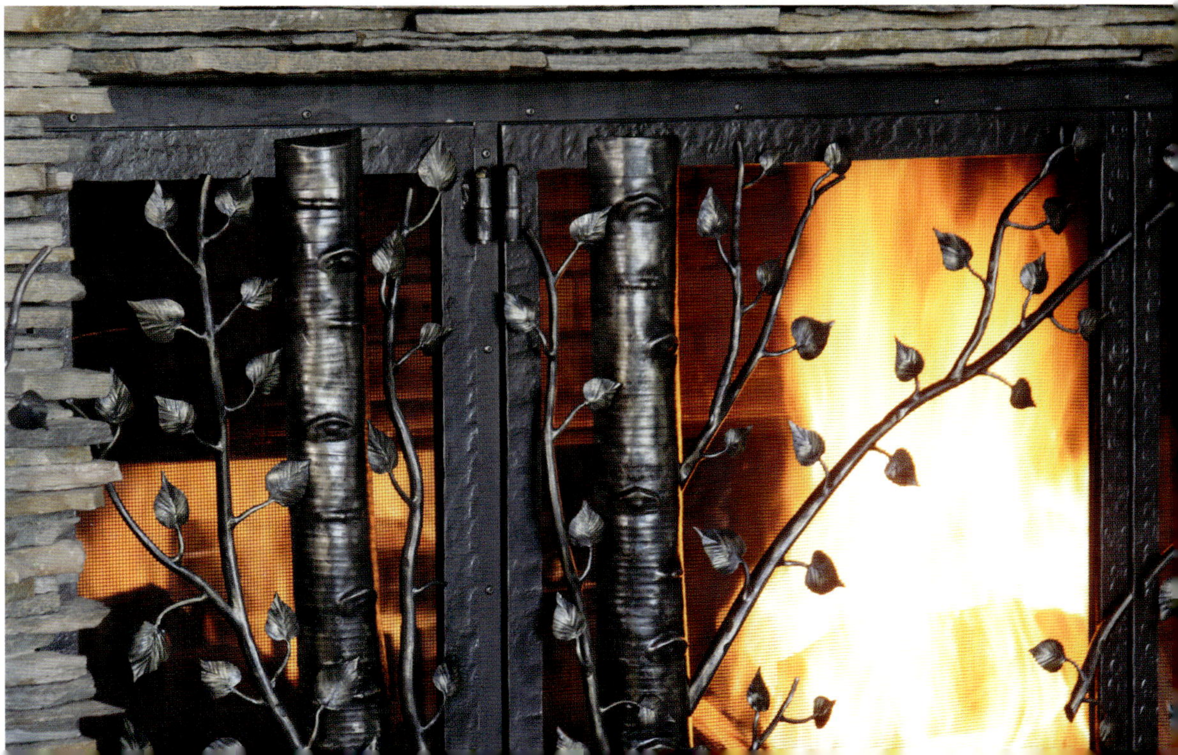

The Aspen Grove

These fireplace doors were inspired by the aspen grove outside the client's great room. The tool set has the aspen branch design, too. The detail photo shows custom-made hinges using bronze brushing and polished pins.

The Aspen Grove. Fireplace doors and tools. 2009. Mild steel, stainless steel. Aspen trunks forged from 12 gauge sheet. Forged solid branches and leaves. Four doors using handmade hinges, with bronze bushings and polished pins. Tool set has the aspen branch design also. Brass highlights and hand-rubbed waxed finish. 8′w x 40″h x 3″d.

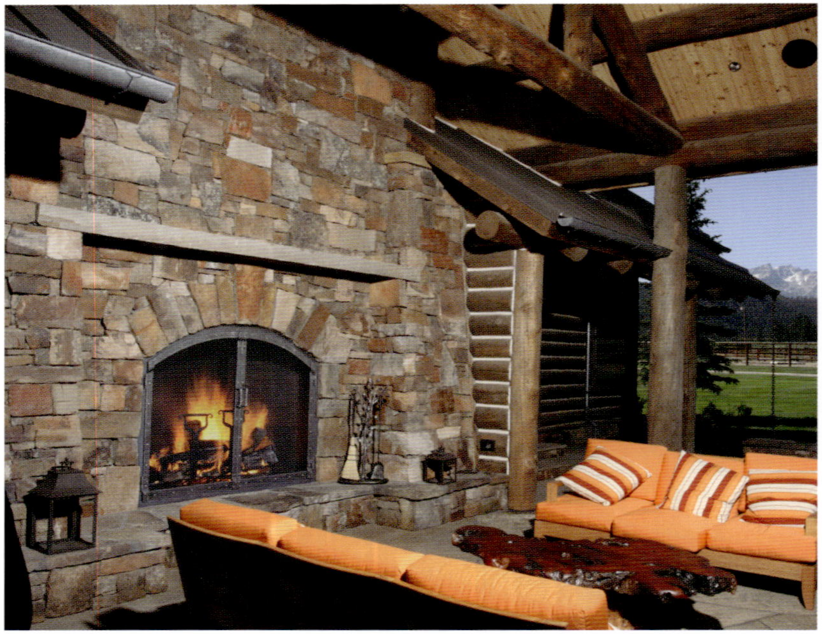

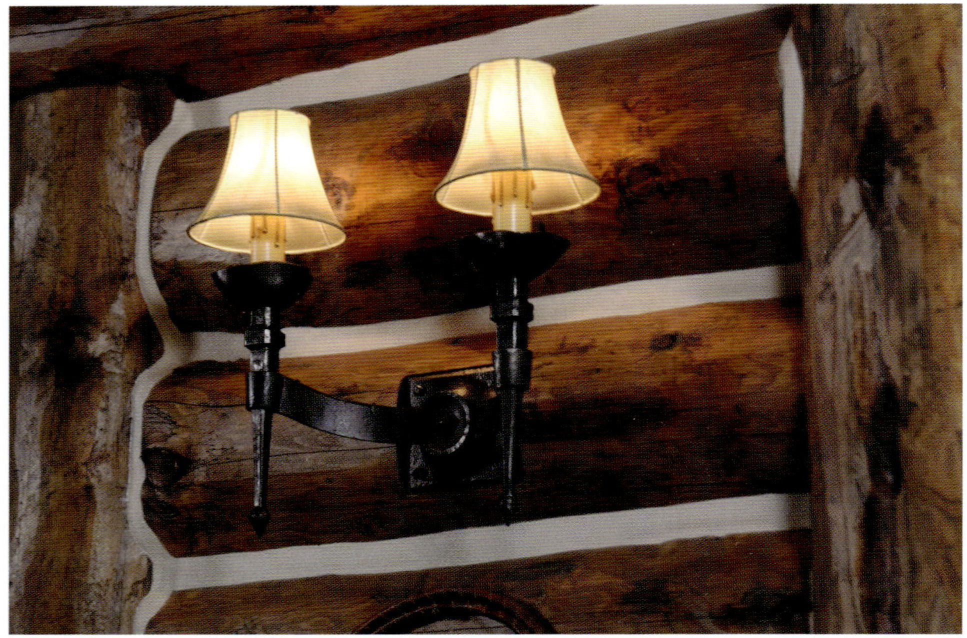

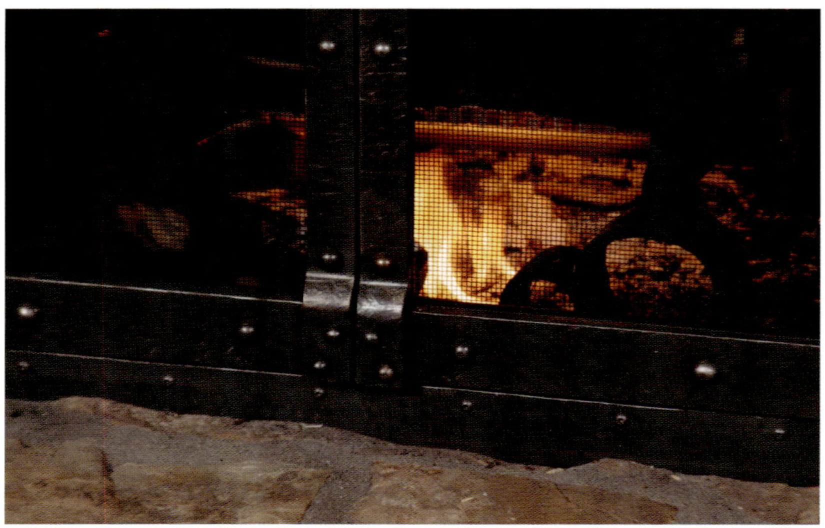

Trapper Peak

These exterior fireplace doors and hearth tool set were made for this stone hearth.

Trapper Peak fireplace doors. 2010.
Mild steel, stainless steel. 60″w x 52″h.

Western Wall Sconce

Western wall sconce with rawhide shades. 2010.
Mild steel, rawhide. 18″w x 12″h x 8″d.

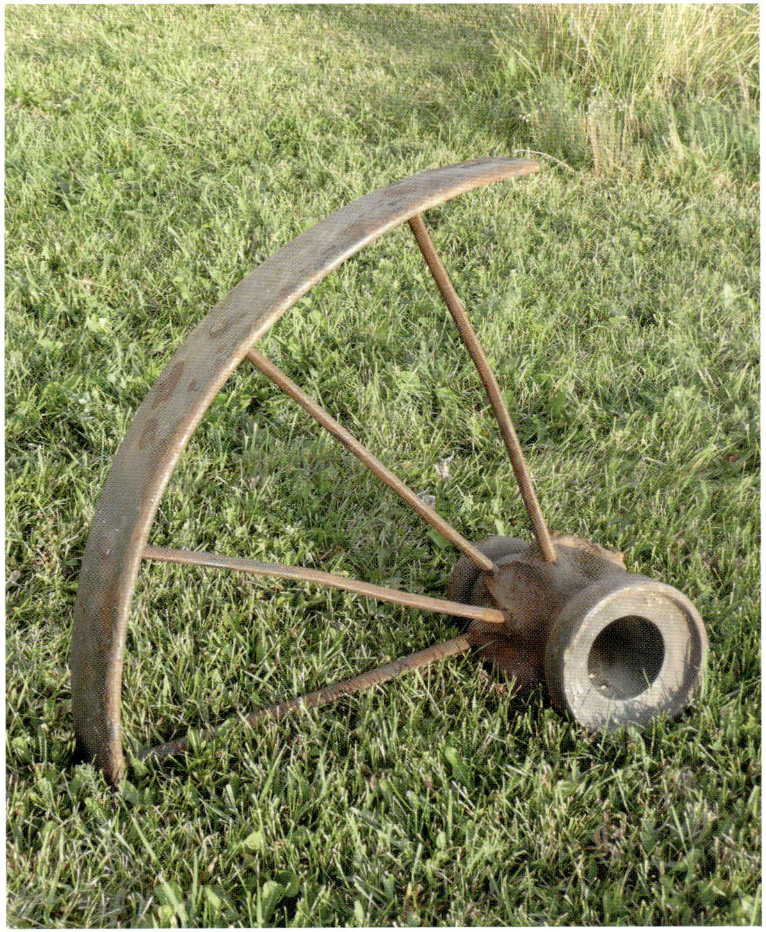

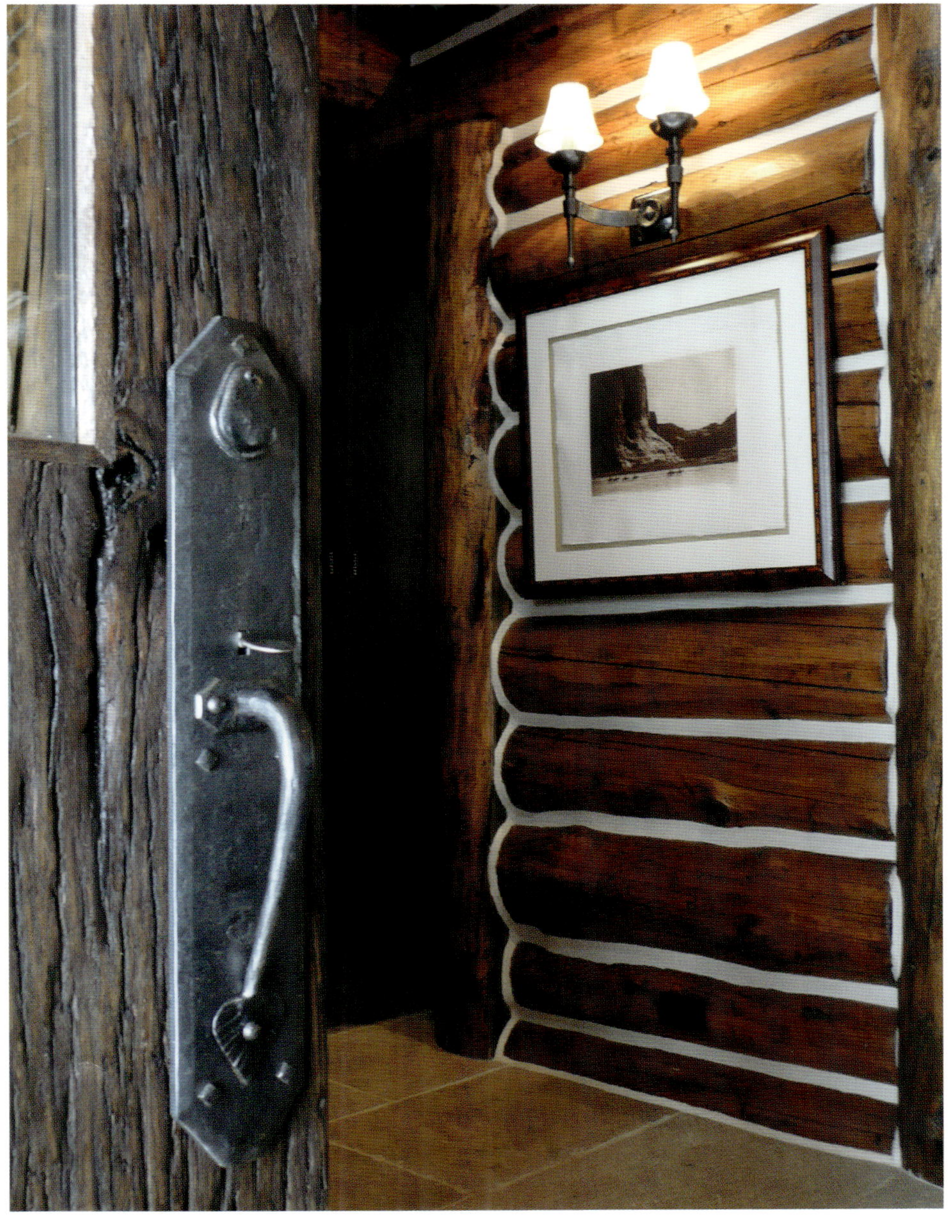

Wagon-wheel Door Hardware

This entry door hardware was made of wrought iron from a hundred-year-old wagon wheel that was used on this ranch. Escutcheon plate was the tire; spoke heads can be seen on the surface. The pull was made from three of the steel spokes, forge welded together and forged to shape. Every time someone enters the home, he or she grabs onto years of the ranch history.

Door hardware. 2009. Wax finish. 28"h x 3 ½"w.

Margaret S.L. Goodman

Memphis, Tennessee
marjit82@gmail.com

ARTIST'S STATEMENT

I have been collecting plant specimens over the past ten years. My collection ranges from North America to Europe, South America, and recently the Central American rainforest. At the beginning of my interest, I was merely attracted to the forms I found in nature. I explored the shapes and old botanical drawings found in textbooks and started to realize what I couldn't see, on the insides and underground, were just as beautiful. This is when I started dissecting and digging up specimens and really studying the characteristics that help them to survive.

This is what brings me to my current body of work, which deals with imaginary plant life. Each one of my creations has a written explanation giving the viewer clues as to what this creature is capable of, what environment it can be found in, and what the plant needs for survival. I explore plant root systems, bulbs and tubers, plant movement and their adaptation to environments, their capabilities to store water, and in some cases parasitic characteristics. I play with the similarities of deep-sea creature characteristics and how plants (that can be carnivore, yet not animal) exhibit some of the same predatory anatomy.

Beggar

Beggar is a domesticated house plant that is dependent on humans for its survival. These plants sometimes do get turned out into the wild when they get too large and outgrow their living space. As a result, the Beggar will develop "pack" mentality much like other bulbs. Examples: daffodil, tulip, iris.

Beggar. Sculpture. 2012. Steel, bronze, copper. Forged and fabricated. 13" x 12" x 17".

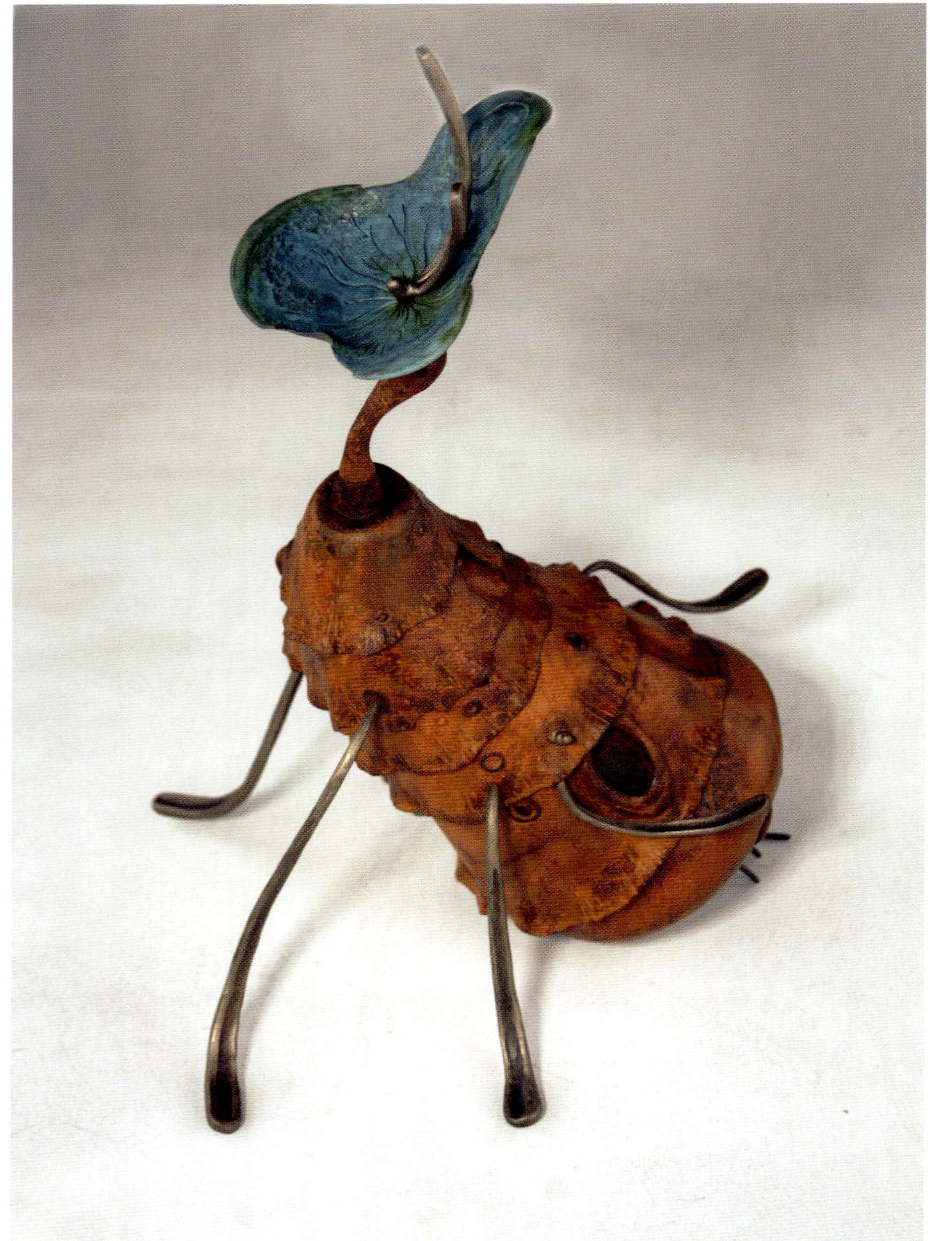

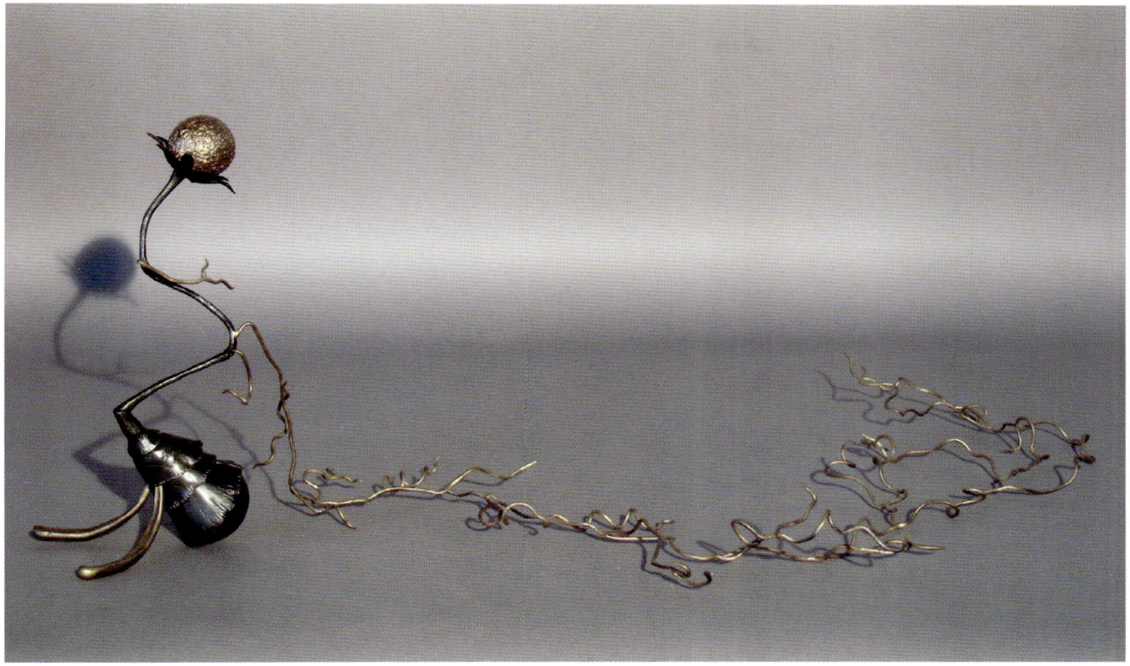

Puddle Jumper

The Puddle Jumper is derived from both aquatic and botanic life—specifically clam and sycamore. Unlike the sycamore, whose seeds fall to the ground, dry, and scatter in the wind, this specimen falls to the forest floor, sprouts the essentials it needs to travel, and picks its own final destination. The sycamore-like seed capsule becomes a mass storage device for water. It soon grows clam-like feet, which aid its movements from puddle to puddle and provide a temporary anchor into the mud and silt. Its roots grow as far as needed to reach the next water source. Once water is found, the Puddle Jumper will relocate to this destination and use its sponge-like device to store water during transport.

Puddle Jumper. Sculpture. 2011. Forged bronze. Forged and fabricated. 35"x 12" x 12".

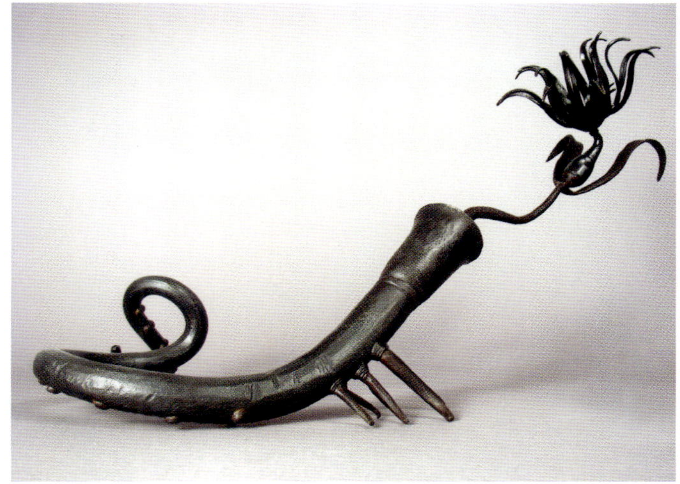

Aquatic Wholer

The Aquatic Wholer is a water- and land-dwelling, amphibious filter feeder, found in shallow water. It is related to snails, caterpillars, and sea anemone. The Whorler relies on the shape of its shell to anchor itself into the silt and sand of lake bottoms. This plant also displays characteristics of the order Lepidoptera; family Pyralidae, or caterpillars, that are able to breathe underwater. Small leg-like protrusions can be found on the underside of its shell, aiding in grasping and crawling.

Aquatic Wholer. Sculpture. 2011. Forged steel. 16" x 10" x 10".

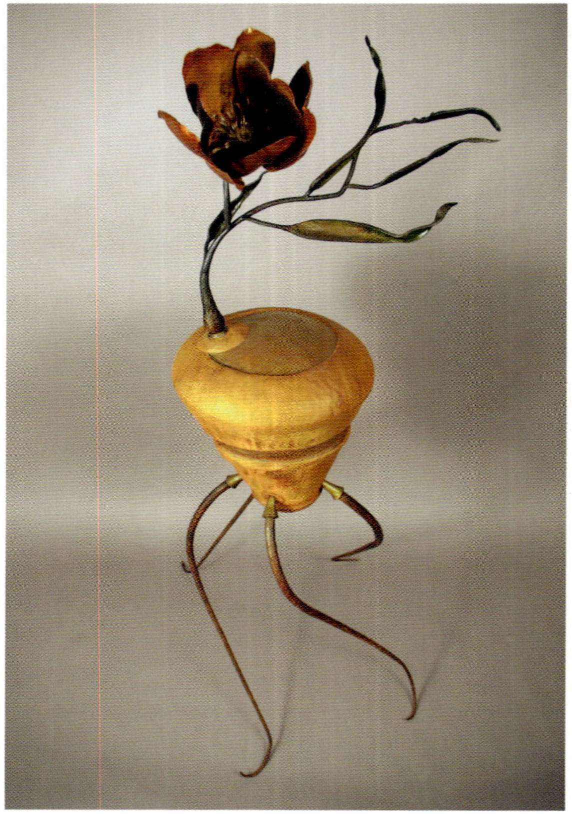

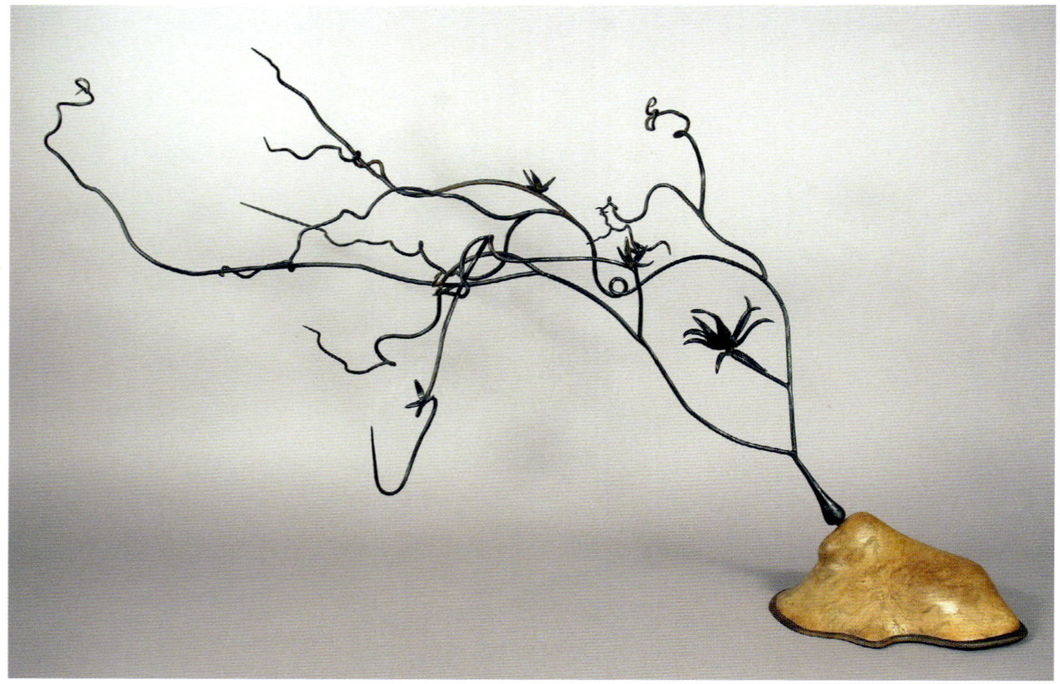

Jellyweed

The Jellyweed is a sea- and land-dwellling, amphibious, predatory carnivorous plant. It is related to both Medusozoa (jellyfish) and Nymphaea (water lily). This creature is allusive and keeps to the depths during the cold months feeding on small fish. In late summer, the Jellyweed migrates to shallow waters to group and reproduce. Once above the surface, the blossoms are used to catch and devour insects and absorb the sunlight needed during its stationary reproduction period.

Jellyweed. Sculpture. 2011. Steel, bronze. Forged and fabricated. 22″ x 19″ x 49″.

Sun Catcher

The Sun Catcher grows in dense forests rooted into the lower limbs of trees. Its long tendrils reach into the heights of the forest canopy and capture nutrients from the sun. What nutrients the Catcher does not use are then released through the root system and absorbed into the host tree, creating a symbiotic relation between the two organisms.

Sun Catcher. Sculpture. 2011. Forged steel, wood. 42″ x 16″ x 36″.

Joshua A. Goss

Berthoud, Colorado
www.joshuagoss.com

ARTIST'S STATEMENT

Topography is subject to pressure; terrain is altered through friction and heat over sustained periods of time. Erosion and deformation reveal the plasticity of substances often considered unyielding. Geological environments are forged, expending stored energy, exposing the fundamental nature of Earth's development.

The Structural Series is characterized by the uplift and faulting that originates from the collision of tectonic plates. As mountains rise, fractures and folds expand through the Earth's crust. With exposure to the atmosphere, organic textures are etched into underlying structures and patterns are revealed. The Structural Series looks to geological processes as an analog to metalworking processes, taking into account the origin of the material being used and embodying the idea of both time and material. Time is shown by the movement and offset of the layers—over millions of years, horizons that were once flat become juxtaposed.

The use of steel and plastic to make these sculptures references geological process and time in several ways: both steel and plastic are products of geological processes. Iron is a result of mineralization. Plastic is made from fossil fuels. In both cases, these transformations are caused by metamorphism of the parent rocks. Metamorphism is a change that sedimentary and igneous rocks undergo when exposed to time, heat, and pressure. These sculptures are a framework in which to make geological time more realistic to the human perspective. Geological processes happen on a magnitude imperceptible to the human scale. Theories of Earth's development are based on hypothesis and objective observation. The investigation of elementary materials, pliable and transferable, informs my understanding of the Earth and processes within.

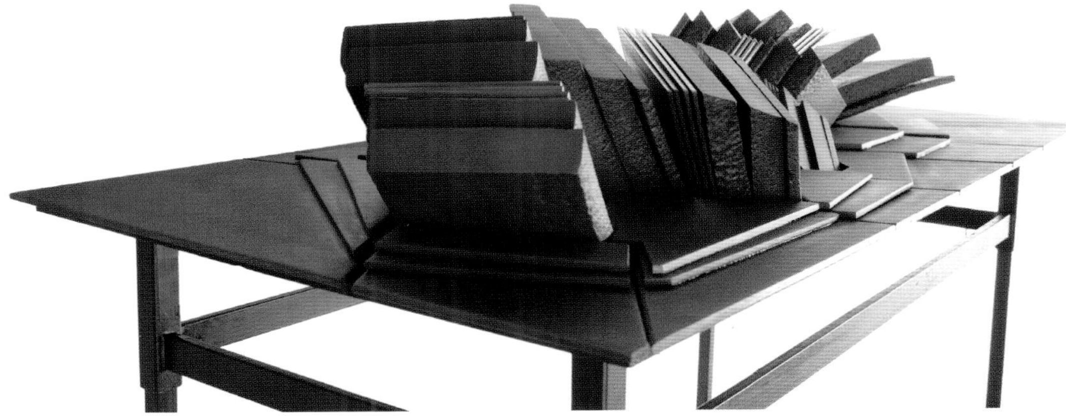

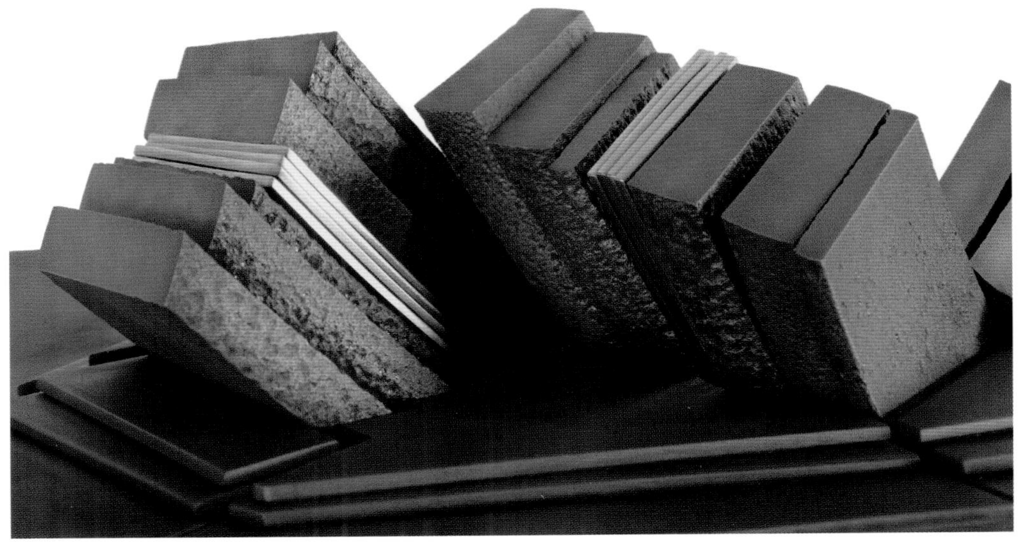

Structural 6 (Uplift). Sculpture. 2012. Steel, stainless steel. 48" x 24" x 53".

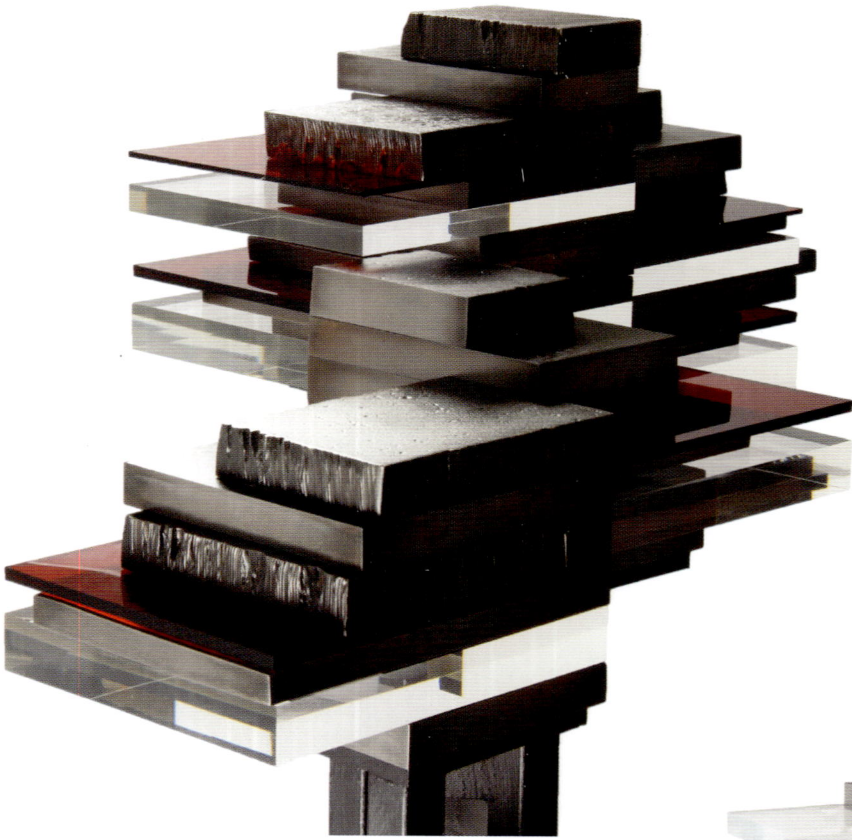

Structural 7 (Normal). Sculpture. 2012. Steel, acrylic. 24" x 36" x 52".

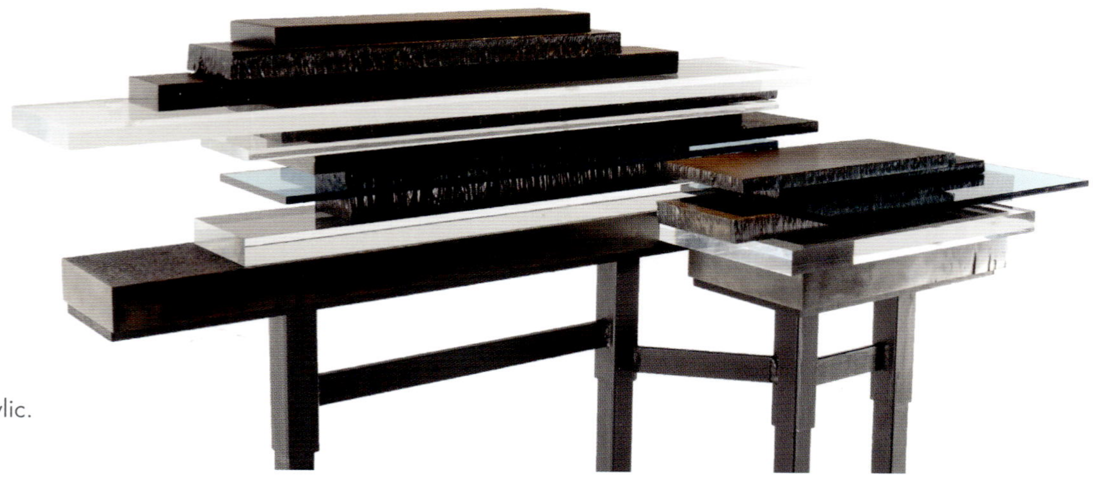

Structural 8 (Reverse). Sculpture. 2012. Steel, acrylic. 27" x 35" x 50".

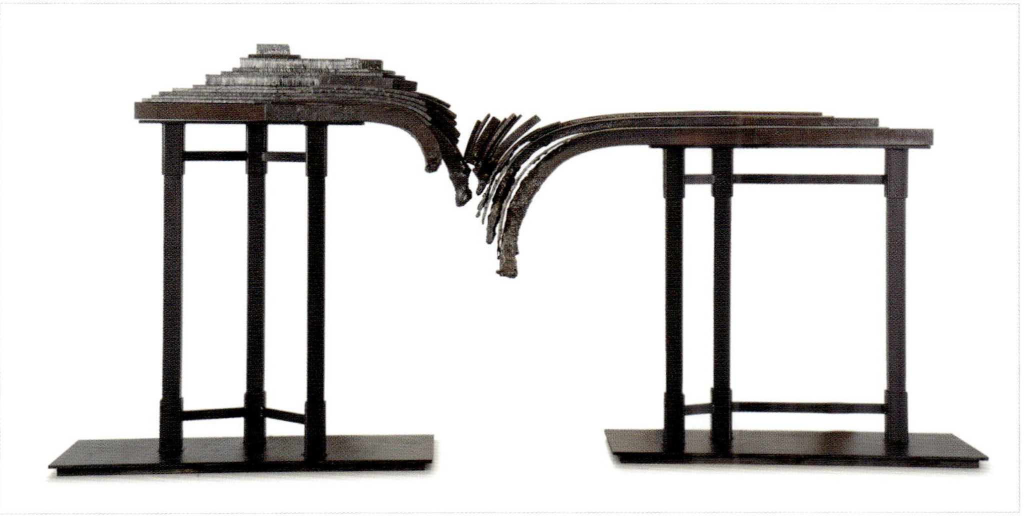

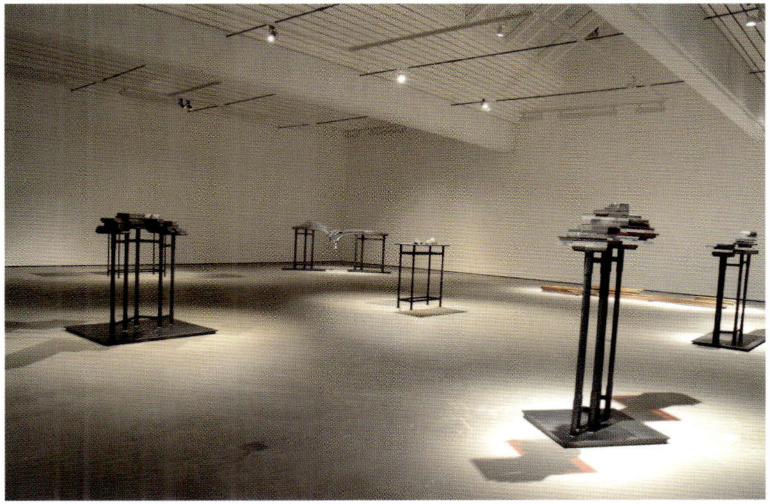

Time, Heat & Pressure solo exhibition. 2012.
Steneby Konsthall, Dals Långed, Sweden.

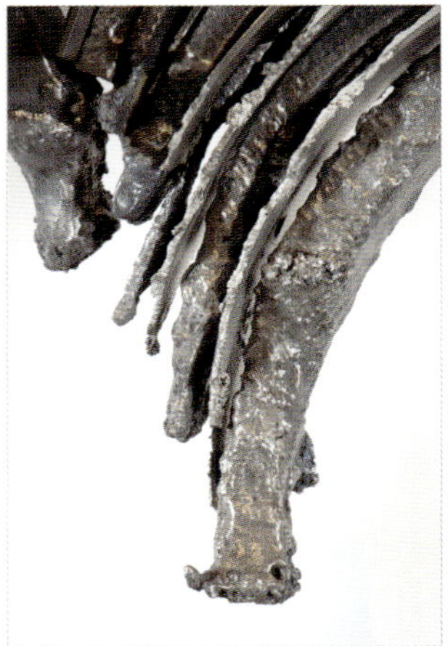

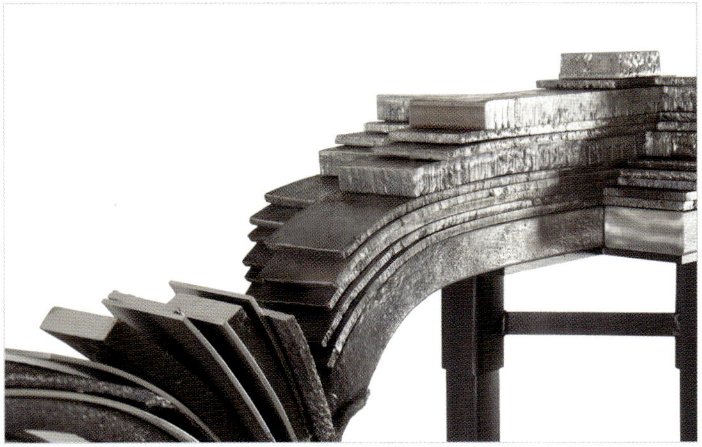

Structural 10 (Subduction Zone). Sculpture. 2012. Steel, stainless steel. 120″ x 30″ x 53″.

Structural 10 (Subduction Zone). Details.

Seth E. H. Gould

Cleveland, Ohio
sethgould.com

ARTIST'S STATEMENT

When I began working in metal I was quickly aware that the tools I was working with were equally attractive as the process of creating. How the file cut, how the handle felt, and how the tool was finished all contributed greatly to the type of experience I had while making. I would pick up old handles and used tools whenever I could. The warn wood always felt more comfortable in my hand, the slightly pitted steel seemed to be more exact.

When I made my first tool, it was the first time I created something that I could use on a daily basis. More than ever, it made me aware of how I was making. The warmth of its oiled handle combined with the strength of its gray steel body; the tool embodied the aesthetics of my grandfather's shop. The functionality of the tools I make is brought into question in different ways. Some tools are highly ornamented on the surface, but still perform their task seamlessly. They are so ornamented that often their function is overlooked. Other tools are rendered useless due to their form, and because of their form they are primarily viewed with function in mind. In each case, the tools I make are very personal objects that question the task at hand, how it is being done, and the worth of doing it.

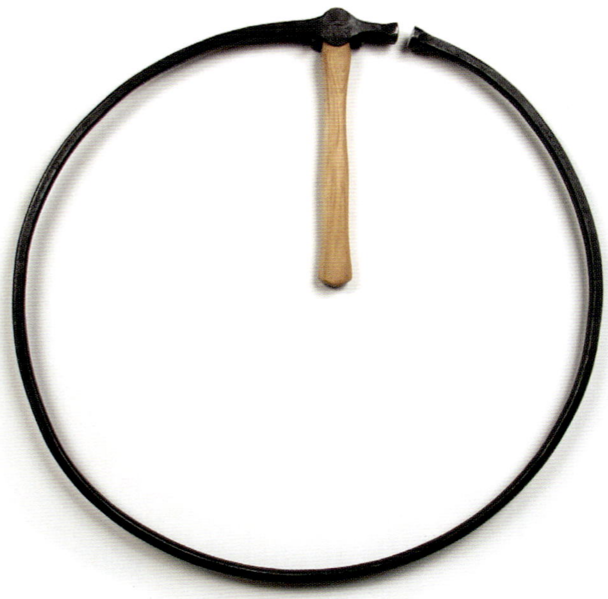

Planishing Hammer No. 3. Sculpture. 2011. Steel, hickory. Forged. 32" x 32" x 1".

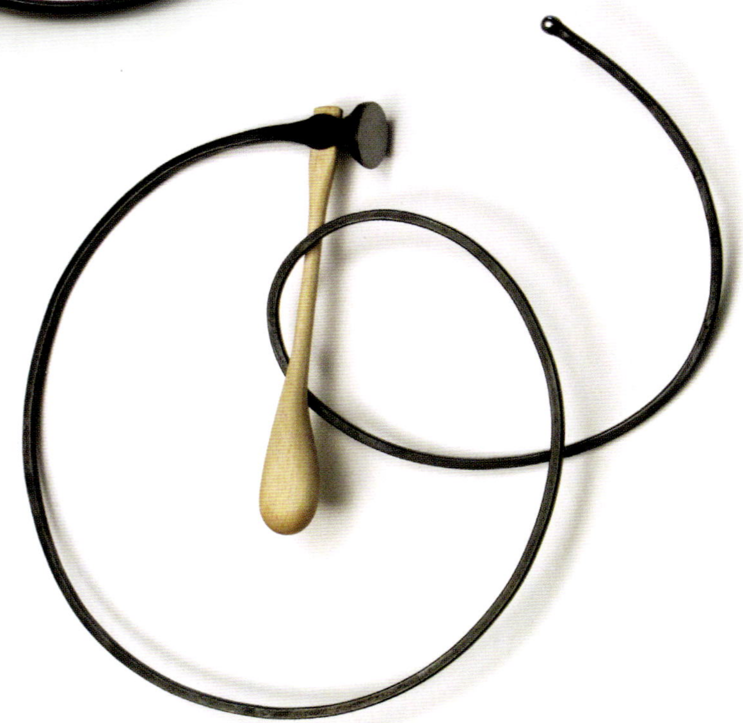

Chasing Hammer No. 1. Sculpture. 2012. Steel, hickory. Forged. 18" x 14" x 5½".

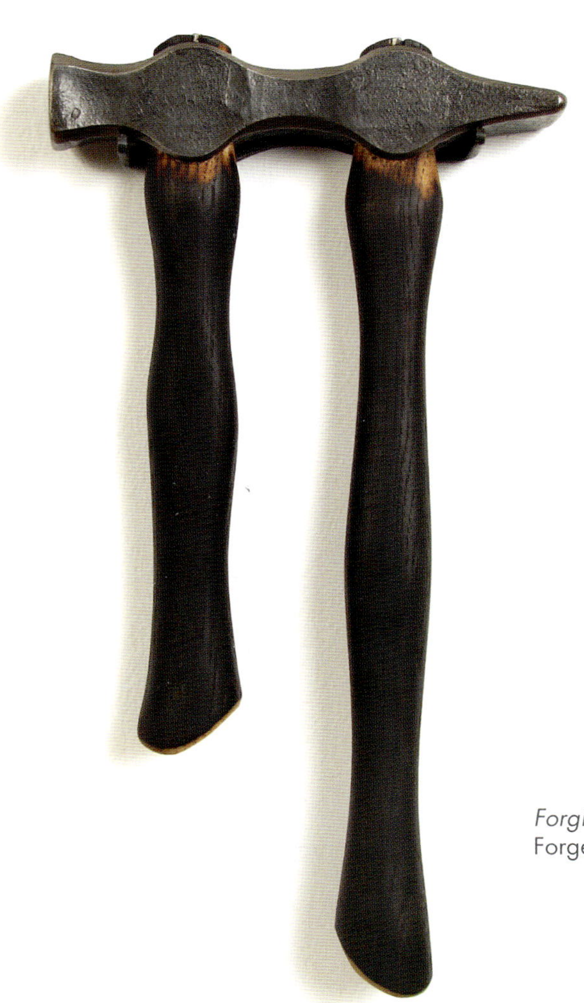

Forging Hammer No. 1. Sculpture. 2011. Steel, hickory. Forged. 11″ x 5½″ x 1½″.

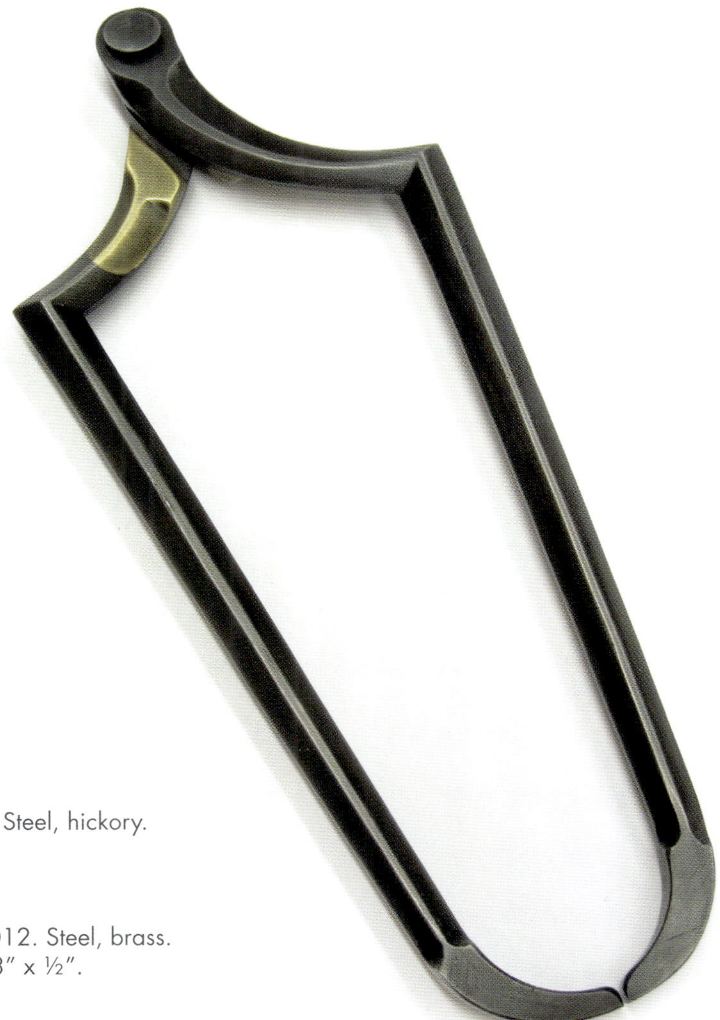

Calipers. Functional. 2012. Steel, brass. Forged and filed. 8″ x 3″ x ½″.

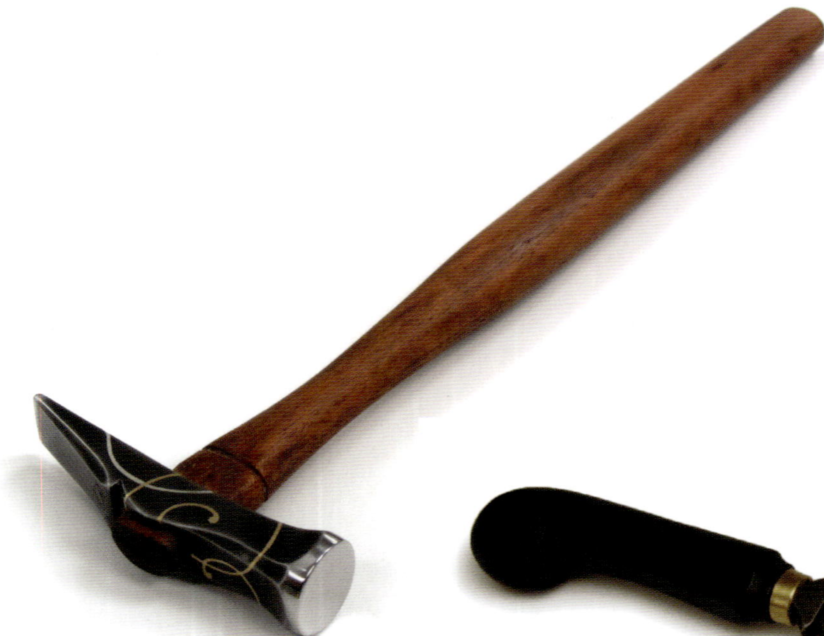

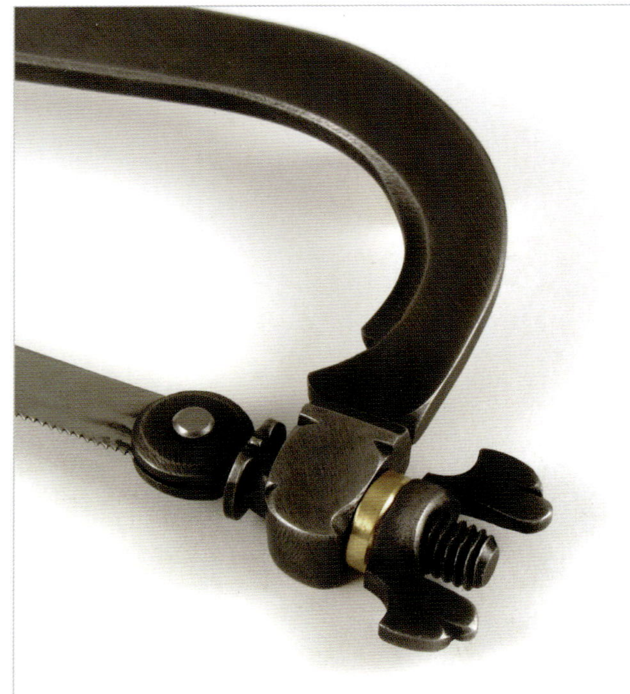

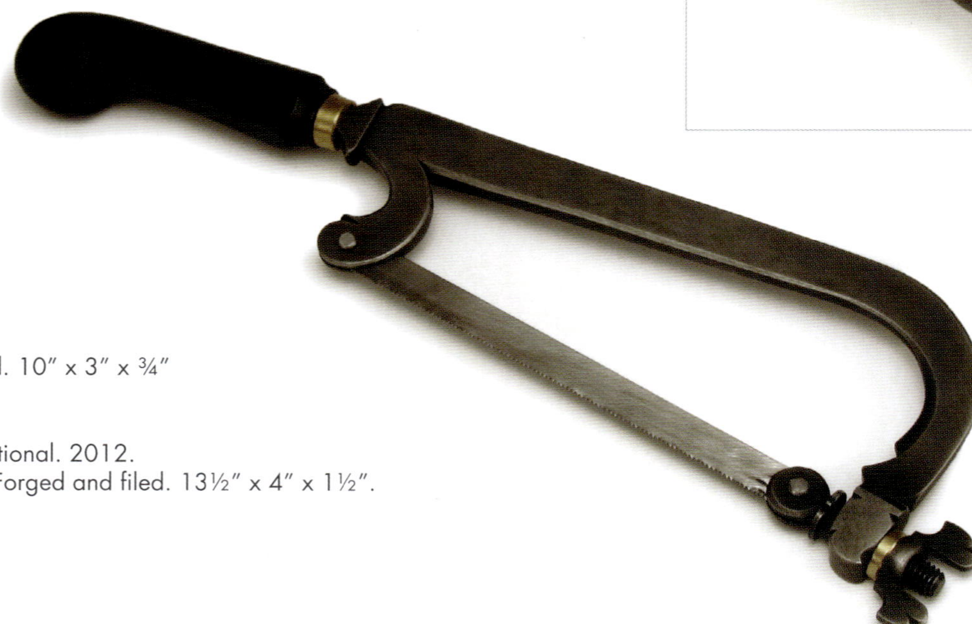

Goldsmithing hammer. Functional. 2013. 4140,
18K, fine silver, snakewood. Forged, filed, inlaid. 10" x 3" x ¾"

Small hacksaw. Functional. 2012.
Steel, brass, ebony. Forged and filed. 13½" x 4" x 1½".

Ekaterina Tatarovich Harrison

La Sal, Utah
www.sculptureadventure.com

ARTIST'S STATEMENT

It seems that our very existence depends on our ability to be creative. This creativity takes many forms, like the sciences, that explore the many sides of our existence and evolution. However, to me, it feels like we as a society have put so much stock into the tangible product that the prevailing tendency is to marginalize the intangible and ethereal. In my opinion, in doing so we are ignoring the very force that drives us. It is like saying the results of creativity, the products, are more important than the desire or drive to be creative. Without the spark, the desire, and the questioning, creativity is impossible. All are essential for moving forward. Today, I believe, art is needed more than ever to help bring back a balanced approach to life within to our society.

Art Railing

One of the most challenging and frustrating things about working with building codes is it can potentially hinder a design. However, sometimes things that appear as blocks can actually push a more creative design. This was the case with this railing. I started on my design and was really liking the elegant lines and the open spaces. The code requirement that a 4-inch ball cannot pass through any part of the railing was weighing on me. I did not want to fill the open spaces with more vines or similar elements as this would have made it too busy. So, I started looking at other design options. I wanted the feeling of light and air. As I was accessing these feelings, I saw images of summertime play and soap bubbles. Then it hit me. Why not use glass, and better yet glass of different colors that can overlap and create other colors? I had seen some fused glass with bubble inclusions by Leona Hawks in a gallery. My clients chose the colors and worked directly with Leona on the final glass pieces, while I made all the templates for the glass and holders for these pieces.

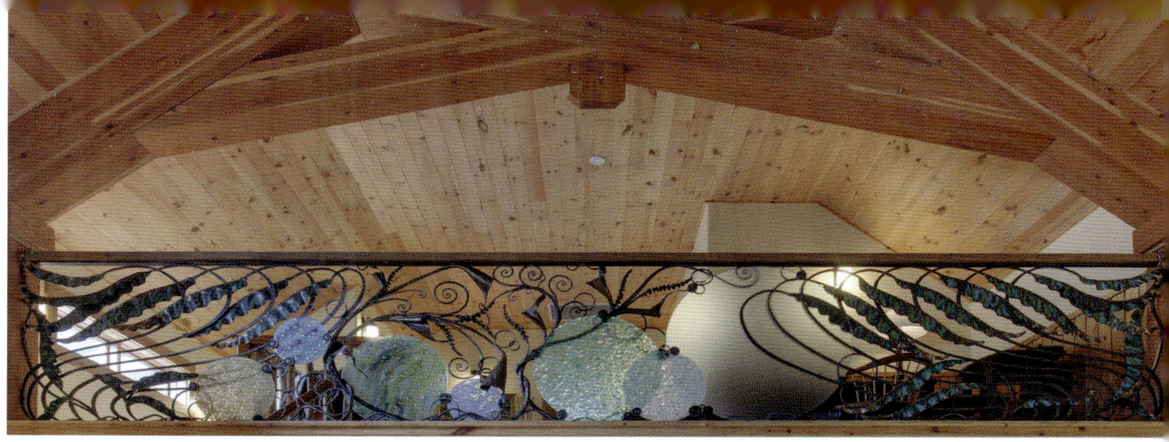

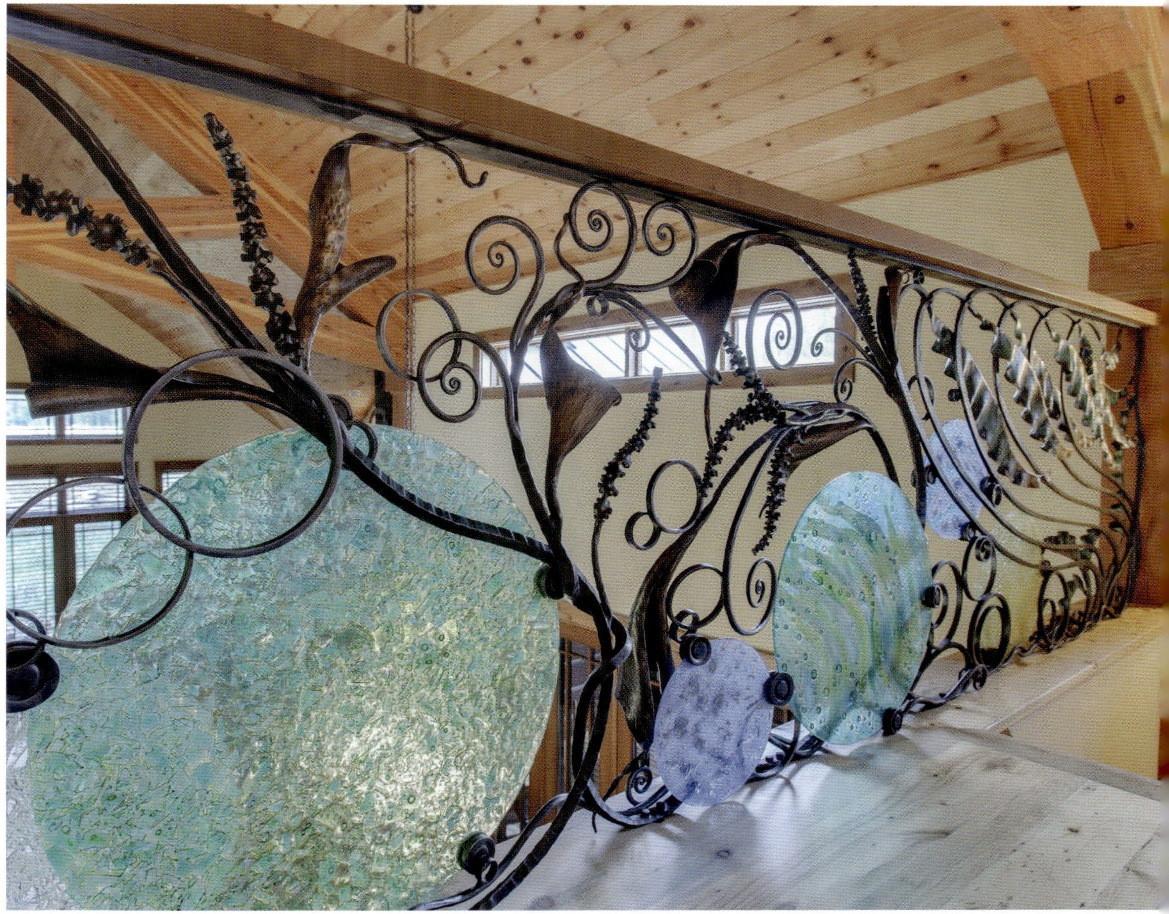

Art railing. 2009. Forged steel, bronze, glass. 20′ x 4″ x 33″. Glass by Leona K. Hawks, Glass Artist, Fused Glass Station. *Photos: George Martin, Jr.*

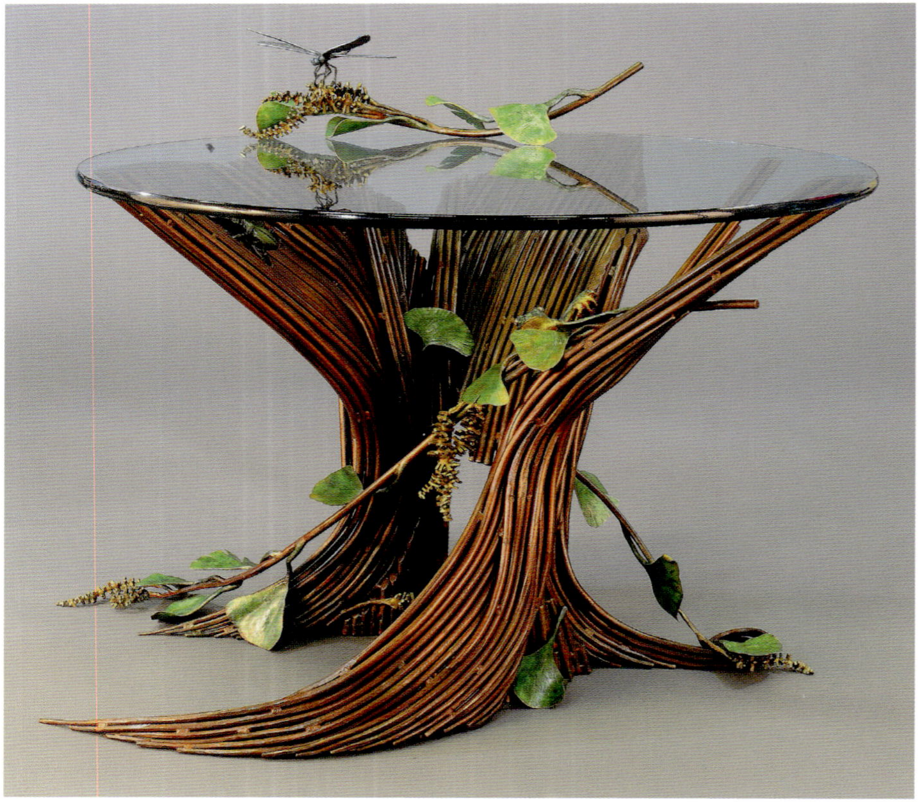

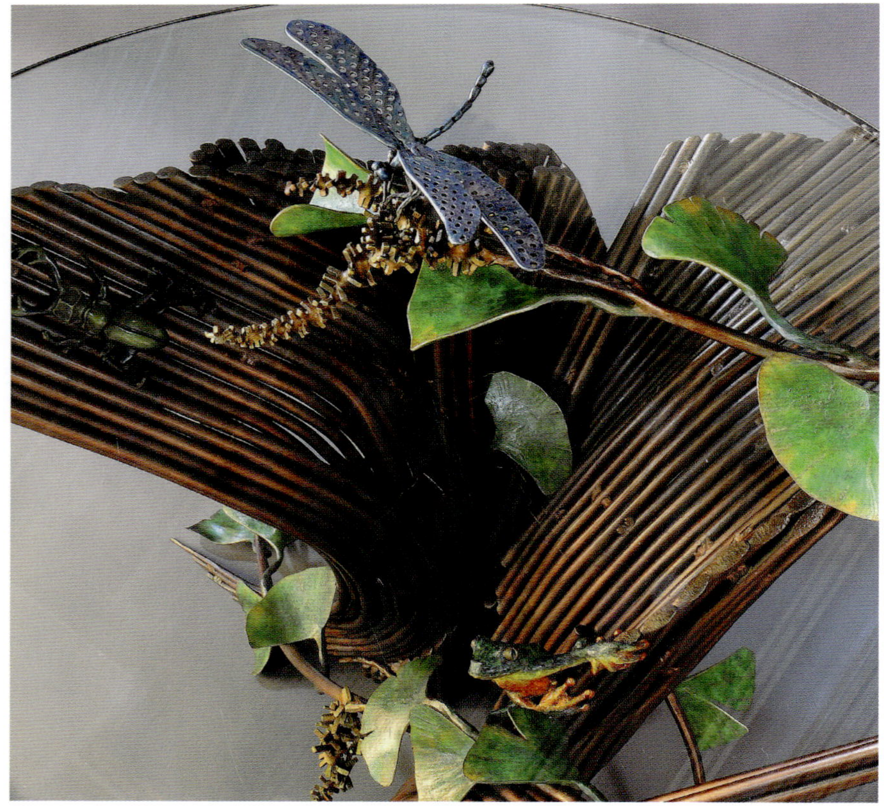

Bedroom table

I collaborated with Barbara G. Browning on the design of this bedroom table. We wanted to incorporate a tree trunk. My idea for the table was one of rebirth. I envisioned a tree stump like the kind you come across in an old forest, half deteriorated and covered in moss. Upon close inspection, one sees all sorts of new life in the stump. The table is quite a mix of various techniques and media. The stump was made from ⅜" steel rods that were tapered and welded together. The dragonfly was forged from steel with wings from ⅛" punch plate, and the frog and beetle were cast in bronze.

Sculptural bedroom table. 2010. Forged steel and bronze castings. 21" x 36" x 36". Design collaboration with Barbara G. Browning. *Photo: Melissa Palfreyman*

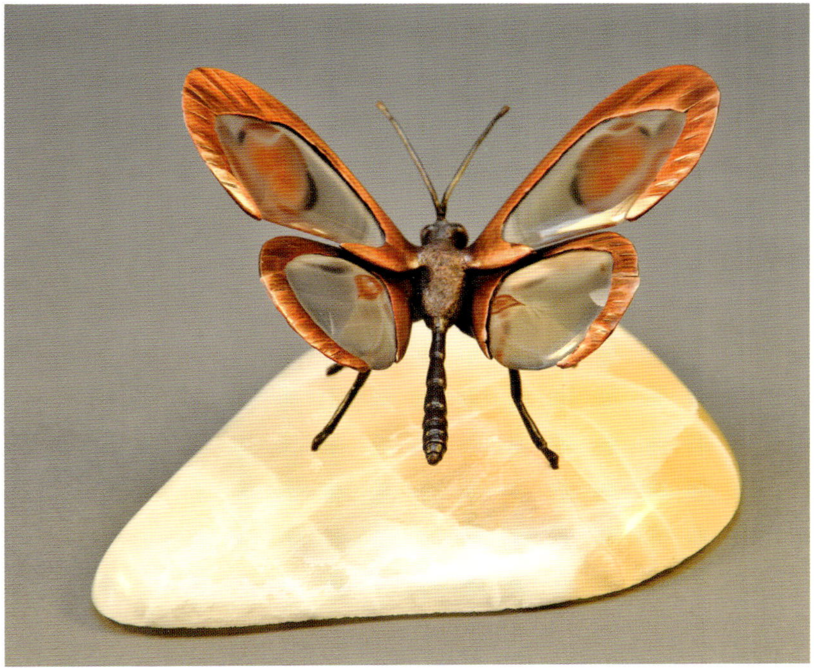

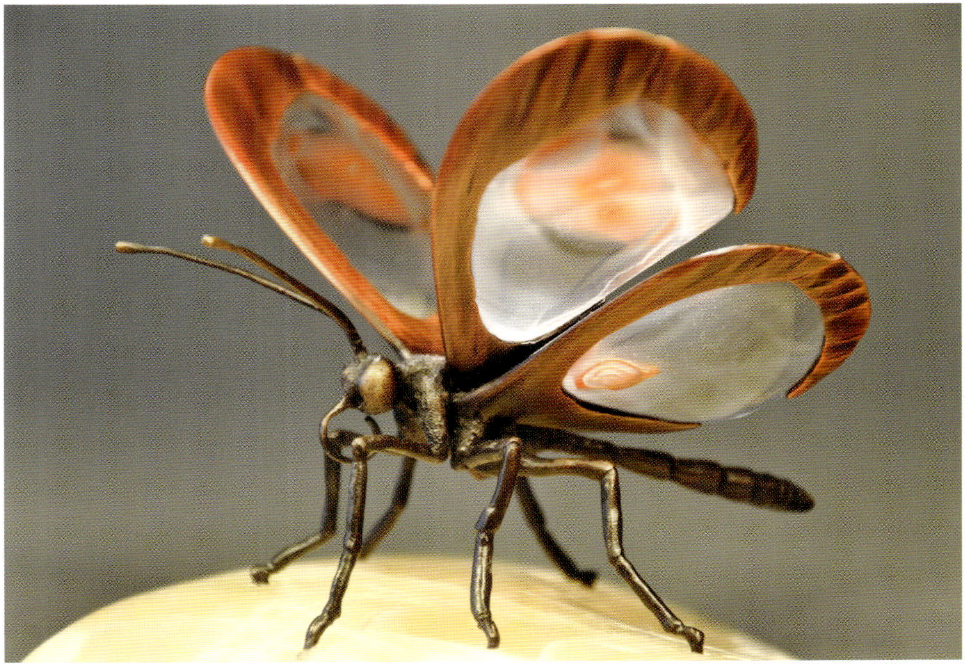

Butterfly

This piece was made to celebrate the university graduation of my good friends' daughter. How inspiring it is to see the love for a daughter in the parents' eyes as they talk of how she fluttered from one task to another as a child and [with] all sorts of beautiful potential opening up for her as she spread her wings. It seams to me a piece of art often wants to be in a certain material. I looked at various pictures of butterflies and I came across one that really stood out for me. This butterfly had incredible translucent wings, but I had no idea how I was going to achieve that look. A little later, the perfect solution came to me at a rock and gem show, where I found two matching slabs of beautiful Apache agate. It was the perfect material for the wings. It was quite a design challenge to incorporate stones in the wings while maintaining the lightness of butterfly wings. I had to cut and polish the stones to very thin dimensions.

Butterfly. Sculpture. 2011. Forged bronze, Apache agate, honeycomb calcite. 10" x 10" x 8". *Photo: Melissa Palfreyman*

Andrew Hayes

Ashville, North Carolina
A.hayes3dart@gmail.com

ARTIST'S STATEMENT

My work combines metal fabrication and paper cutting. I work with sheet steel that is cold formed and welded into hollow constructions. These shapes are then attached to sculpted book pages. The paper moves in a very similar way to the steel. The similarities and differences of these two materials, along with discovering and refining new ways to work the steel and paper, drive this body of work technically. Conceptually, this work remains formal in many regards. The books I use become paper void of content; the text blocks become a new surface where the words become pattern. The steel shapes are referential to industrial forgings and other details I find in metal that are simple in shape but keep me coming back for more.

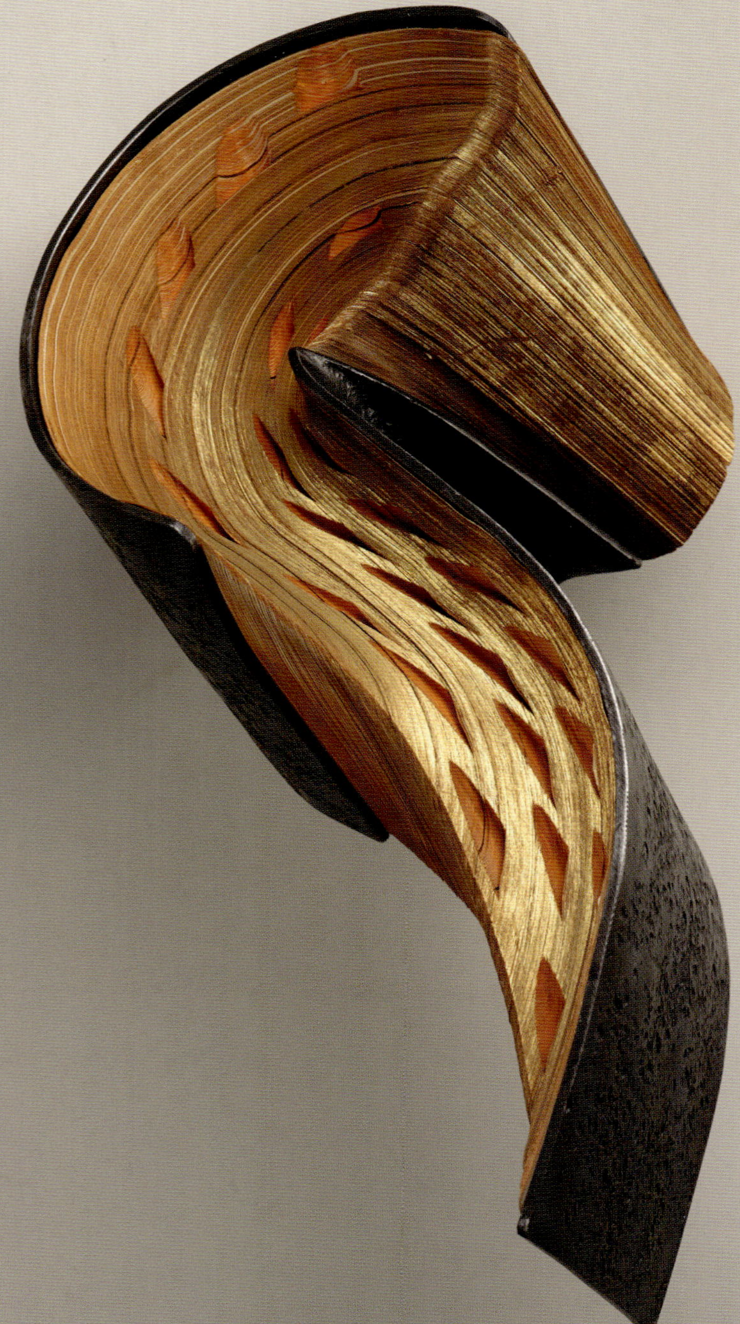

Placer. Sculpture. 2013.
Steel, book pages, and brass. 10''l x 7"w x 9''d.
Photo: Steve Mann, Black Box Photography

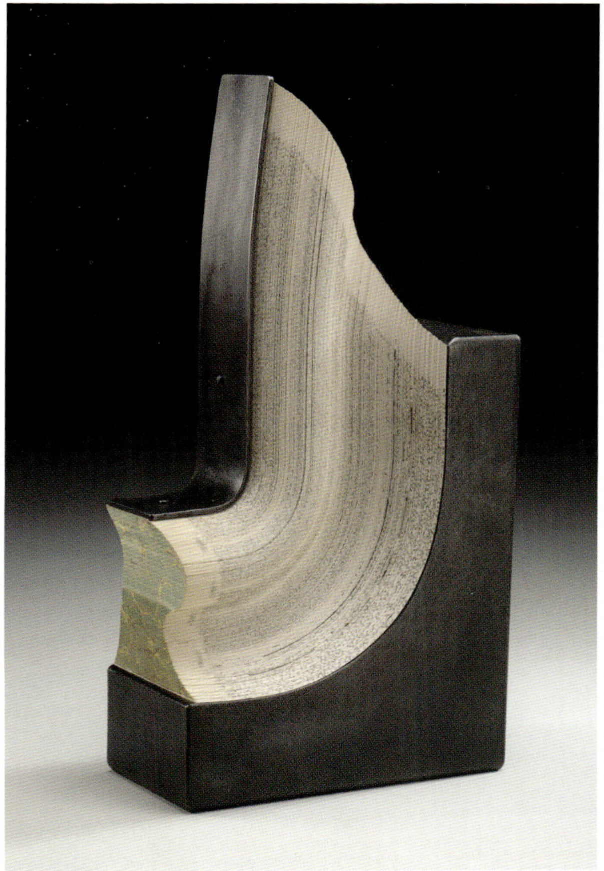

Inhere. Sculpture. 2013. Steel, book pages. 15" x 7½" x 2½". *Photo: Steve Mann, Black Box Photography*

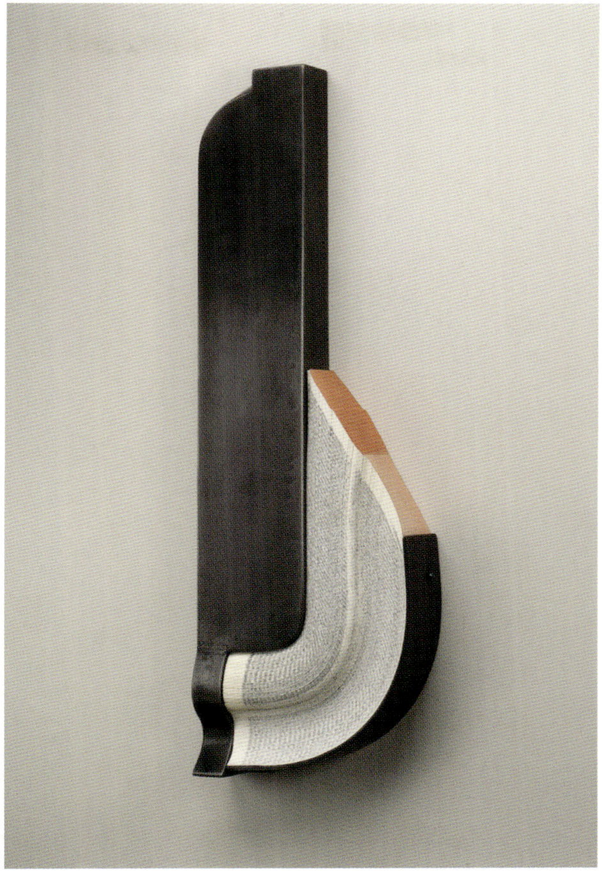

Path. Sculpture. 2013. Steel, book pages. 18" x 6" x 2". *Photo: Steve Mann, Black Box Photography*

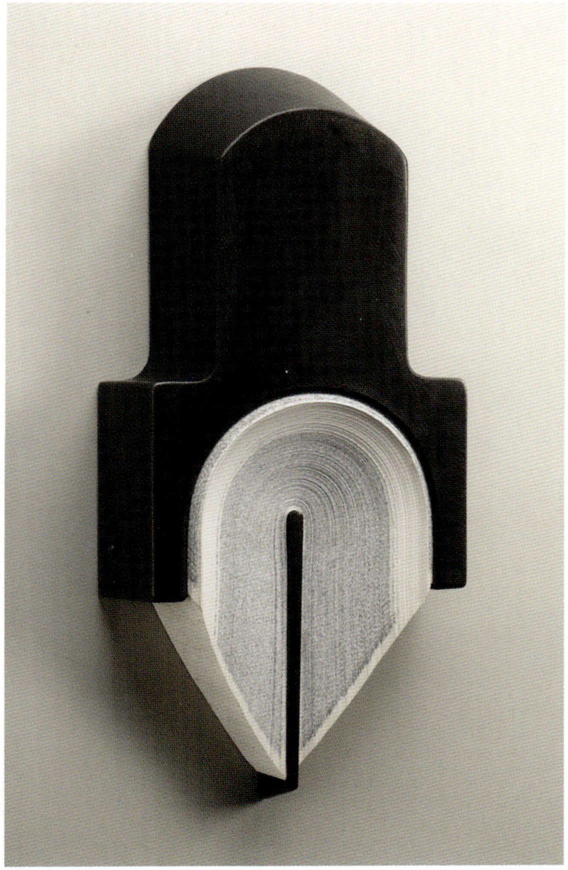

Oxbow. Sculpture. 2013. Steel, book pages. 13" x 6" x 3". *Photo: Steve Mann, Black Box Photography*

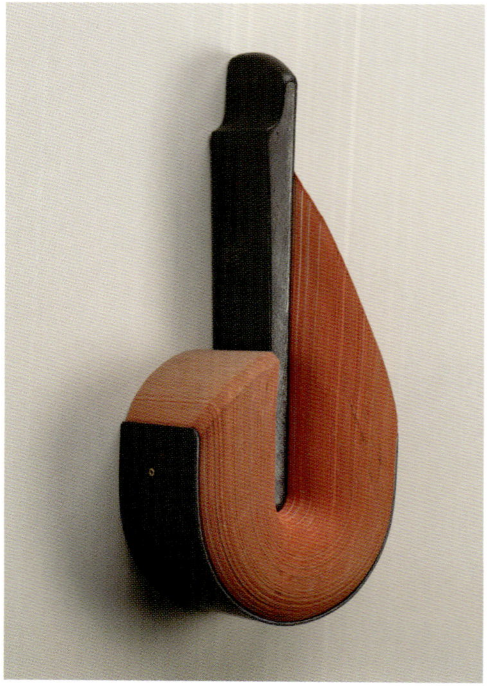

Hone. Sculpture. 2013. Steel, book pages. 7½" x 3" x 2". *Photo: Steve Mann, Black Box Photography*

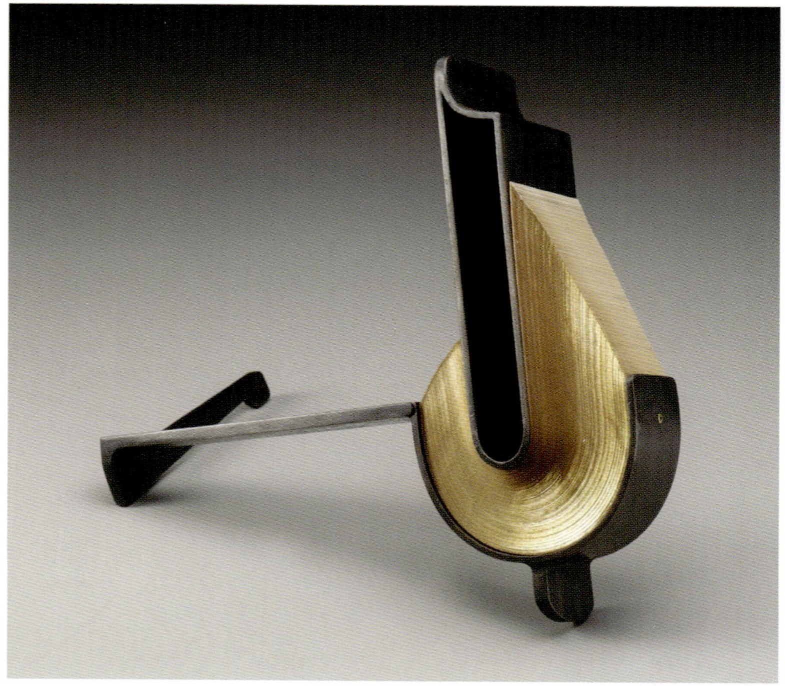

Approach. Sculpture. 2013. Steel, book pages, brass. 8½" x 10" x 6". *Photo: Steve Mann, Black Box Photography*

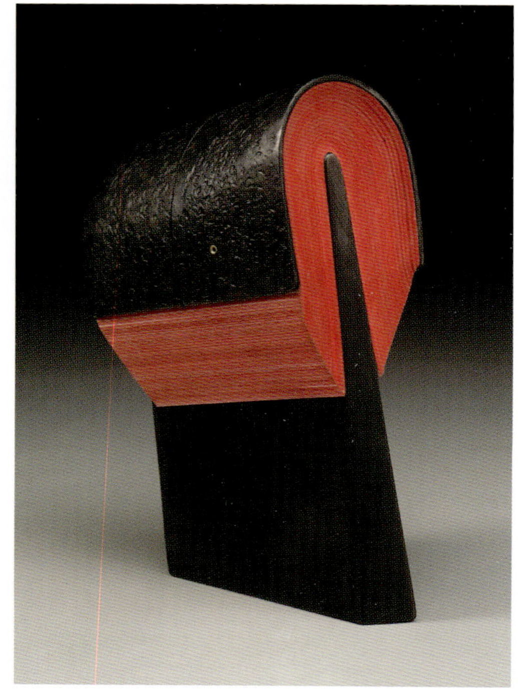

Cadre. Sculpture. 2013. Steel, book pages, brass. 9" x 6" x 4". *Photo: Steve Mann, Black Box Photography*

Lauren Head

Bethel, Maine
headl@gouldacademy.org

ARTIST'S STATEMENT

I cannot help but notice the natural world. I am drawn and bound to the textures and forms and the beauty. I love working with metal. It is a material that can be hard and strong yet malleable and accepting of marks when the element of heat is applied. I can draw on metal with fire and create interesting shapes—intentional and random, depending on the mood of the piece. Taking forms that were never intended to be together and experimenting with their relationships lends a serendipitous approach referencing that which can be found in nature. Mostly, I like making things. I get exciting by the possibilities that lie ahead: an adventure. You begin and see what you can find.

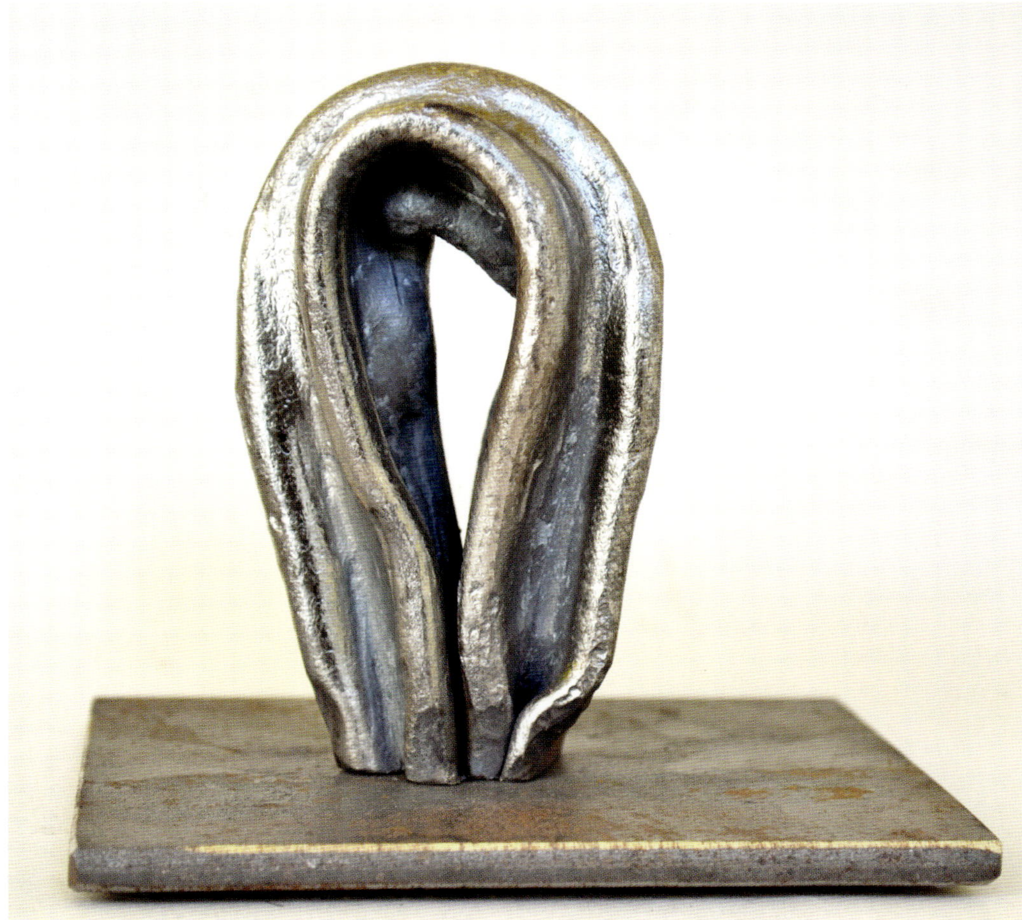

Untitled

This piece is about the transformation of hard, angular form into a softened sensuous form.

Untitled. Sculpture. 2012. Steel. Square tubing indented on all four sides, heated and bent. 5″ x 4″ x 4½″. *Photo: Lauren Head*

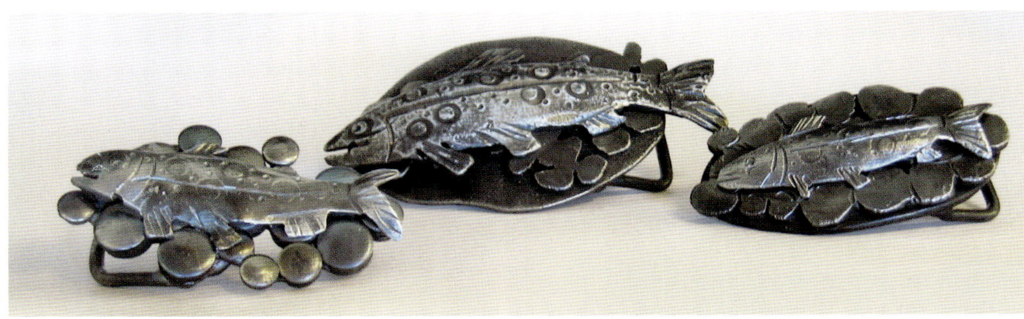

Trout Belt Buckles

These belt buckles were made to capture the image of a brook trout and the pebbled surface of a stream bed.

Trout belt buckles. 2011. Steel. Plasma cutting, MIG welding, texture applied with cross peen hammer, chisels, and punches. 3″ x 2″ x ⅜″. *Photo: Lauren Head*

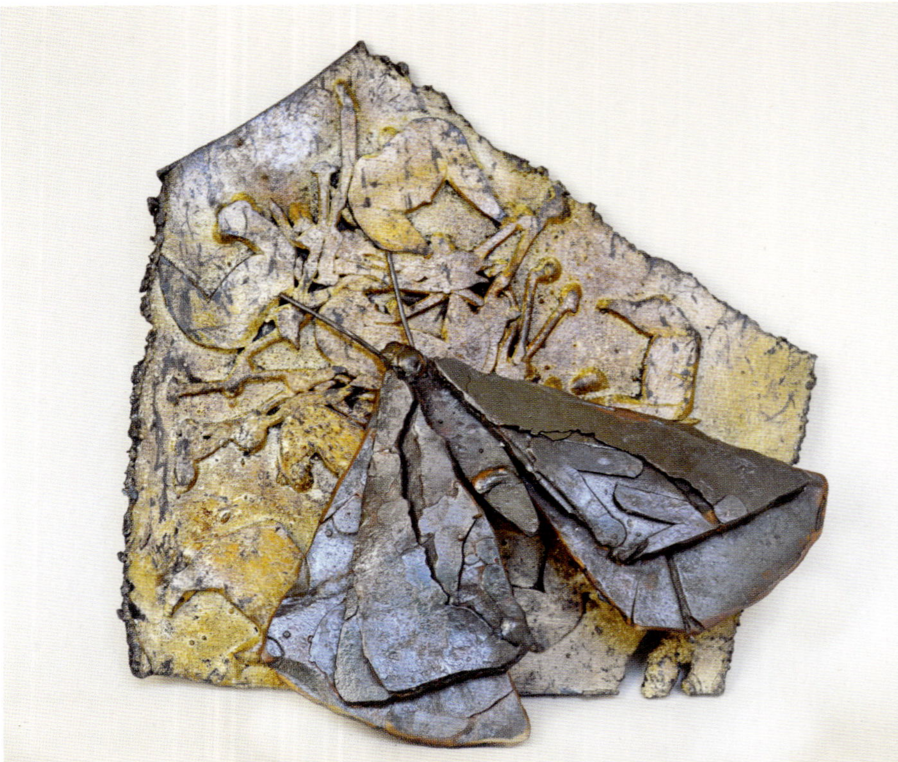

Moth

The moth lands on something it can cling to, an interaction of the two textured forms. The texture reflects the beauty and patterns often found on the wings of a moth. The form the moth has landed on has a gesso patina. The shapes were created by selecting random scrap pieces, welding them on to a plate and flattening the forms with a power hammer.

Moth. Sculpture. 2011. Steel with gesso patina. MIG welding, forging and plasma cutting, gesso patina. 8″ x 8″. *Photo: Lauren Head*

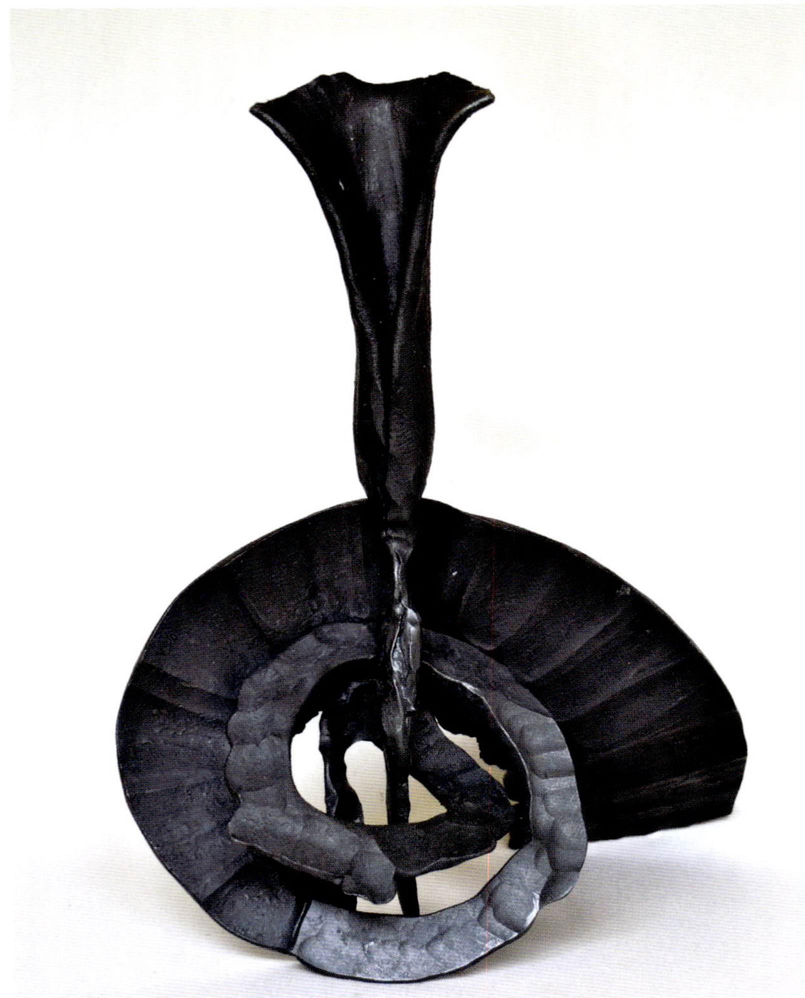

Untitled. Sculpture. 2011. Steel. Pieces of square and round tubing twisted and altered, pieces of flat and round stock MIG welded together and flattened in a power hammer, and all pieces later assembled with MIG welding. 14″ x 6″ x 9″.

Arman Hostikyan

Sochi, Russia
http://hostikyan.com/en

ARTIST'S STATEMENT

I've been forging iron for twenty-eight years. It all started when I was fifteen years old. By accident, I got into a blacksmith's workplace in the town of Ashtarak (Armenia), and I first saw how iron is forged. That same moment I felt wild desire to make things out of burning iron, and this desire still hasn't let me go. Iron is often overlooked and underestimated—people tend to think that only cheap things can be made of it. I prove that wrong. Working with iron is very hard physically, but physical hardships are almost nothing compared to the creative process. I'm very self-critical, and I approve only a small percentage of my works.

I don't think there's one work I have finished completely—all are incomplete, more or less. I'm much more open in my works than in my life—if you look at them you can see much more of me than if you look at Arman. And I believe when one is alone and sad, he/she is honest and vulnerable enough which is the right point to start making something beautiful. It's level zero, it's where the real thing starts.

Mask of Winter Queen

This was inspired by Michael Whelan's famous painting. Mr. Whelan and his wife Audrey saw this sculpture and were absolutely astonished. Winter mask was made by fingertips from iron garbage. Summer Queen's Mask (also inspired by Whelan) is coming later.

Mask of Winter Queen. Wall art. 2010. Only iron, no special tools used. Manual forging, welding. About 40" x 40".

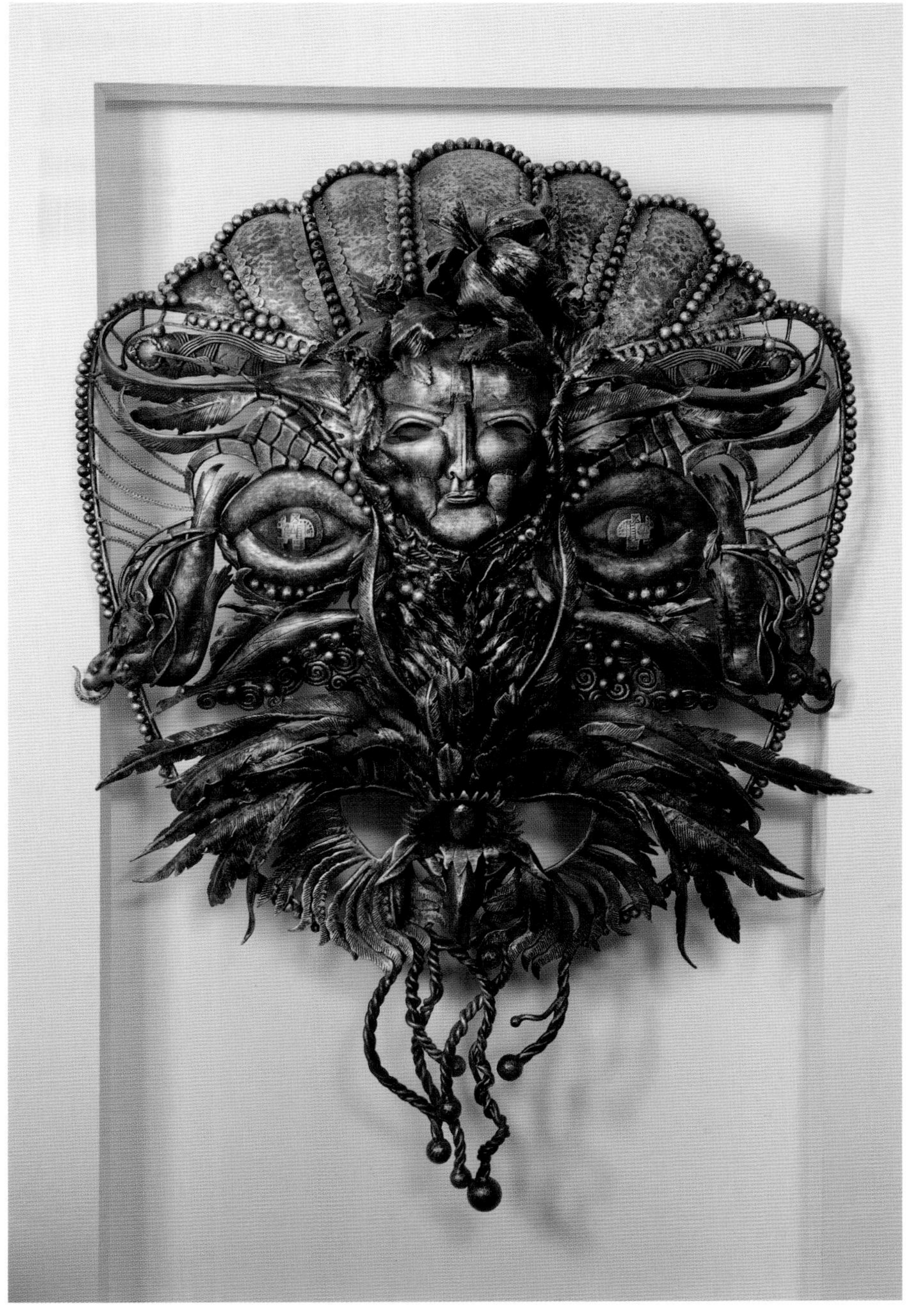

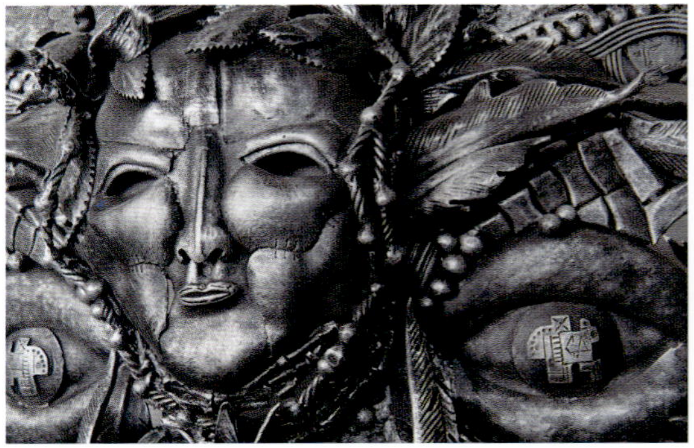

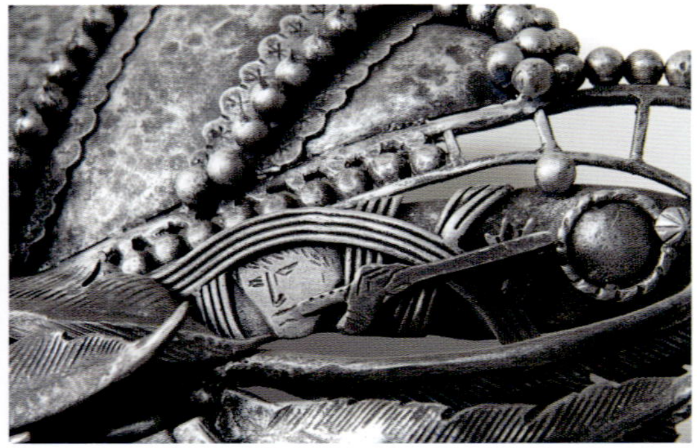

Mask of Winter Queen. Detail.

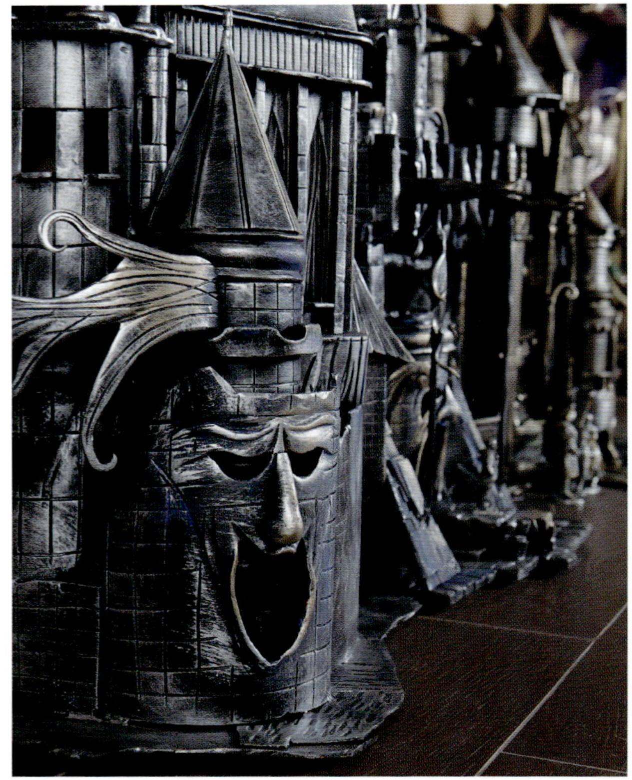

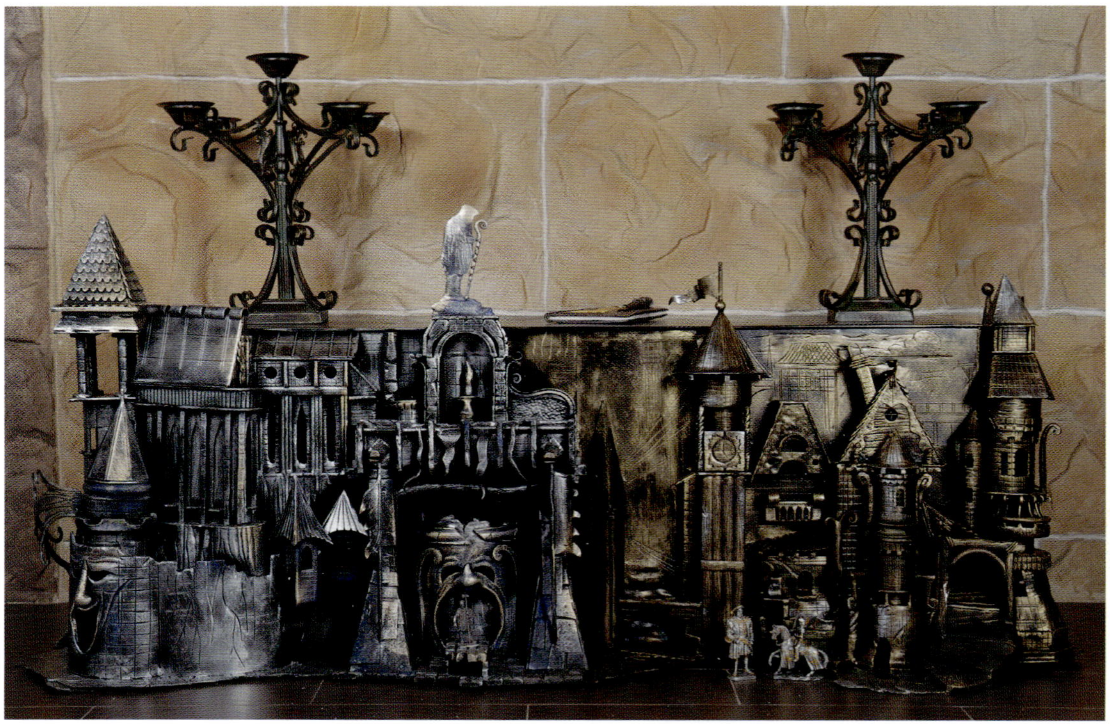

Castle of Montague & Capulet

This is part of a wall composition inspired by the plays of William Shakespeare and paintings of James C. Christensen. The whole composition is in a private museum in Adler (Sochi area). I like to think that there's eternal struggle, ancient grudge, and mutiny happening in this dual castle: the left part fights the right part, good fights evil, and some disturbed souls may appear in its windows sometimes.

Castle of Montague & Capulet. Sculpture. 2011-2012. Part of wall composition *Cogito Ergo Sum*. Only iron, no special tools used. Manual forging, welding. About 20" x 20" x 60".

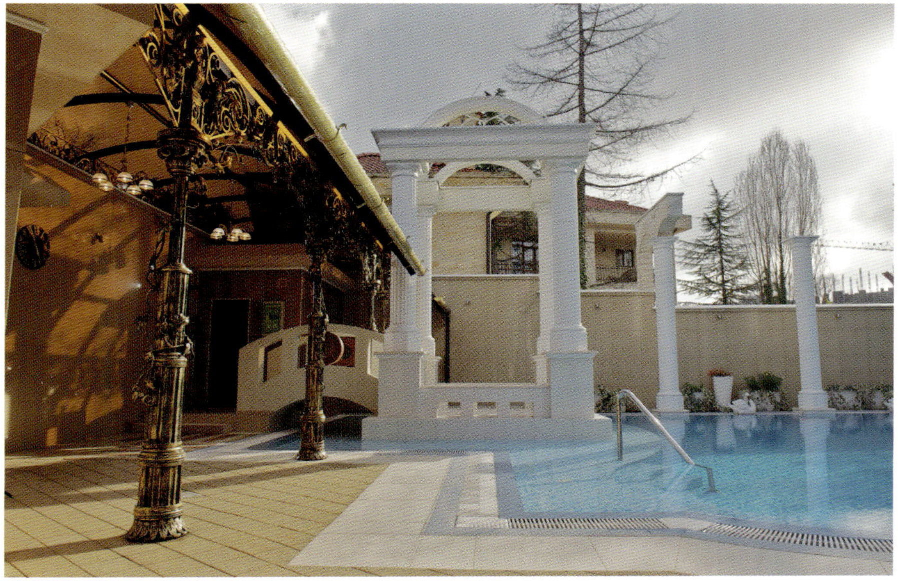

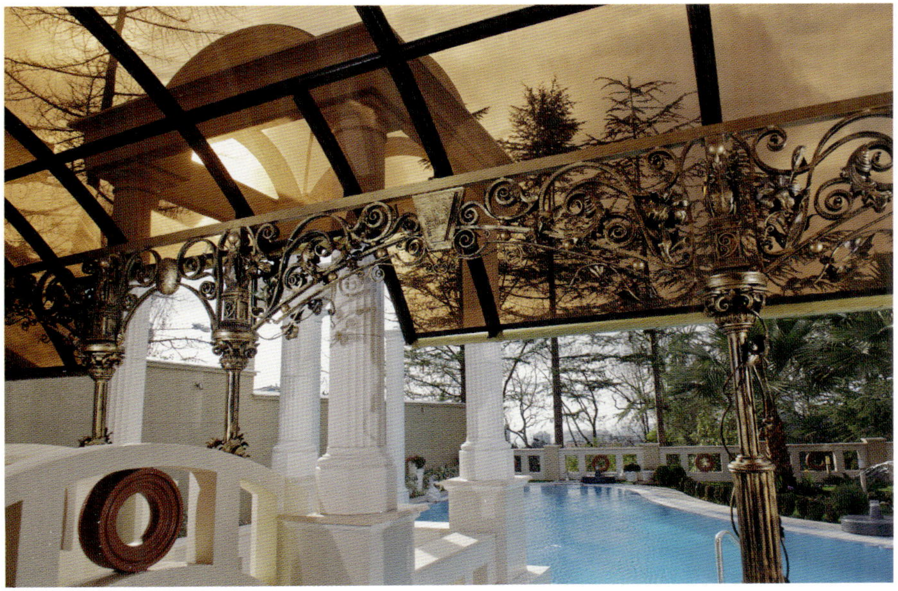

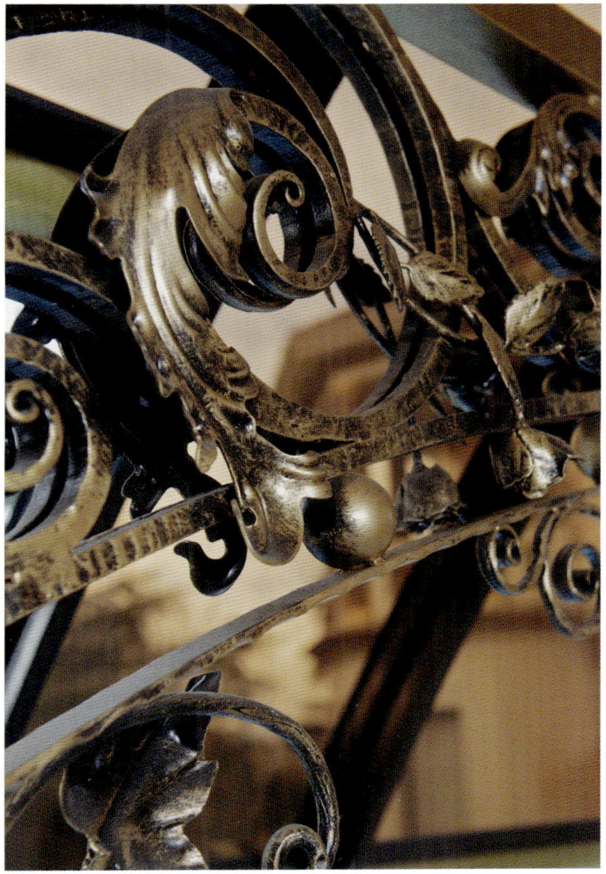

Poolside Pavilion

This was made for a very important person in Sochi. Roof made from glass; pillars are not molten. At first, the pillars had bronze color but then a brave and expensive decision was made to cover them with real gold! Four layers of premium car paint containing gold and two layers of premium car paint containing silver cover the pillars now. Silver was added because it gives bliss and depth. The contrasts among the gold pillars, the blue pool water, and the gray skies and surroundings is especially shocking at sunset.

Poolside pavilion. 2013. Only iron, no special tools used. Manual forging, welding.

Nicholas Ireys

Paw Paw, West Virginia
ireyssne@gmail.com

ARTIST'S STATEMENT

As I develop my work as a blacksmith and art-maker, I look for language in my work, a way of expressing my ideas. I have discovered a language that is based on how shape can communicate emotion and movement. The pieces that I make are meant to convey certain emotions through shapes and gesture. I draw much of my inspiration from natural forms, both animal and plant. I find it interesting how specific shapes can trigger a viewer's unconscious reaction and can express certain emotions, much like the movement of dancers.

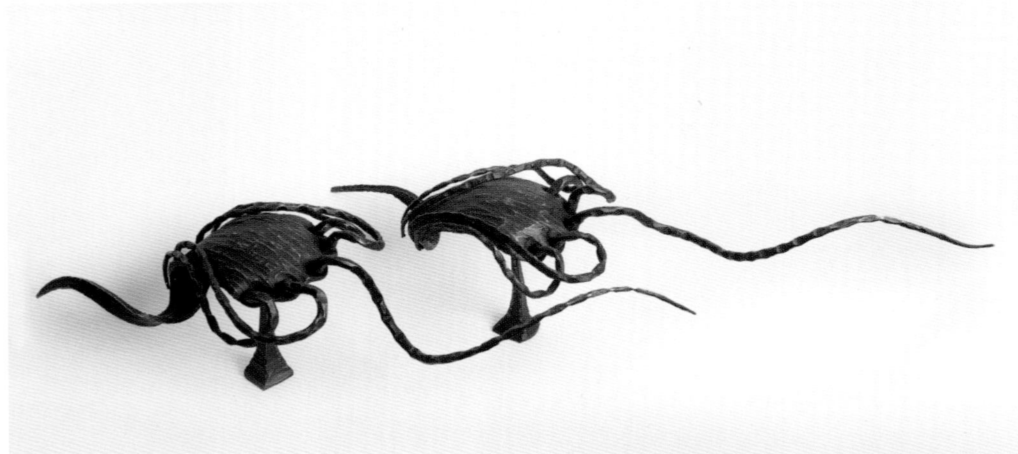

Twin Erchant

I once heard the phrase, "An artist can make something once; a craftsman can make it twice." This led to me making two of the same sculpture. Finding the shapes for these pieces was very spontaneous and achieved through the construction process. There was little planning involved. They both balance on a stand so that the slightest movement or wind will make them turn or sway.

Twin Erchant. Sculpture. 2013. Steel. 12" x 26".
Photo: Elizabeth Ellenwood and Mercedes Jelinek

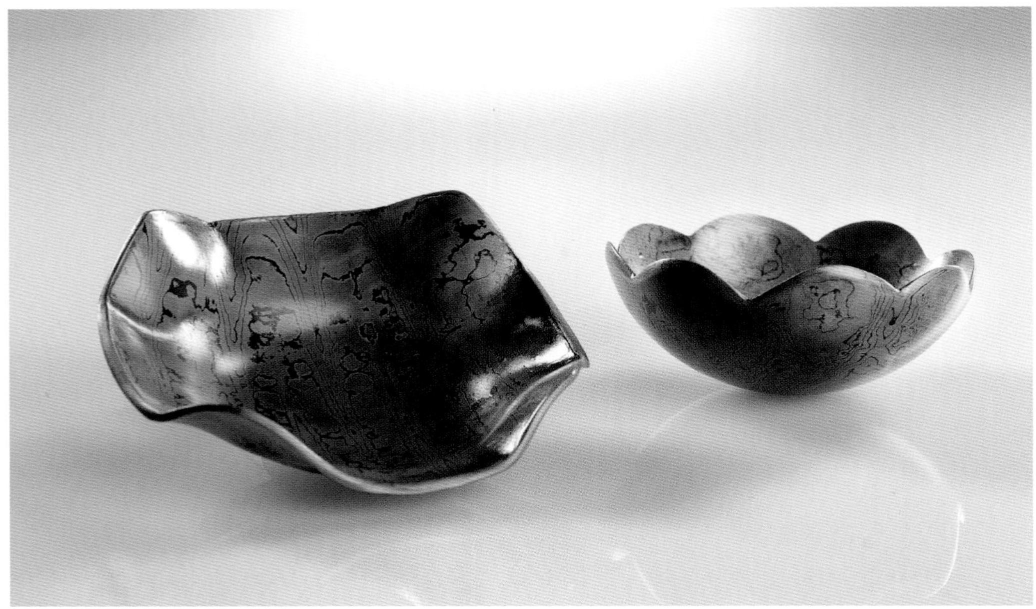

Damascus Vessels

I wanted to focus on surface and quality of lines. I have always admired the technique and results of pattern welded steel. These vessels are experiments using the lines of pattern-welded steel along with the lines of the shape of the bowl.

Damascus vessels. 2013. Damascus steel.
8" x 8" x 3"; 7" x 7" x 3". *Photo: Sherry Elliot*

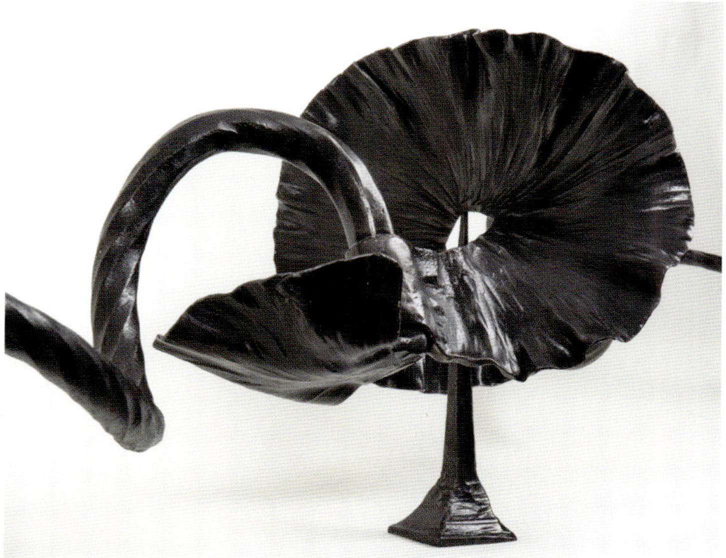

Balance Study

I wanted to make a piece that used some of the best qualities of steel. One of those qualities is that it can hold much of its own weight. In this piece, I tried to show the fluid grace that this material can achieve. By using the language of shapes, I am expressing swift, graceful movement. This piece also balances on its stand and will move and spin in the wind.

Balance Study. Sculpture. 2012. Steel. 8′ x 18″ x 18″.
Photos: Elizabeth Ellenwood and Mercedes Jelinek

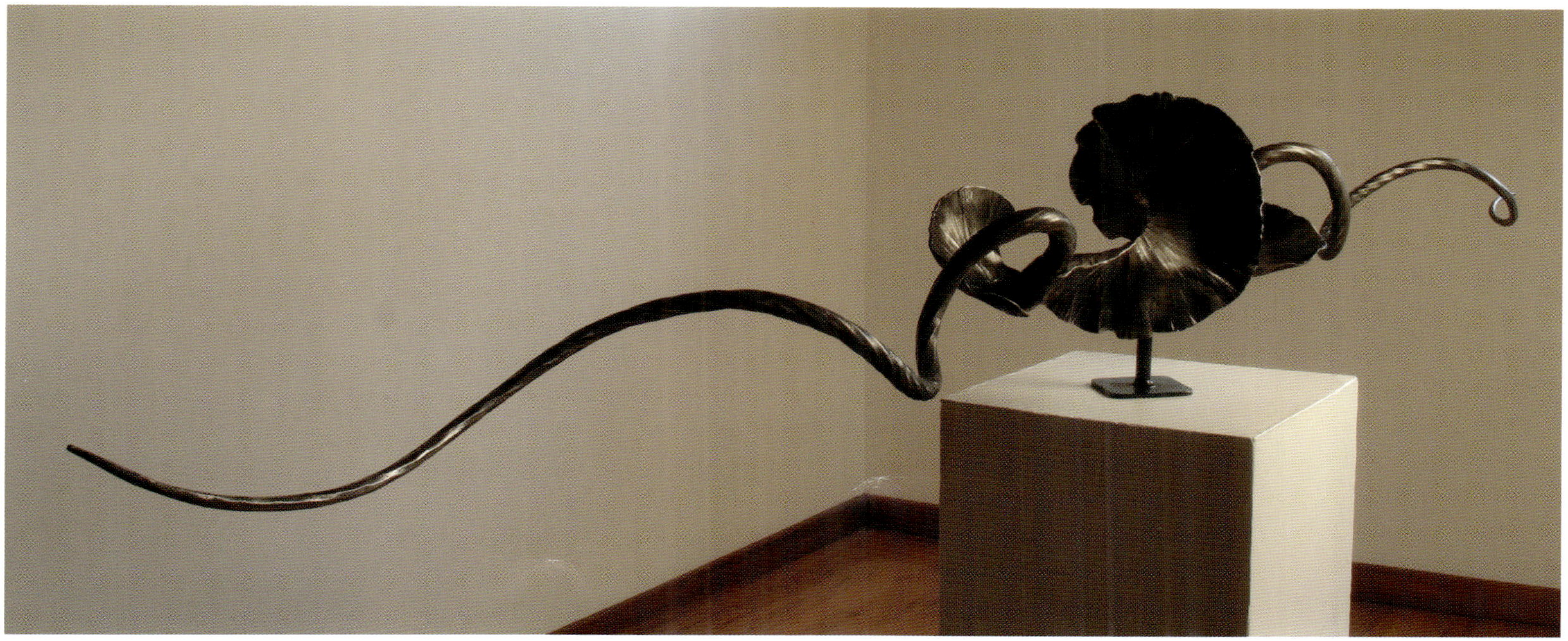

NICHOLAS IREYS

Parents' Basket

This piece straddles the line between sculpture and utilitarian object. It can be used as a centerpiece on a table, as decoration, or holding other objects. There are only two parts to the piece—the hanging basket and the stand. There is a symbiotic relationship between the two parts: neither can survive without the other.

Parents' basket. 2013. Damascus steel and mild steel. 18" x 14" x 20".
Photo: Sherry Elliot

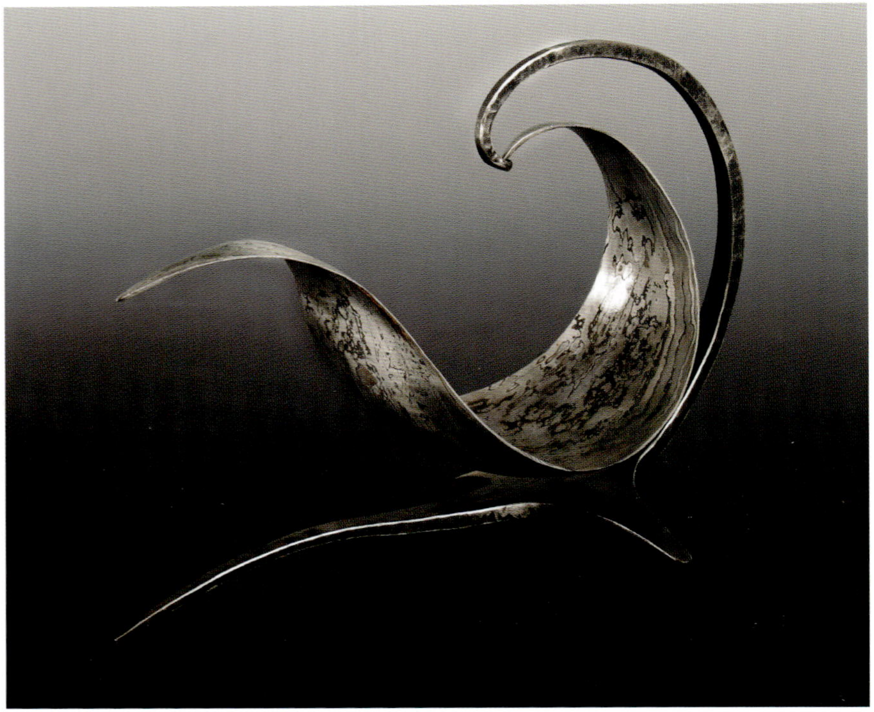

Glass Hammer

This is part of a performance piece where the crank on one wheel is spun, turning the other wheel and then lifting the long arm with the glass hammer head on the end. An anvil (not shown) is placed at an appropriate height so that the long arm must reach critical speed. Once going fast enough, the long metal arm flexes enough to strike the waiting anvil, causing the glass hammer head to explode.

Glass Hammer Machine. Sculpture. 2013. Steel, leather, blown glass.
14" x 14" x 72". *Photo: John Payne*

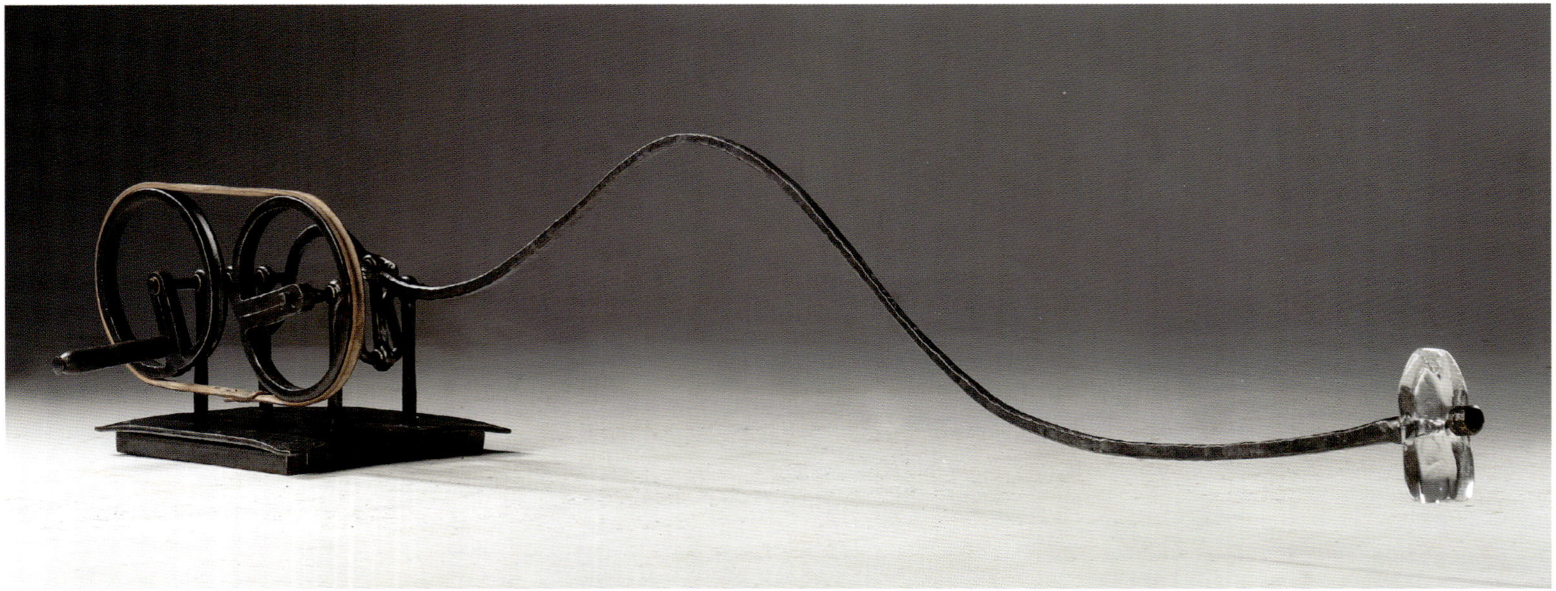

David Kamenicek

Euro Metal Art Studio, Riverside, California
www.eurometalartstudio.com

ARTIST'S STATEMENT

I began my journey as an artist-blacksmith over twenty years ago, upon entering into an apprenticeship at the shop of Ilja Behal in the Czech Republic. With the completion of apprentice, I set out to learn from the current masters of the craft in Europe. I have worked and studied under the Italian Master Claudio Bottero, the late Master Sculptor Toni Benetton, and graduated from the Art School in Luhacovice Czech Republic as an artist-blacksmith. Since 2005, my Euro Metal Art Studio has built a reputation for creating unique, hand-crafted designs influenced by both traditional and contemporary European metalwork.

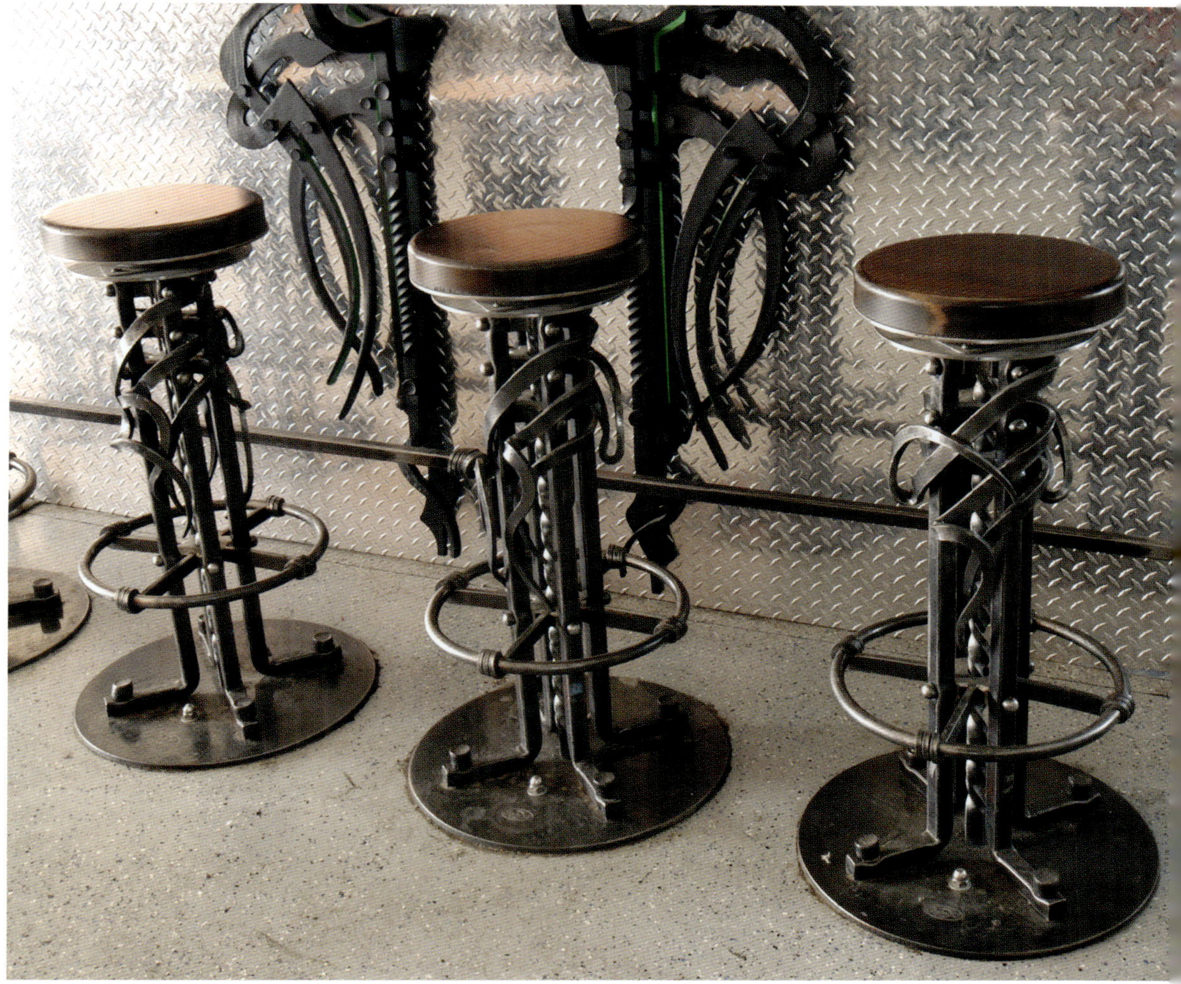

Entertainment-area stools. Forged steel. Private residence in San Bernardino, California.

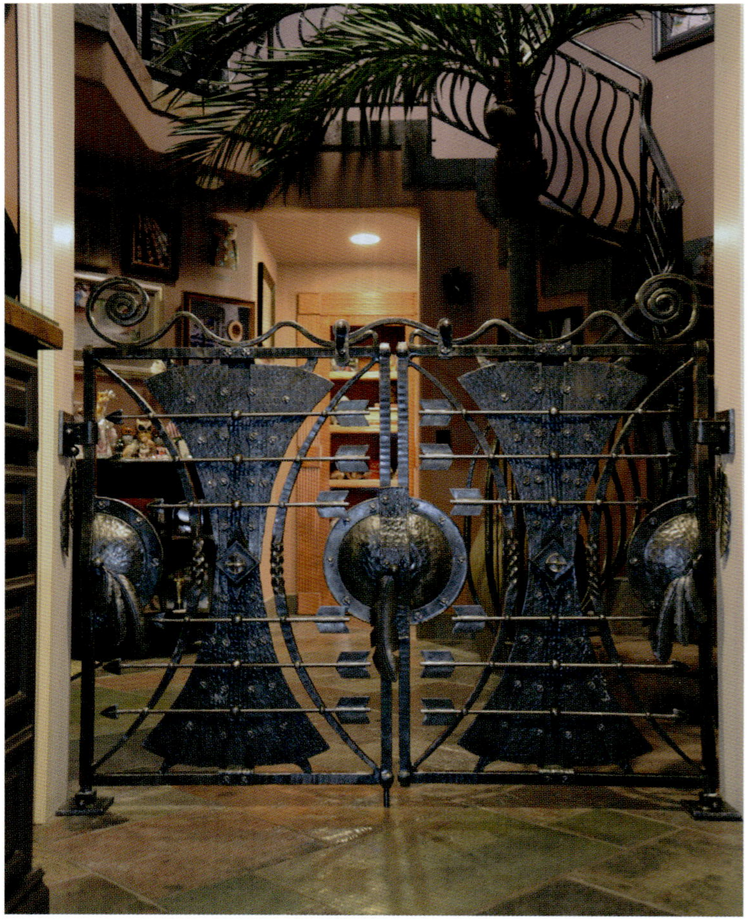

Interior gate. Forged steel. Private residence in San Bernardino, California. About 4′ x 5′.

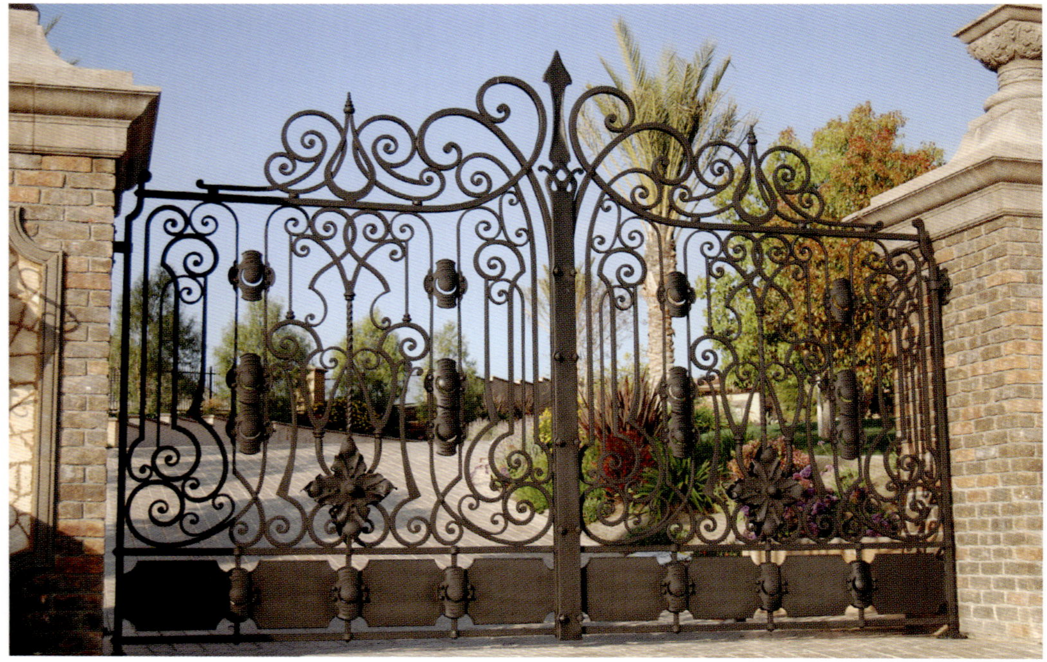

Gate. 2011. Forged steel. About 16′ x 11′. Private residence, Riverside, California.

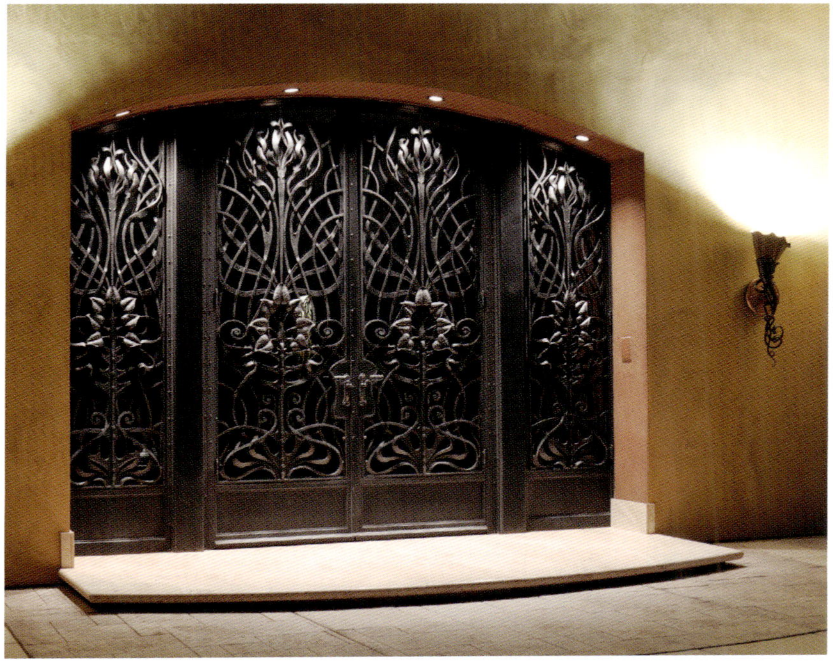

Entry door. Forged steel. About 14′ x 11′.

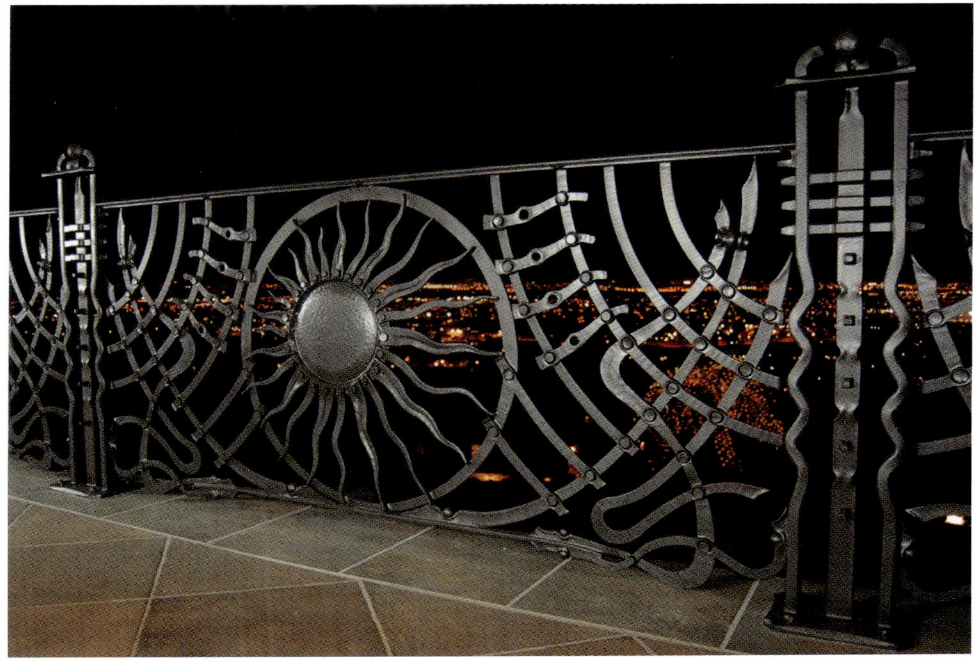

Balcony railing. Forged steel, panel about 4′ x 8′. Panels represent sun, moon, air, water, earth, and animals. Private residence, San Bernardino, California.

Craig Kaviar

Kaviar Forge & Gallery, Louisville, Kentucky
www.craigkaviar.com

ARTIST'S STATEMENT

I have been making cool classical work from the inferno of my forge in Louisville for over thirty years. Throughout my career, I have developed and refined my style, which combines sleek lines with rough textures often inspired by nature. I follow the natural flow of the material and forge it into organic forms. My work is inspired by the works of celebrated artists Alberto Giacometti and Alexander Calder.

Originally, blacksmithing provided the founding of material culture. However, industrialization eventually replaced the utility need for blacksmithing, thus transforming the craft into a sophisticated and ancient form of artistic expression. I work relentlessly to honor the long line of blacksmiths who came before me, including my great-grandfather, who was a wheelwright in Russia.

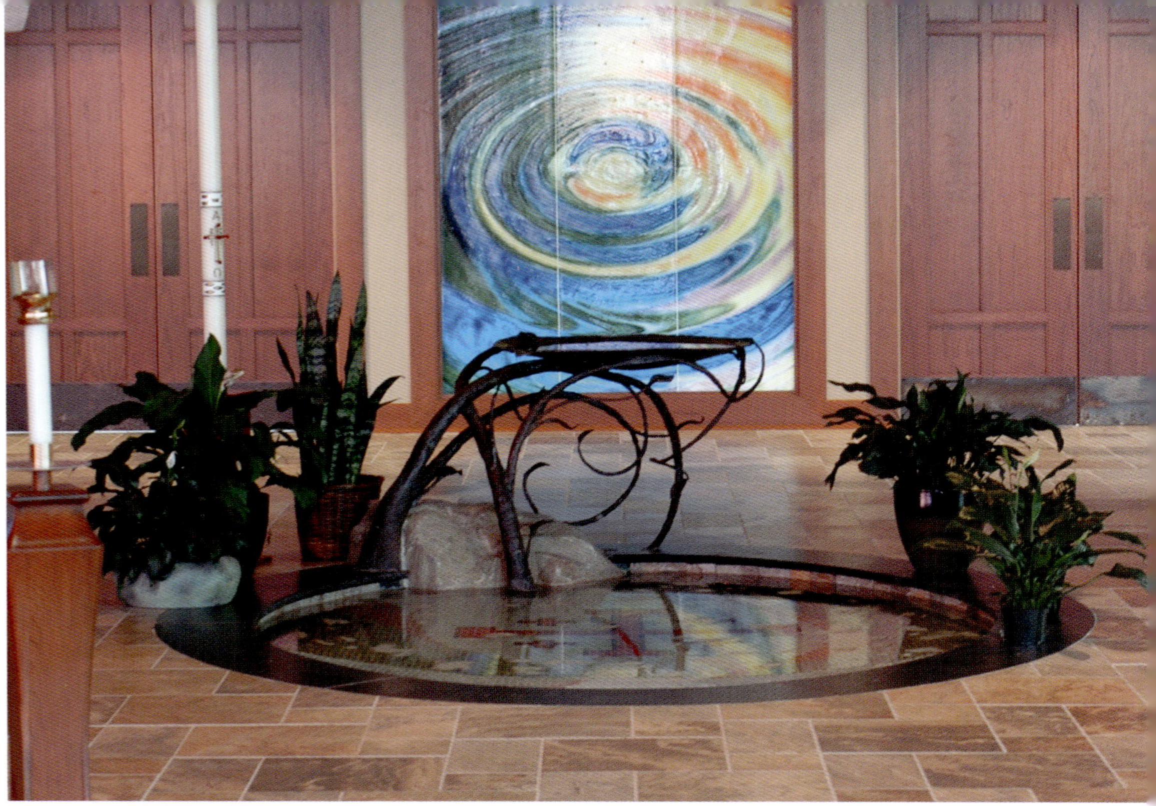

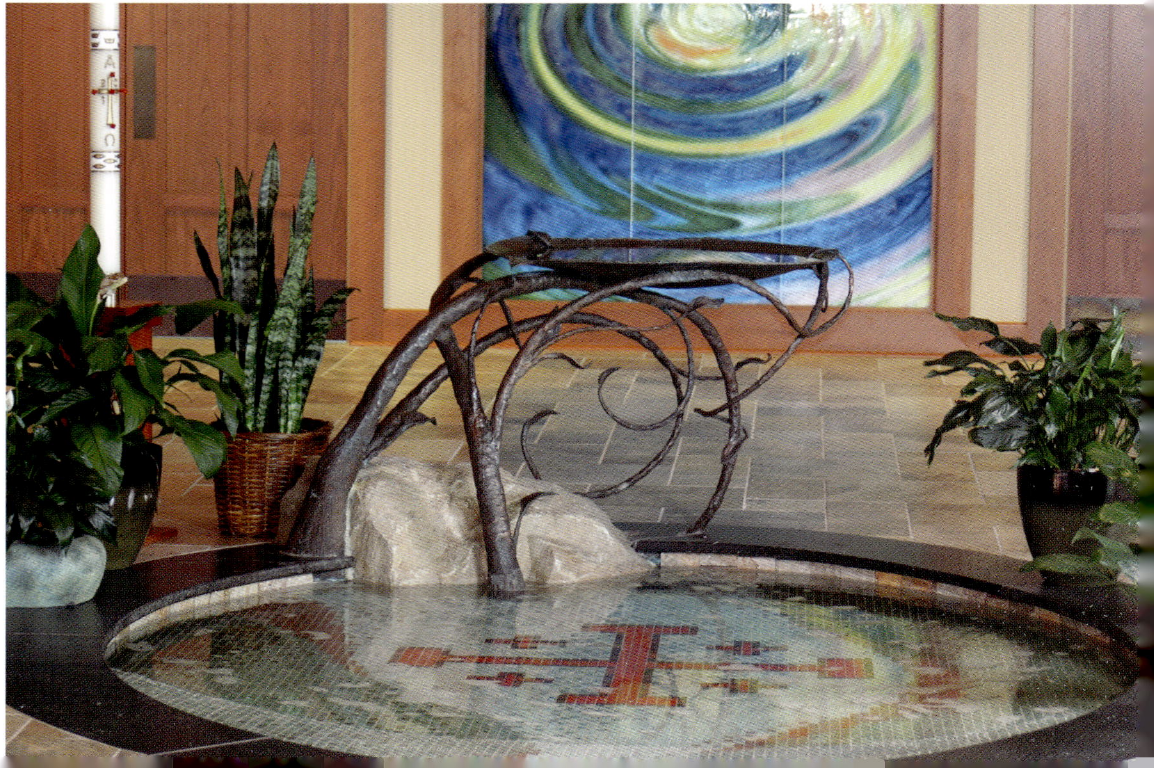

Baptismal Font

The boulder the font rests on was found at the site where the church was originally built. The patina of the copper was set to complement the stone, as though it grows through the tiles around the boulder. I spent a great deal of time hammering the circle of copper into a bowl shape, alternating between working with my own hands and using my 200 pound Chambersburg Air Hammer, which was originally built for use on battleships in WWII. By using this machinery of war to create art, I feel I am, in my own way, helping to turn swords into plowshares. In addition to the font, there are four holy water containers with slumped glass.

Baptismal font. 2013. Forged copper on boulder base. Installed at St. Michael's Church, Jeffersonville, Kentucky. 64" x 40" x 36".

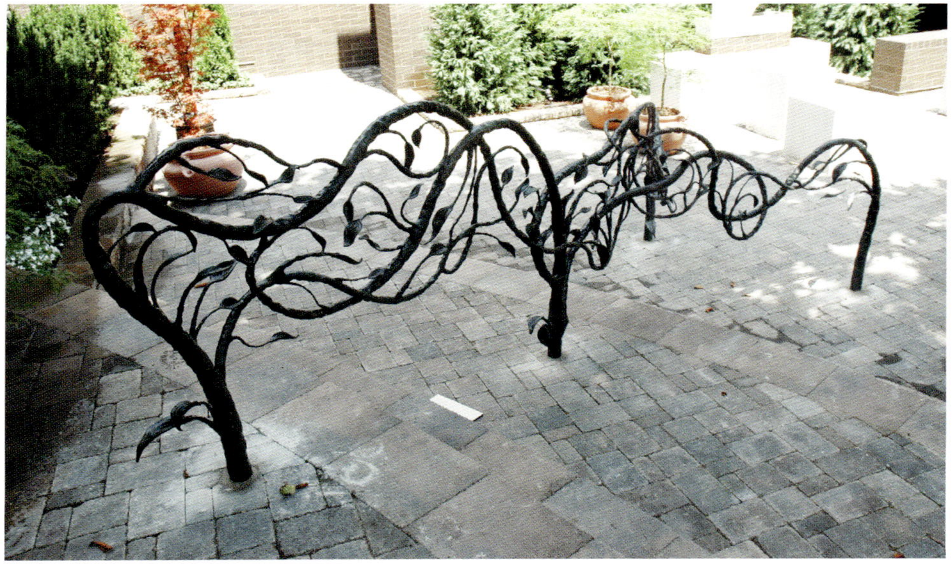

Healing Garden Handrail

This handrail was commissioned in 2011 by Norton Hospital for the Healing Garden, an area designed specifically with cancer patients in mind. For this piece, the texture of the ironwork invites you to experience the forged iron on both a visual and tactile level that is soothing because it interacts with the viewer. It suggests the order within chaos, as the branches split and twist, seeking more room to grow. The trunk of the curving vine leads the viewer down a set of stairs into the Healing Garden.

Healing garden handrail. 36′ x 8′ x 18′.

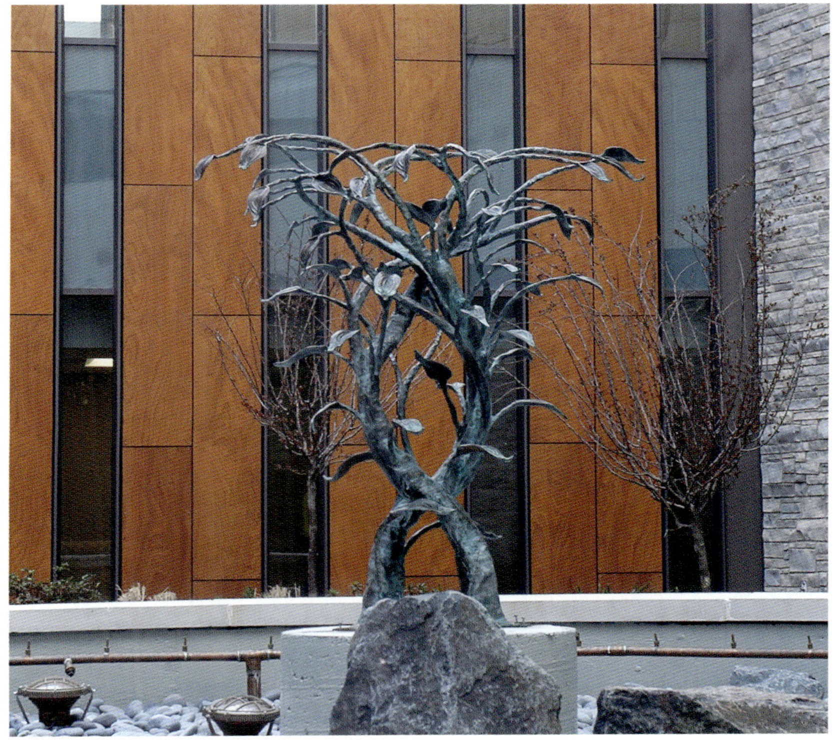

Reaching for Balance

Created in 2013 to be installed in Owensboro Hospital courtyard fountain, this sculpture was displayed before installation at Kentucky Crafted, The Market *as well as at my gallery, The Kaviar Forge & Gallery. I wanted to give people the opportunity to see the work up close, to examine the metalwork and to see the clearly visible grooves in the hand-forged copper that recall a tactile nature of both the medium and the tree branches rendered. The overall impression is of touch—and I cannot imagine a more appropriate home for such a message than a hospital, where healing hands are always touching ailing people. Built for a place of contemplation, reflection, and relaxation, the hospital courtyard is grounded by the innate strength of forged copper. The tree's limbs weave in between each other, creating a sense of steady rhythm and movement as they ascend vertically into the sky.*

Reaching for Balance. 2013. Sculpture. Forged copper. 54″ x 48″ x 45″.

Corporate Retreat Handrail

This forged-iron staircase complements the stone walls of an Oldham County home. The use of glass visually increases the space of the room. The rail displays my signature combination of sleek lines with the tactile, hand-forged texture of the iron. In addition to the pictured railing, I built two outdoor balcony railings, a main entrance rail, and an entire room themed to a New Orleans street scene, complete with three interior balconies and several repoussé pieces based on classical paintings.

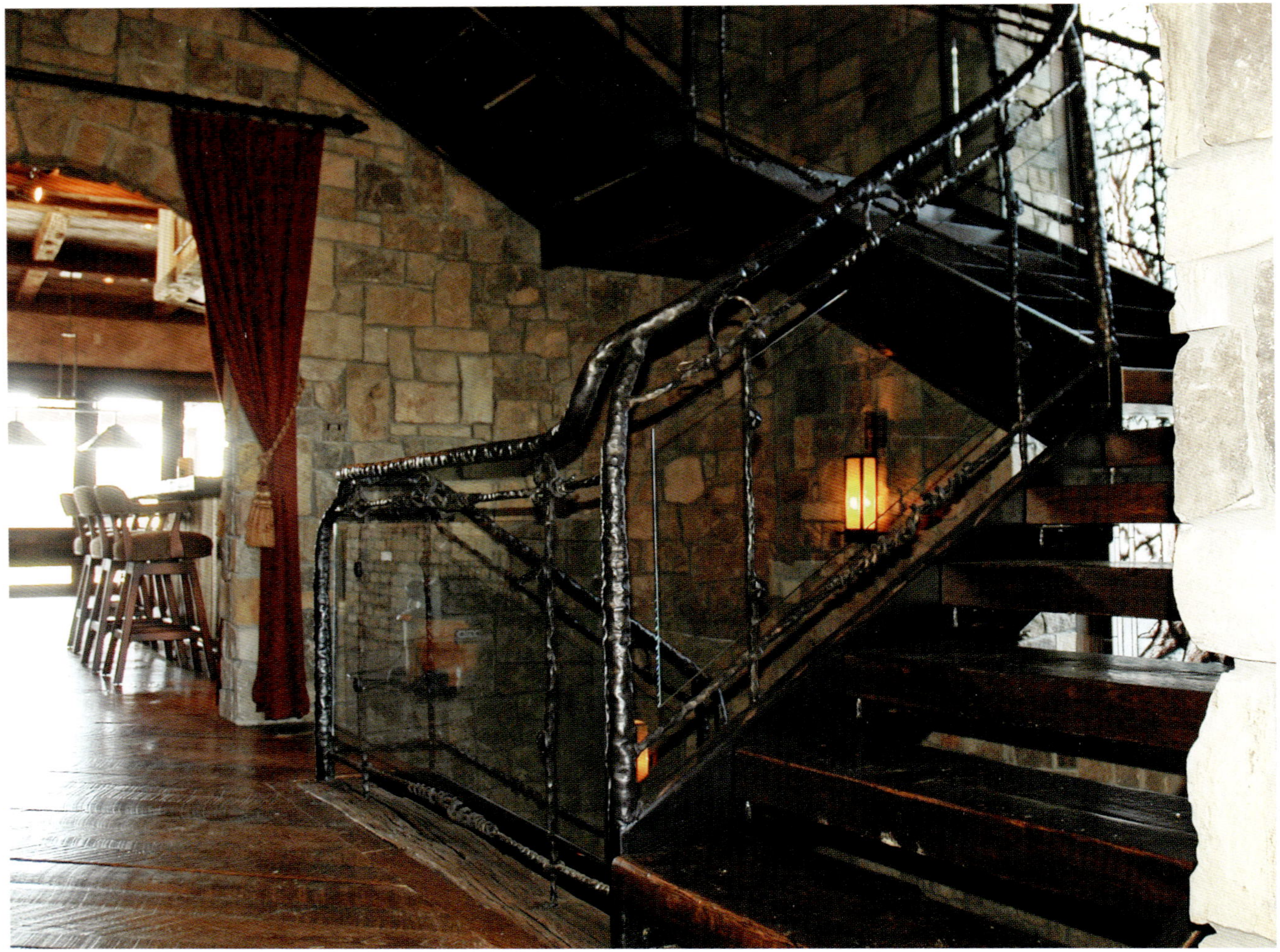

Corporate retreat handrail. 2011.
Forged iron. 248′.

Star of David Memorial

This Star of David made of forged iron was created for a Jewish family to commemorate a loved one. The strength of the iron symbol of Judaism is particularly striking in the snow of Adath Jeshurun Cemetery. The Star of David is representative of the connections between this life and the hereafter, making it an appropriate monument for a cemetery. 40" x 48".

Star of David memorial. 2010. Forged iron. 40" x 48".

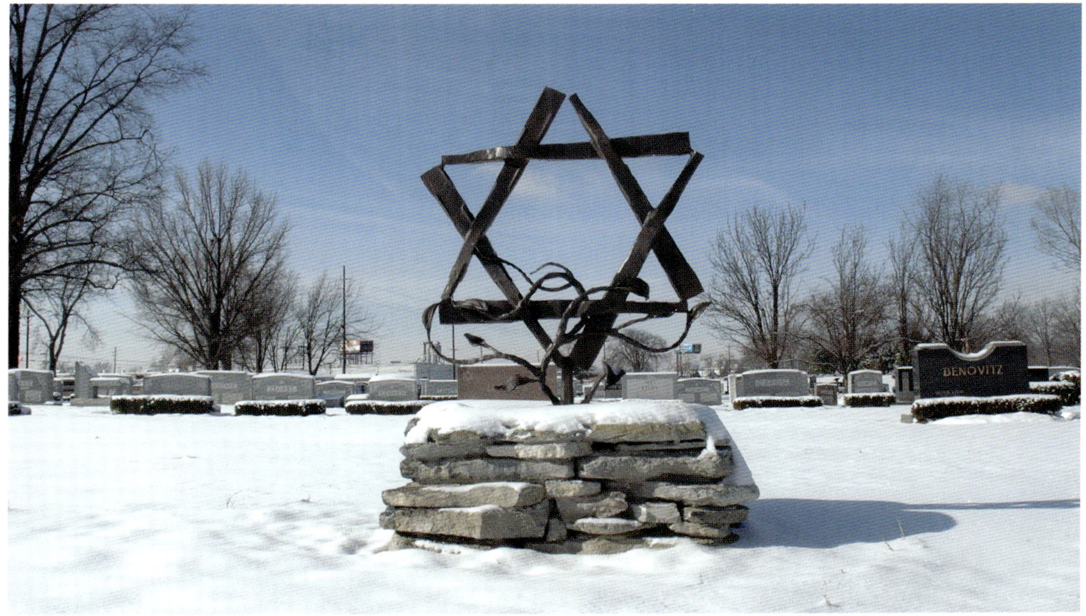

Library Desk

In 2009 I was commissioned by the Louisville Free Public Library to create a centerpiece for the newly renovated library entrance. The desk's ironwork frame combines elements from the library's scrollwork staircase as well from my own textural style. The countertop is black, polished concrete with brown vein-work throughout, accompanied by recycled glass pieces. The main branch of the Louisville Free Public Library, in downtown Louisville, sustained over $8 million in damages with the torrential rains that ravaged the city, causing extensive flooding in August 2009. The library took in over six feet of water, damaging the lower level and claiming over 50,000 books, as well as causing extensive interior, electrical, and mechanical damage.

Library desk. 2009. Iron, polished concrete, recycled glass. 72" x 33" x 40".

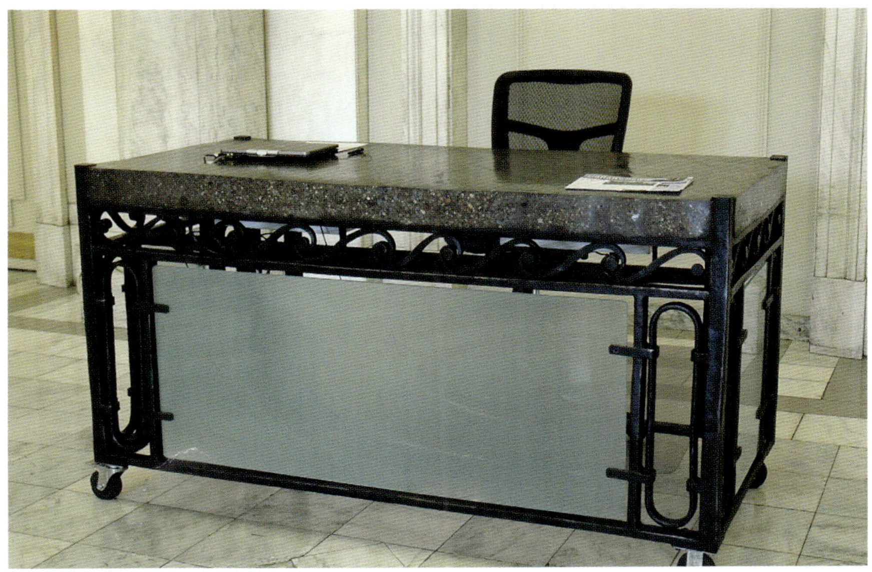

Mark Kent

Traditional Iron, Queensland, Australia
www.traditionaliron.com

ARTIST'S STATEMENT

To me, hand-forged iron work, using traditional blacksmithing techniques and processes, is a way of life. I love creating unique pieces that give my clients as much joy using them as I get creating them.

My blacksmithing is an individual journey to be creative and strive to improve with every piece. I don't think that one ever conquers this medium; you just get very comfortable with it. I get inspiration from nature. Forging organic pieces from iron gives me the freedom to release my thoughts and visions. I always ask myself the question "What if I do this?" or "What if that was turned around?" My other concerns are proportions and making sure lines are fluid. That's what I do.

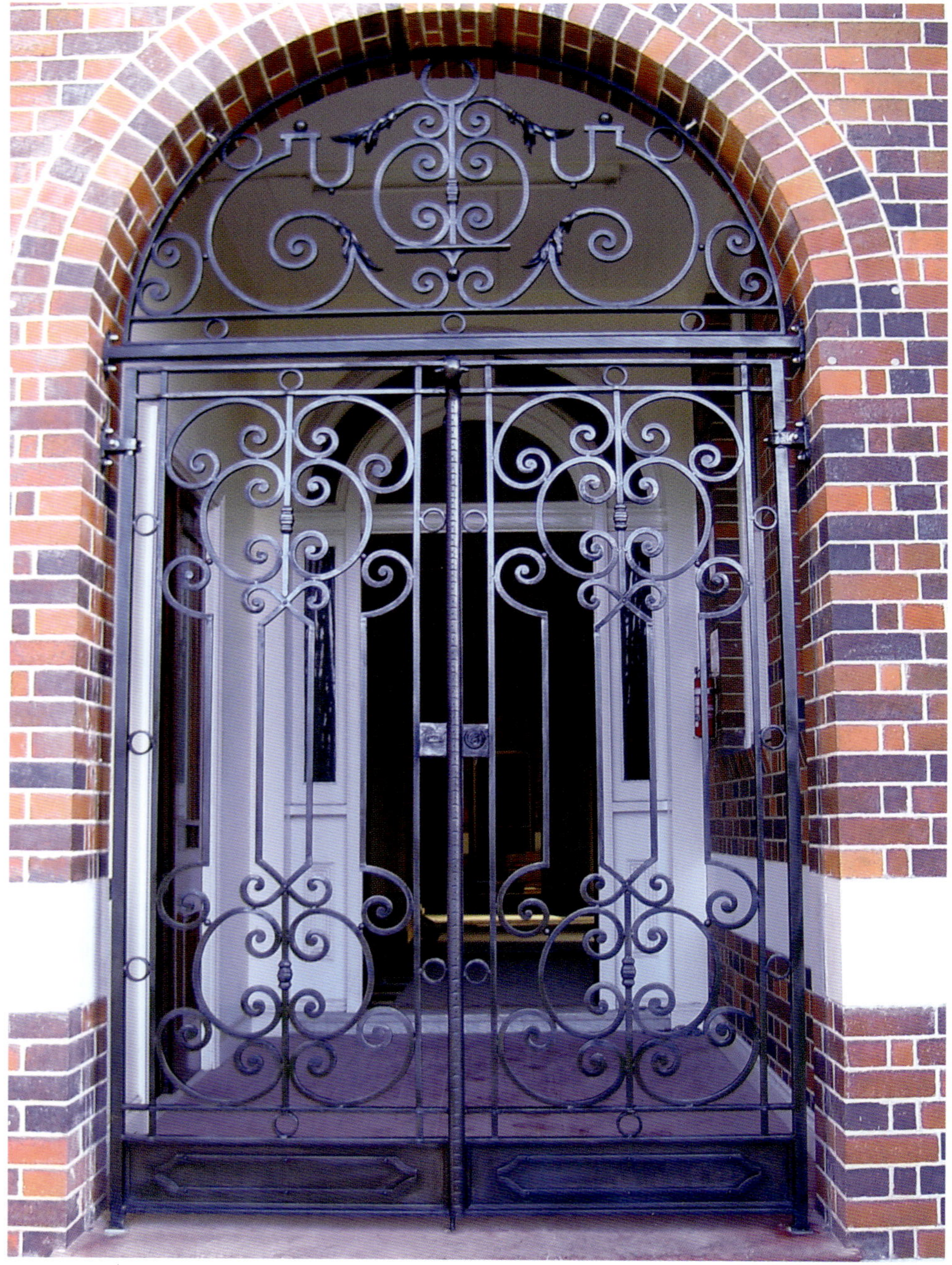

Front entrance gates for a heritage house. Hot-punched, snub-end scrolls are joined by pinned balls with forged acanthus leaves and handmade hinges. Hand forged from 16 mm steel. Back styles: 32 mm (about 1¼") solid steel with forged hinge journals and forged drop bolts. Zinc sprayed and hand polished with graphite wax and sealed with clear lacquer.

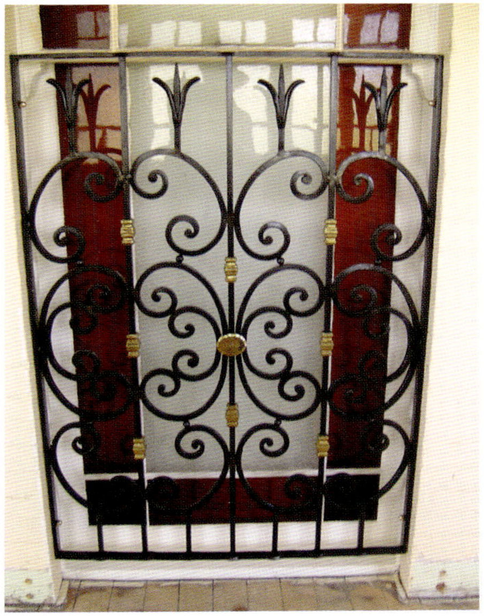

Window grill, using forged, snub-end scrolls joined with forged ball and pin riveting through the middle. Forge welded fleur de lis and polished cast brass ornaments. Graphite and wax finish.

Organic table. Top of polished Huon pine burl with forged vine legs and an organic candle holder with five candles to symbolize parents and three children. The table legs weres inspired from a plant root I pulled out one day after tripping over it one time too many.

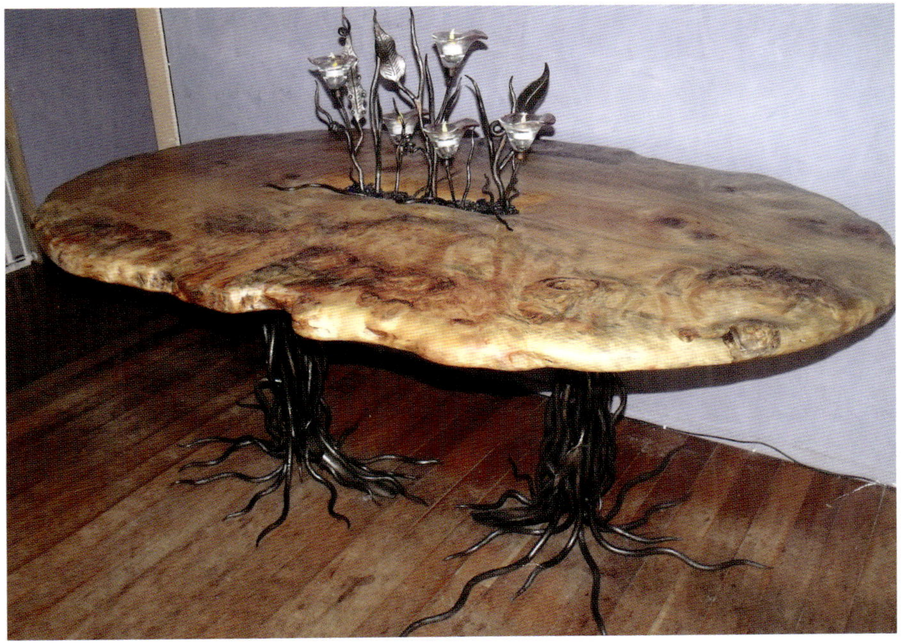

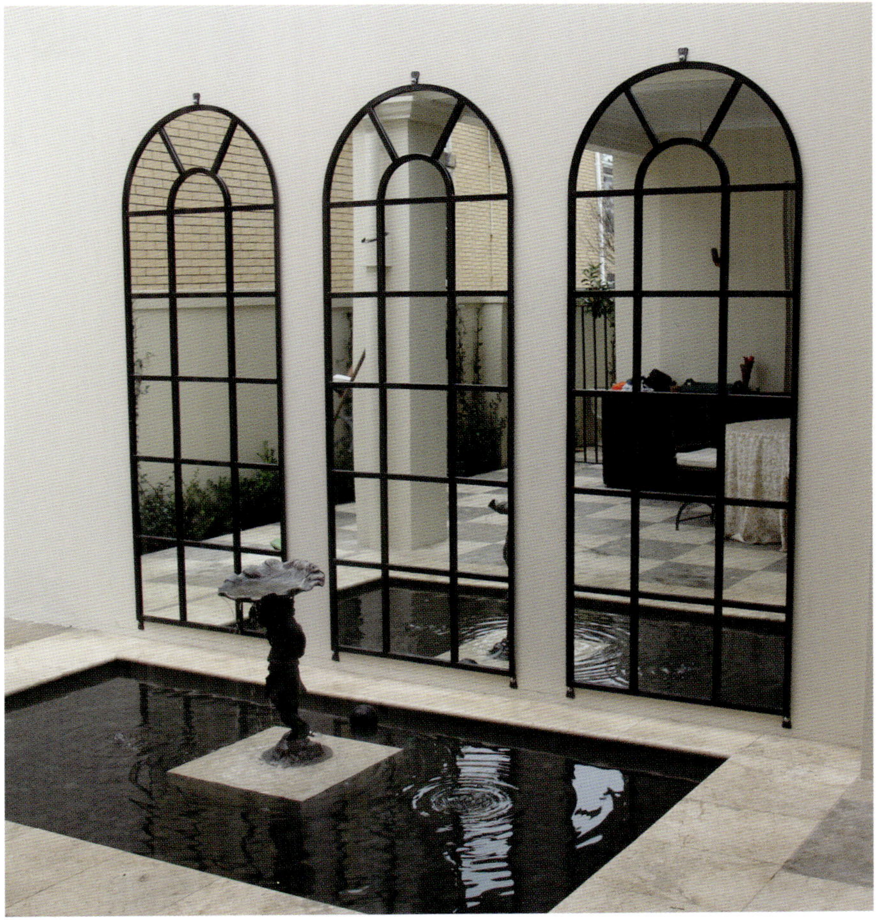

Garden mirrors. Fabricated from 25 mm (1") x 10 mm (3/8") steel. Galvanized and hand polished. Private residence.

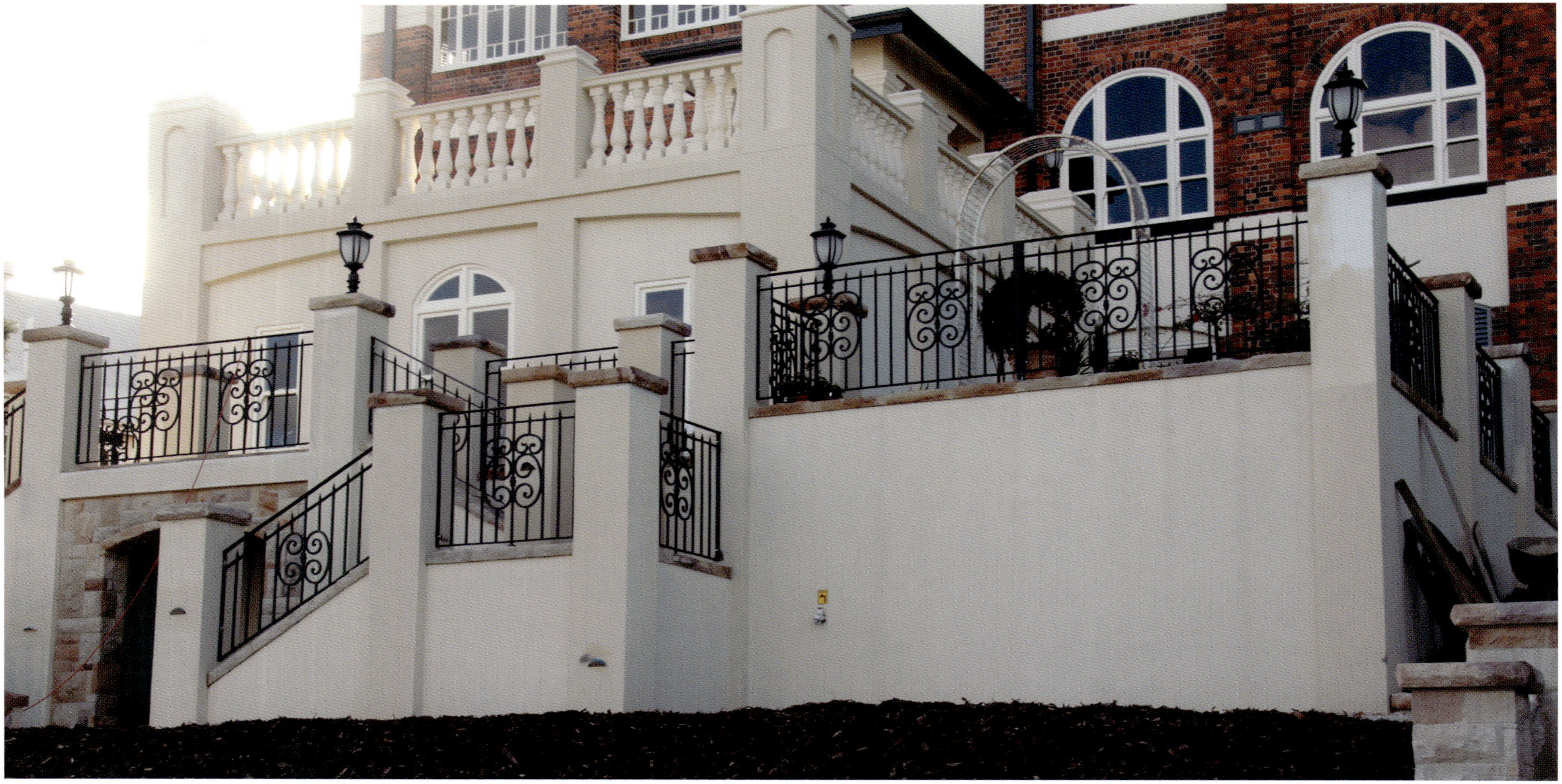

Forged ironwork for a heritage house. Hot punched top and bottom rails, forged pickets, and forged snub-end scrolls. Galvanized and hand painted.

Rodger & Jason LaBrash

Grizzly Forge, Phoenix, Arizona
www.grizzlyiron.com

ARTISTS' STATEMENT

Grizzly Forge produces architectural metal products as well as sculpture and artwork. Our company was started by Rodger "Grizz" LaBrash in 1987 as a small fabrication shop. It now includes Rodger's son Jason, working side-by-side. Grizzly has evolved into one of the largest blacksmith shops in Arizona by designing and forging original parts for its projects. Most of our projects tend to be of traditional style and design, but we are always trying to develop fresh and innovative designs.

Entry Gate

This entry gate was designed by Grizzly for a customer who wanted an organic, yet traditional, style of gate. We included elements of both through joinery details, scroll work, and the calla lilies that are throughout the gate.

Entry gate. 2011.
Forged and fabricated steel. 6′ x 9′.
Photo: Tim Harper

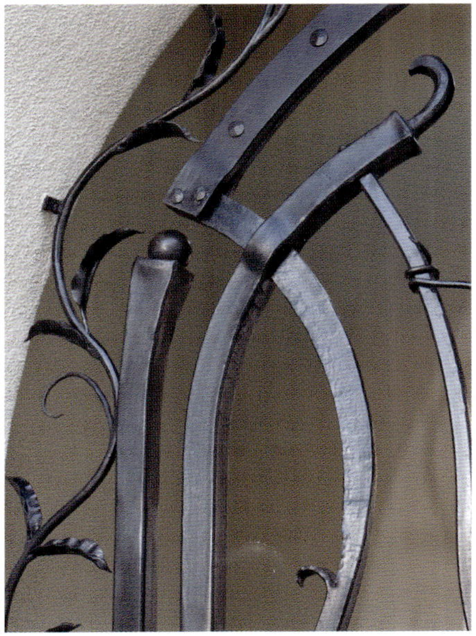

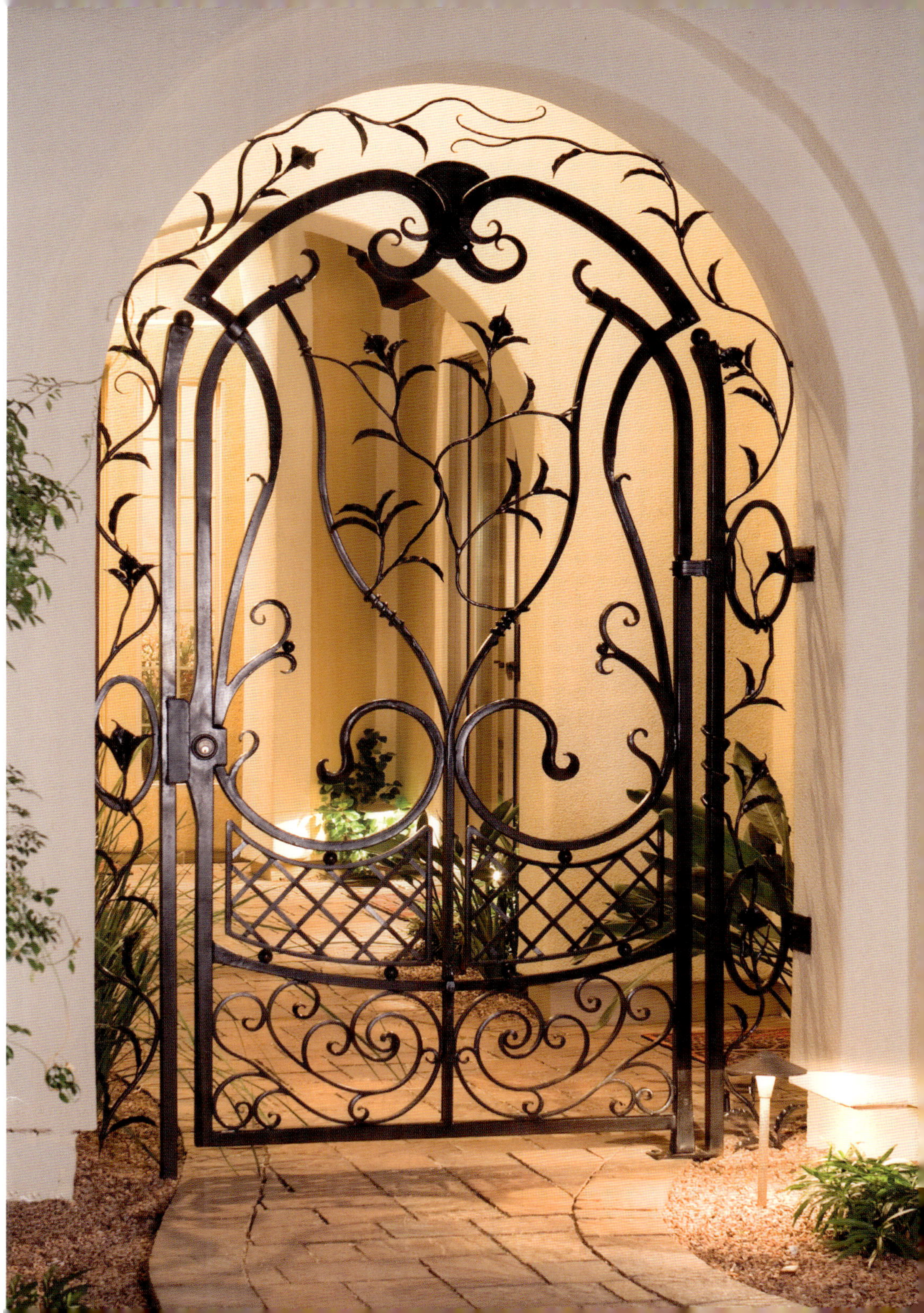

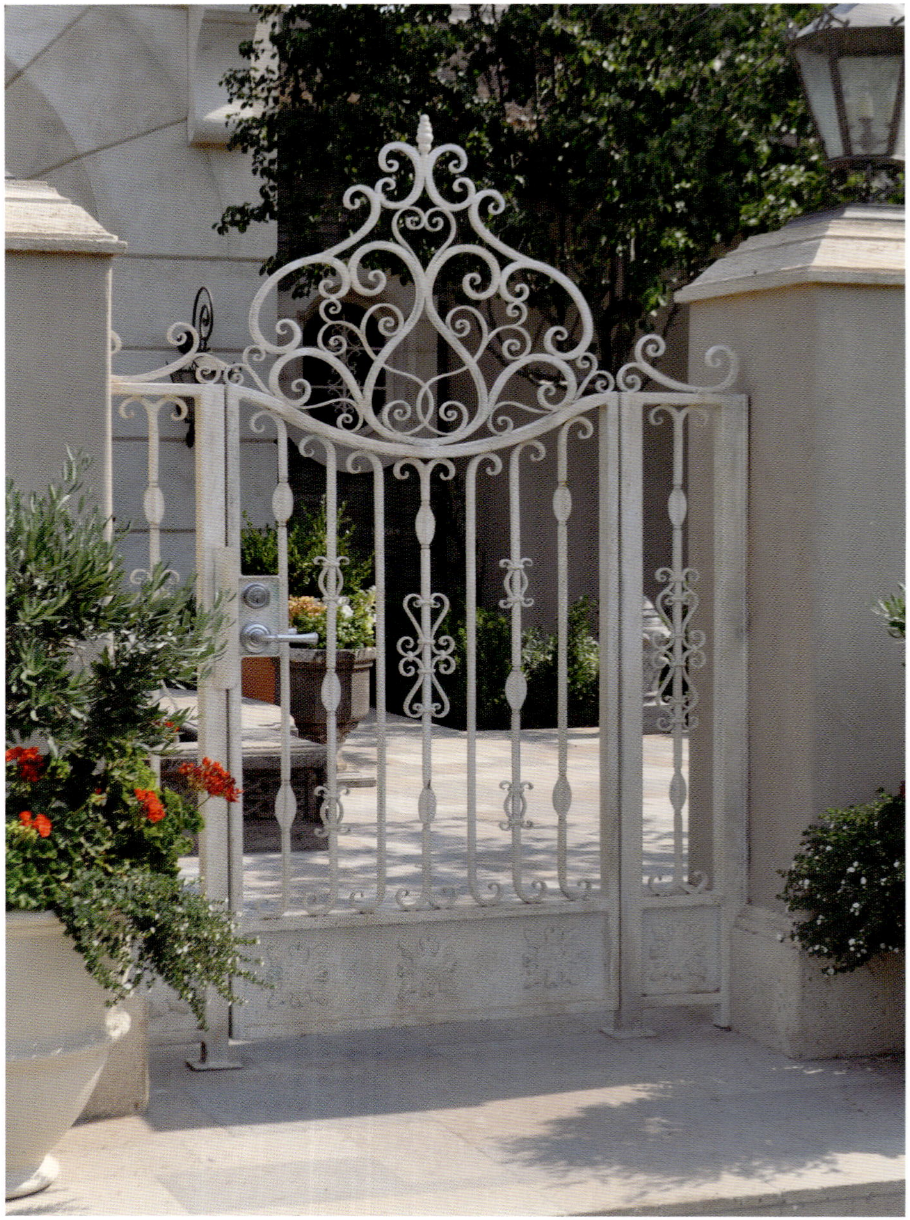

Courtyard Gate and Entry Door Grill

These ironwork pieces were designed for a French home in Paradise Valley, Arizona. We designed and hand forged each piece.

Courtyard gate. 2012. Forged and fabricated steel. 5′ x 7′.
Photo: Jason LaBrash

Entry door grill. 2011. Forged and fabricated steel. 6′ x 9′.
Photo: Jason LaBrash

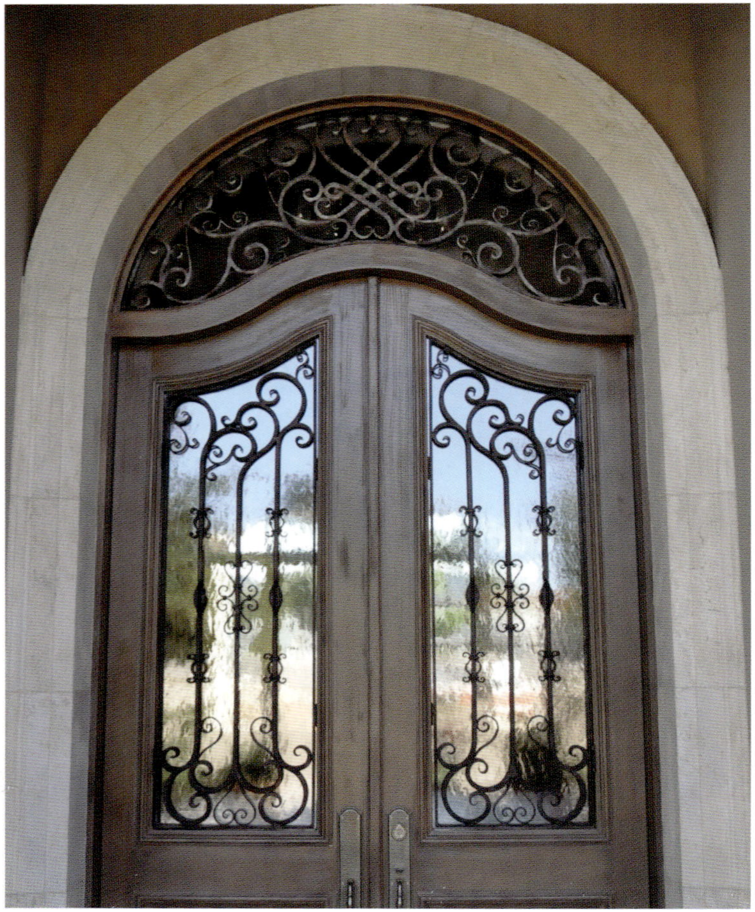

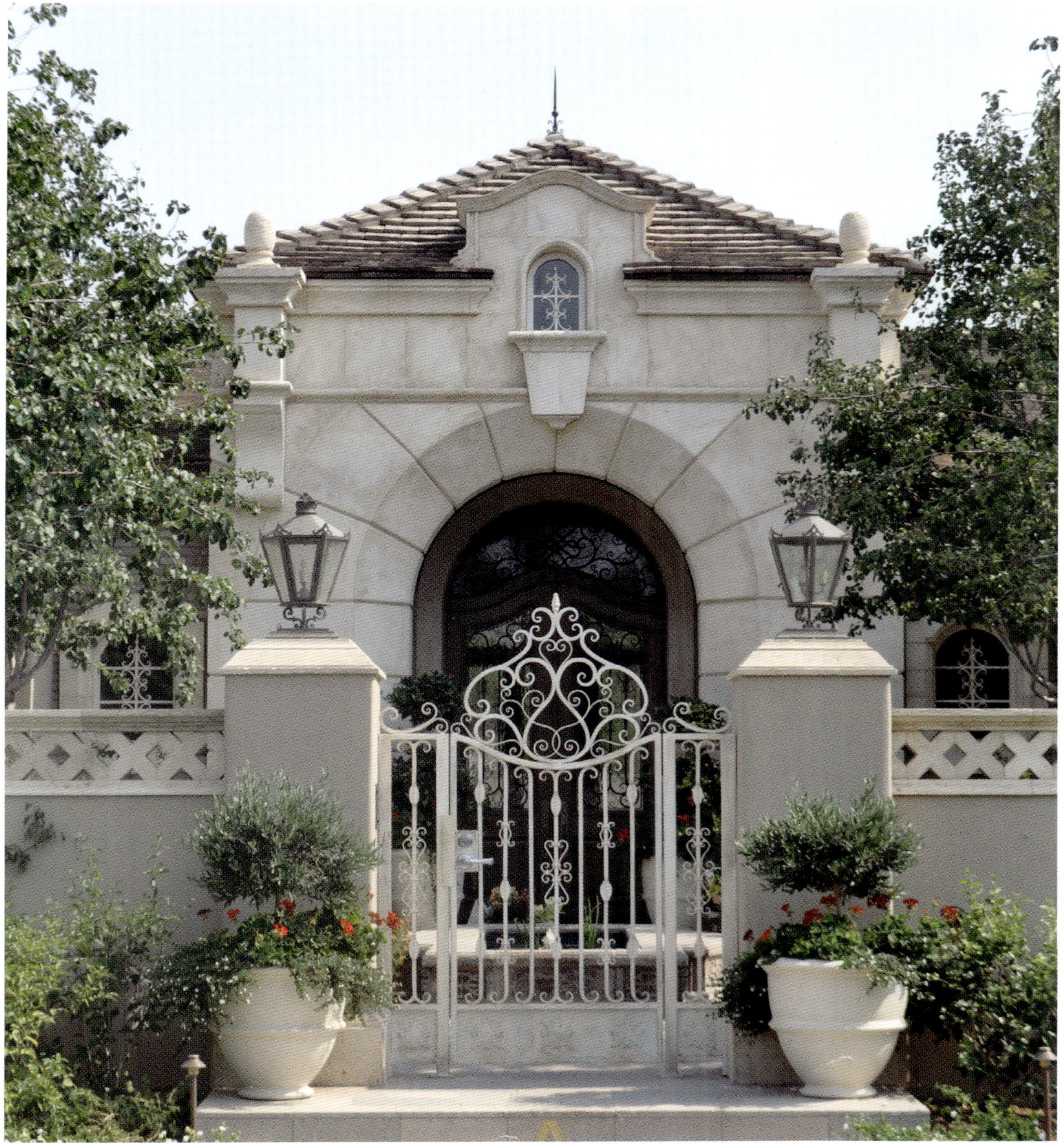

Front entry. Forged and fabricated steel. *Photo: Jason LaBrash*

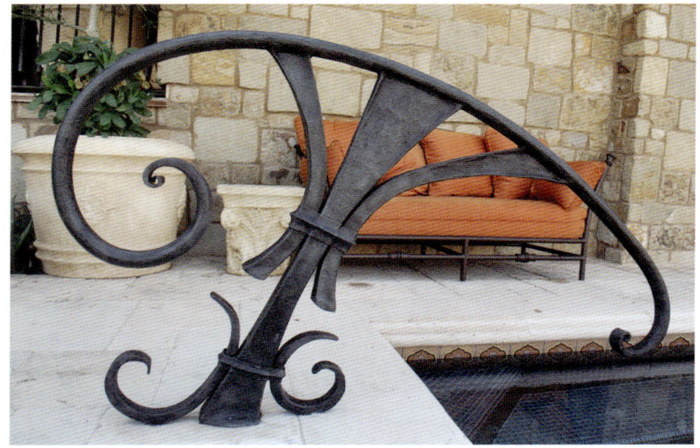

Spa Railing

This spa railing was designed to stand apart from a standard pool rail, yet have a sculptural appearance. Grizzly Forge created the initial concept and presented it to the designer, who let us design it completely. The main post of the rail started as a 2″ x 4″ solid bar stock. The base was upset to approximately 4″ x 6″ and the top was fullered to over 8″ wide. The hand rail is forged from 1½″ square bar into an oval profile. The finish is zinc metalizing, which was then blackened and sealed with a clear coat.

Spa railing. 2010. Forged and fabricated steel. 5′ x 36″. *Photo: Jason LaBrash*

Sue Lampert

IronShore Studio, Jupiter, Florida
www.ironshorestudio.com

ARTIST'S STATEMENT

Art begins as a vision, a sound, or a movement in the mind of the artist. It is then translated from the mind and expressed by the artist's technical ability to create the physical art. I am constantly amazed at how incredibly talented and clever artists can be in manifesting and transforming their thoughts into visual or performing works of art. I am humbled by this process and so very thankful that I have the opportunity to create art as an expression of my own visions.

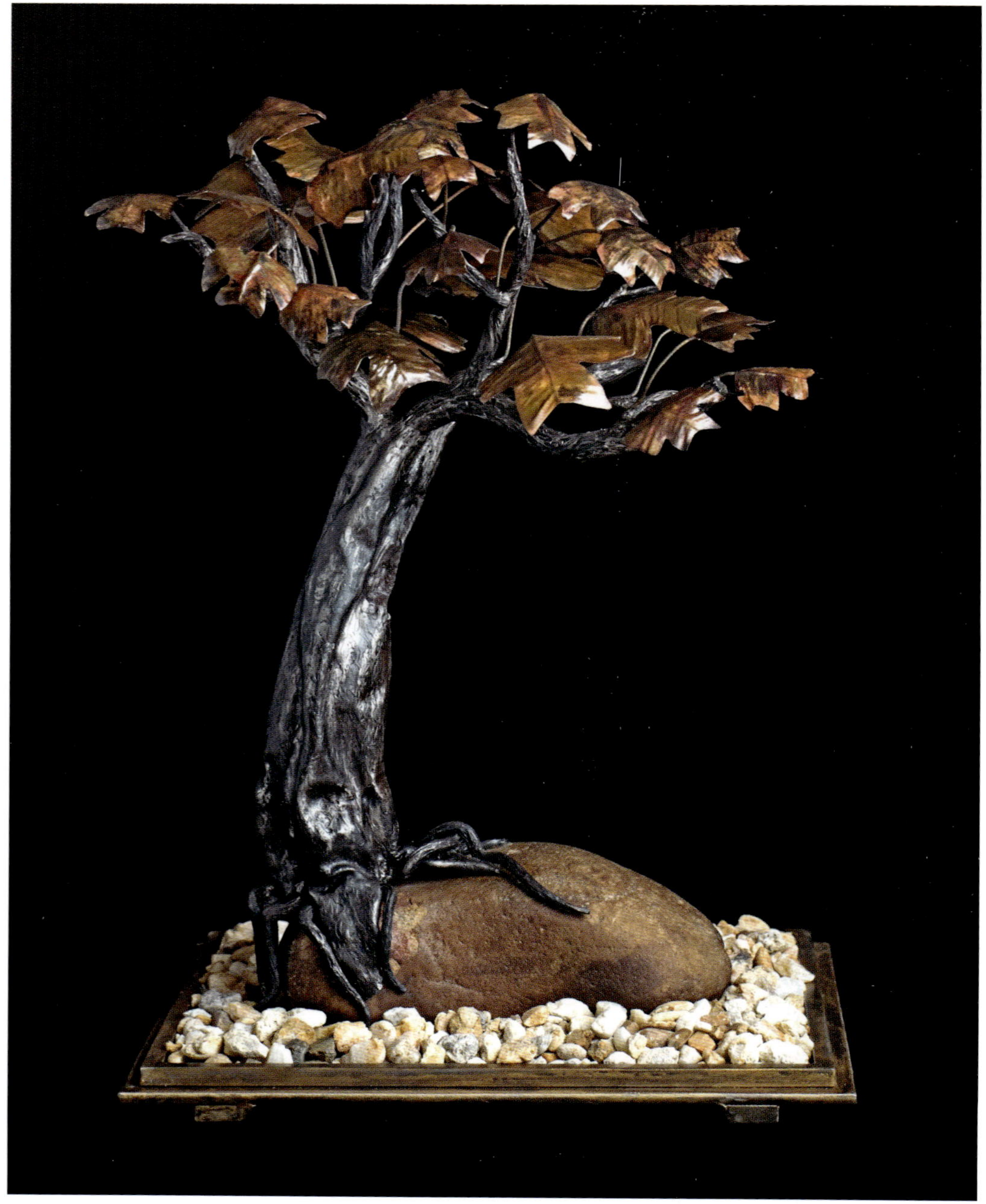

Blacksmith Bonsai

Forged and fabricated steel and copper bonsai tree sculpture, mounted on a river rock with fabricated steel pot. Natural heat patina on the copper leaves. Guilders paste highlights on the steel tree trunk and pot.

Blacksmith Bonsai. Sculpture. 2010. Steel, copper, rock. Private collection, Greenville, South Carolina. 20"h x 14"w x 12"d. *Photo: Robert Swinson*

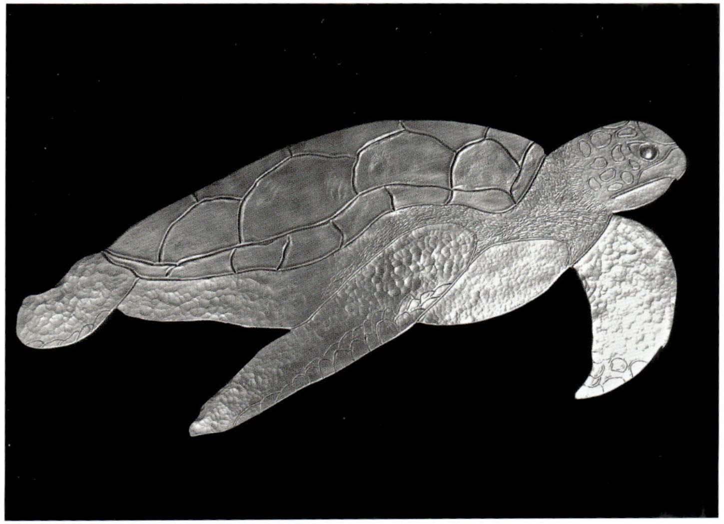

Sea Turtle

This sea turtle was created as part of a public art project I was awarded in Martin County, Florida. The projected consisted of an 1,800-square-foot waterfront pedestrian plaza with seascape railing. I designed, hand forged, and installed nearly 100 detailed pieces of sea life for this project. An oxy-acetylene torch with a heating tip was used as the heat source, which allowed for greater control of the heat on the aluminum. Texturing was done using a variety of methods, including power-, treadle-, and hand-hammers, texture tools, and air chisels. This image shows the amount of detail that was consistent throughout the project.

Sea Turtle. Sculpture. 2012. Forged ½" aluminum plate. Public art project: Gateway To Port Salerno, Pt. Salerno, Florida. 12"h x 20"w. *Photo: Sue Lampert*

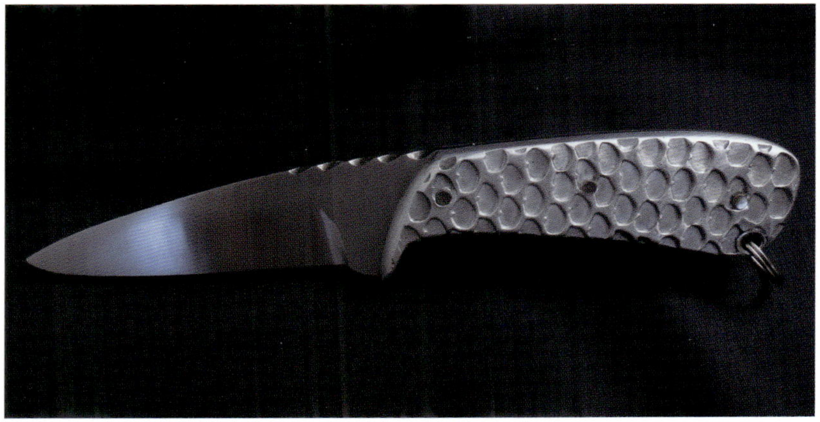

Knife (full tang) with fish scale handle. 2013. Forged 1075 carbon steel, forged aluminum slab handle. Overall length: 7 ½". *Photo: Sue Lampert*

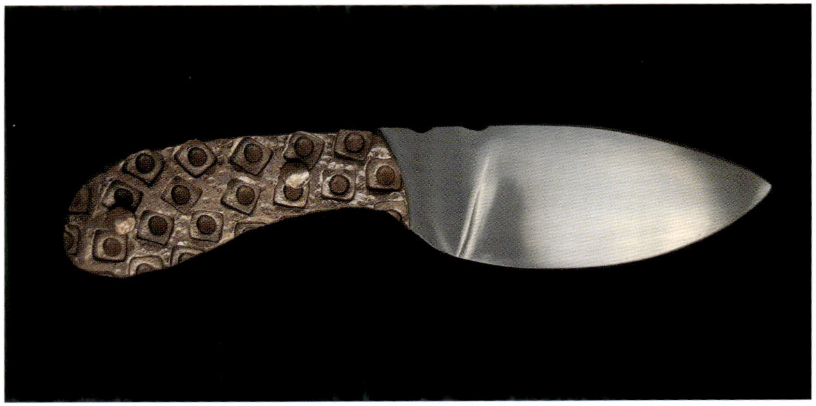

Knife (full tang) with copper slab handle. 2013. 01 tool steel, forged copper slab handle. Overall length: 6". *Photo: Sue Lampert*

Knives

Recently, I started producing some knives for fun, and they have generated a lot of interest. These knives are forged, ground, filed, heat treated, and tempered to produce a serviceable cutting blade. The handle slabs are custom designed and forged using punches I made in-house to produce a unique look. There are endless possibilities in the decoration of the handles, and I am looking forward to producing more knives, including pattern-welded, blade knives.

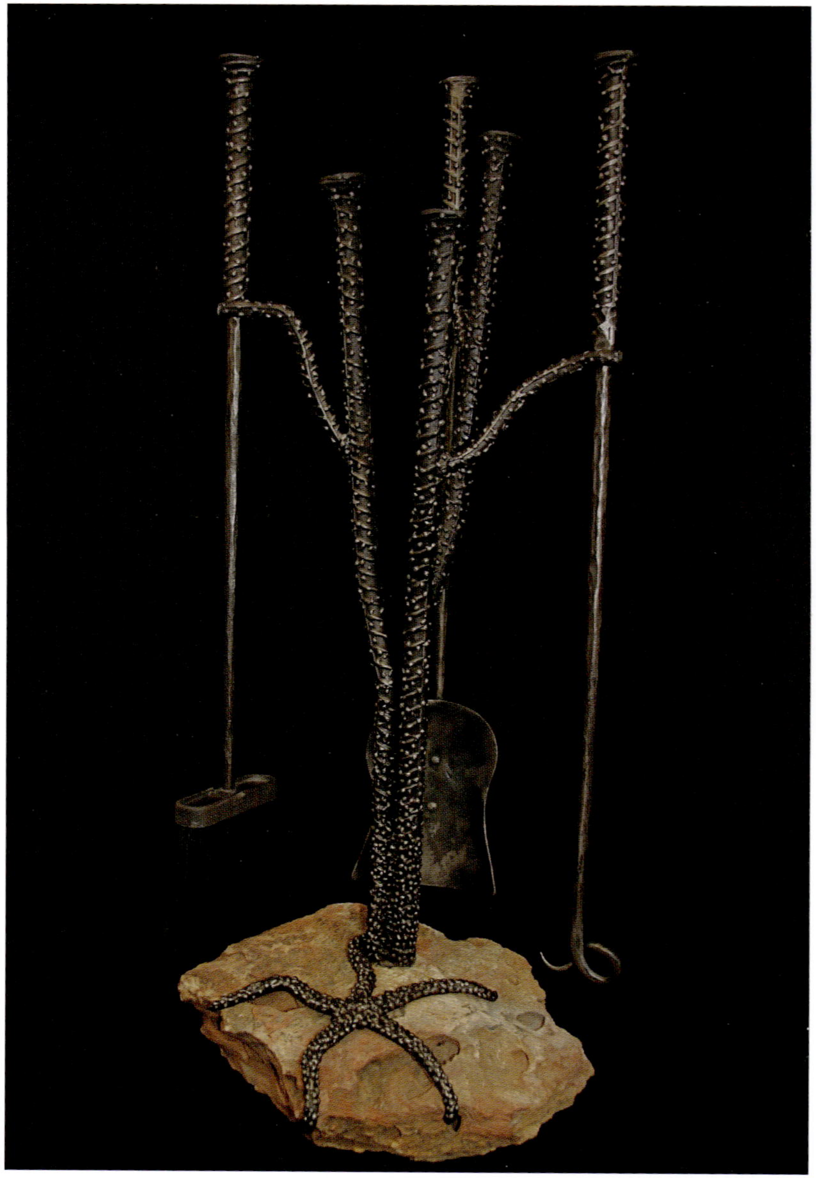

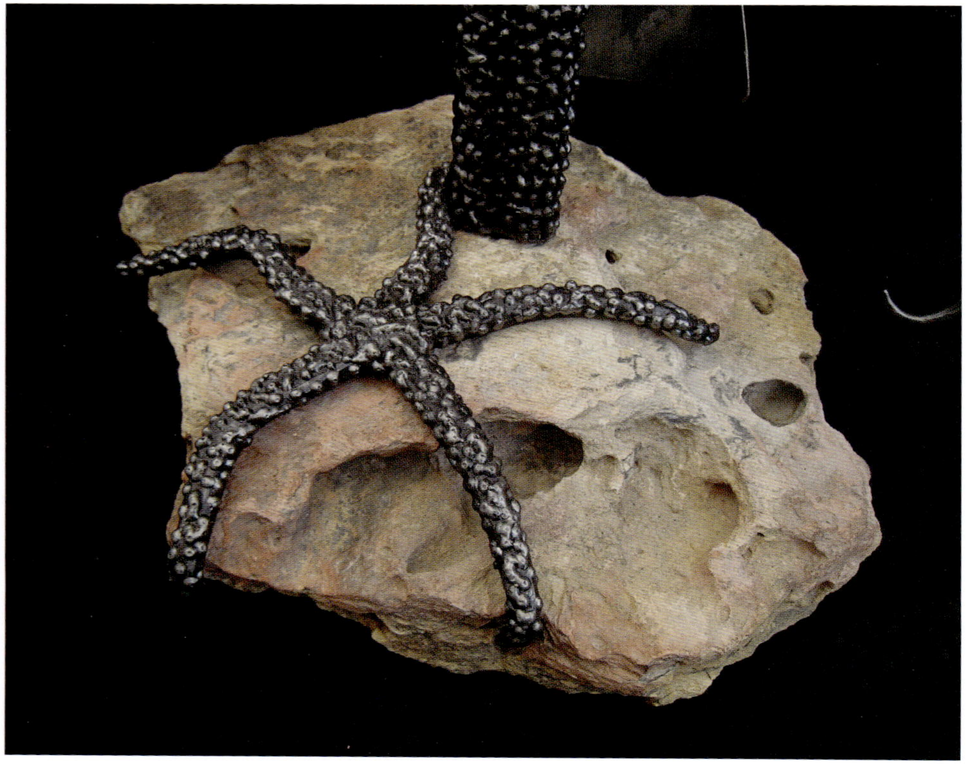

Starfish Fireplace Tool Set

This fireplace set was commissioned for a client in Florida. The main stanchion and tools are forged rebar decorated with a MIG welder. The starfish is forged from half-inch, round bar, decorated, then contoured to wrap around the rock. There are hundreds of weld spots covering this project.

Starfish fireplace tool set. 2011. Forged and fabricated steel mounted on a rock base. 36"h x 15"w x 15"d. *Photo: Sue Lampert*

Greg & Tiana Leavitt

Leavitt Studios, Berks County, Pennsylvania
www.GregLeavitt.com

ARTISTS' STATEMENT

Leavitt Studios creates commissioned sculptural metalwork. All work is forged, fabricated, and created in-house. This hands-on approach allows for the love of material and process to be imbued into the spirit of the work. The viewer responds to this time-honored process steeped in the blacksmithing tradition. Greg Leavitt heads up the studio with over forty years of experience. Since 1997, his wife, Tiana, has worked in the studio with Greg as a designer, consultant, and production manager. Greg's daughter Camille has been working on projects with Greg for fifteen years.

Macromergence. Sculpture. 2013. Hand-forged and fabricated steel, copper, and bronze. 15'h x 38' diameter. Designed by Tiana Leavitt; created by Greg Leavitt. Created for the demonstration gardens at the Conard-Pyle Co.

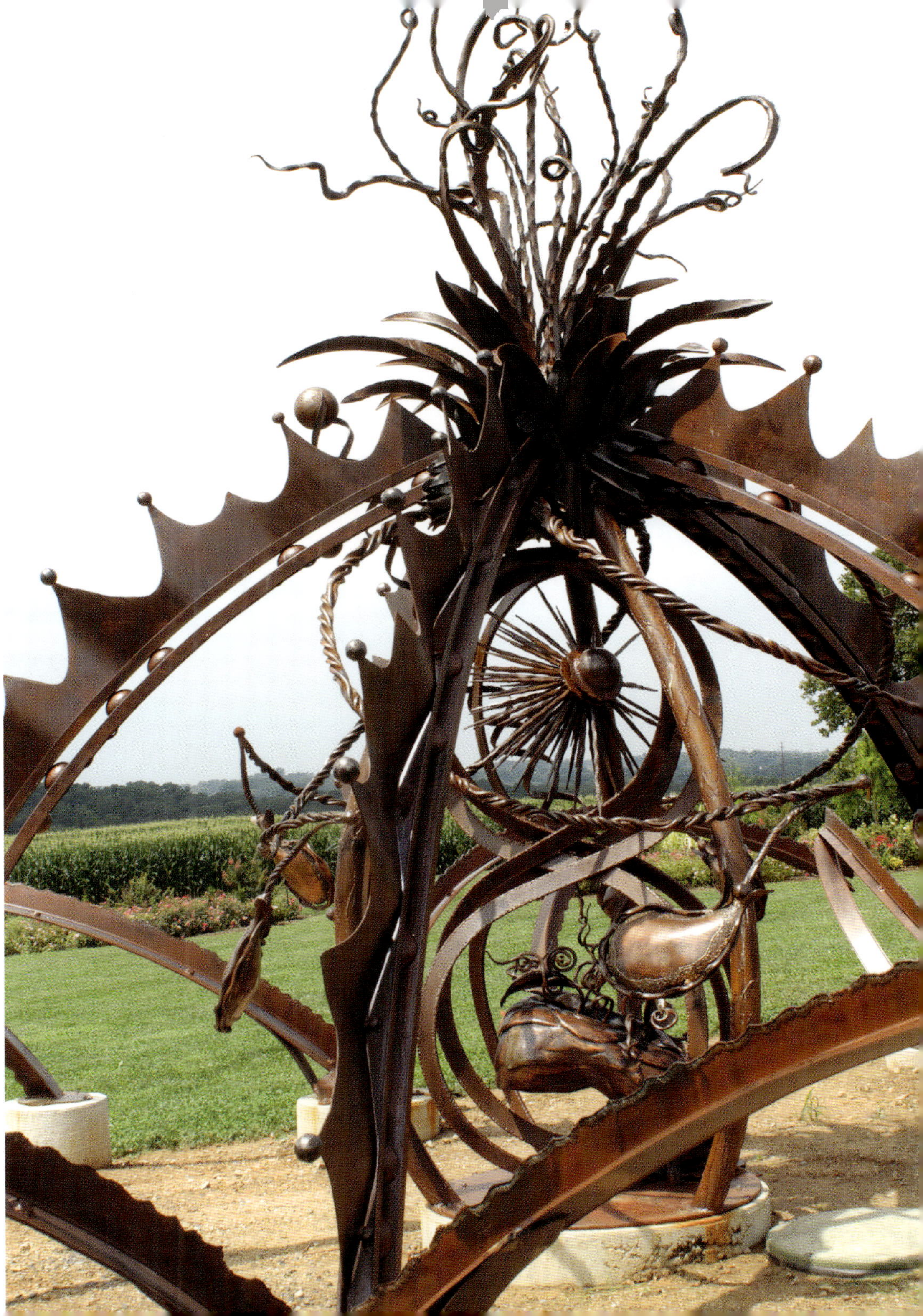

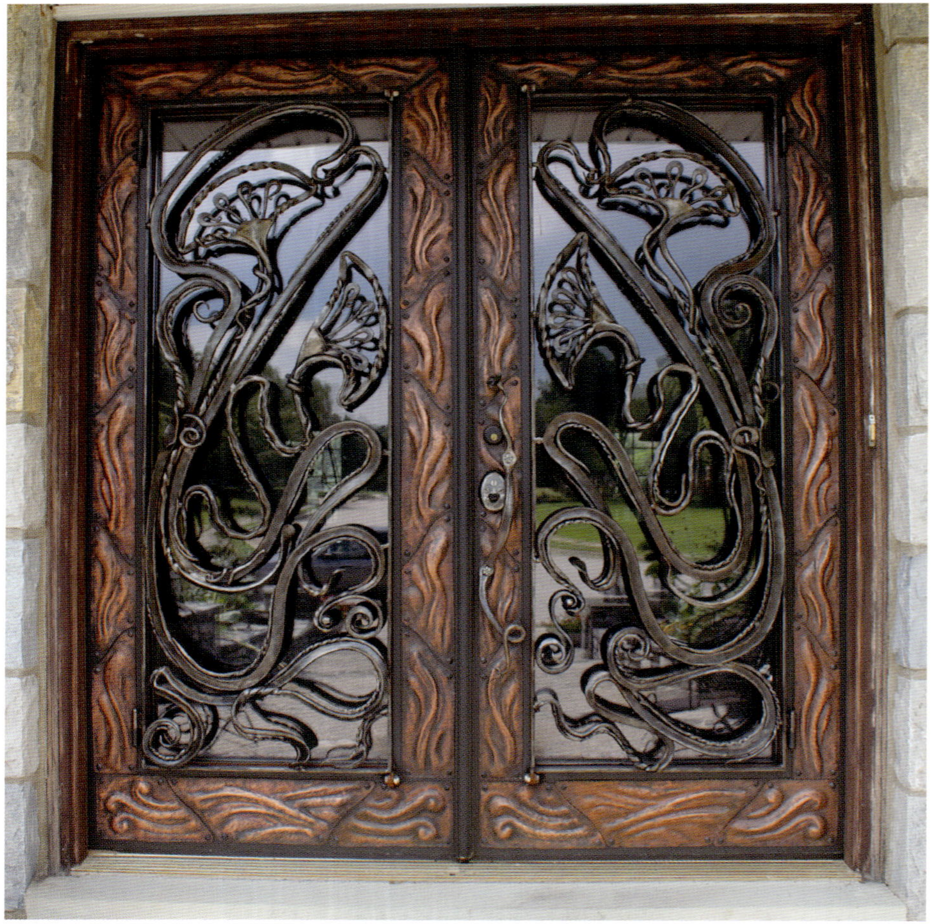

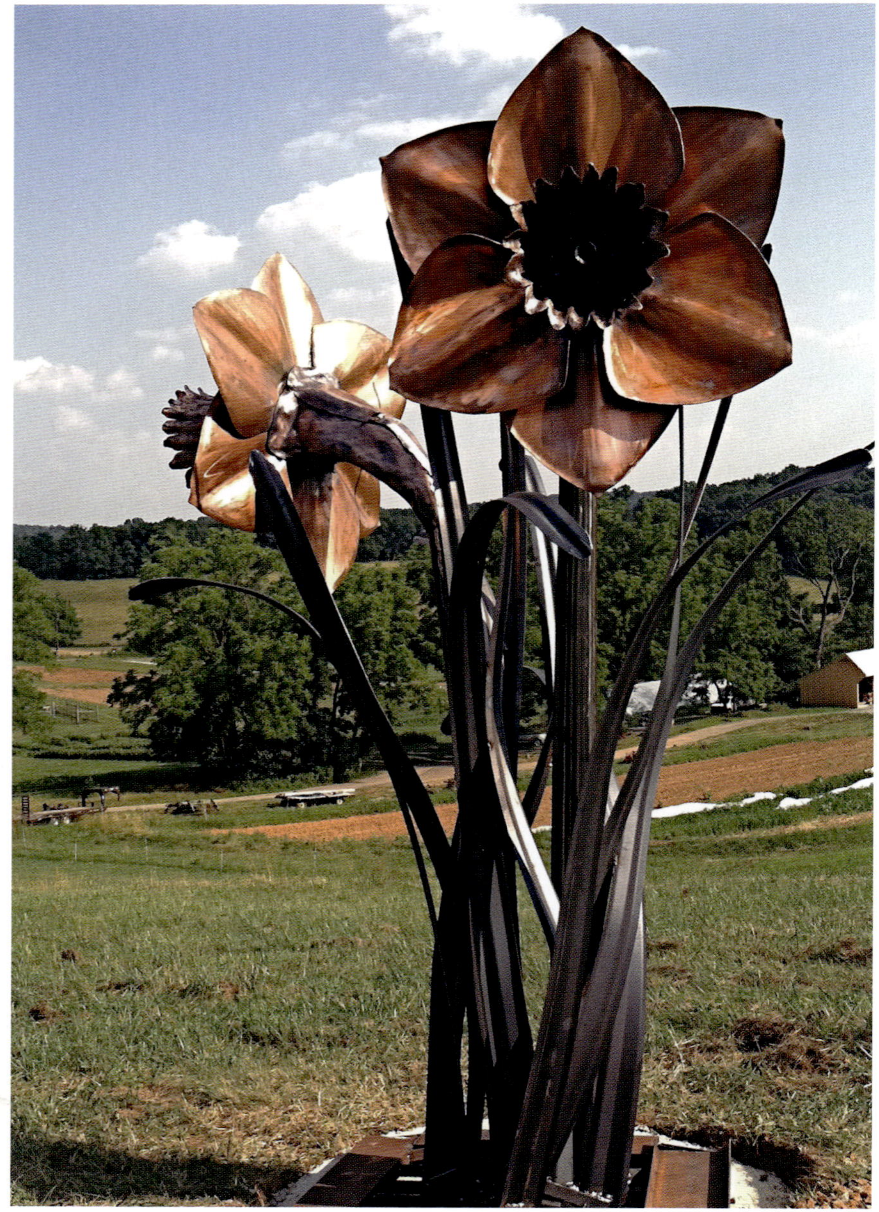

Art nouveau doors. 2013. Forged steel and copper. 7′h x 6′w. Designed and created by Greg Leavitt and Camille Leavitt. *Photo: Bob Yungma*

Daffodil. Sculpture. 2011. Forged copper and steel. 13′ h x 10′ diameter. Designed by Tiana Leavitt; created by Tiana and Greg Leavitt. *Photo: Tiana Leavitt*

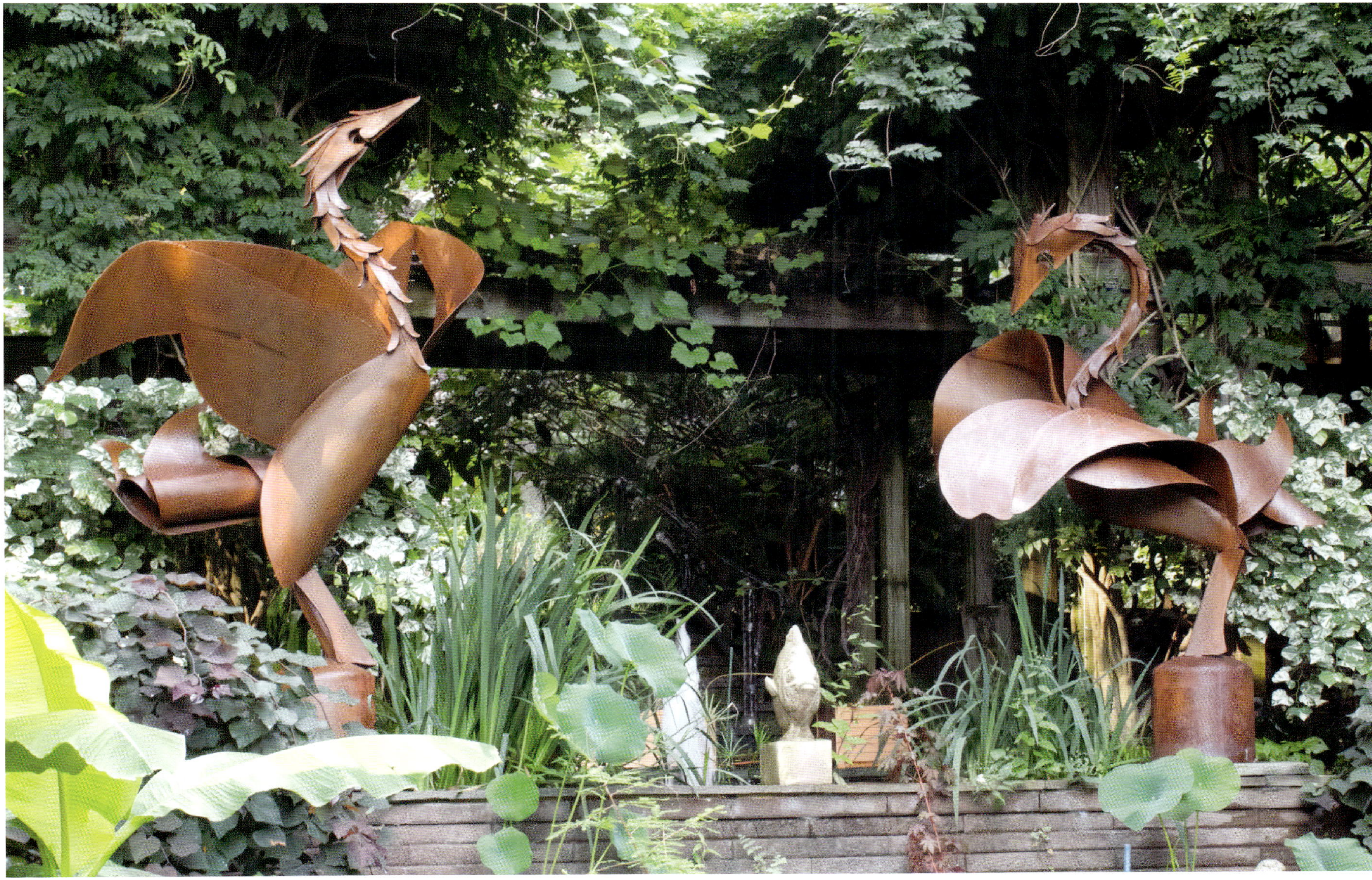

Feng and Shui. Sculpture. 2012. Forged and fabricated steel. Each 9′h.
Designed by Tiana Leavitt; created by Greg Leavitt. *Photo: Bob Yungman*

Shawn Lovell

Shawn Lovell Metalworks, Alameda, California
www.slmetalworks.com

ARTIST'S STATEMENT

As a teenager I used to go out to our garage and try to make things out of the random parts I found there. It was so mysterious to me how anything got made at all. I was a suburban kid and rarely saw anything being produced. I wanted to peek behind the curtain and discover how everyday objects were conceived.

Curiosity and a desire to create a richer, more vibrant environment than the one I experienced growing up in mass-produced track houses compelled me to explore the world of making and eventually led me to art school and degrees in design and sculpture. I gained experience working in metal through welding and foundry work, first in school, and later, while working as an artist assistant to a local sculptor. I was not, however, exposed to much in the way of forged iron. When I came across books with pictures of historical ironwork while doing some design research at the library, I was immediately interested. It was so beautiful. How was it made? I began exploring…first on my own and then through the help of a wonderful group of experienced smiths who gather together twice a year to share their knowledge and experience with each other. I found, through the craft of blacksmithing, an endless frontier to explore.

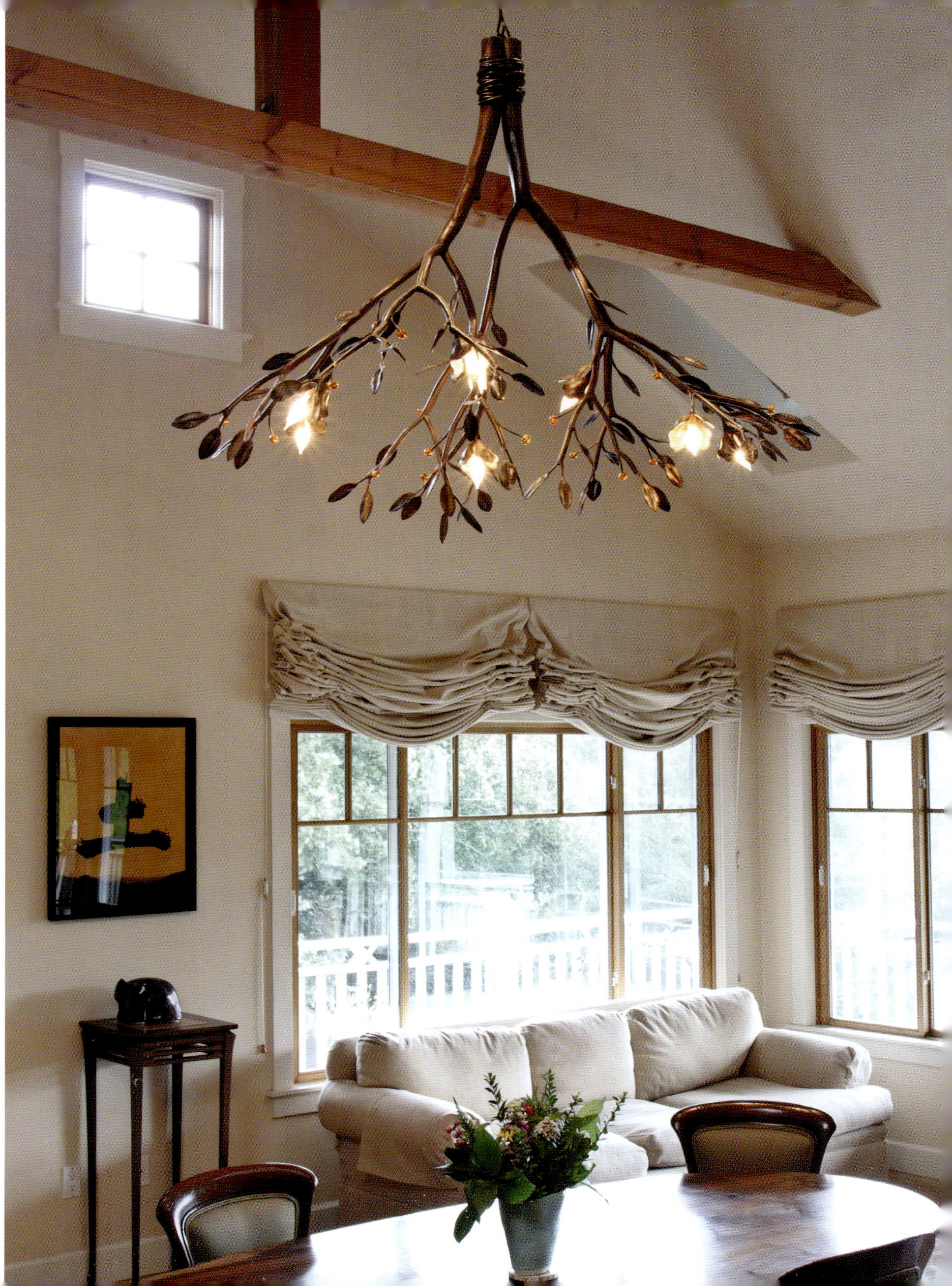

Branch chandelier. 2010. Forged and fabricated steel, fused glass. 36" x 36" x 36". *Photo: Anita Bowen*

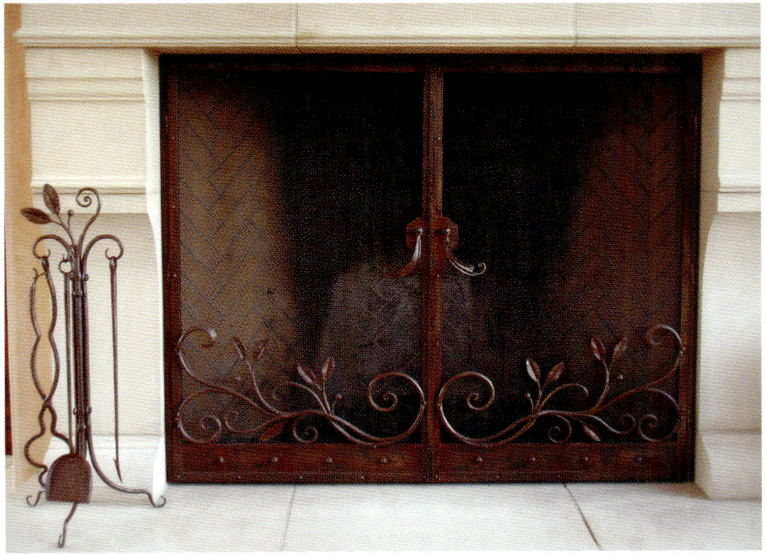

Fireplace screen and tool set. 2010. Forged steel.
Screen: 49″h x 59″w. Tool set: 36″h x 16″w x 10″d.

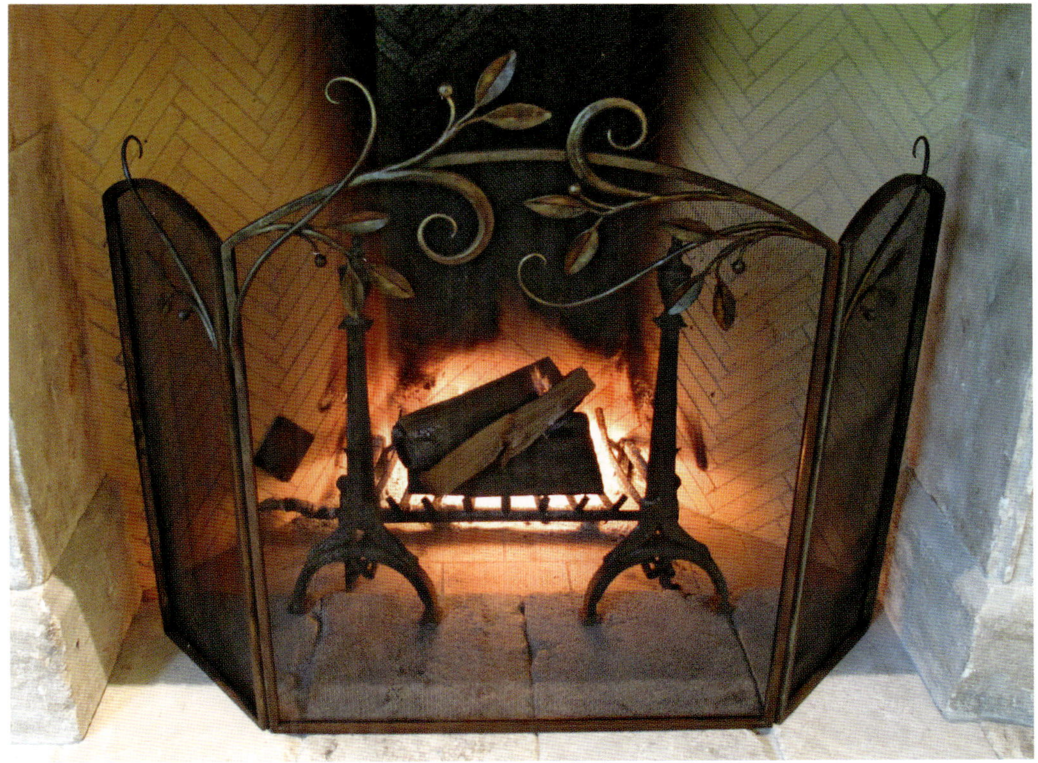

Orinda residence fire screen. 2010.
Forged steel. 29″h x 39″w.

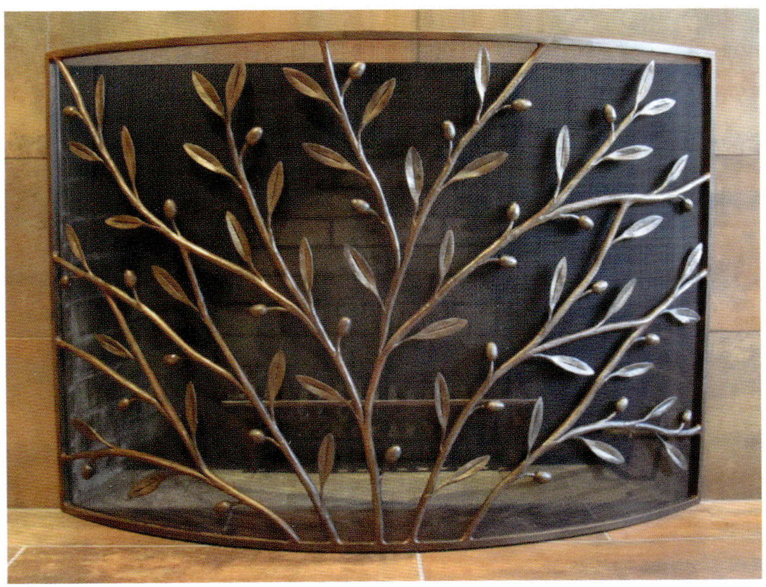

Olive branch fire screen. 2011.
Forged steel. 27″h x 37″w.

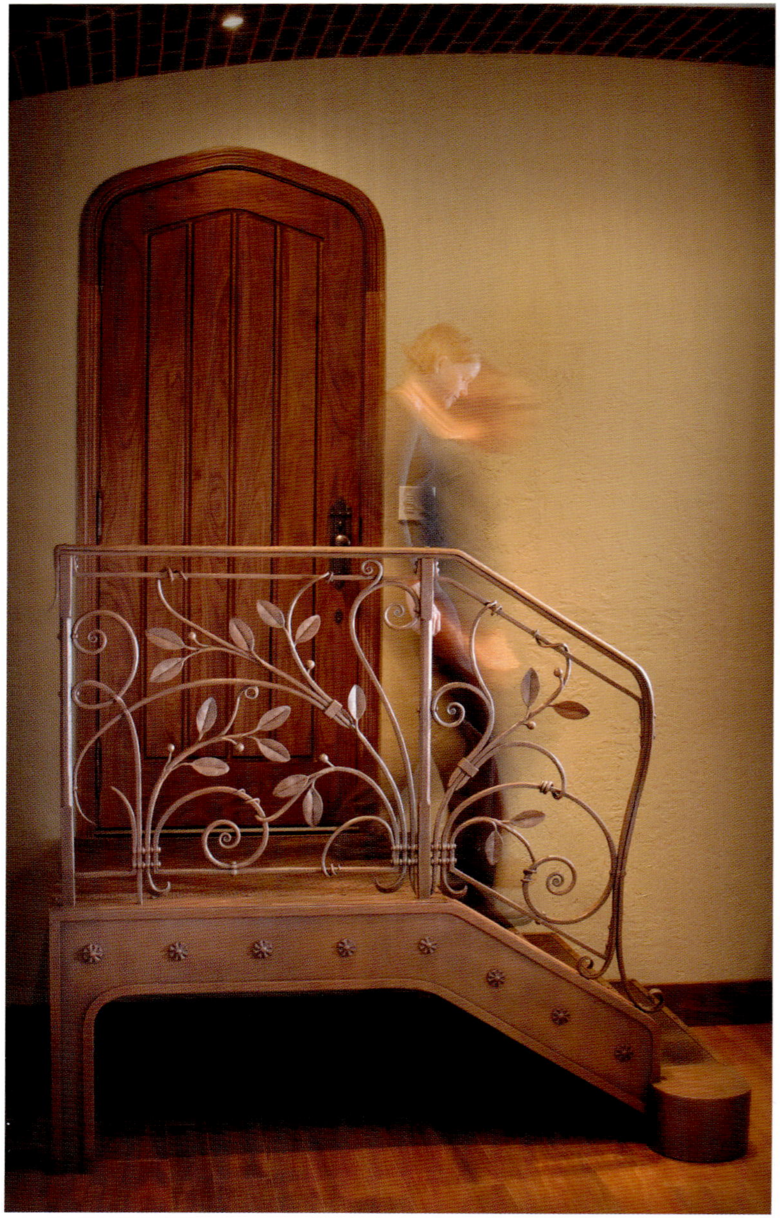

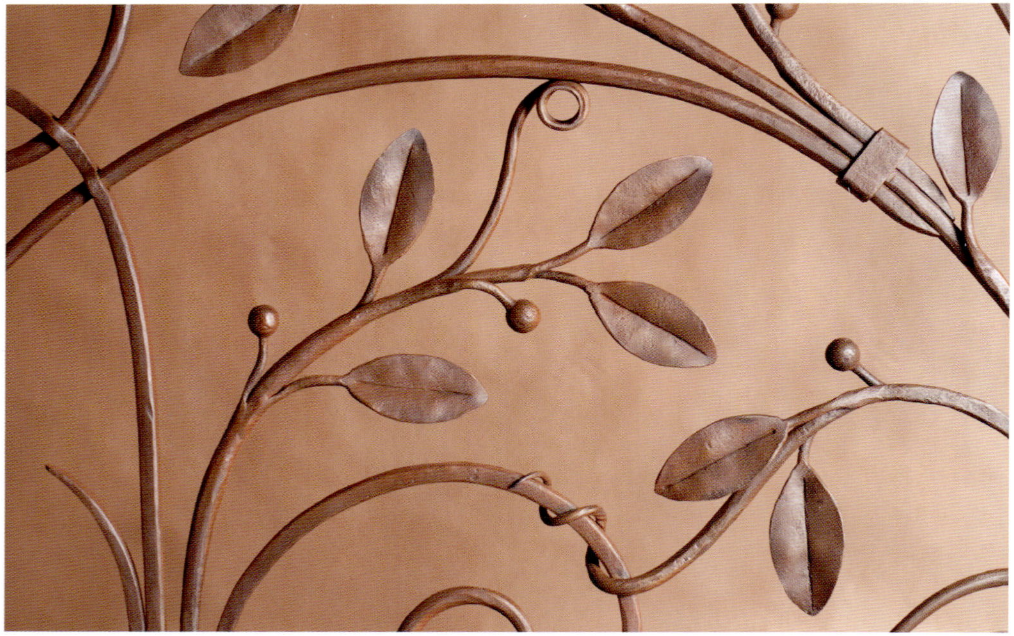

Residential wine cellar railing and staircase. 2011. Forged steel. Forge welding, punching, riveting, and collaring. Leaves, scrolls, and other elements forged from solid bar stock, using a coal forge, hammer, and anvil. Railing: 36"h x 66"l x 1.5"d. Staircase: 28"h x 40"w x 80"l. *Photos: Anita Bowen*

Susan Madacsi

Ledyard, Connecticut
http://susanmadacsi.com

ARTIST'S STATEMENT

I work with steel in the traditional forging manner of a blacksmith. When steel is heated to forging temperatures of approximately 2200 degrees, it can be manipulated in the same ways as clay. I explore and push the plasticity of the material in this hot state achieving a variety of layered textures and patterns. I begin a piece by making a multitude of elements to work with. I then intuitively arrange the pieces until I have a composition that I find interesting and that captures an element of beauty. Once a piece carries these aesthetic qualities, I begin to join the work together by means of welding and riveting. I then apply aerosol enamel paint and use a variety of techniques to distress the surface. By using pigment, I have found I am able to emphasize the many textures that evolve from forging. The result is an interpretation of a contemporary art form that hints toward nature and is an attempt to capture entropy. Although steel is usually first thought of as an industrial material, I like to draw attention to our connection with it on a human level by creating objects that reveal organic forms. My work is the result of my desire to use steel as a substitute for texture and form and as a palette for exploring color.

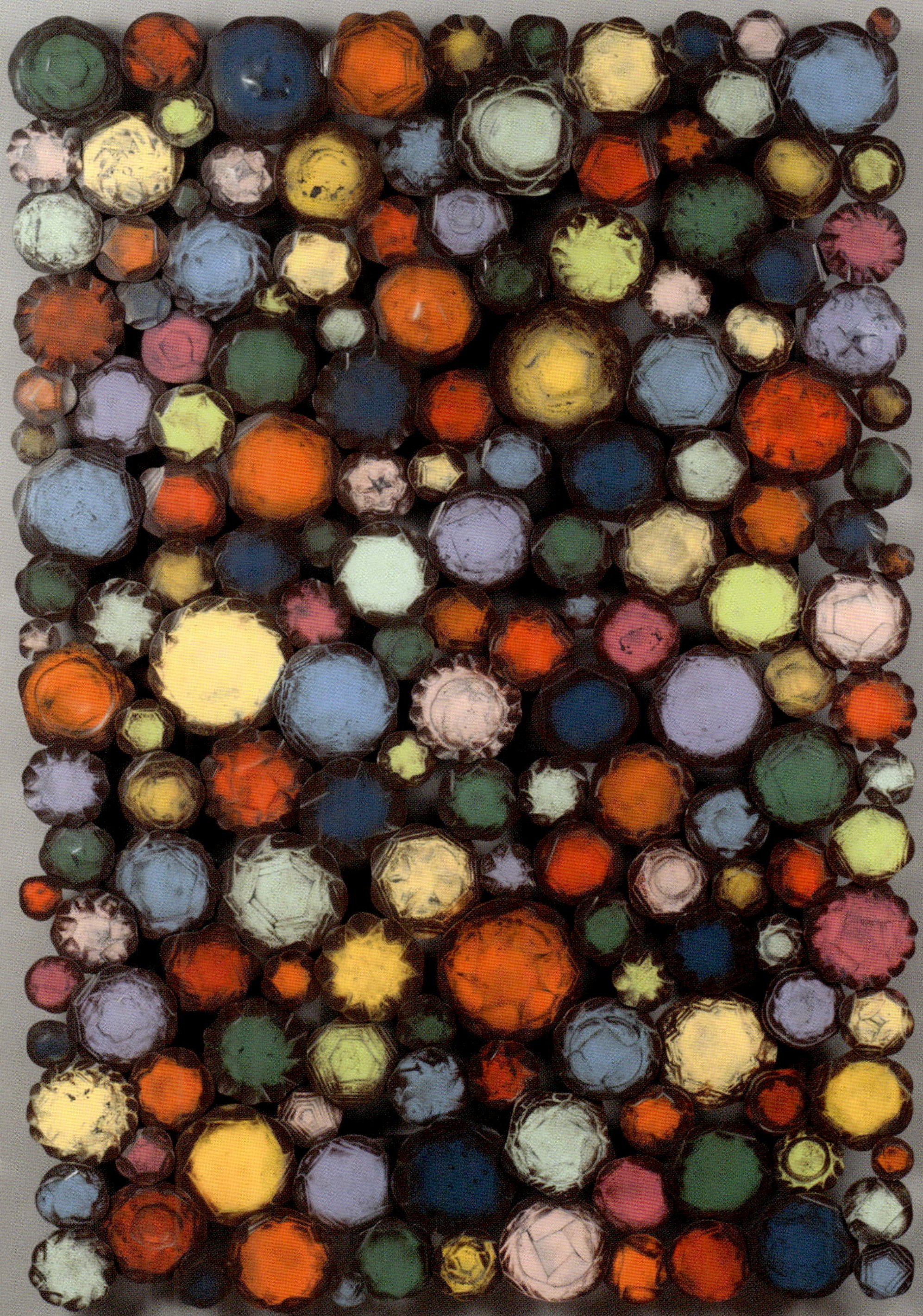

Confectioner's Flag. Wall-hung piece. Forged and fabricated steel with enamel paint and wax. Purchased by the U.S. Embassy and hanging in Monrovia, Liberia. 34"l x 57"w. *Photo: Ralph Phil*

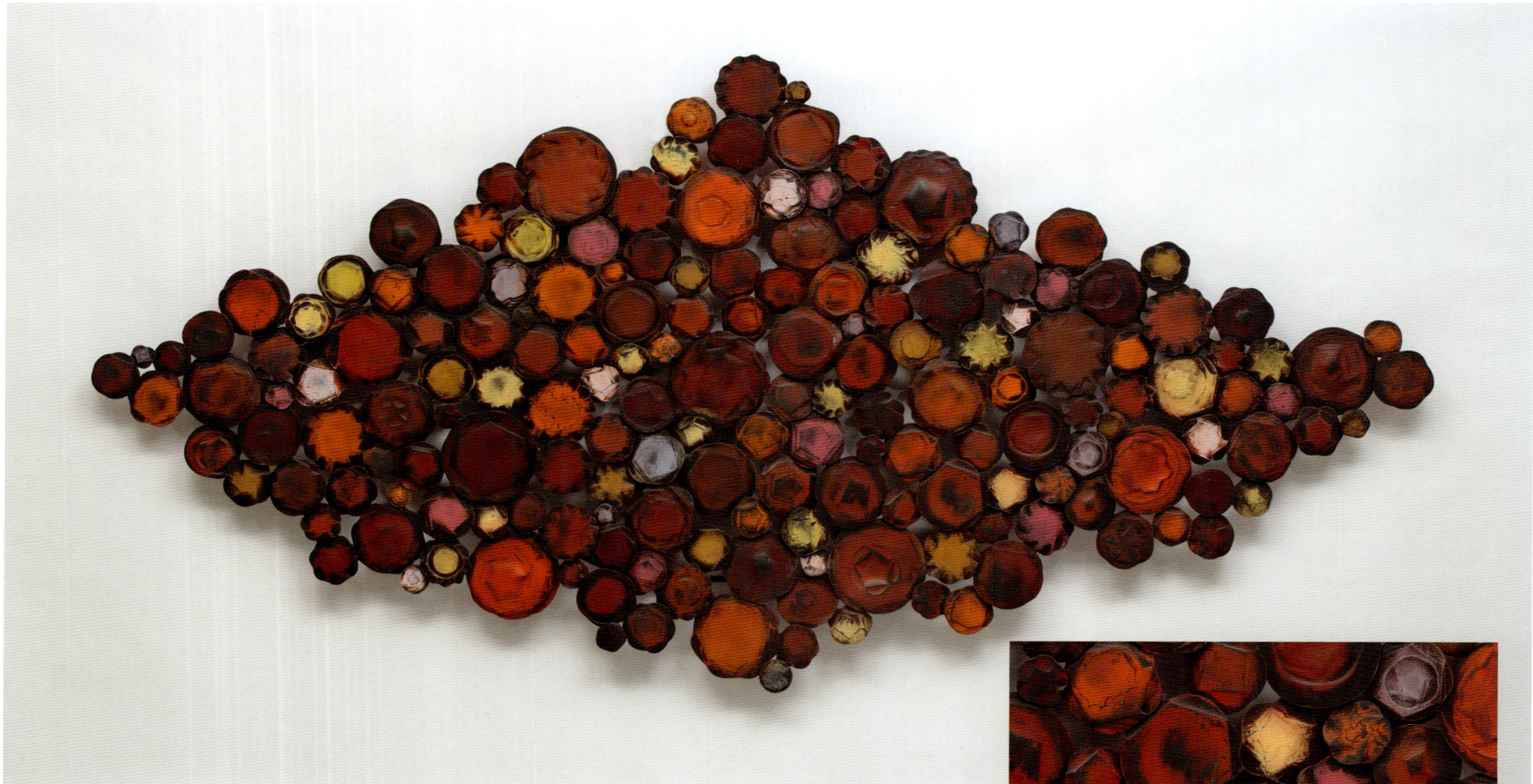

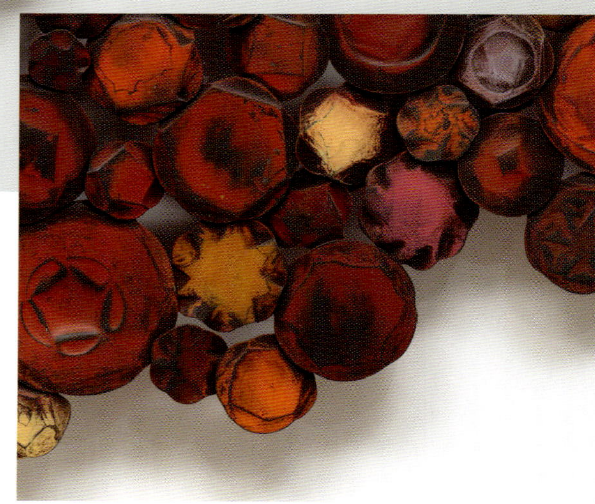

Big Red. Wall-hung piece. Forged and fabricated steel with enamel paint and wax. 74"l x 36"w. *Photo: Ralph Phil*

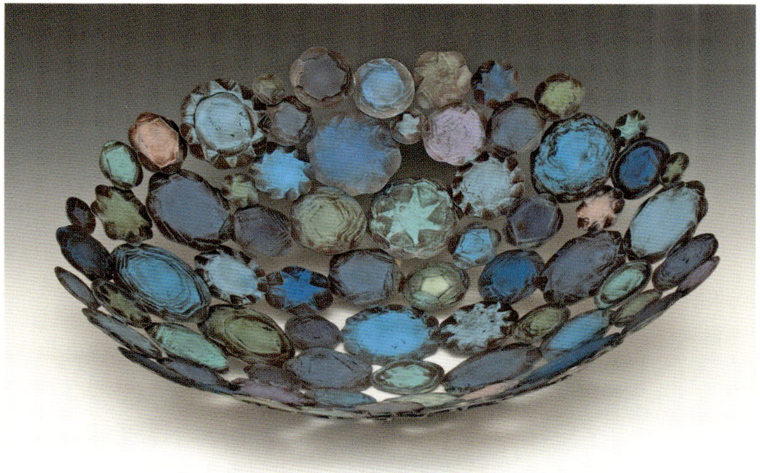

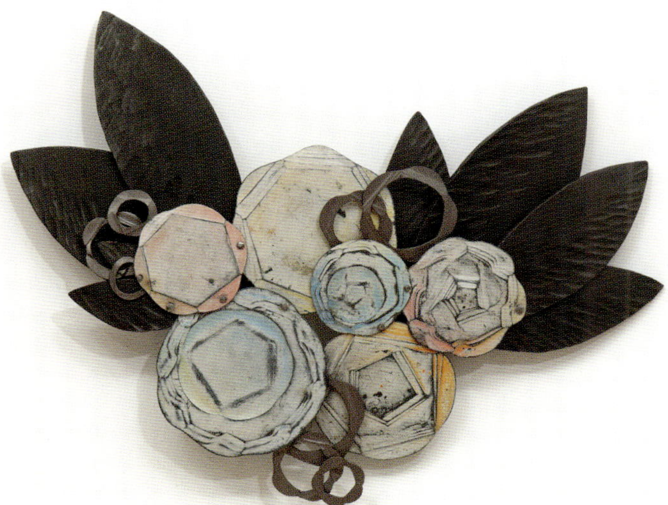

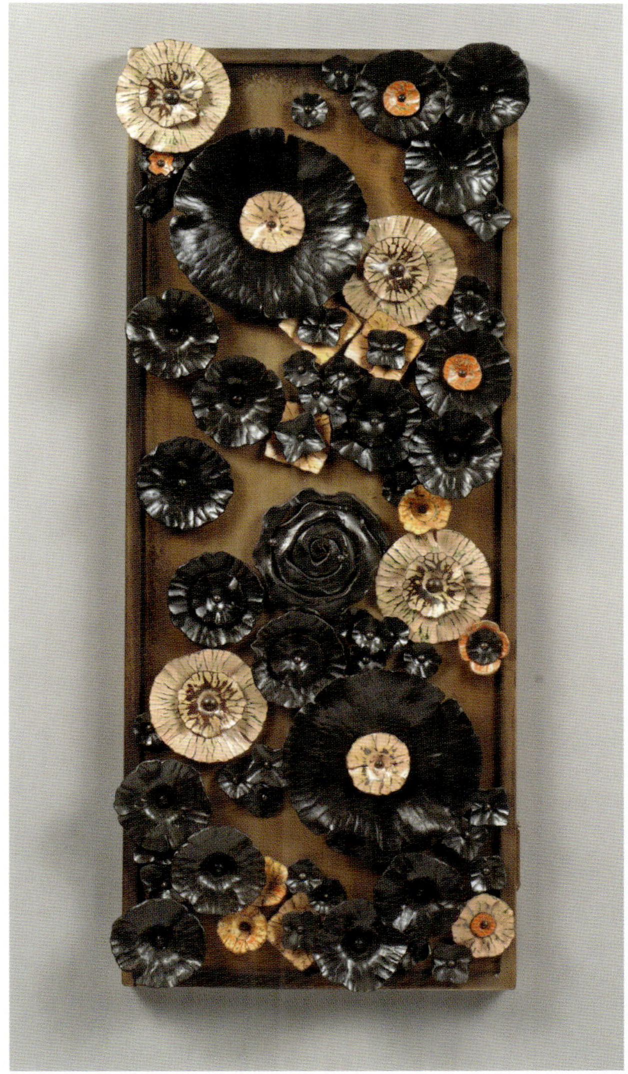

Far left, top: *Blue Splash*. Bowl. Forged and fabricated steel with enamel paint and wax. 26″ diameter x 8″ h. *Photo: Ralph Phil*

Far left, bottom: *Headdress #2*. Wall art. Forged and fabricated steel with enamel paint and wax. 18″ l x 14 ″ h. *Photo: Ralph Phil*

OBI Field. Wall art. Forged and fabricated steel with enamel paint and wax. 12″ l x 24 ″ h. *Photo: Ralph Phil*

Darrell Markewitz

The Wareham Forge, Proton Station,
Ontario, Canada
www.warehamforge.ca

ARTIST'S STATEMENT

Now with over thirty-five years in the forge since I started as a college student in the late '70s, my work has shifted direction several times. My starting interest in the objects of the Viking Age has served me well, leading to my involvement in major museum projects and to professional relationships (and friendships) with more academic researchers. These would link back into the past decade's work in rediscovering the lost techniques of bloomery iron smelting. A chance meeting with Lee Sauder of Virginia (his work seen in past volumes in this series) resulted in my role as one of the instigators of the current 'Early Iron' movement here in North America.

In 2012, I was fortunate to receive a project grant from the Ontario Arts Council, enabling me to concentrate for a full three months on consolidating a decade-high pile of individual blooms into working bars. *Bloom Bowl 2* (at right) is an early example of my reaction to the textures and physical properties possible by forging bloomery iron. *Hector's Bane* (see page 140) is the first artistic blade I forged from this unique material. My intimate relation with direct process bloomery furnaces, especially as a working blacksmith undertaking experimental archaeology and historical process, certainly gives me a different perspective on these methods and materials.

Much of my previous work has been marked by designs dominated more by line than texture. I have striven to create one-of-a-kind objects that are clearly beautiful, but always with functionality at their core. I have recently shifted to new projects of a more sculptural nature. The current *Hallucigennia* series of sculptural pieces (see page 139) is certainly the best example.

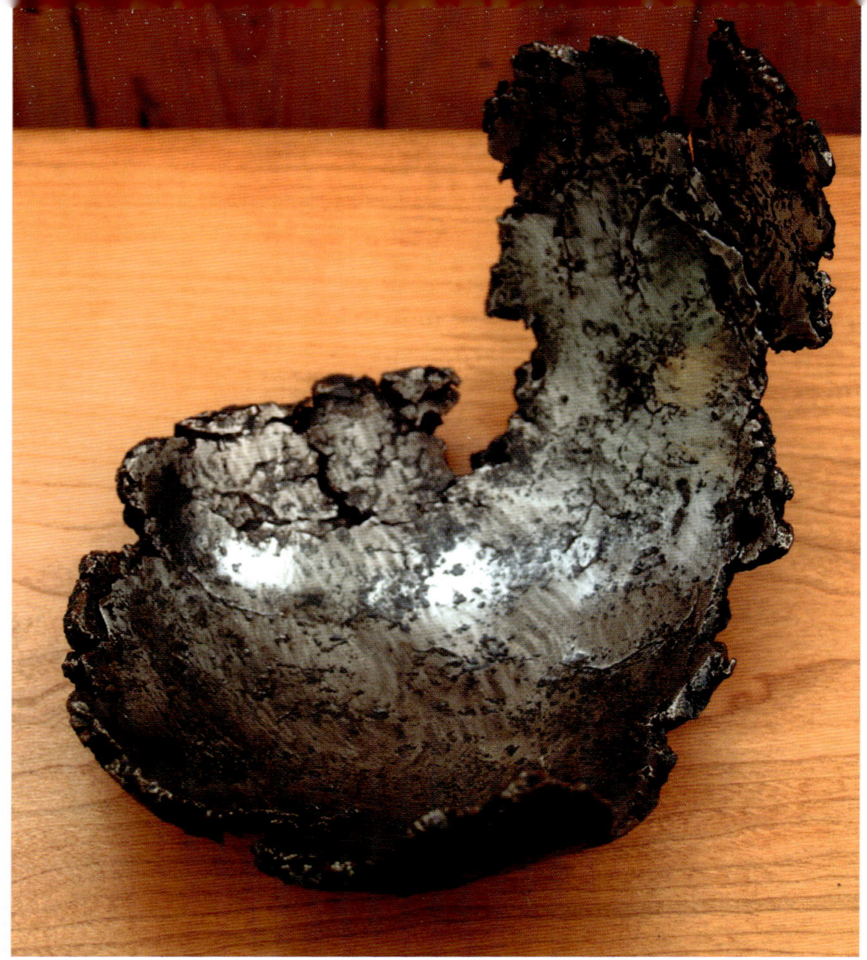

Bloom Bowl 2

The bloomery iron used here was itself made from ore smelted using a direct reduction furnace, based on those from the Viking Age. The starting mass was created at the 2008 'Smeltfest' research workshop, held each year at Lexington, Virginia. The original bloom mass of roughly 5.5 kg was quartered by hot cutting. One piece was selected and then flattened under a small air hammer, working at welding temperature. Only one compaction series was undertaken, intentionally to allow cracks and fissures to develop along the margins of the plate. The roughly rectangular plate was then dished hot to create the bowl's shape. The inner surface was roughly polished with a flap sanding disk. The outer surface was given a fast wire brush to remove any loose scale. To finish, the piece was sealed with a spray matte varathane.

Bloom Bowl 2. 2011. Sculpture. Forged bloomery iron. About 20 cm (7 ⅞") long.

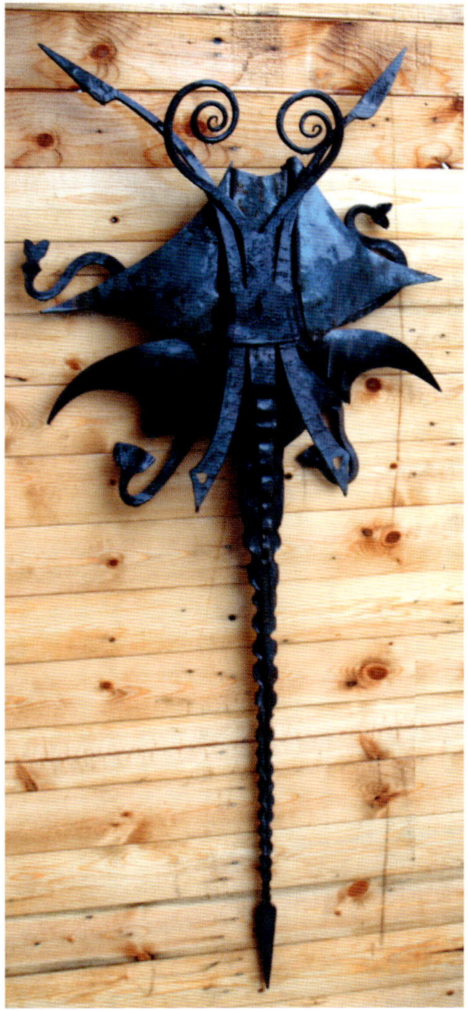

Burgess Crab - Hallucigenia No. Three. Sculpture. 2011. Forged mild steel bar and sheet. Approximately 125 cm (50") long.

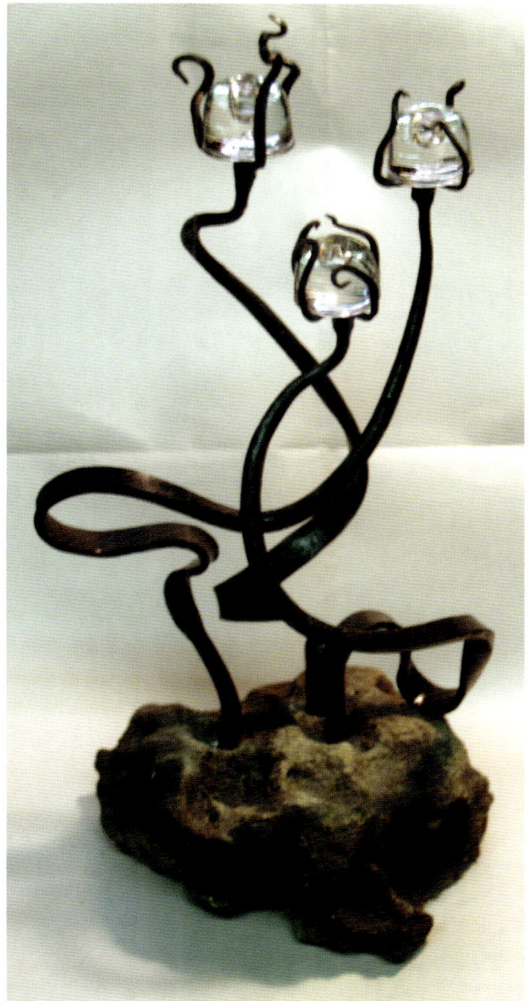

Crinoid - Hallucigenia No. Four. Sculpture. 2012. Forged mild steel with commercial glass, natural stone base. Approximately 30 cm (12") high.

Hallucigenia

The Burgess Shale in southeastern British Columbia, Canada, is an absolutely unique deposit, rich in fossils, which dates to roughly 500 million years ago. First, the fine silt that eventually turned to stone has faithfully recorded even the soft tissues of the animals that once lived there. And what animals! Creatures from the Cambrian Explosion show a bewildering array of types and body plans. The result of sudden evolution after a major extinction event, most types never survived into later ages. Some are so strange, so outright bizarre, that to our modern eyes they look to be the product of a crazed dream. The pieces in this recent sculptural series are inspired by these wonderful fossils.

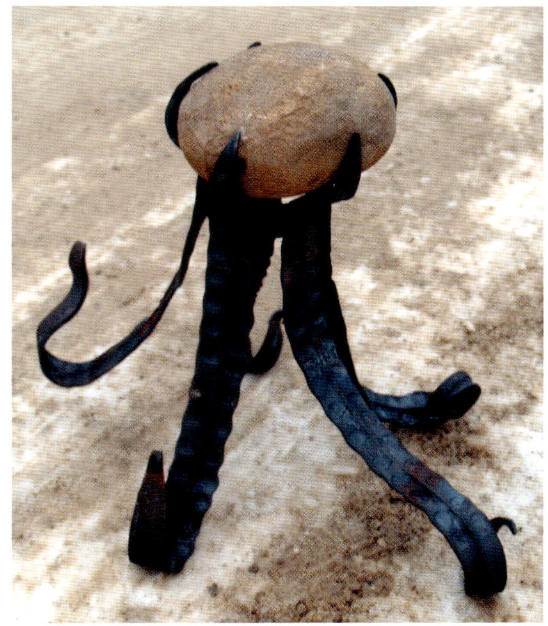

Pentapus - Hallucigenia No. Six. Sculpture. 2013. Forged structural mild steel, natural stone. Approximately 35 cm (14") high.

DARRELL MARKEWITZ

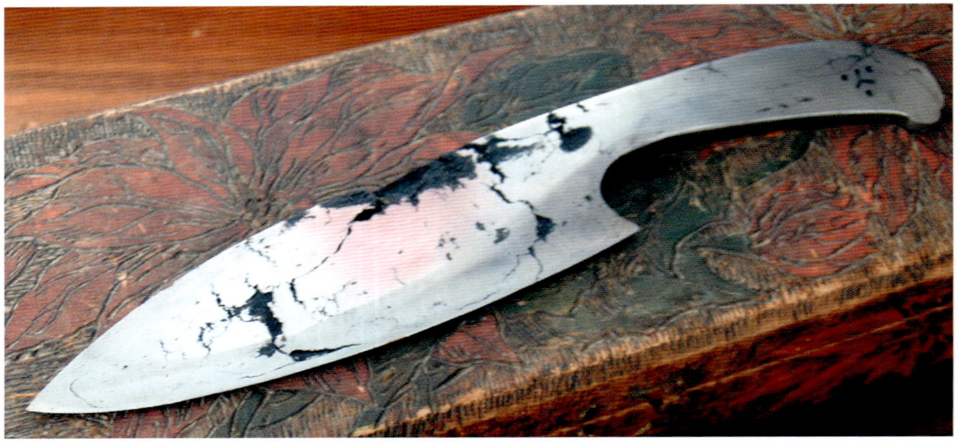

Hector's Bane

The source of inspiration for this rather large knife was two-fold. A portion of an early bloom (2006) was drawn into two slabs, straight from the bloom without the normal folding and welding to seal flaws. These pieces were forge welded to a spring steel core, with the more ragged outside edges of the bloom intentionally left along the back of the blade. As the blade was forged and polished, the hard core was exposed to create a durable cutting edge. The lines are suggested by bronze knives used by the Greeks during the Trojan Wars. The finished knife is over 6 mm (more than ¼") thick along the back. The rough surfaces and surface fissures that remain as part of Hector's Bane *rejoice in the creation and qualities of the bloomery iron it is composed of.*

Hector's Bane. Knife. 2012. Forged bloomery iron and spring steel. Approximately 28 cm (11").

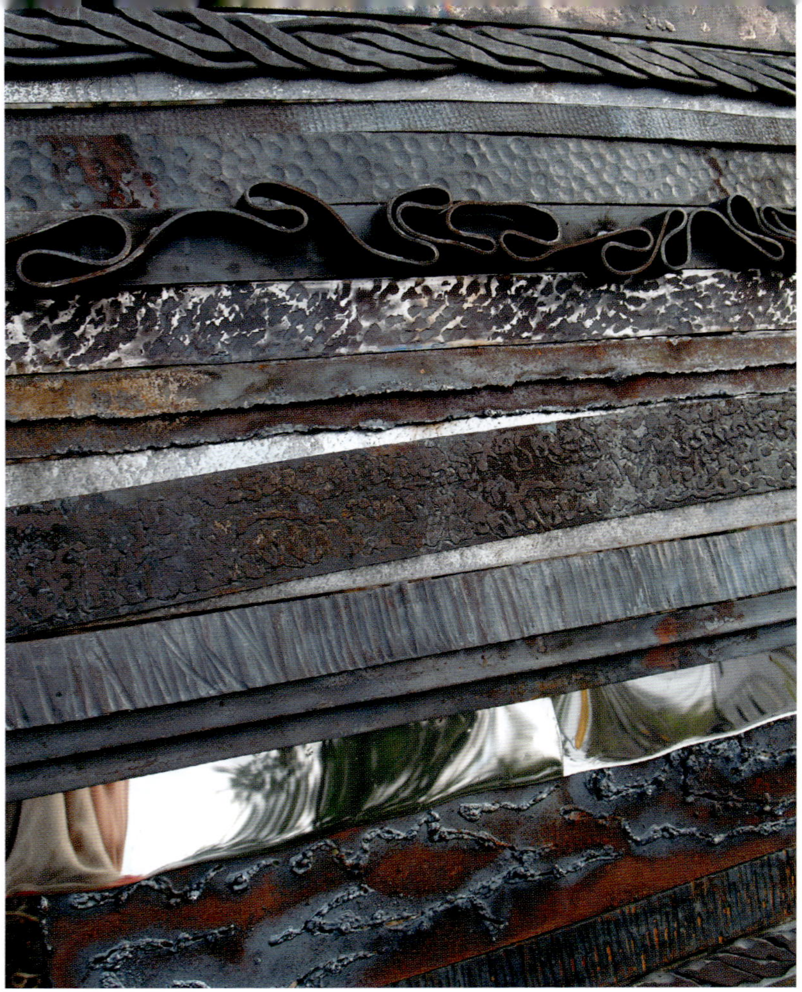

Layers

Layers *is part of the 2013 Elora Sculpture Project, a set of ten individual artists' contributions on display in Ontario, Canada.* Layers *was originally inspired by images of weathered granite from eastern Georgian Bay, the ground-down and exposed stubs of ancient mountains. The sculpture takes the form of a large panel, set tilted back on one edge. The panel is composed of a series of individual metal bars. Each is composed of differing metals, from antique wrought iron to modern stainless steel. All are hot forged in various ways, with additional surface textures and treatments added as well. These bars are left untreated and are intended to weather naturally. Exposed to the elements, the differing metals and surfaces age with differing rates and effects.*

Layers. Sculpture, detail. 2013. Forged steels, wrought iron, stainless, use of bronze patina. Approximately 130 x 120 cm (51" x 47 ¼")

Clark Martinek

Mitchell, South Dakota
www.clarktheblacksmith. com

ARTIST'S STATEMENT

I've always been drawn to art's creative process and working with metal encourages this process and gives me the power to harness some of the oldest art techniques known to man. Being able to create my own tools, as well as to create formative art, is very appealing to me. In today's world, having access to modern-day tools while holding true to the time-honored quality and craftsmanship of blacksmiths before me is what makes my sculptural work unique and interpretive. Because iron is so hard to manipulate, it demands dedication in order to make it move properly. But once the final product is achieved, it is very rewarding.

The Seahorse

As a father and blacksmith, I often have a unique desire to educate the younger generation about blacksmithing, just as a seahorse plays a unique role in the upbringing of their own young. They are strong and graceful creatures with unusual form, elegance, and imaginative beauty. The techniques I used to create this piece are very simple form and joinery. No welding was used to create this item. It is complemented with rock and copper. I will often choose to complement my items with rock, for the natural yet strong look it gives to a very delicate-looking iron piece. The copper, I feel, adds an element of elegance to the nostalgic creature.

Seahorse. Sculpture. 2013. Iron, rock, copper. Blacksmithing. Total approximately 30"h with base; seahorse is approximately 10"h x ¾" at belly. *Photo: Charola Martinek*

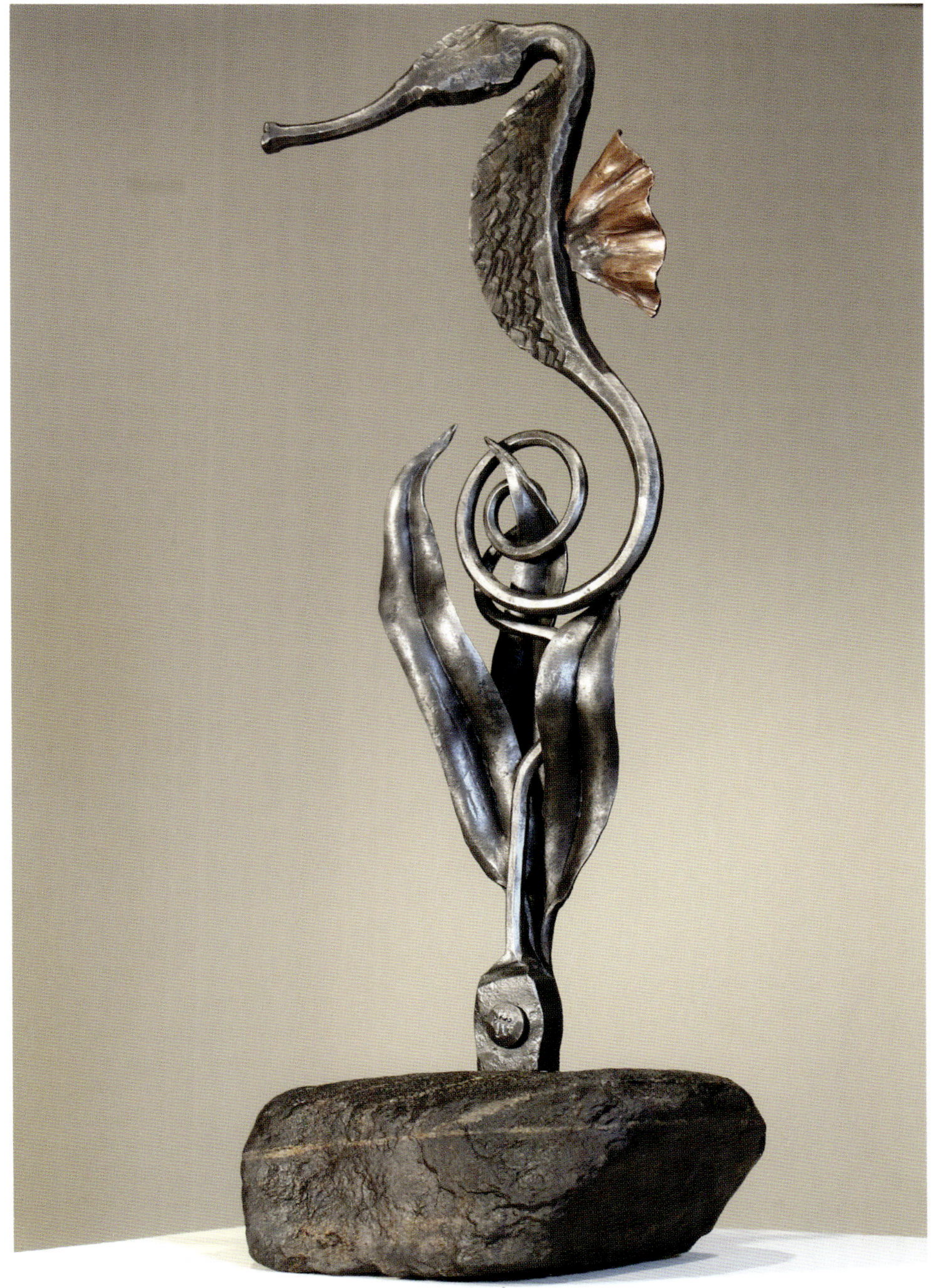

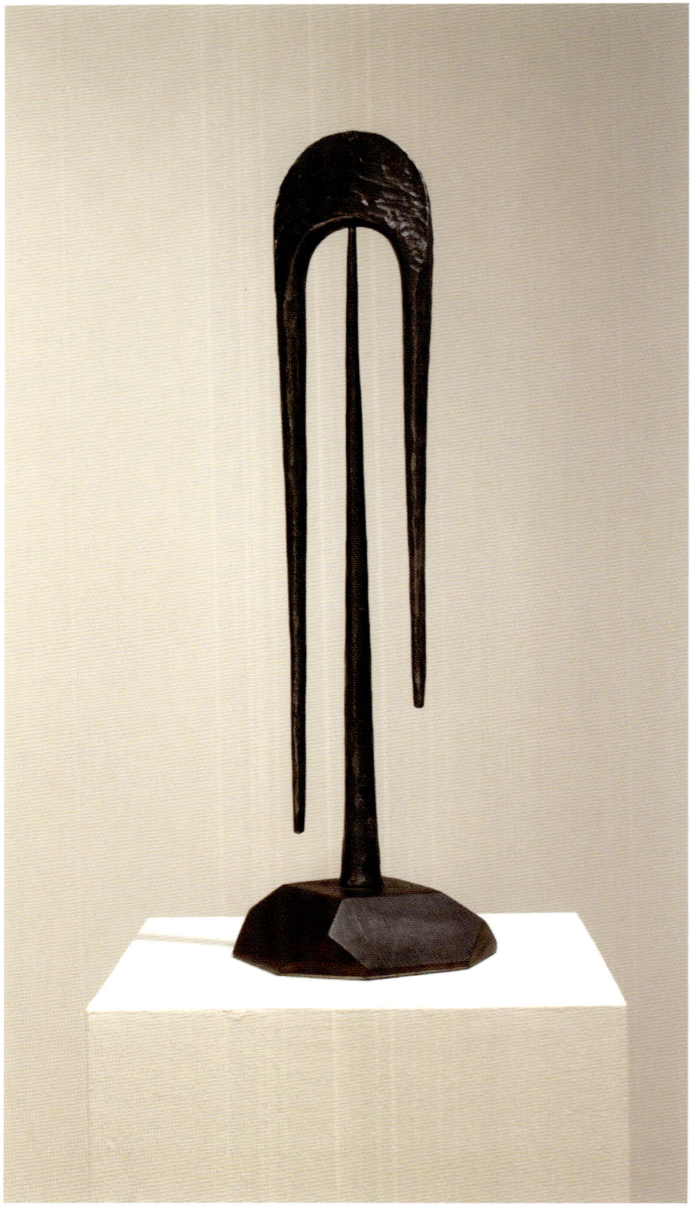

Bilancio

Bilancio—Italian for hanging in the balance—was created to show that we can all balance art and life. This is a two-piece sculpture. The top portion is set on the tip of the center portion and is in true balance. The center portion was then positioned in a piece of wood. I chose wood for this item because it is one of the elements that bring balance to our lives. For the center post, I used traditional hand tapering techniques but added the element of a power hammer to give texture and depth to the piece in balance. The wood is hand cut and hand stained to compliment the iron.

Bilancio. 2013. Sculpture. Iron and wood. Traditional blacksmithing and joinery. Iron center, 1″ round bar tapered to ¼″. Balancing iron piece, flattened 3″-tall tapered to ¼″. Total height, approximately 28″ with base. *Photo: Charola Martinek*

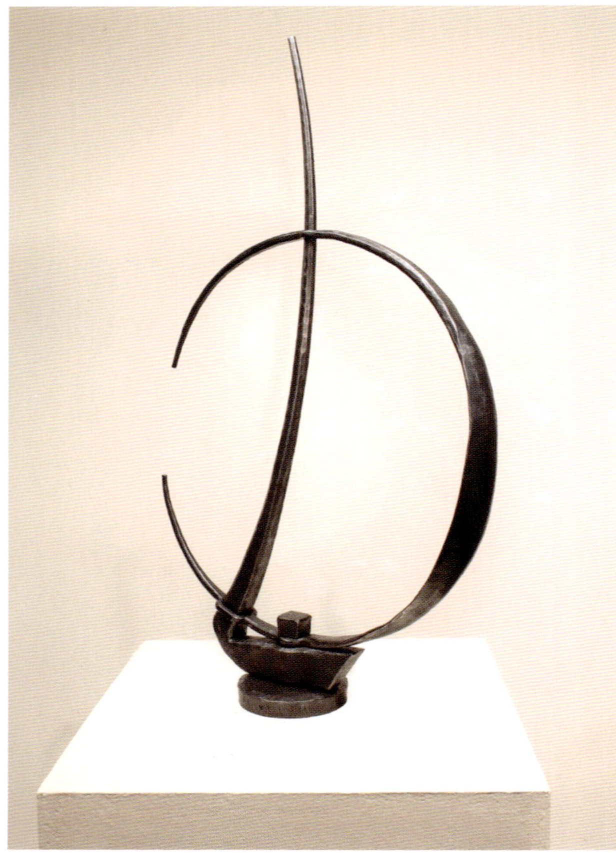

Sevin's Sail

The inspiration for Sevin's Sail comes from many places. The first one, and one I'd like to recognize the most, is my mentor, Peter Sevin. I created this piece to inspire him as he inspired me, over the years. The techniques I used to create this piece are very simple joinery and pass throughs. I also formed a group of friends into a small, striking team, and with each one's hammer blow we were able to create the large upset you see in the middle. The item was then pieced together and joined traditionally at the base. No welding was used to create this item.

Sevin's Sail. Sculpture. 2013. Iron.
Traditional blacksmith joinery.
Total approximately 36″h x 24″w.
Sail approximately 24″h x 5″w.
Photo: Charola Martinek

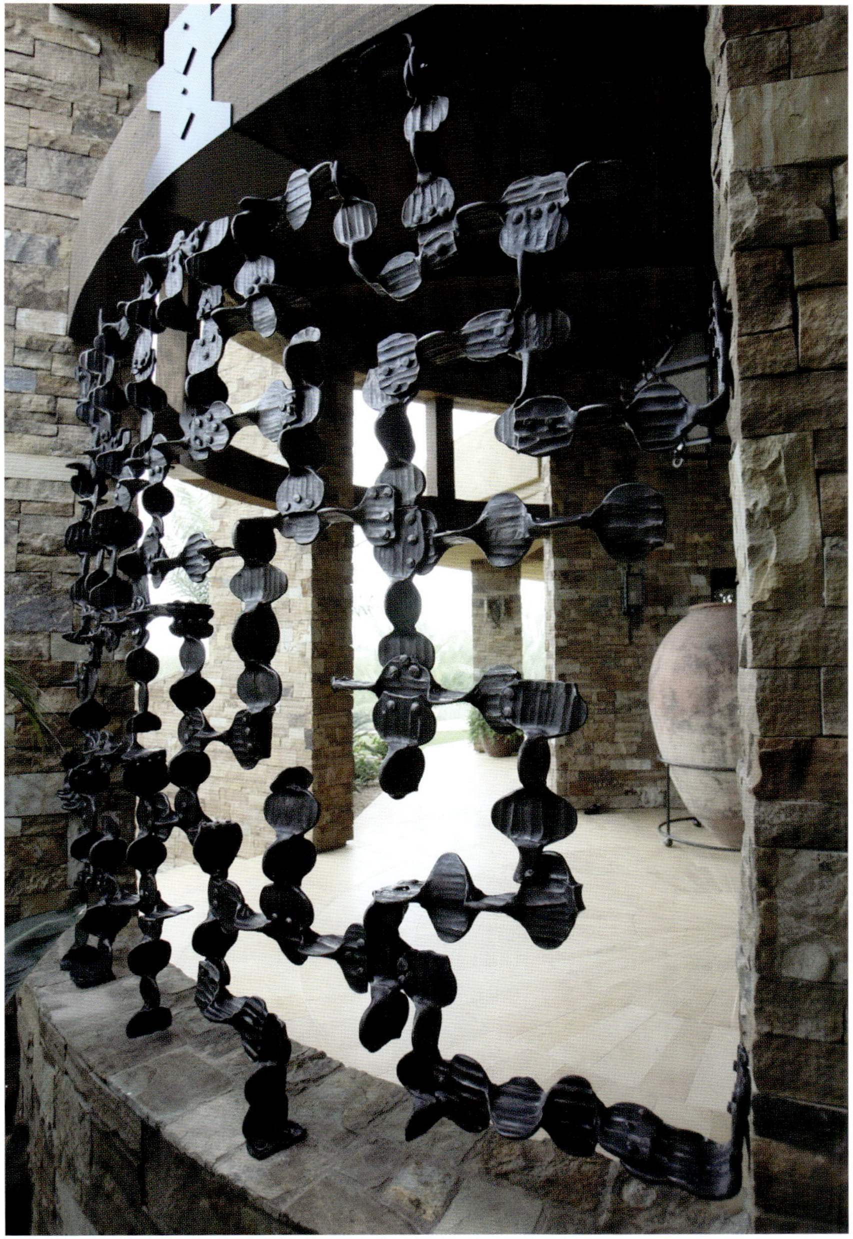

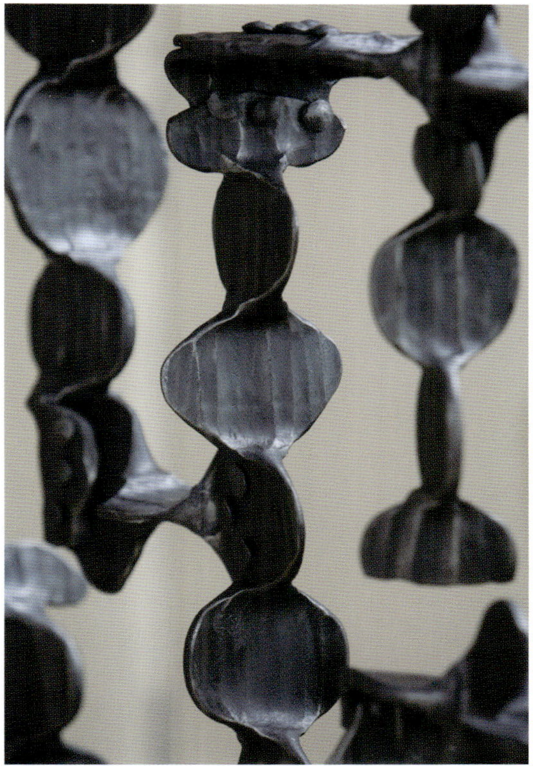

Viscous

This work stems from the idea of viscosity, the property of a fluid that resists the force tending to cause the fluid to flow. This large sculpture was commissioned for a gentleman in Arizona for a large outdoor area. It consists of very large iron pieces placed in an order to create a puzzle-like pattern, revealing both positive and negative space with the iron. The "iron puzzle" is pieced together with iron rivets and hand forged staples and is approximately 8' wide by 8' tall on a curve. In order to create something of this scale, many specialized blacksmith tools were needed, including an iron press to "squish" the iron into the desired shape and thickness, and large air-powered hammers to give it detail and fine-tune the textures.

Viscous. Sculpture. 2009. Iron. Hand forged and pressed. 8'h x 8'w x approximately 5"d. *Photos: Lisa Olson*

Pete Mattila

Mattila Studio, Launceston, Tasmania, Australia
www.petemattila.com

ARTIST'S STATEMENT

The meaning of the pieces I produce is, for me, inextricably entwined with process, material, physical engagement, and technical ability. It is only through open-ended activity that new works can emerge. The way I view my work is like a continuous thread in a larger fabric. I am a maker; what I am making is new to me. I am not viewing it from the outside, I am viewing it from the inside. My conceptual framework comes from that act of doing, making, thinking. I make objects out of steel. Each new moment emerges from its history and could not be arrived at without it. In this way, the object is continually emerging. To me, they are not resolved static things; within each is a growth of understanding.

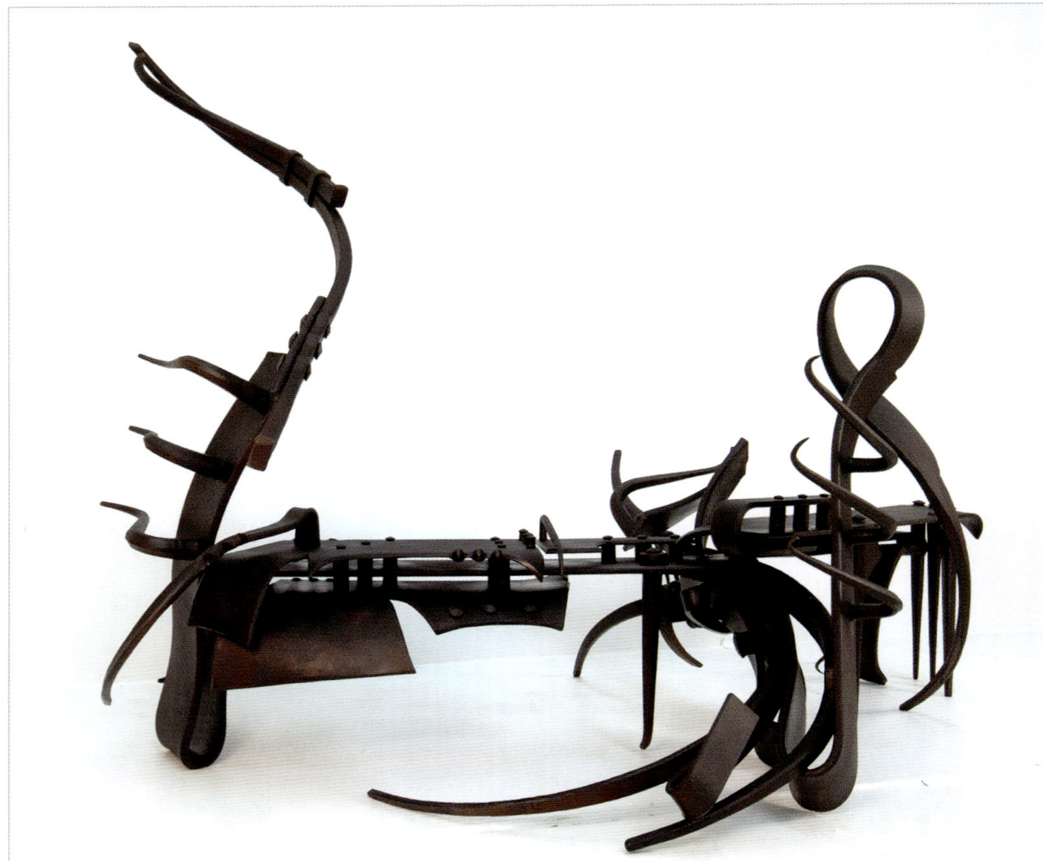

Object 1

Surface Study V. 2013. Steel, brown and black patina.
50"d x 83"w x 67"h.

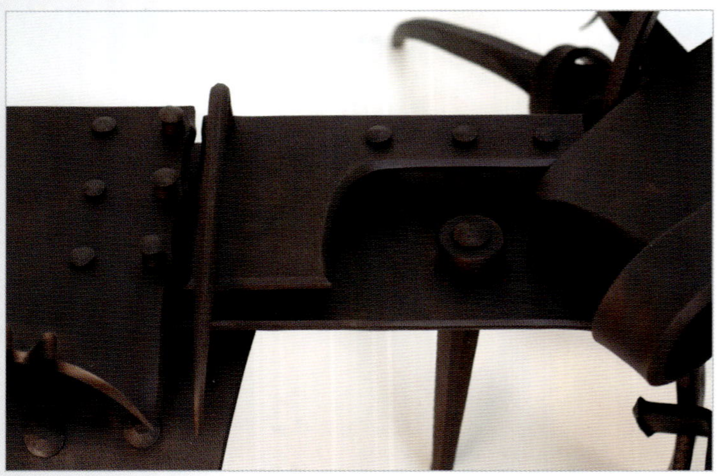

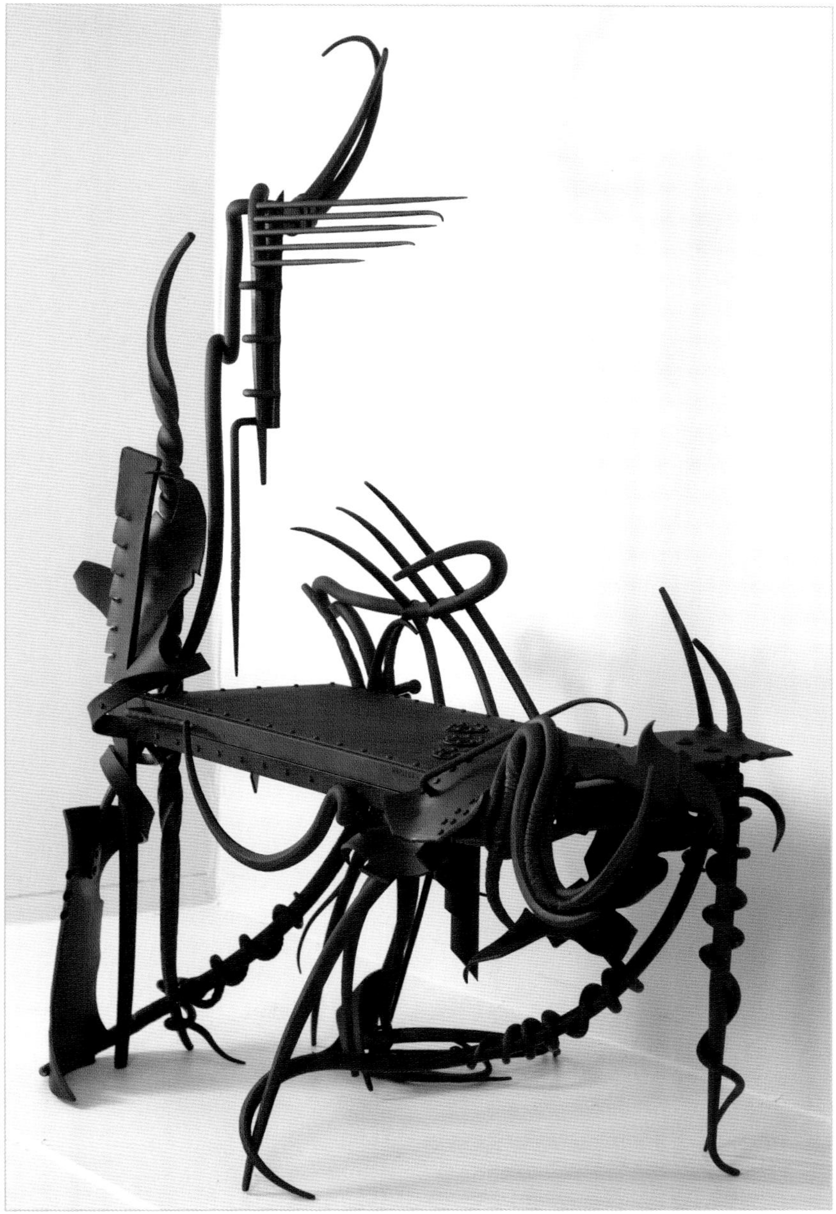

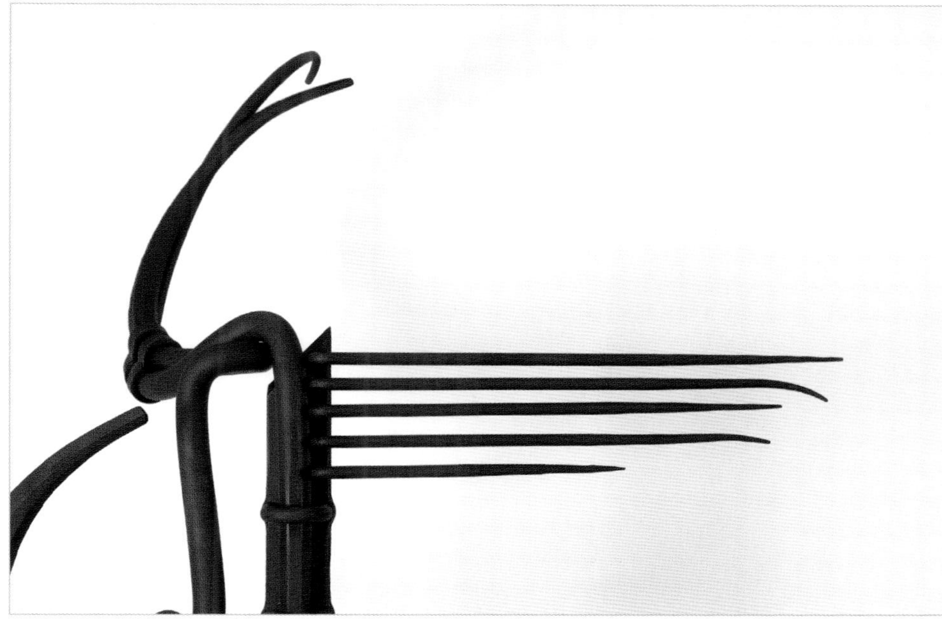

Object 2

Surface Study IV. 2013. Steel, brown and black patina. 41"d x 67"w x 80"h.

Craig May

Dragon Forge, Ltd., Pine, Colorado
www.DragonForgeltd.com

ARTIST'S STATEMENT

"By hand and hammer, all art doth stand."
— William Banks Fortescue

The art of blacksmithing allows me to express myself in a venue that feeds the creative drive in my spirit, creating a vision with fire and hammer that transforms an idea, a feeling, into instant gratification.

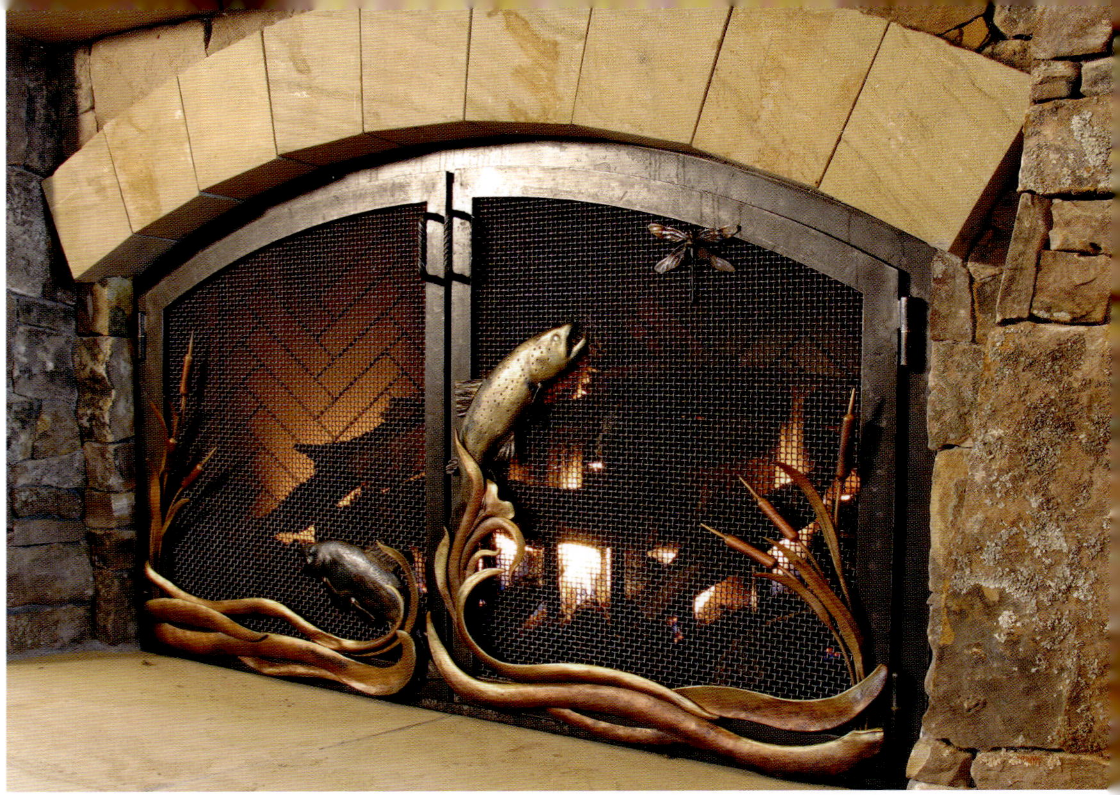

Fish fire doors. Hand forged using air hammers and repoussé techniques. *Photo: Rory May*

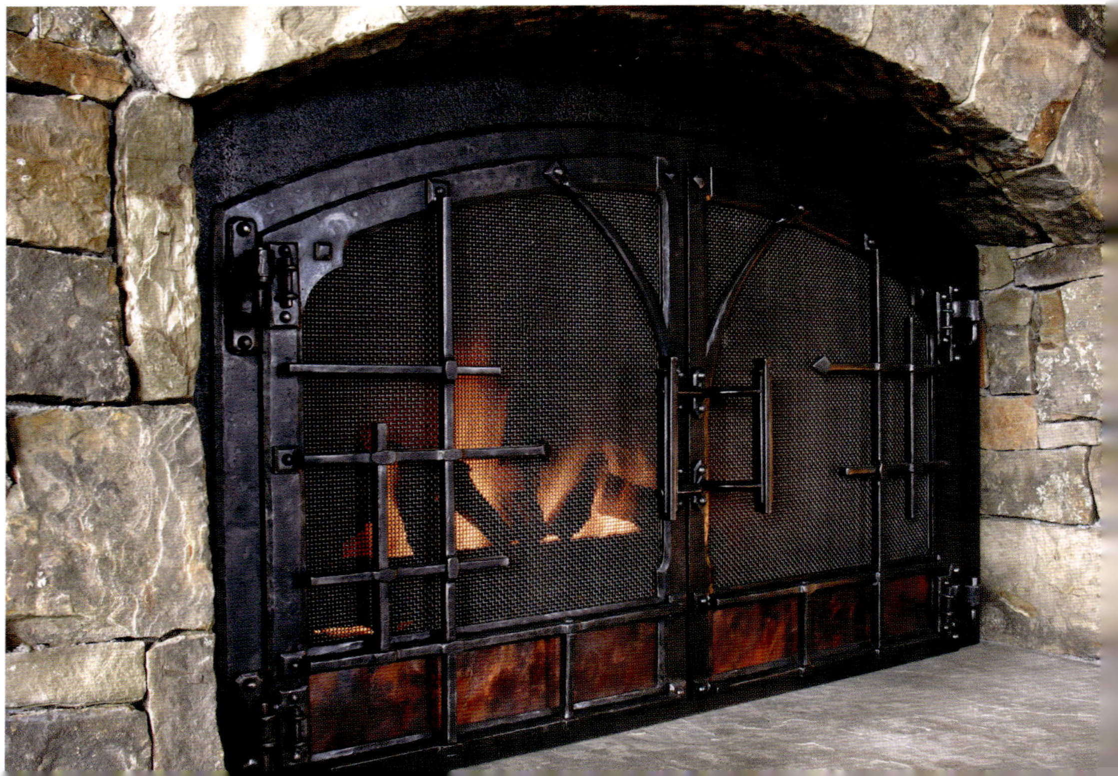

Fireplace doors. Copper panels on the bottom.
All details hand forged: hinges, pulls, frames. *Photo: Rory May*

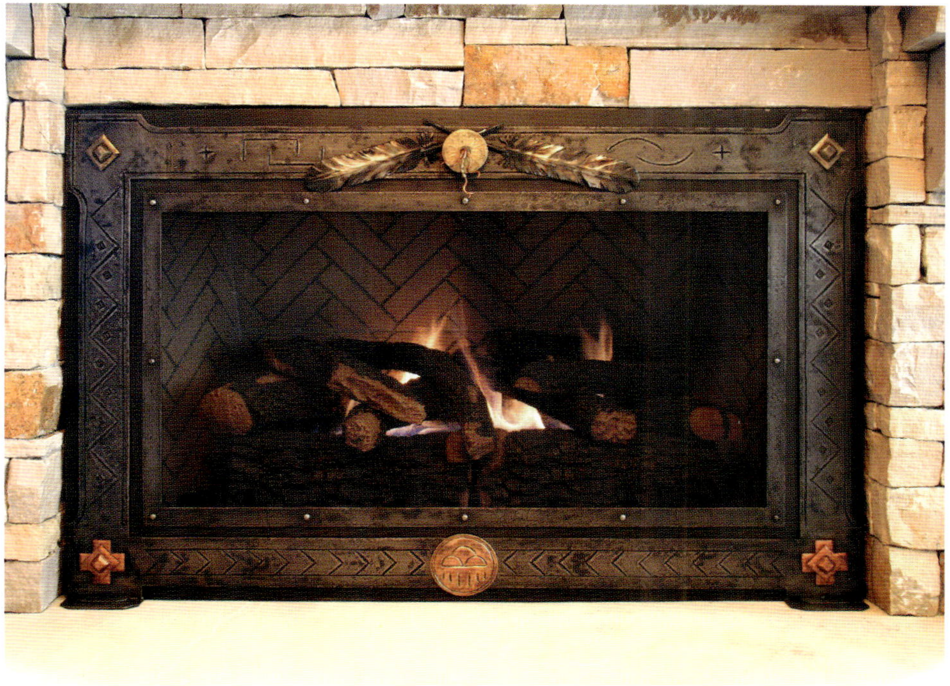

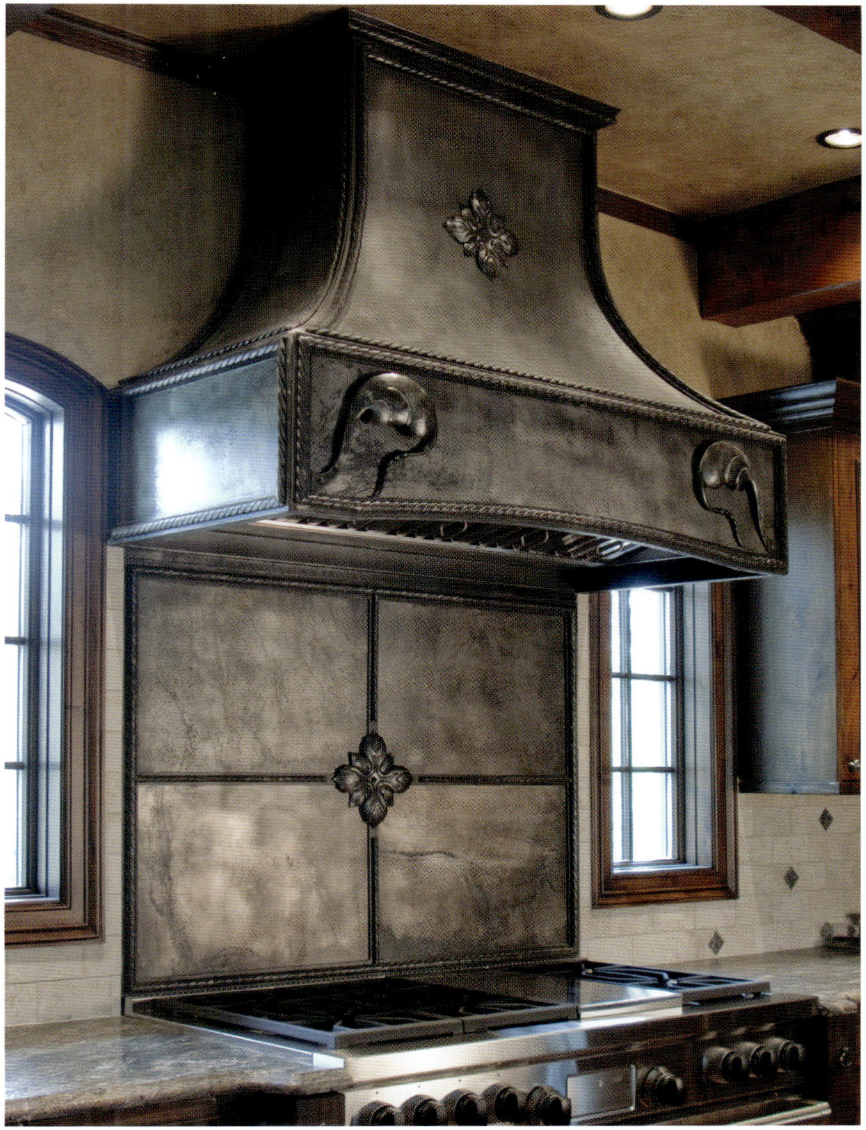

Pueblo deco fireplace screen. 6′ wide with forged Native American ideograms. *Photo: Rory May*

Stove hood and backsplash. Steel with repoussé acanthus leaves. *Photo: Rory May*

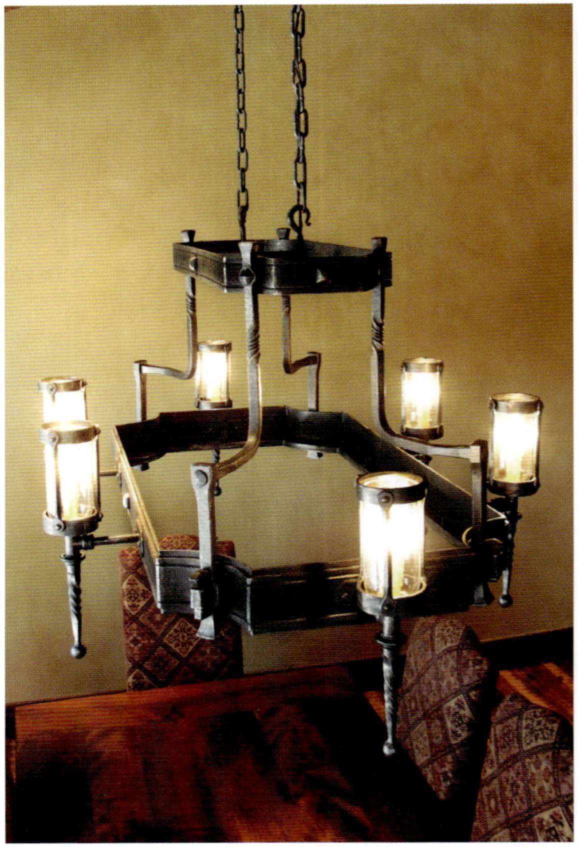

Dining room chandelier. Forged steel.
Slit and drift with tenons and rivet joinery.
Photo: Rory May

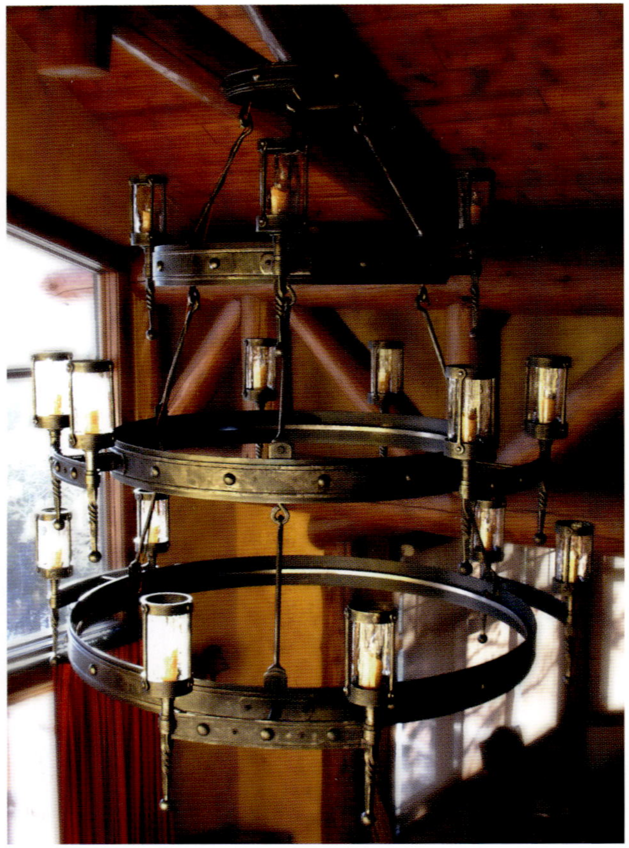

Great room chandelier. 10'h x 8'w.
Photo: Rory May

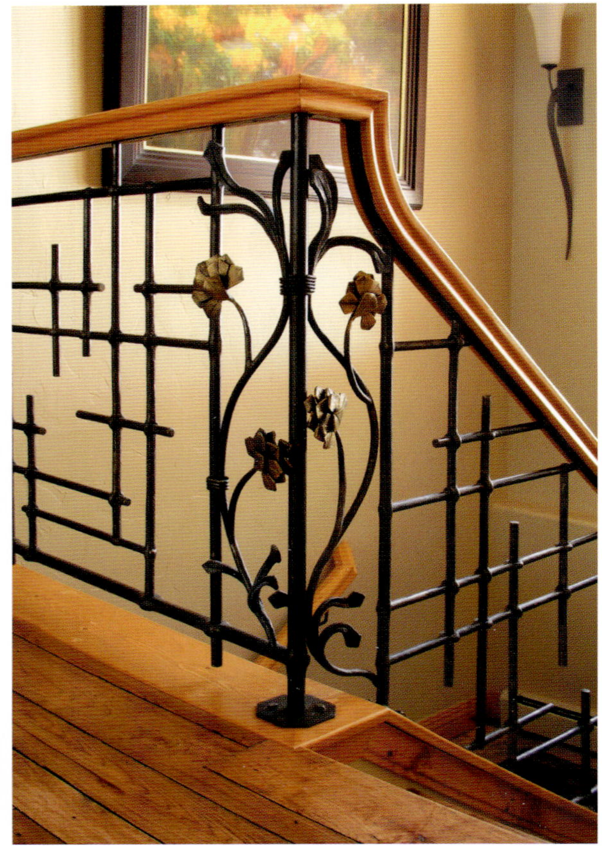

Art deco railing. Slit and drift joinery through the round bar panels, with stylized art deco, pine cone theme. *Photo: Rory May*

Matthew & Karine Maynard

Maynard Studios, Lawrenceburg, Kentucky
www.maynardstudios.com

ARTISTS' STATEMENT

Our approach is relatively simple. We feel that everything surrounding us has an effect on our lives and that if something is worth building, it is worth building to last. We believe that practical items should serve their function well, but also reflect creative and aesthetic form. These principles should be acknowledged in the design of any product, especially one that will be part of your life, day-in and day-out. Our pieces are made to be enjoyed not only by this generation but by those who come after.

If our hands make something that gives you joy, it is our sincerest hope that a bit of that travels with you out into the world. Heat and muscle shape the metal, but the true, successful product of our efforts is our client's happiness. It simply feels wrong to conduct ourselves in any other fashion.

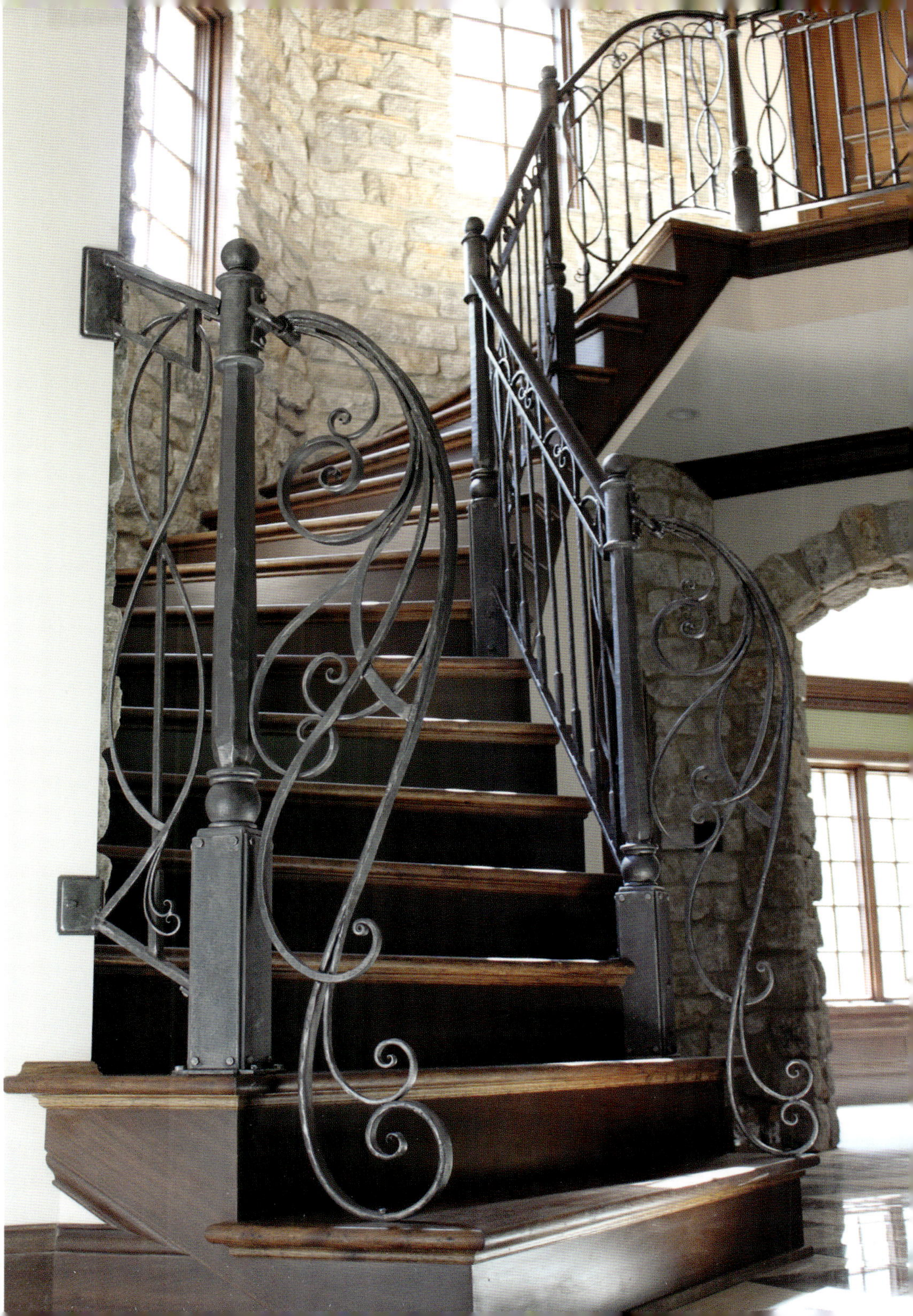

Custom Railing

Cascading newel drops provide an extended handgrip to this railing, for a steadier approach to the stairs.

Custom railing for private home. 2012. Forged and welded mild steel. Wire-brushed with clear enamel finish.
Photo: Maynard Studios

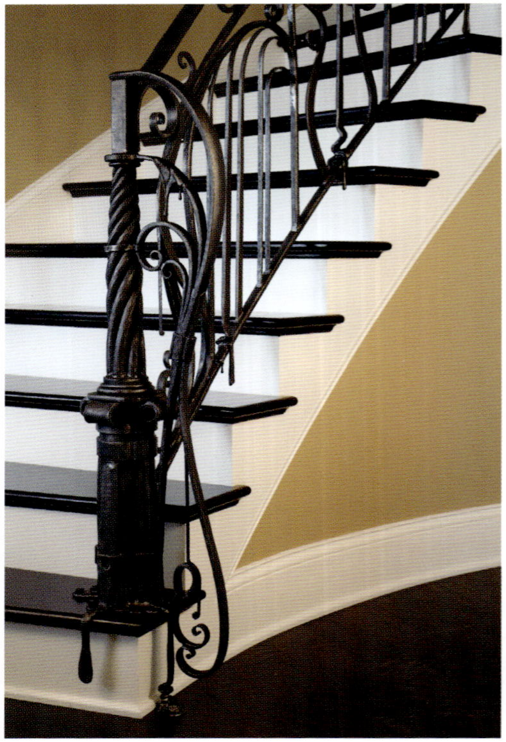

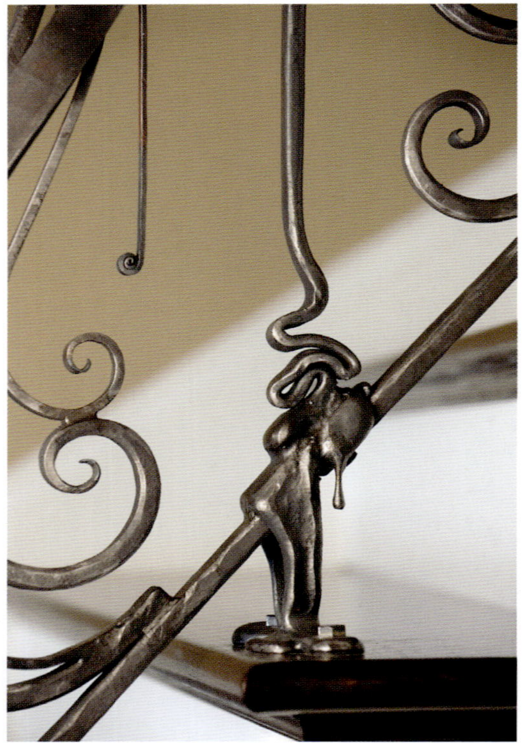

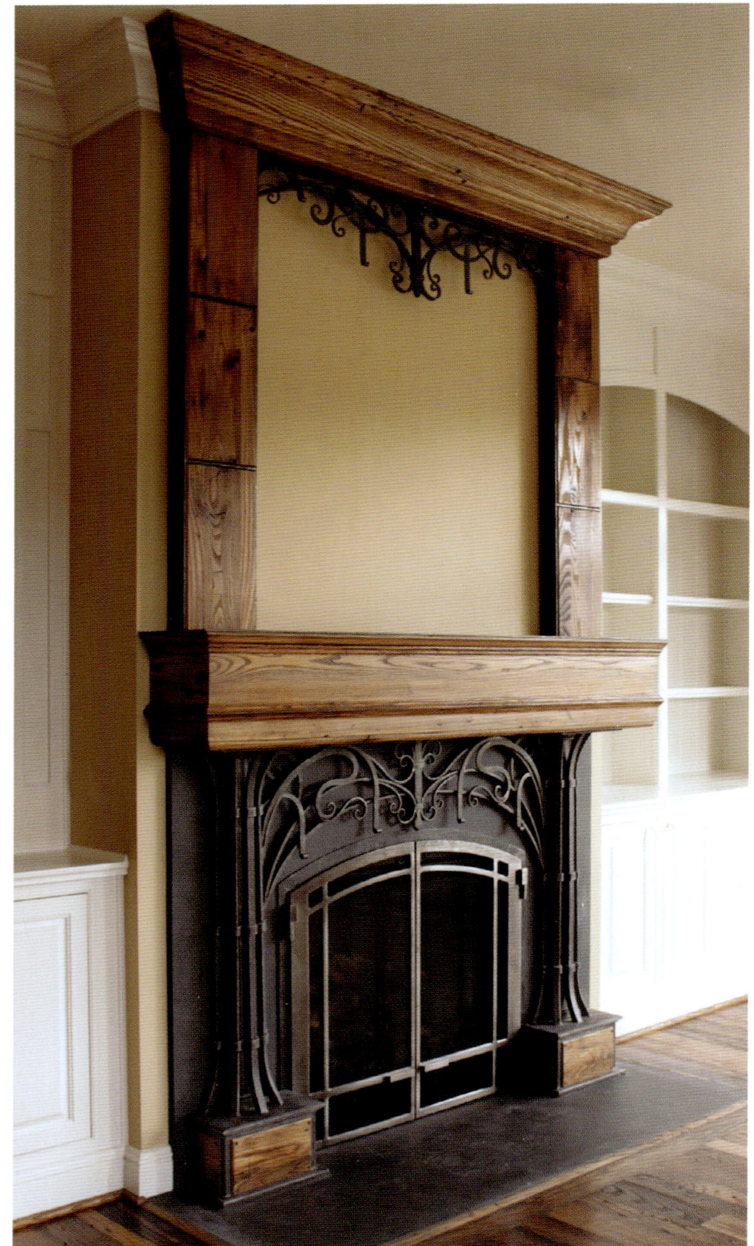

Dali Railing

This railing was designed for clients who have a collection of work by the artist Salvador Dali. With this railing, we attempted to blend nouveau and classical elements in a way that we had never done before, while also accepting the challenge from our client to create portions of the rail that appear to be melting, as if made of wax.

Dali railing. 2011. Forged, formed, and carved mild steel. Wire-brushed with clear enamel finish. *Photo: Ryan Bowles*

Mantle Surround

The mantle surround and over-mantle ornamentation incorporate wormy chestnut panels.

Mantle surround. 2012. Forged and formed mild steel, wire-brushed with clear enamel finish. Wormy chestnut panels incorporated. *Photo: Maynard Studios*

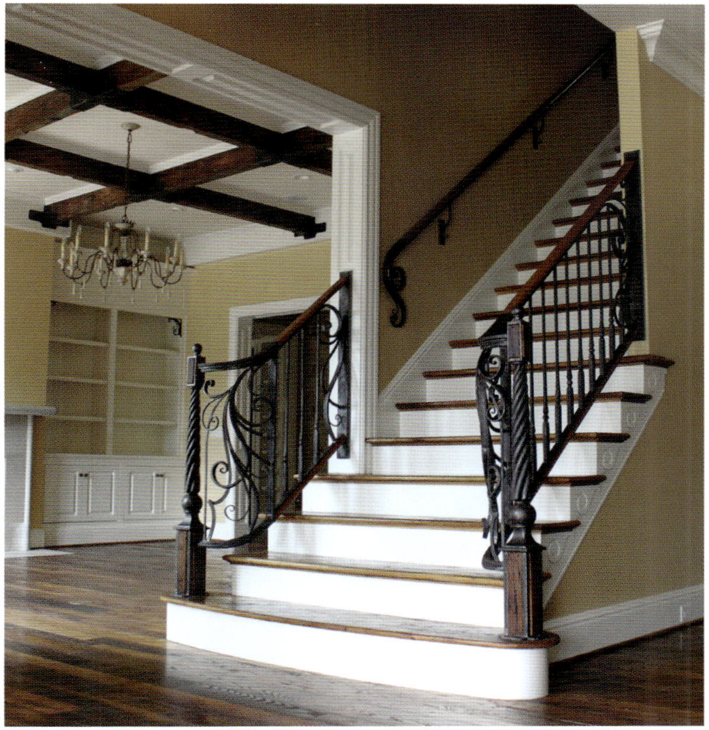

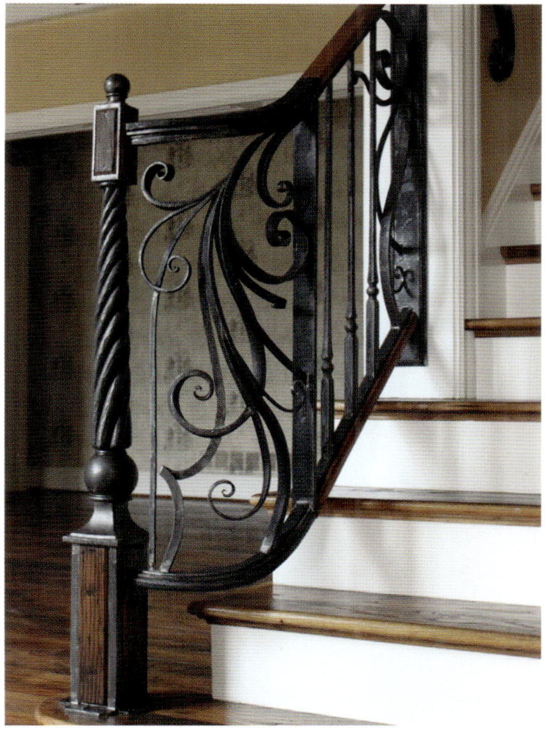

Railing with Wormy Chestnut

This railing incorporates wood in the newels and on the top and bottom rails as a way to frame the metalwork. The design uses components forged in a shape reminiscent of wood spindles in conjunction with scrollwork at the ends to create a juxtaposition of styles.

Railing with wormy chestnut. 2012. Forged mild steel and wormy chestnut. Wire brushed with clear enamel finish. *Photo: Maynard Studios*

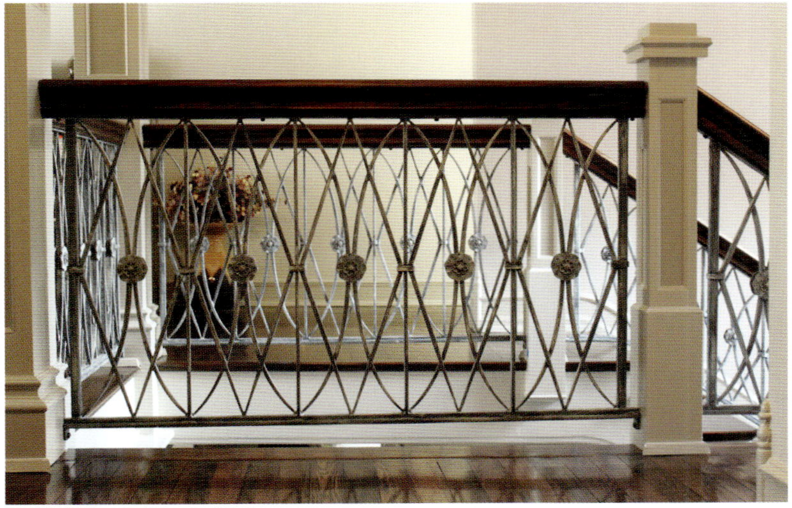

Historic Remodel Railing

This railing was part of a remodel of a historic residence. One of the design criteria was that everything had to fit to the existing newels and mahogany handgrip that were original to the home. Each piece was tapered to add visual interest and lighten the overall appearance of the metal work.

Historic remodel railing. 2013. Forged steel with hand-rubbed pigmented wax. *Photo: Maynard Studios*

Randy A. McDaniel

ExPRESSive Metals, Reading, Pennsylvania
rams4g@msn.com

ARTIST'S STATEMENT

Creating works in metal is a way for me to express a three-dimensional feeling of motion, life, and fun. Creating with the hydraulic forging press is another way to show the life that hot metal exudes as it displays a clay-like quality. Even after forty years in this art, I am in a state of constant growth as new methods and ideas keep me creating new works. This allows my whimsical designs to perpetuate a lighter heart for all—for myself while creating and for the client over the years.

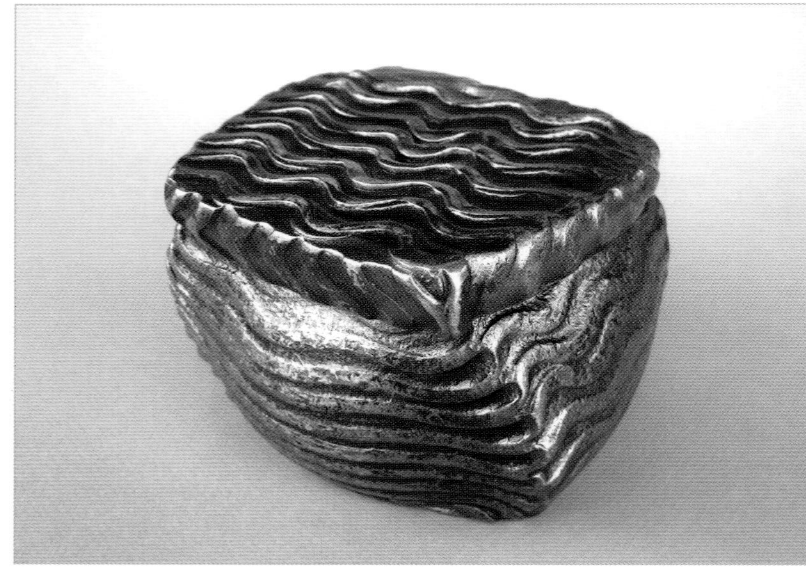

Squished Box #444

I used pure iron to start with a softer material and to get more detail in my work. The sides were textured with hand-made dies to show the life of the squish and then the opening of the box was punched. The lid was pressed into the opening using a texture die on top, which produced the design as well as a perfectly fitting lid.

Squished box #444. Box. 2012. Hot forged pure iron.
4½" x 4¼" x 3¼". *Photo: Randy A. McDaniel*

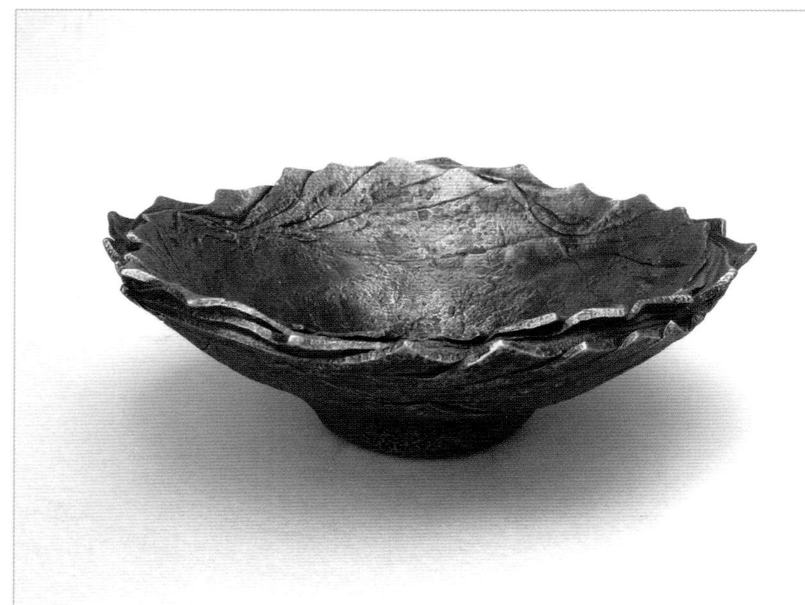

Stacked Bowl 11

My goal with this bowl was to produce a serrated edge. I created a stack of eleven pieces around a central post and rotated each layer to make the edge detail. I then forge welded the mass into one piece using the hydraulic forging press. This was then drawn out and formed in the press to produce the bowl.

Stacked bowl 11. Bowl. 2010. Mild steel. Hot forged.
8" (diameter) x 2¾" d. *Photo: Randy A. McDaniel*

Flames Candle Holder

I picked some old wrought iron to recycle for this item. I wanted it to crack to show the grain structure of the material. In using this with my flame dies, it is like a crack in the ground with volcanic action. Uniting this with the flame of the candle ties it all together.

Flames candle holder. 2013. Wrought iron. Hot forged using texture dies and punches. 2" x 2" x 2¾". *Photo: Randy A. McDaniel*

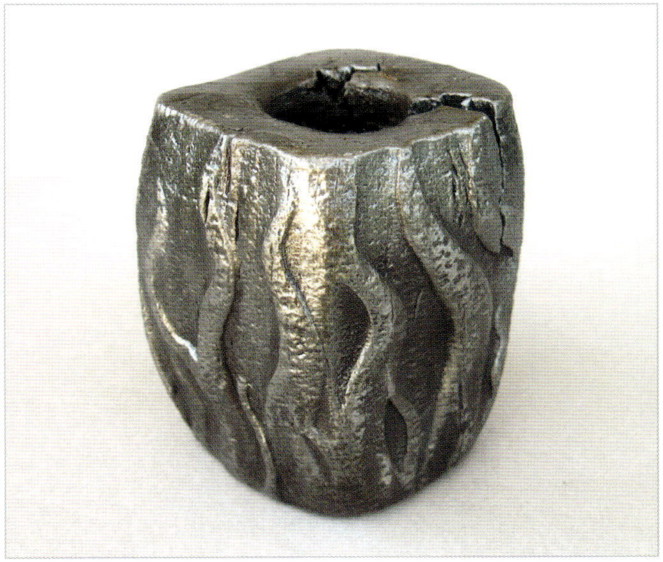

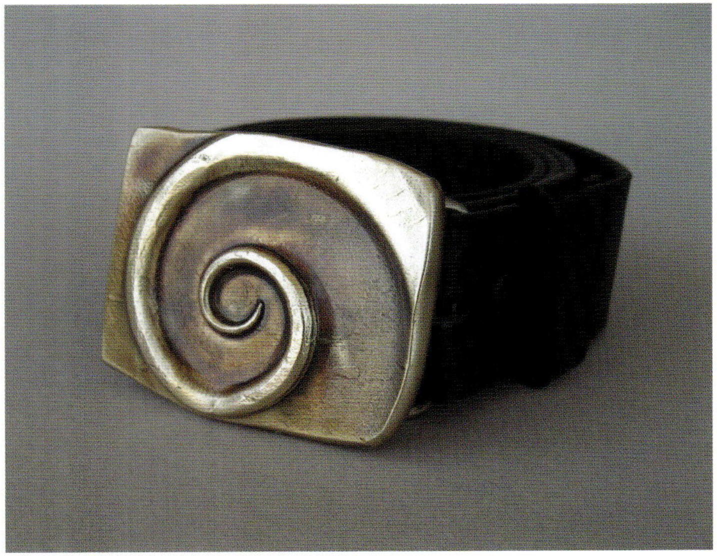

Snakeskin Candle Holder

The texture pattern dies I created for this effect do not look like snake skin. By squishing the steel by about forty percent after texturing, this look is achieved. I like the life and motion that this produces.

Snakeskin candle holder. 2010. Mild steel. Hot forged using texture dies and punches. 2¾" x 1¾" x 1⅞". *Photo: Randy A. McDaniel*

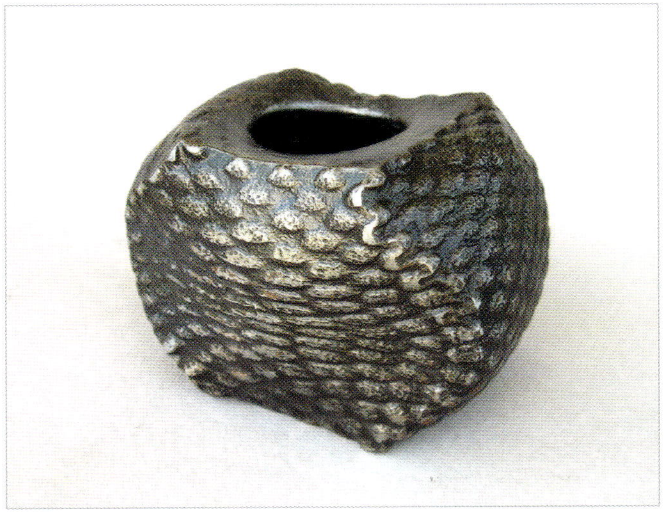

Scroll Belt Buckle

As with the other designs that I use in my press, I hand forge the tooling for this design. Scrolls represent nature with its connection to snails, ocean waves, water going down a drain, curves in plant life, and other similarities. Because of this, it creates life and motion.

Scroll belt buckle. 2012. Bronze. Hot forged using hand-forged dies. 2¾" x 2¼" x ½". *Photo: Randy A. McDaniel*

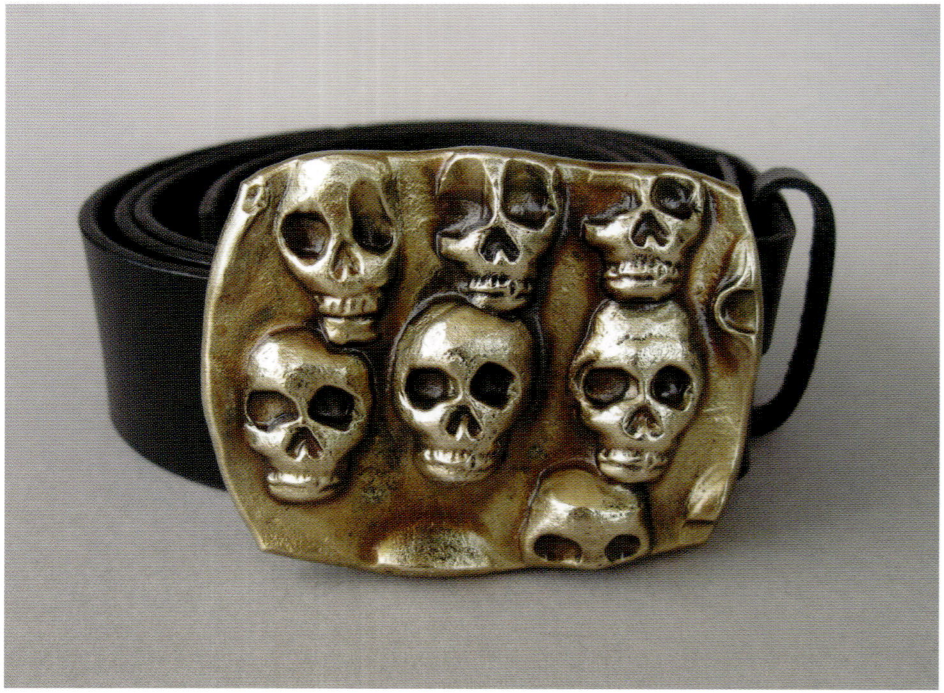

Skulls Belt Buckle

My skull buckles have been a popular item. I have several configurations of them using a variety of skull shapes, sizes, and details. This has even morphed into pirate coins and buckles.

Skulls belt buckle. 2012. Bronze. Hot forged using hand-forged dies. 2 15/16" x 2 7/16" x 7/16". *Photo: Randy A. McDaniel*

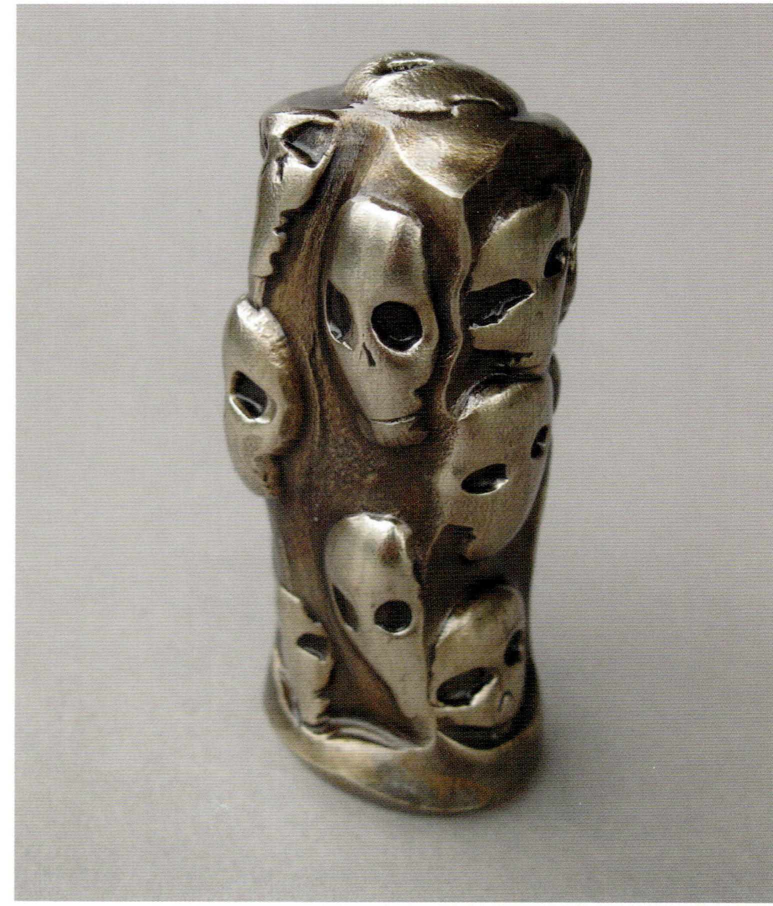

Spirits Cane Topper

Sometimes I get ideas and then it is a matter of trying them to see what happens. Sometimes they work out better than planned. I was thrilled how this idea turned out. The spirits seem to float and drift upward. Not only are there spirits on the sides, but there is also one on the top.

Spirits cane topper. 2012. Bronze. Hot forged using hand-forged dies. 1 3/8" diameter x 3 3/8". *Photo: Randy A. McDaniel*

Heather McLarty

Steel Crazy, Los Angeles, California
www.steelcrazy.biz

ARTIST'S STATEMENT

I take steel, get it hot, hit it with a hammer on an anvil, and make it beautiful. I continue to explore the endless ways to transform hard, industrial materials into lively, organic pieces of sculpture and functional art. After learning steel fabrication as a props artisan in the theater, I began working backwards technologically. I use a mixture of modern and ancient methods to create my pieces.

I have found a special affinity for sheet work, particularly repoussé and high relief chasing. In 2001, I won a CBA grant to study high-relief chasing with Kirsten Skiles at the Campbell Folkschool. After winning a Bedayn grant in 2005, I spent several transformative weeks in the Czech Republic and studied Louis XVI ornament and tooling from master smith Alfred Habermann. In May of 2010, I traveled to Ivano-Frankivsk to participate and exhibit in the Union of Ukrainian Blacksmiths Festival with blacksmiths from around the globe.

I am grateful for the generosity of my husband and the blacksmithing community in helping me along this path.

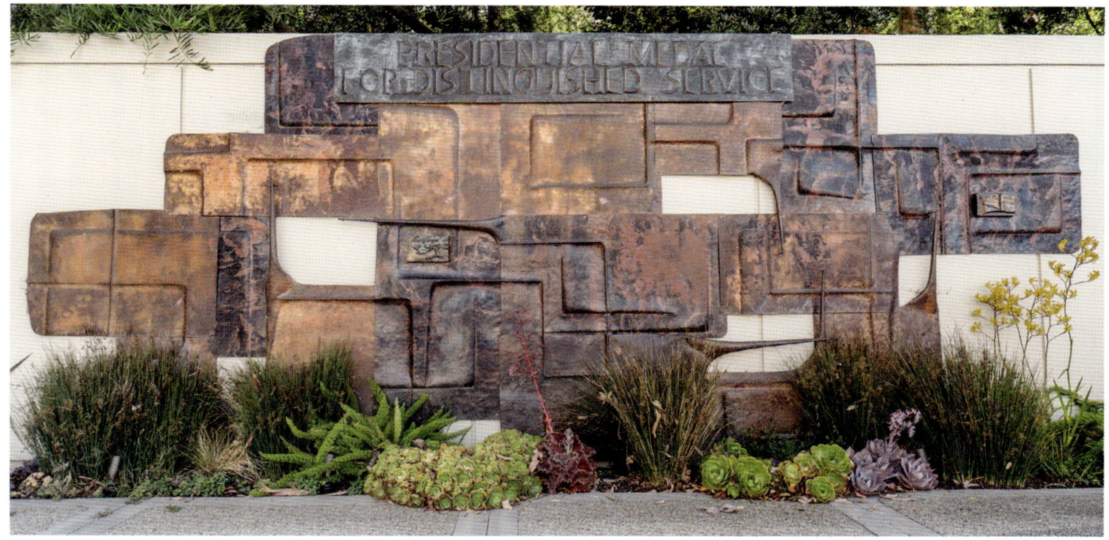

Presidential Medal for Distinguished Service Wall

This is the first commission I completed for Occidental College. The president of the college asked me to design a wall to put plaques for an ad hoc medal for outstanding contributions to the college. It needed to be able to be added to over time. They had a place selected just outside the administration building on a painted cement wall. My first thought was to design individual bronze plaques. Next, I realized I really needed to design the wall as a piece. I wanted it to attract attention from afar and draw people closer, without distracting from the plaques themselves. I did a drawing, then a copper material sample that evolved into a scale model. Forming the entire piece in one-inch scale allowed me to figure out the tooling and techniques I would need when I scaled up.

Presidential Medal for Distinguished Service wall. Copper, bronze.
Commissioned by Occidental College, Eagle Rock, California.
10'h x 25'l. *Photo: Martha Benedict*

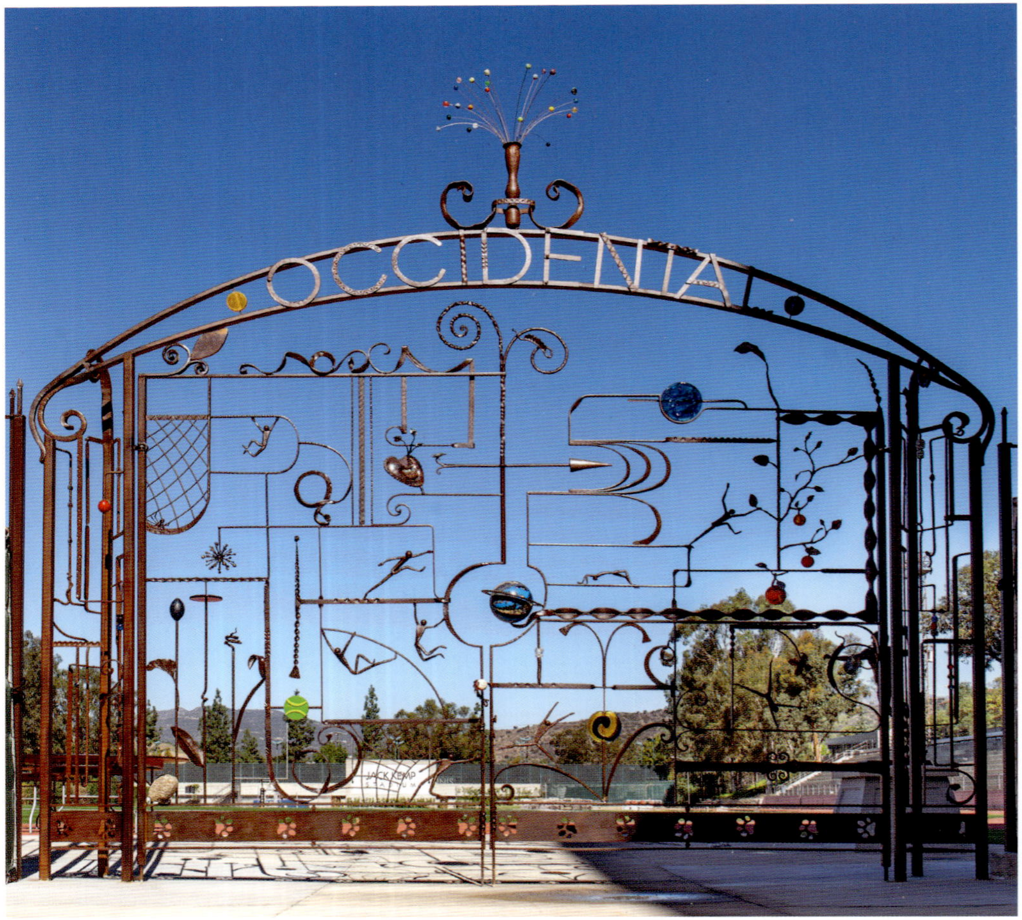

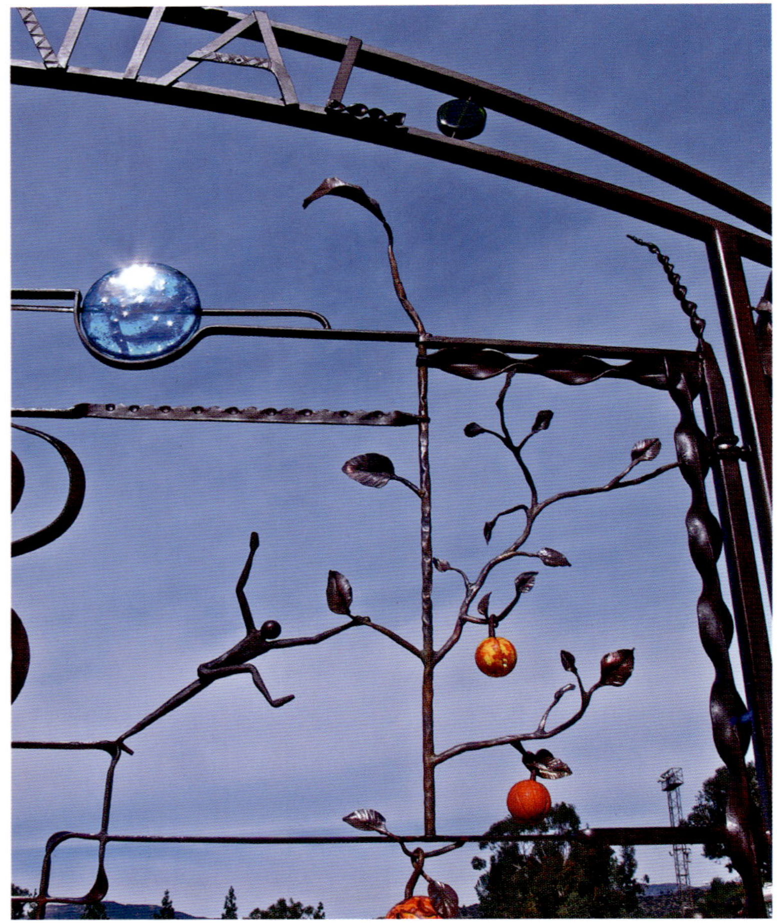

Enter the Field of Play

My second commission for Occidental College were these gates leading to the athletic field.

Enter the Field of Play. Gates. Steel, copper, glass (by Cathi Milligan), bronze, stone, bowling ball, pool ball. Commissioned by Occidental College. *Overall photo: Marc Campos, Occidental College; Detail photo: Troy Evans*

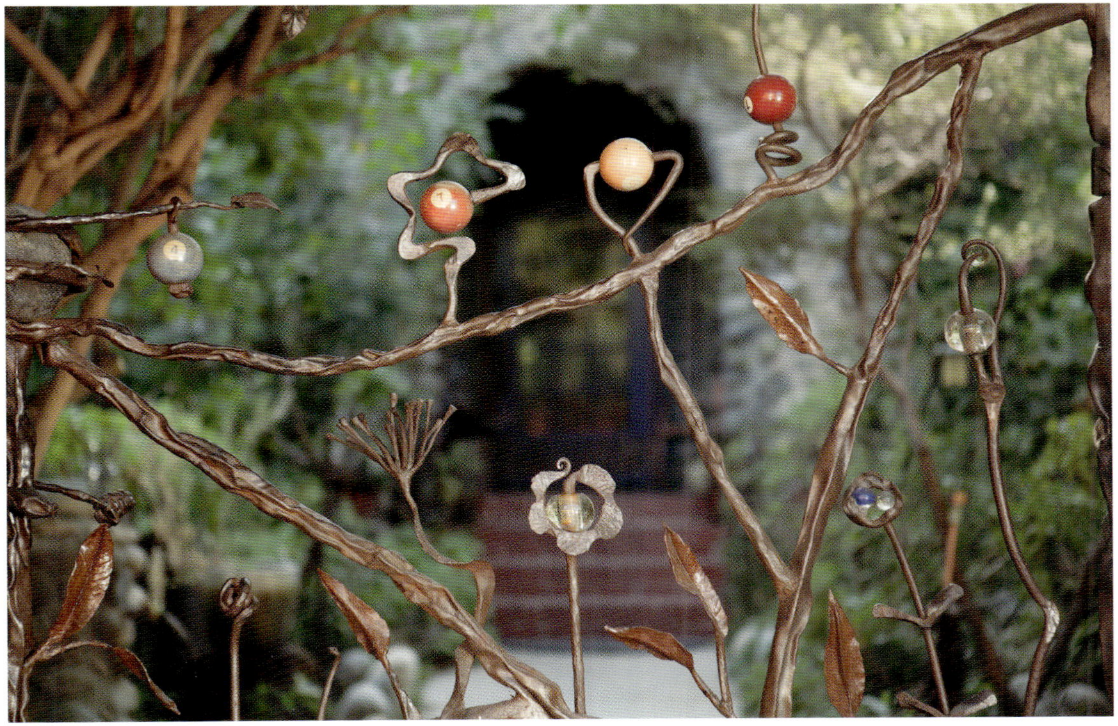

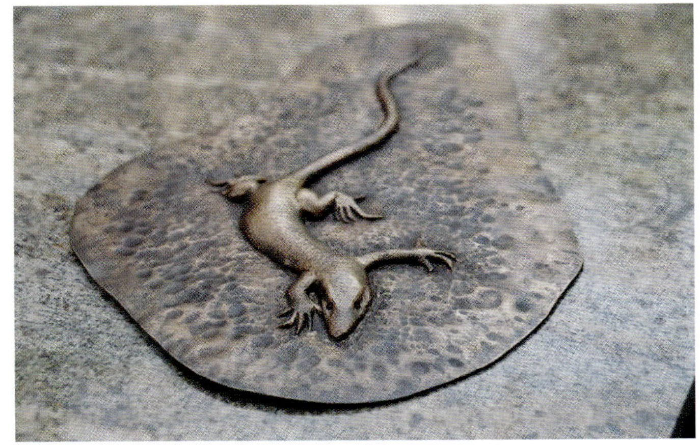

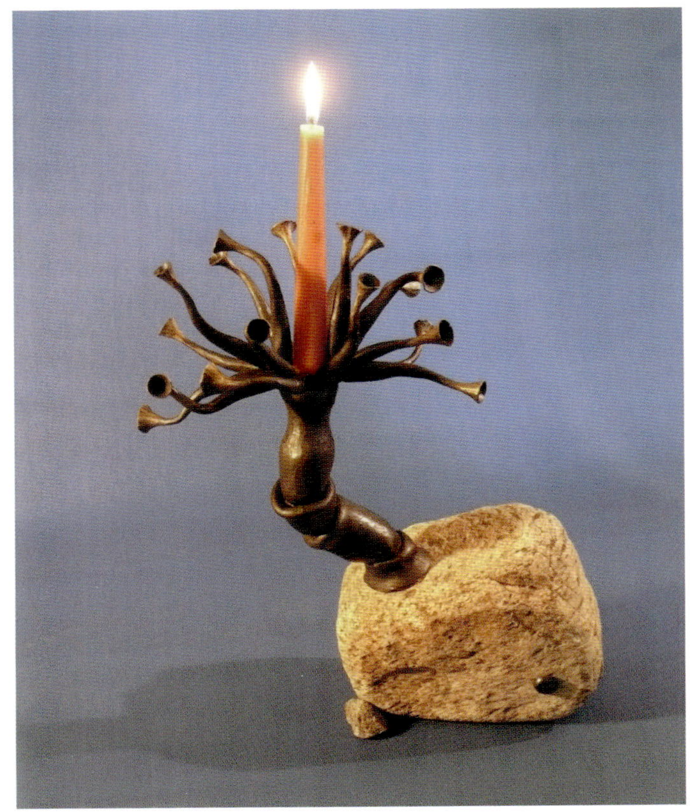

Artist's Gate

Artist's own gate, detail. Steel, glass, pool balls, stone, bronze, copper. *Photo: Stella Kalina*

Lizard

Lizard. Sculpture. Bronze. High relief chasing. Commissioned by the Audubon Center in Debs Park, Los Angeles, California. *Photo: Troy Evans*

Seastick

Seastick. Candlestick. One of a series of underwater-inspired candlesticks using steel tubing and pipe with stone. 16″h x 12″w x 9″d. *Photo: Troy Evans*

Lynda Metcalfe

Brasstown, North Carolina
www.lyndametcalfe.com

ARTIST'S STATEMENT

My personal interests in ironwork are structure, the graphic lines of a piece, and visual rhythm. We can often decode a handmade piece by looking at the joinery, which speaks of a human involvement in the work from start to finish, and it can lead to some innovative and creative solutions. As I am usually forging bar stock, making 3-D lines in space, I pay close attention to the graphic feel of a design. The visual rhythm in a piece can be very formal and progress in a predictable manner, or it can be varied and evolving through the length of a piece so that there is an element of time in taking in the whole of the artwork.

I go in to the workshop and get hot/cold/sweaty/dirty/tired because I enjoy the practical side of making ironwork and the problem-solving that goes along with it. At this stage I am not only executing the signed-off design but I am also making aesthetic judgments about details of form, surface texture, and finish all the way through. I feel lucky that my job enables me to wear so many hats and be involved in all aspects of producing a piece of work.

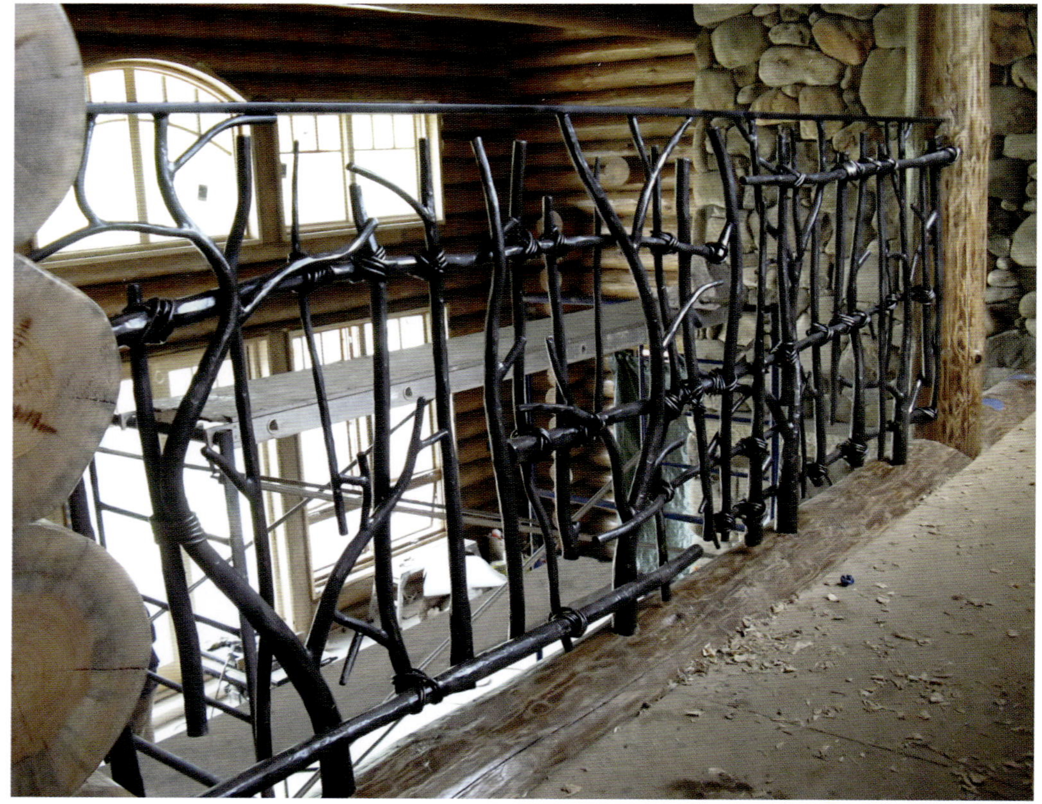

Railings, Log House

The railings made for this large log home were all forged from bar stock to look somewhat like branches in different forms. The balcony railing and stair railings all fastened directly into the wood beneath them and presented particular technical challenges.

The balcony railings were mounted on a single large log that ran the entire length of the balcony and that tapered from one end to the other. The railing's top surface had to remain level so the panels had to graduate in height to accommodate the tapering log surface.

The four flights of stair railings were designed such that each picket was bolted through the open stairs. This created the interesting dichotomy of needing the pickets to look organically forged while the base needed to be precisely perpendicular to the vertical so that it could be drilled and tapped to accept a ½″ bolt.

Laurel and lattice balcony railing. 2010. Forged and fabricated steel.
27′ x 36″ x 6″. *Photo: Lynda Metcalfe*

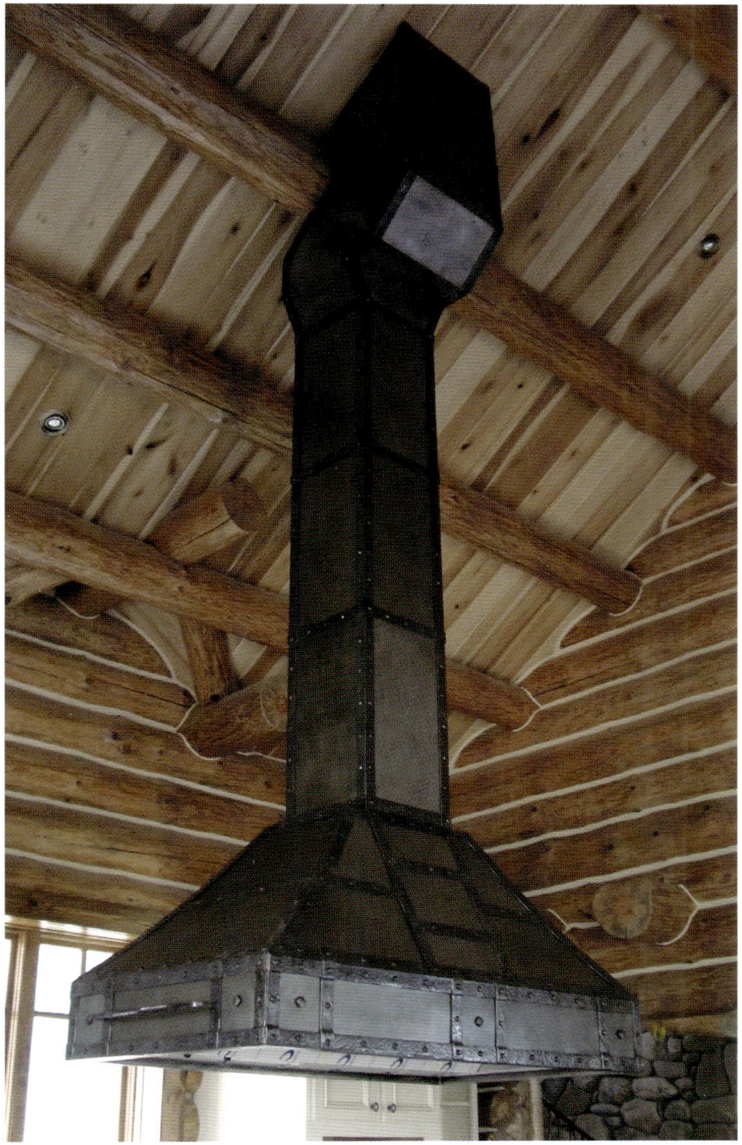

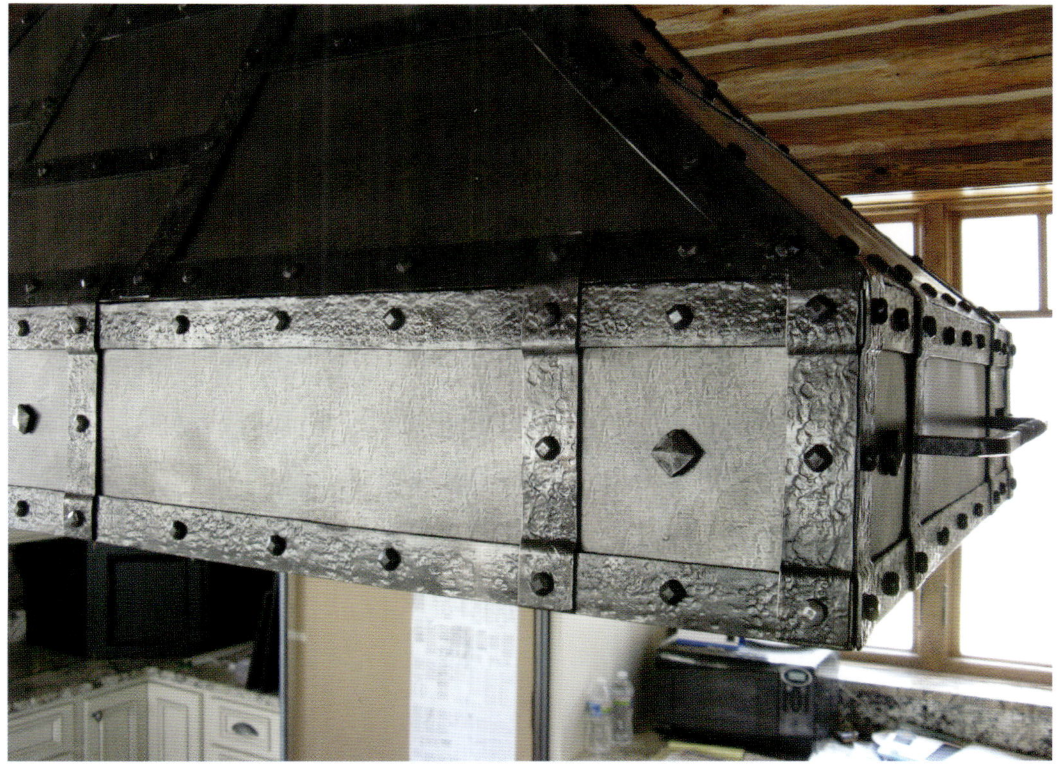

Range Hood

The range hood for the kitchen of the log house was an exciting departure from my usual work with solid bar stock. It was a large, hollow structure to contain the commercial extractor fan unit and cover the ductwork going into the 20′ ceiling. I made a full-size mock-up in cardboard that I mounted on-site, before beginning to work in steel. This gave me a full understanding of the bends in the interior pipe and how to piece together the decorative shroud around the pipe when it was installed.

Range hood. Forged and fabricated steel. 136″ x 56″ x 31″. *Photos: Lynda Metcalfe*

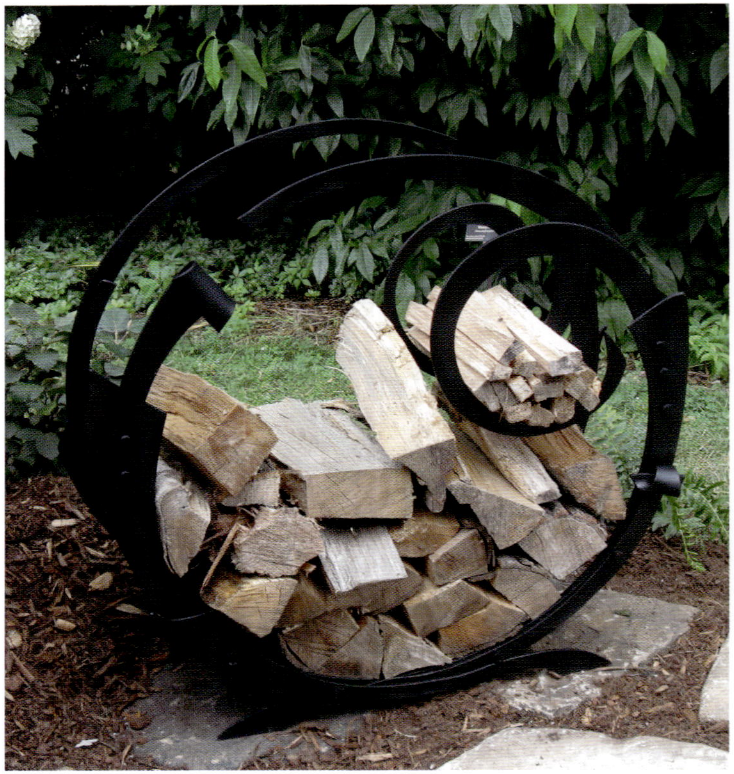

Circular Log Holder

Circular log holder. 2010. Cut, forged, and riveted steel. 32″x 32″x 18″. *Photo: Lynda Metcalfe*

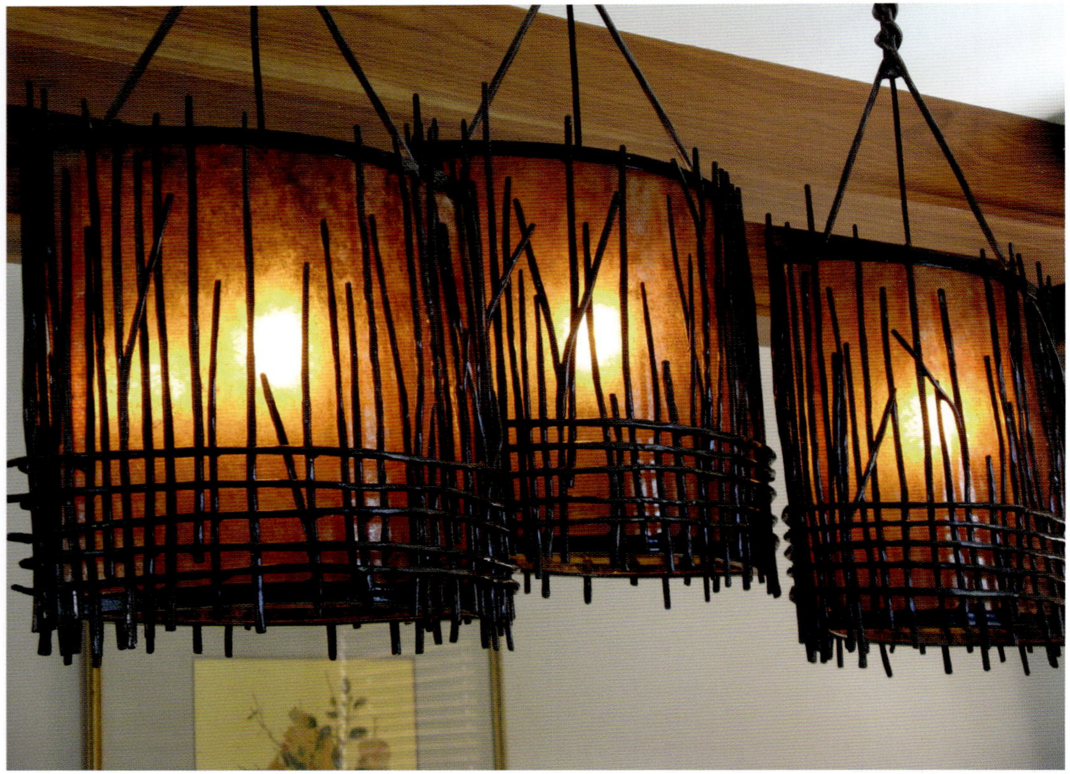

Ceiling Light Fixture

Triple ceiling light fixture. 2012. Forged and riveted steel and mica. 36″ x 30″ x 8″. *Photo: Lynda Metcalfe*

Daniel Miller

Waynesville, North Carolina
millermetalsmith@gmail.com

ARTIST'S STATEMENT

I'm so often astonished, when I look at a finished piece of mine—standing there in its august completeness, smiling—at how haphazard and almost spasmodically reactive my creative process usually is. So often, it is unexpected occurrences in my own life and in the lives of those around me that lead to my choices of the direction I'll follow in a piece, and which then finally result in the forms I'll employ. It leaves me feeling—with a slight grin—rather tangential, a bit like a hired hand, while the piece decides what it wants to be, dictating its form by deciding to embody whichever elements or occurrences in my life apparently catch its fancy.

Thurible for All Souls' Cathedral

This is an incense burner made of wrought iron. The chain is a replica of chain used in the sixth-century Byzantine thuribles found in the collection of the Metropolitan Museum of Art, NYC.

Thurible for All Souls' Cathedral. Incense burner. From the collection of All Souls' Cathedral, Asheville, North Carolina. 37"x 8"x 8".
Photos: Steve Mann

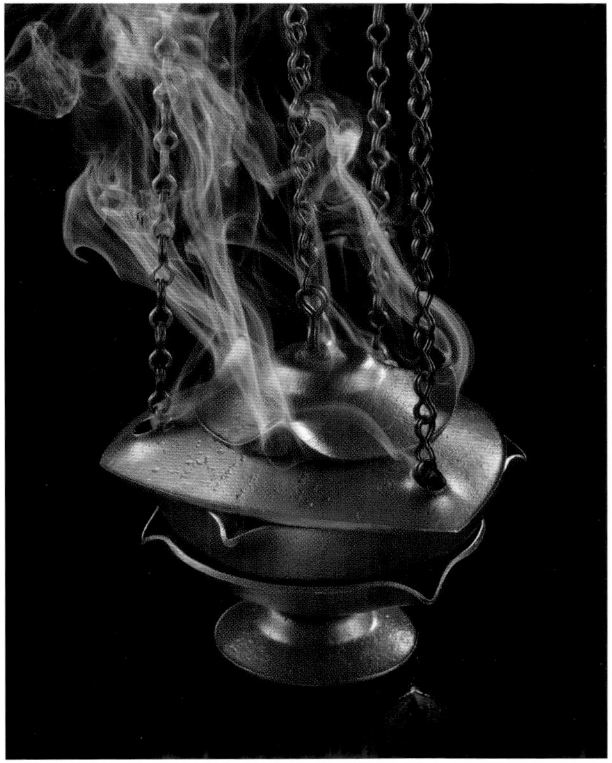

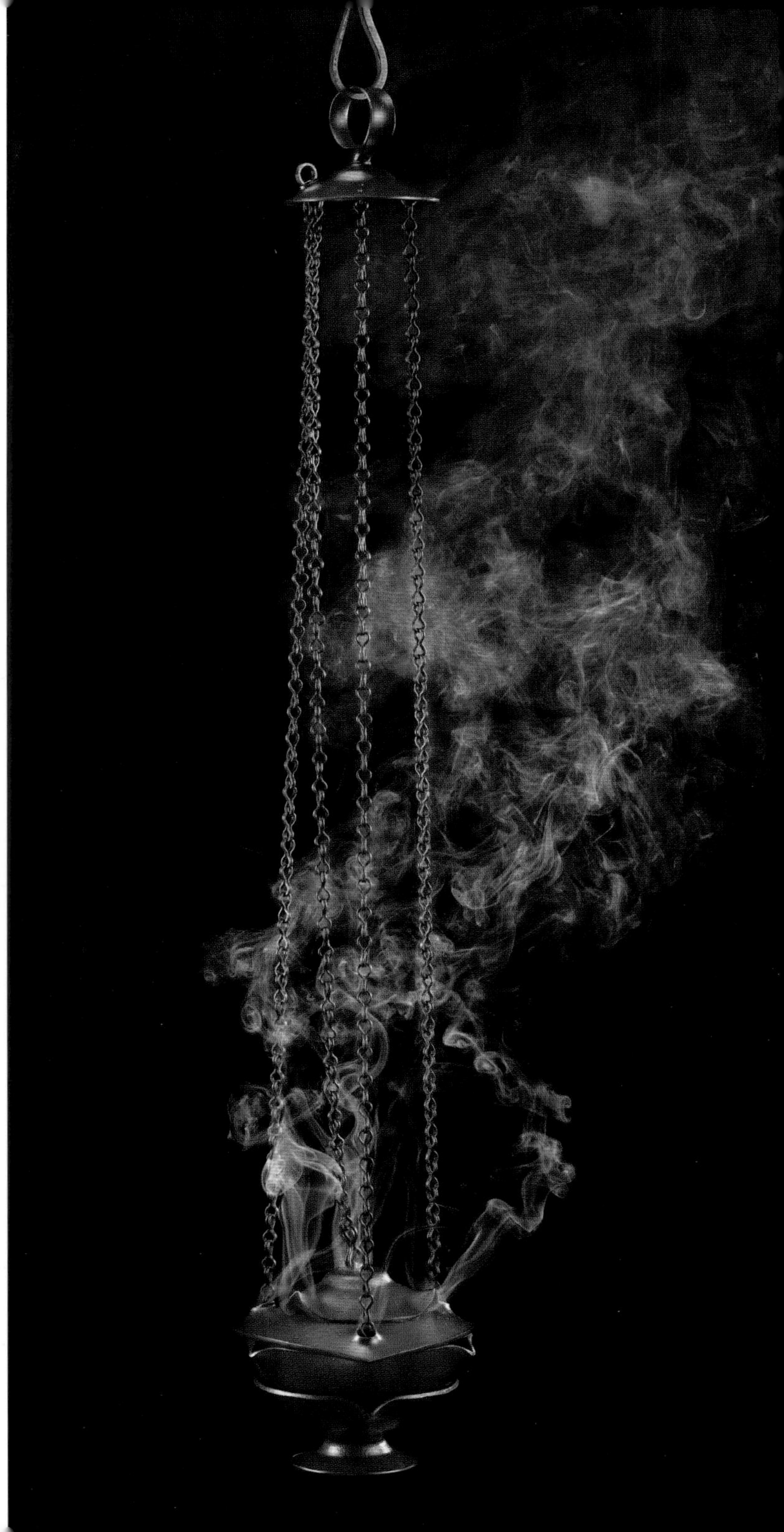

Ways of Eros

This set of fire tools, Ways of Eros, was commissioned by an astonishing friend of mine, who also happens to be a brilliant scholar, writer, and teacher in the fields of medieval drama and the works of Shakespeare. Had she not been working on a manuscript about Shakespeare's "invention of a new 'grammar of forgiveness' " in his last four plays, and had the injection of those deeply human ideas and concerns not resulted in my frenzied study of that manuscript, and of the four plays involved, I surely wouldn't have been driven into the kind of rabid search for new kinds of joints to convey the new means of human connection and the new ways of human relating as explored in these plays.

Another, more specific occurrence in my life that affected this set can be seen in the rather complex form at the top of the stand. That form and that joint came into being in response to an emotional jolt of grief, delivered to me by my grandson, August. Since his family lives next door (lucky me), he immediately got to know and fall in love with an apprentice who worked with me for a few months. August's two-year-old eyes saw in Eric—the tall, strong, blond, handsome visitor—some kind of deity for little boys. When he got word that his blond god would soon have to return to Valhalla,Montana, he couldn't hide his first heartbreak.

The form at the top of these tools was my attempt to portray—to represent—the complex embracing and penetrative nature of a very sweet love. The making of it was my feeble attempt to cut the pain I was feeling, too. It worked a little. Now it stands as a silent, smiling witness.

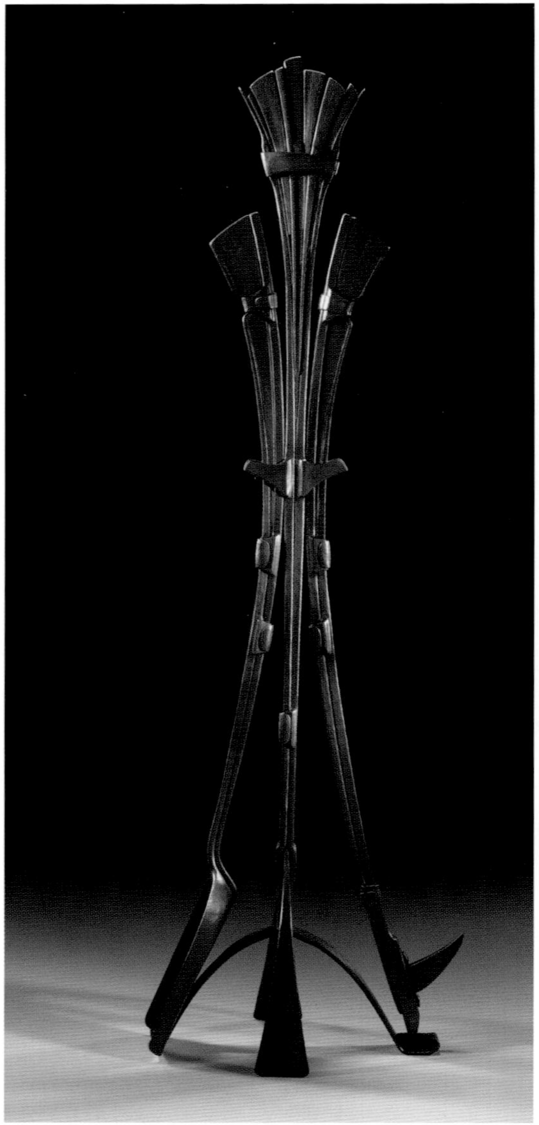

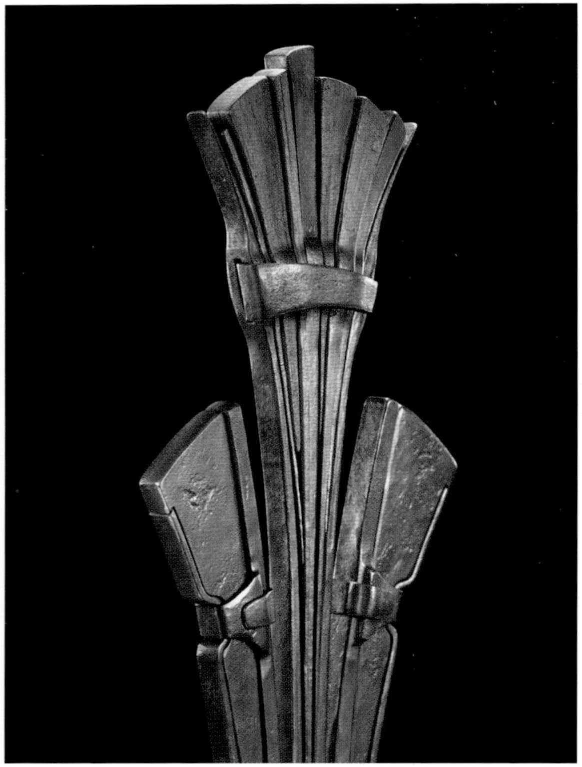

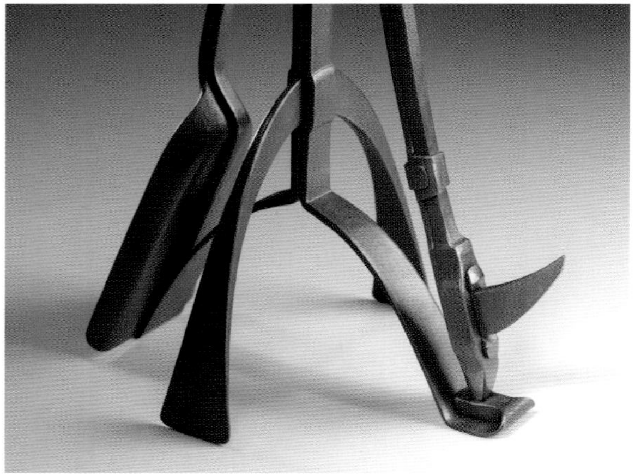

Ways of Eros. Set of wrought iron fire tools. This set of tools employs, in four of its joints, a new approach to joinery, which I call "embracing joints." The material for the "embracing" elements is drawn out of the parent stock, not welded on. The object was to accomplish a joining of two pieces without the introduction of a third element. 38"x 9"x8". *Photo: Steve Mann*

Detail of top joint, referred to as a "piercing embrace." *Photo: Steve Mann*

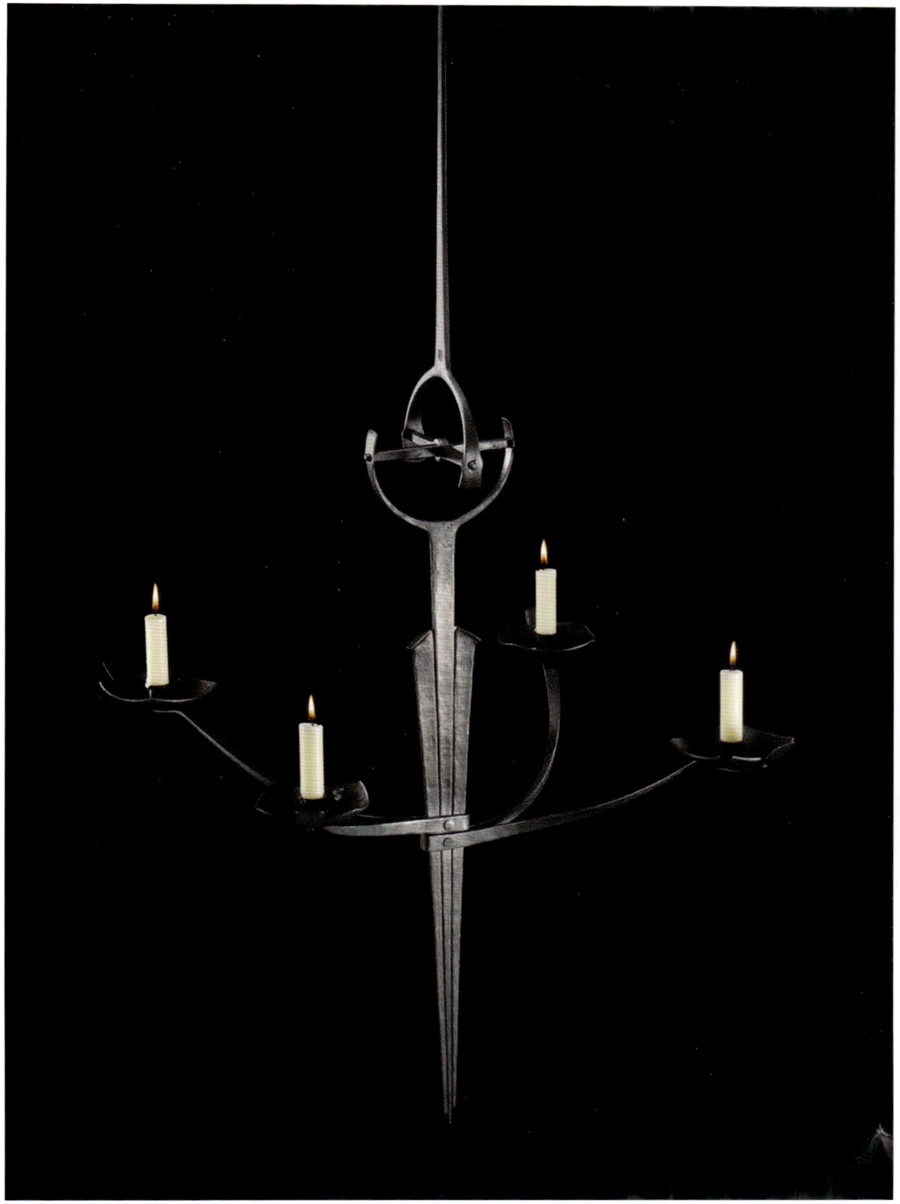

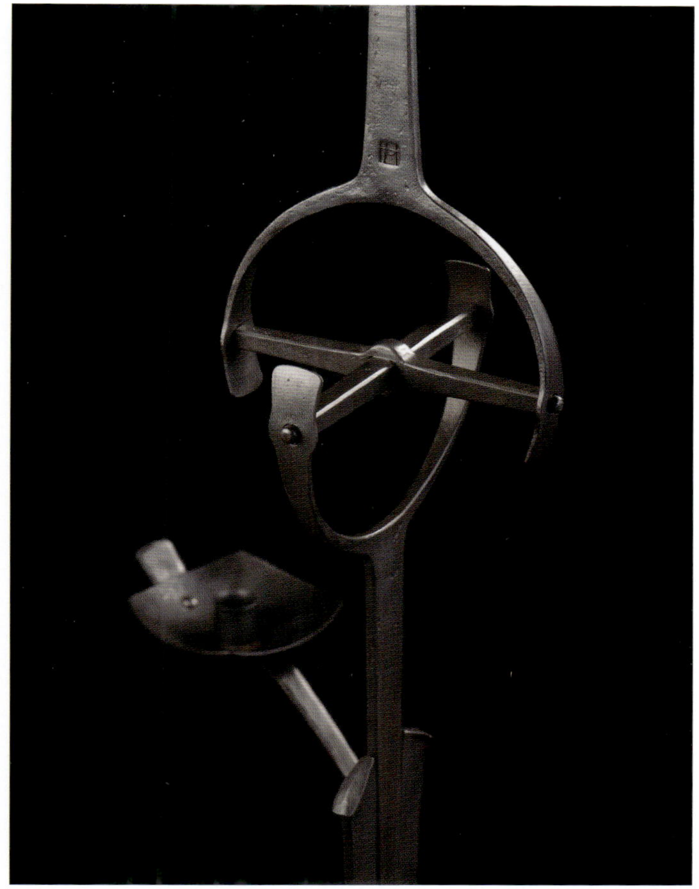

Light from August, bearing Long Awaited Intimations of a Universal Joint. Wrought iron chandelier. From the collection of August Lucca Menck. 38′ x 24″x 22″. *Photos: Steve Mann*

James W. Moseley

Heirloom Hand Forged Design, Campobello, South Carolina
www.heirloomstairandiron.com

ARTIST'S STATEMENT

"Hang around people that are better at it than you are." That was my father's advice when I first got into this craft and decided that I wanted to commit my professional life to it. Being a relatively young artist, I have a deep respect for those who have gone before me, not only because working with metal is challenging, but because of the life discipline required to be very good at it. As a result, I'm always seeking out other artists, getting their opinions, and asking advice. I think it's very important to have a "pay it forward" kind of attitude. Because our culture today pushes young people in a white-collar direction, I try to do all I can when someone younger than me expresses an interest in doing what I do.

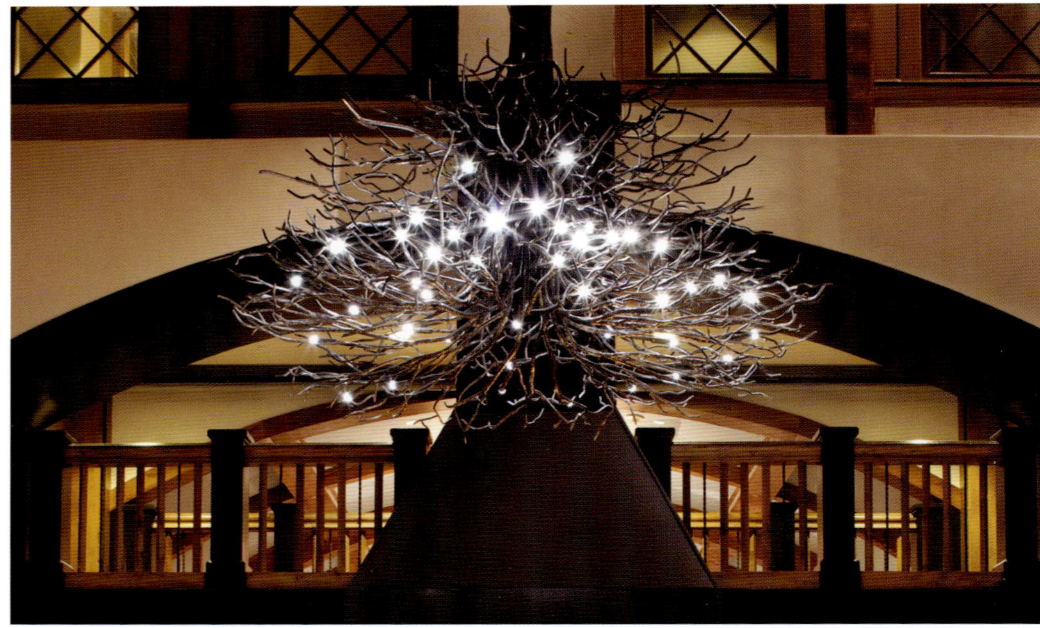

Sebastian Hotel lobby chandelier. 2011. Iron. Hand forged. Ski lodge, Vail, Colorado. 92" diameter.

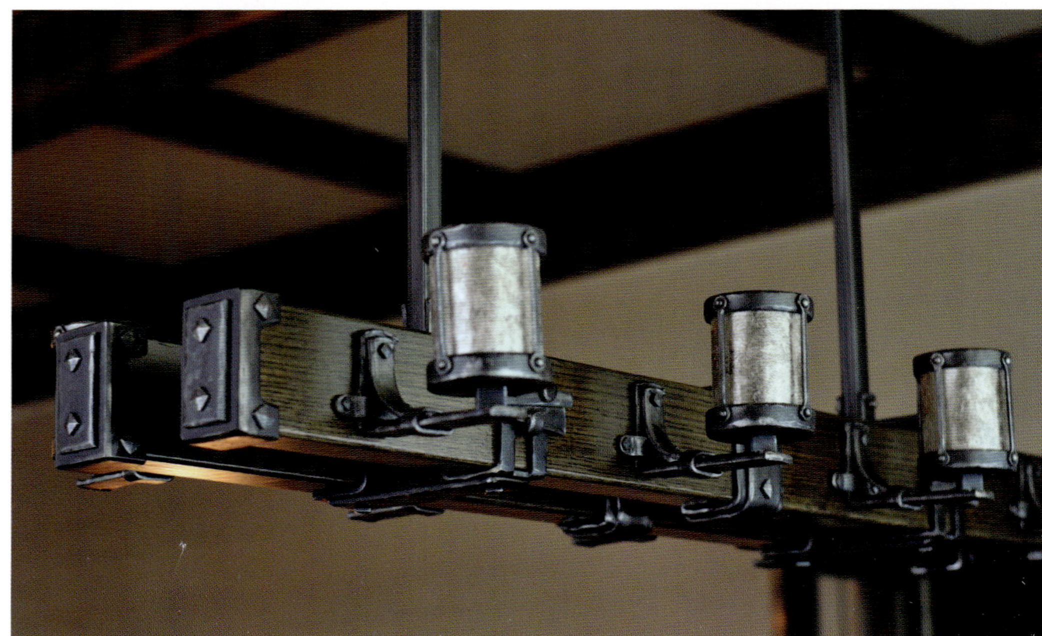

Dining light. Residential hanging light fixture. 2012. Iron and wood. Hand forged. 18" x 54".

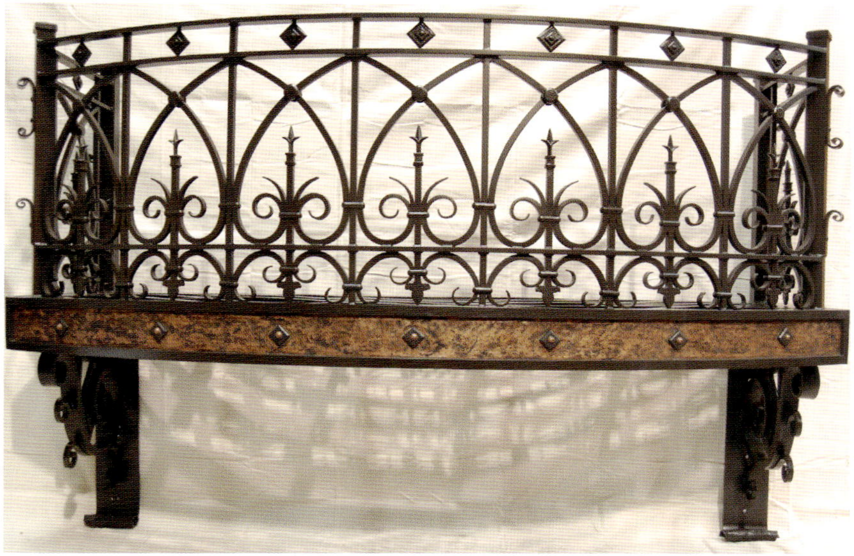

Chicago balcony. 2011. Iron and copper. Fabricated and hand forged. Private residence. 8′l x 3′w.

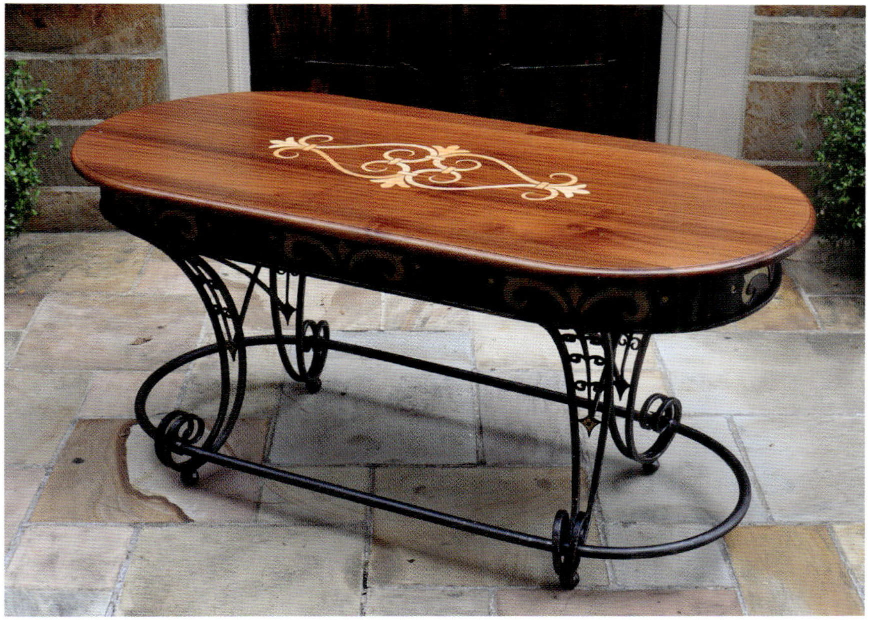

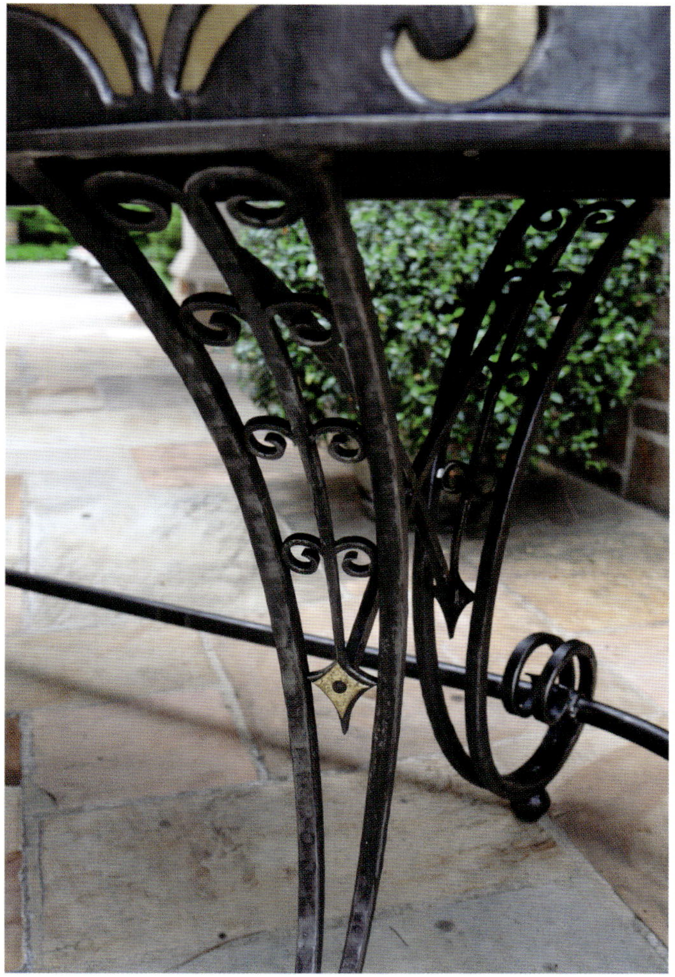

Wine-tasting table. 2012. Iron and wood. Hand forged. Private residence. 72″ x 42″.

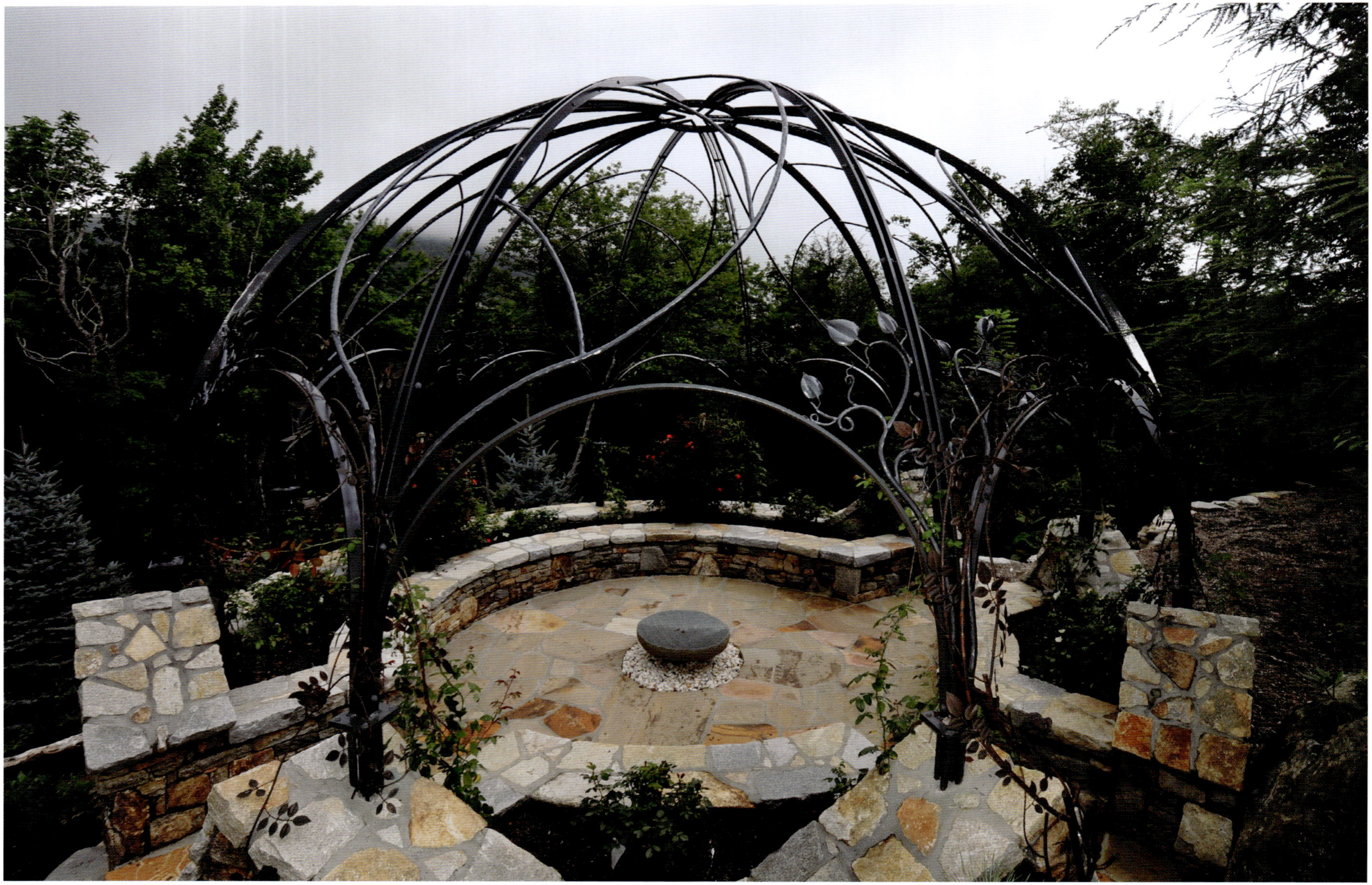

Rosarium. Garden gazebo. 2011. Aluminum and copper. Fabricated and hand forged. 24′ diameter.

Suraiya Murray

Seguin, Texas

ARTIST'S STATEMENT

Being a gardener most of my life, I began learning traditional blacksmithing techniques in 1999 so that I could create cool trellises and functional garden bling in my own, funky style, to add character to my garden. I found that I loved the art, the creative outlet, and the labor of blacksmithing as much as I loved gardening. I built a shop, retired from my "day job," and now I spend my time as a working blacksmith. I use traditional joinery and forging techniques in combination with more contemporary wraps and forms to add life, movement, and attitude to my pieces. I often decorate even small rivets to add little surprises or incorporate tendrils and swirly shapes for movement and to add life to the metal. It is amazing how something so rigid can become fluid and lifelike. Although I am not able to spend as much time as I would like creating things for my own garden now, I love being able to work on projects that add my character to other people's homes and outdoor spaces.

Garden Gate

I created this mild steel gate to match a trellis that I made for a private garden in 2010. The space between limestone garden walls was approximately 71", filled by two 10½"w x 49½"h panels and the 42" w x 51¾"h gate, supported by 2" square pipe. Hand forged rivets were used to secure all pieces at outside joints and wraps secured all interior joints. Corner wraps connecting horizontal to vertical exterior joints keep the gate and panels square. Tendrils of ½" round wander along the top of the gate and they include several steel, ball-mill balls. The gate is closed using a cannonball closer attached between tendrils on the gate and tendrils on a separate post. The gate is intended to rust naturally.

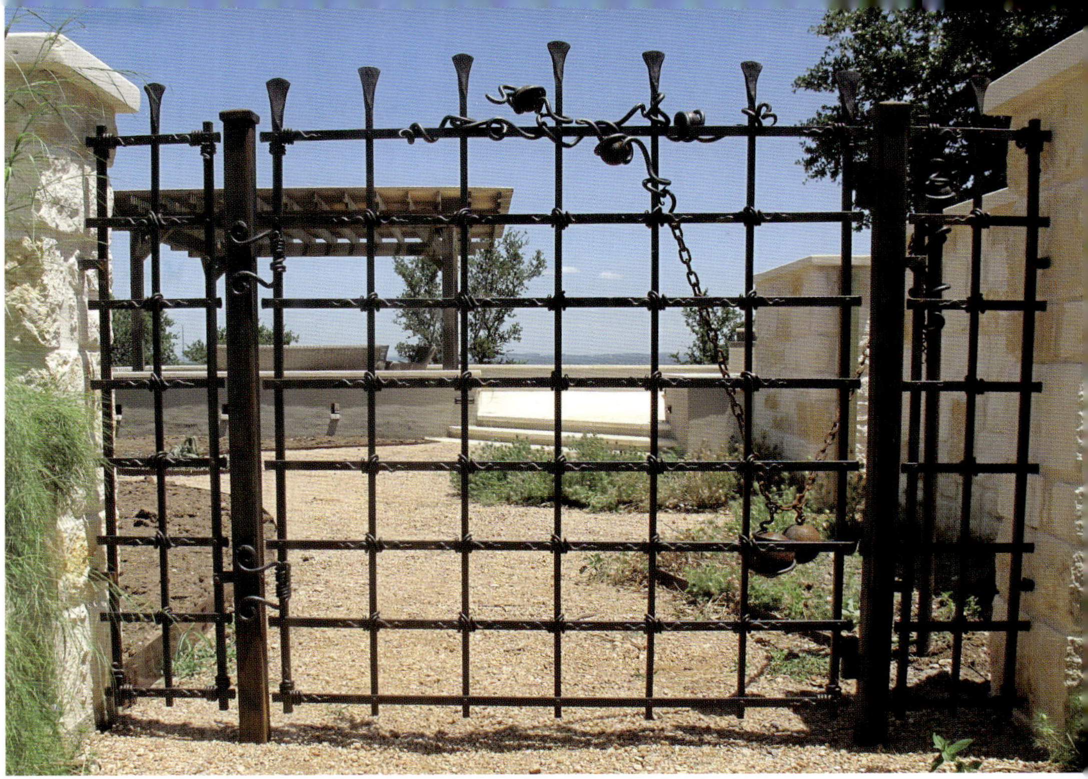

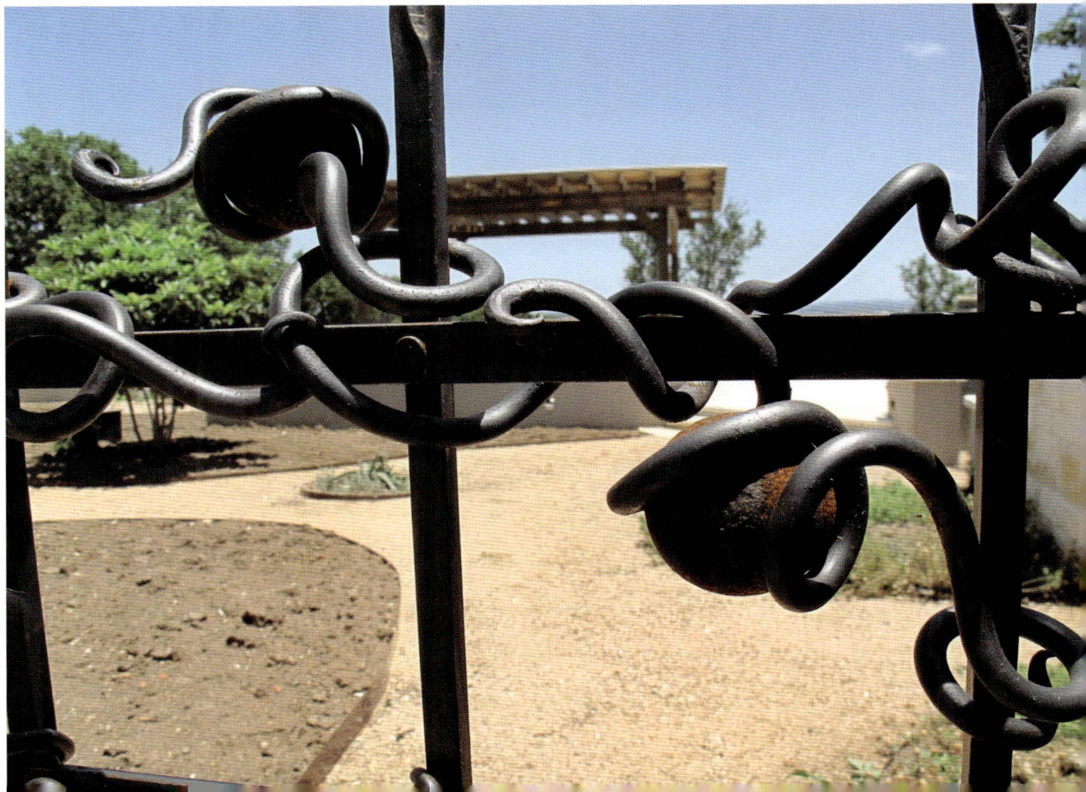

Garden gate. 2013. Hand forged, riveted, and wrapped. Private residence. 71"w x 51¾"h.
Photos: Suraiya Murray

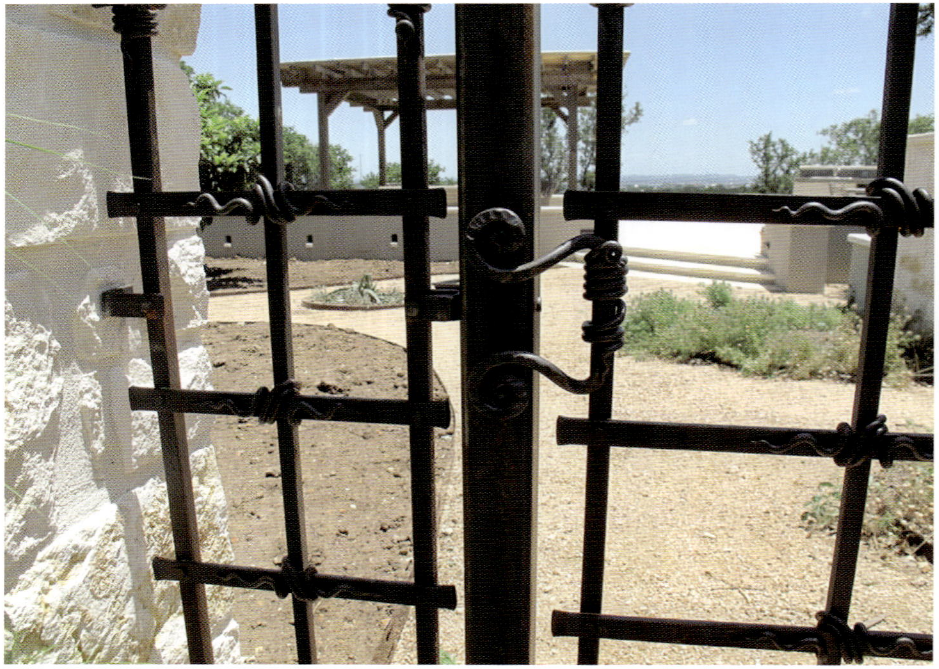

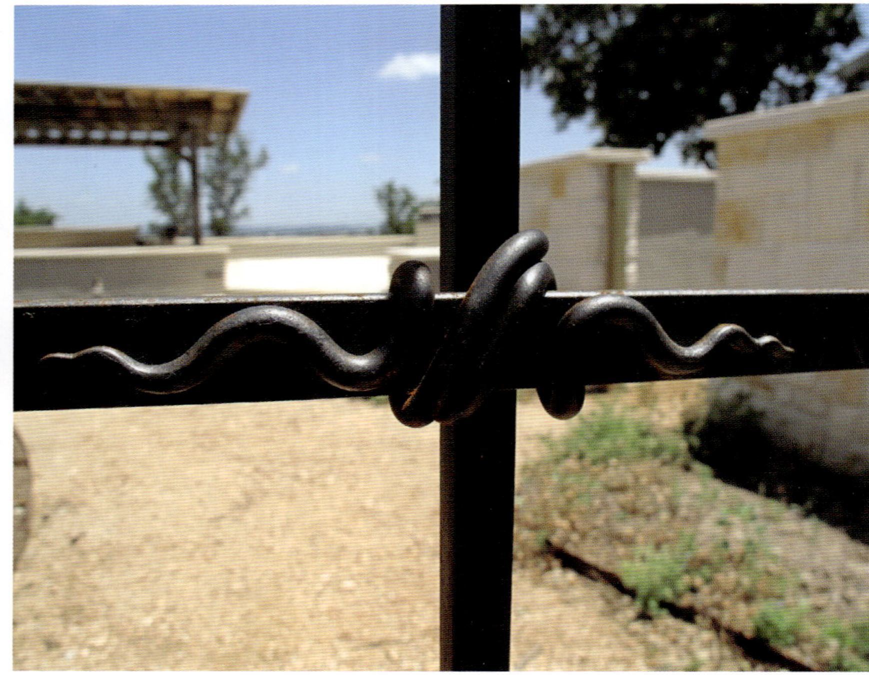

Garden gate. 2013. Hand forged, riveted, and wrapped.
Private residence. 71"w x 51¾"h. *Photos: Suraiya Murray*

Brad Nichols

La Crosse, Wisconsin
bnichols@uwlax.edu

ARTIST'S STATEMENT

A blacksmith needs to explore the boundaries of the craft in order to forge new processes. These discoveries then become part of the contemporary dialogue with tradition. The promotion of these new approaches asks tradition to embrace innovations. In time, applying novel approaches can become part of the larger body of traditions allowing the craft to evolve.

Alloying both traditional and contemporary techniques allows me to pursue a modeling process using forged and welded steel. The forged and fabricated objects created in this process reveal the fluid nature of steel when manipulated with a blacksmith's expertise and finesse. Works in steel narrate my ideas and demonstrate my love of the craft. The combination of narration and craft engage the audience in a playful, visual dialogue. This fluid dynamic requires extraordinary effort and skill, due to the nature of my medium. Steel's inherent characteristics demand a forceful, calculated act in order to achieve a desired form. Every mark created by a hammer, grinder, file, or flame demonstrates evidence of a labor-intensive process. I permanently alter this rigid material into animated objects to change the viewer's experience of steel's blue-collar pedigree.

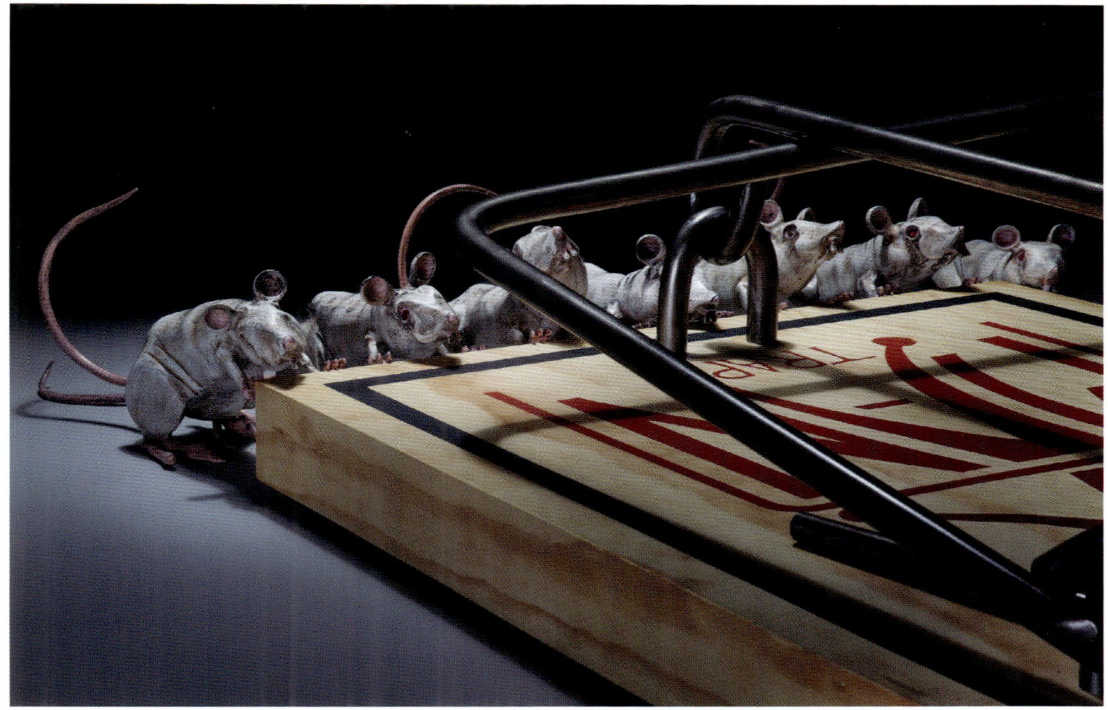

Wrath of the Rodents. Sculpture. 2012. Forged and fabricated steel, wood, paint. 76" x 33" x 15½". *Photo: Regan Photography*

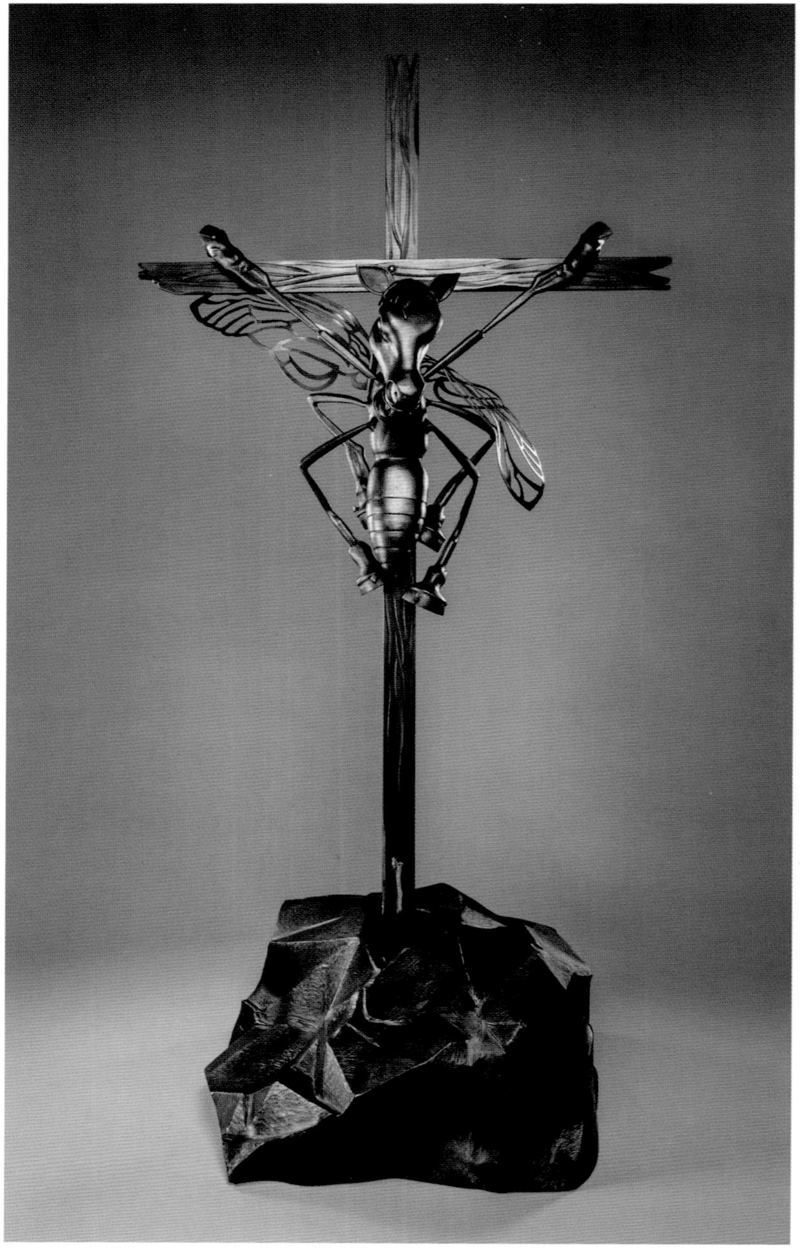

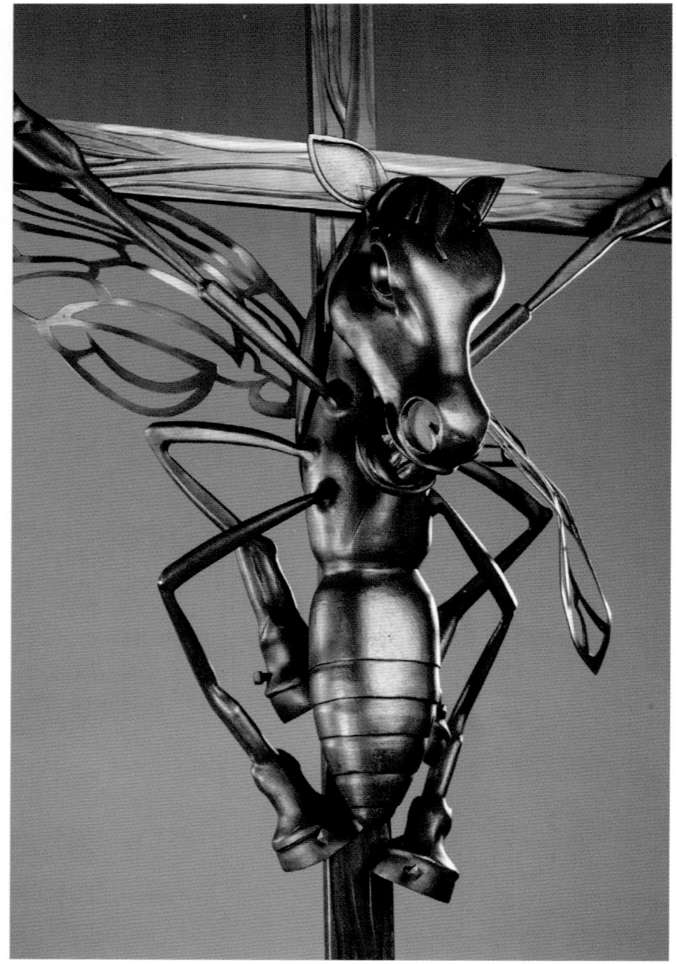

Crucifixion of the Horsefly. Sculpture. 2012.
Forged and fabricated steel, wood, paint. 81" x 28" x 32".
Photo: Regan Photography

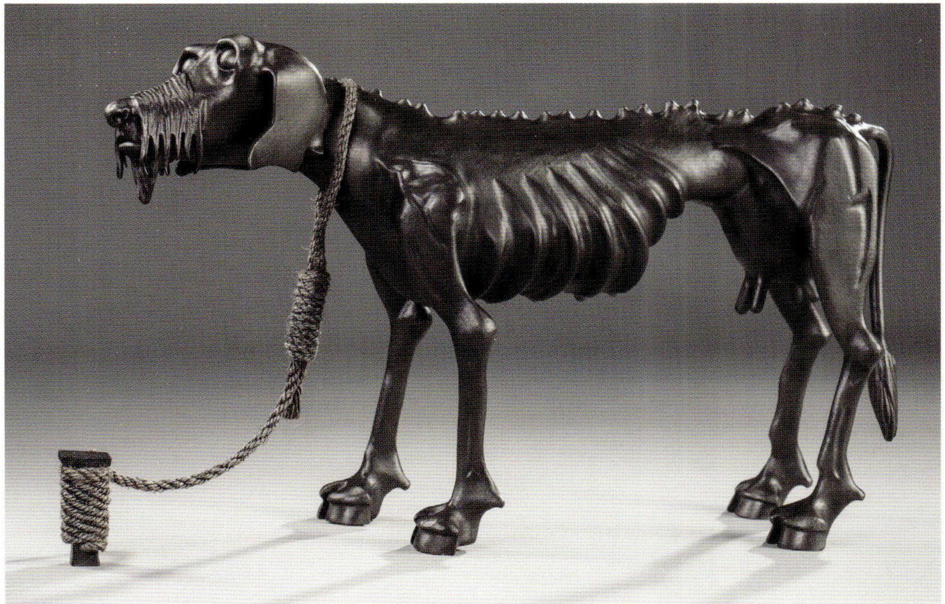

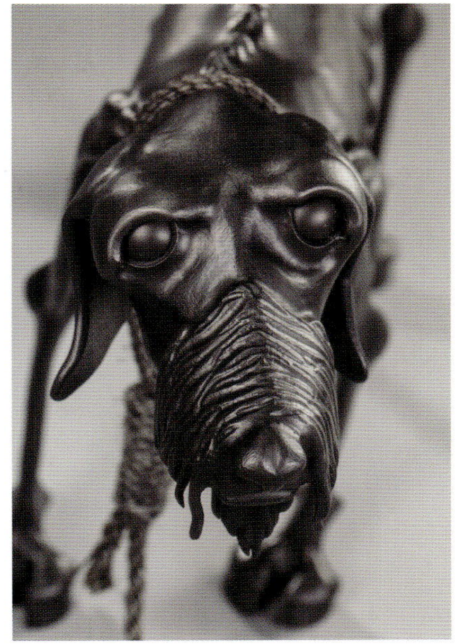

Forgotten Pet. 2012. Sculpture. Forged and fabricated steel, rope. 16" x 9" x 29". *Photo: Regan Photography*

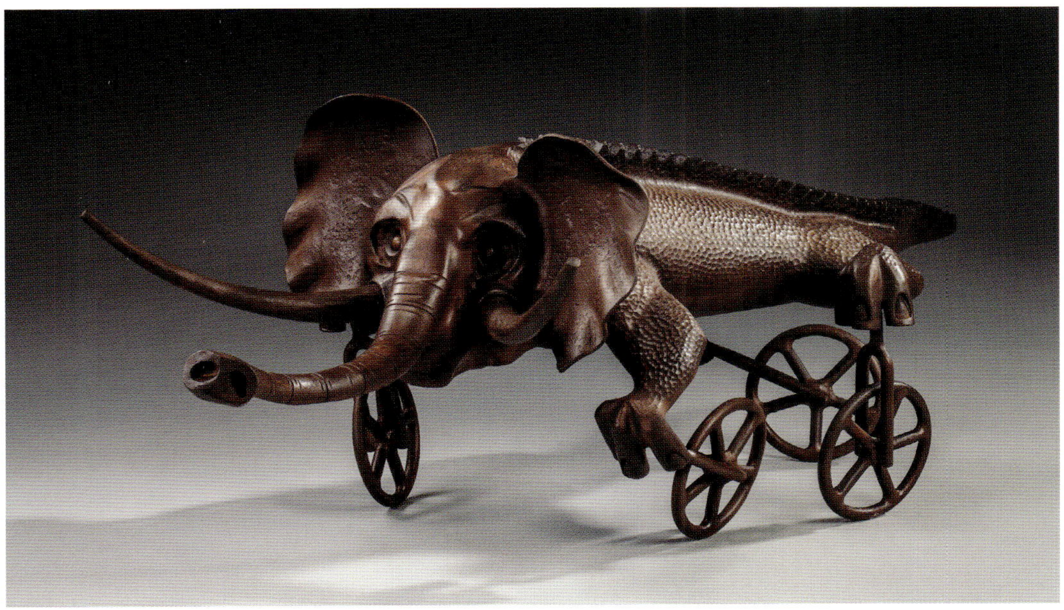

Circus Freak. Sculpture. 2012. Forged and fabricated steel. 12" x 16" x 34". *Photo: Regan Photography*

Zachary Noble

Bakersville, North Carolina
www.zacknoble.com

ARTIST'S STATEMENT

My current work involves stretching and expanding on traditional techniques in an effort to create modern designs with a focus on craftsmanship. I make sculptural, functional, and architectural work and enjoy challenging myself with each new project. I grew up in Brooklyn, New York, where I was educated in a number of things, including graffiti writing, photography, poetry, film making, and just looking. I was awarded a Core Fellowship for two years at the Penland School of Crafts in Penland, North Carolina. I also worked in Great Britain with Brian Russell and with Chris Topp of the Real Wrought Iron Company. My home is in Bakersville, North Carolina, where I maintain my workshop and live with my wife, Darrah, and our daughter, Celia Sky.

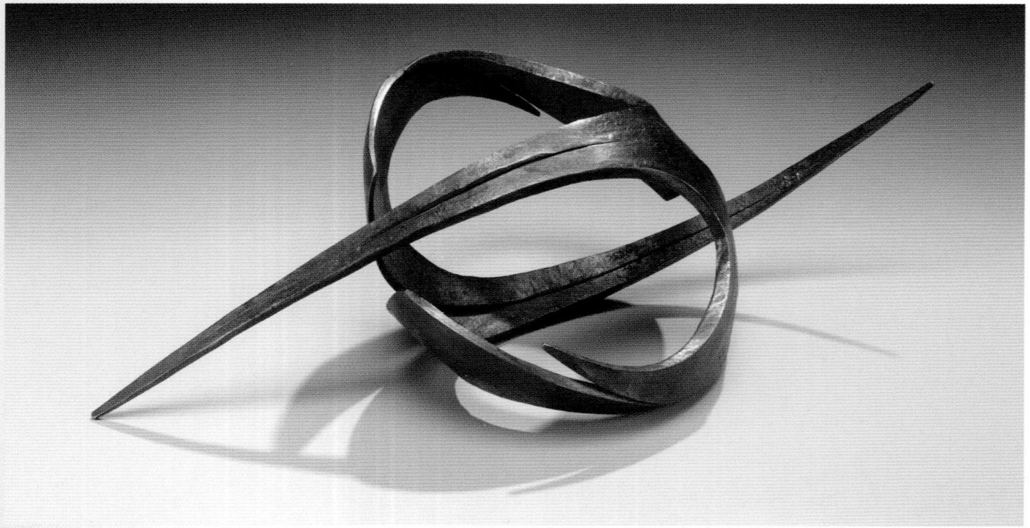

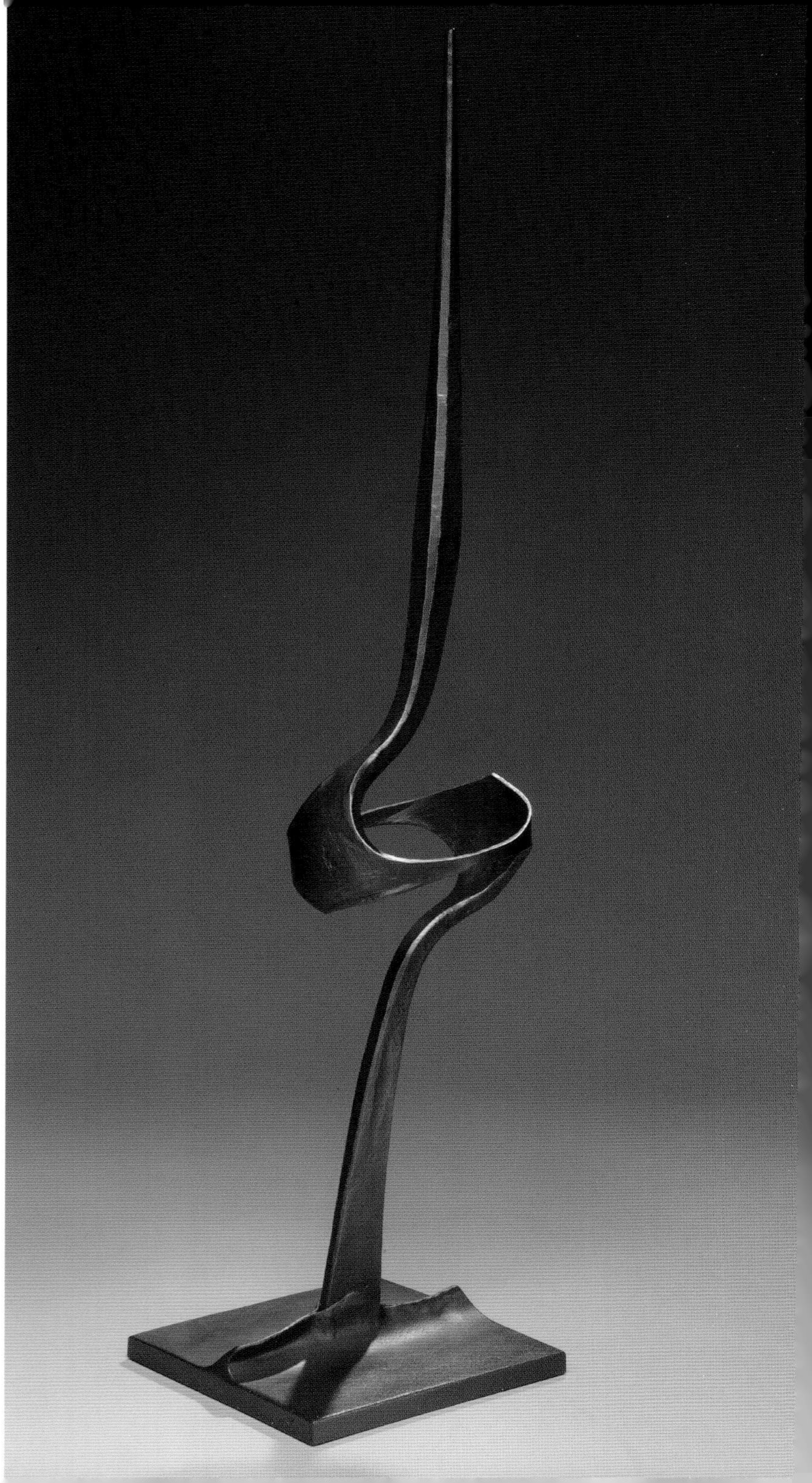

A Mating, Aloft

A Mating and *Aloft* are both from a series of work based on solid forms around a central space: Using large and small forged elements to create a unique negative space, while keeping the forged elements interesting as well, the series is an on-going exploration.

A Mating. Sculpture. 2012. Forged iron. 12″ x 8″ x 10″. *Photo: Tim Barnwell*

Aloft. Sculpture. 2012. Forged iron. 12″ x 40″ x 12″. *Photo: Tim Barnwell*

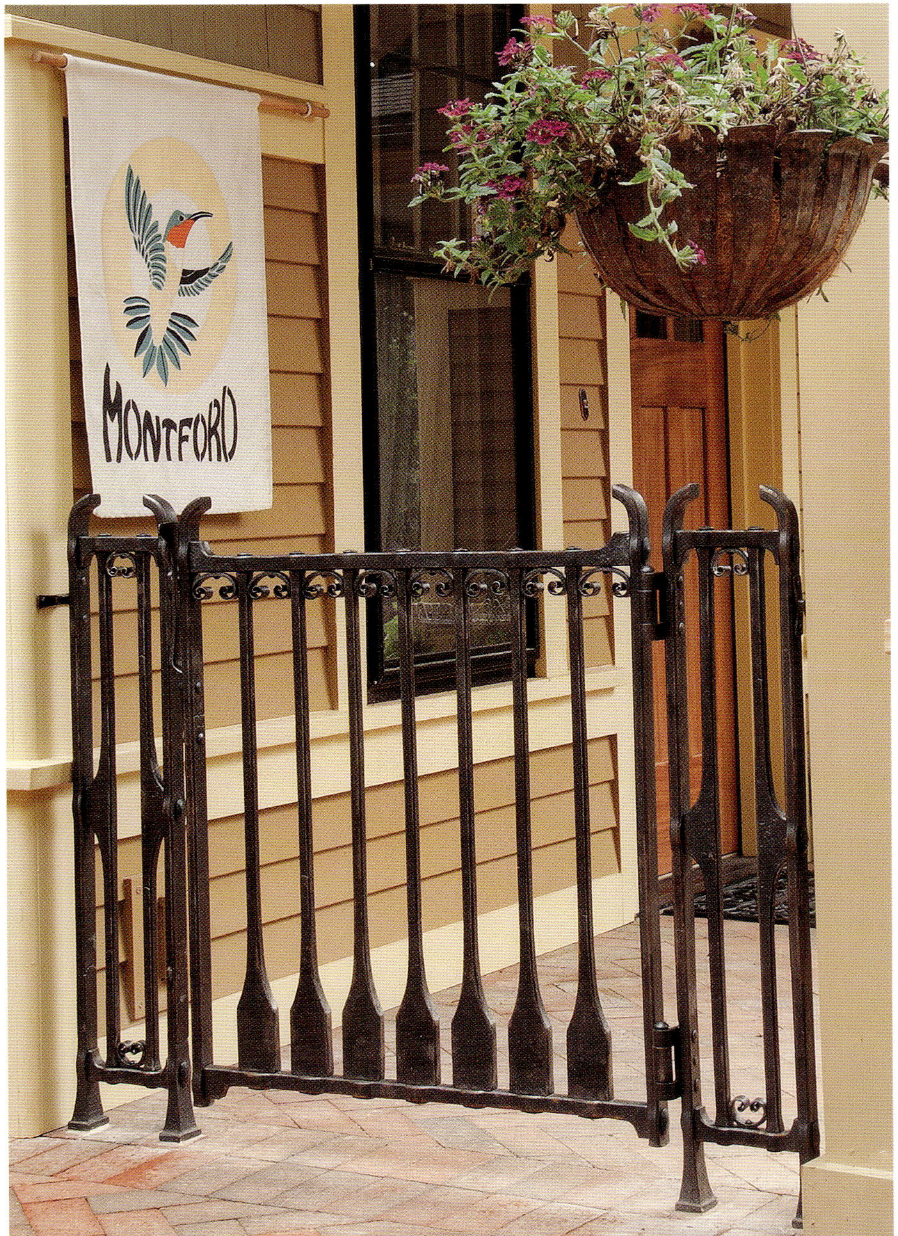

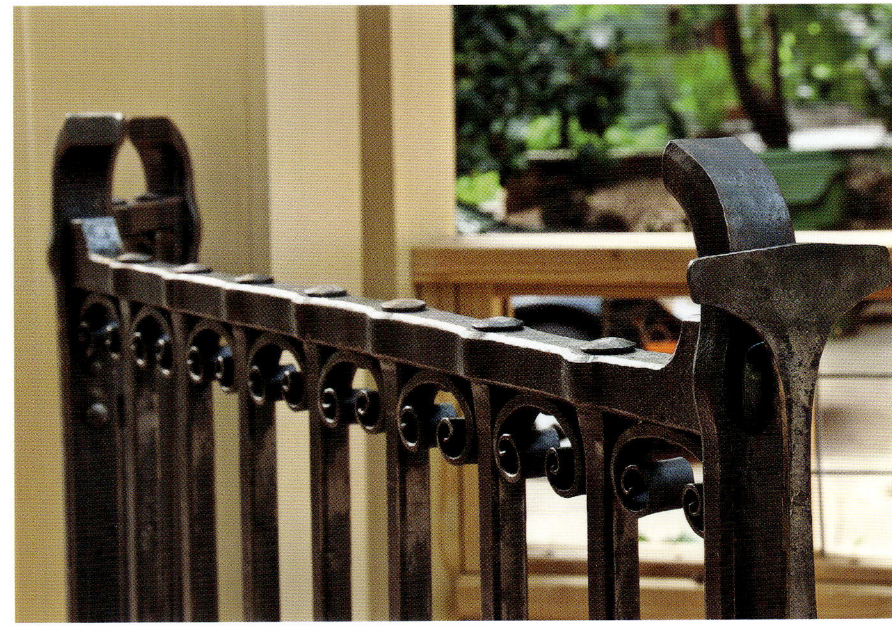

Montford Gate

This gate was commissioned by a couple who renovated a beautiful, Victorian home in the Montford neighborhood of Asheville, North Carolina. To make the project more interesting, I used only traditional techniques to create the gate. All the vertical bars have several forge welds on them, and all the tenons were fitted hot,with no help from a grinder or welder.

Montford gate. 2010. Forged iron. 42"h x 54"w x 3"d. *Photos: Mary Vogel*

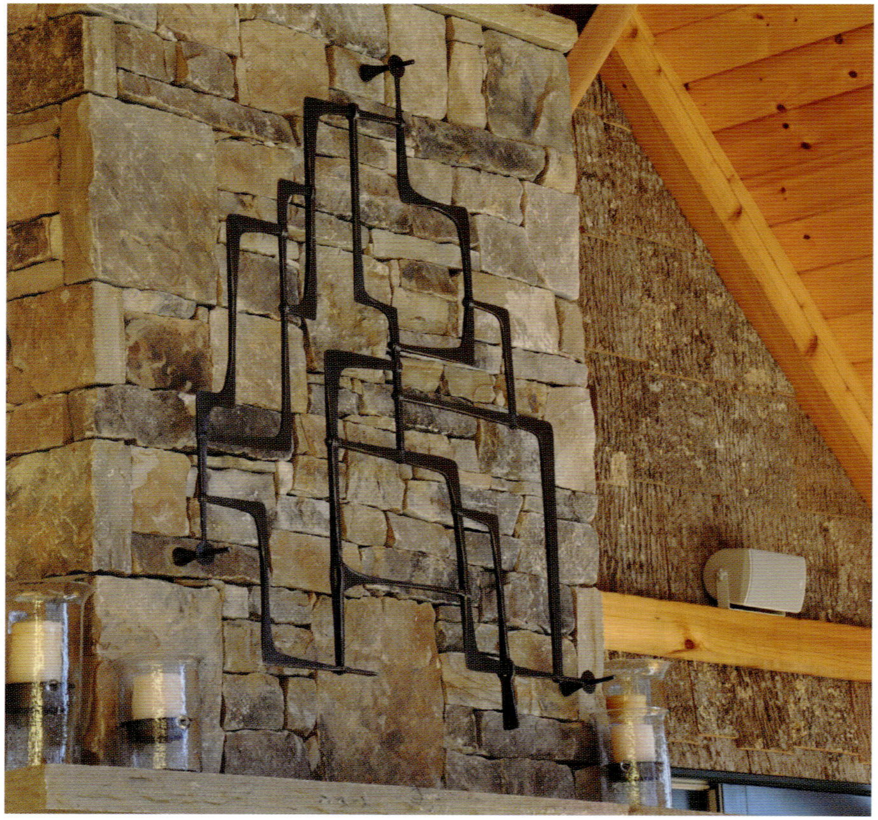

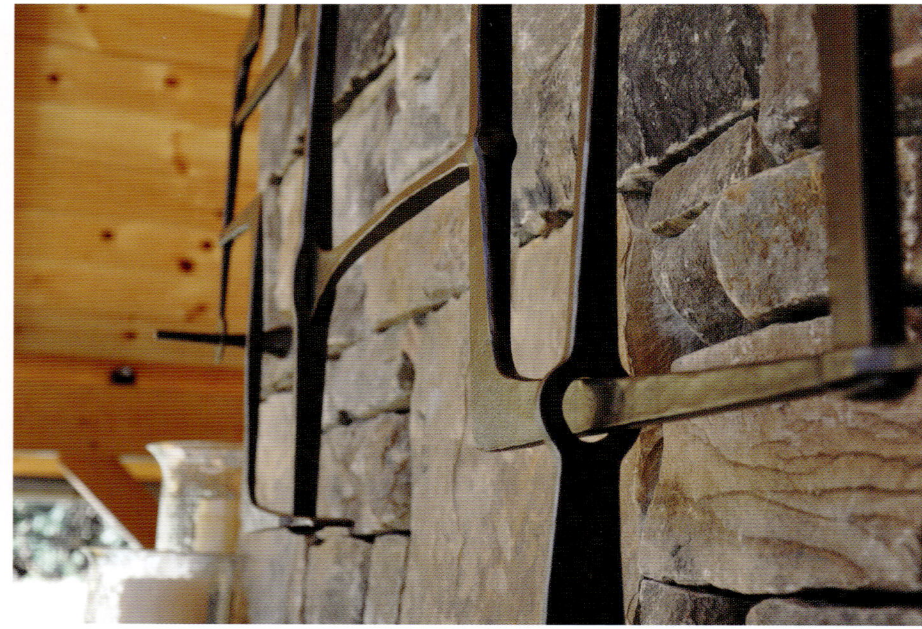

Painting #6

This piece was made for some clients who like my sculptural wall pieces. I started making pieces for the wall and calling them paintings because the linear form resembles a brush stroke, if you will. I love the look of traditional joinery in iron work, but it seems to me that only metalsmiths notice this joinery. So, with these works, I decided to put the work on the wall as you would a painting. Hopefully, the beauty of the forged line will be noticed.

Painting #6. Wall art. 2012. Forged iron. 46″ x 78″ x 5″.
Photos: Zachary Noble

David W. Osmundsen

Arrowhead Forge, Buffalo, Wyoming
www.arrowheadforge.com

ARTIST'S STATEMENT

The process of creating functional art through the confluence of earth, fire, and water has been a passion of mine since the 1970s. The fulfillment of shaping hot iron, with direct and deliberate hammer blows, leads to a desire to create fresh designs using new techniques that further challenge me. My goal is not to duplicate nature, but to borrow designs from the environment and incorporate them into functional iron objects. I never tire of this process.

My life as a blacksmith has shifted from working solely as a commissioned artist to a blacksmithing instructor. Mentoring students from all parts of America and Canada has pushed me to further explore and perfect the techniques I have been using over the years.

As an artist-blacksmith living at the base of Wyoming's Bighorn Mountains, I feel fortunate to be able to work with my own designs—influenced by nature and the traditions of my craft—and to possess the ability to pass the craft on to others.

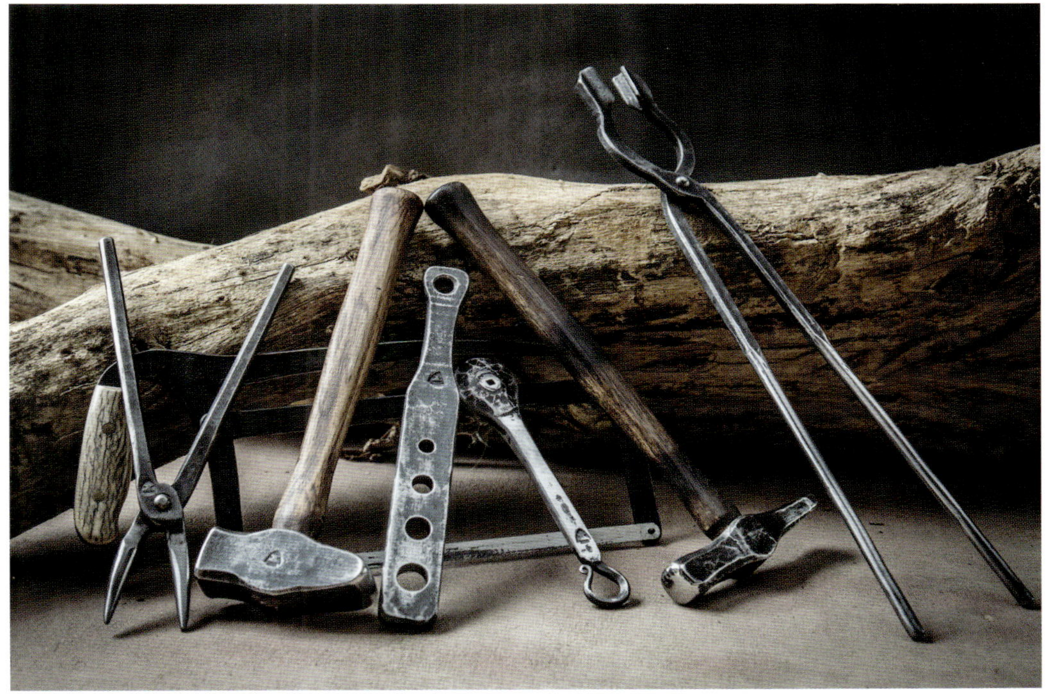

Forged Tools

The blacksmithing trade is unique from other trades in that blacksmiths can make their own tools as well as the metal tools for other craftsmen. Having the knowledge and skill to make one's own tools allows the blacksmith to make a tool used to make yet another tool. For example, a slot punch and eye drift have to be made first in order to punch and drift the handle eye when making a hammer head. This concept has inspired me to make many of my own tools that are used in the forge shop. Pictured are (left to right), hack saw, scroll tongs, cross pein hammer, bolster block, nail header, leafing hammer, and bolt tongs.

Forged tools. Mild steel, medium carbon steel, hickory, and deer antler. Wax finish. Lengths of tools vary from 10" to 20". *Photos: Lanna Wing Photography*

Church Railing

Father Pete, of the local Catholic church, approached me with a vision of inspiring the parishioners by adding four railings with a communion theme to the entrance of the church. The wheat and grape design was decided upon with installation to be complete before the steps were made icy with the onset of winter. My desire was to use traditional joinery, mortise, and tenon joints, but to stay within budget. The main construction was MIG welded with all welds ground and heated to add scale for coloring. Another goal was to design railings that looked as if they had been installed during the original, 1950s construction of the church.

After many attempts at fabricating different wheat facsimiles without success, I implemented a simpler, more traditional approach. Square bar stock was tapered on one end and flattened to spread the wheat head. The balance of the bar was drawn out to create the narrow round stem. Then the detail on the wheat head was hot cut.

Church railing. One of four railings. Mild steel. Linseed/wax finish. 2′ 10″h x 6′l. *Photos: Lanna Wing Photography*

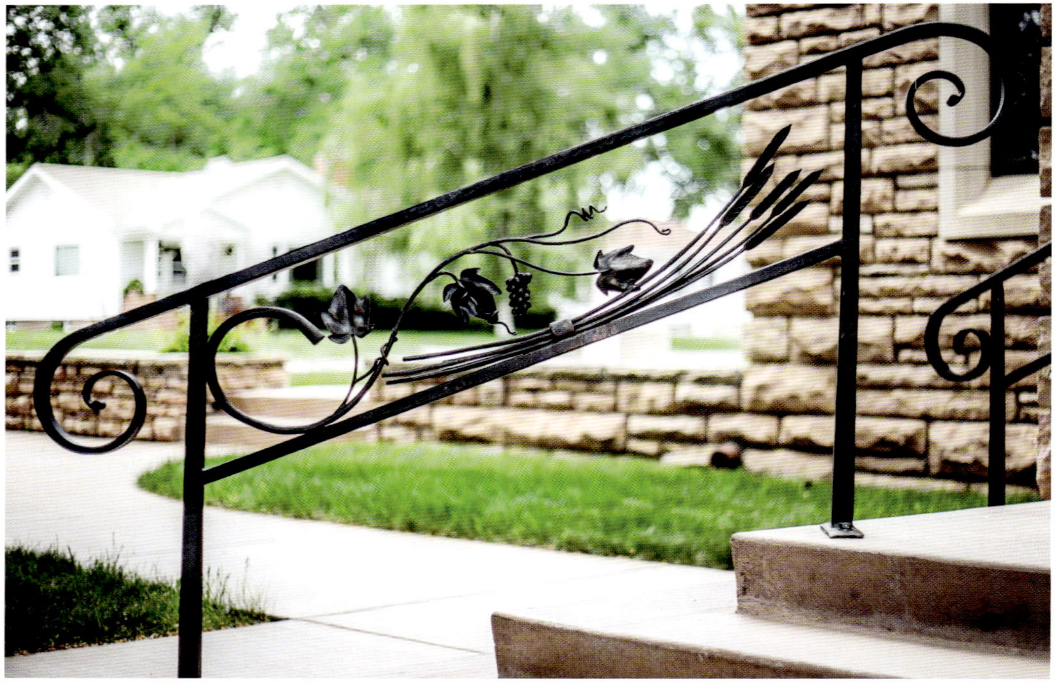

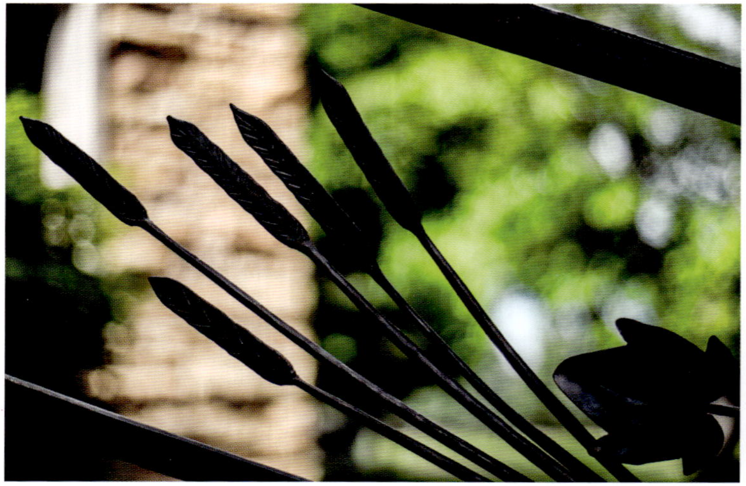

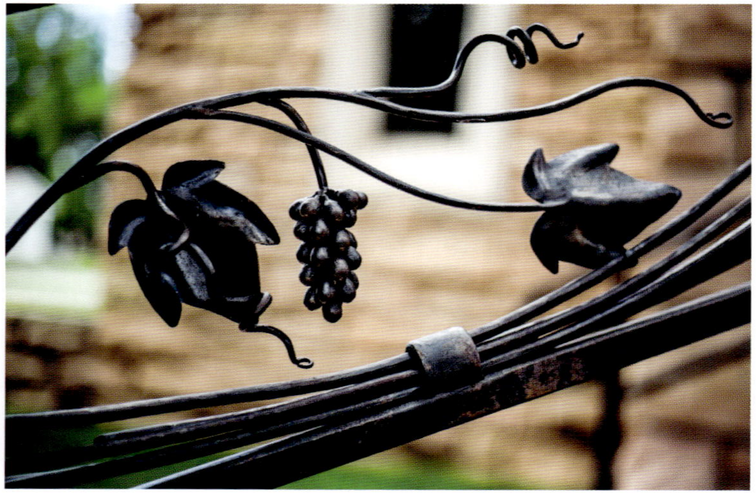

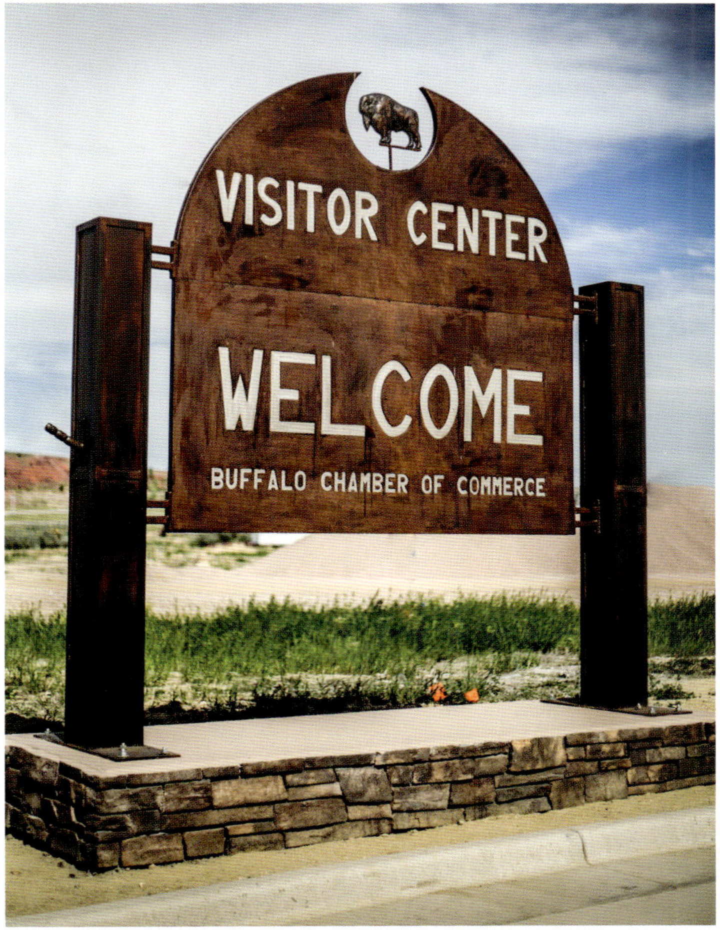

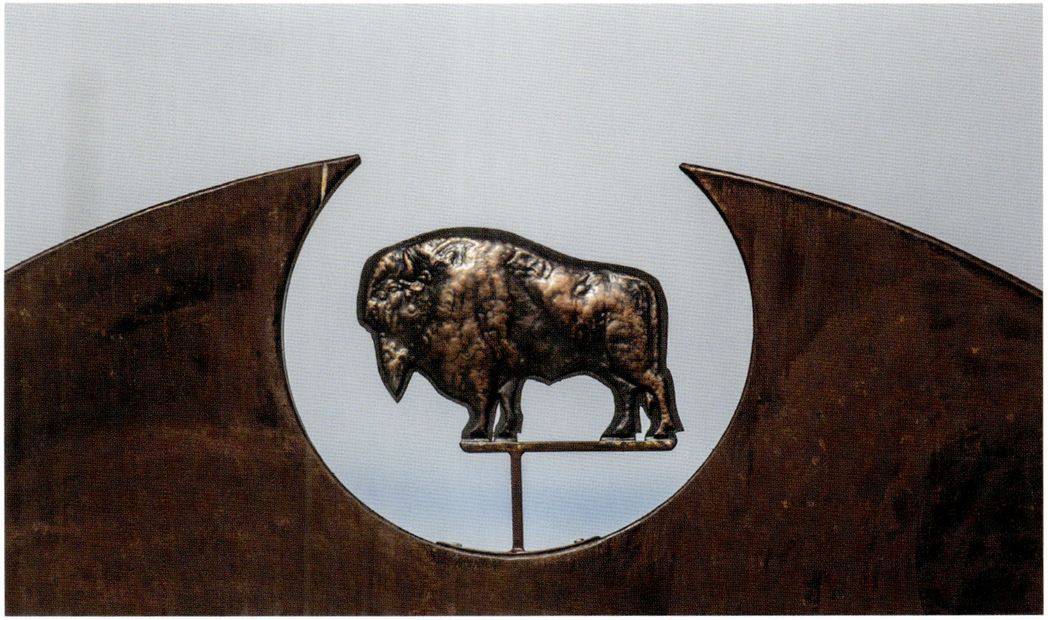

Visitor Center Sign

This sign welcomes visitors to Buffalo, Wyoming. The basic shape resembles the walking trail kiosks I made several years earlier for the city. Ten-inch square steel tubing, trimmed with angle iron, supports the 8′ x 8′, double-sided sign. A 1 ½″ square steel tubing frame provides support for the mild steel and stainless steel sheets. The copper repoussé buffalo and the stone work mimic the bronze sculptures and stone landscape that share the site.

When I design jobs for customers I try to incorporate something I haven't done before. In this case, it was copper chasing and repoussé. The customer's logo was enlarged and transferred to the copper sheet. The work was done by using steel and hardwood tools, made on the fly as needed, and a four-ounce ball pein hammer that I upset the face of to make a chasing hammer. The copper was annealed several times during the process to avoid cracking from work hardening. The finished buffalo is double-sided, colored with cold gun blue, and sealed with car wax.

Visitor center sign. Mild steel, stainless steel, copper and cultured stone. Natural rust patina and linseed oil finish. 14′w x 13′h. Buffalo: Copper sheet. Bluing and wax finish. 10″h x 14″w.
Photos: Lanna Wing Photography

Chad A. Otis

Northfield, Minnesota
goodhue@cpinternet.com

ARTIST'S STATEMENT

Working with metal has been a pleasure for me since the first time I welded two pieces of metal together. One of the reasons I enjoy working with metal is that I can create unique shapes that are instantly strong in structure, allowing endless possibilities for creation. Another reason I enjoy working with metal is that metal can be altered by many methods, including bending, twisting, hammering, and the application of heat. When creating artwork in metal, I know that the time and details I put into the piece will more than likely remain for quite some time, as metalwork is very durable. I look forward to continually learning new ways to create through metal. As for a work philosophy with metal, I look at the desired result as a finished puzzle. First, I focus on building a strong foundation, then begin creating each piece of the puzzle to reach the end result.

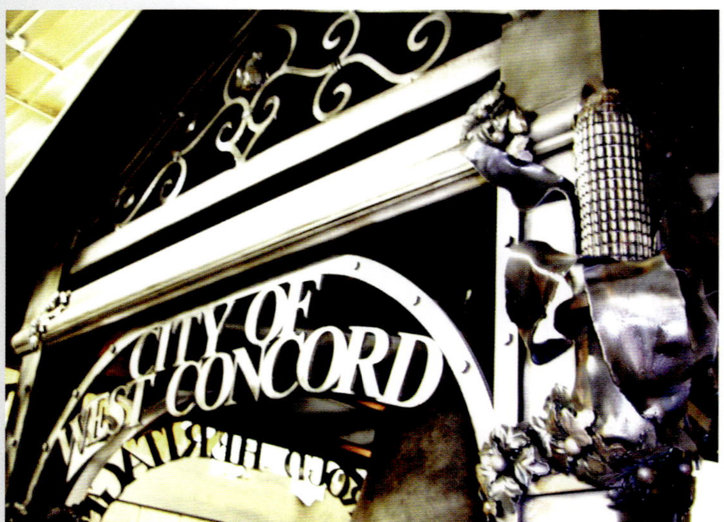

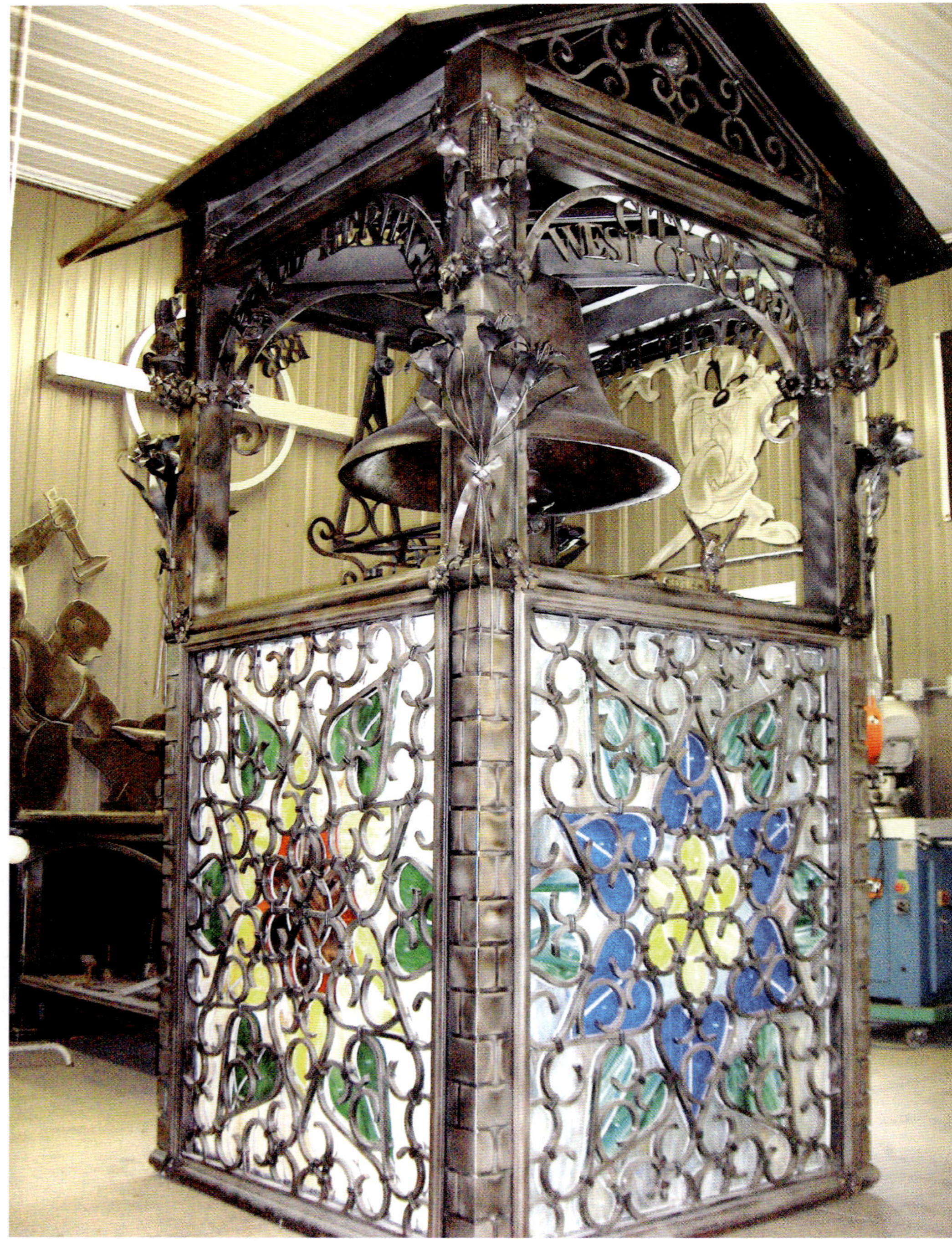

Bell Tower

I was provided an old, civil bell by the City of West Concord, Minnesota, and asked if I could design something to support its massive weight and, hopefully, have it be able to ring again. I wanted this bell tower to appear as if it would be at home in a time when there were horse-drawn carriages, cobblestone streets, and gas street lamps. I wanted to incorporate the appearance of both wood and brickwork, besides steel, but yet wanted it to be made from steel.

To accomplish these design aspects, I overlapped numerous pieces of flat pieces of steel and welded them from the backside, creating a wood-shake appearance for the roof. I plug-welded numerous pieces of steel to the outer frame in a brick-and-mortar pattern. I also wanted to incorporate the city's agricultural history into the bell tower. The tower features hand-crafted steel ears of corn representing the city's agricultural background, hand-crafted steel lilies representing the city's flower and hand-crafted, life-size steel cardinals representing the city's local school mascot.

Once the bell tower structure had been finished, I thought it would be incredible to be able to light it up at night. I had already designed and made custom scrollwork panels on the four sides of the bell tower. I thought stained-glass panels would dim the light and also offer beautiful colors to the structure. Rochester Stained Glass made the stained-glass panels, following the pattern of the scrollwork and organizing the glass with color patterns representing the four seasons.

Bell tower. Displayed in Centennial Park, West Concord, Minnesota.

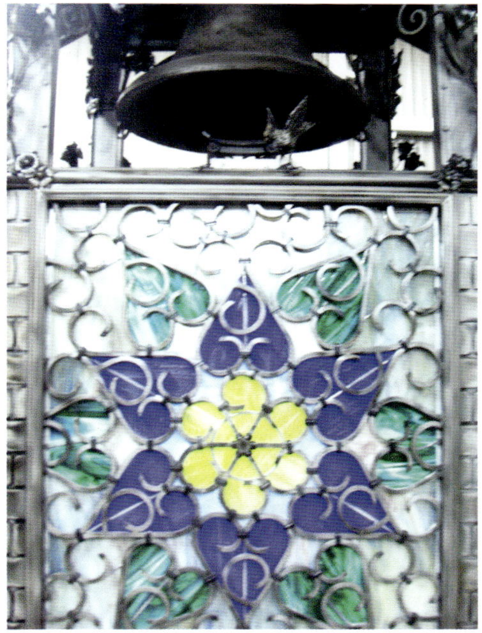

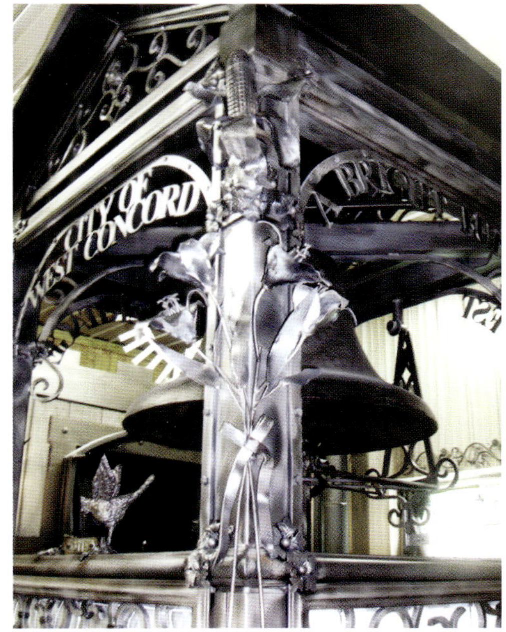

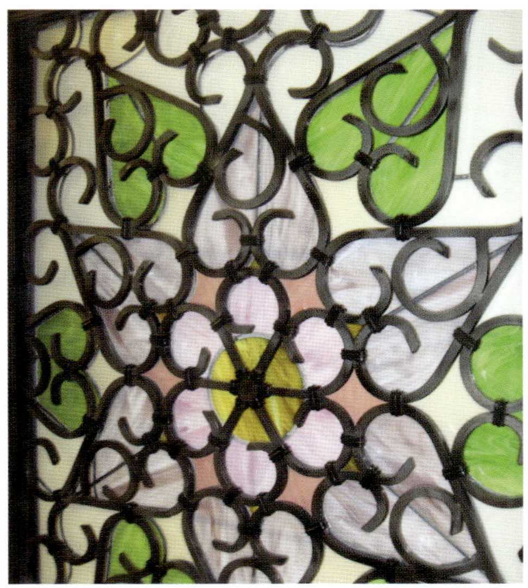

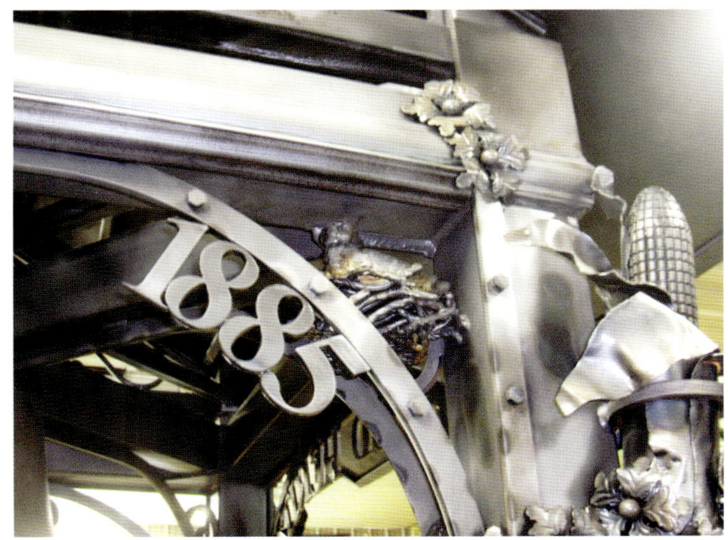

Laura Parker

Sacramento, California
www.metalobsession.com

ARTIST'S STATEMENT

I am passionate about the creative potential of metal. What attracts me to the working of steel is the exploration of its plastic qualities through direct process: bending, twisting, riveting, joining, etc. There is something sustaining and true about shaping hot metal in much the same way as it was done centuries ago. My work is an exploration of movement or motion. The immediacy and directness of the process encourage spontaneity in my idea development. The forge fire is my "inner center."

My work is usually personal in nature, emulating my own trials and tribulations as well as my responses to the fragility of human interaction and relationships. Even so, I have been surprised how many of my "musings" are universal. Often as artists we feel we are somehow more sensitive than the rest of the world. In reality, we all have soft underbellies. Some of us just choose to express those thoughts and feelings through art.

I am a tenured professor in the art department at American River College in Sacramento, California. Conveying my work process and thoughts in an educational environment keeps things fresh.

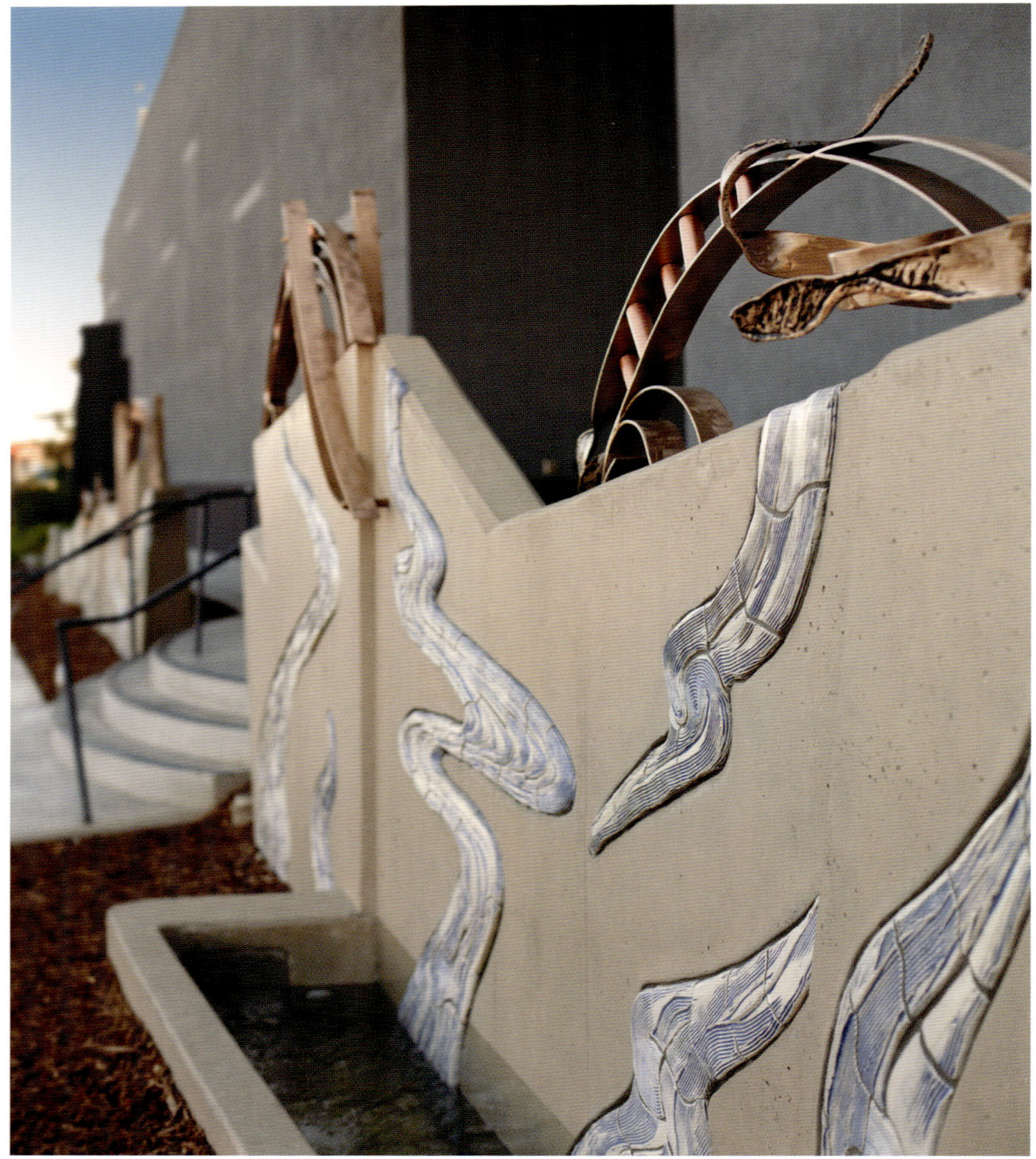

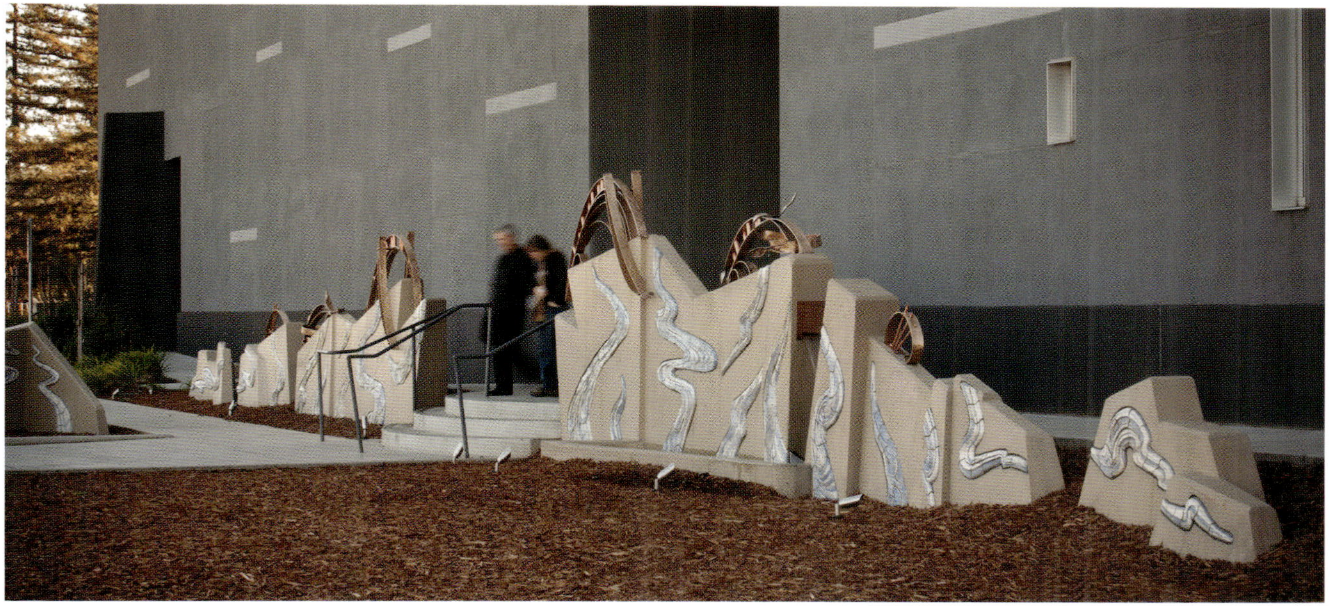

Confluence of the Arts

This public installation was created by me and ceramic artist Sam Tubiolo. The intent of this work was to design an environment that would be inviting as well as complementary to the front of the new music and theater building at American River College. Sam's ceramic tiles were inspired by the flow of rivers and waves. I wanted to illustrate, conceptually, the staccato and allegro of music and the movement of performance art.

This installation took several years from conception to completion. Working large scale in bronze was a new experience for me. I had to build a temperature-controlled forge for the project because bronze is sensitive to overheating and will literally just crumble if overheated.

Confluence of the Arts. Music and theater building public art project. Sculpture. 2011. Forged bronze. Full installation approximately 60'l x 48"h x 15"d. *Photos: Kent Lacin*

Equilibrium

I once read that if only one component of your life is missing, you will feel out of sorts. This artwork moves back and forth with the slightest touch to symbolize how easily we can lose our sense of being grounded. The seedpod shapes represent all the aspects of our lives that we are always trying to juggle.

Equilibrium. Sculpture. 2011. Forged steel. 19"h x 55"w x 16"d. *Photo: Kent Lacin*

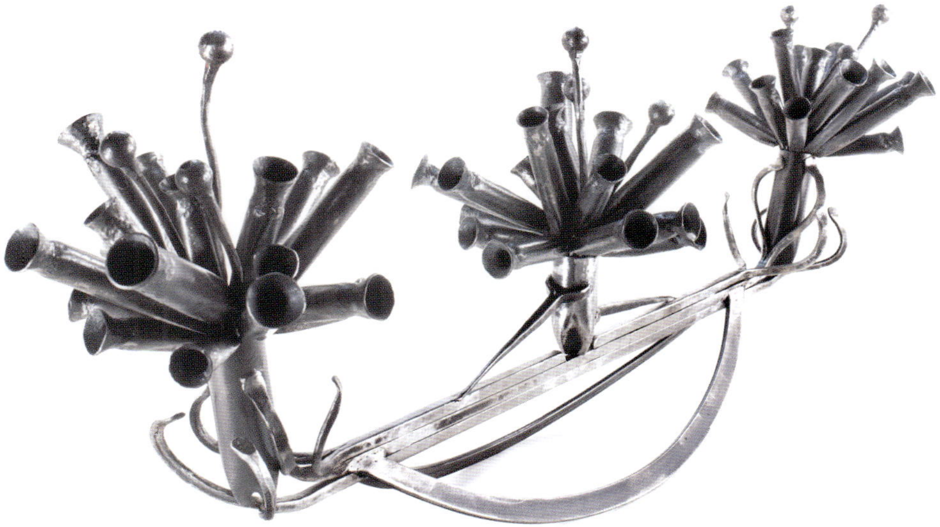

Opposing Views

The function of a boat rudder, to control the direction of the boat, reminded me of how people argue. Each person has a sincere interest in controlling the outcome. If there is no compromise, you end up with two rudders and the boat just goes in circles. As luck would have it, I had to ask my husband to help steady the work while I set one of the rivets and he stated he should be the one to hit the rivet since he was stronger. The piece had already earned its name before it was even complete.

Opposing Views. Sculpture. 2011.
Forged steel, exotic wood (laminated).
14″h x 33″w x 16″d. *Photo: Kent Lacin*

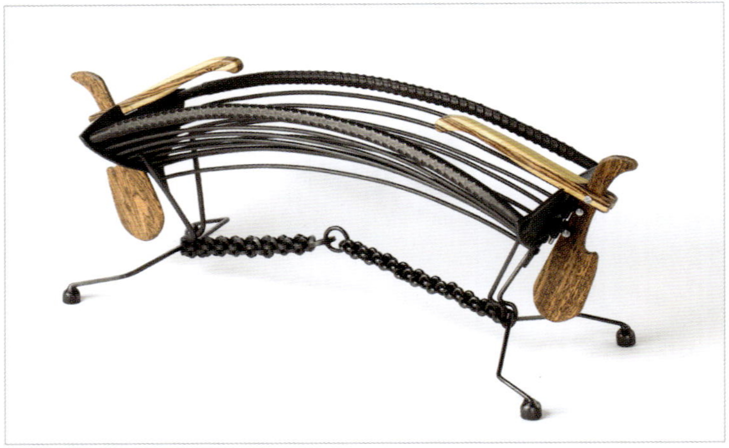

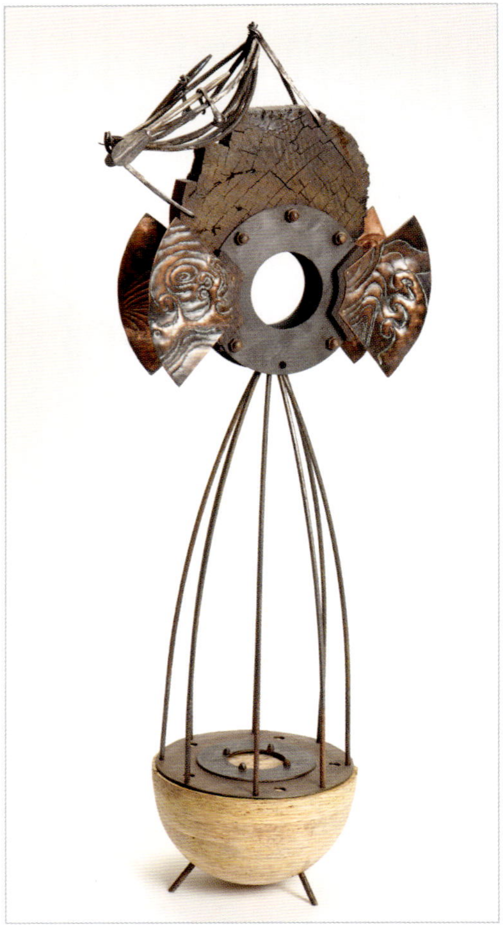

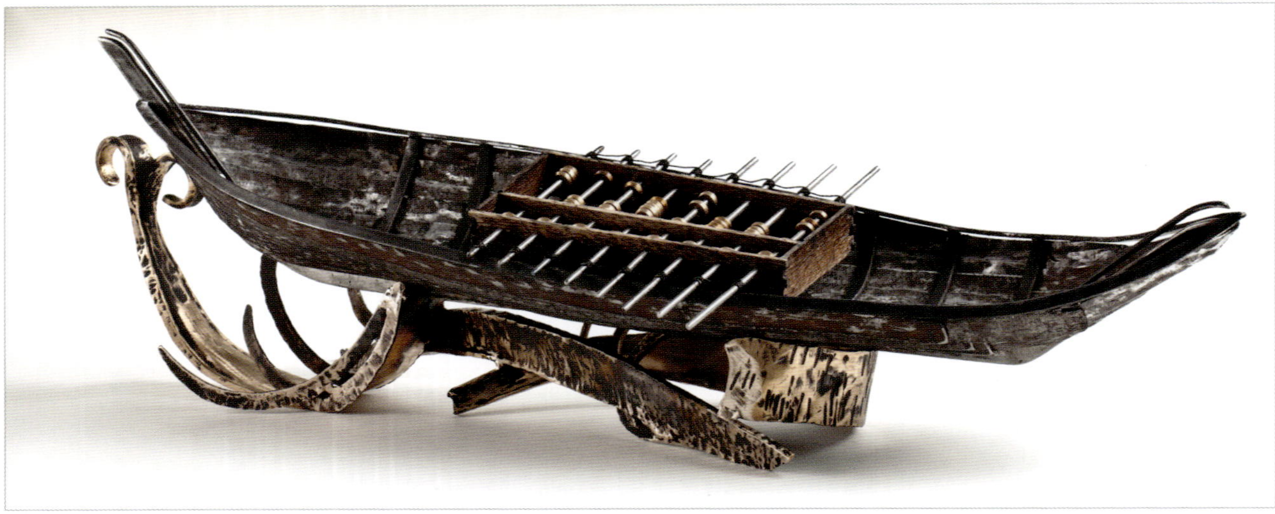

The Wisdom of Insecurity

The boat has come to symbolize for me not only my own artistic journey but also the state of the economy. As a baby boomer, I have become aware of how we are struggling to make sense of what our futures will look like. The boat is unstable, but is still afloat. The abacus represents our obsession with whether we are ready financially for retirement.

The Wisdom of Insecurity. Sculpture. 2013. Forged steel and bronze. 22″h x 38″l x 16″w. *Photo: Kent Lacin*

Losing Ground

The small boat is precariously perched above the waves, with the buoy swaying back and forth. The work symbolizes how, as a nation, we are responding to the downturn in the economy.

Losing Ground. Sculpture. 2012.
Forged steel, wood, copper repoussé.
45″h x 17″w x 11″d. *Photo: Kent Lacin*

Peter Parkinson

Oakhanger, Bordon, Hampshire, UK
www.peterparkinson.co.uk

ARTIST'S STATEMENT

Having studied industrial design at the Royal College of Art and worked as a designer, I became an Art College Lecturer, then, later, a blacksmith. Making objects has been a compulsion since childhood, so working hot metal—playing with fire, like my mother told me not to—came as a revelation.

The combination of problem-solving, visual judgment, and sheer physical effort is endlessly rewarding. Somebody once said to me that he didn't like painting because it didn't make enough noise—and I know what he meant. Taking an unprepossessing piece of metal and turning it into something of beauty and interest is constantly challenging—and ultimately satisfying when it goes right.

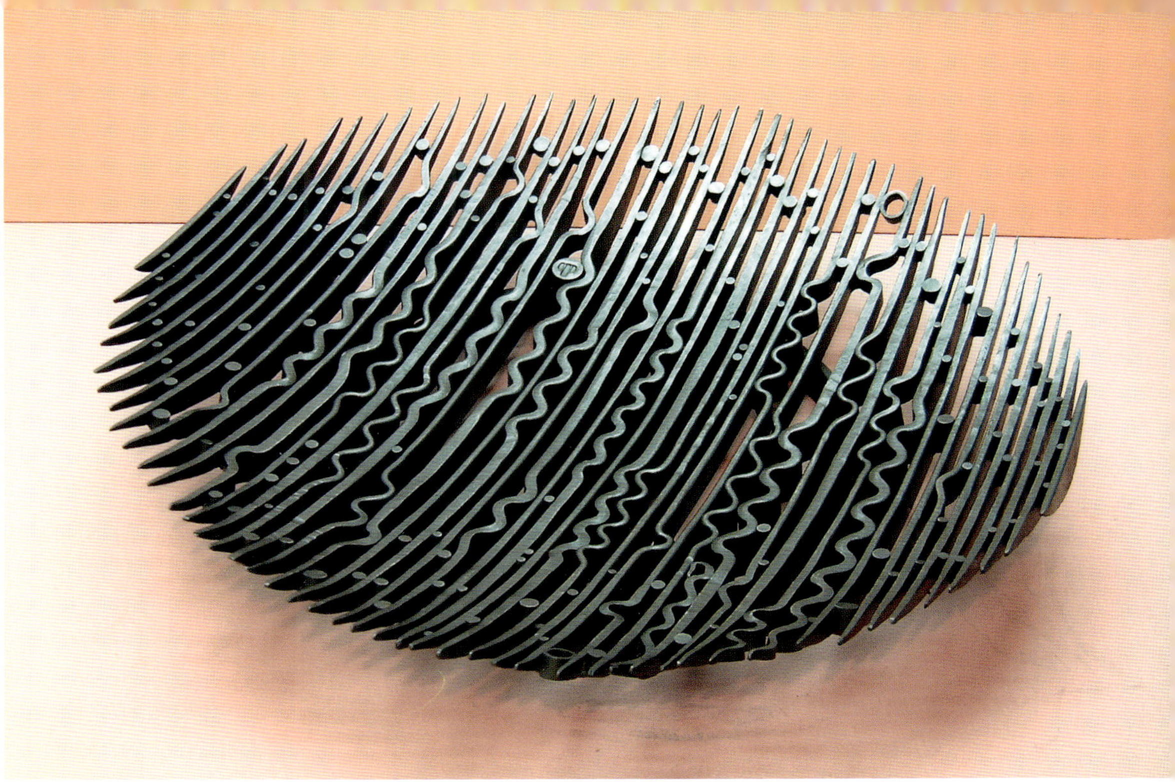

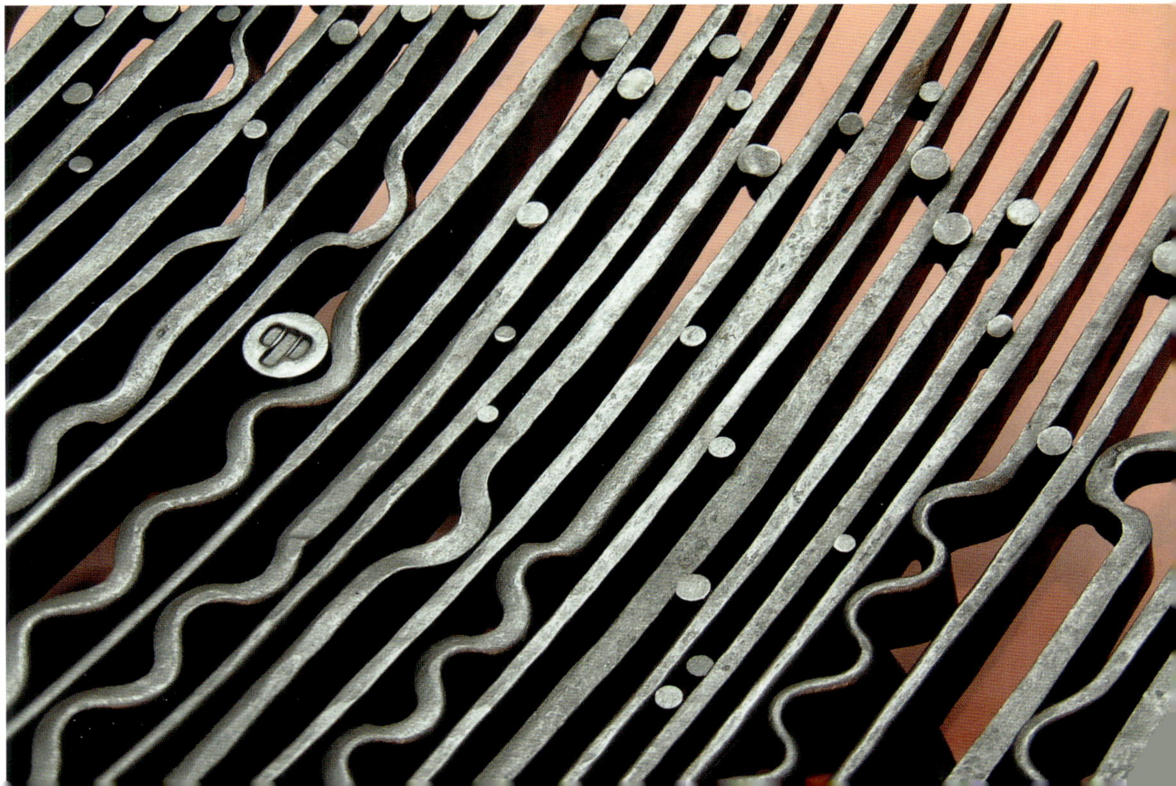

Ripple Bowl

The pattern of the bowl derives from the ripples in sand when the tide goes out. The detail shows "pebbles"—spacers TIG welded between the rippled bars.

Ripple bowl. Mild steel. 300 mm (12") diameter.

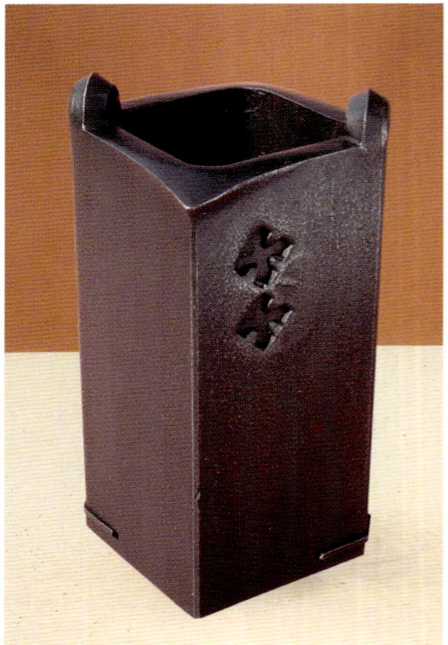

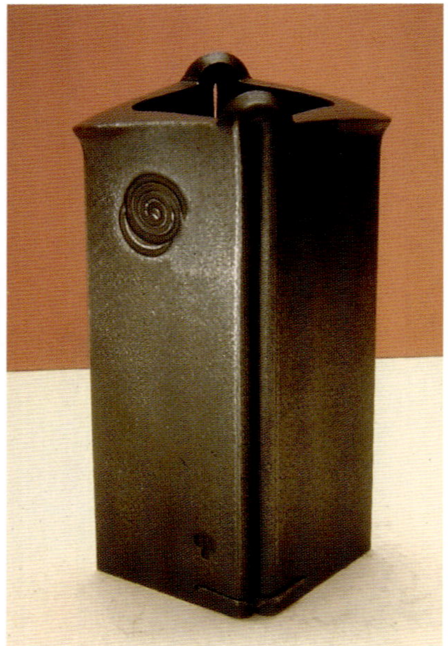

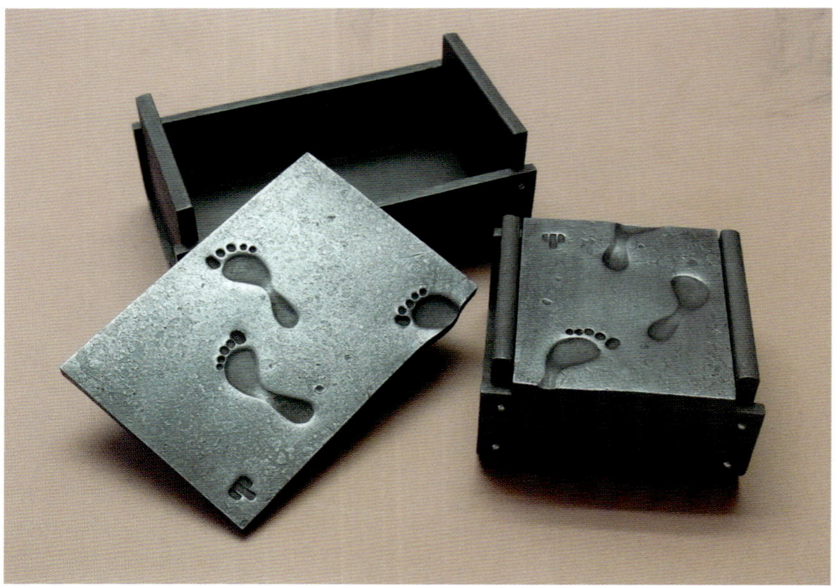

Angle Containers

Cut and formed from one piece of angle iron, the sides are hot bent, trapping the base in slots. Punched decoration in the design is the result of exploring uses of more unusual steel sections.

Angle containers. Mild steel. 180 x 55 x55 mm (7″x 2¼″ x2¼″). *Photos: Peter Parkinson*

Footprint Boxes

There is an essential humanity about footprints—they are what we all leave behind.

Footprint boxes. Mild steel with stainless steel rivets. Punched footprints. Larger box, 140 x 80 x 50 mm (5½″ x 3¼″ x 2″). *Photos: Peter Parkinson*

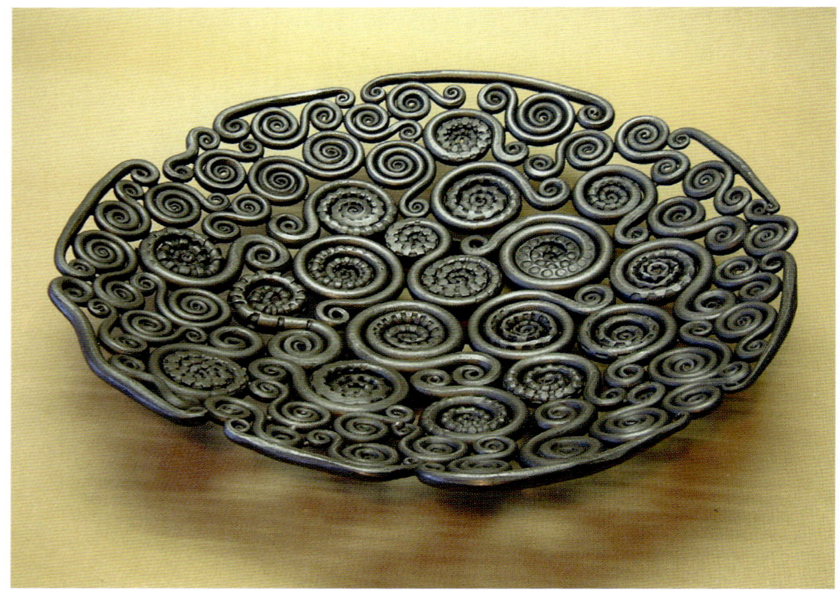

Coil Bowl

Coil bowl. Mild steel. Forged, punched and coiled elements TIG welded together. 320 mm (12.5″) diameter.

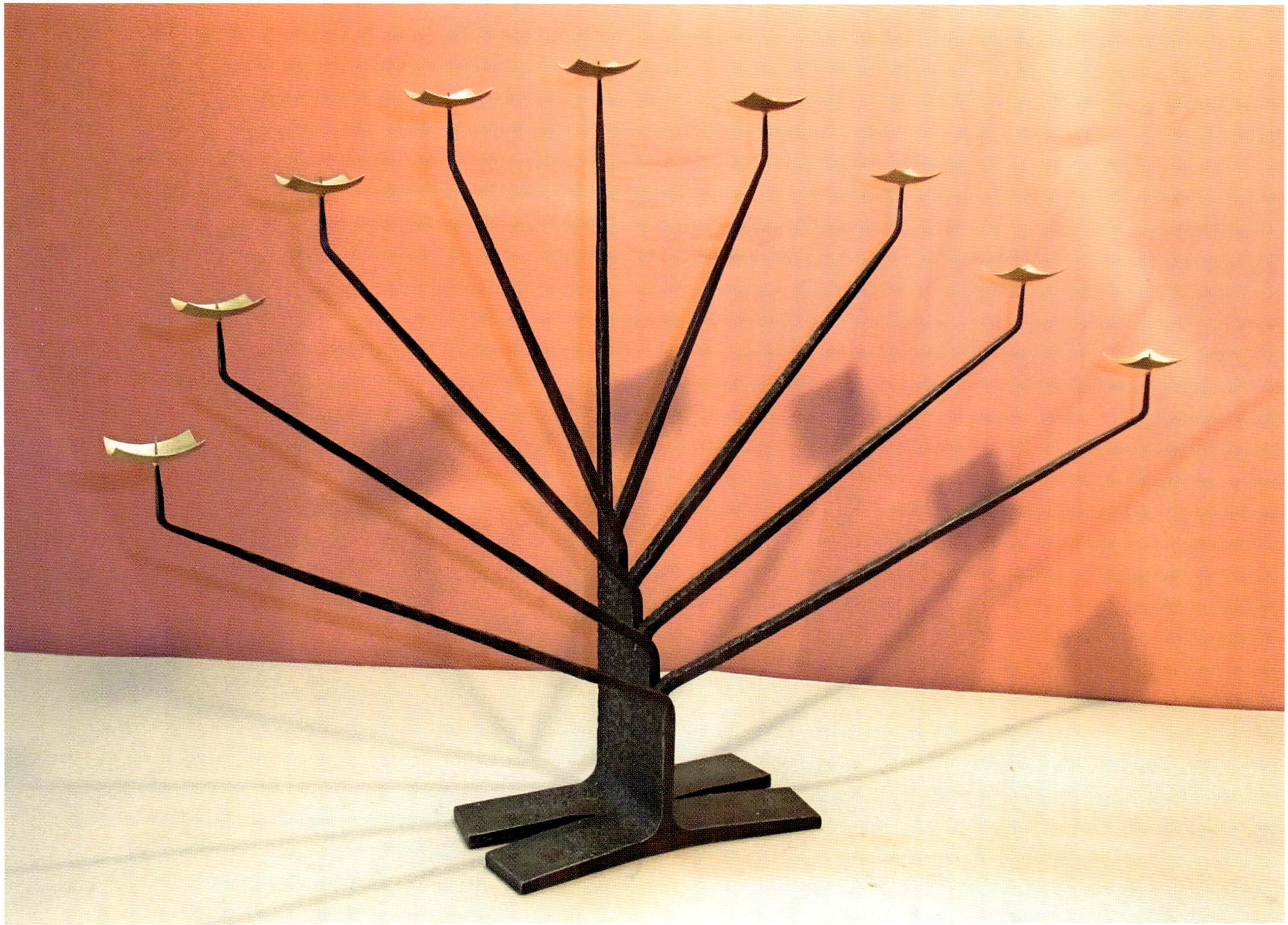

Candelabra

Like the angle containers, this is a result of investigating uses for unlikely steel sections.

Candelabra. Mild steel and brass. Forged from one piece of 'I' beam. 300 x 350 x 150 mm (12"x 14"x 6"). *Photos: Peter Parkinson*

John Phillips

Phillips Metal Works, Montgomery, Alabama
www.phillipsmetalworks.com

ARTIST'S STATEMENT

My inspiration for architectural metalwork comes from centuries of hand-forged ironwork. Historic European craftsmen transformed raw bars of iron into breathtaking architecture for royalty, protective suits for their knights, and tools for the working people. The fluidity, personal nature, and mystical properties of historical ironwork are the qualities that I attempt to capture in my work.

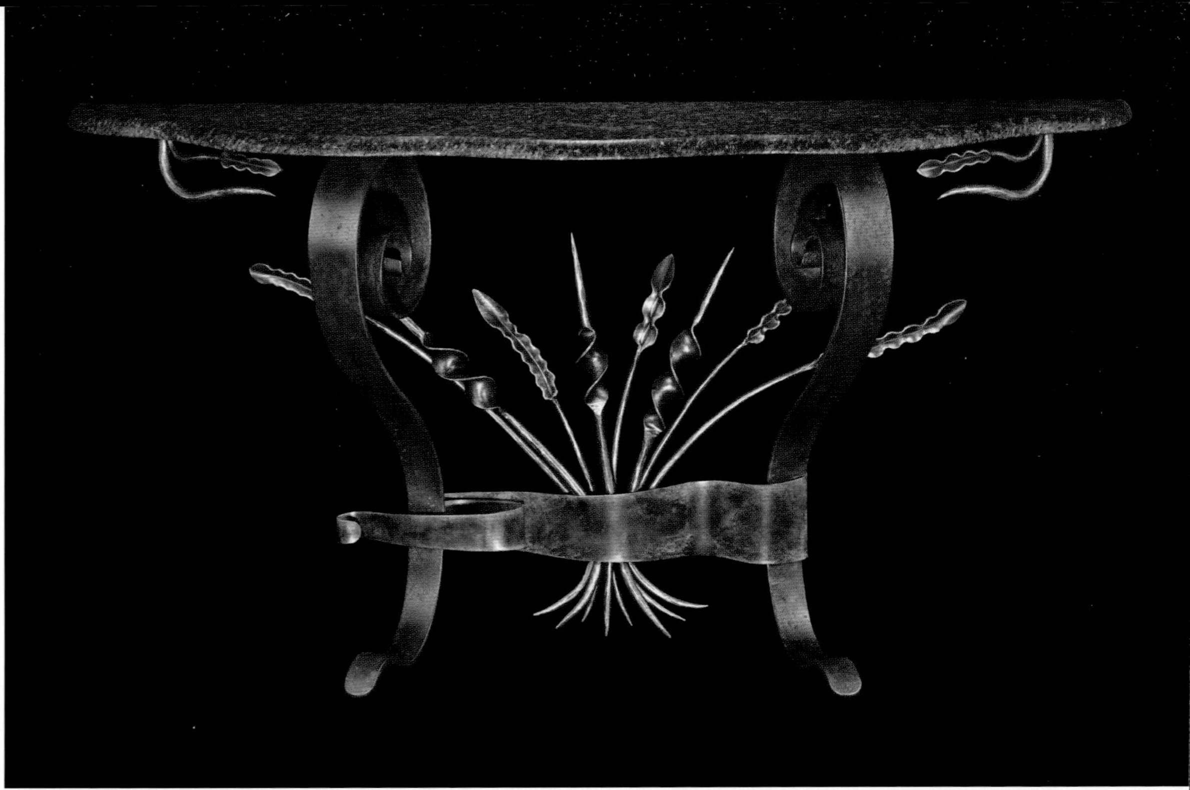

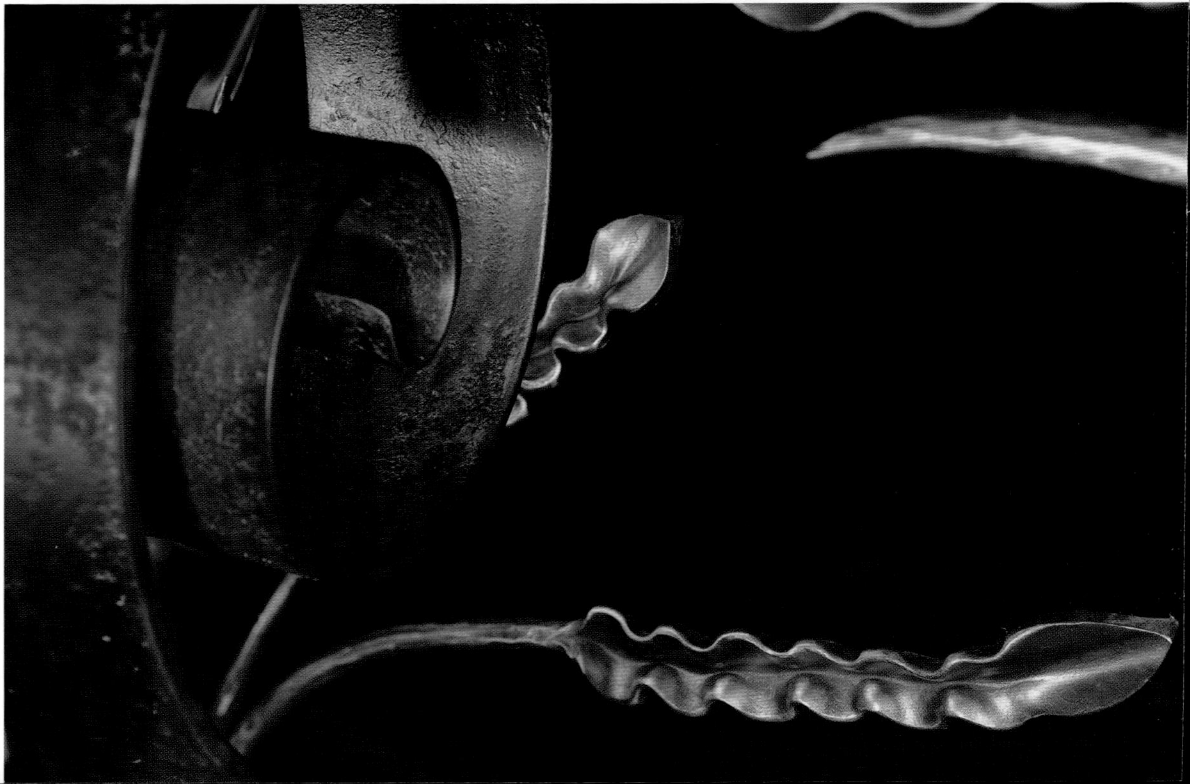

Baka's Garden

Baka's Garden *is a piece from my* Wetlands *series. The design was conceived in my late aunt's beautiful backyard garden, and the console table is named after her. The base is forged and fabricated from steel, with a chemically blackened finish and patina highlights. The top is flamed granite.*

Baka's Garden. Table. Steel, granite. Forged and fabricated. 36"h x 18"d x 68"w. *Photos: John Phillips*

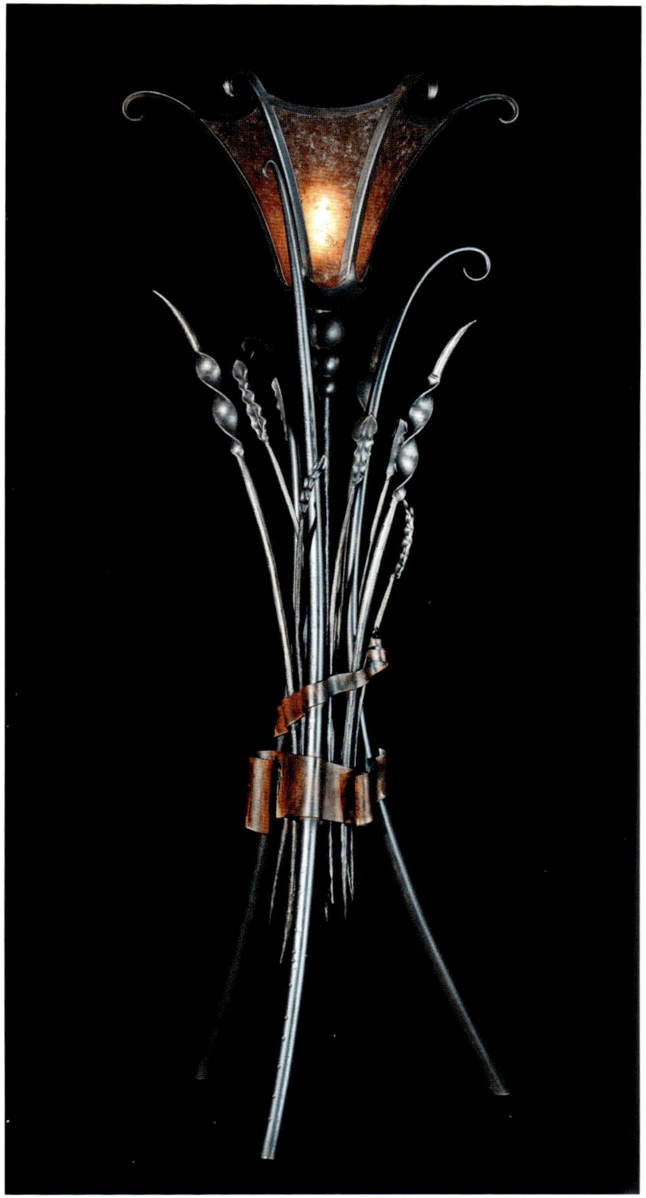

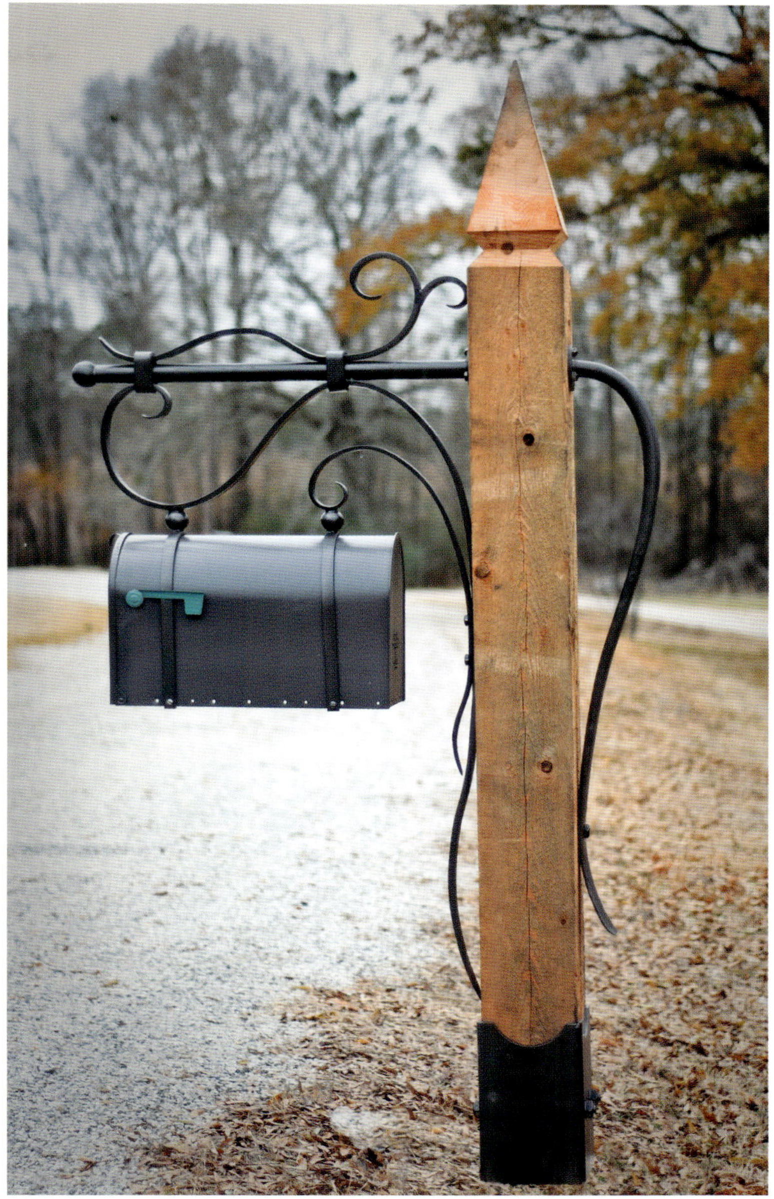

Lighting Lake Marie

Lighting Lake Marie *is the beginning of a series of pieces inspired by the wetlands of the South. The lamp is forged and fabricated from steel and has a chemically blackened finish with some patina highlights. The shade is constructed from formed mica sheets.* Lighting Lake Marie *is named after my late mother, and the name was inspired by a John Prine song.*

Lighting Lake Marie. Lamp.
Steel, mica. Forged and fabricated.
84"h x 36" diameter.
Photo: John Phillips

Flowing Winds Mailbox

The Flowing Winds *mailbox was designed for a client in rural Mississippi who wanted a mailbox that would not fill up when his family left on their frequent trips. The design was inspired by the equestrian history of the area.*

Flowing Winds. Mailbox.
Steel, cypress. Forged.
98"h x 51"w.
Photos: John Phillips

Joseph Christopher Porcarelli

Porcarelli Studio, Fengersfors, Sweden
www.porcarellistudio.com

ARTIST'S STATEMENT

Interpersonal communication, sculptural forms, metal working techniques, and sound are sources of investigation and inspiration. My practice weaves interests in social dynamics and material- based objects in hopes of developing opportunities for user creativity and face-to-face relations. I am currently focusing on developing social platforms for indoor and outdoor spaces. Sites and objects are designed to evoke curiosity and to encourage physical activity with one or multiple users. When engaged, objects mechanically transfer the energy of users´ movements into auditory signals. Interactive motions actuate layers of sound and rhythm that compose a unique event created by those present.

Sound, 6.11

Sound, 6.11. 2011. Sculpture. Forged and fabricated mild and spring steel. Rubber, nylon, felt and leather components. Pine decking.

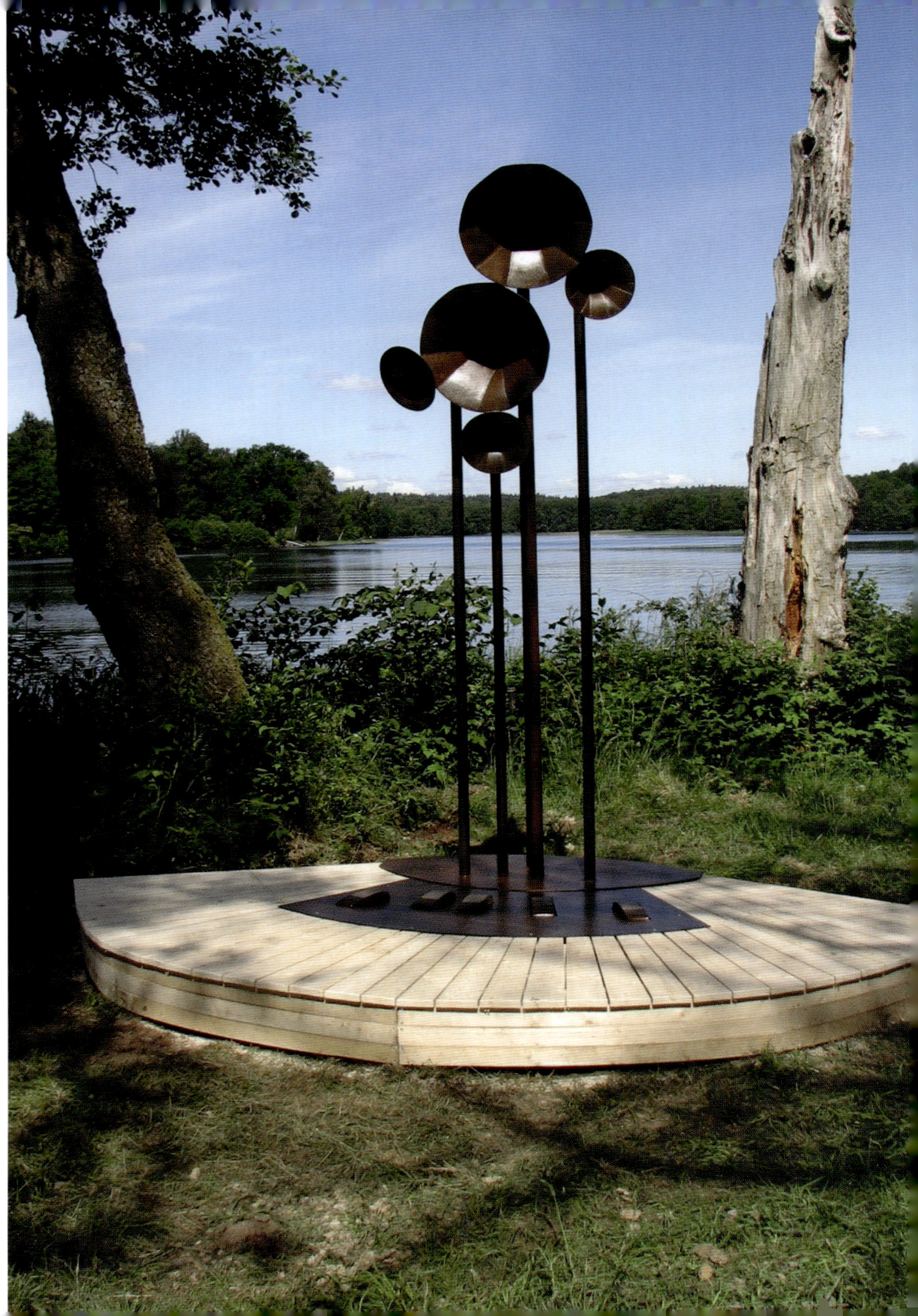

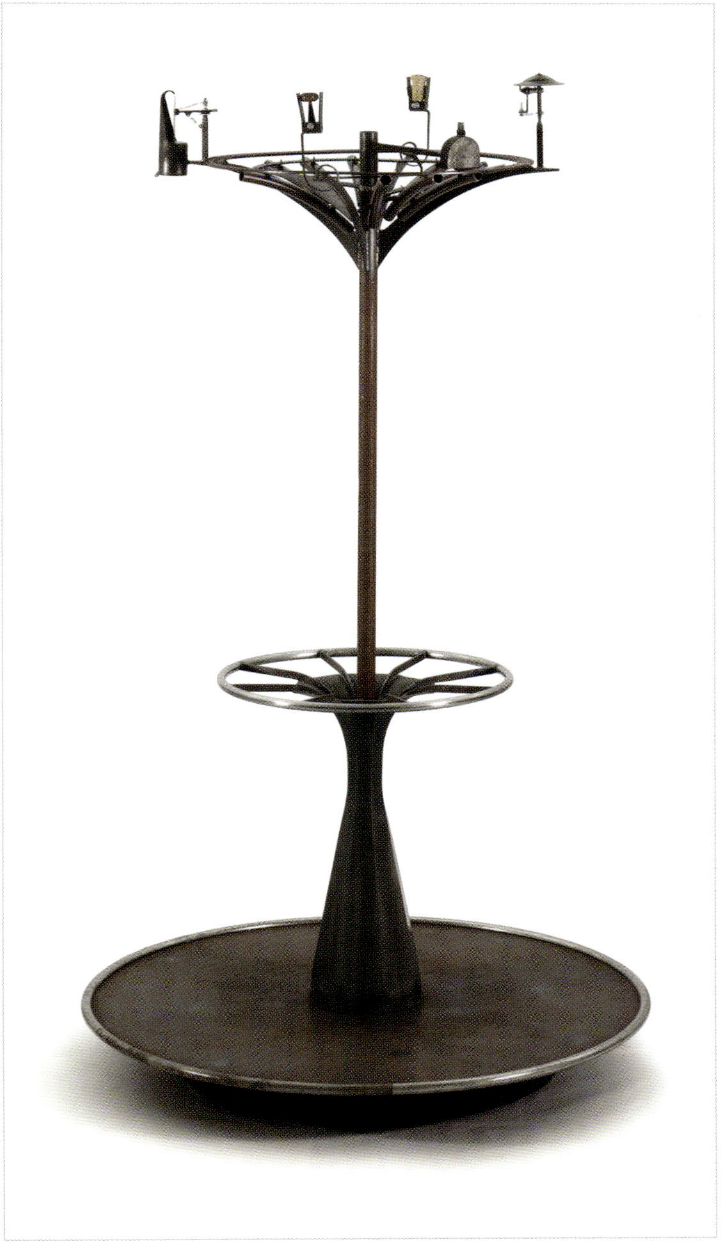

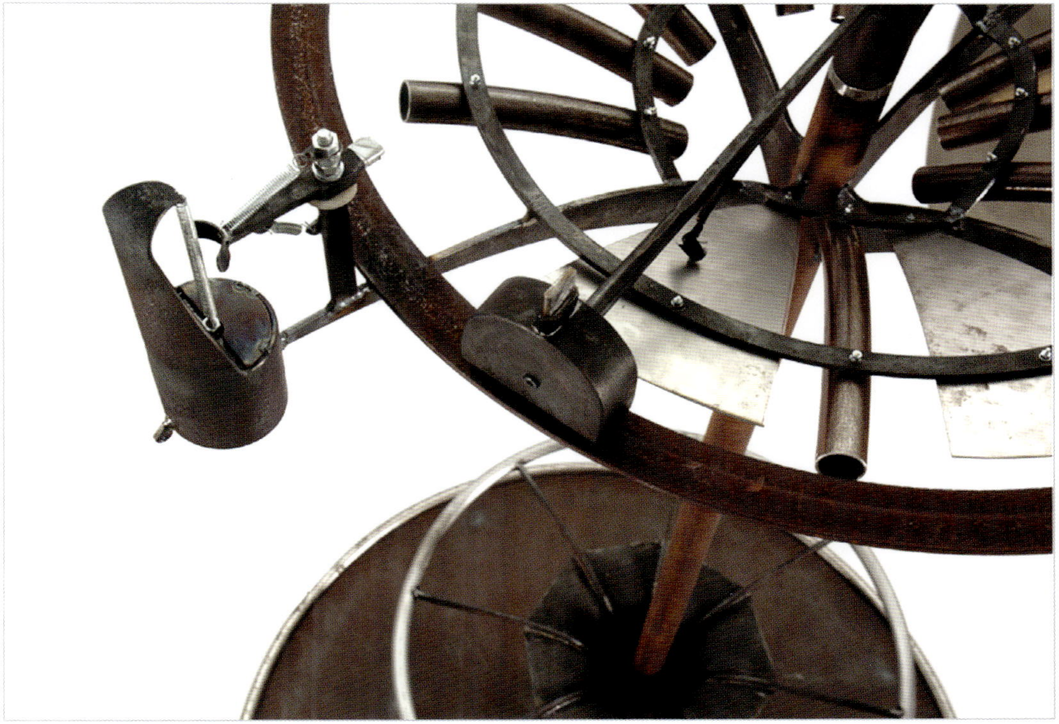

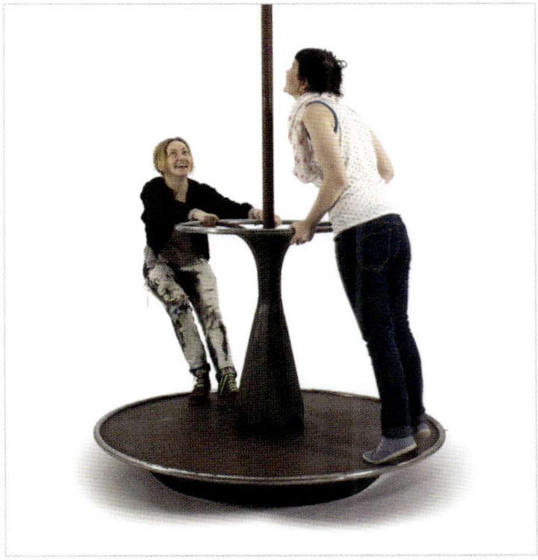

Sound, 4.12

Sound, 4.12. 2012. Forged and fabricated mild and spring steel. Rubber, nylon, foam, and felt components.

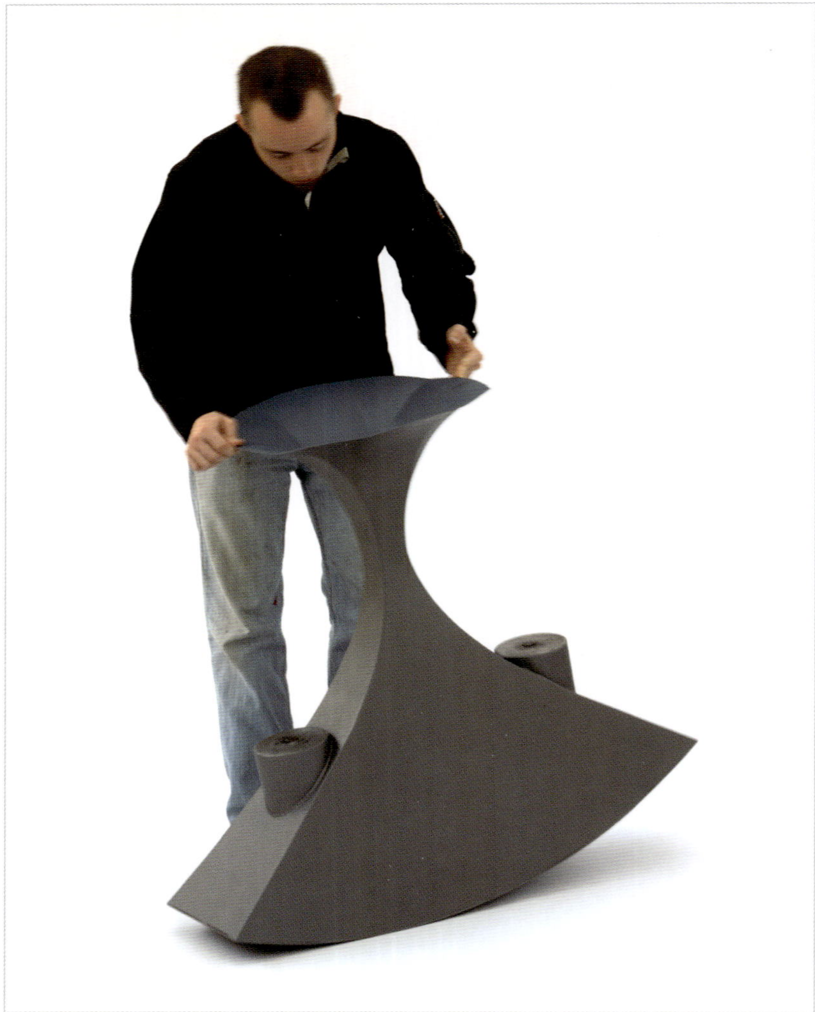

Sound, 11.11

Sound, 11.11. 2011. Forged and fabricated mild and spring steel. Rubber, nylon, and felt components.

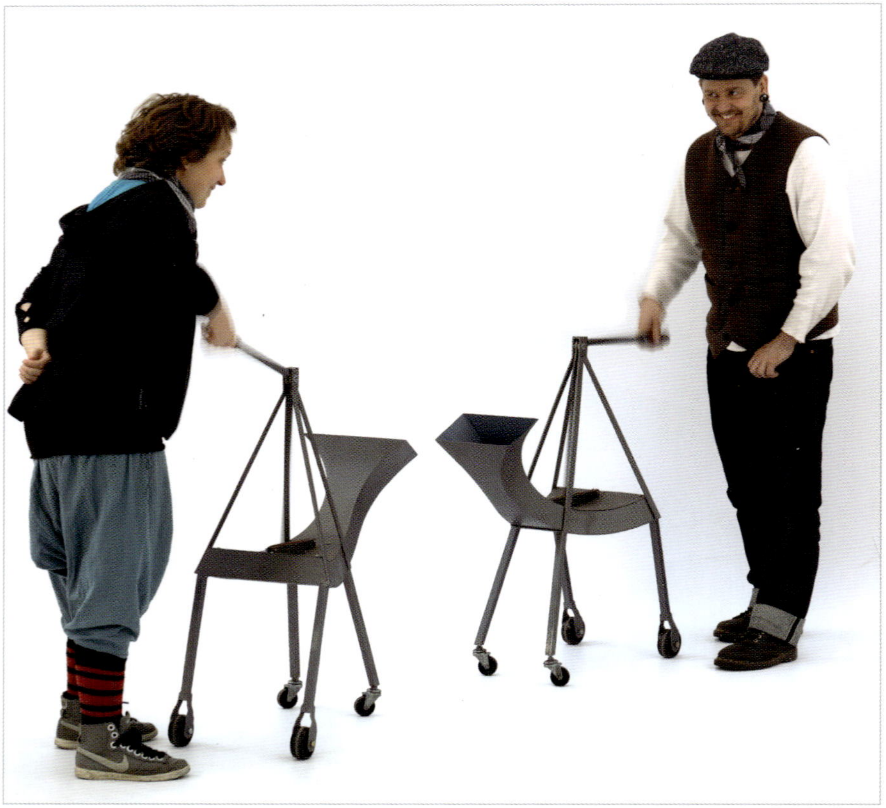

Sound, 12.11

Sound, 12.11. 2011. Forged and fabricated mild and spring steel. Rubber, nylon, felt, and leather components.

Bill Price

Memphis, Tennessee
billpricemetalarts.com

ARTIST'S STATEMENT

My sculptural work draws inspiration from natural forms, predominantly birds. Some pieces are purely representational studies, taken from direct field observations, while others are interpretations exploring the posture, gesture, action, and linear nature of the avian species.

Research has led me to include components from discarded firearms into the "gunduck" series. These sculptures address the issue of hunter vs. prey and explore role reversal within the context of man and nature. By giving the hunted the tools to defend themselves, and exchanging the roles of aggressor and quarry, I consider the concept of prey evolving greater, more equal means of protection and revenge.

Night Hawk

Night Hawk *captures a moment in time at the end of a dive performed by the common Nighthawk during courtship rituals. This piece is made from silicon bronze. The body was cast as a blank and then forged into its final shape. The wings are made from bar stock tapered at either end with fuller marks along their length to imply primary wing feathers.*

Night Hawk. Sculpture. 2011. Forged and cast silicone bronze, steel. 14" x 12" x 10".

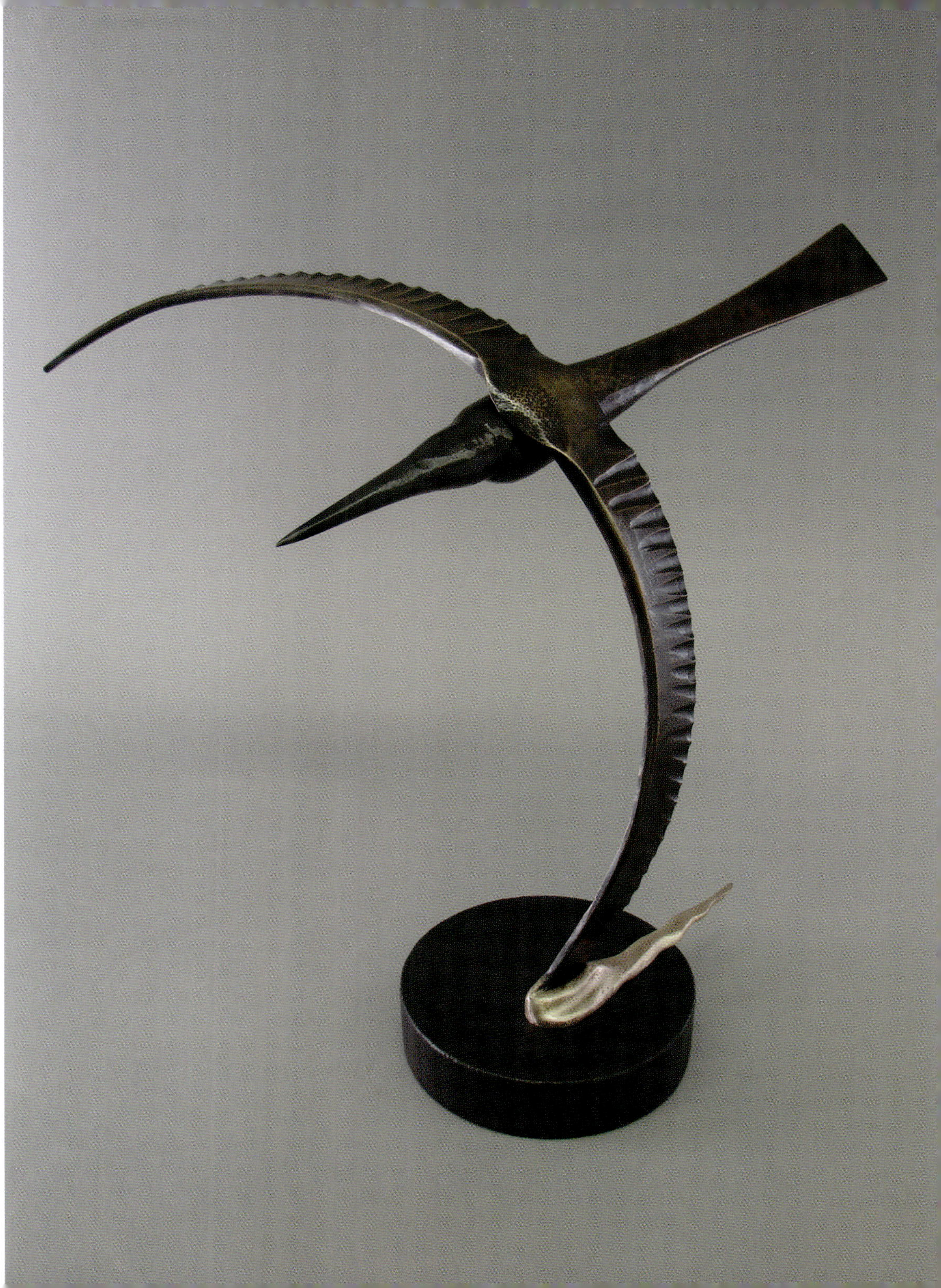

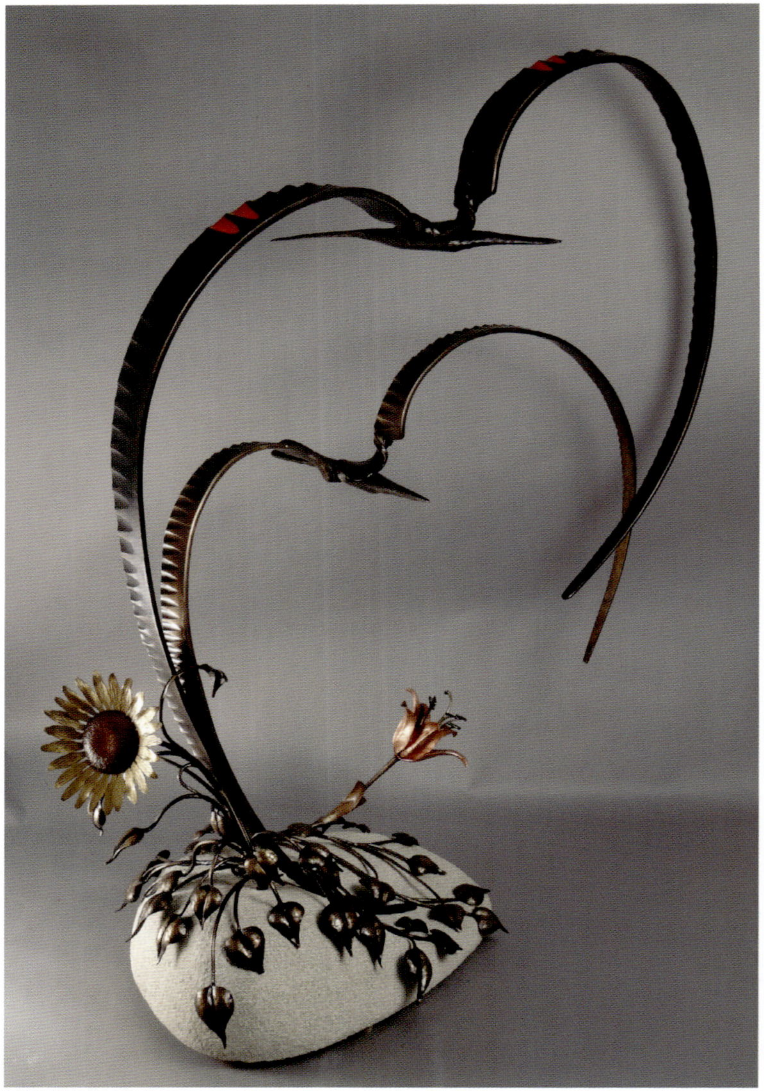

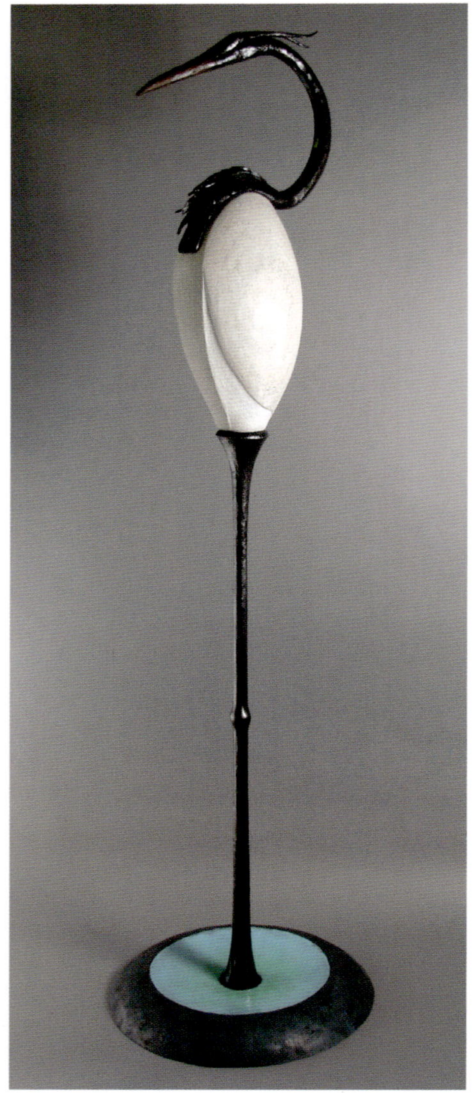

40

This commissioned piece was completed in the summer of 2013. The client had seen another recent piece and liked the fuller details in the wings and the simplified contours of my Redwing Blackbird forms. She wanted a piece for her husband to commemorate their fortieth anniversary. The male and female Redwing are stand-ins for the couple. The forty heart-shaped leaves on the limestone base reference each year of their marriage, while the Sunflower and Lilly personify their two daughters.

40. 2013. Forged silicone bronze, NuGold, copper, limestone. 44" x 46" x 14".

Great Blue

Great Blue *is one of many from my Wader series. It depicts the Great Blue Heron wading in a pool of water. The head and neck are one piece folded and forge welded to make the beak and crest feathers. The beard is a series of split pieces stacked and forge welded to the neck. I embrace the challenge of minimizing the number of pieces used to depict a particular species of bird. The body of this piece is carved limestone fitted into a socket at the top of the leg. The base is steel sheet with enamel fired onto its center to depict water.*

Great Blue. 2010. Forged steel, limestone, vitreous enamel. 44" x 12" x 12".

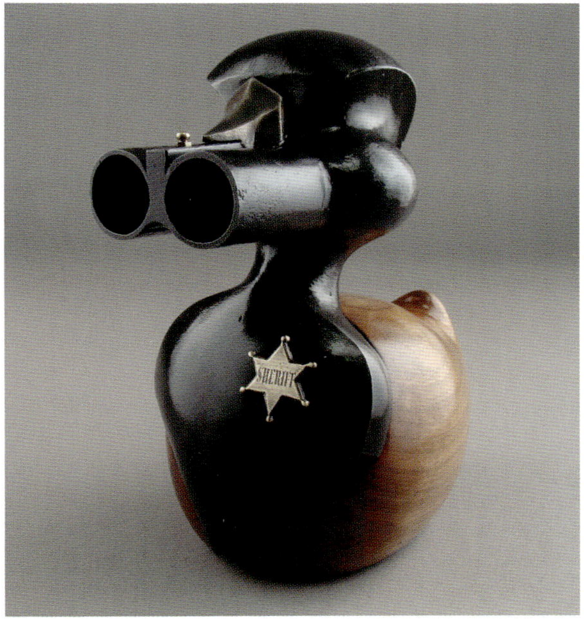

Sheriff Rubber Ducky

Sheriff Rubber Ducky *is one of the ongoing* Gunduck *series. I love the irony and humor his piece conveys through what is normally seen as such a benign object, the rubber ducky.*

Sheriff Rubber Ducky. 2010. Forged steel, cherry, white bronze, 20 gauge steel shotgun barrel. 4" x 4" x 2½".

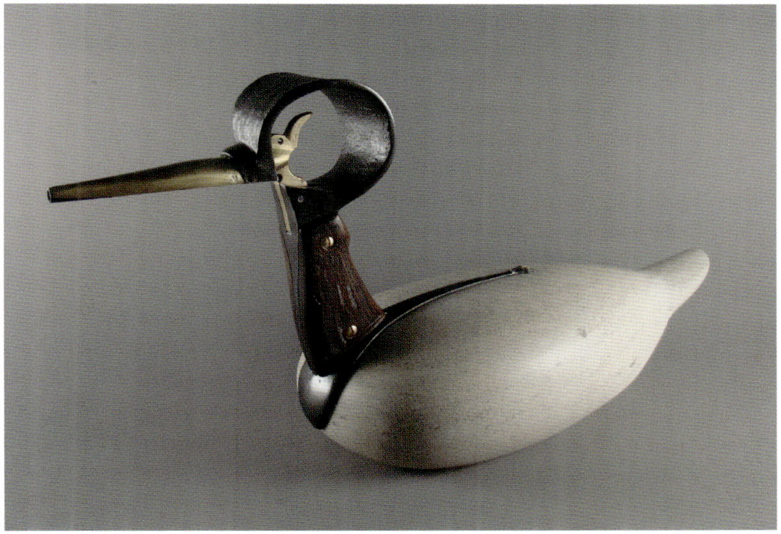

22 Caliber Canvasback

This piece was a fun challenge. It is part of the Gunduck series but differs from the others because it does not use any recycled gun components. The forge work was challenging, but not nearly as much as fitting the metal parts to the stone and the carved walnut handles to the steel. Combining materials like this lets me develop the mass I want without the need to generate hollow forms.

2 Caliber Canvasback. 2010. Forged steel, limestone, brass, walnut. 9" x 16" x 7".

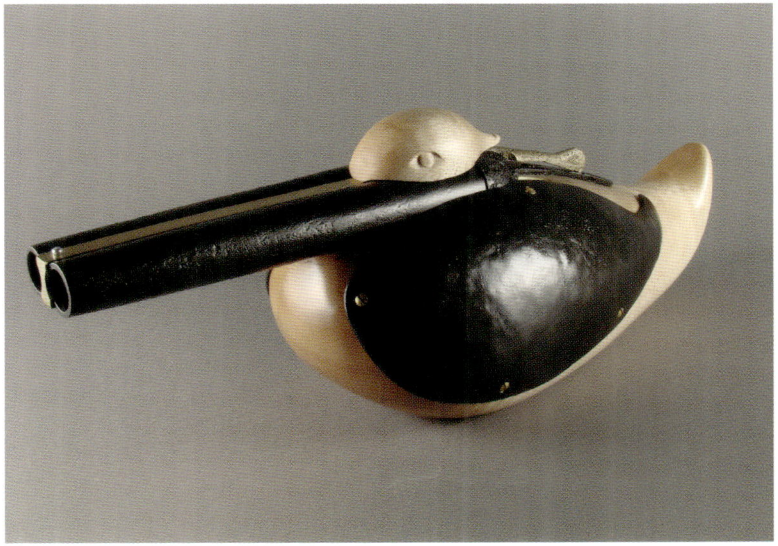

Double Improved Break Action Drake

This piece started with the body and trigger assembly from an old double-barrel shotgun a friend salvaged from a dilapidated barn in North Mississippi. The gun body can be seen just below and behind the head. With a piece like this, I carve the wood first and then fit the 12 gauge sheet metal to the form. The barrels are forged from pipe and fitted with brass to accurately depict a break-action shotgun.

Double Improved Break Action Drake. 2010. Forged/fabricated steel, maple, brass, recycled shotgun components. 5 ½" x 14" x 6".

Margo & Dennis Proksa

Blackrock Forge, Pocatello, Idaho
blackrockforge@cableone.net

ARTIST'S STATEMENT, MARGO

I am a material girl. I draw and paint; I use clay, willow, textiles, and all sorts of objects that find me. I have metal work in my family history and a life and business partner with extensive metal working skills. So I imagine and manifest in metal, too.

I am inspired by the natural world and patterns. I find art history, from prehistoric to contemporary, exhilarating.

Whatever material is in my hands when I have an idea of what I think I'm doing is a thrill. Sometimes I mess something up because I'm predicting success. Some pieces happen in a flurry of activity, others take months, or years to complete. I don't care. The process can be a source of pleasure or pain. The body of work I have generated in my lifetime amazes me because it is diverse, some of it's large scale, some is small, both 2-D and 3-D. My work is driven by worldly concerns and interests, this day and age. It's hard to explain the joy that comes from nothing evolving into something. It's magical. It is one of the benefits of being human.

Enfolded

This sculpture represents a new direction for exploring form with steel. Enfolded *began as a ⅜" x 1' x 1' steel plate that was folded and forged repeatedly under the Chambersberg hammer until the desired number of layers were achieved. After studying the form, cutting began in order to see the layers revealed: a somewhat unpredictable process with a very organic outcome. Surfaces were polished and finish was applied.*

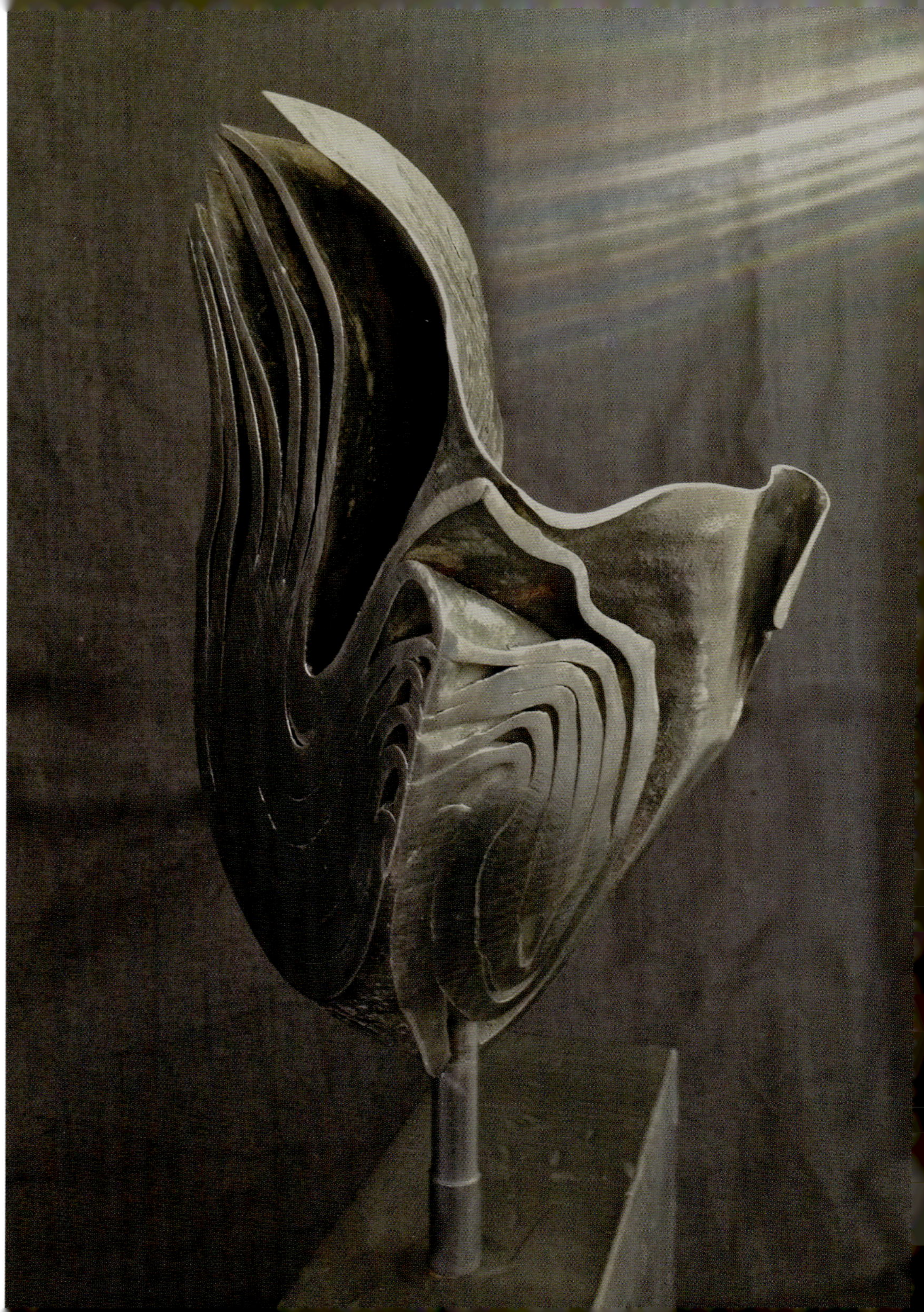

Enfolded. 2013. Sculpture. Steel. 5" x 7" x 4".

MARGO & DENNIS PROKSA

ARTIST'S STATEMENT, DENNIS

I forge and fabricate steel sculptures, build architectural ironwork, and design contemporary furniture because it's the way I choose to express myself artistically. I prefer steel because of its strength and plasticity as well as its organic nature when properly treated. Metal work has a long history and has served humanity in many useful and beautiful forms. A close look at the past inspires the present.

I believe in freeing myself by using modern technology if it is appropriate, but I employ historic methods, too. Most often the work I do is an efficient use of the full spectrum of possibilities. Modern metal smiths are just part of the continuum that began thousands of years ago.

Litharacnium

The Litharacnium was identified and drawn by scientist Ernst Haeckel (1834-1919) in the mid-1800's. It is a single-celled, aquatic protozoan, just 0.5 mm in diameter. We used Haeckel's drawing to create this sculpture 11½' in diameter cut from ½" steel plate. The City of Boise commissioned this artwork to help raise awareness of biodiversity and the interdependence of all life forms on earth.

Oceans cover 70 percent of the Earth's surface and the exquisite Litharacnium is part of the free-floating, plankton community, whose plant members (phytoplankton) are responsible for 50 percent of the oxygen on Earth through the process of photosynthesis. Phytoplankton and zooplankton (the free-floating animals, including Litharacnium) provide life support for the whole marine food chain, from fish and whales to crabs, worms and starfish, from the seabed to the seabirds in the sky. Climate change and changing ocean currents are affecting the abundance and distribution of the plankton, with ramifications for the ecology of the entire planet. This sculpture of an oceanic life form in Boise provides a reminder that we are all connected to the distant oceans.

The Litharacnium is an introduction to the stunning beauty, complexity, and importance of the sea world. DaVinci said "Art is not merely an investigation of beauty, but a path of understanding." (Submitted by artists Margo & Dennis Proksa with architect Bruce Poe)

Litharacnium. 2014. Steel. 11½' diameter. Installed in Boise, Idaho.

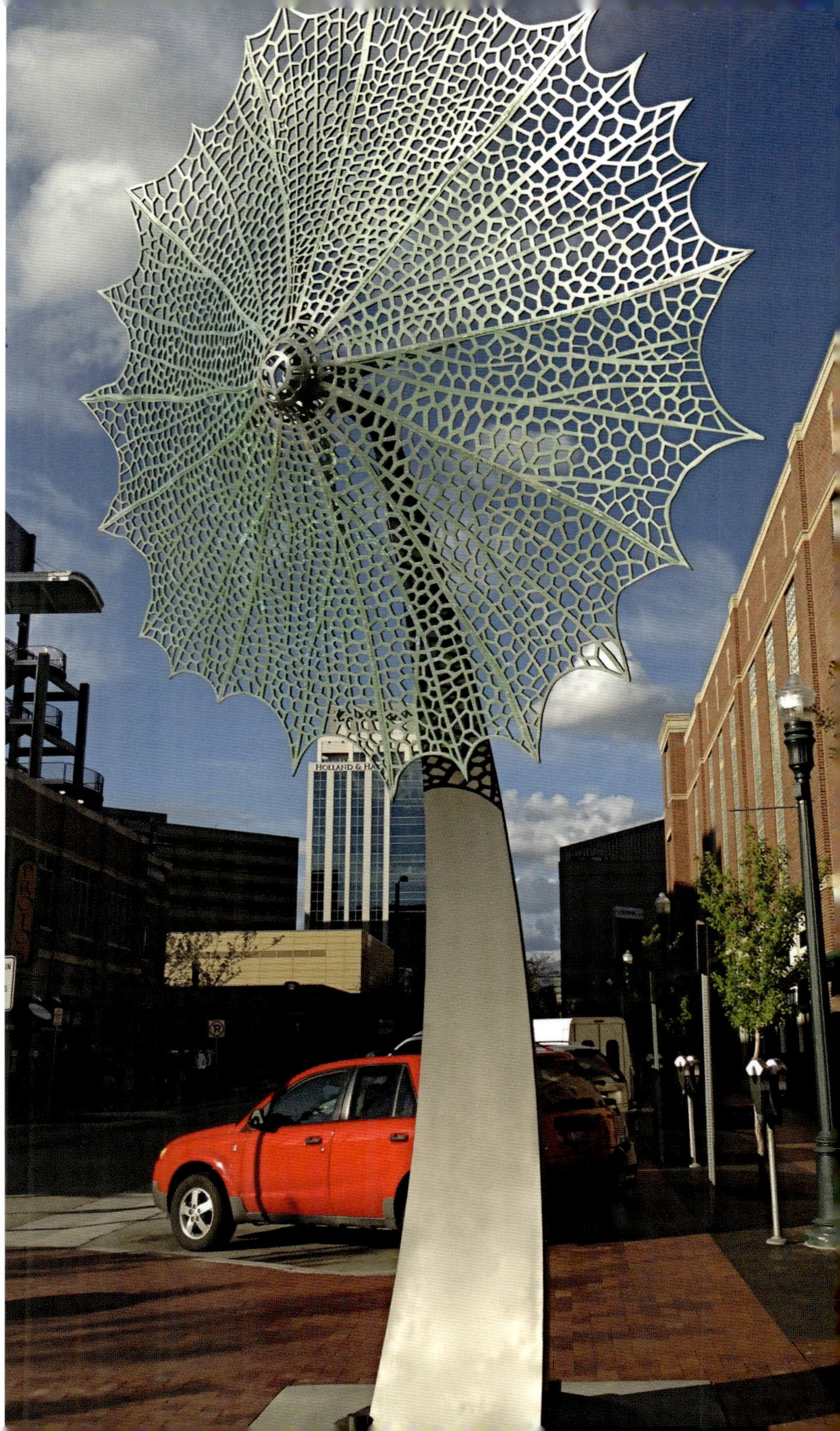

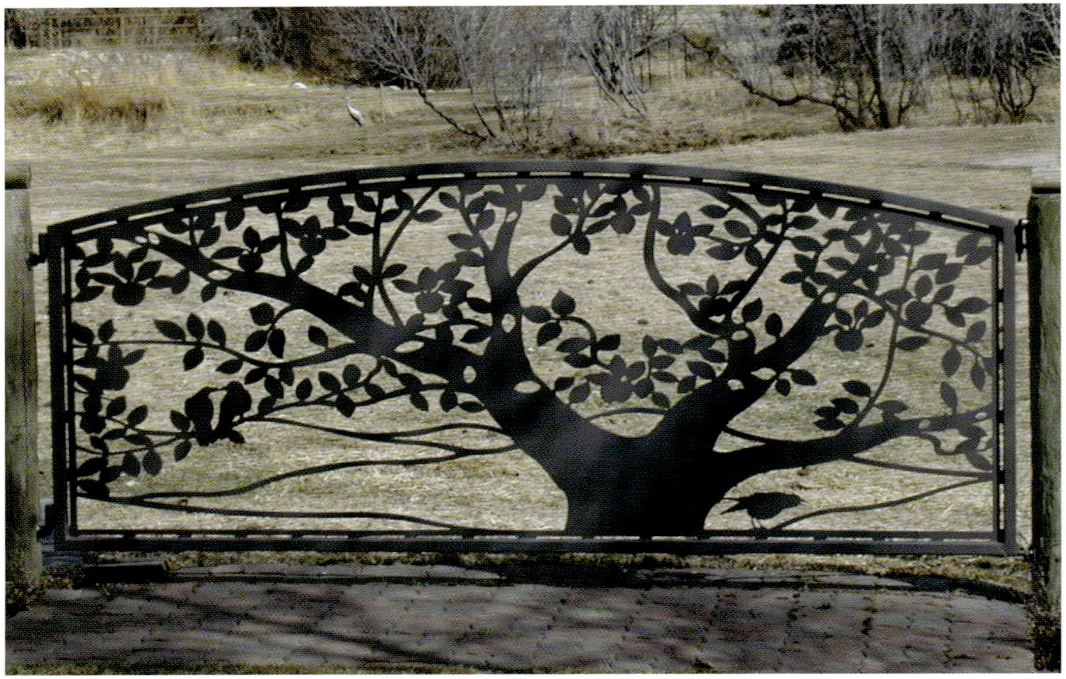

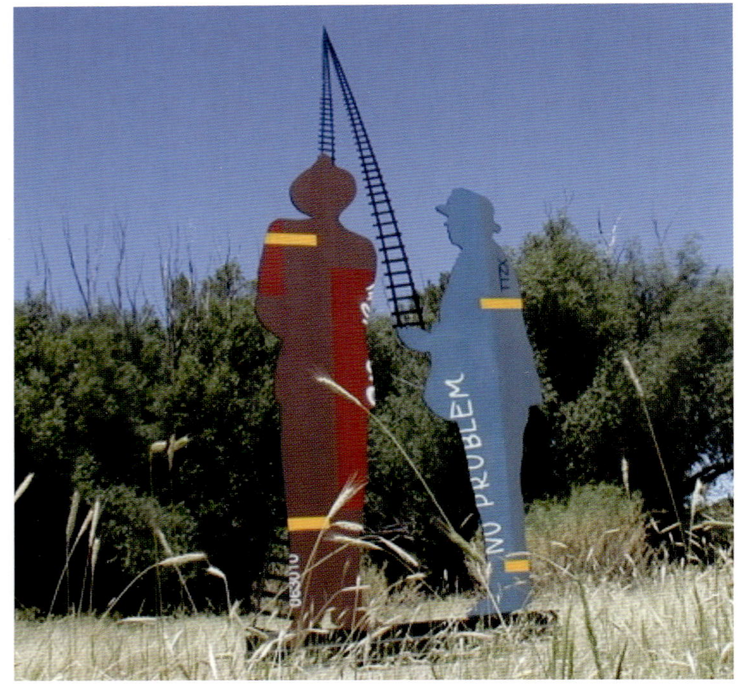

Mink Creek Gate

This gate for a horse pasture was adjacent to an apple orchard which became the image the owners wanted to reflect in a gate. There were many sketches and ideas presented before the final drawing of an apple tree with crows came about. The piece was cut from one sheet of 5/16" plate using a cnc plasma, a frame was built with 1-½" tubing, then it was cleaned, painted and installed.

Mink Creek gate. 2009. Designed by Margo Proska. 9'6"w x 46"h.

The Hobos

This sculpture was commissioned by the Portneuf Greenway Foundation. The sculpture marks the site where hobos camped and hopped on and off trains during the Great Depression in Pocatello, Idaho. They are larger than life for emphasis of their "super" human qualities and to draw attention to their ambition to travel the hard way, and perhaps the only way, to a better life. They are made of steel plate because the hobos were strong and they used the railroad as their mode of transportation. They stand upon a piece of track, which carried them on their journey. The figures hold in their hands and lean on tracks that come together in one point perspective above their heads, symbolizing their view and determination to make it to a better life. Two figures, companions, acknowledge their interdependence.

The Hobos *reminds us that human nature in the face of adversity is resourceful, tenacious, and courageous.*

The Hobos. 2010. Designed by Margo and Dennis Proska. 20'h x 10'w.

Mark Puigmarti

Port Perry, Ontario, Canada
www.sparkswillflyforge.ca

ARTIST'S STATEMENT

Hot forging metal appeals to me on many levels, including the interaction of energy and design. You really get a chance to understand the material on a very basic level while working with it hot. Inspiration comes from all the things in my life. I like to mix concepts together to come up with crazy things that don't exactly mimic/repeat nature or reality. The forging process and resulting details are very important to me...I would also say that the overall impact or sum of all the parts of a piece is equally as important.

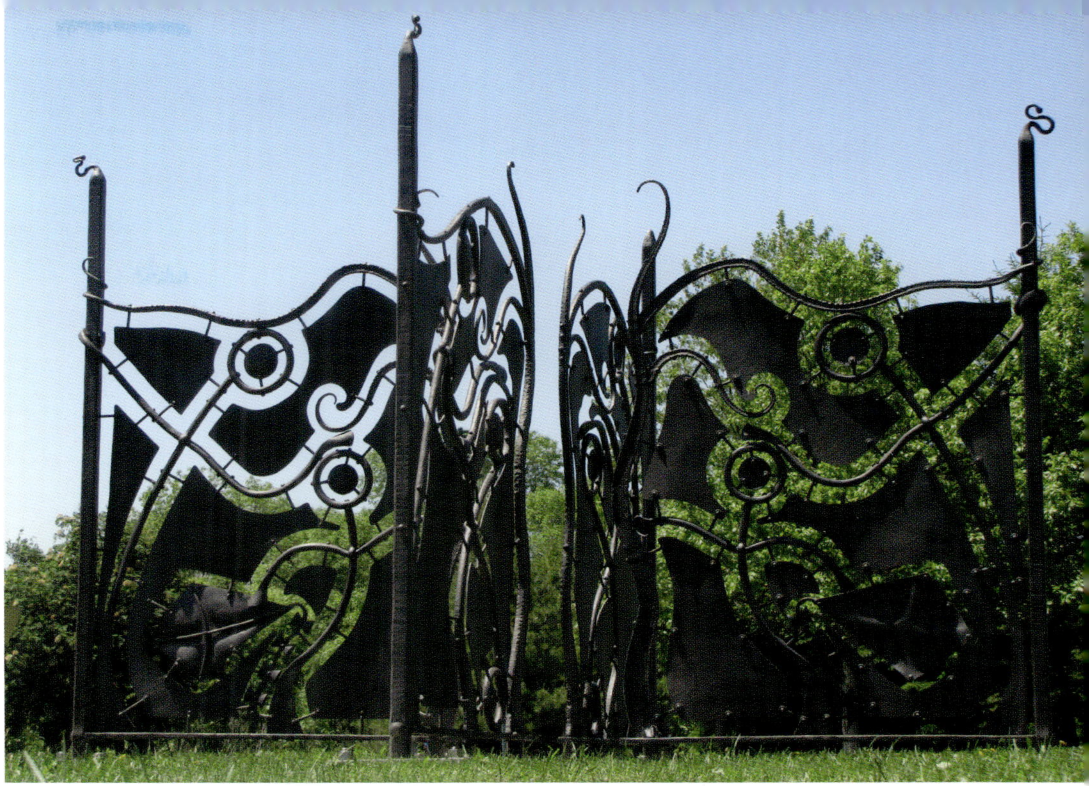

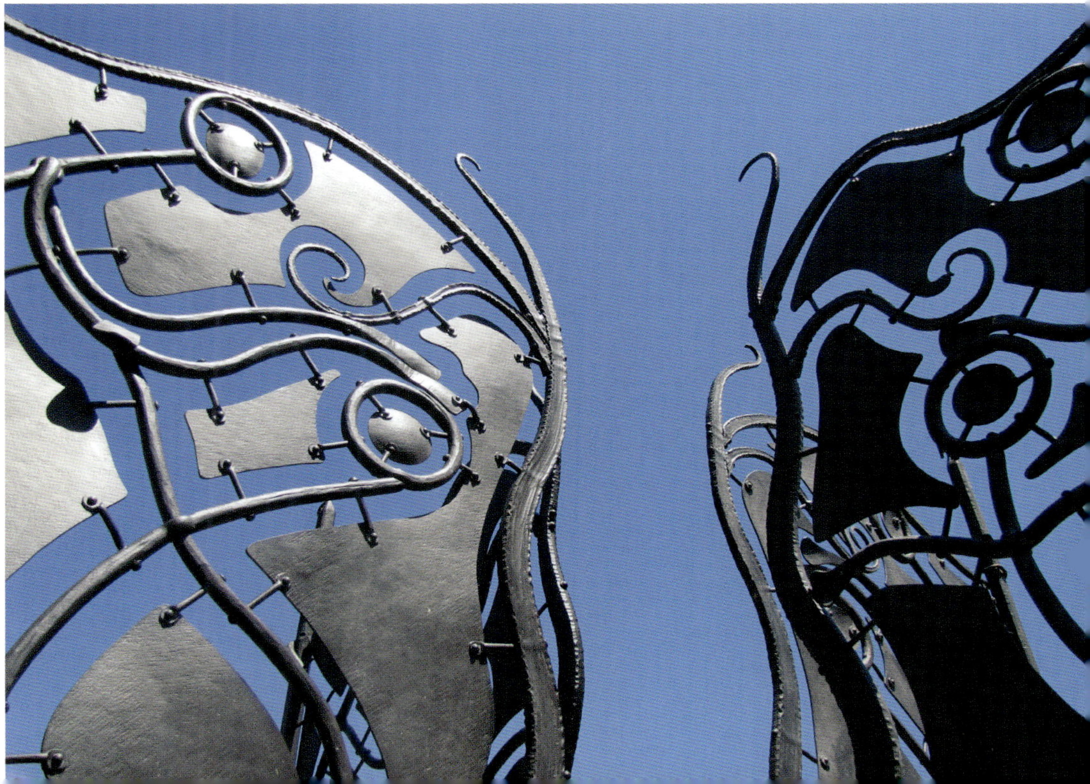

WoodHaven

This public sculpture is in Carruthers Marsh Pavilion in Ajax, Ontario. These perspectives show light and shadow working with positive and negative.

WoodHaven. Sculpture. 2013. Ajax, Ontario.

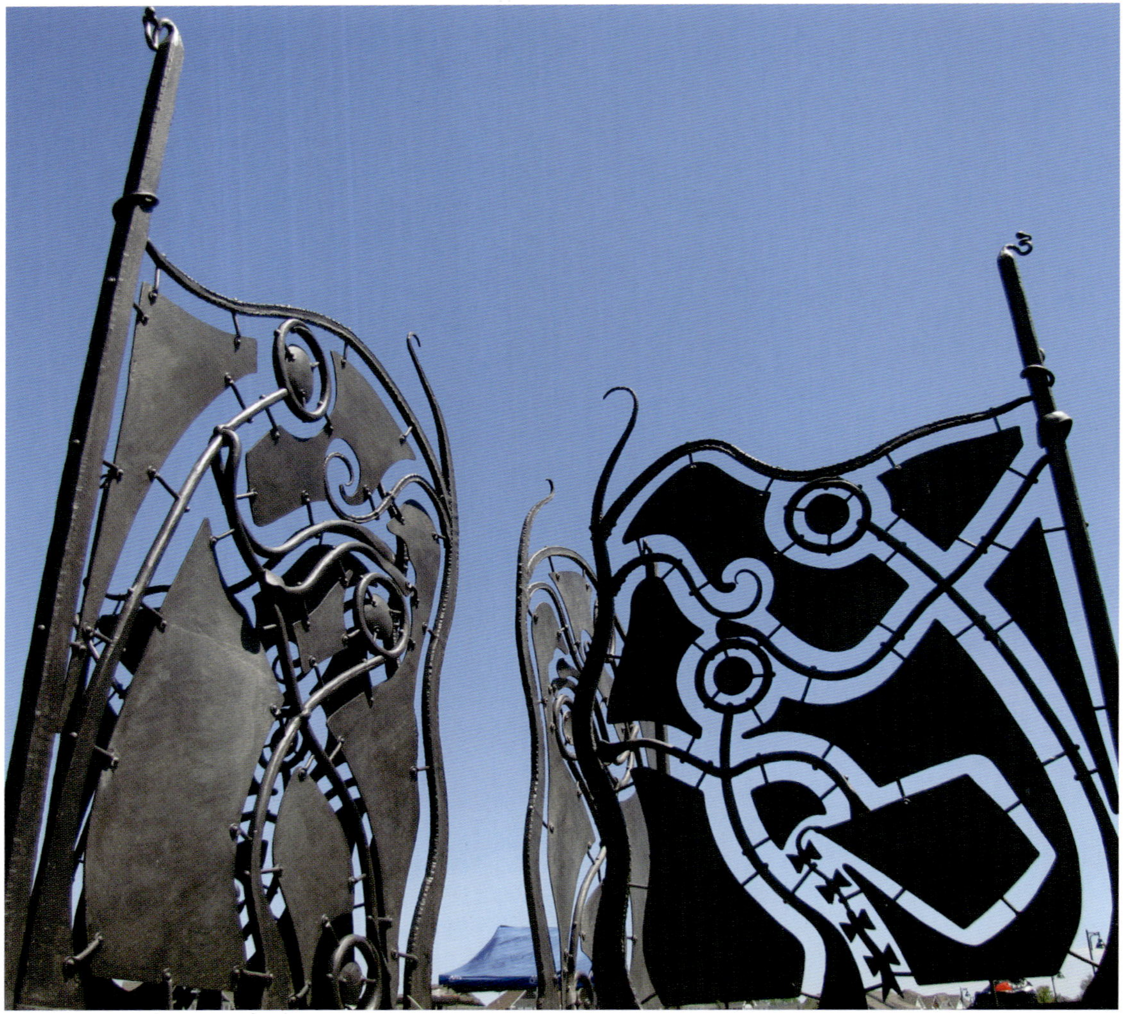

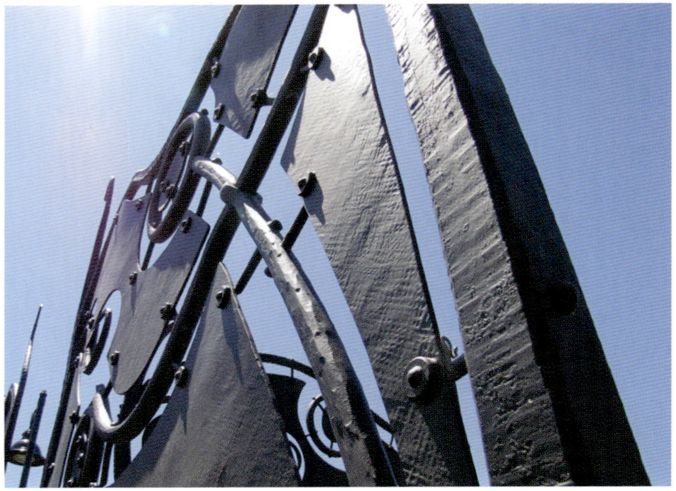

WoodHaven. Sculpture. 2013.

Dawn Raines

Rusty Belly Forgeworks, Austin, Texas
rustybellyforgeworks@yahoo.com

ARTIST'S STATEMENT

It wasn't until after I completed my bachelor's degree in art at Texas State University in 2006 that I began my career as a blacksmith. After graduating, I stumbled upon a custom, ornamental-iron shop called Mind over Metal and apprenticed under a gentleman by the name of Richard Schultz. I worked at Mind over Metal for many years creating gates, hand railing, architectural hardware, furniture, and a slew of other things. On weekends, I found another ornamental iron shop called San Gabriel Forge. At that point I was anxious to learn as many different techniques as possible. Finishing, joinery, attention to detail, and mere equipment use varied significantly between the two shops, and I was more than happy to learn both approaches to the art.

Later, I took a job finishing and assembling semi-automatic pistols in the finish shop at S.T.I. International, a custom and competition pistol manufacturer. S.T.I. allowed me to learn a far different approach to metalwork.

The romance that is involved in hand forging a piece of sculpture is what draws me to the trade.

Everyone Has To Go

The bathroom is a universal place where our fronts are put aside, and this piece is a tribute to the humor and subtleties that can be found within our struggles, if we choose to look at them in a different light.

The toilet paper was fabricated out of 12 gauge sheet metal. It was textured by using cold chisels and a set tool that was modified to make a quilted pattern. The components for the base were shaped using Hossfeld Universal Bender and then welded together. The patina on the base is M38 Antique brown that was applied cold.

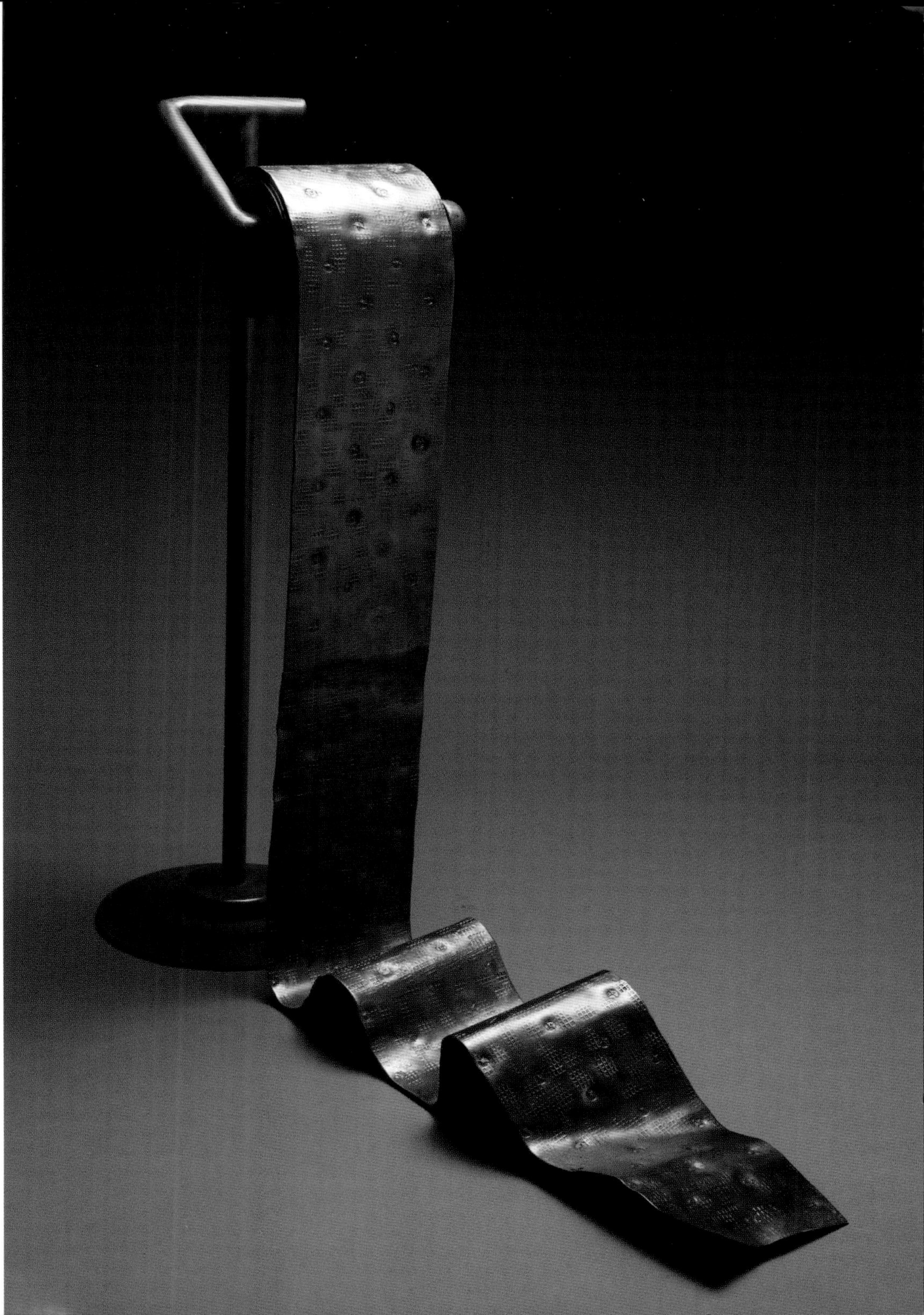

Everyone Has To Go. Sculpture. 2012. Forged and fabricated steel. 38" x 36" x 12". *Photo: Boland Photography*

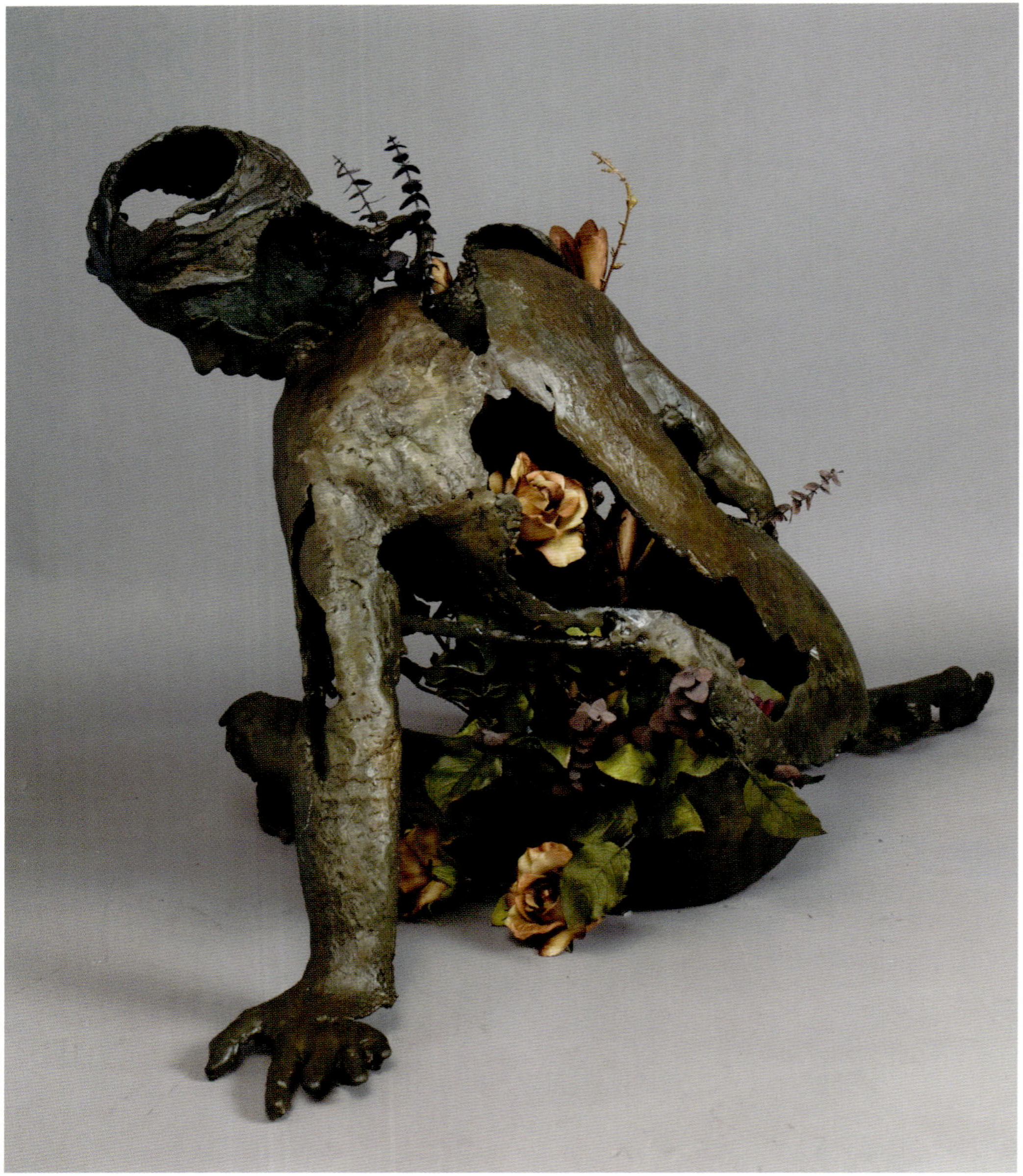

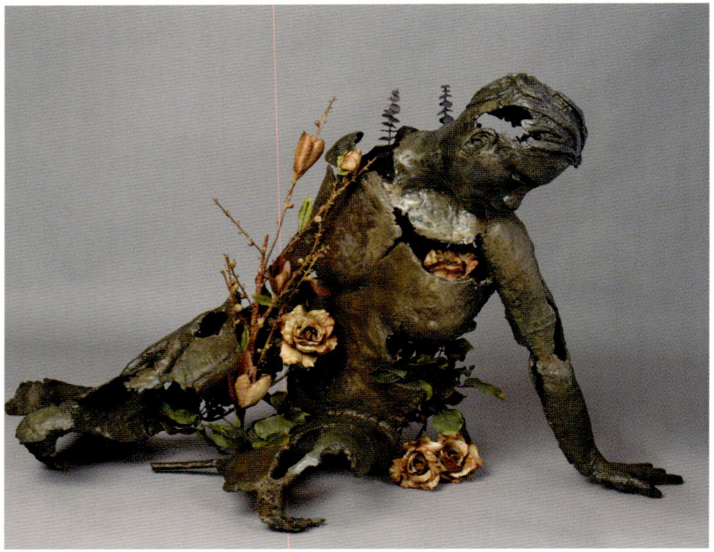

Withering and Life

I began making this sculpture by making a plaster of Paris cast of my body so I could later make a wax mold and cast it in bronze. I soon found myself plastered, quite literally, to the floor of my studio apartment. Fortunately there was little unintentional damage to the plaster mold when I broke myself out. Withering is a feeling most of us have experienced. Whether we find ourselves stuck in a metaphorical rut, are dealing with health concerns, or simply have apprehensions about growing old and changing, it is all part of the journey.

A Cupric Nitrate patina was applied once the sculpture was completed. She was heated with a rosebud propane torch and the Cu(NO3)2 – 3H20 solution was sprayed onto the heated bronze to achieve the final variety of colors.

Withering and Life. Sculpture. 2011. Cast bronze. 30" x 48" x 24". *Photo: Margaret Norris Design*

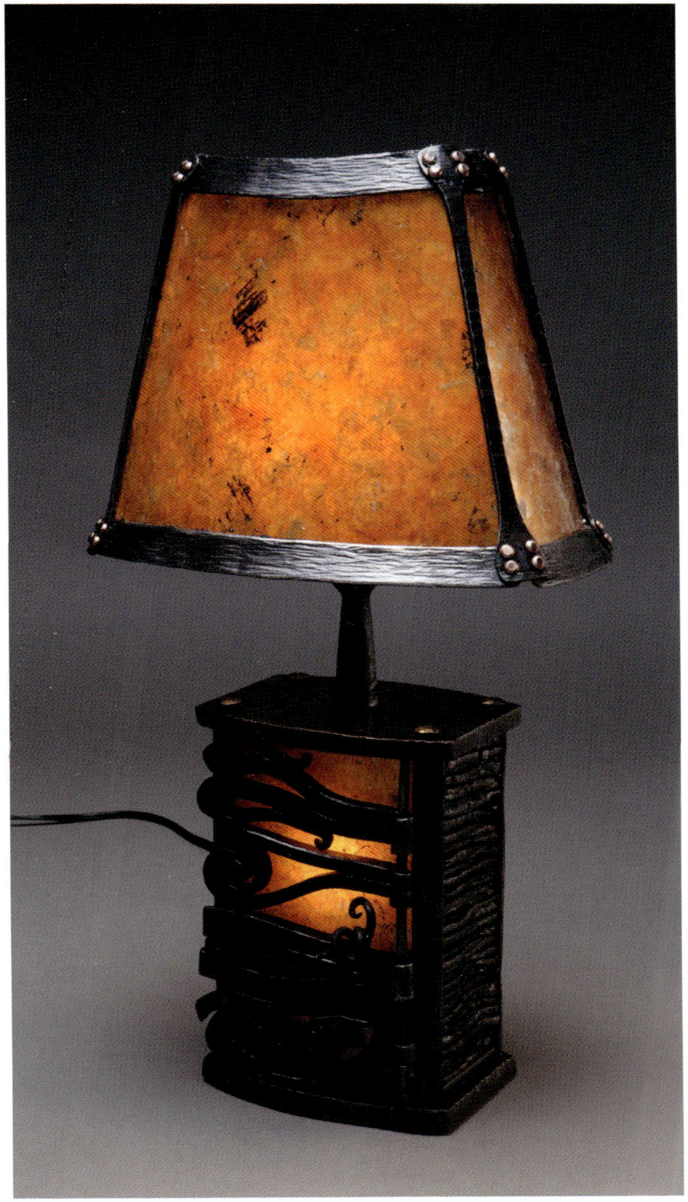

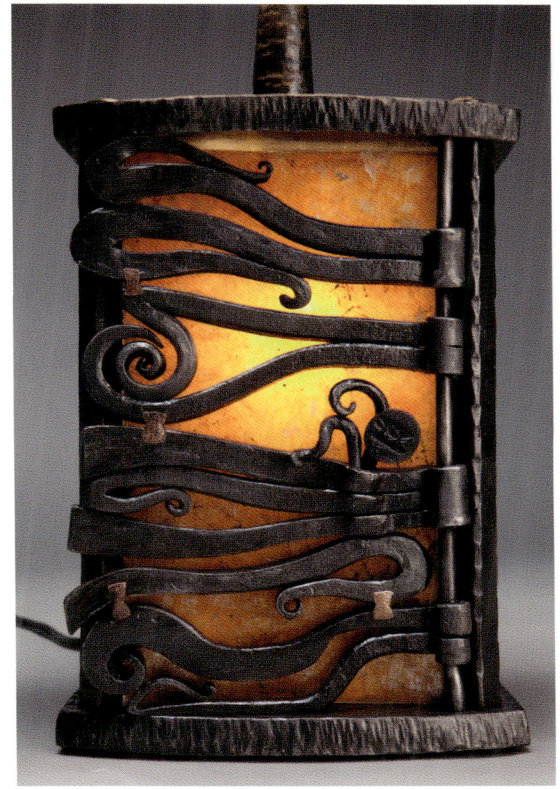

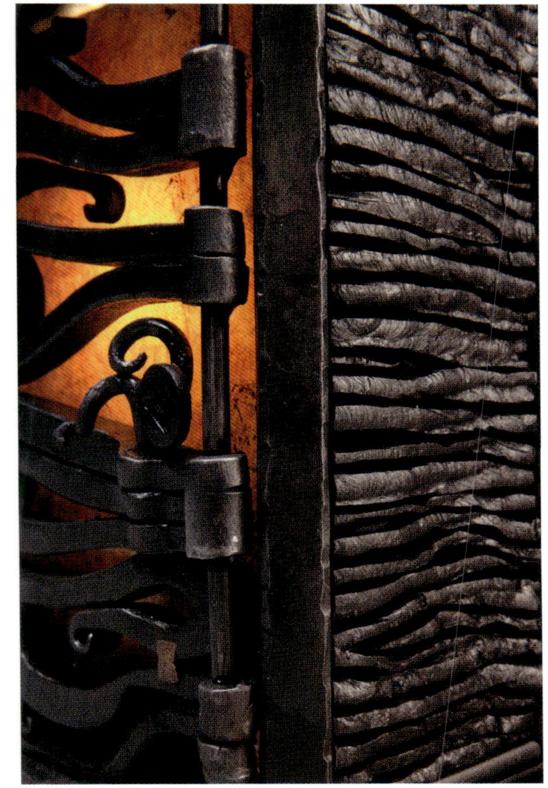

Una Luz de Noche Pesada

When creating this light fixture, I wanted to try several different forging techniques and approaches to texture and joinery. The side panels were formed by making horizontal cuts around the face of 2½" schedule XX-Hvy pipe, which was then opened and flattened. The back panel embraces this process as well. The front panel was designed to make use of negative space and is comprised of several linear forge welded elements. These elements form the hinges on the right hand side and are joined with double-dovetail copper keys on the left. For the joinery on the side panels, I made a vertical, 90 degree, groove down both sides of the textured plates to allow them to nest within the corresponding angle of the ⅝" pillars on the base of the lamp.

Una Luz de Noche Pesada. Lamp. 2013. Forged steel with copper accents. 21" x 14" x 12". Photo: Margaret Norris Design

David Robertson

Cargill, Ontario, Canada
www.artistblacksmith.com

ARTIST'S STATEMENT

Part of the beauty of the blacksmithing craft is that there is always room to grow and develop both techniques and design interests. For many years, I have been drawn to organic forms and shapes. In some cases, my works are very representational of flowers found in nature. In other cases, such as the *Spring Tide* sculpture, the fluid lines are maintained but leaves and flowers are absent. My personal goal is to explore, using the forged steel, a creative statement either of emotion or of interest.

The *Font* series that I am engaged in lends itself for technical exploration: how to create traditional and interesting joint structures to hold everything together. Much is worked out on paper, while some ideas still require small test pieces in the steel to make sure everything will work. Aesthetics are taken into account for the interaction of the base and the bowl form, in both proportion and balance.

After working with the hot steel for over twenty-five years, I still get a huge amount of satisfaction from taking plain bar stock and transforming it into something beautiful and interesting.

Spring Tide

Spring Tide *captures my enthusiasm for the return of spring after a long winter. It symbolizes a burst of growth of life with the new season.*

Spring Tide. Sculpture. 2013. Forged from mild steel with riveted and hot wrap construction. 33"h x 17"w. *Photo: David Robertson*

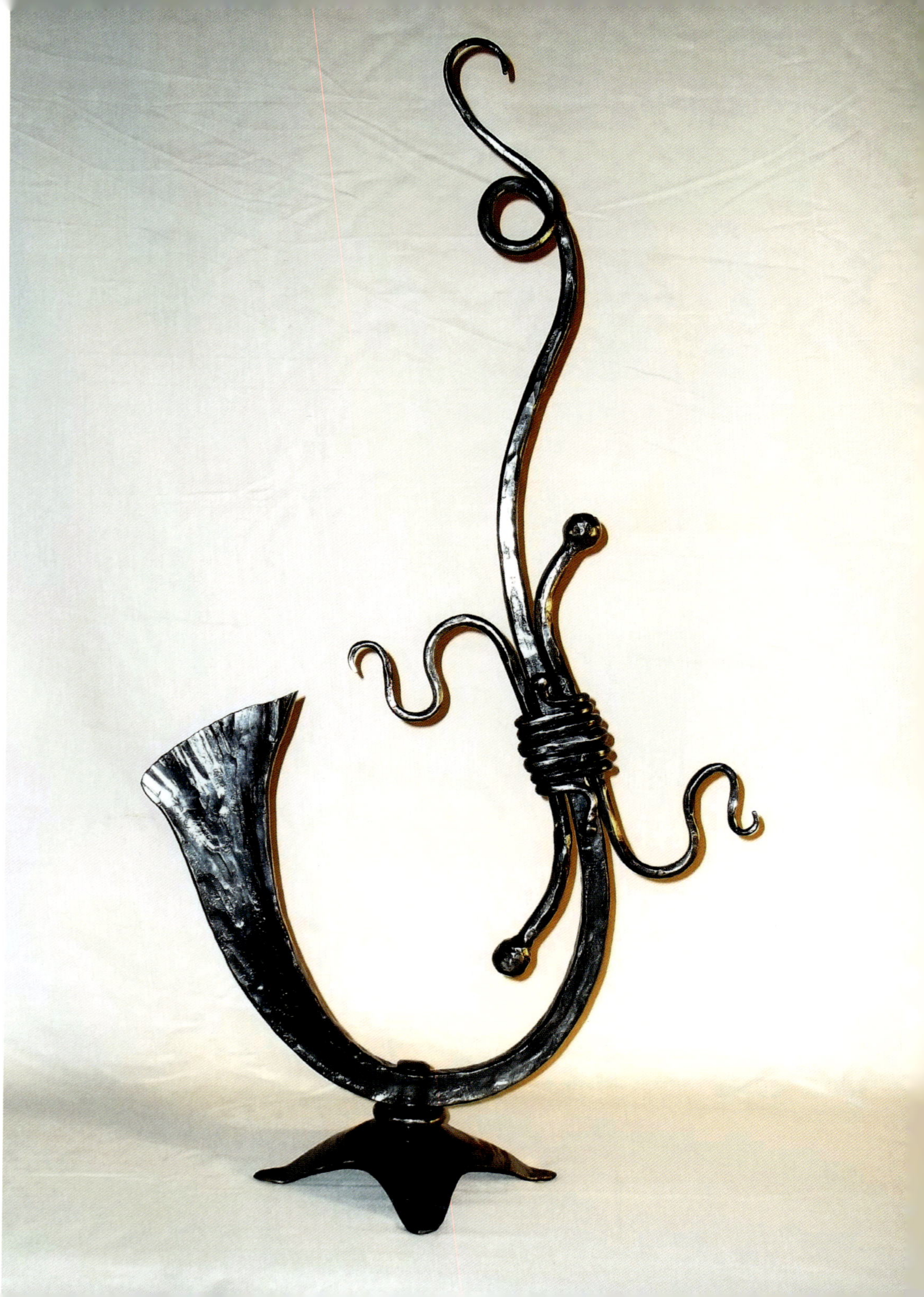

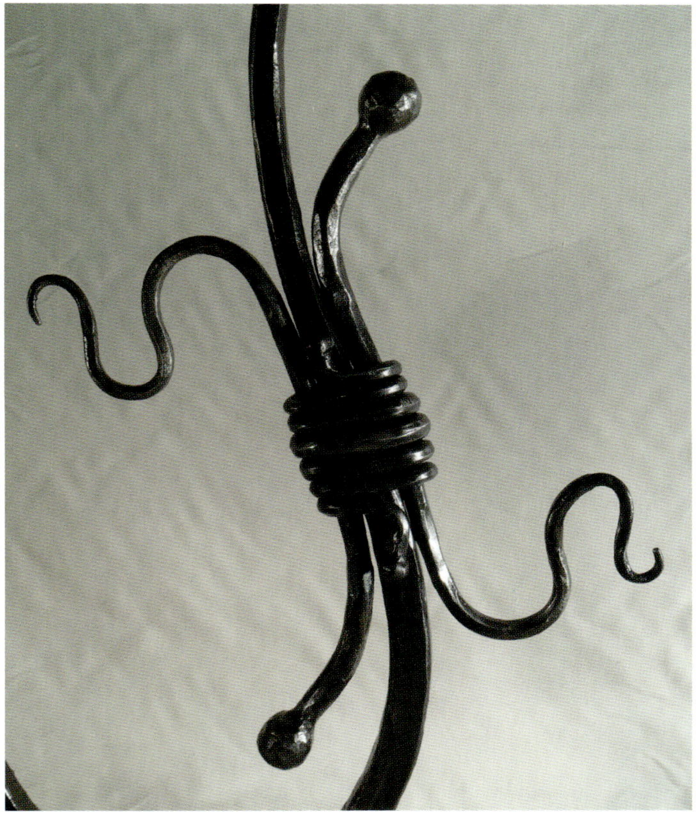

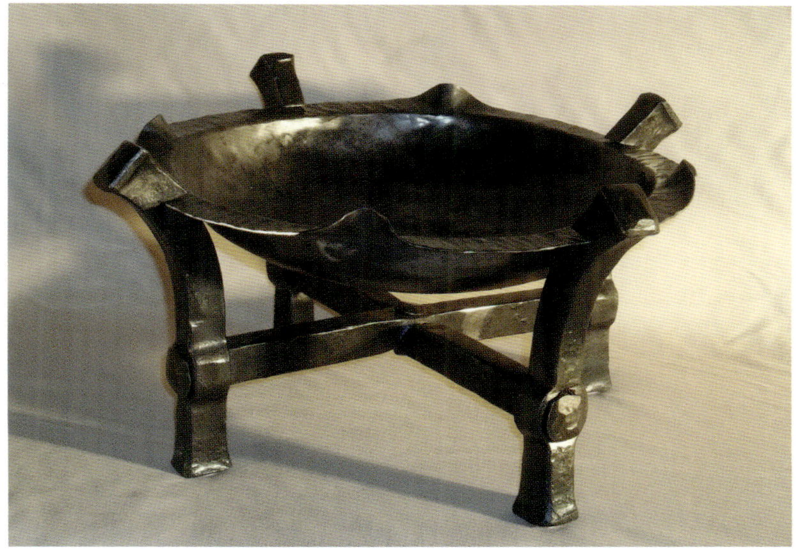

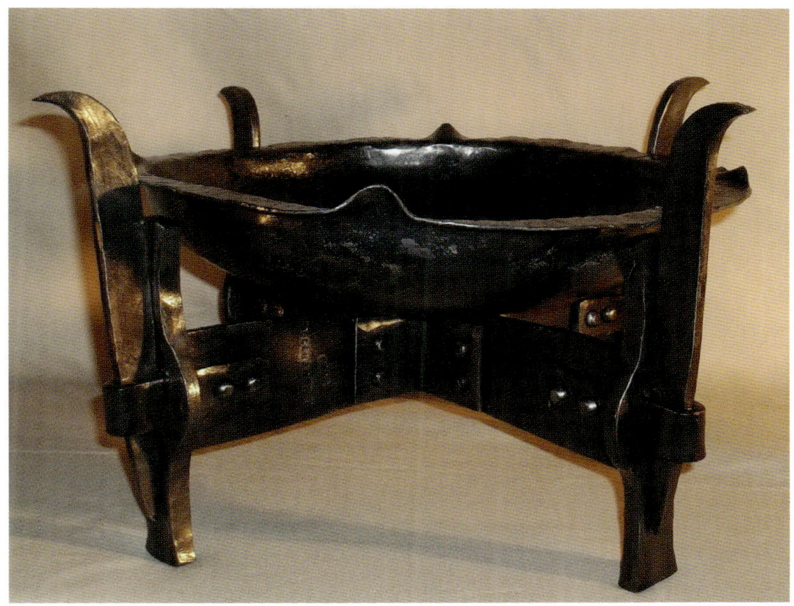

Reckoning Font

The focus on this piece was the use of heavy mortise-and-tenon joints to construct the base of the bowl. The mortise-and-tenon is made out of ¾" x 1" mild steel. Sequence of events is important, since locking the bowl in the last mortise-and-tenon joint is done with the bowl in place. The ends of the legs of the base are upset as well.

Reckoning. Font. 2011. Mild steel. 14" diameter, 8"h. *Photo: David Robertson*

Richard Rozinski

Flying Sparks Studio, Inc., Mesa, Arizona
rrozinski@cox.net

ARTIST'S STATEMENT

I use forged and fabricated abstract shapes to create geometric and organic sculptures. My creations convey the impression of movement and life. These images are inspired by rock formations, the motions of water, aquatic habitats, astronomical patterns, and life cycles of plants and animals. The simplicity inherent in these forms is both inspiring and breathtaking. Through the various techniques of metal smithing, fabrication, and welding, I produce sculptures that are infused with neon. They illuminate an entire space in luscious lights and shadows, bathing and embracing the viewer. Eruptions of the metal's surface represent the emergence of life. Neon speaks of the awakening spirit.

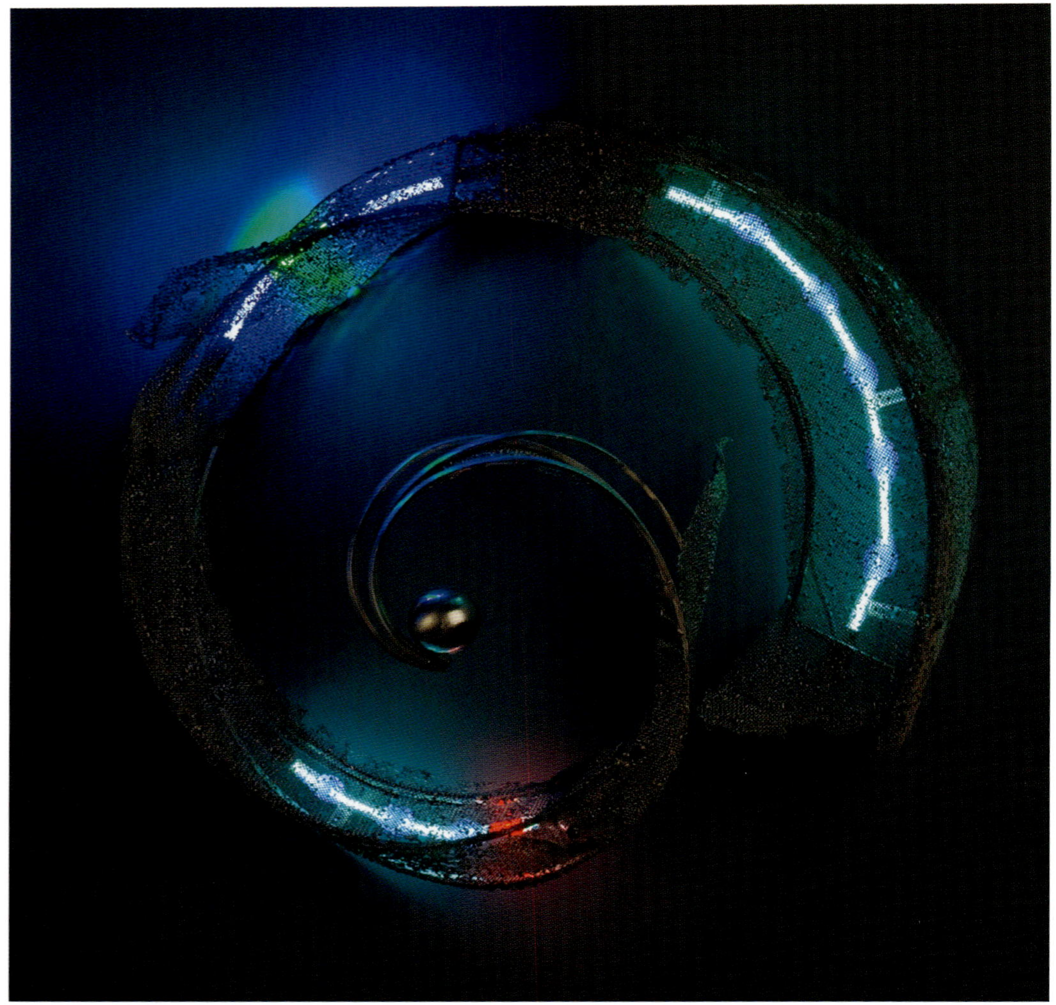

Nebula. Sculpture. Neon, stainless steel. Wall mounted, forged and fabricated. 35½" x 34" x 8".
Photo: Michael Thompson

Top: *Eclypz III.* Sculpture. Neon, steel, brass, Wall mounted fabricated steel, brass, and neon. 48″ x 28½″ x 11″. *Photo: Michael Thompson*

Bottom: *Homage VIII.* Sculpture. Neon and steel. Wall mounted, forged and fabricated steel, and neon. 56″ x 16″ x 4″. *Photo: Sean Kapra*

Right: *Live Force IV.* Sculpture. Neon, steel, stainless steel. Wall mounted, forged and fabricated steel, stainless steel, and neon. 19″ x 12″ x 3″. *Photo: Red Rock Studio*

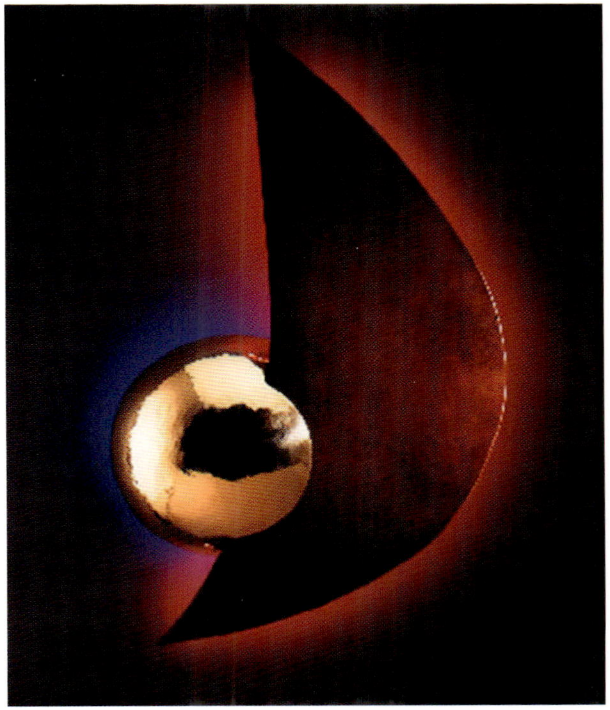

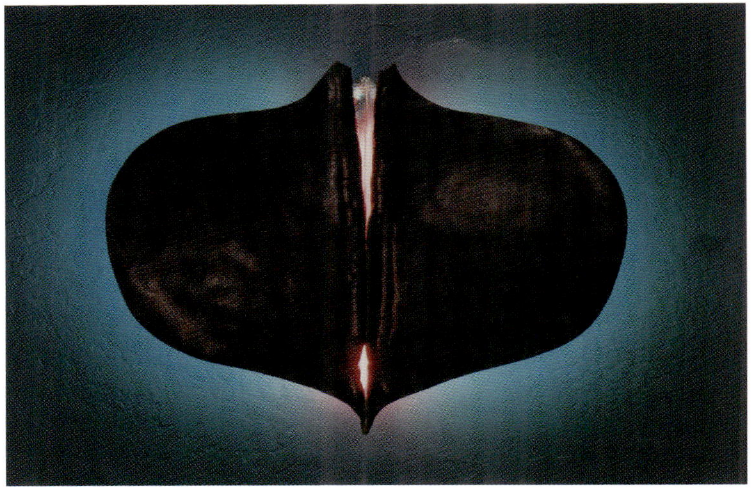

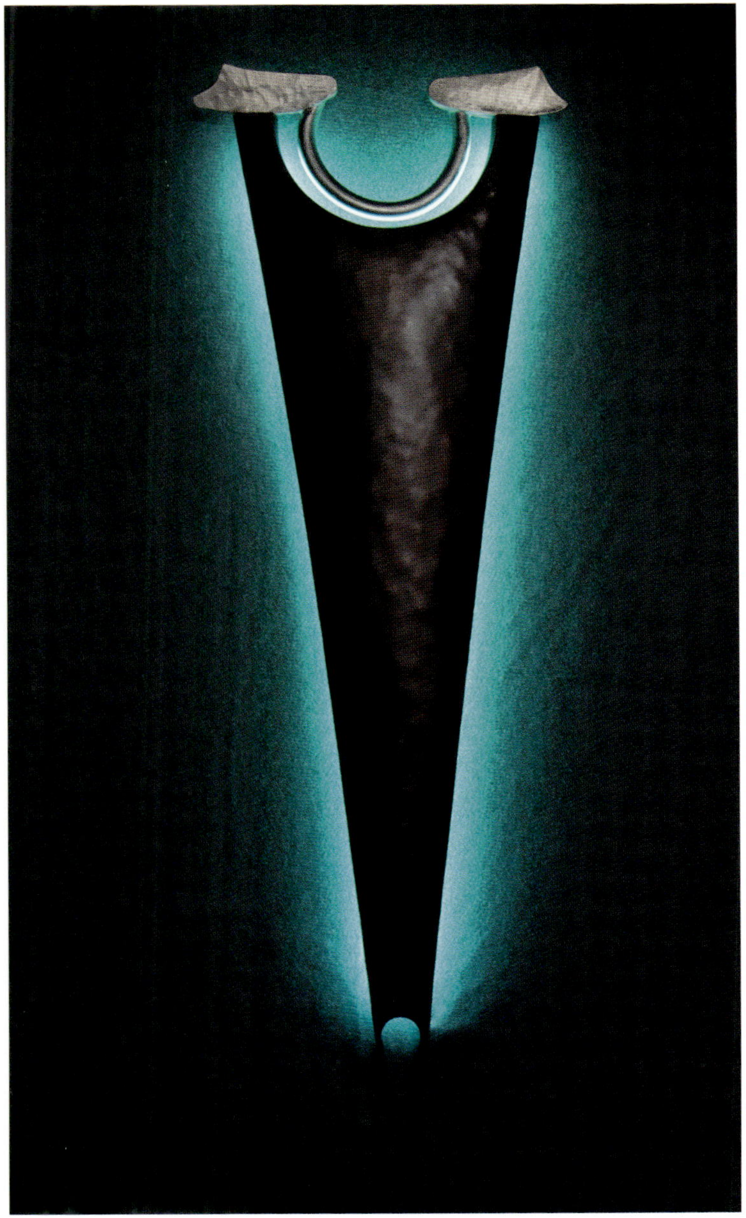

Robert A. Rupert

Clinton, PA

ARTIST'S STATEMENT

My interest in metals and knife-making was awakened in the 1980s. I was fortunate to live near a knifemaker who peaked my interest enough that I enrolled in a knife-making class at Rochester Institute of Technology, taught by Bill Moran. I went on to learn more when I joined the local ABANA chapter, Pittsburgh Area Artists and Blacksmith Association (PAABA). Attending classes in Missouri led me to write and self-publish a book, *Fundamentals in Blacksmithing*.

My goal is to produce lasting works of art and share that love and ability with others through my teaching.

Tenebrae Candle Holder

This work was completed for a special service at Four Mile Church near Beaver, Pennsylvania. This candle holder of eight is supported by arched, bolted legs that taper upward to the pierced, slanted bars holding each candle. The snuffer is of copper with a handle forged from a discarded railroad spike.

Tenebrae candle holder.

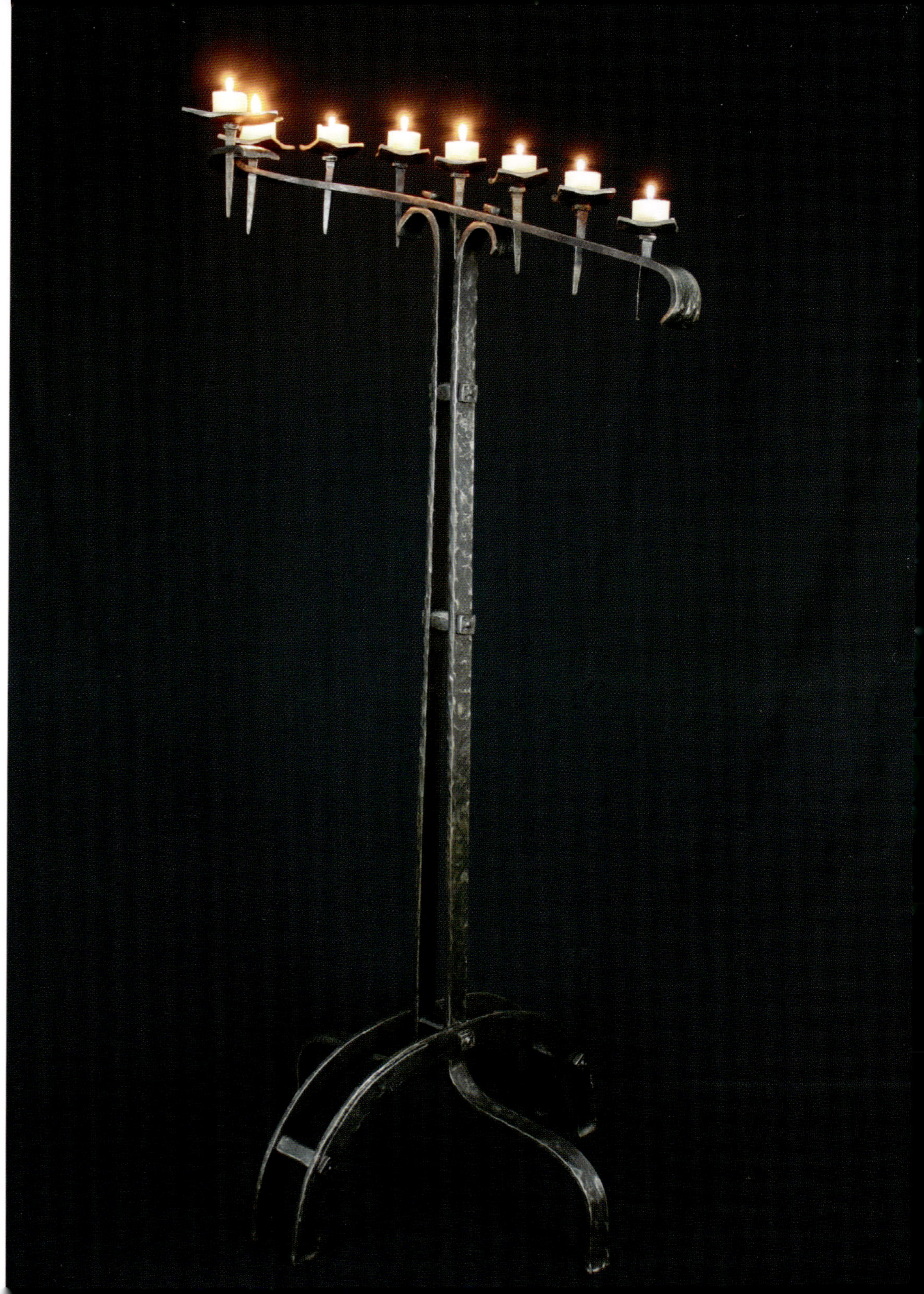

Top: *Eclypz III*. Sculpture.
Neon, steel, brass, Wall mounted fabricated steel, brass, and neon.
48" x 28½" x 11".
Photo: Michael Thompson

Bottom: *Homage VIII*. Sculpture.
Neon and steel. Wall mounted, forged and fabricated steel, and neon.
56" x 16" x 4". *Photo: Sean Kapra*

Right: *Live Force IV*. Sculpture.
Neon, steel, stainless steel. Wall mounted, forged and fabricated steel, stainless steel, and neon.
19" x 12" x 3".
Photo: Red Rock Studio

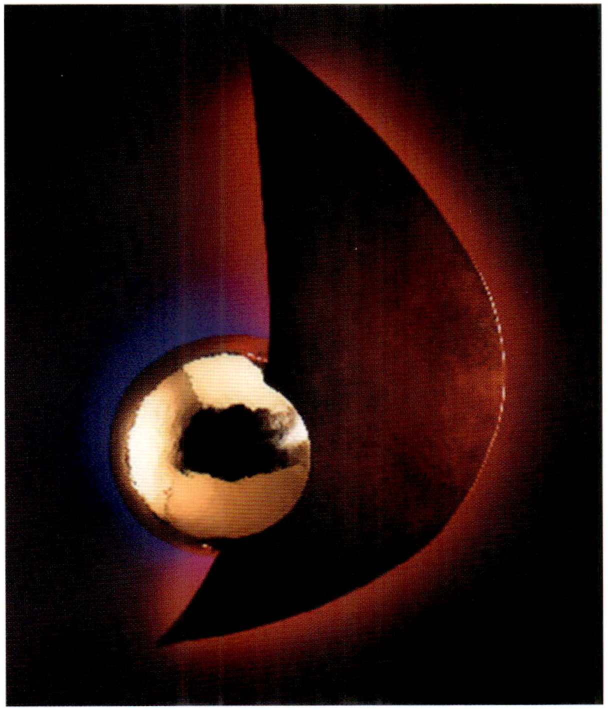

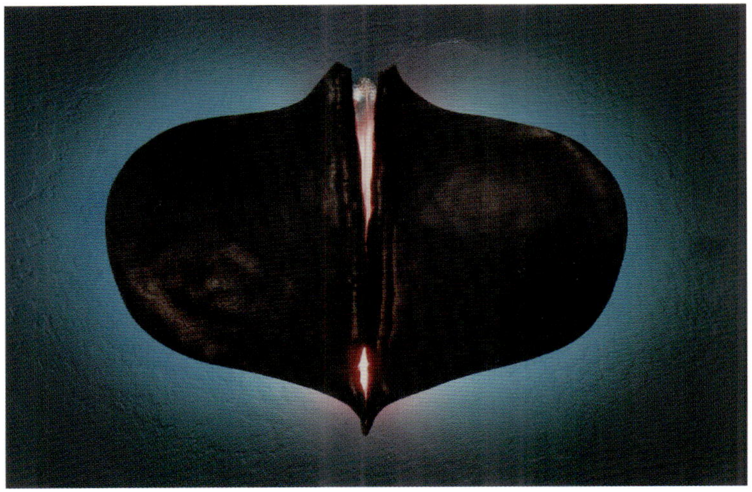

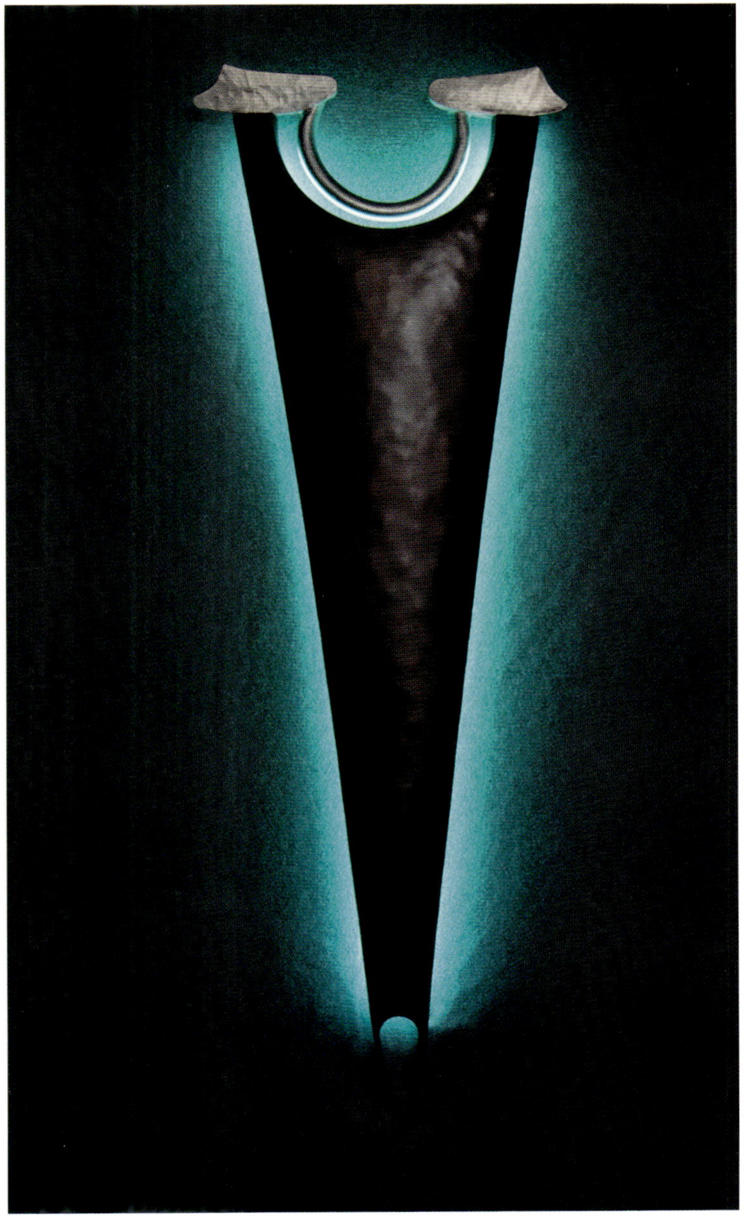

Robert A. Rupert

Clinton, PA

ARTIST'S STATEMENT

My interest in metals and knife-making was awakened in the 1980s. I was fortunate to live near a knifemaker who peaked my interest enough that I enrolled in a knife-making class at Rochester Institute of Technology, taught by Bill Moran. I went on to learn more when I joined the local ABANA chapter, Pittsburgh Area Artists and Blacksmith Association (PAABA). Attending classes in Missouri led me to write and self-publish a book, *Fundamentals in Blacksmithing*.

My goal is to produce lasting works of art and share that love and ability with others through my teaching.

Tenebrae Candle Holder

This work was completed for a special service at Four Mile Church near Beaver, Pennsylvania. This candle holder of eight is supported by arched, bolted legs that taper upward to the pierced, slanted bars holding each candle. The snuffer is of copper with a handle forged from a discarded railroad spike.

Tenebrae candle holder.

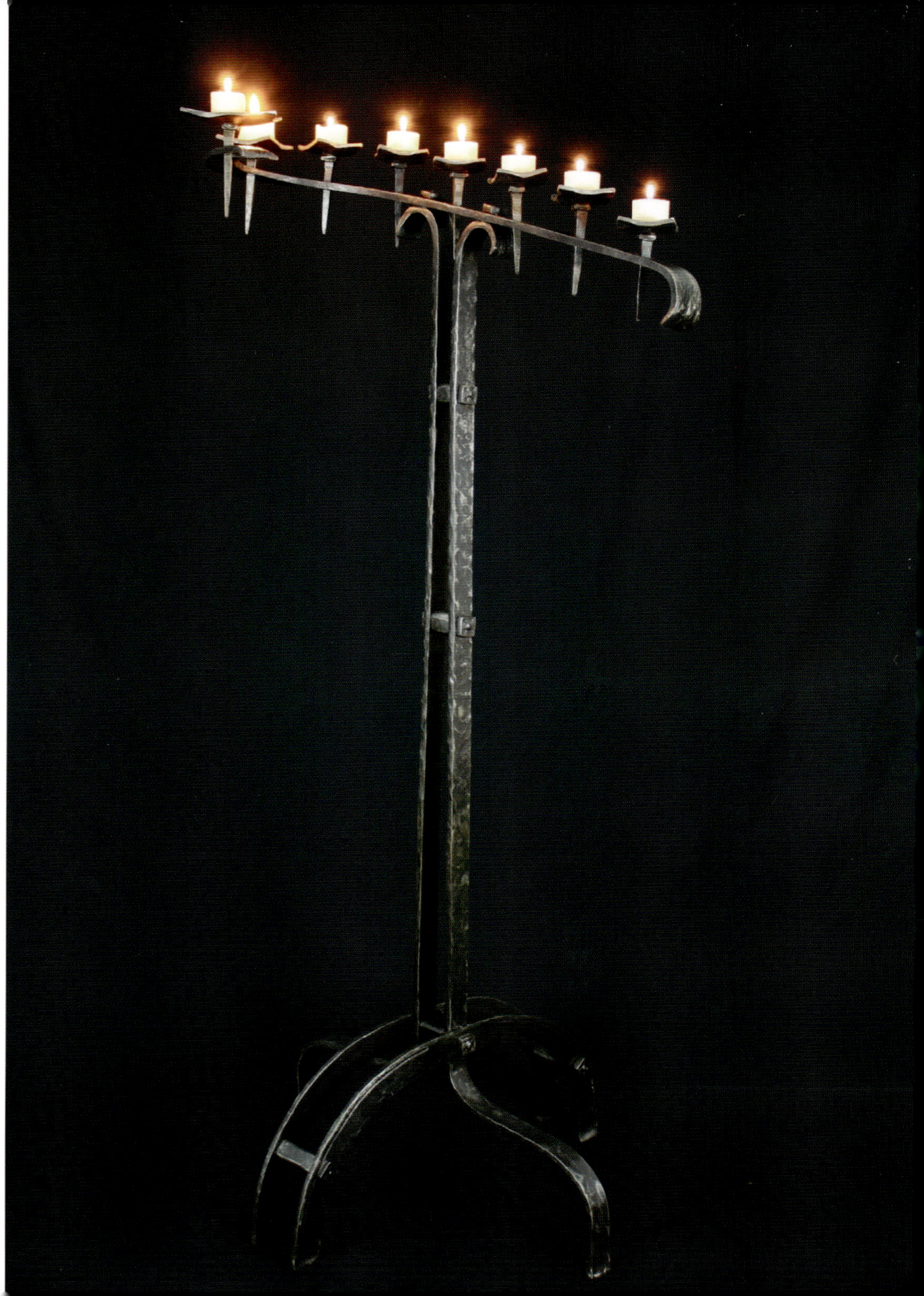

Top: *Eclypz III*. Sculpture.
Neon, steel, brass, Wall mounted fabricated steel, brass, and neon.
48" x 28½" x 11".
Photo: Michael Thompson

Bottom: *Homage VIII*. Sculpture.
Neon and steel. Wall mounted, forged and fabricated steel, and neon.
56" x 16" x 4". *Photo: Sean Kapra*

Right: *Live Force IV*. Sculpture.
Neon, steel, stainless steel. Wall mounted, forged and fabricated steel, stainless steel, and neon.
19" x 12" x 3".
Photo: Red Rock Studio

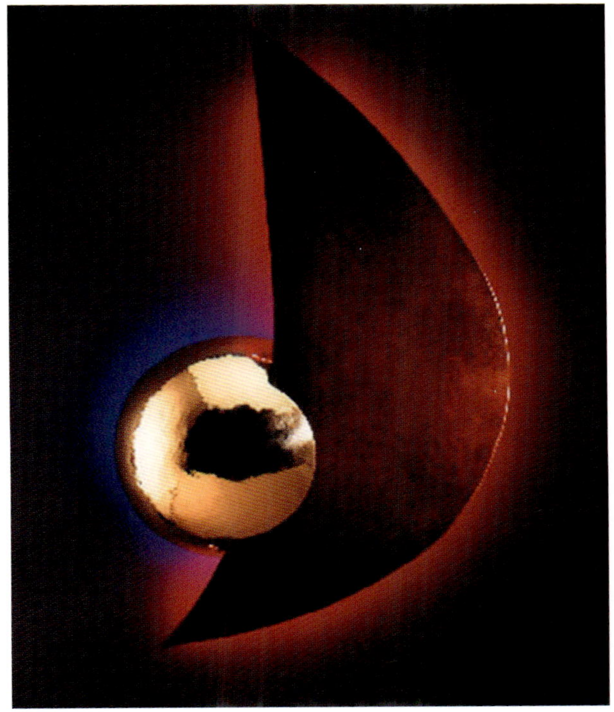

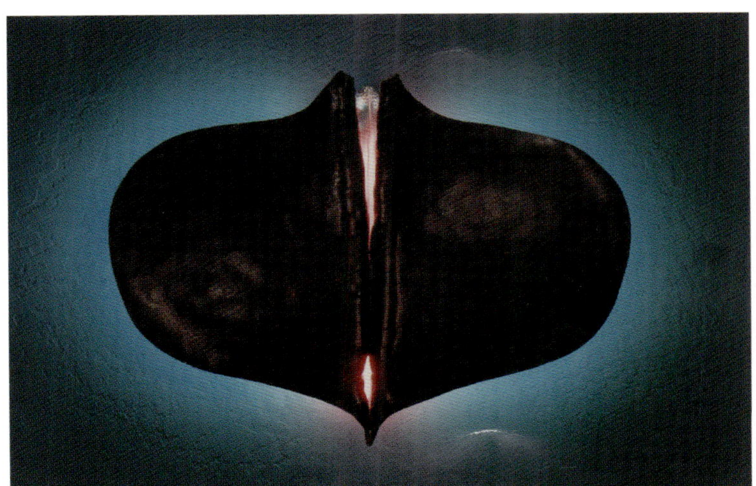

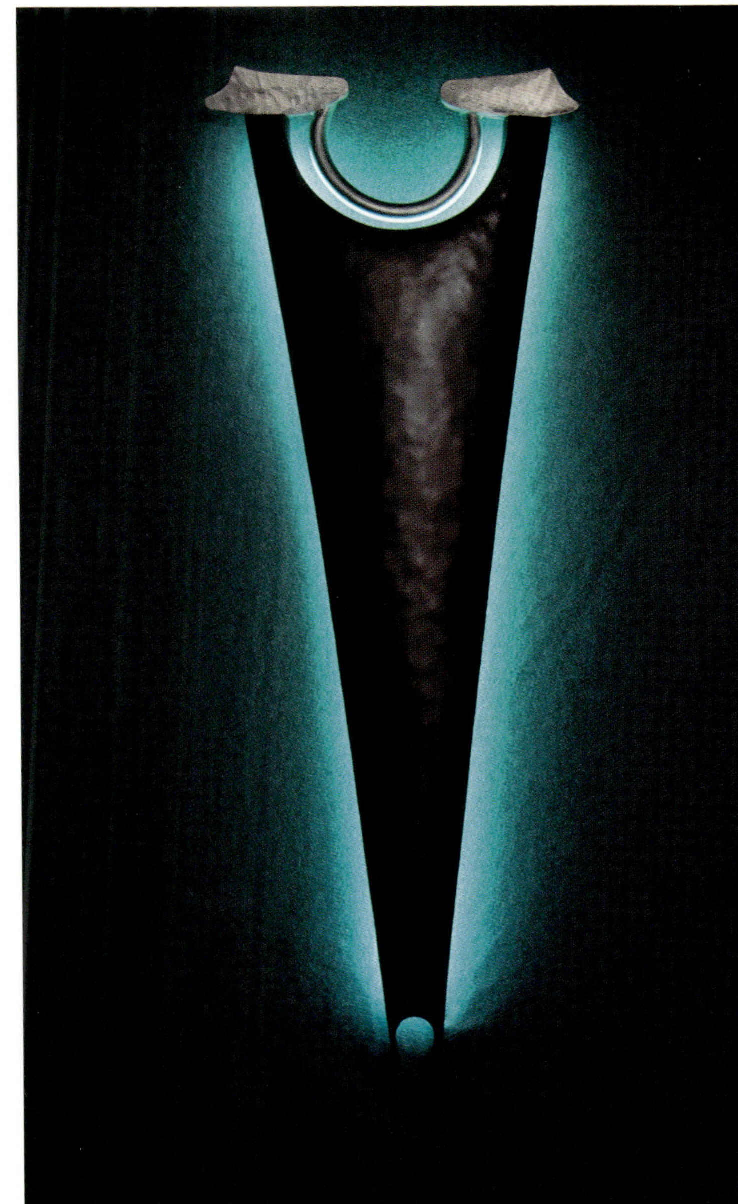

Robert A. Rupert

Clinton, PA

ARTIST'S STATEMENT

My interest in metals and knife-making was awakened in the 1980s. I was fortunate to live near a knifemaker who peaked my interest enough that I enrolled in a knife-making class at Rochester Institute of Technology, taught by Bill Moran. I went on to learn more when I joined the local ABANA chapter, Pittsburgh Area Artists and Blacksmith Association (PAABA). Attending classes in Missouri led me to write and self-publish a book, *Fundamentals in Blacksmithing*.

My goal is to produce lasting works of art and share that love and ability with others through my teaching.

Tenebrae Candle Holder

This work was completed for a special service at Four Mile Church near Beaver, Pennsylvania. This candle holder of eight is supported by arched, bolted legs that taper upward to the pierced, slanted bars holding each candle. The snuffer is of copper with a handle forged from a discarded railroad spike.

Tenebrae candle holder.

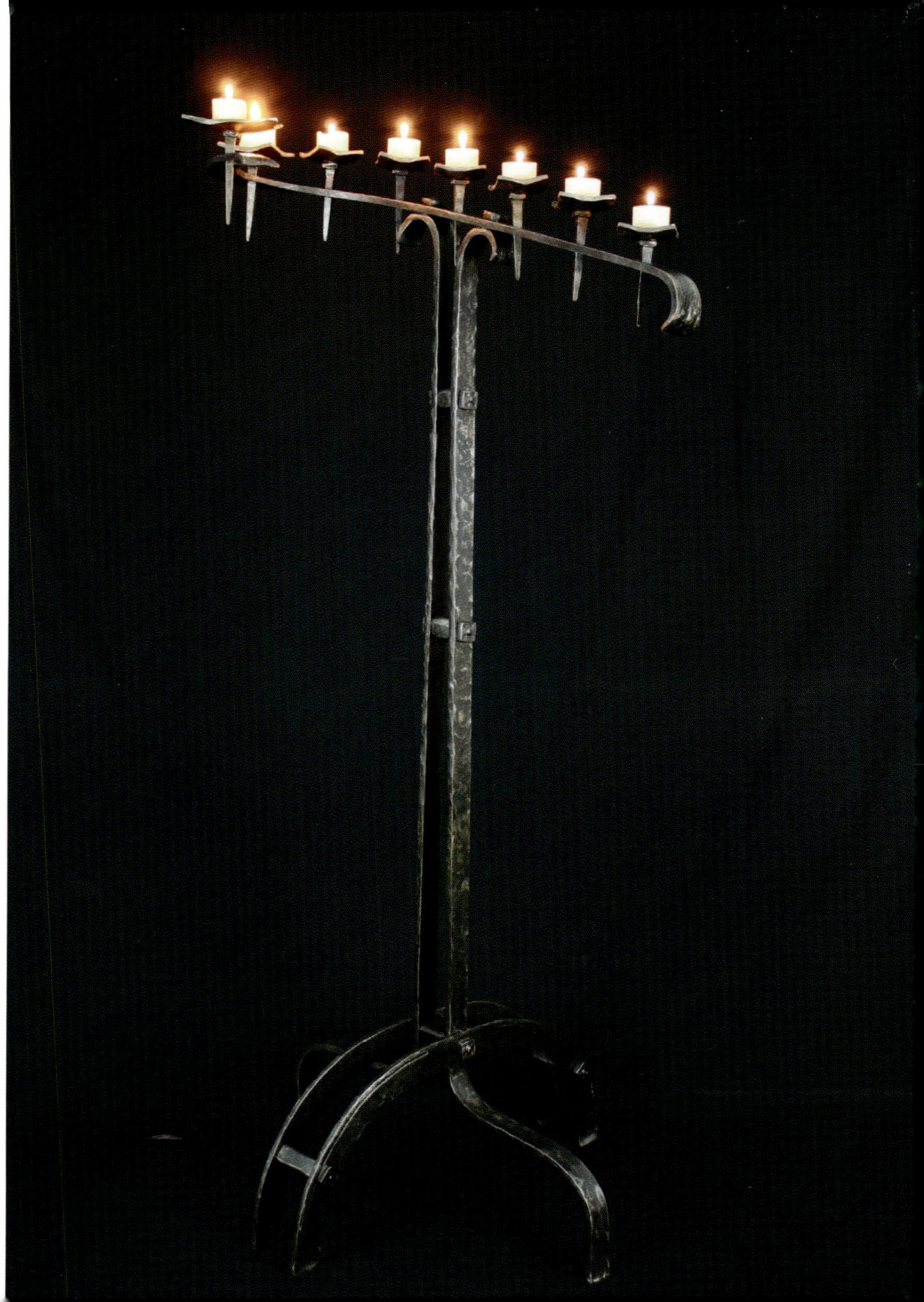

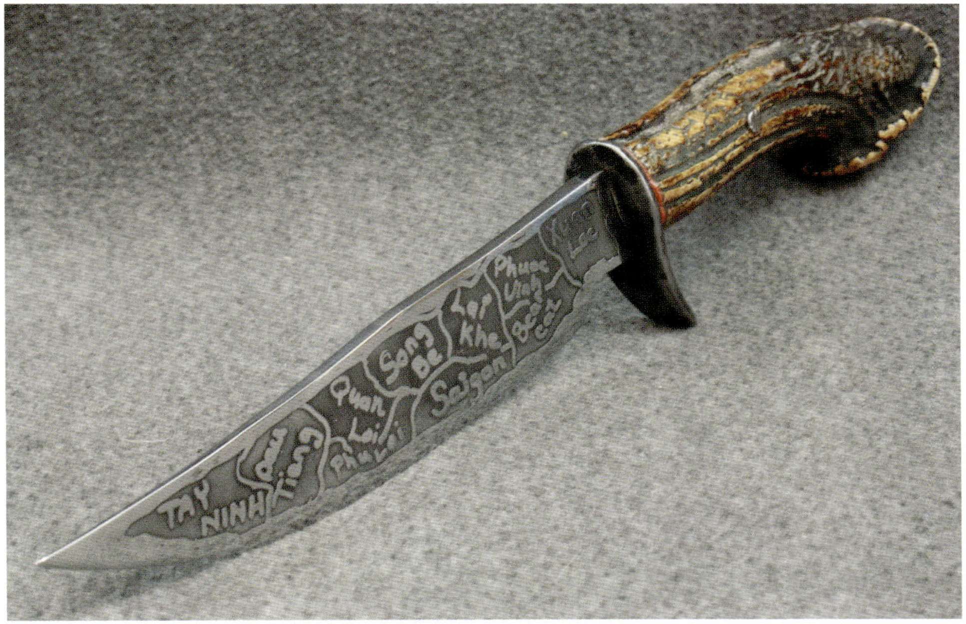

Vietnam

This knife depicts my tour of duty serving with the Army's 1st Air Cavalry in 1969. Each province where I served is etched on this carbon steel blade, made of 1095 steel. The grip is of stag horn and can be removed using the decorated pin of monel at the middle of the handle.

Vietnam. Knife. Carbon steel, stag horn.

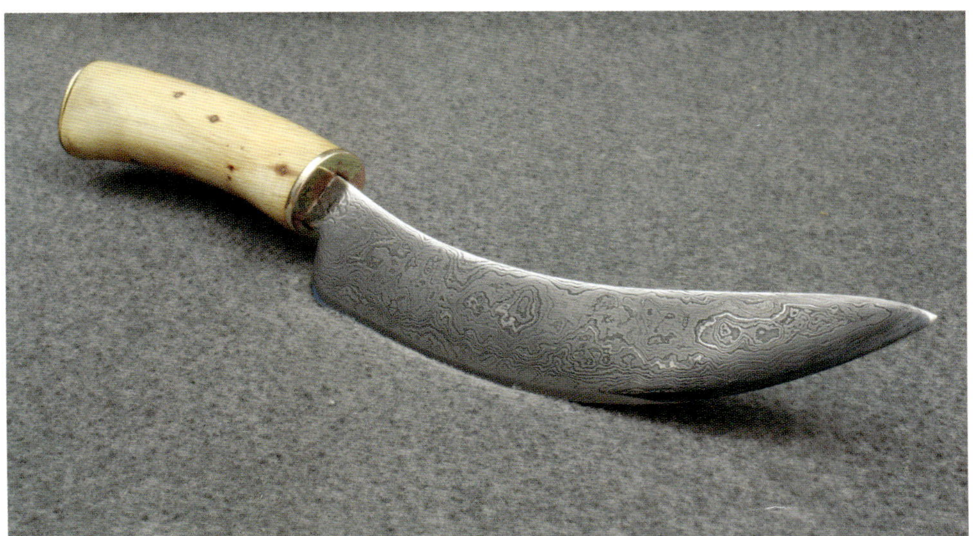

Damascus

This blade uses a combination of 5160 steel with L6 and nickel to create a random decorative pattern made in 320 layers. The blade's Damascus steel was made as a demonstration piece at Touchstone Center for Crafts, where I was teaching a class on forge welding. The hidden tang has a grip of yew bush with mokum`s fittings. The handle is held in place with a coned nut at its hilt.

Damascus. Knife. Damascus steel, yew bush.

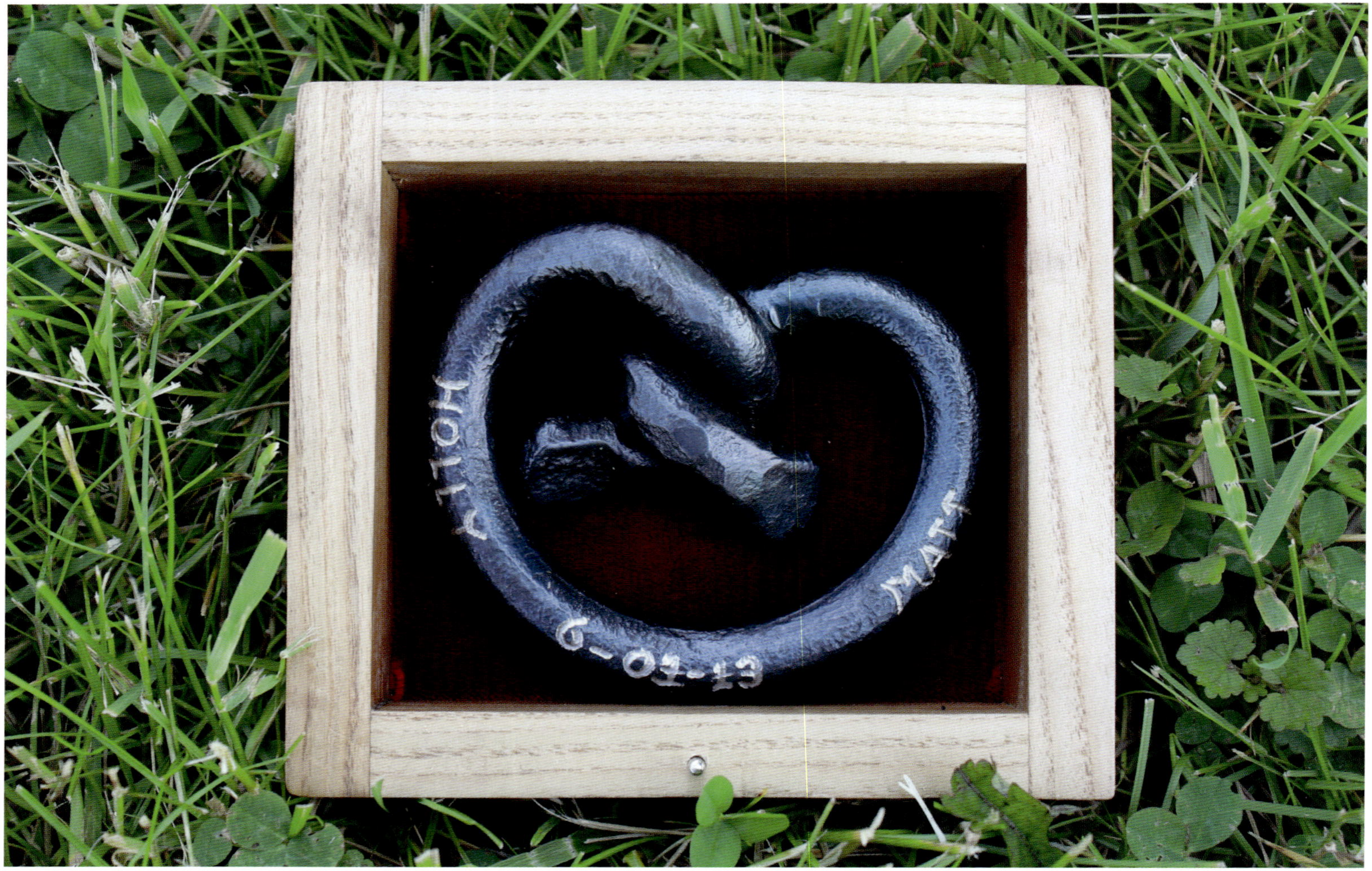

The Nuptual Knot

This piece was designed and created as a wedding gift; the announcement decreed that the couple was "tying the knot." The work is made from one piece of ¾" round steel. It is seated in a handmade box of sassafras wood and embellished with carving and a wire inlay in the shape of the letter D, for the couple's name. I wrote the history of the "Nuptial Knot" tradition on the inside of the box lid.

Nuptual knot. Sculpture. Steel.

Eric A. Ryser

Ryser Forge and Design, Manhattan, Kansas
www.ryserforge.com

ARTIST'S STATEMENT

While having been a traditional object maker in nonferrous metals, my past eight years have been strictly focused in iron and steel. One process in particular is the use of nitric acid to etch detailed patterns in plate steel. Previous experience with intaglio printmaking has resurfaced in my metal work. I use the same process as a printmaker would in dealing with multiples. Once the pattern is determined, it is then etched into steel while still in plate form. When the selected numbers of prints are made, the plate is then struck. The striking then becomes the actual act of forging or fabricating the material into a physical object. Doing all of this allows me to explore the realm of two dimensions, while continuing to be a three-dimensional artist.

Emily's Box

The inspiration for Emily's Box *evolved through a series of conversations and research ideas with a close colleague at the Penland School of Crafts. The purpose here was the exploration of textile patterns shifting from a two-dimensional surface to a three-dimensional surface. The rationale of this exercise was to determine if volume, materials, and color would vary or alter the visual quality of the overall pattern. As the pattern shifted from a digital printed surface to a hard etched ferrous surface, it was concluded that the loss of color and pattern volume greatly affected the viewer's perception of the overall value of the pattern.*

Emily's Box. 2012. Forged and fabricated steel, acid etched pattern, Prismacolor. 9½" x 5½" x 6½".

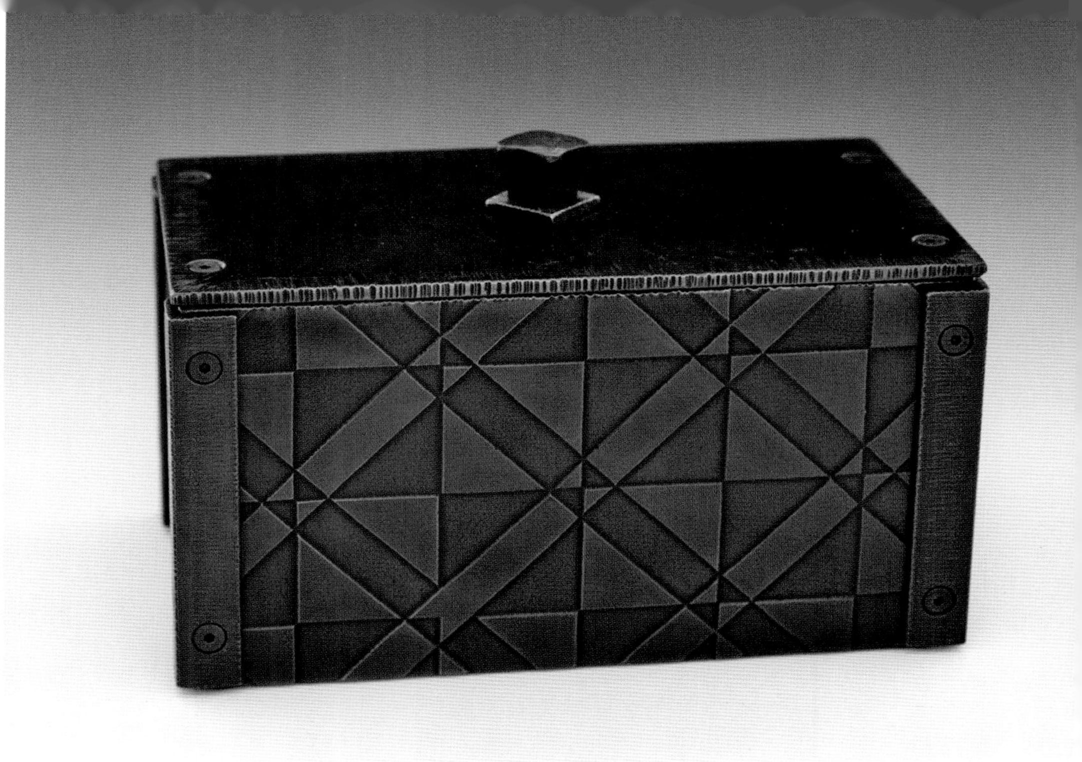

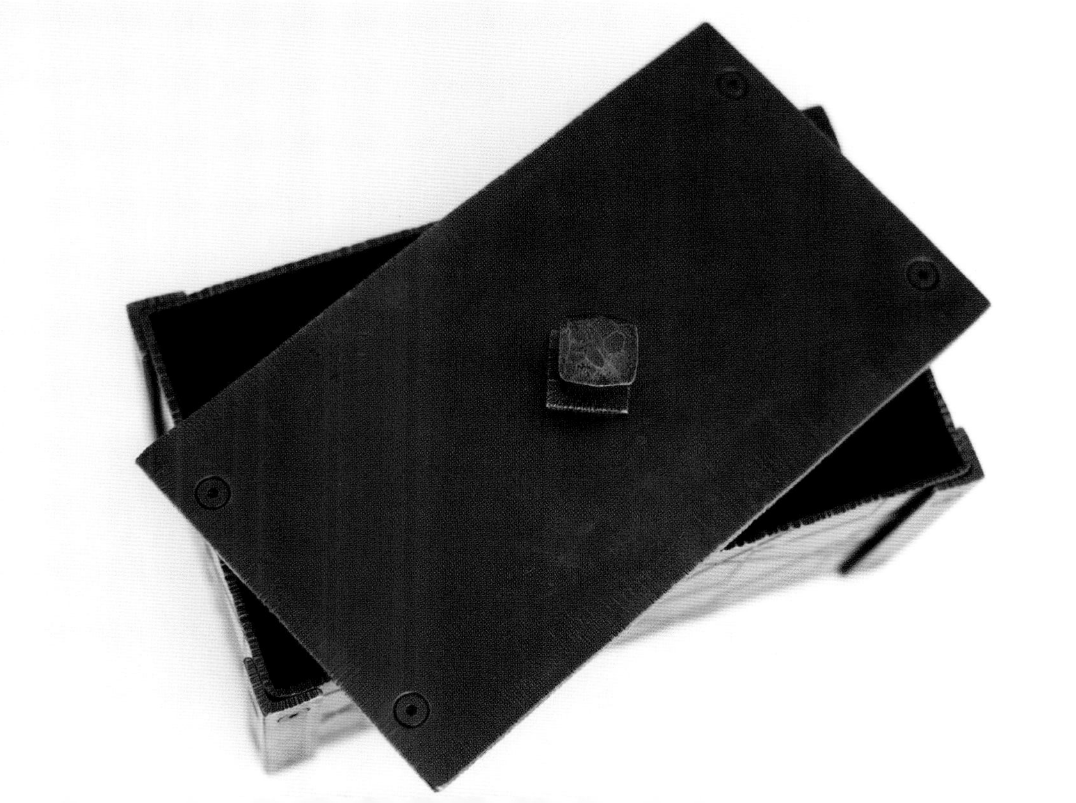

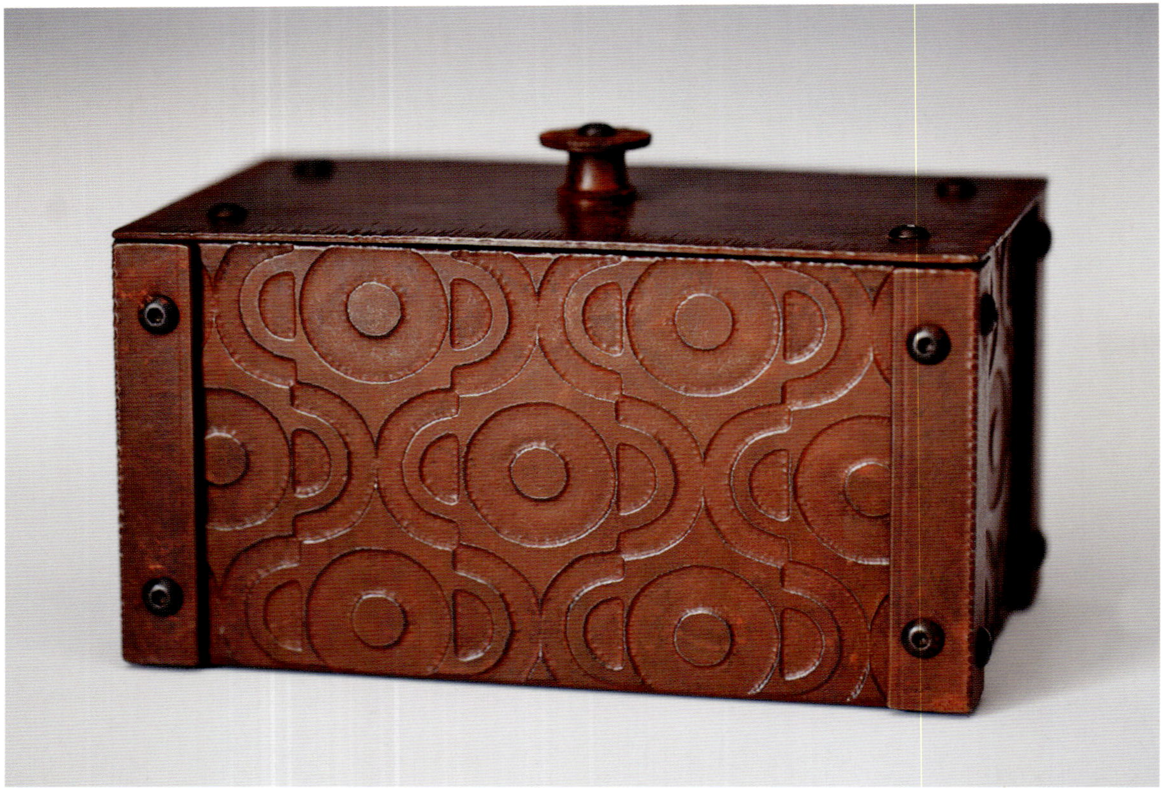

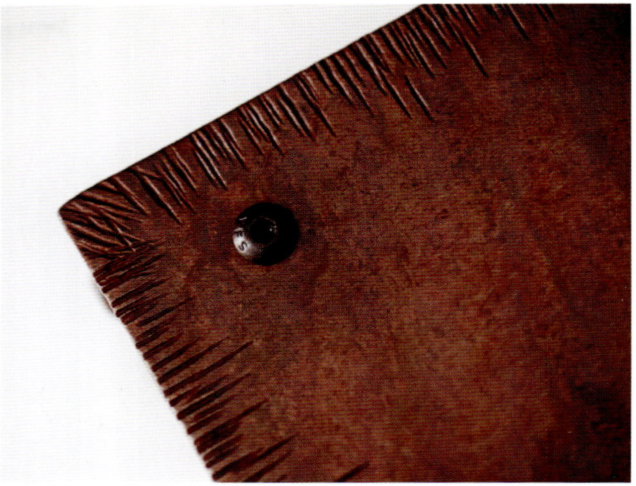

Circle Pattern Container #4

Circle Pattern Container #4. 2012. Forged and fabricated steel, acid etched pattern, colored wax. 8½" x 4½" x 5".

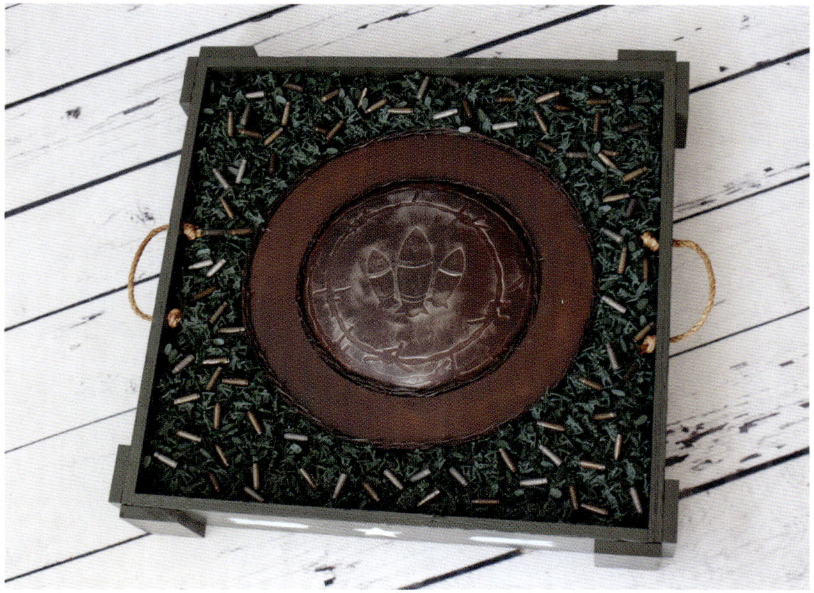

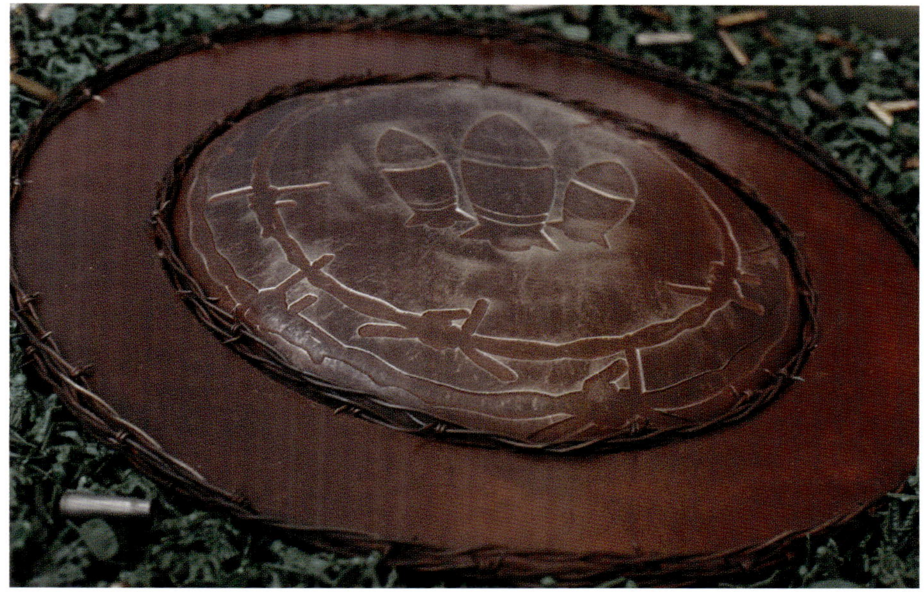

Self Destructive Existence

Self Destructive Existence. 2013. Sculptural object. Forged, fabricated steel, wood, acid-etched image, found objects, rust patina. 31" x 31" x 5".

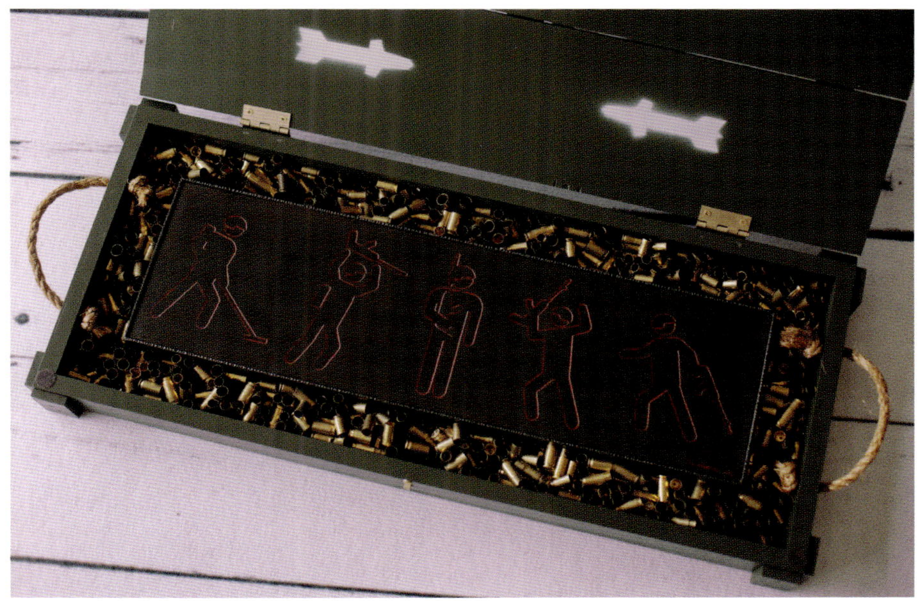

Calibrated Ammunition

Calibrated Ammunition. Sculptural object. 2012.
Fabricated steel, acid-etched image, wood, brass shell casings, Prismacolor. 31" x 14" x 4".

Jon Shearin

Jon Shearin Forge LLC, Brooklyn, New York
www.jonshearin.com

ARTIST'S STATEMENT

The majority of my work features clean lines and smooth forms. Using both traditional and nonconventional blacksmithing and fabrication techniques, I strive to manipulate the metal into organic shapes in both my production work as well as my art pieces. Drawing inspiration from natural forms helps to give these new shapes a sense of familiarity and accessibility. Through the incorporation of different patinas, weathering processes, and materials, such as pattern-welded steel, I have found I can use more subtle means of surface treatment to create a new dimension on the metal itself—bringing 2-D and 3-D together. Whether I use solid planes to create mass, lines to suggest movement, or finishes to enhance surfaces, I want the end result to be a graceful, flowing form that is both pleasing to the eye and to the hand.

,

Composite Wing—Maquette

This piece is made up of forty-two individual forged and fabricated feathers each piercing a central armature. Each feather was forged out to its rough shape. Next, a piece of round rod was welded on for the quill. Finally, it was ground down and filed. The feathers were then put back through the fire to build back a layer of fire scale. Holes were drilled in the solid armature to receive the quills. Side holes were drilled and tapped for thumb screws, which were made by forging down the heads of standard machine screws. The stand is made from forged steel pipe, with the central armature attached with a single pin. The square base is a scale model of the install platform that was provided by the juried public art competition for which this piece was entered. It was accepted and then recreated to scale, at a height of 9 ½' (see page 214).

Composite Wing—Maquette. Sculpture. 2011. Mild steel. Forged and fabricated. 27" x 17" x 7" (without base). *Photo: Jon Shearin*

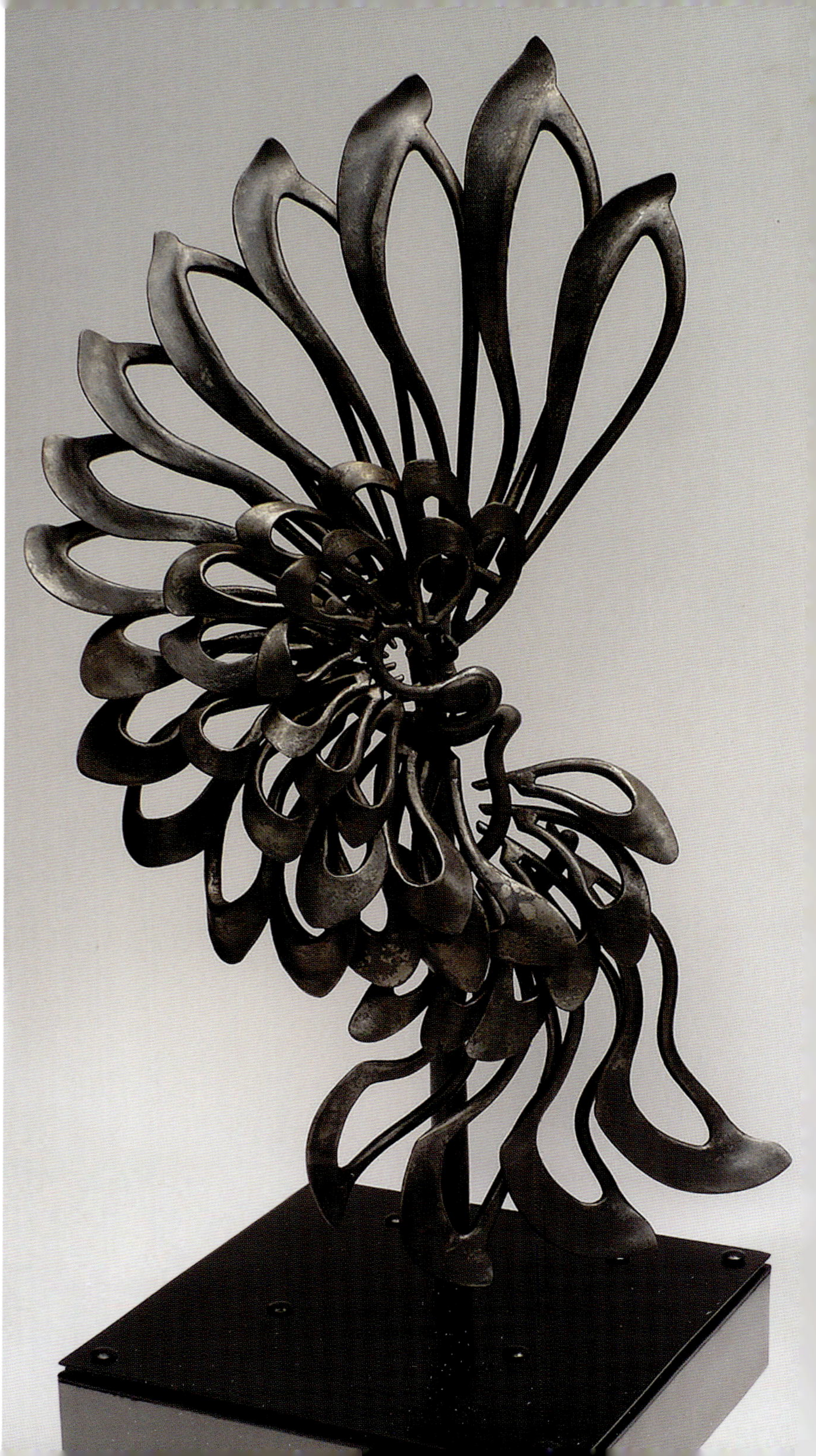

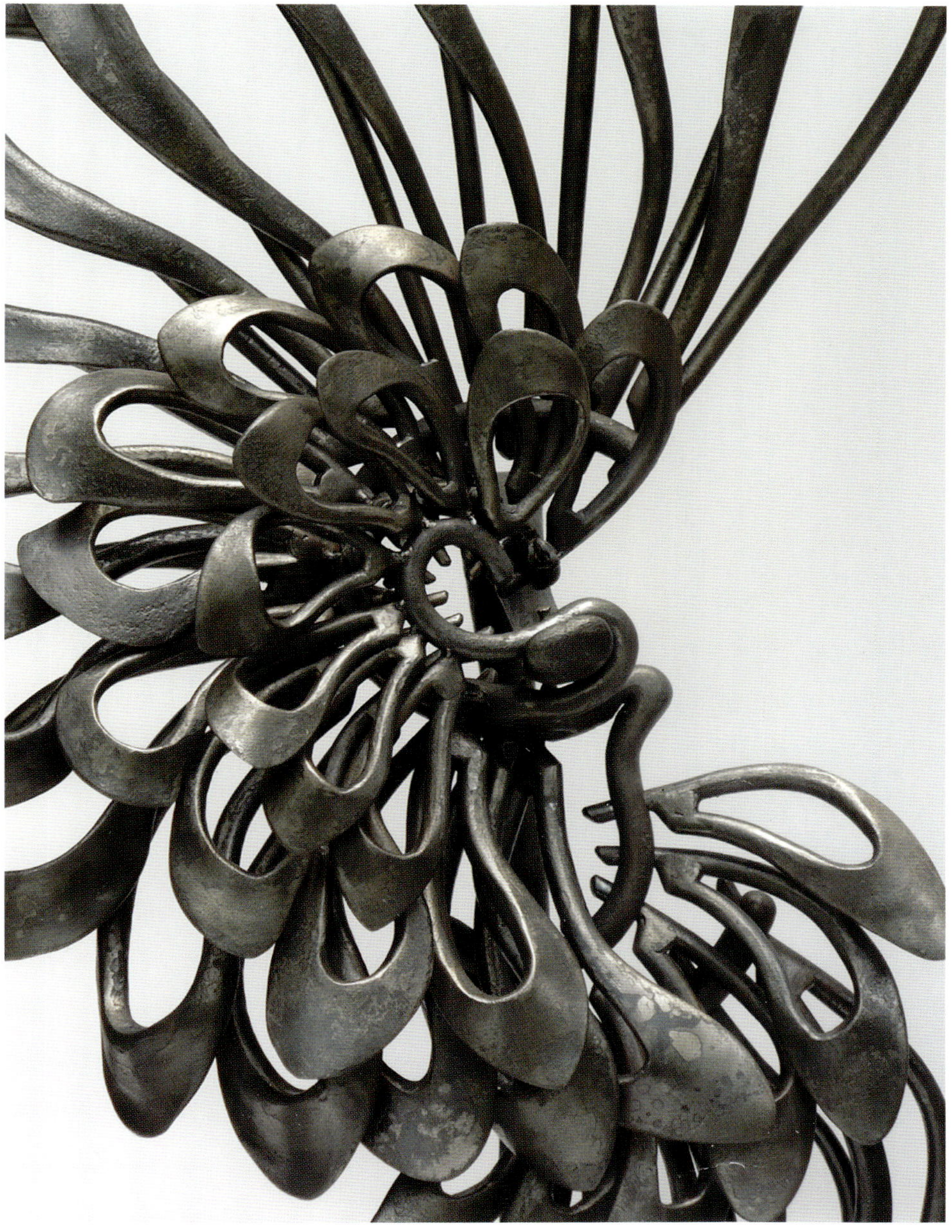

Damascus Engagement Ring

This ring was made by both me and my fiancée, though without her knowledge. We met at the Penland School of Crafts in the mountains of North Carolina. I was in charge of the smithy at the school and she came to take a two- month concentration in blacksmithing with Jay Burnham-Kidwell. During the class, she made a billet of Damascus with 1095 & 15N20 tool steels with a twisted star pattern under the expert guidance of April Franklin. We also fell in love and have been ever since. Flash forward a few years. I remembered the billet when brainstorming ideas for an engagement ring. I found it and cut off a piece that I then sanded and filed facets onto it to create the look of a cut stone—also her idea. I made the band from stainless steel and welded itto the Damascus "stone." She said "Yes," loves the ring, and hasn't taken it off since.

Damascus engagement ring. 2013. Damascus steel and stainless steel. Forged and fabricated. Ring size 6.5. 27" x 9" x 9". Contributing artist: Pilar Gonzalez. *Photo: Jon Shearin*

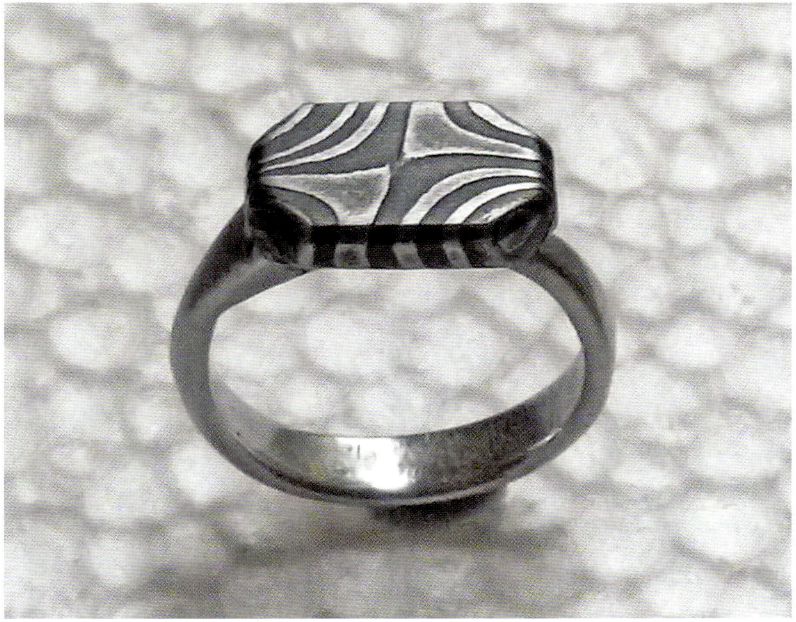

JON SHEARIN

Composite Wing

Since I had already worked out the shapes and proportions that I wanted in the maquette (see page 212), I took the original line drawing and blew it up to scale on a photocopier in a tile format. From there I had my rough blueprints for each feather. I used as much scrap material as possible to reduce cost. The flatter, wider half of each feather is solid steel and for the most part forged from cut offs of large stock. The thinner, round half is made of forged steel pipe, which helped to cut down on the overall weight of the piece. This time, the central armature was also made from steel pipe. I did this for the following reasons: First, to reduce both weight and cost while keeping the proportions in check. Second, to get a "pucker" effect where the feather penetrated the armature and came out the opposite side. Instead of drilling and tapping a ¾" hole, I drilled a hole and welded on a stainless steel nut. The use of stainless hardware was to minimize the risk of the bolts seizing up in the elements. For a finish, I wire brushed each piece, gun blued it, scrubbed it with acetone, and then immediately coated it with multiple layers of lacquers. It was purchased for the foundation's permanent collection and is on display on Main Street in Chattanooga, Tennessee.

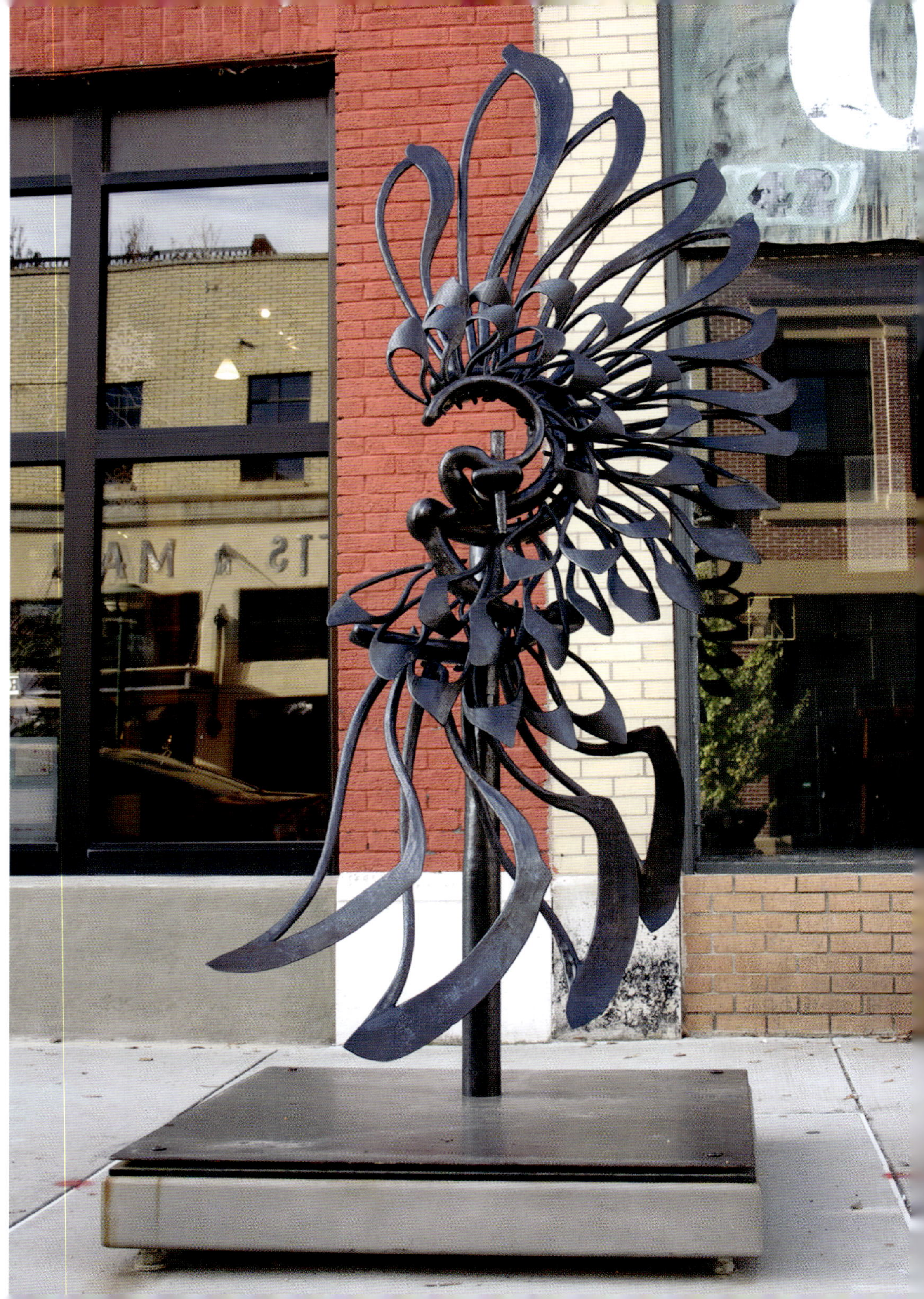

Composite Wing. Sculpture. 2011. Mild steel. Forged and fabricated. Installed in Chattanooga, Tennessee. 9½′ x 5½′ x 2½′ (without base). *Photo: Shane Darwent*

Spire

This is the latest in a series of sculptures I've been doing for years. I stumbled upon this aesthetic when I tried to figure out ways to recreate some of my forged pipe vessels at a much larger scale. I ended up taking a fabricator's approach and transformed them into forms with truncated sides made of sheet metal and ribs to cover the resulting seams. I cut pieces of angle iron into tapers and started the piece by building a cage form. I then took patterns from the openings in the cage to figure out the shapes that needed to be cut fromthe sheet. Those pieces were attached to the interior in order to hide the welds. The long taper on the top of the vessel is forged from solid stock, ground down, and filed to shape. It was finally placed vertically, with the base in the coal fire, so that the scale and heat colors would run up the sides. The taper was then welded to the vessel and blended. The whole piece was treated with gun blue and a lacquer finish.

Spire. Sculpture. 2011. Mild steel. Forged and fabricated. 27" x 9" x 9". Photo: Jon Shearin

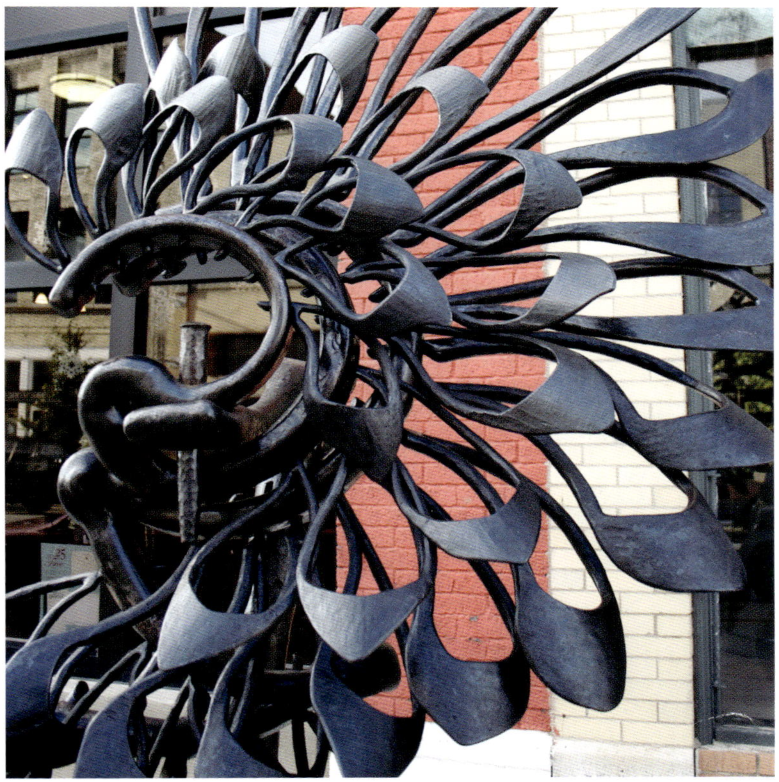

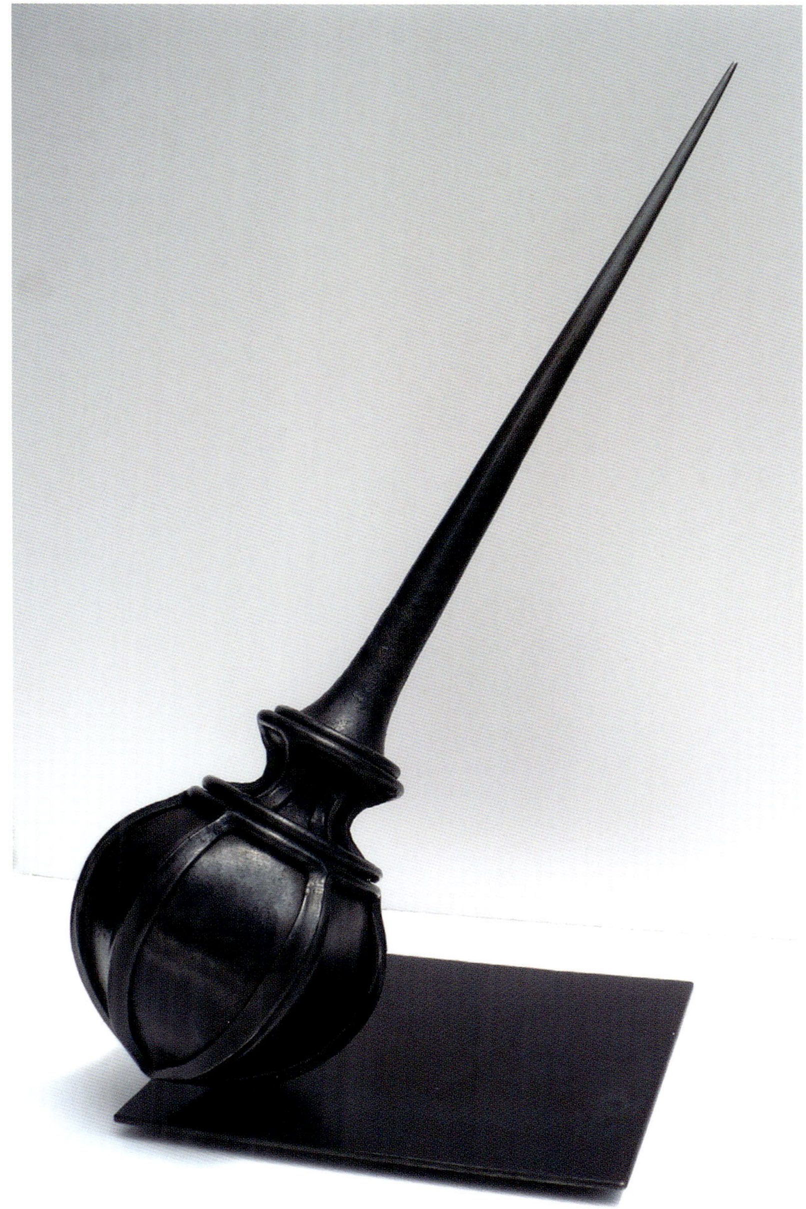

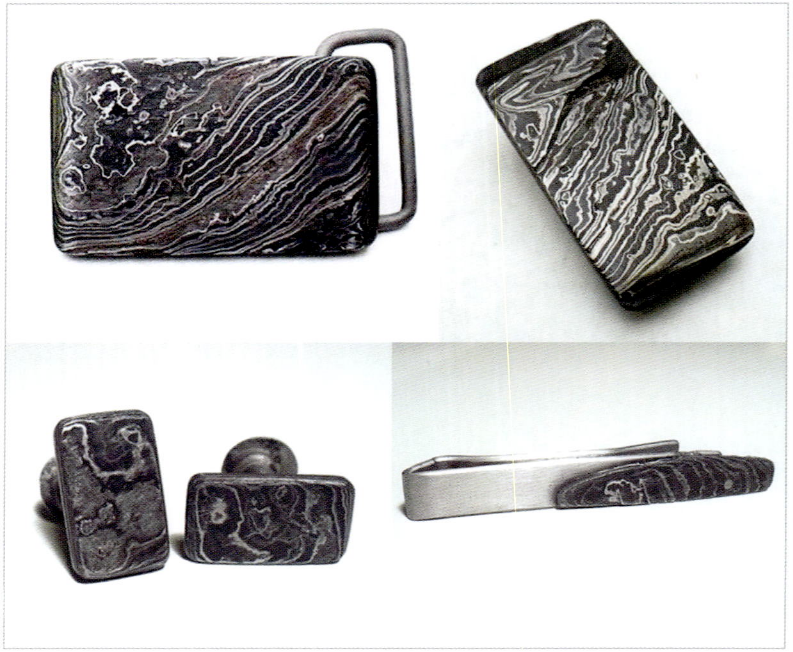

Damascus Men's Accessories Set

This set includes a belt buckle, tie clip, money clip, and cufflinks. They are all made from the same billet of Damascus steel that combines wrought iron from a graveyard fence, a huge blade from a sawmill, and other scrap metals. The rather scattered pattern emerged while making this billet. I just couldn't seem to get it to fully weld. It kept delaminating. I tried and tried until I finally ended up twisting the whole piece in order to keep it together. I took one last welding heat and it stuck. The whole ordeal resulted in one of my favorite pieces of Damascus due to its strange depth of field with overlapping and intertwining layers. I couldn't do it again if I tried.

Damascus men's accessories set. 2012. Damascus steel and stainless steel. Forged and fabricated. Varying sizes. *Photo: Jon Shearin*

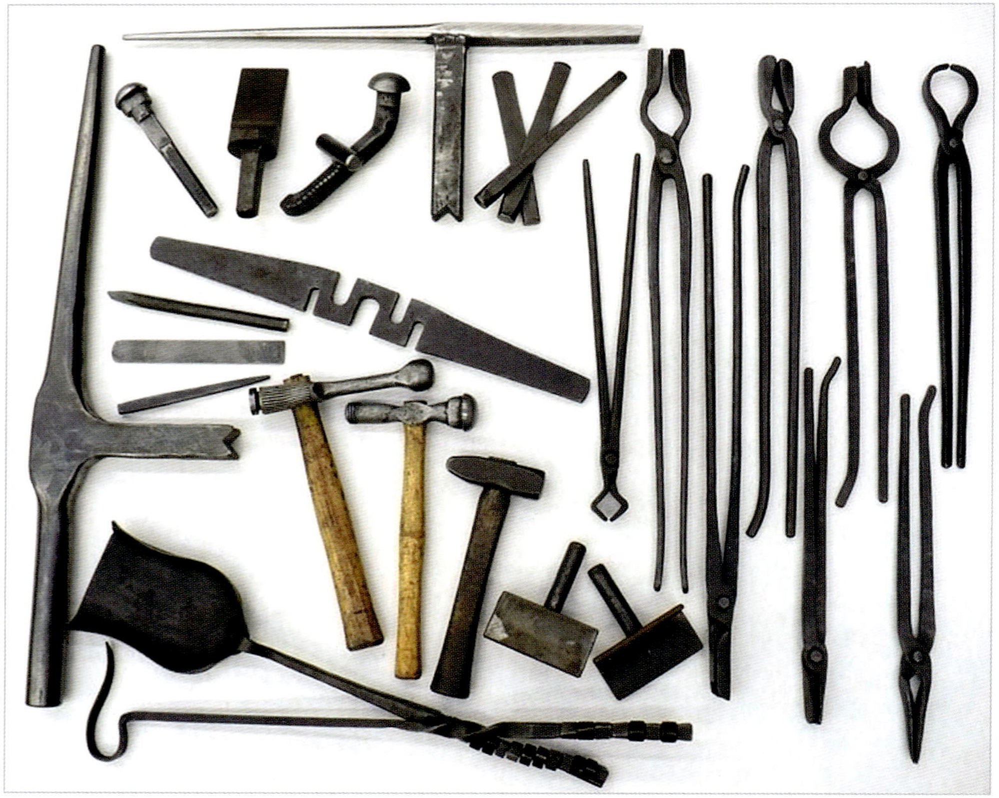

Forging Tools

Most of the tools pictured here were made from various kinds of repurposed tool steel found in local scrap yards. There are hammers and stakes made from old bolts, a chisel made from a used file, and a bick anvil forged from a section of an I-beam.

Forging tools. 2009-2011. Mild steel. Forged and fabricated. Varying sizes. *Photo: Jon Shearin*

John Boyd Smith

John Boyd Smith Metal Studios, Moore, South Carolina
www.johnboydsmith.com

ARTIST'S STATEMENT

As a young child, I watched my mother nurture plants, flowers, and animals. Her keen interest in nature and the outdoors must have had a profound influence on my fertile mind, since I now forge, shape, and sculpt solid steel into forms that emulate the natural world. I have fashioned various flowers, plants, animals, trees, and insects from hot-forged steel for more than thirty years. I characterize my style of artistry as "realism in metal" and attempt to depict realism by capturing key details from nature.

Trump Decorative Screen

This screen was a commission for Donald Trump's Ocean Club Resort Hotel in Panama City, Panama. It is forged from mild steel with a polished and waxed finish. The tropical flora design included the national flower of Panama.

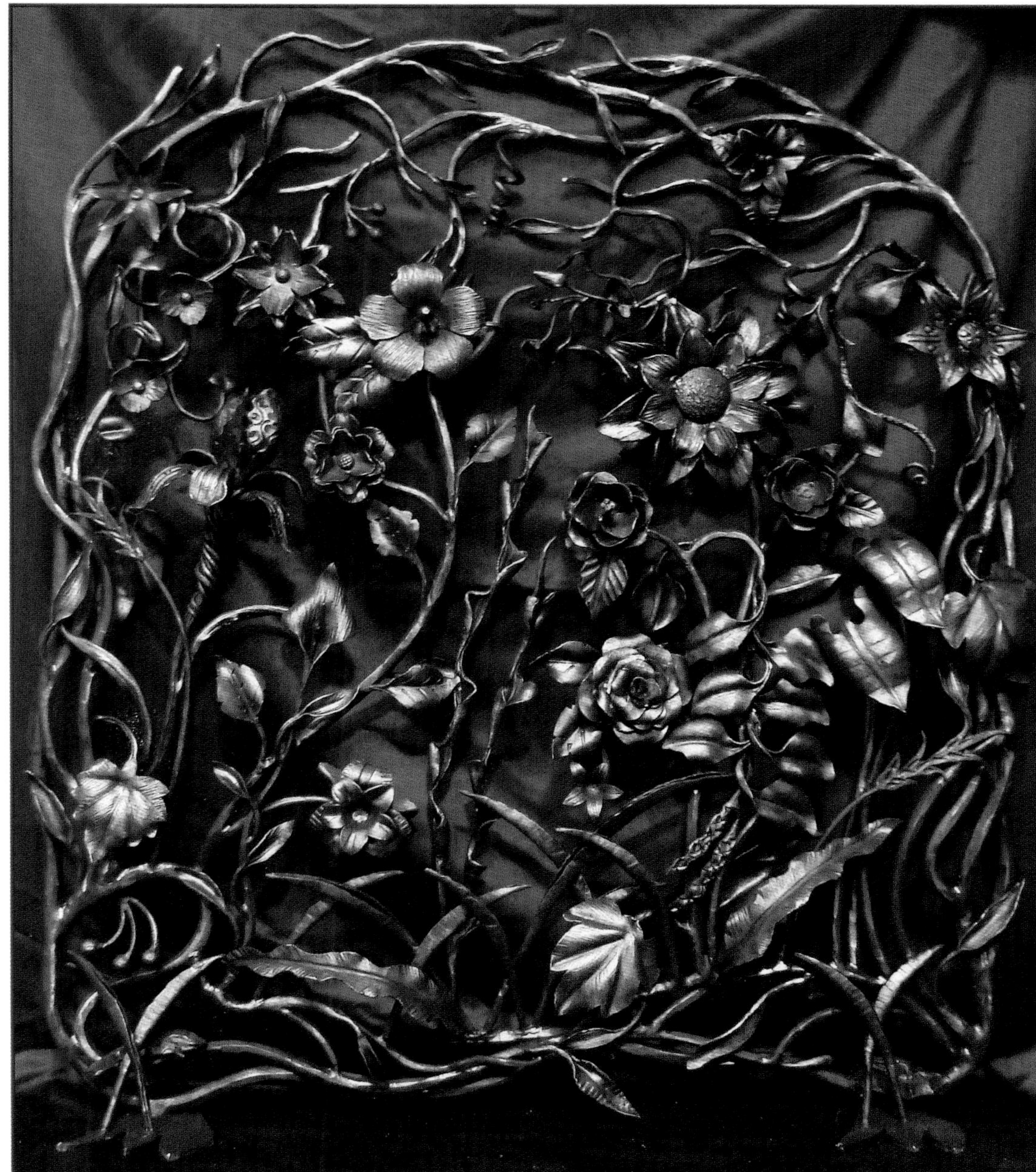

Trump decorative screen. 45"w x 51"h.
Photo: Rhonda Nell Fleming

JOHN BOYD SMITH

Dogwood Gate

This forged steel gate depicts a dogwood tree in full bloom. The gate was commissioned for a private residence in Savannah, Georgia.

Dogwood gate. 30″w x 84″h. *Photo: Rhonda Nell Fleming*

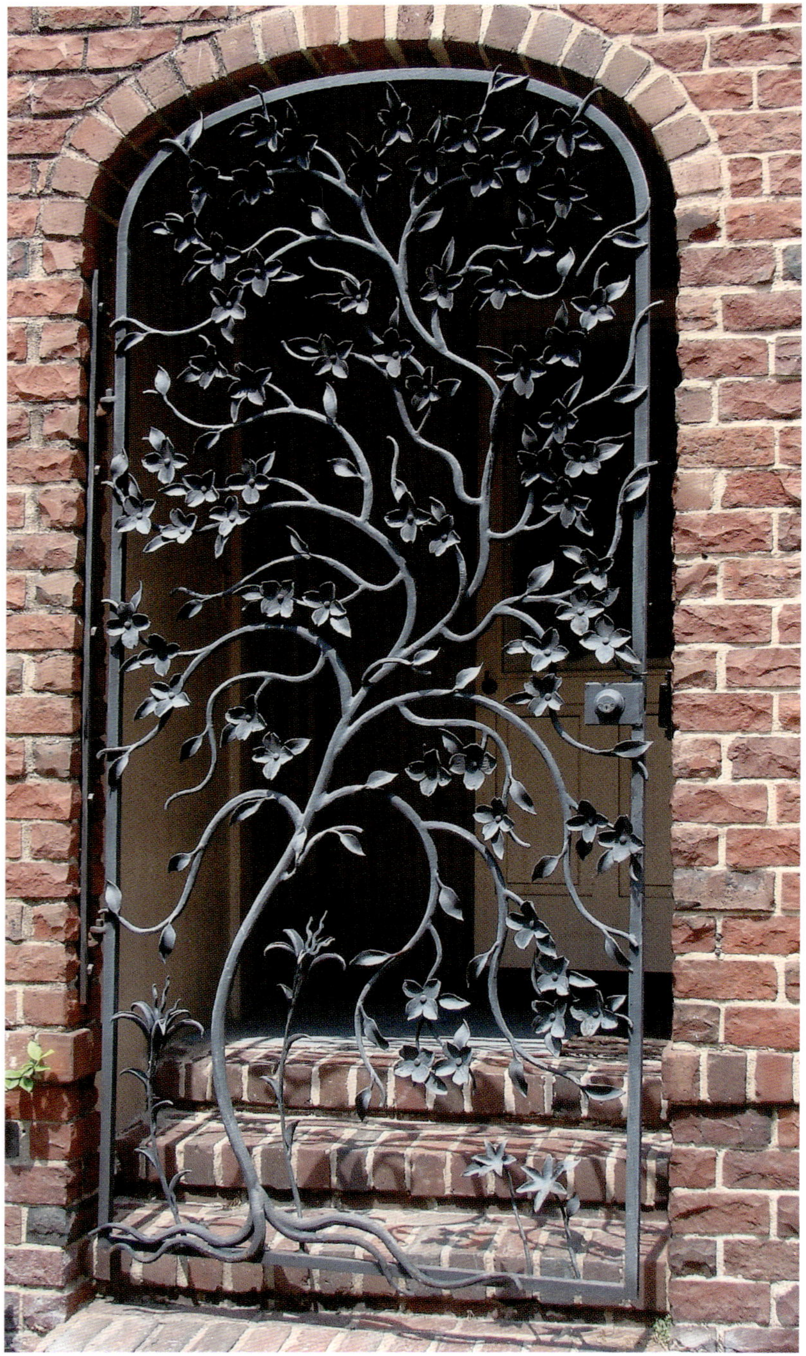

Traditional Organic Gate

The interior of the forged steel double gate is riveted bar (traditional). The exterior of the gate is forged limbs and leaves (organic). The gate was commissioned for a private residence on Hilton Head Island, South Carolina.

Traditional organic gate. 60″w x 84″h. *Photo: Rhonda Nell Fleming*

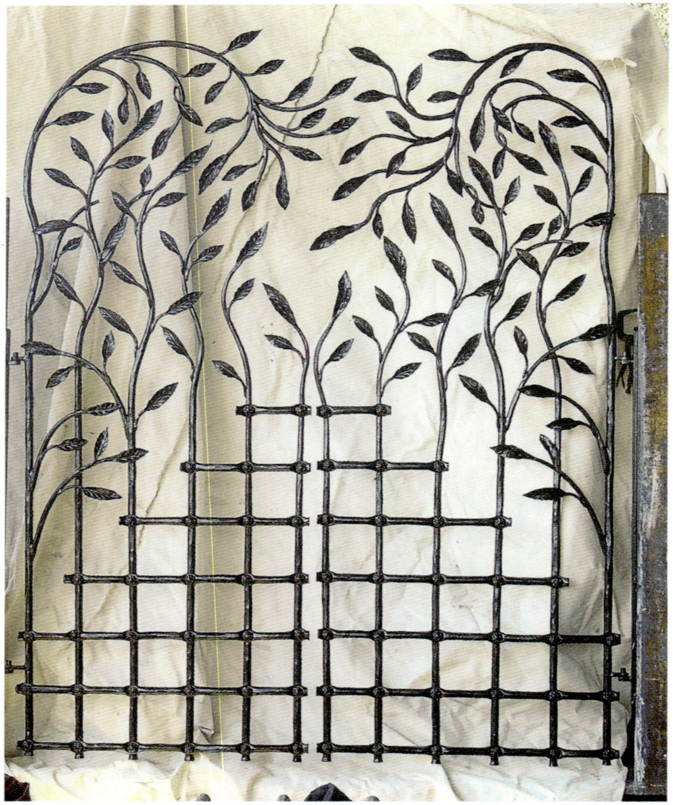

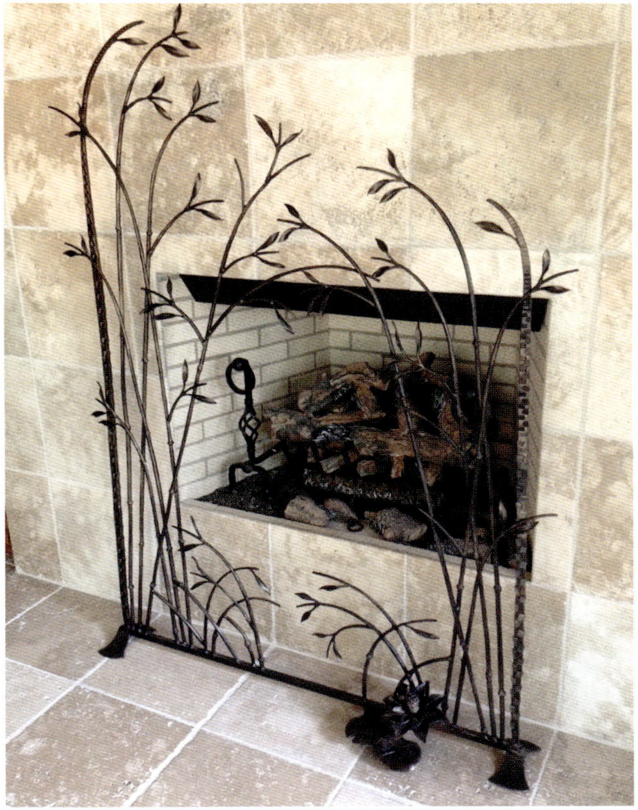

Bamboo Fire Screen

This bamboo motif was forged of mild steel for a meditation room that included a wall fountain, wind chimes, and open-air whirlpool. A forged lotus blossom adorns the base of the screen. The piece is in a private residence on Kiawah Island, South Carolina.

Bamboo fire screen. 48"w x 76"h.
Photo: Rhonda Nell Fleming.

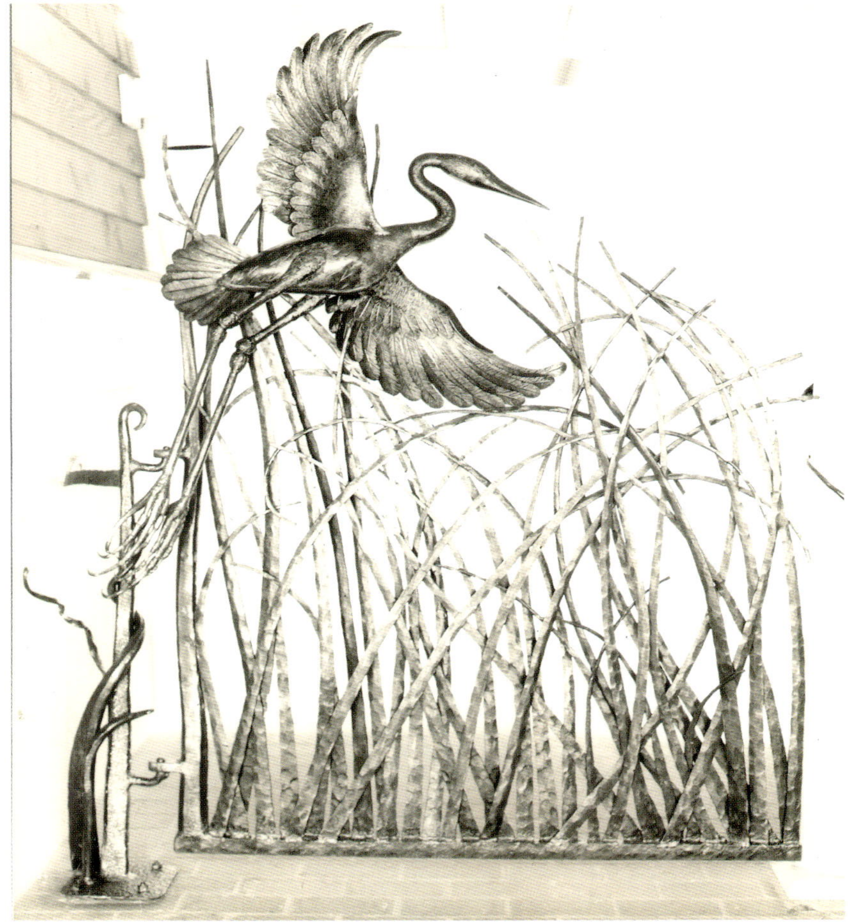

Pool Gate

This swimming pool entrance gate depicts a flying heron in a sea of marsh grass. The gate is essentially "frameless," with the marsh grass serving as the structural framework. The bird is realistic in nature with all individual feathers and claws. The material is forged mild steel with a natural finish. It is located at a private residence in Savannah, Georgia.

Pool gate. Approximately 72"w x 48"h. *Photo: Rhonda Nell Fleming*

Mike Sohikian

Genoa, Ohio
sohikian@aol.com

ARTIST'S STATEMENT

Forging and fabricating steel offers me unlimited possibilities to communicate my thoughts and visions to others.

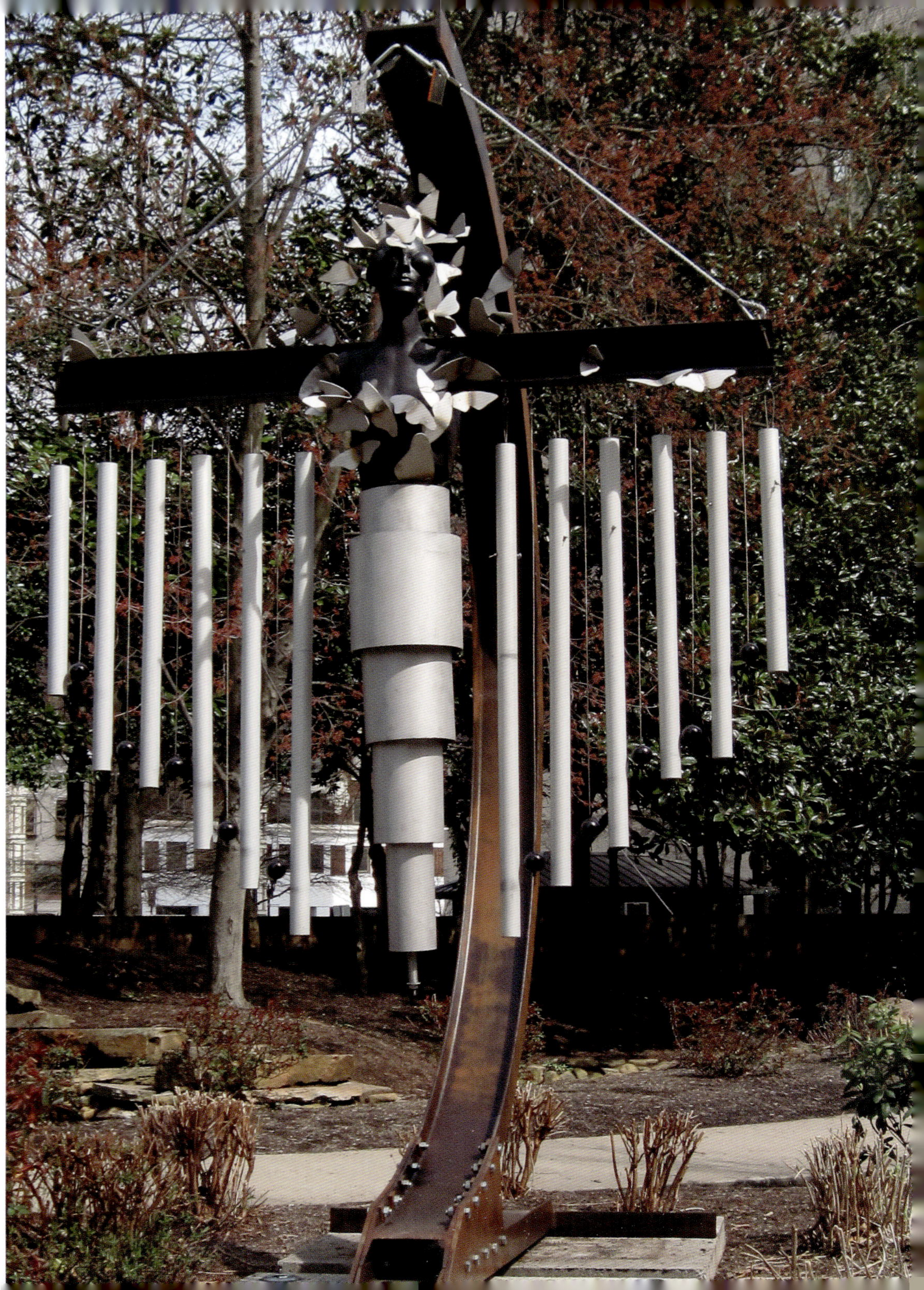

Madam Butterfly. Kinetic sculpture. Steel, stainless steel, aluminum, wood. Produces sound. 10′ x 8′ x 7′.

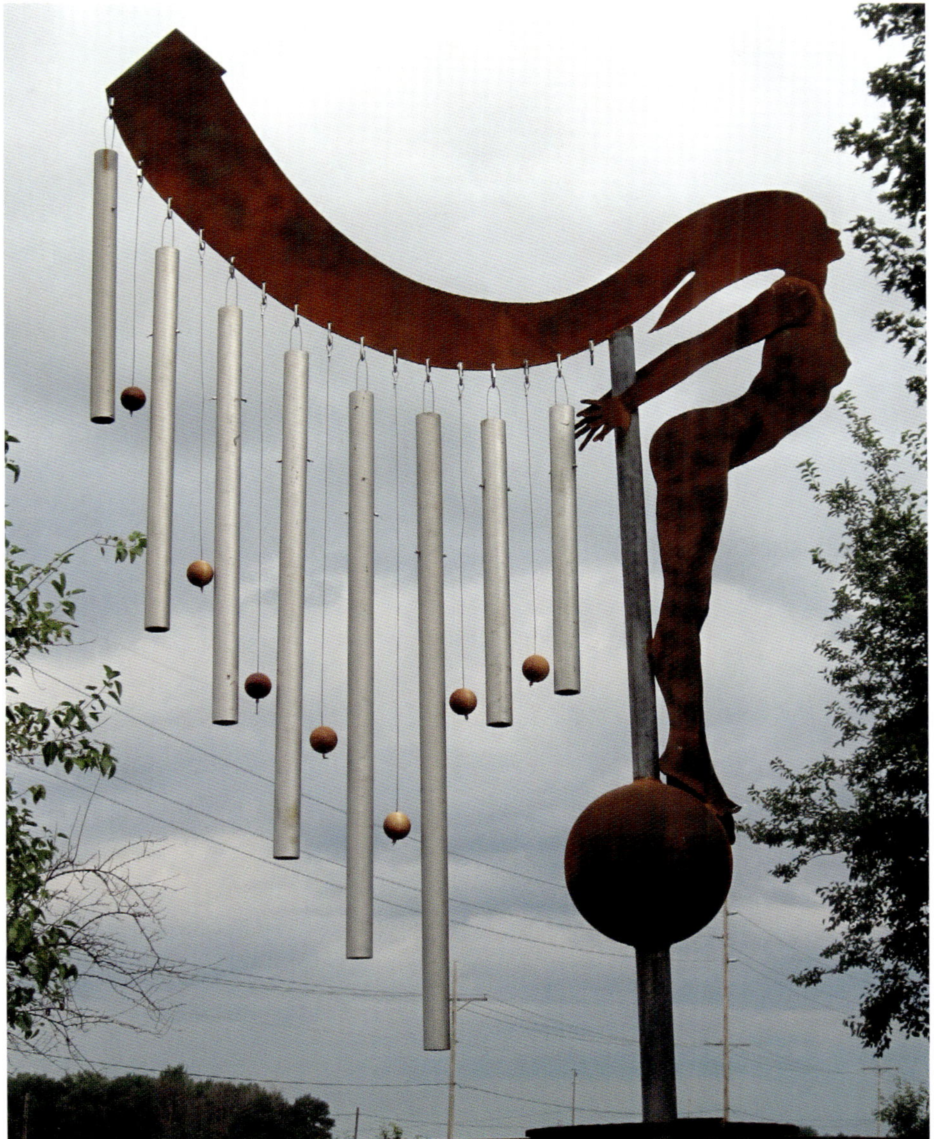

Harp (Chimes). Kinetic sculpture. Steel, stainless steel, aluminum, wood. Revolves 360 degrees and produces sound. 9′ x 5′ diameter.

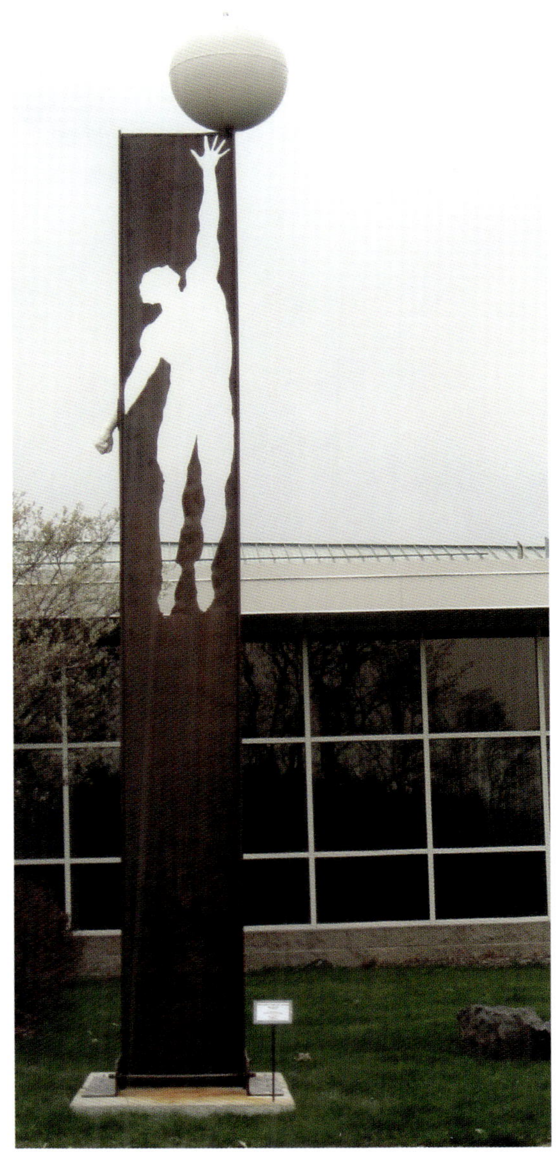

Reaching for the Moon. 16′ x 2′ x 2′.

Anton Standteiner

Truckee, California
www.mtnforge.com

ARTIST'S STATEMENT

In 1968, Hans Standteiner, a blacksmith from Austria and a ski coach for the 1960 Olympics, came to Squaw Valley and fell in love with the place. Forty years later, we find our home nestled in the high mountain snow country of the Sierra Nevada in Truckee, California. Here we have grown into a state-of-the-art workshop employing the age-old techniques of traditional smithies from around the world. Our family's strong Austrian heritage is responsible for our philosophy of time-honored craftsmanship forged with modern tools and materials to produce unique functional art.

Propeller Railing

The owner of this house is an aviation aficionado. The design replicates propellers. The changing flat surfaces create a windy effect when passing through the entry staircase area.

Propeller railing. Mild steel. 42"h x 53'l.

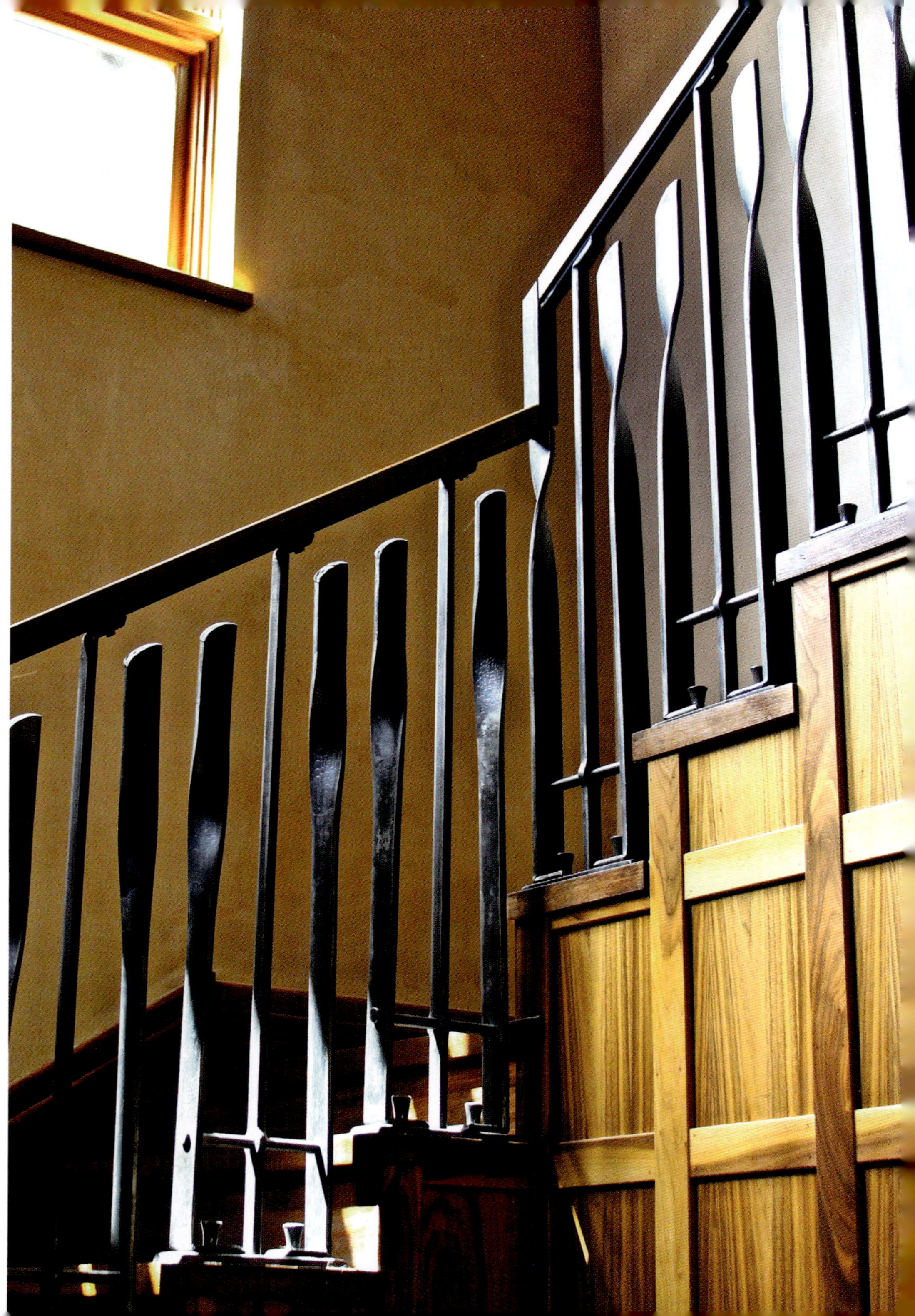

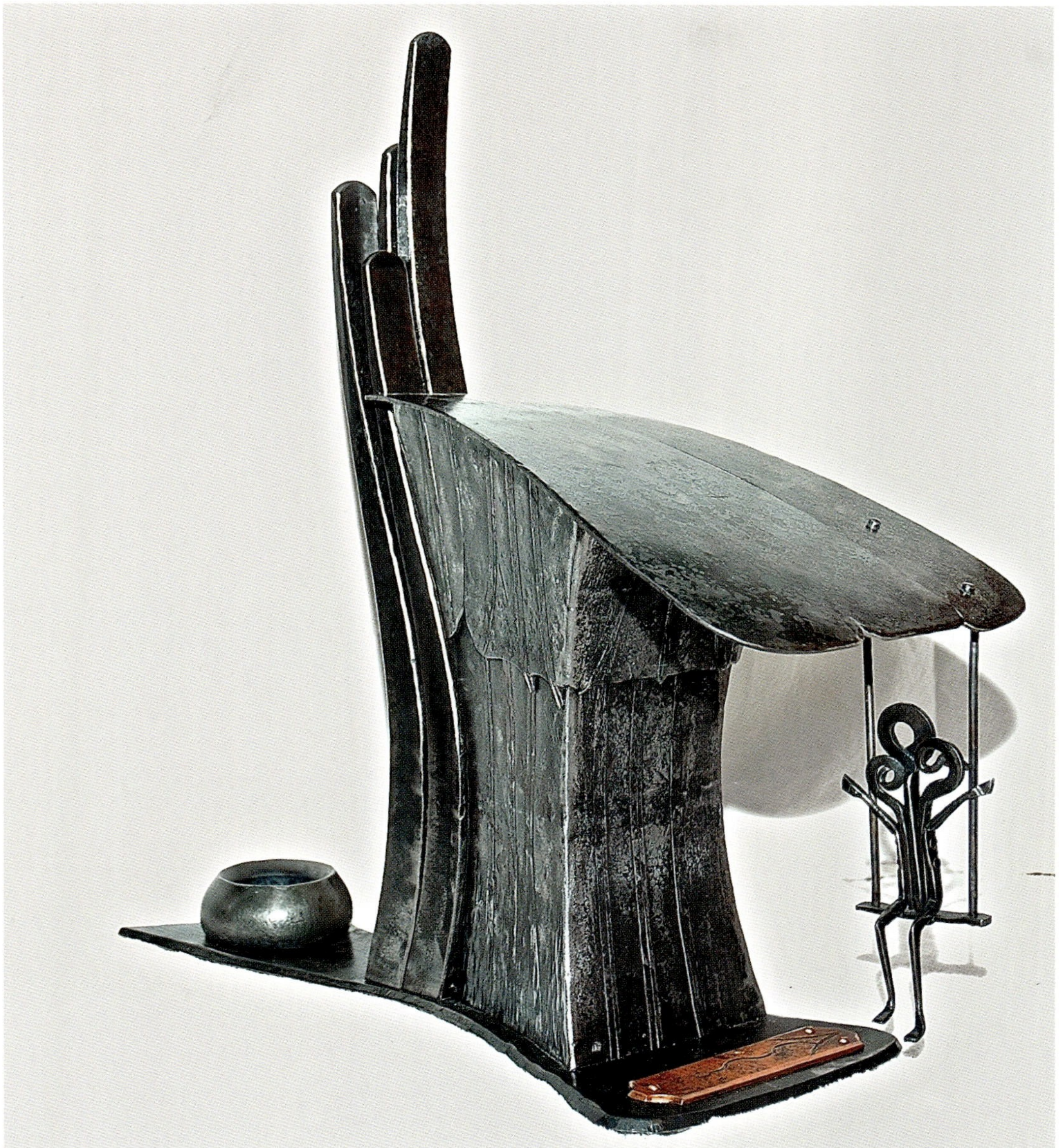

Swing Urn

A legendary ski icon tragically died base-jumping off a large cliff with skis on. He left behind his four-year-old daughter and wife. I designed this urn to be an interactive sculpture for his daughter. The lid of the main cavity opens. The bottom half contains his ashes, while the top half creates a storage space much like a jewelry box. The wife came by the forge and chiseled in a personal message on the inside of the lid. I hung a swing from the parachute-like material hanging over the cliff. The swing has three figures, all riveted together and representing the father, mother, and daughter. I used the steel edges from a favorite pair of the owners skis as inlay material on the cliff wall. The tall curved pieces represent ski tracks. The wife owns a candle business, so we pressed a large chunk of round metal to create a candle spot. The copper plate bears the family's emblem.

Swing urn. Mild steel, ski edge material, copper. 26"h.

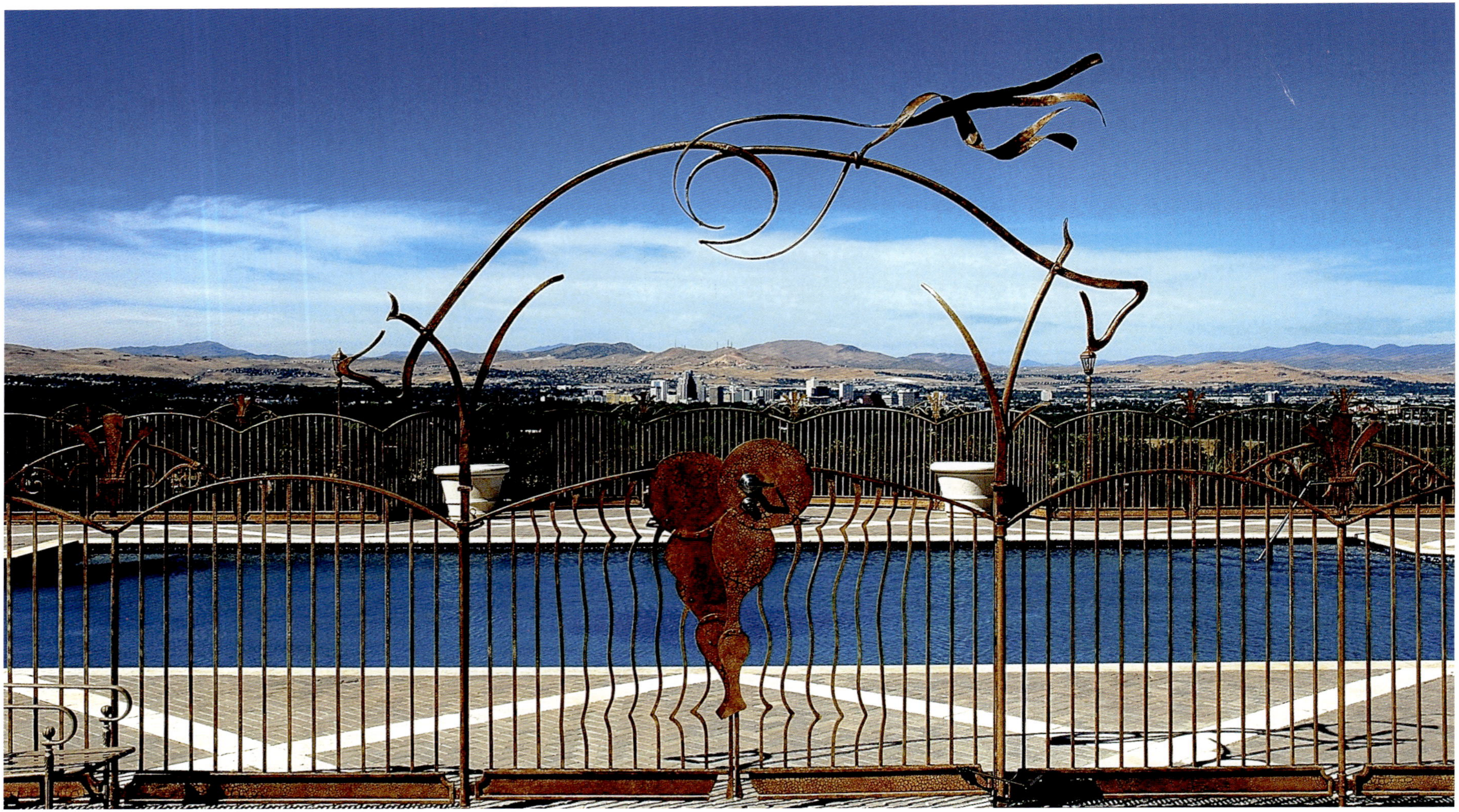

Wind Gate

This pool area is located in an area known for its dry and hot weather. These wind gates were designed to show some movement, mimicking the wind. Hopefully, people looking at the gates might mentally cool themselves down.

Wind gate. Mild steel, stainless steel, patina finish 14'h x 16'w.

John Steel & Chris Holt

Steel Welding, Freedom, Pennsylvania

ARTISTS' STATEMENT

John Steel is a retired Ironworker Local #3 and I, Chris Holt, am an art teacher and master gardener. We have been working together for over ten years and have made a wide range of projects, including driveway gates, furniture, celestial items, bowls, large wall sculptures, unique railings, etc. We work primarily with mild steel but have worked with copper, bronze, and aluminum. Our projects are custom designed for our clients and, when possible, a little whimsy is added in the design, such as a bar of soap for a birdbath and even secret compartments in railings.

Baptismal Font

This baptismal font lid was made from copper sheet that was spun. It was completely hand hammered using a custom planishing hammer to make the hammering even. We made four of the decorative plates with a leather finish using an air hammer and needle gun. Each rose-head rivet had four to five klops (indentations). There are 92 handmade rivets. The baptismal font bowl was also hand hammered from sheet. The lion's feet were made first in clay, then cast in copper. The finial was also cast in copper in a design based on a traditional finial, but we clarified the detail by chasing.

Baptismal font. Copper. Lid: 22″ diameter x 13″h.
Bowl: 18″ x 4″ deep with 1″ rolled rim.

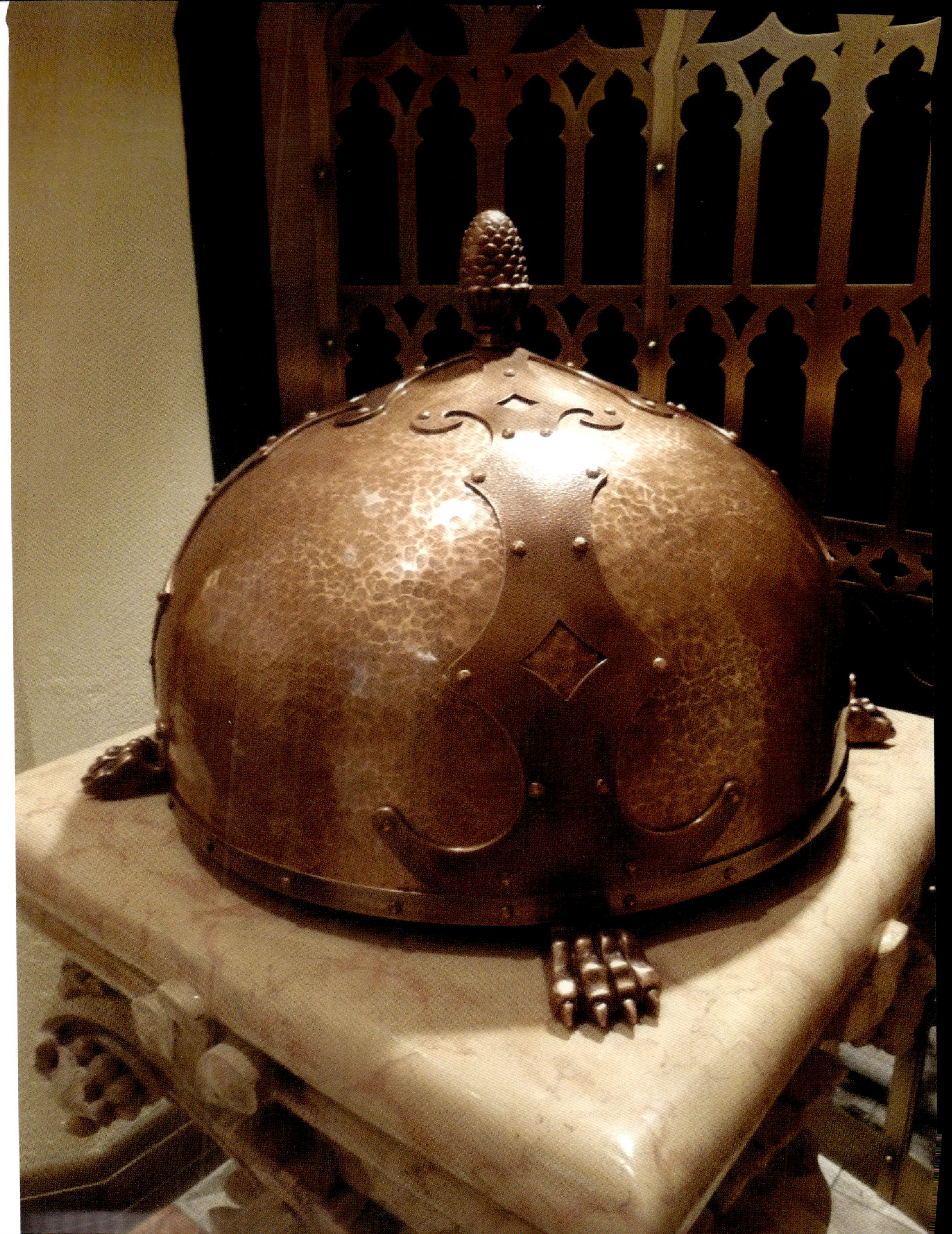

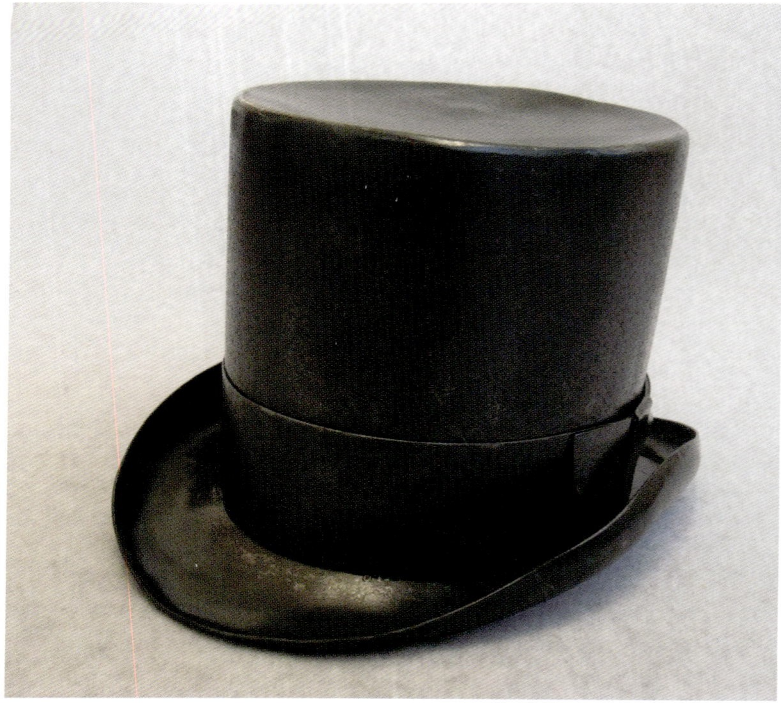

Top hat

This top hat was made close in size to a "real" top hat. It is made from mild steel with a ribbon of the same material. It was made for an individual who was promoted to a top job position. The owner decided to donate it to a local theatre where it feels right at home.

Top hat. Sculpture. Mild steel.

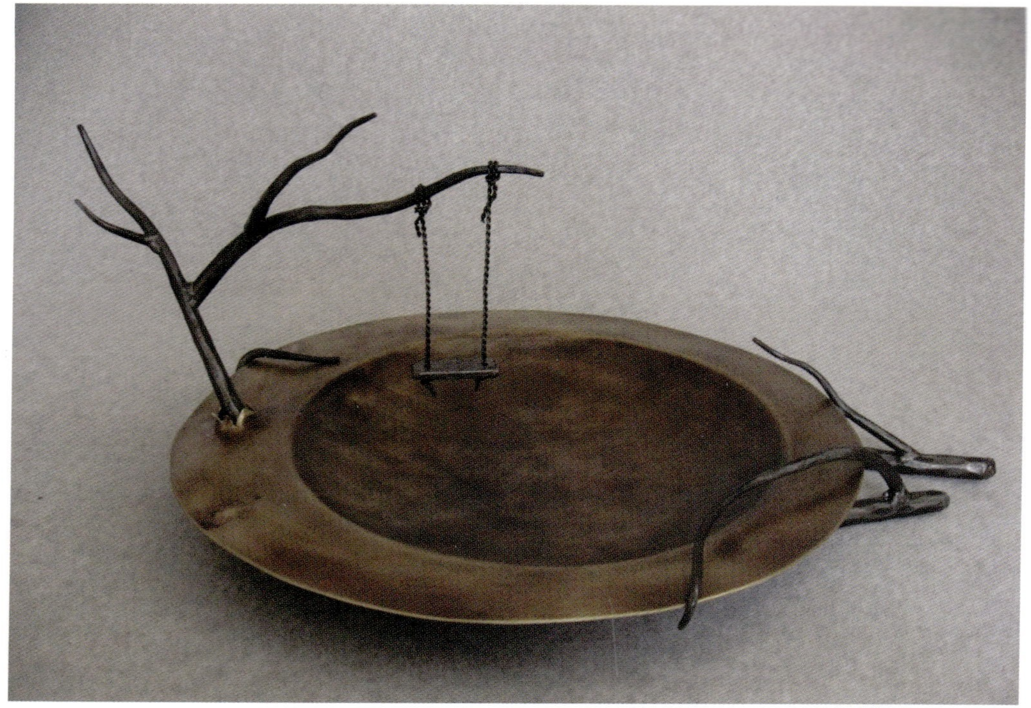

Swimming Bowl

John and I wanted to make a series of bowls but wanted to make them different than heavily textured steel containers. We thought about bowls and what they mean. Everybody has fond memories of a favorite vegetable soup or a family recipe served in a bowl, so we decided our bowls would also tell a story. This particular bowl is a nostalgic nod to lazy days spent at a favorite swimming hole. We titled our collection Serial Bowls, each with a story. We hammer large sheets of bronze into a bowl and then add elements to give them character. This bronze bowl has a mild steel tree and swing. The rope is also made from mild steel.

Swimming bowl. Bowl. Bronze, mild steel. 24" x 16½" x 10".

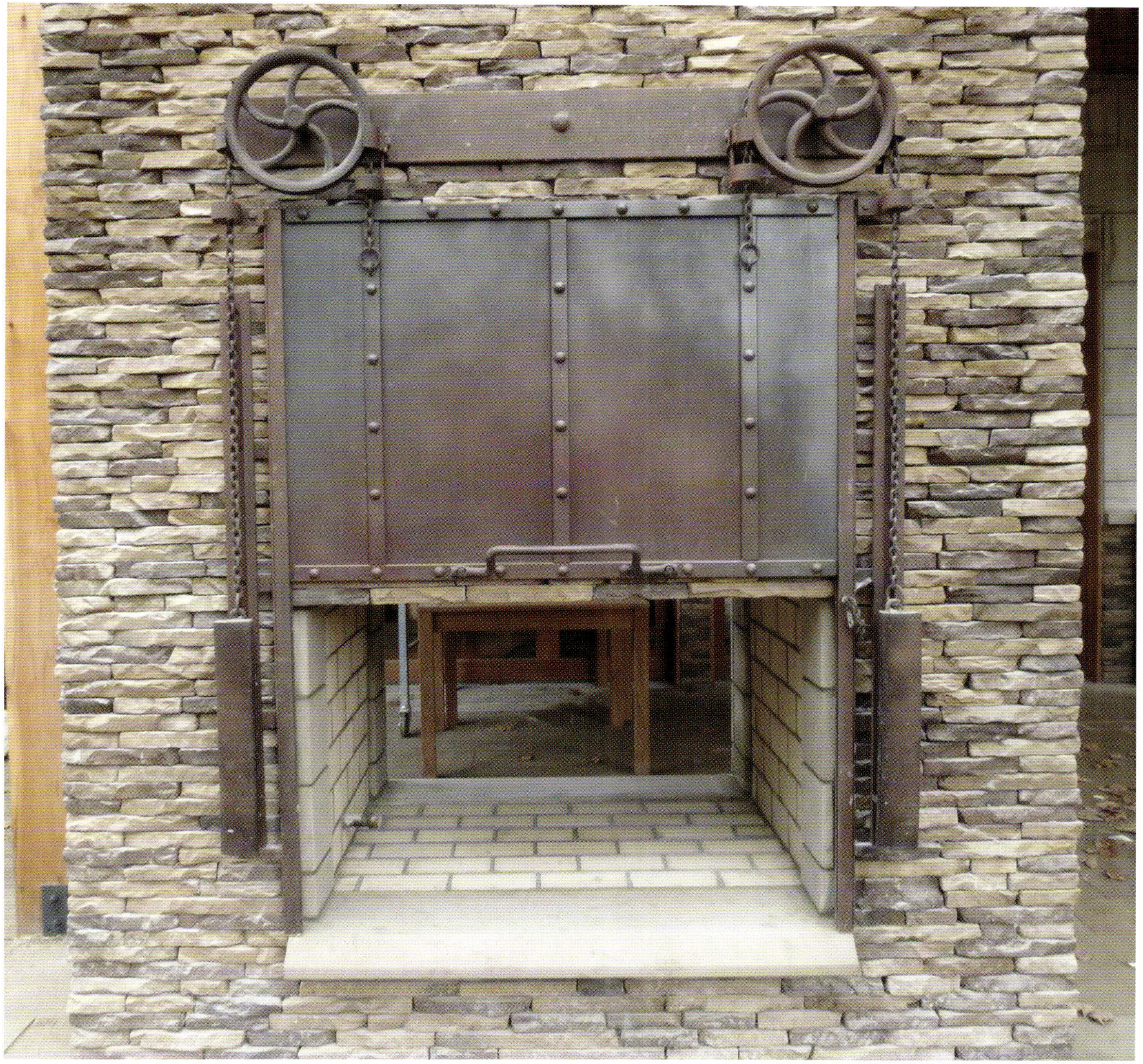

Fireplace Door

A new bistro-type restaurant was opening and needed an unusual fireplace covering for an outdoor eating area. The architect wanted it to imitate the look of a skip hoist on a blast furnace. Their wish was for it to look like it was actually removed from a steel mill and "upcycled" into use as a fire screen. Since we were familiar with blast furnaces, our design was readily accepted. The door was made from 10 gauge plate with ⅜" X 1⅜" buggy tire reinforcing straps. We used authentic rivet construction with 80 pounds of ore-bridge rail counter weights. We believed it was important to use materials that would help give an authentic look to the door. Safety guards were also installed around the chains to keep hands a safe distance from the pulleys. A safety lock and pin were also installed to keep the door in an upor down position. The door can be easily opened and shut with one hand. To give it a "used" look, we added high-temperature paint as well as a variety of spray paints. This door won a NOMMA (National Ornamental Miscellaneous Metals Association), 2013, Gold Top Job Award.

Fireplace door. 4'1" x 34".

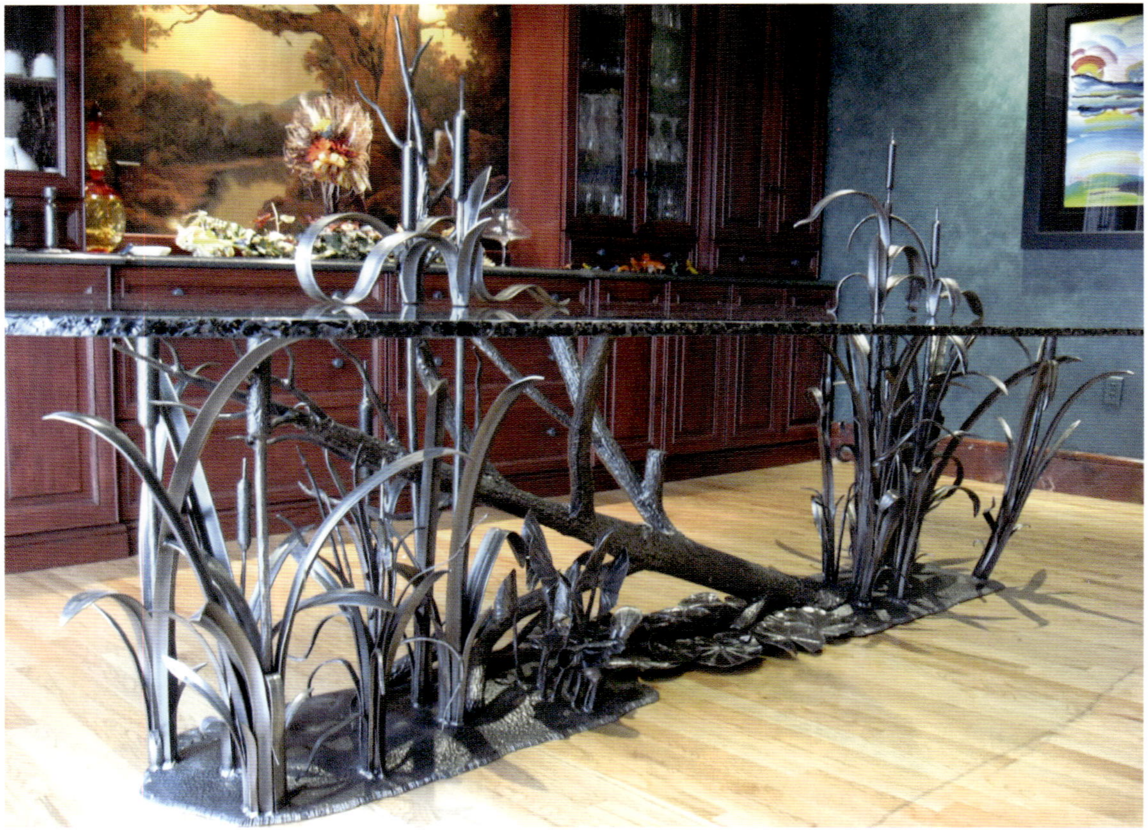

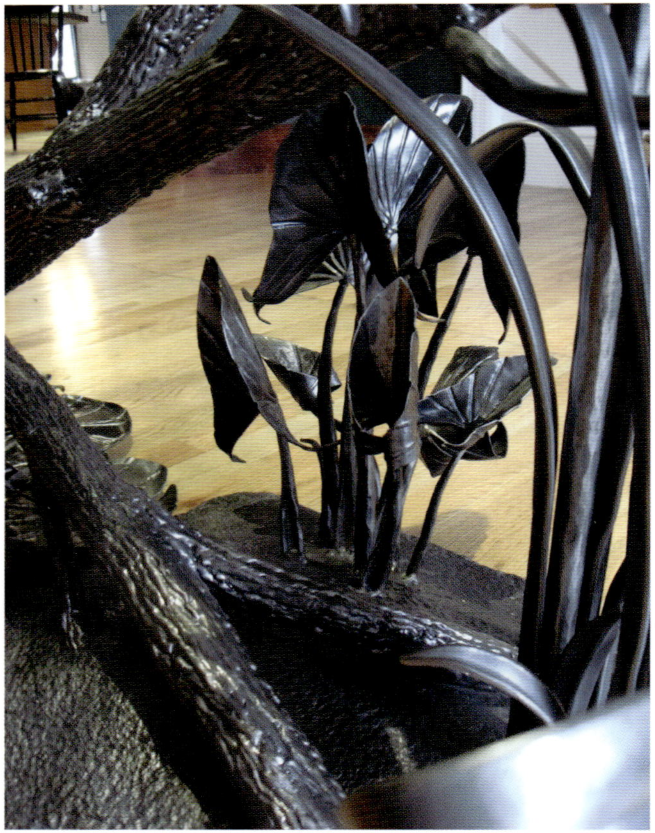

Dining Room Table

This dining room table for twe've was created to suggest a bog environment. The two ⅜" base plates were hand forged and textured to add variety to the design. The plants were made to accurately depict cattails, harts tongue, water lilies, arrowhead, etc. The cattails and one branch appear to go through the glass top, but actually rest on the glass and line up with the corresponding stems beneath the glass. This makes for easy removal and the clients can use the table without the additional centerpieces. The clients own two large Labrador dogs, so their footprints were forged into the "mud" base plates to personalize the table. The tree was made from welded textured pipe to connect, stabilize, and support the glass top. The project took 432 hours. This table won a Silver NOMMA (National Ornamental Miscellaneous Metals Association) Top Job Award in 2009.

Dining room table. Mild steel. Table base approximately 21" x 108" x 30".

Kenneth M. Thompson

Blissfield, Michigan
www.kenthompsonsculpture.com

ARTIST'S STATEMENT

I see each project as a clean sheet of paper that presents new opportunities to discover sculptural solutions. Beyond content and suitability, my sculpture concentrates on the fundamental issues of form and how negative space defines it, as well as the techniques employed to create it.

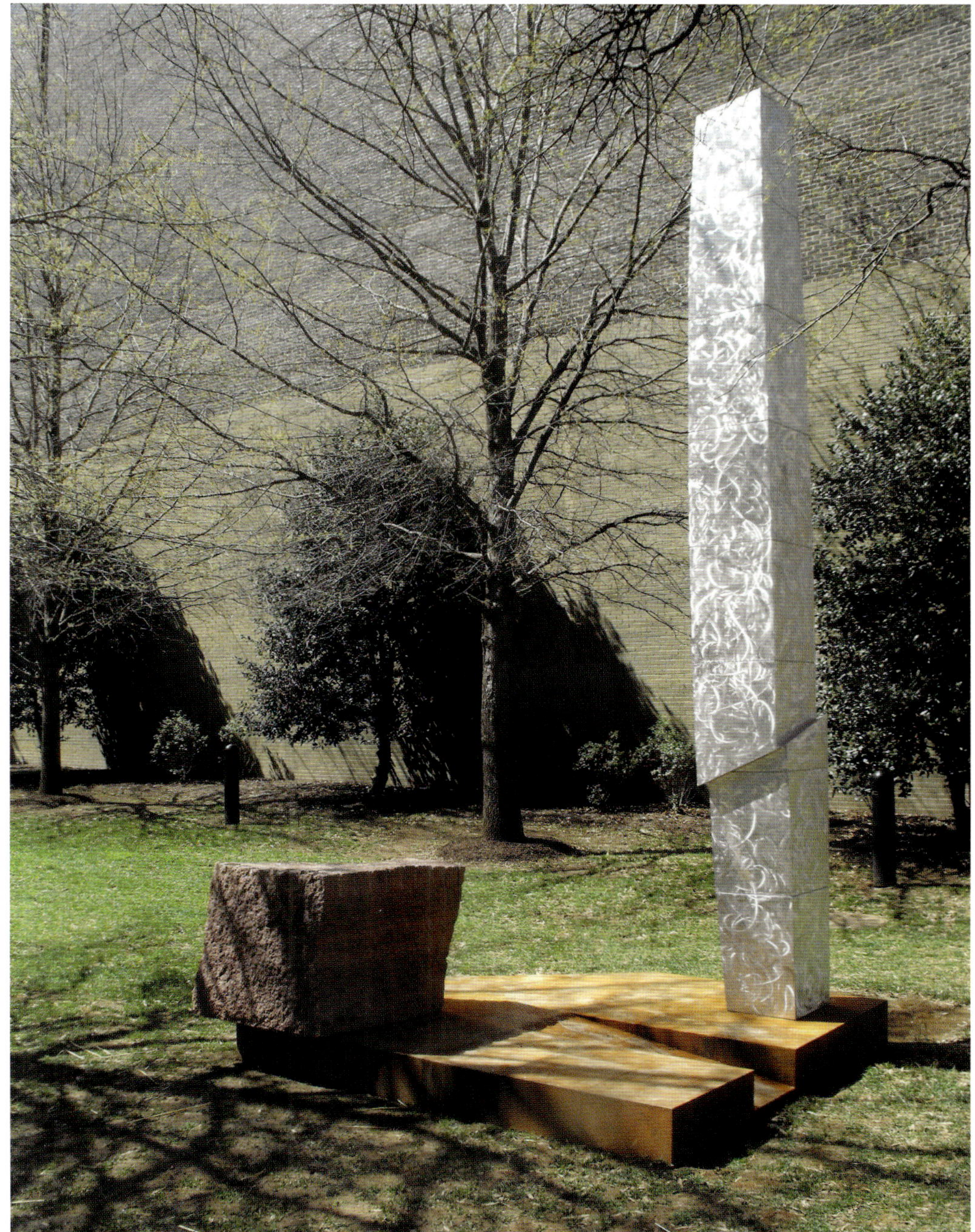

Column, Block and Base 2

This sculpture is about the relationship between dissimilar materials, the forms they take, and the negative space that surrounds them.

Column, Block and Base 2. Sculpture. 2013. Corten steel, aluminum, granite. 7′ x 8′ x 16′ 6″.

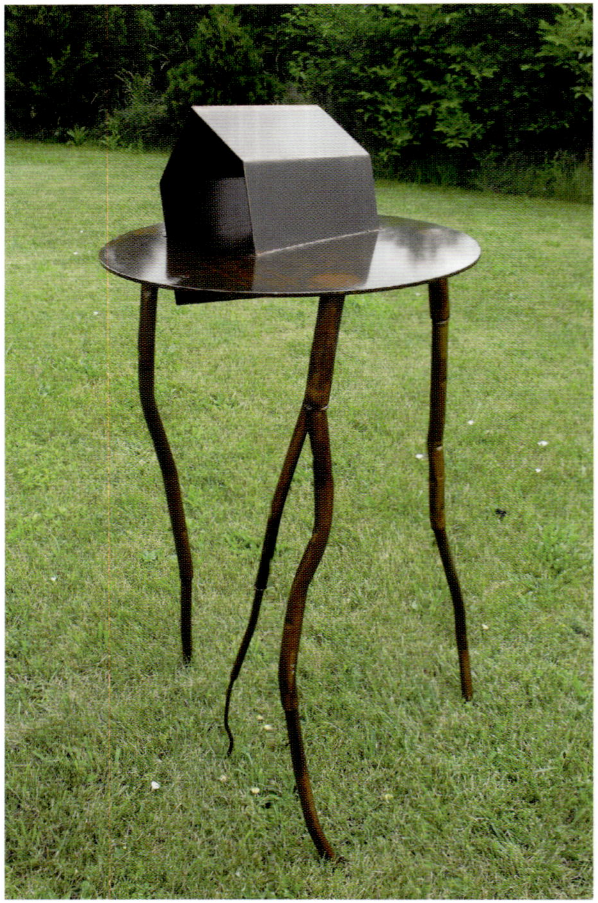

The Illustrated Facts of Global Warming: Washed Away

This is part of a series, inspired by Hurricane Sandy of 2012, that illustrates the negative effects man has on his environment. The series features sixteen emblematic works completed in mild steel.

The Illustrated Facts of Global Warming: Washed Away. Sculpture. 2013. Mild steel. 5′ 6″ x 1′6″.

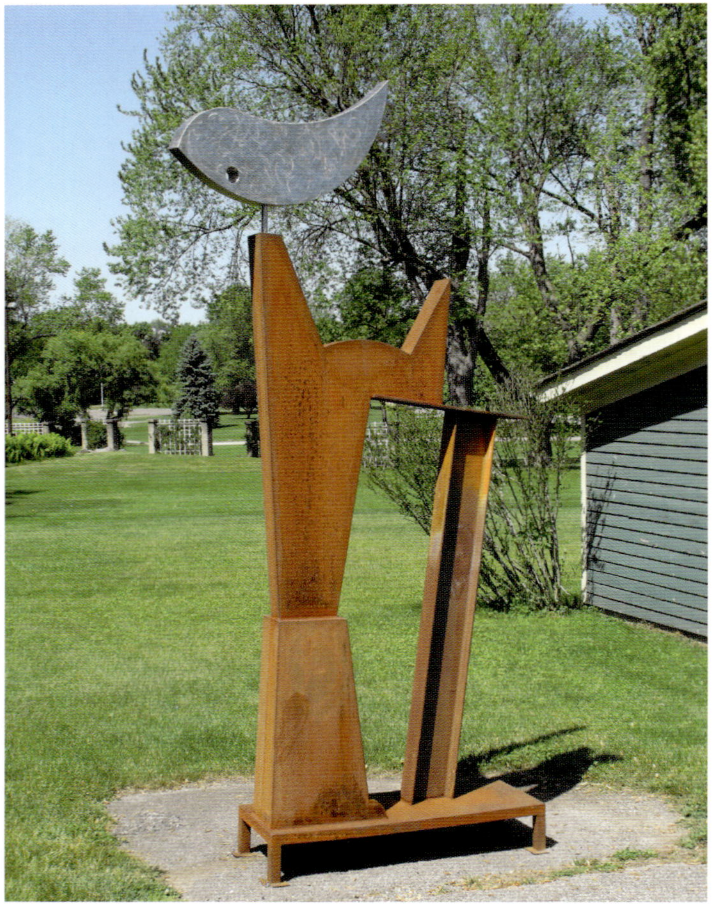

Catfish

This is part of a series exploring basic table form with the added features of "it spins" and "shiny."

Catfish. Sculpture. 2011. Corten steel and stainless steel. 11′ x 5′ x 1½″.

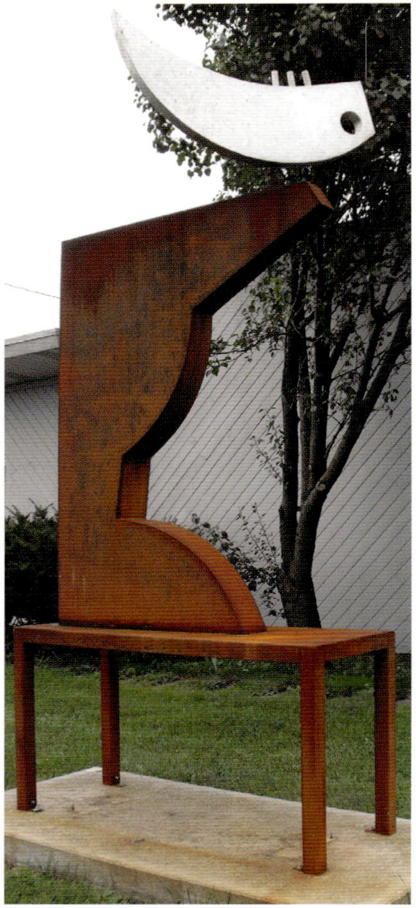

El Fishbird

This is another work from the series exploring basic table form and what to put on it. Again, the added features are "it spins" and "shiny."

El Fishbird. Sculpture. 2011. Corten steel and stainless steel. 13′ x 6′ x 2′.

Christopher Thomson

Christopher Thomson Studio and Gallery, San Jose, New Mexico
www.christopherthomsonironworks.com

ARTIST'S STATEMENT

I forge sculpture, architectural lighting, and home furnishings in white-hot iron and bronze. Forms initially explored for their own sake find their way into my gates, railings, chandeliers, lamps, candle sticks, fireplace tool sets, tables, and chairs. Three employees and tools, from ancient to modern, help me with these creations. Life experiences subconsciously blend with the rich traditions of my craft to push the work in new directions.

Over the last forty years, I have spent much time hiking, kayaking, and camping in the deserts and canyons of the Southwest. Often, I go alone in search of vision and am transported by the light, vastness, and geologic time made visible. The monumental rock formations captivate me. Carved by wind and water, by faulting and geological upheavals, they appear marvelously random and yet unerringly reveal the character of their material. They stretch my ideas of beauty and rightness.

Spiral Pajos #2

Pajos are a series of sculptures that have been evolving for several years. I pull long pieces of dripping-hot steel from the fire and hammer them to shape under large power hammers in the moments before they cool or before the next piece overheats. The immediacy, physicality, primal force, rhythm, and repetition often induce the mindless, totally aware state from which I like to create. In magic moments, all I know and care about flow through me, untranslated to conscious thought. The forgings are executed without the constraints of preconceived ideas on how they will fit into the final composition. I forge the individual sticks in groups of forty to eighty at a time. Then, in a more contemplative mindset, I compose them into groups of three, attaching them to a spiral base. The interplay between the elements is lyrical, meditative, and unpredictable. I've been making them in many sizes, up to 9' tall, and the compositions are becoming more elaborate. I foresee them getting still bigger.

Recently, I discovered the interplay is further enhanced by arranging the sculptures in groups, and I am offering them in different configurations. They move nicely in the wind. Spiral Pajos #2 is composed of four groups of three stalks attached to an Archimedean spiral base.

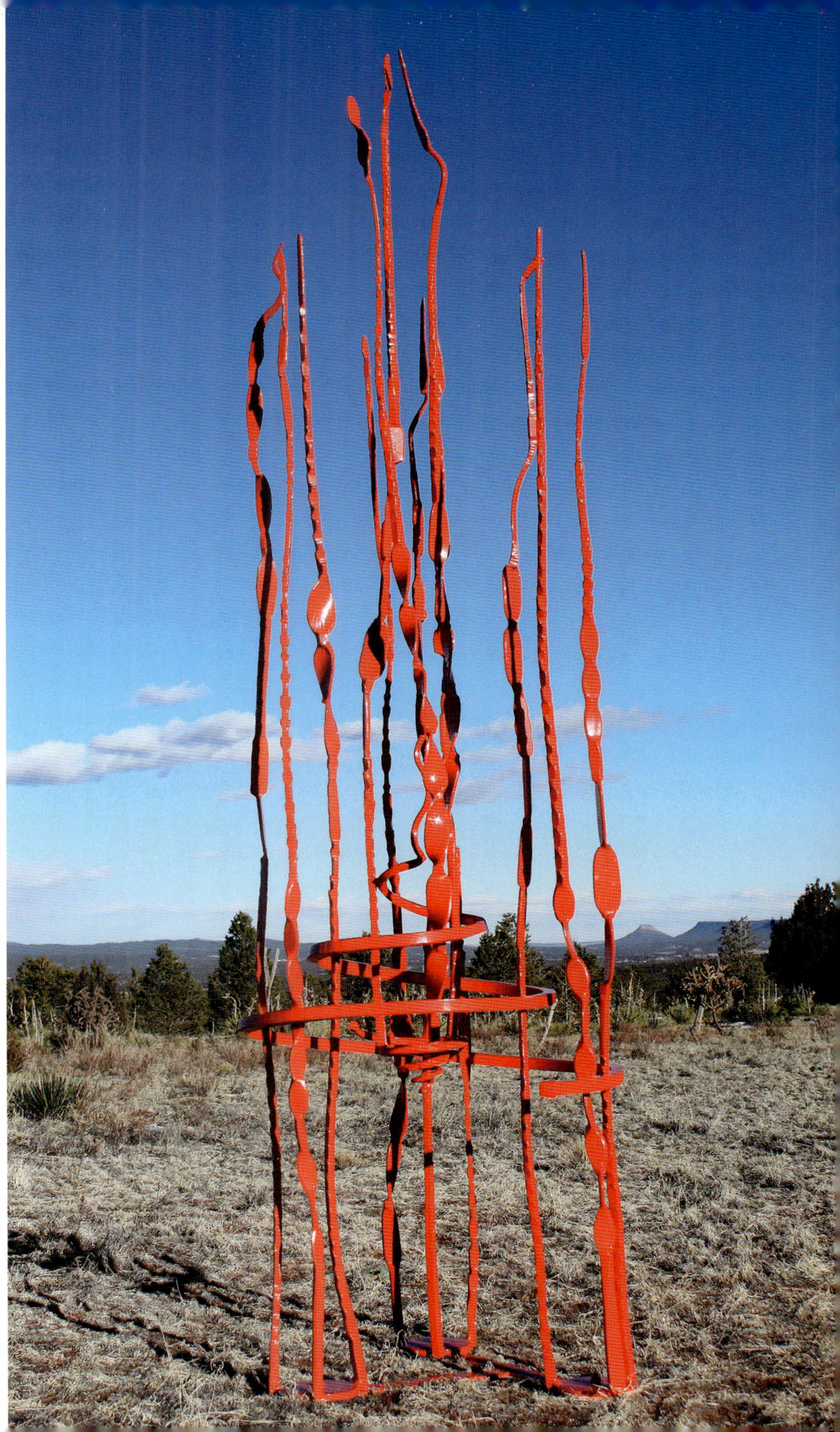

Spiral Pajos #2. Sculpture. 2013. Forged steel and red powdercoat. 108"h x 32"w x 32"d. *Photo: Susan Livermore and Christopher Thomson*

Chinlone Orb Group

In 1954, my political-scientist father returned from a year of study in Burma. His present to me was three woven wicker chinlone balls. I was six years old. They fascinated me. I enjoyed looking at them almost as much as kicking them.

As an adult, these spherical projections of icosidodecahedra, the Archimedean solid composed of six great circles defining twenty equilateral triangles and twelve regular pentagons, still fascinate me. I am not alone with my fascination. Though Archimedes's original treatise was lost, all twelve of his solids were rediscovered by Renaissance mathematicians and artists. More recently, Buckminster Fuller has written extensively about this form.

I am thrilled that elegant design in folk crafts, science, mathematics, and nature frequently converge. My childhood fascination with looking at these orbs has not diminished. I still keep wicker and steel renditions close at hand.

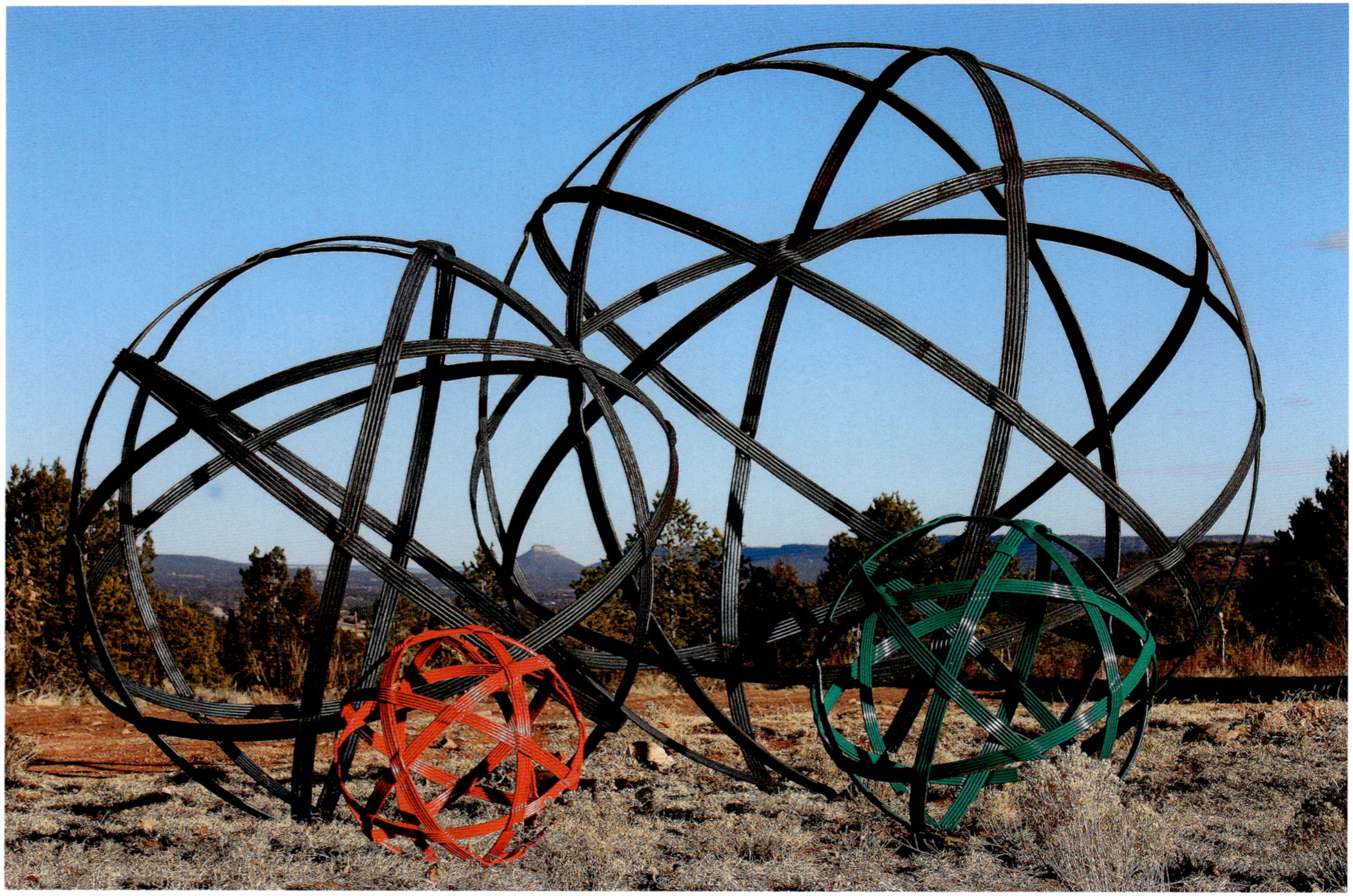

Chinlone Orb Group. Sculpture. 2012. Multi-strand woven steel and powdercoat. 72"h x 112"w x 98"d. Orbs: 18" diameter, 25" diameter, 51" diameter, and 72" diameter. *Photo: Susan Livermore*

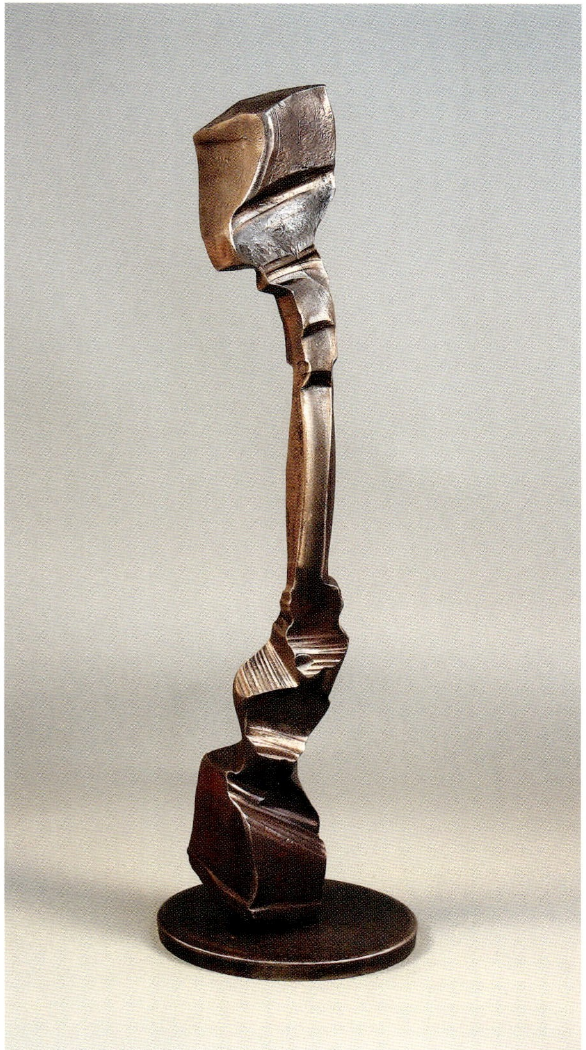

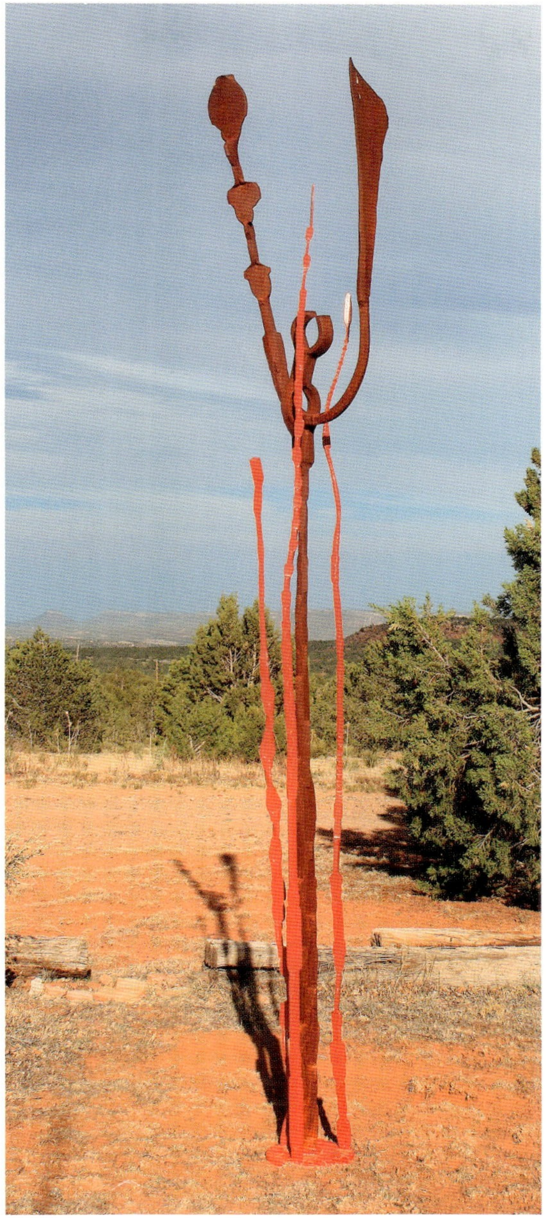

Essence of Akaba #3

Hiking alone, climbing Mount Akaba in the Grand Canyon, I was paying more attention to the wonder of the rock forms than to the time. I became lost in a snowstorm with only the clothes on my back. I knelt on my rope, shivering under an overhang for hours. Luckily, the moon would show through the clouds from time to time, and I was able to use its light to hike rapidly among the rock spires and keep my body heat up waiting for dawn. The full moon, glistening rock, and my own feeling of vulnerability enhanced these spectacular precariously balanced spires—physical manifestations of great geologic forces over ages of time. At first light, I rappelled back down to my pack. On my return to my shop, I forged chunks of steel reminiscent of the energy I felt exuding from those rocks.

Essence of Akaba #3. Sculpture. 2012. Forged steel. 20″h x 6″w x 6″d. *Photo: Susan Livermore*

Spirit Pajos #1

When I was young, I worked for many years as a potter. When steel is hot, under heavy blows, it moves very much like clay. Beautiful forms blossom naturally from the internal forces generated by the heavy hammer and, to my eye, have a natural rightness difficult to plan or achieve by any other means. Chisel-slit holes are a traditional way of passing one bar through another without weakening either. I used unrefined versions of this joinery in Spirit Pajos*. The wispy, willowy, powder-coated stalks of my regular pajos contrast with the heavier, rusted forgings.*

Spirit Pajos #1. Sculpture. 2013. Forged steel, red powder coat. 65″h x 13″w x 8″d.
Photo: Susan Livermore and Christopher Thomson

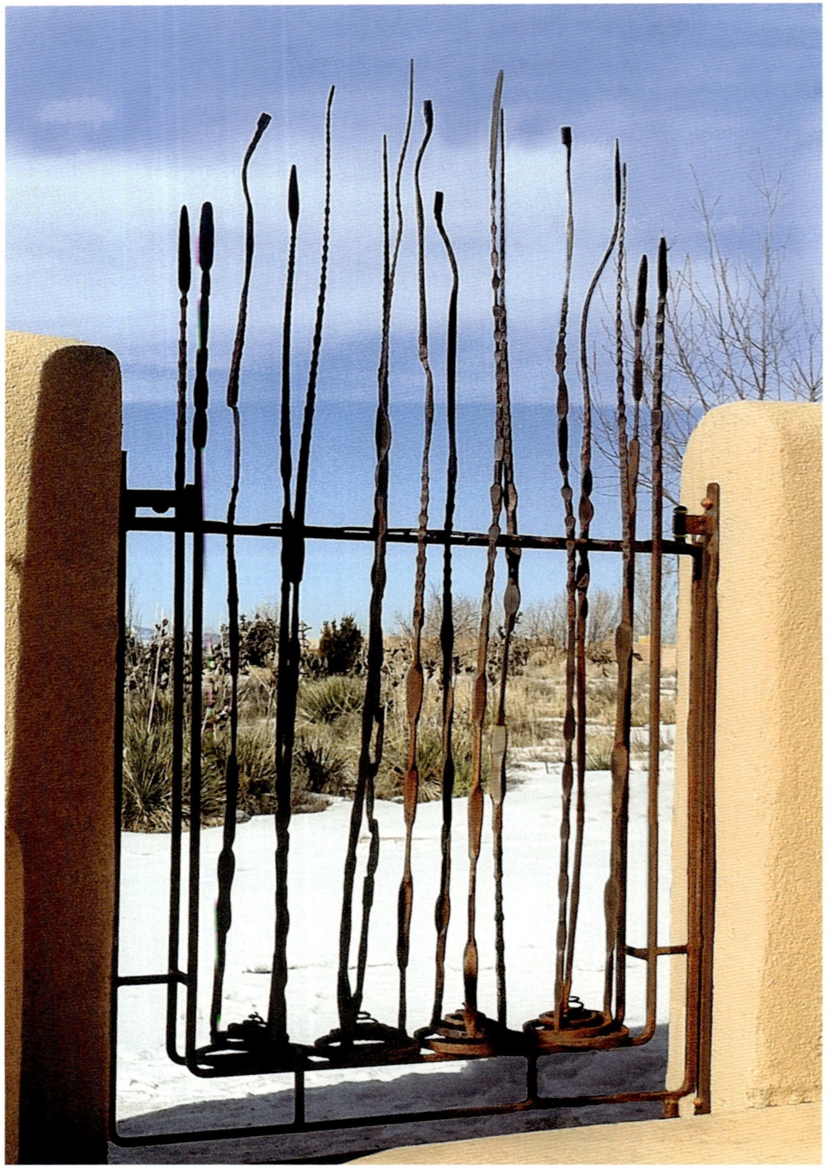

Pajos Gate

I forge the individual "sticks" of my pajos sculptures quickly, passionately, mindlessly. Later, I compose them in threes attached to a spiral base. The random interaction of shapes and textures intrigues me in the individual sculptures. I was pleased when an art- collecting couple commissioned me to incorporate pajos into gates for their courtyard. The groupings in their gates enhanced the interplay—like clumps of grasses in a field or willow thickets along the river. This functional sculpture defined the entry to their courtyard and also kept their dog in. I kept the gate frame very simple but added detailing such as the bronze-bushed hinges. The finished piece was sand blasted and allowed to rust naturally.

Pajos gate. 2012. Forged steel, rust finish. 46"h x 43"w x 6"d.
Photo: Susan Livermore and Christopher Thomson

Bart Turner

Flying Anvil Studio, Seattle, Washington
flyinganvilstudio.com

ARTIST'S STATEMENT

I have drawn since I can remember, constantly exploring positive and negative shapes. An idea or inspiration can happen at any time and come from anything. When this happens, I try to draw the image in its simplest form at that moment and, when I have time, come back and refine or expand on the idea. Sometimes it leads in a completely different direction. And sometimes it turns out exactly as I first imagined.

When working in both glass and metal together I like to find interesting ways to attach the pieces, to bring the focus and attention to how they are connected. I find the difference between metal and glass compelling. The translucence of glass and the strong presence of metal are opposites, but support each other. Metal and glass allow me to explore this relationship between the two mediums coming together, connecting with one another.

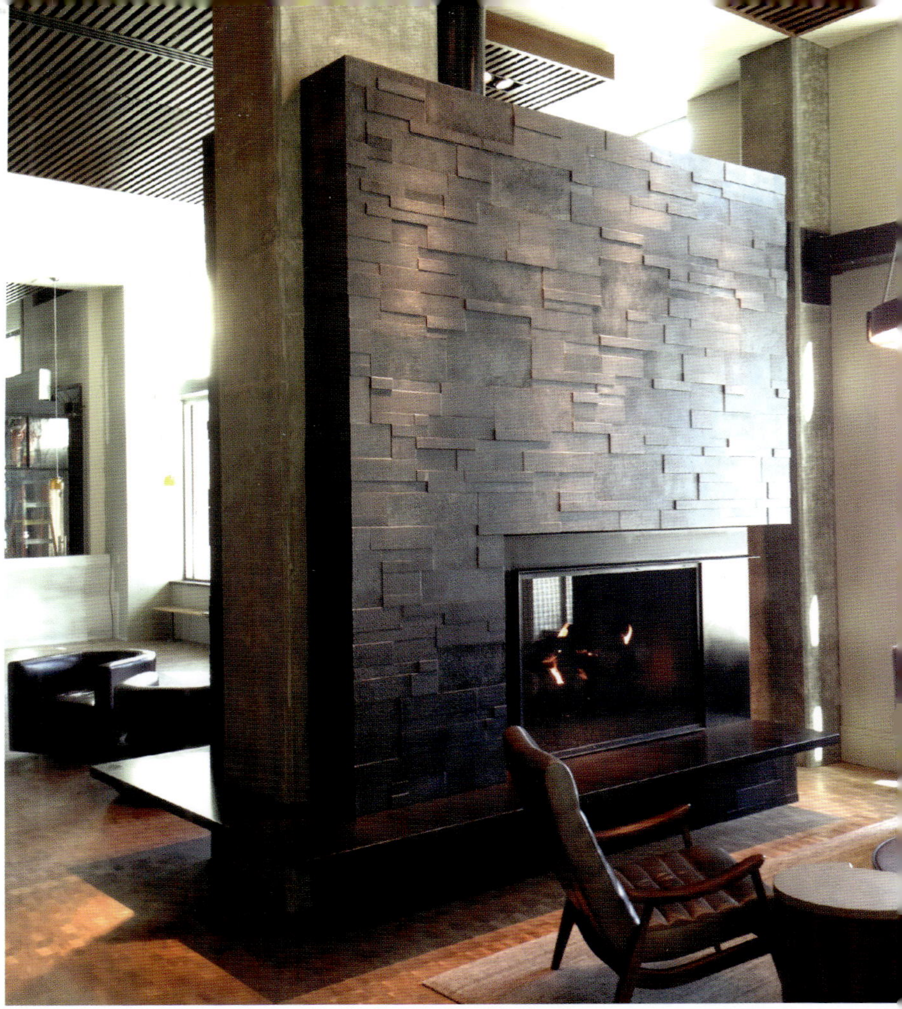

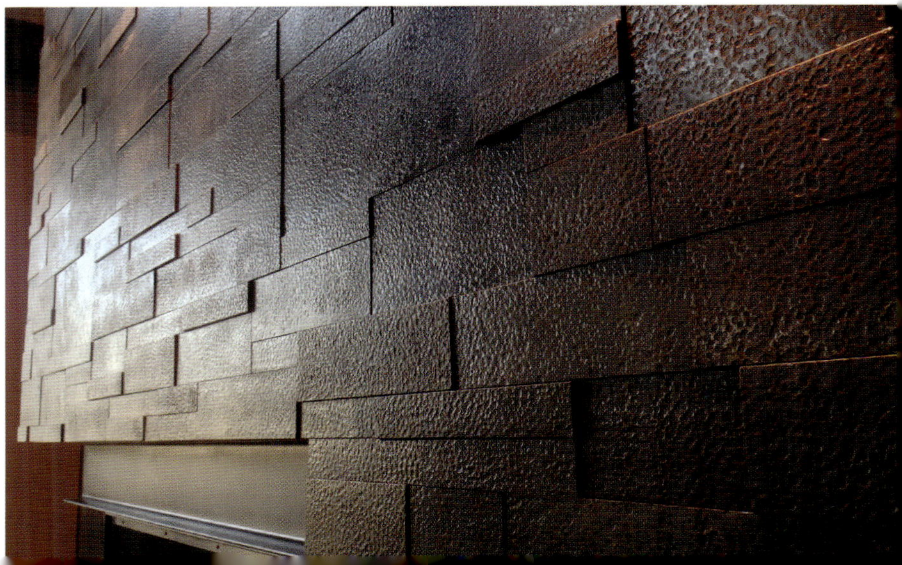

Fireplace Surround

Forged, textured-steel tile surround and a 2"-thick steel hearth. I was in a design meeting for this fireplace,and the designer brought up the idea of having a 2"-thick by 7' by 11' solid -teel hearth plopped in there. I laughed out loud as my mind quickly went through the install of this giant piece of steel. Then I noticed he was serious, and I said, "Okay, I can do that." It worked out well, I think.

Fireplace surround. 2013. Forged textured steel.
12'w x 4'd x 13'h.

BART TURNER

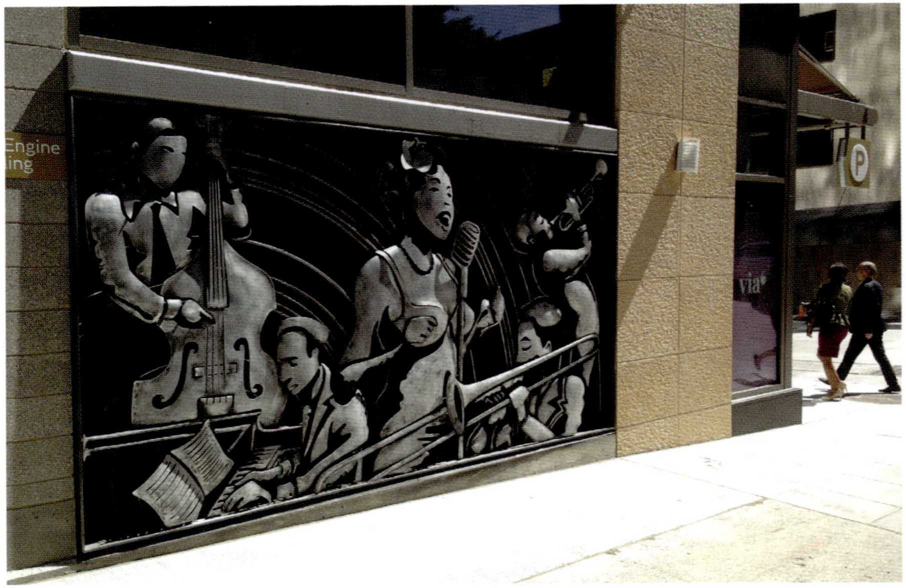

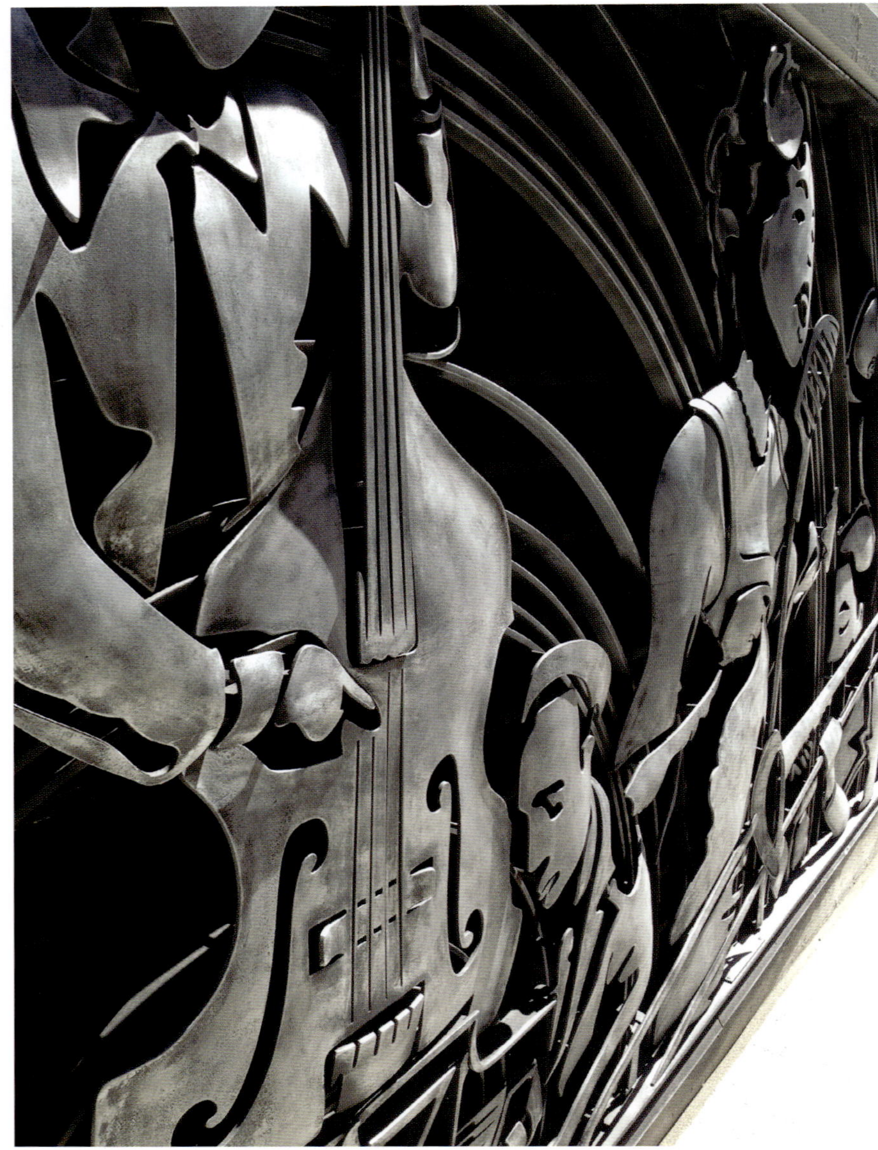

Jazz Band

The folks hiring me for this public art panel in downtown Seattle wanted it to have a jazz feel and it had to have a certain amount of air flow through it in order to cover a vent louver. I wanted to do exploded views of several jazz instruments, all forged then welded on different planes to give it depth. They wanted to see people in it. So we agreed on the band scene This was a fun project to design and make.

Jazz Band. Public sculptural panel. 2013.
Forged galvanized steel. 13′w x 6″d x 8′h.

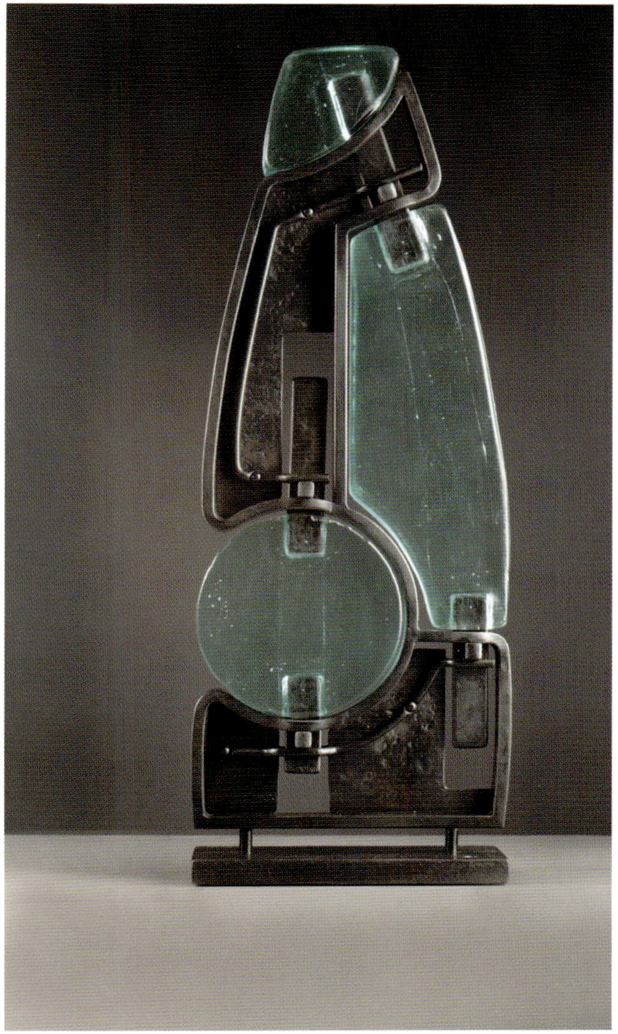

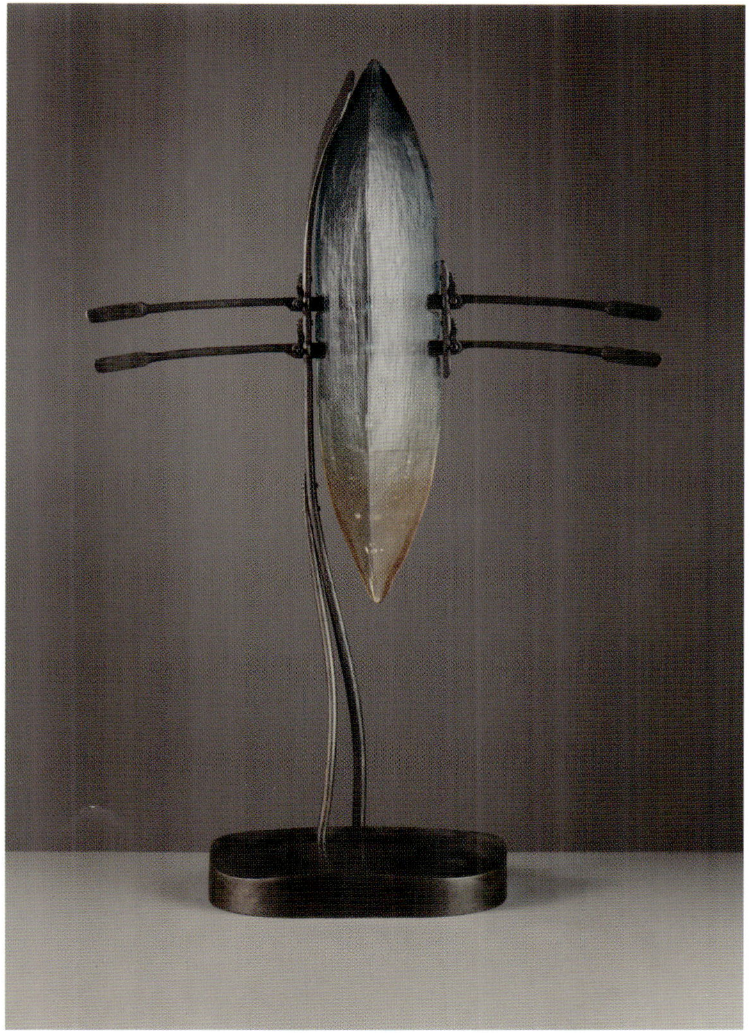

Untitled and Boat

My most recent sculptures have been designed to bring focus to the coupling of forged metal and cast glass, and to integrate these very different mediums fluidly, as equal parts of the whole piece.

Untitled. 2011. Kiln-cast glass and forged steel. 34″h x 13″w x 5″d. *Photo: Horst G. B. Kiessling*

Boat. 2011. Kiln cast glass and forged steel. 24″h x 14″w x 6″d. *Photo: Horst G. B. Kiessling*

Andy Upright

Andy Upright Metal Works, Philadelphia, Pennsylvania
AndyUprightmetalworks.com

ARTIST'S STATEMENT

I love working with iron, and I love the satisfying swing of a hammer. Using the classical element of fire to bring iron to a malleable state is quite gratifying.

It's taken many years to learn the language of forging iron, and now I'm starting to tell my own story with it. I strive to explore humor and levity through the medium, to illustrate in iron the stories written in the architecture—books filled with wonder, curiosity, horror, fantasy, and beauty to be read while walking down the street.

I live and work in an urban environment, where iron is a given part of many people's lives and has been for centuries. Philadelphia has a rich history of decorative ironwork. It's a gratifying experience to get to add my own flavor and variation to the world around me. Random people interact with my work on a daily basis, and as a result, I feel very connected to my community through my work.

Dragonfly, Spider, and Grass

The spider, dragonfly, and grass pieces are from a series I refer to as my ten-year plan. There are multiples of each in a 40′ fence surrounding the courtyard of the Satellite Café in West Philadelphia. I was inspired to do this project on a preexisting fence that had no adornment. I saw the fence as a blank canvas to work with and set about making a series of spiders. I informed the building owner, a friend of mine, that something would be happening to the fence and went about my work. The spiders were received well and I have continued to add a new series of work each year when I have downtime from my other projects. It is unique to get to work on a project that evolves with my work over a period of time.

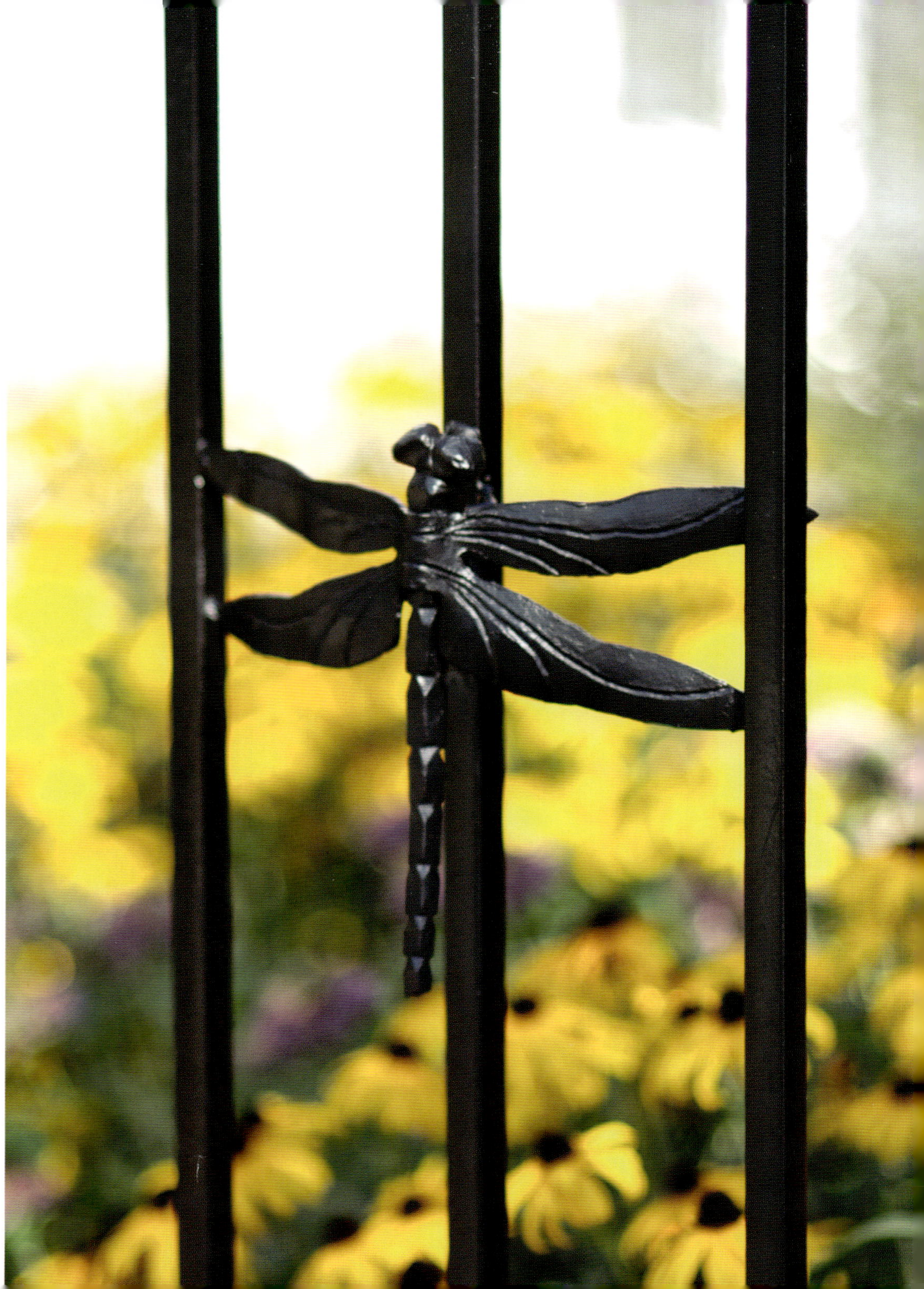

Dragonfly. Sculptural detail on fence. 2011. Forged steel. 9″x 9″.
Photo: Daniel Raaf

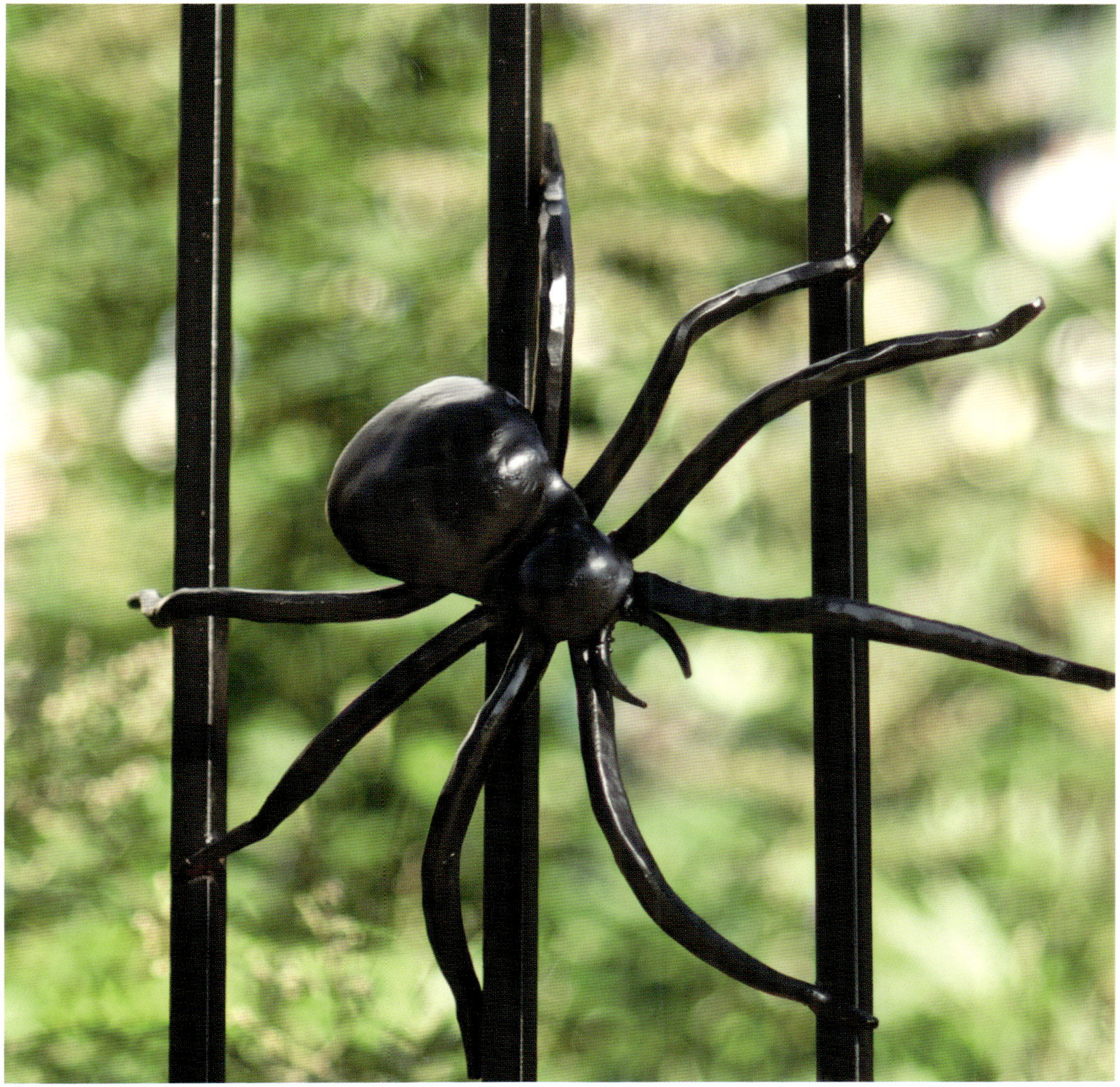

Spider. Sculptural detail on fence. 2010. Forged steel. 16″ x 16″. *Photo: Daniel Raaf*

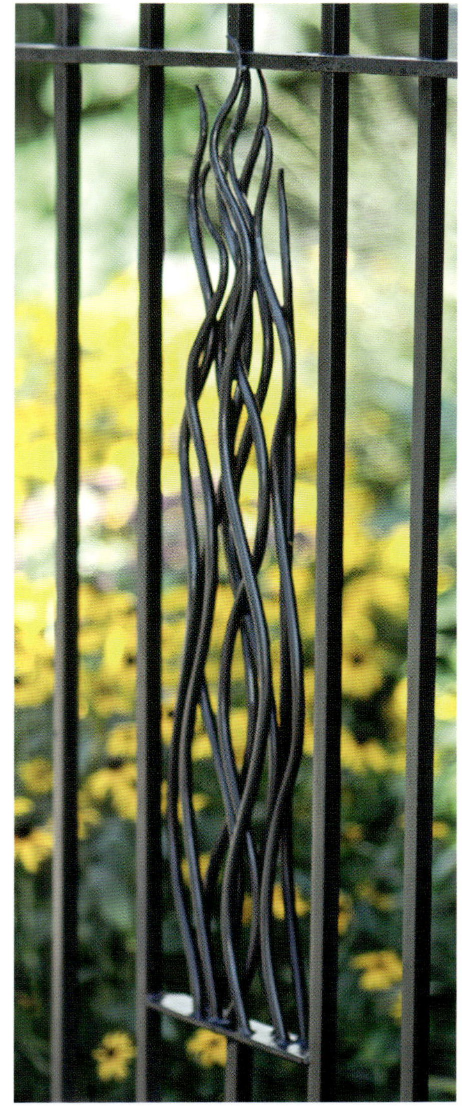

Grass. Sculptural detail on fence. 2012. Forged steel. 9″x 30″. *Photo: Daniel Raaf*

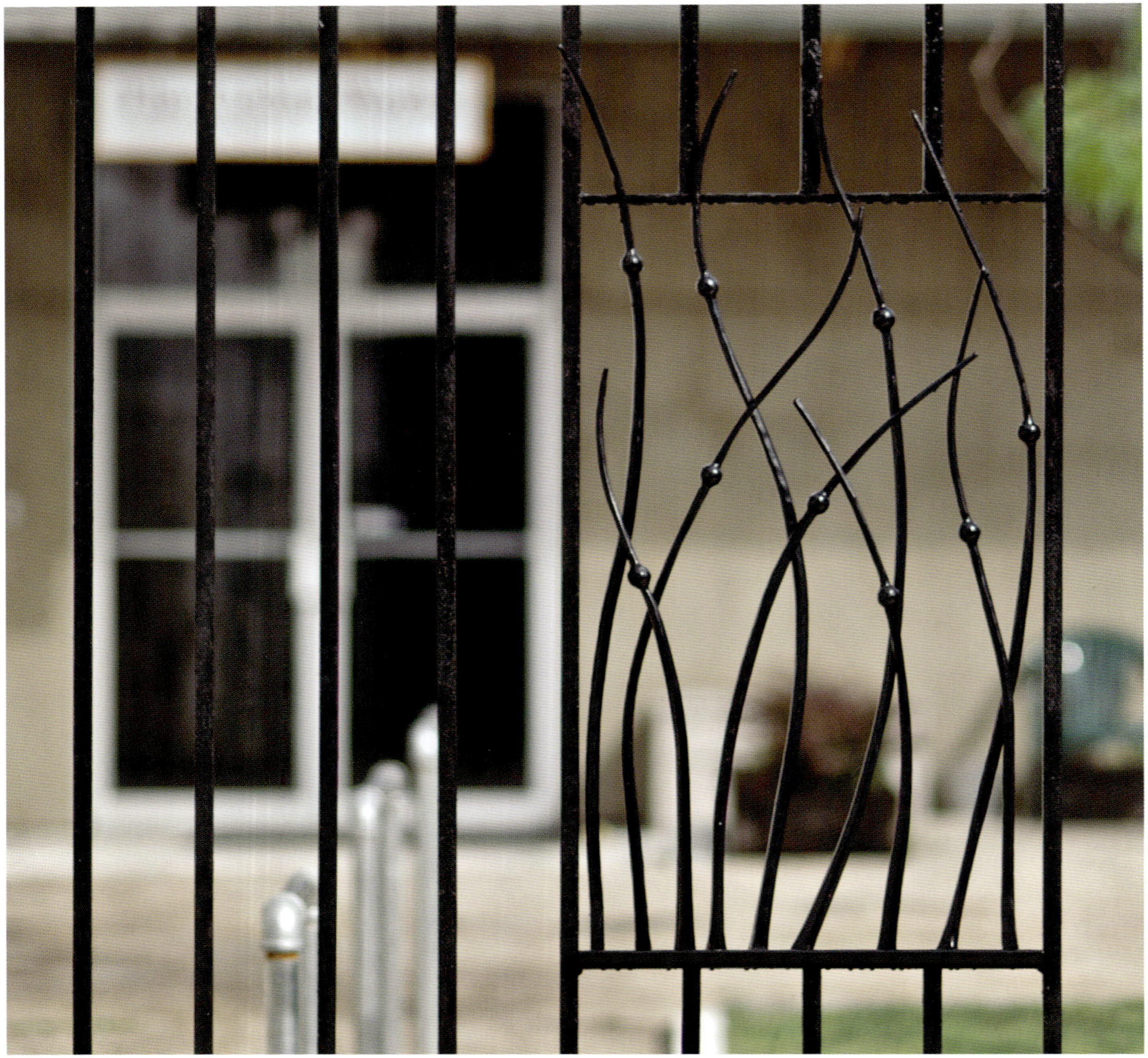

Grass with Egg Sack, Arches

These pieces are part of a fence outside the Cedar Works Studios in West Philadelphia. I was approached to do the project and asked to find a way to reuse/reinterpret a preexisting fence brought in from another location. Again, this is a fence that had no adornment aside from the spiked tops on the pickets. I took on the idea of starting with the same material thickness as the pickets for the source of my forged pieces. They articulate different forms that come out of a standard ¾" square material. I designed the pieces as they were being forged, using techniques I wanted to experiment with.

Grass with egg sack. Sculptural detail on fence. 2012. Forged steel. 19" x 36". *Photo: Daniel Raaf*

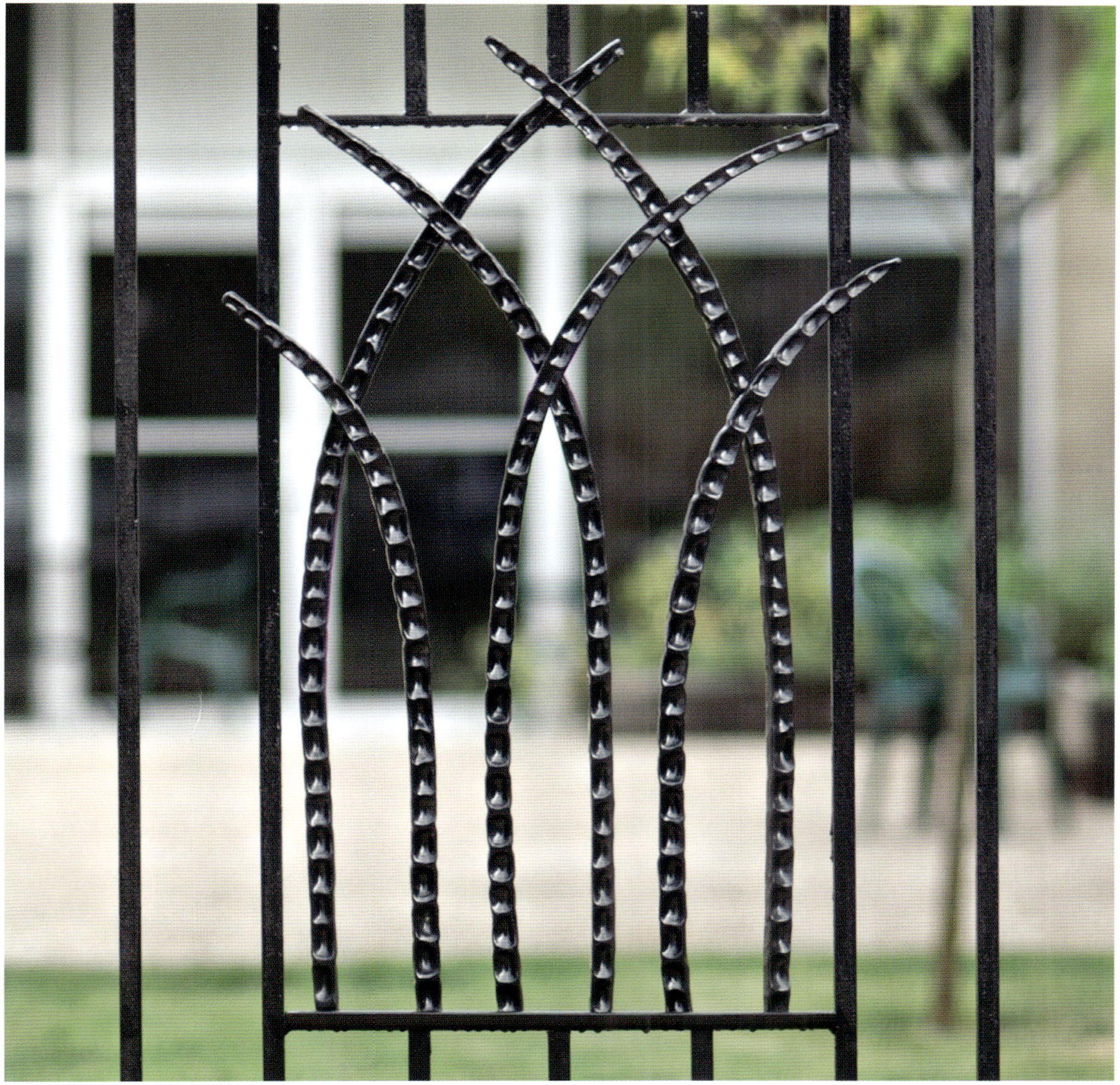

Arches. Sculptural detail on fence. 2012. Forged steel. 19″ x 36″. *Photo: Daniel Raaf*

James Viste

Edgewise Forge, Hamtramck, Michigan
edgewiseforge@hotmail.com

ARTIST'S STATEMENT

My vessels are created using both traditional and contemporary blacksmithing processes. Through traditional forging, power assisted forging, die forging, and metal fabrication techniques, I am creating steel vessels that are decorative objects of desire and contemplation. I do not employ any casting/foundry techniques.

I work in series, like a potter. I always have several pieces in process at the same time. I allow the work to influence itself, one piece inspiring new elements in the next. Unlike my commissioned works, where detailed drawings and mechanical drafts must be offered, my vessels are based on loose sketches and a playful approach to making: spiraling flattened iron into a cylinder, attaching handles, a lid and a rolled foot, infusing it with color. In ceramics, the essence of throwing is a sequence of manipulations followed by firing; in steel, ironically, it is heated first to form it and wetted last with patina.

The vessel is my folly, imitation, impression, my muse.

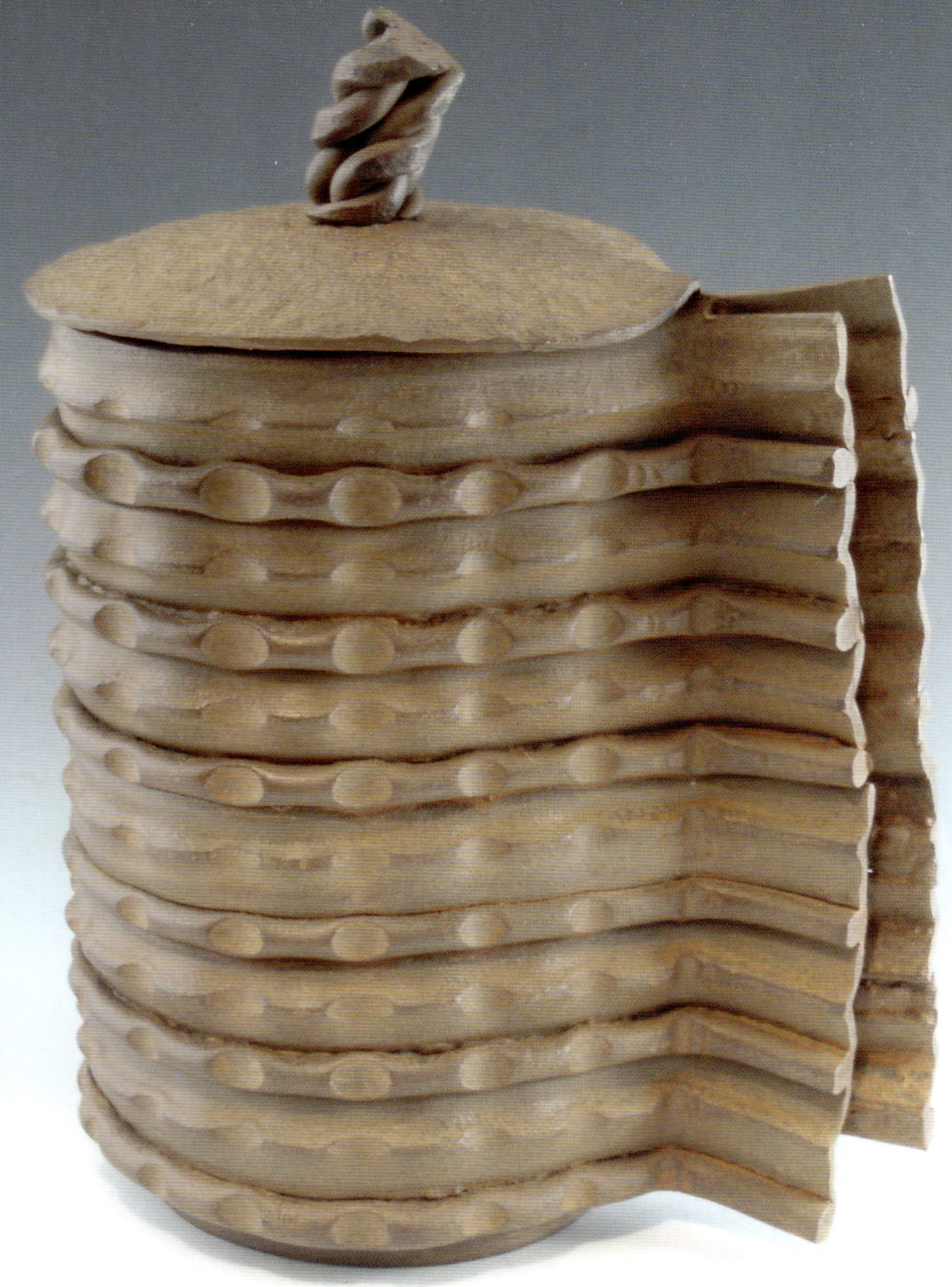

Burlap Flap. Vessel. 2011. Steel.
Forged and fabricated. 11″ x 7″ x 6″.

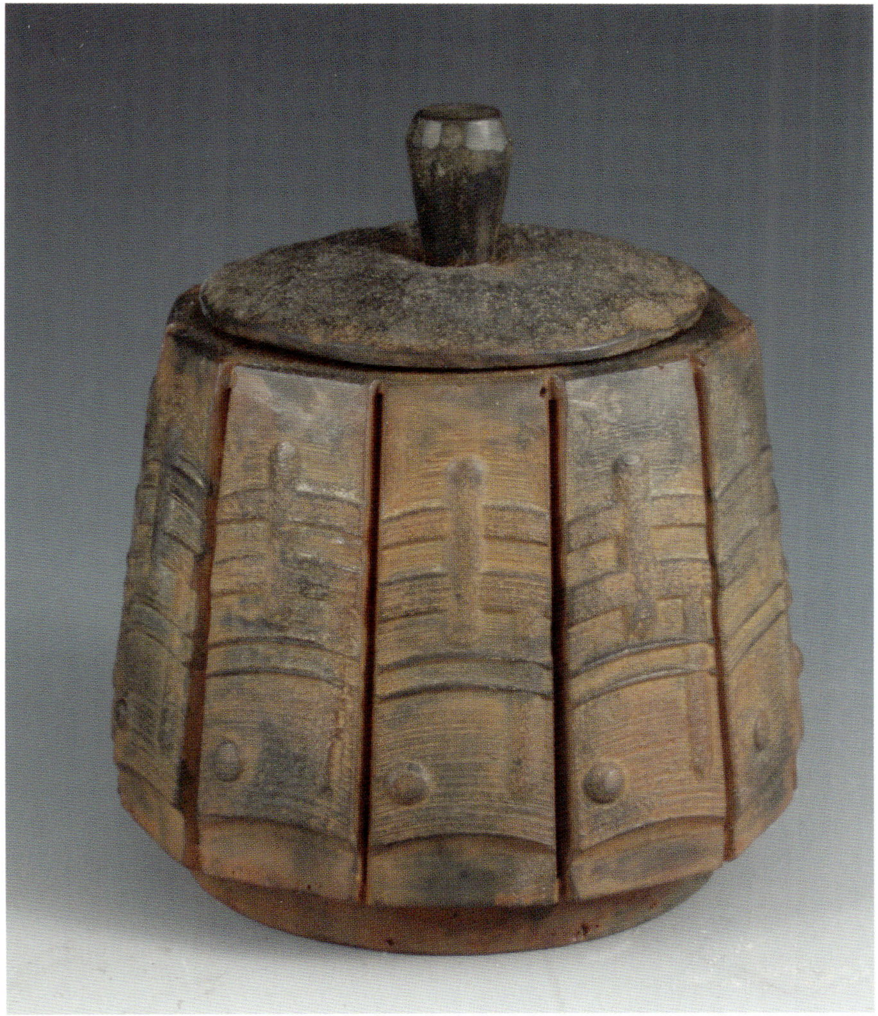

Monsieur Nemoy. Vessel. 2012. Steel. Forged and fabricated. 11″ x 9″ x 9″.

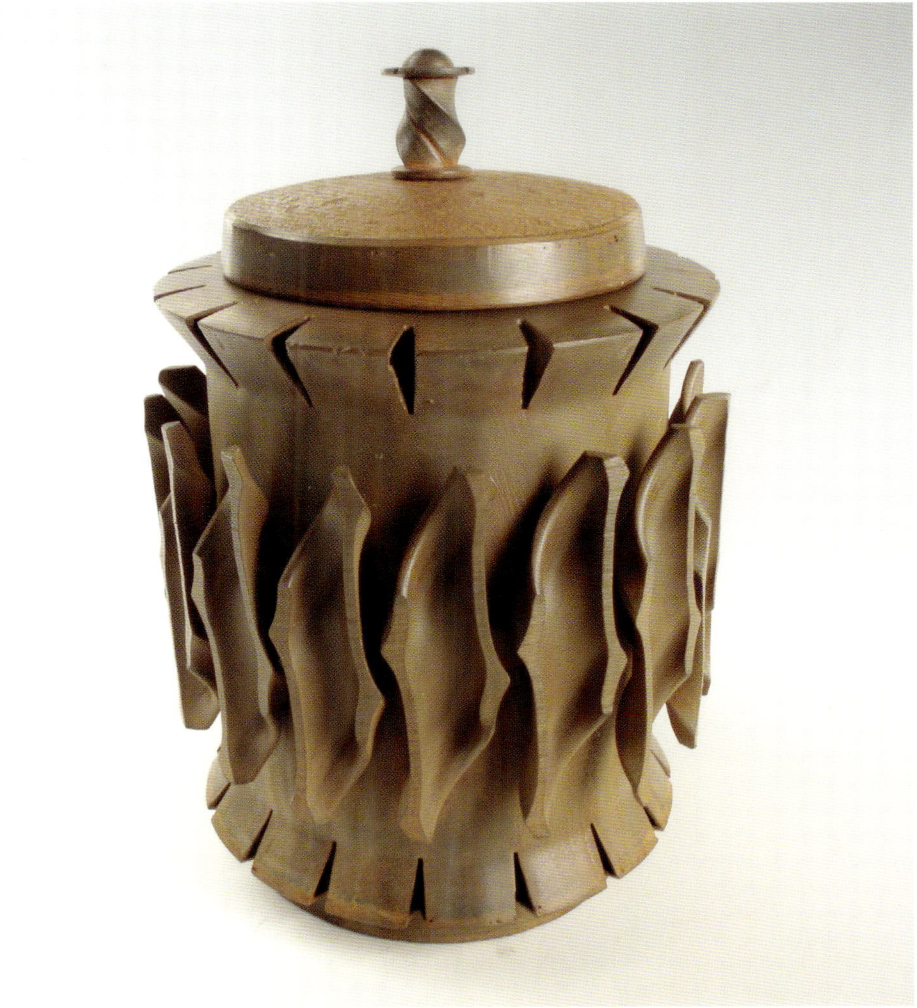

Ink Well. Vessel. 2012. Steel. Forged and fabricated. 4″ x 3″ x 3″.

Jack Wylestone

Williamstown, Victoria, Australia
jdwhilestone@bigpond.com

ARTIST'S STATEMENT

Forging objects from steel is the means that I use to externalize thought and emotion. At the core of my practice is a self-imposed parameter, that the work is achievable with basic blacksmithing techniques. Interpreting ideas into the pure and recognizable language of forged ironwork is a clarifying process at the heart of my design method, an essential tool for pairing back to the basic forms that capture the energy or essence of an idea.

Garden

The initial inspiration for this lock came from the title of the story The Secret Garden *by Frances Hodgson Burnett. The concept of a mysterious and secret garden room, just out of reach, was something that I wanted to explore in a small and tactile object. The form of a lock, the keyhole, and the key are highly suggestive symbols evoking mystery, adventure, or even the forbidden. The large proportions of both the lock and the key give the objects a fairytale feel, while the organic accents and heavily textured surface hint at the wild and overgrown place that lies just beyond.*

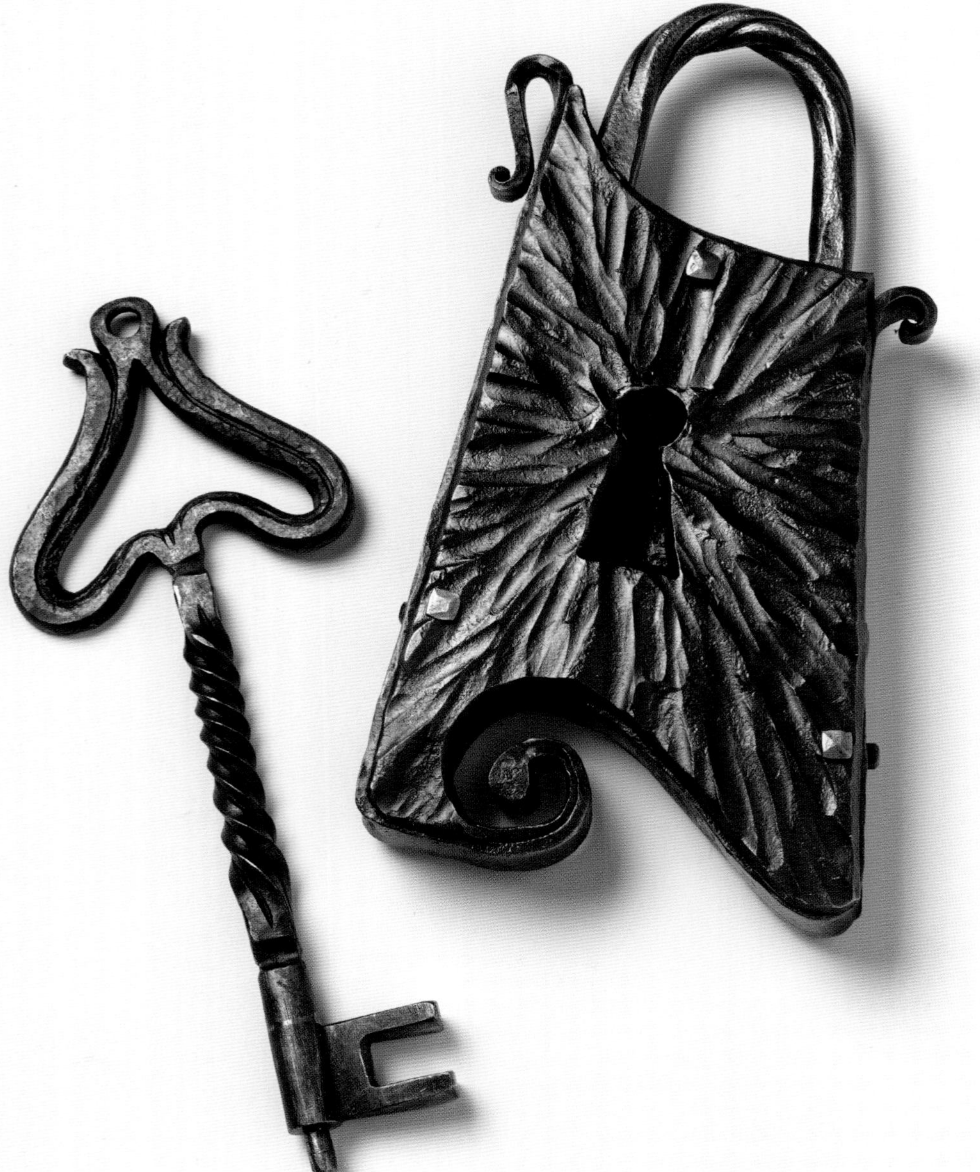

Garden. Large padlock and key. 2010. Hand forged, mild and spring steel. Forge welded and riveted with heavy radiating hammer blows, texturing to front and rear cover plates. Hot blued in oil, wax finish. Lock: 8″ x 4″. Key: 8″ x 3″. *Photo: Jeremy Dillon*

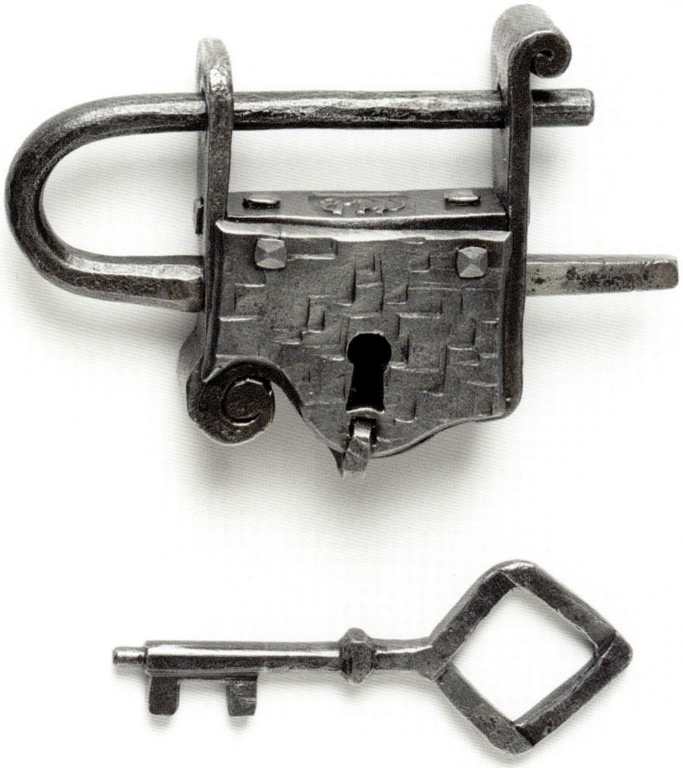

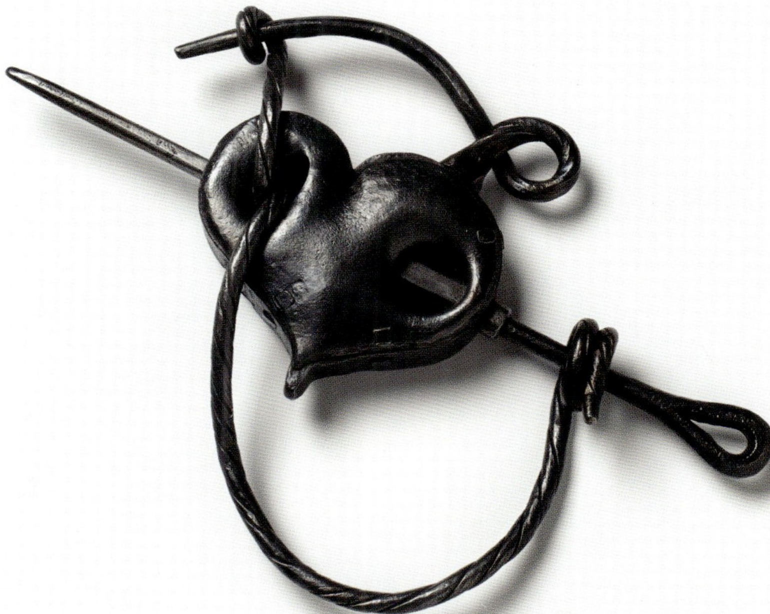

Labyrinth

I find the symbolism associated with padlocks fascinating. These small objects themselves can be interesting vehicles for exploration. I drew upon a few visual ideas of a fictitious place with stone walls and spiral stairs, a labyrinth where memory and emotion are hidden or discovered. I tried to put some of these visual elements into the design of this lock and key in both the choice of the object and the shapes and surface texture employed.

Labyrinth. Two-position padlock with key. 2010. Hand forged mild and spring steel. Forge welded, riveted, and bound. Hammer-textured front and rear cover plates. Wire brushed and waxed finish. Lock: 4″ x 6″. Key: 2″ x 5″. *Photo: Jeremy Dillon*

Heart Stitch

Exploring conditions of the human heart using a lock as a vehicle of expression led to many variations of design, including the complete abandonment of having a separate key. Spring steel barbs on an oversized sewing needle that pierces the heart serve to keep this piece in a locked position. A delightfully interactive action of placing your fingers into a hole in the heart, squeezing the barbs together, and pulling out the needle allows the twisted steel cord to be removed and the lock is opened.

Heart Stitch. Heart-shaped lock pierced by sewing needle and cord. 2011. Forged mild and spring steel, forged welded and riveted. Flame blued with furniture oil and wax finish. 10″ x 11″. *Photo: Jeremy Dillon*

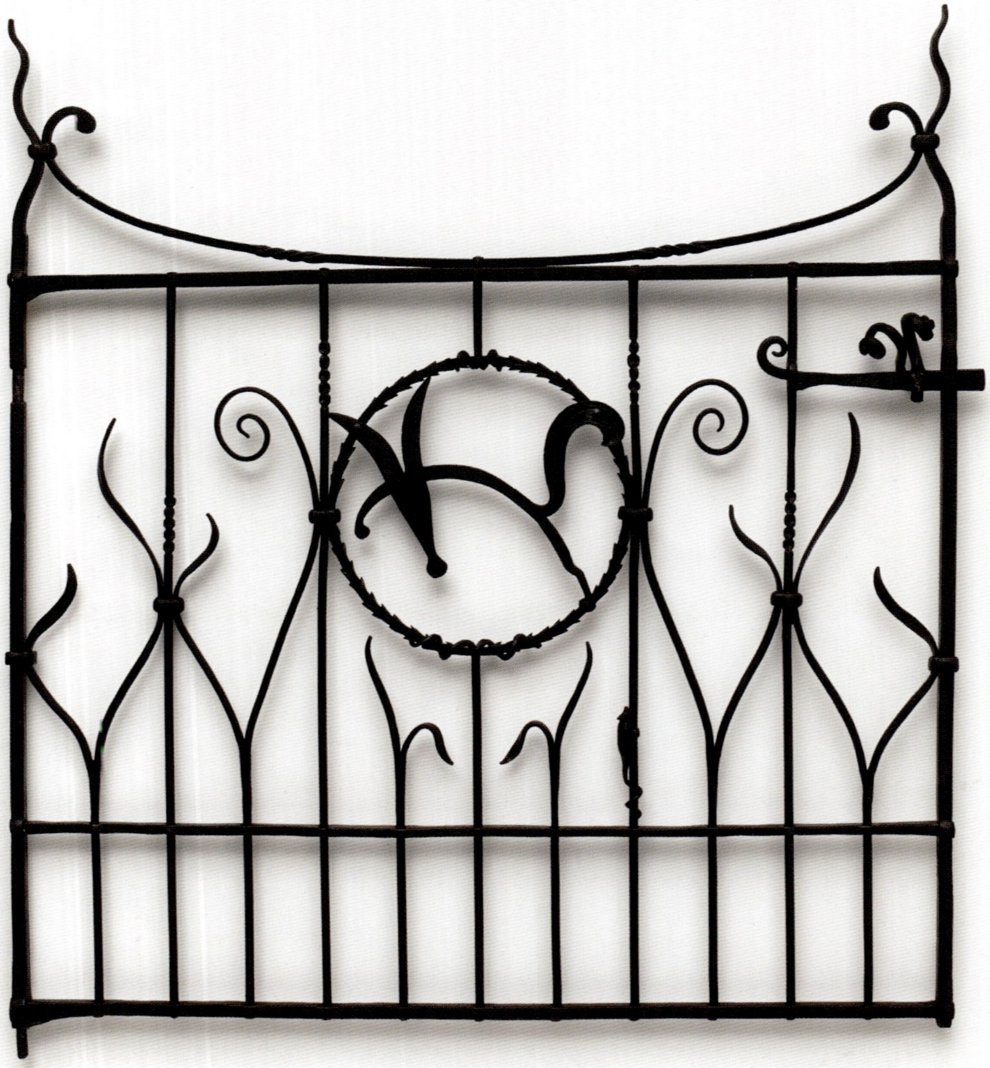

Secret Garden Gate

I really love small gates! There is an intimate communication between the gate and the user. The gate is touched, and over time, a patina of human use imparts onto the work and tells a story about place and time. This Secret Garden gate marks the entry into a small, inner-city, garden retreat. The use of a "mousing fox" surrounded by a circle of thorns represents a place of freedom from the world of man and protection for derided, yet beautiful, creatures.

All parts of this gate are hand forged, not for some stoic adherence to tradition but to effectively convey a personal warmth. A bold decision from the outset of this commission was that the work would not be painted or galvanized, despite being located in a marine environment. A simple treatment of linseed oil diluted with paraffin seemed more in keeping with the premise of the garden and has proved completely successful.

Secret Garden gate. Small garden gate comprising botanical elements and featuring a leaping fox and mouse. Forged mild steel assembled with pure forging techniques. Oil finish. Approximately 4′ x 4′. Private collection. *Photo: Jeremy Dillon*

Stephen Zawistowski

Jacksonville, North Carolina
stephenzmetaldesigns.com

ARTIST'S STATEMENT

I still remember the first time I saw an ironworker forge two pieces of steel into one. The sparks, the noise, and the heat all became a symphony of creation. Somewhere in the midst of all the heat, dust, and noise, I found an outlet for my craftsmanship and imagination.

I have assembled a unique collection of new, vintage, and custom-made tools to aid me in my work. This enables me to work in the time-tested, old-style methods, all the while incorporating the freedom of creativity allowed by modern techniques. I consider myself a modern blacksmith, celebrating the old and embracing the new.

In nature, we can see fantastic designs, the perfect blending of beauty and function. Our world is full of great natural art. We just need to take time to see it. As an artist, I take pride in making pieces that do not attempt to replicate nature but rather reflect its essence. The fluid forms of nature are my inspiration

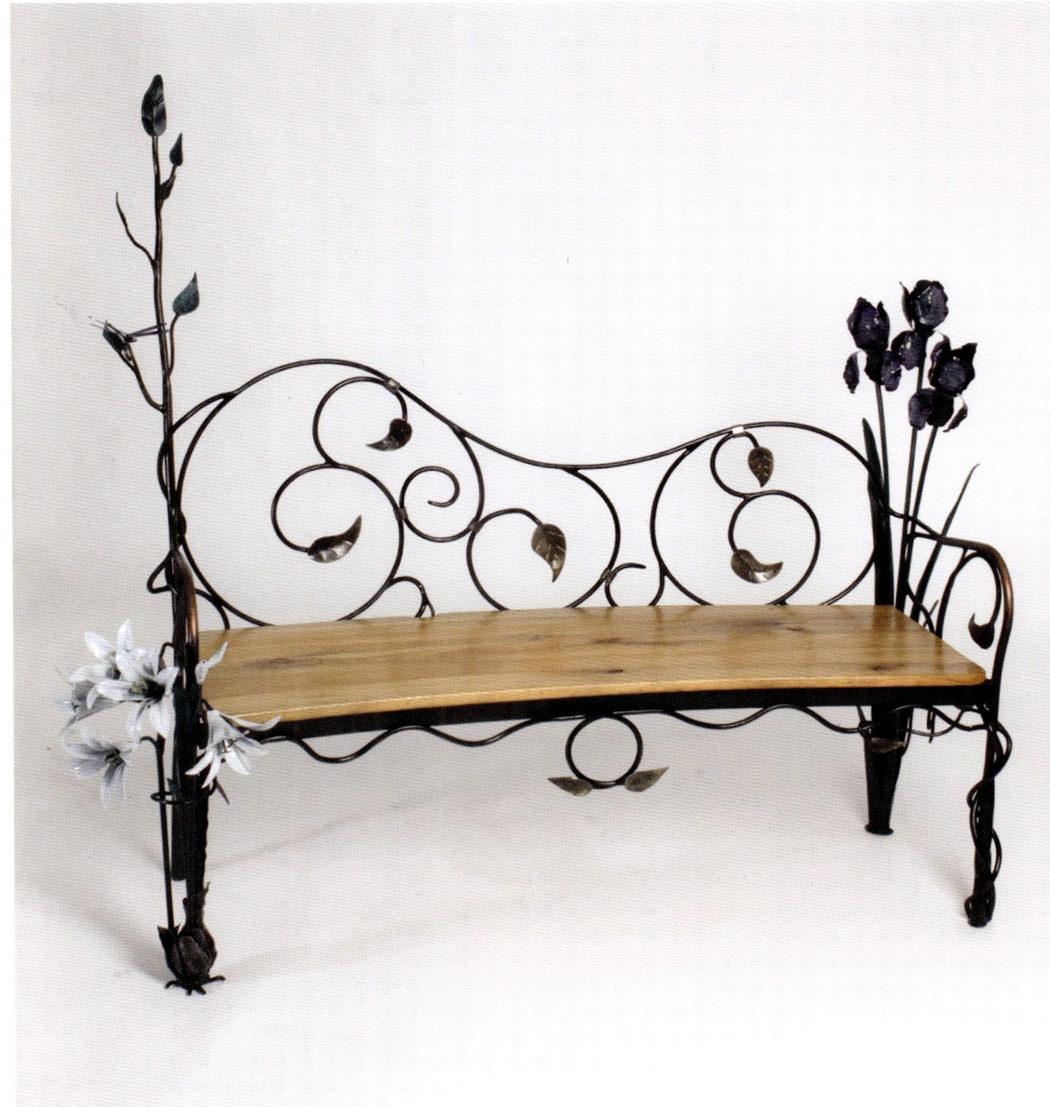

Garden bench. 2013. Steel, rust patina, metal dye, brass impregnation, vintage wood, black enamel. Cold and hot forged, electric welded. 60" x 46" x 20". *Photo: Melissa Russell of Melissa and Co. Photography*

The Art of Nature

The designs in nature are so perfect. They are totally functional, yet nature has imparted them with astounding beauty. Utility was the original purpose, but beauty is the result.

The native plants of North Carolina and the southeastern United States are both fascinating and beautiful. Using them as part on my work is a nod to the design power of nature. To separate the form from the function would be contrary to the natural laws so evident all around us. The beauty instilled in these plants helps me carry my work in a direction dictated by the materials I will use and nature itself.

In The Art of Nature, *I have created pieces that showcase the marriage of form and function that is so obvious in the natural world.*

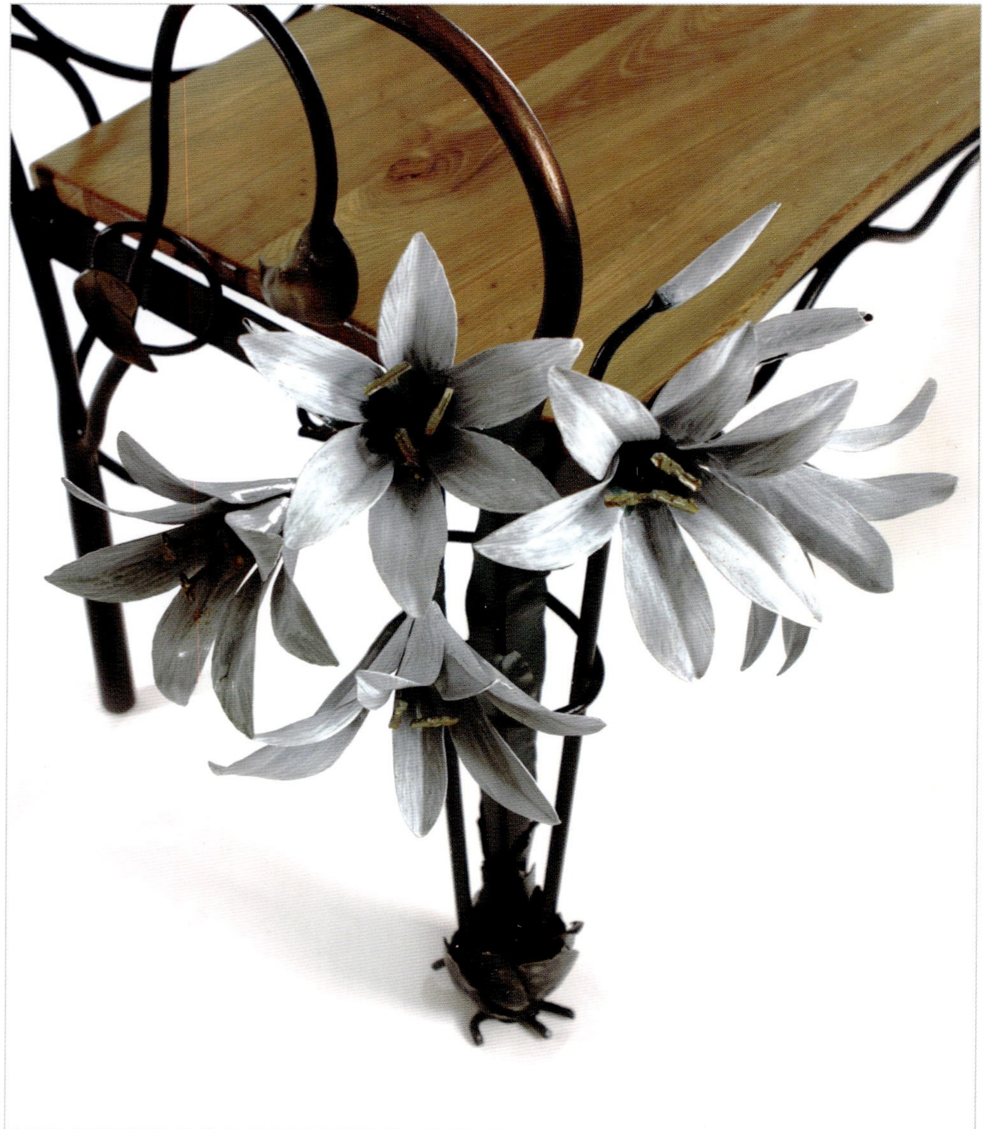

Garden bench. 2013. Detail.
Photo: Melissa Russell of Melissa and Co. Photography

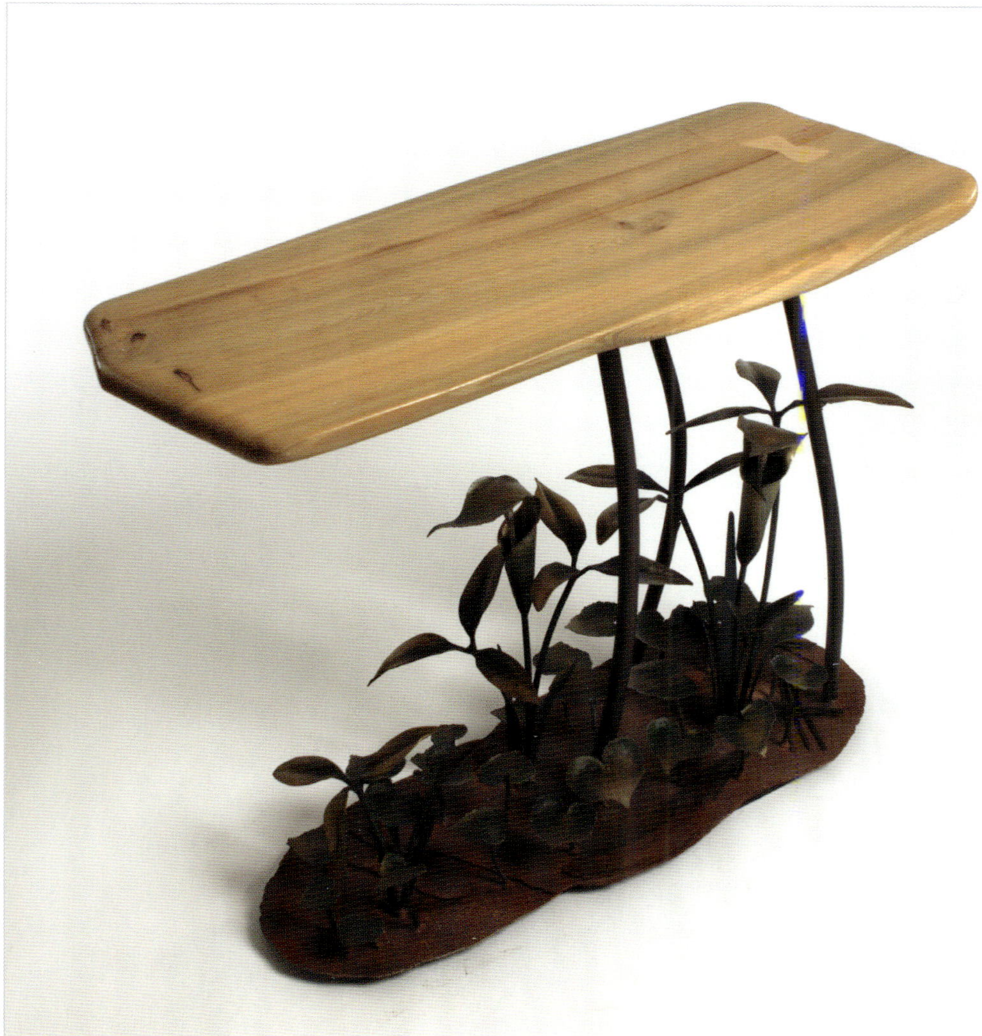

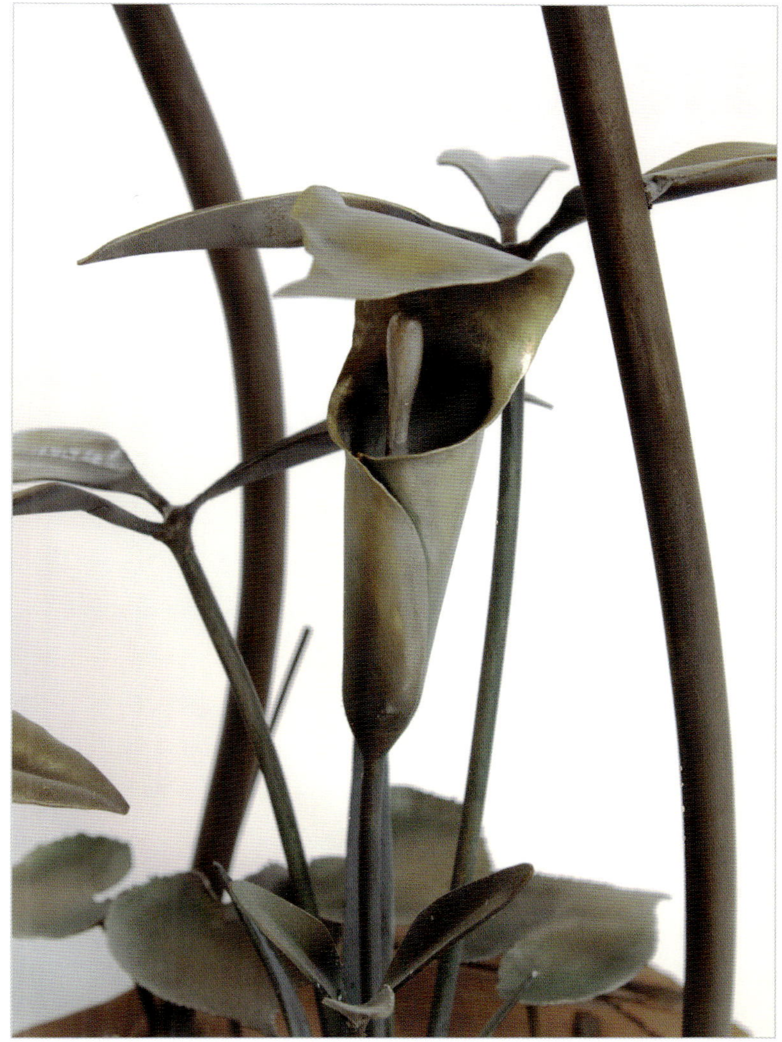

Jack in Pulpit. Table. 2013. Steel, rust patina, metal dye, colored wax rub, brass impregnation, vintage wood. Cold forged and electric welded. 26″ x 24″ X 12″.
Photos: Melissa Russell of Melissa and Co. Photography

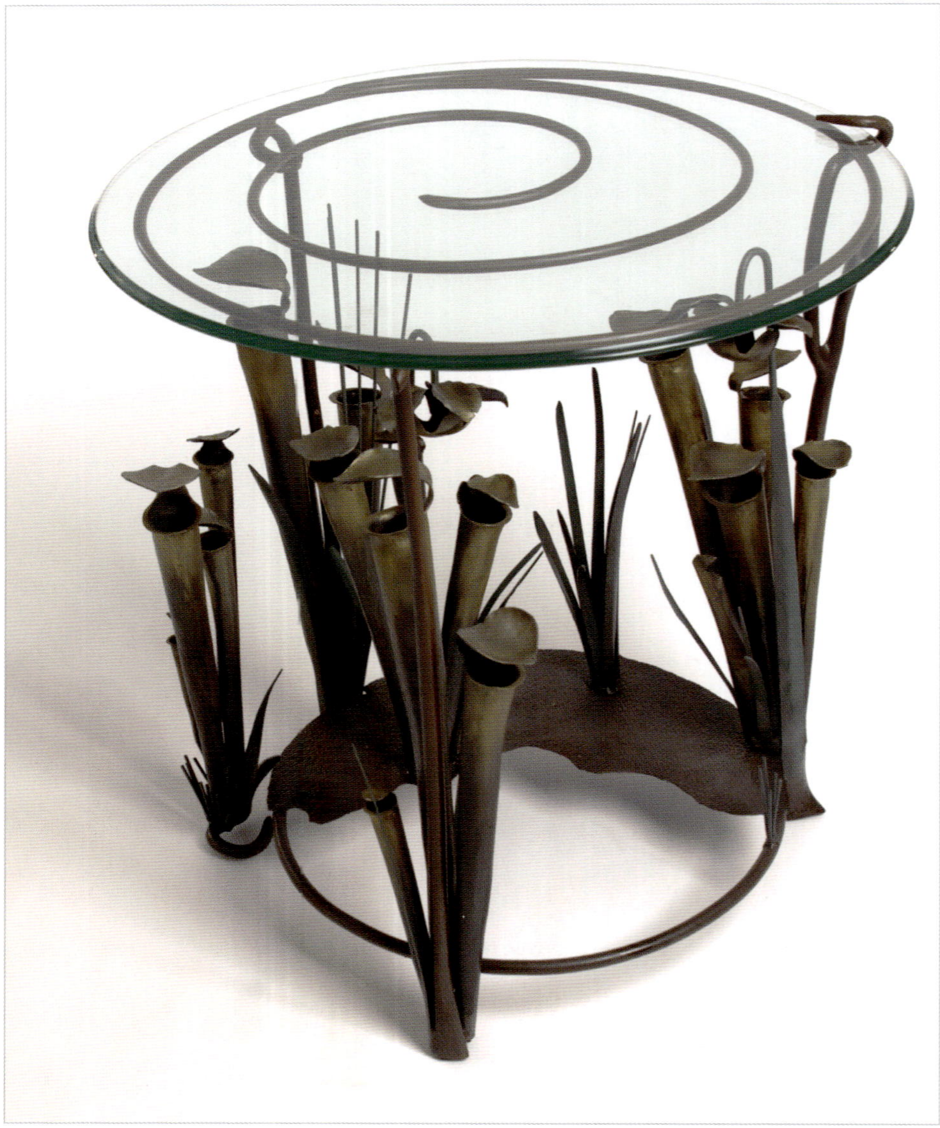

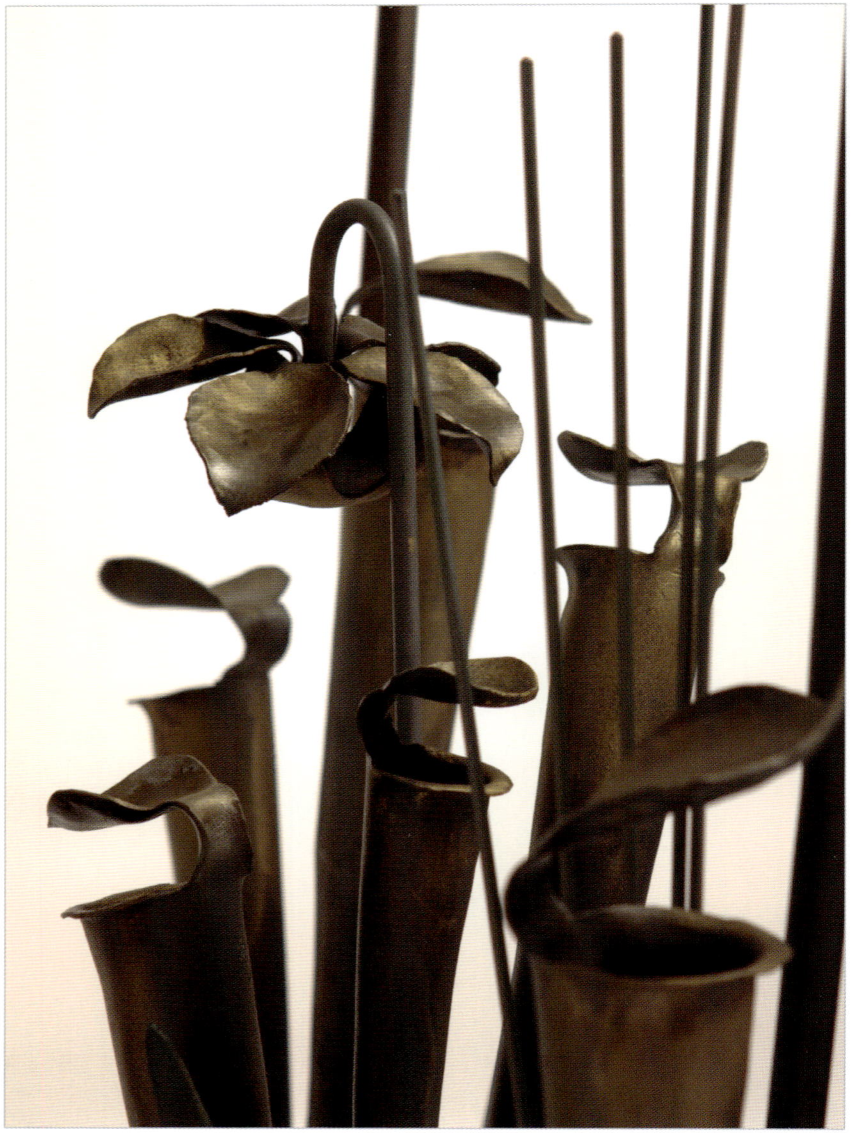

Pitcher Plant. Table. 2013. Steel, brass impregnation, oil patina, metal dye, rust patina, glass top. Cold and hot forged, electric welded. 20″ x 20″ X 24″. *Photos: Melissa Russell of Melissa and Co. Photography*

Heiner Zimmermann

Pliezhausen, Germany
www.heinerzimmermann.de

ARTIST'S STATEMENT

With *Light Artifacts*, the objects talk about material and time. Using two materials—on the one hand, metal, and on the other, acrylic glass—opens up a dialog between the materials and helps each demonstrate its unique qualities. In these objects I create a confrontation between the light-transmitting qualities of the materials. In this confrontation, the materials talk about light.

The objects also talk about time. Metal has been used throughout history as a precious material for our civilization. Through the burning surface that creates iron oxide, I reference the process of iron extraction historically. Meanwhile, acrylic glass is a rather modern material. Nowadays, all our communication is based on it, so it references the present.

Forging metal is an organic movement of an inanimate material and allows for expression of life and growth. Light encompasses and reveals steel but is resisted. The symbiosis creates energy and the continuation of life.

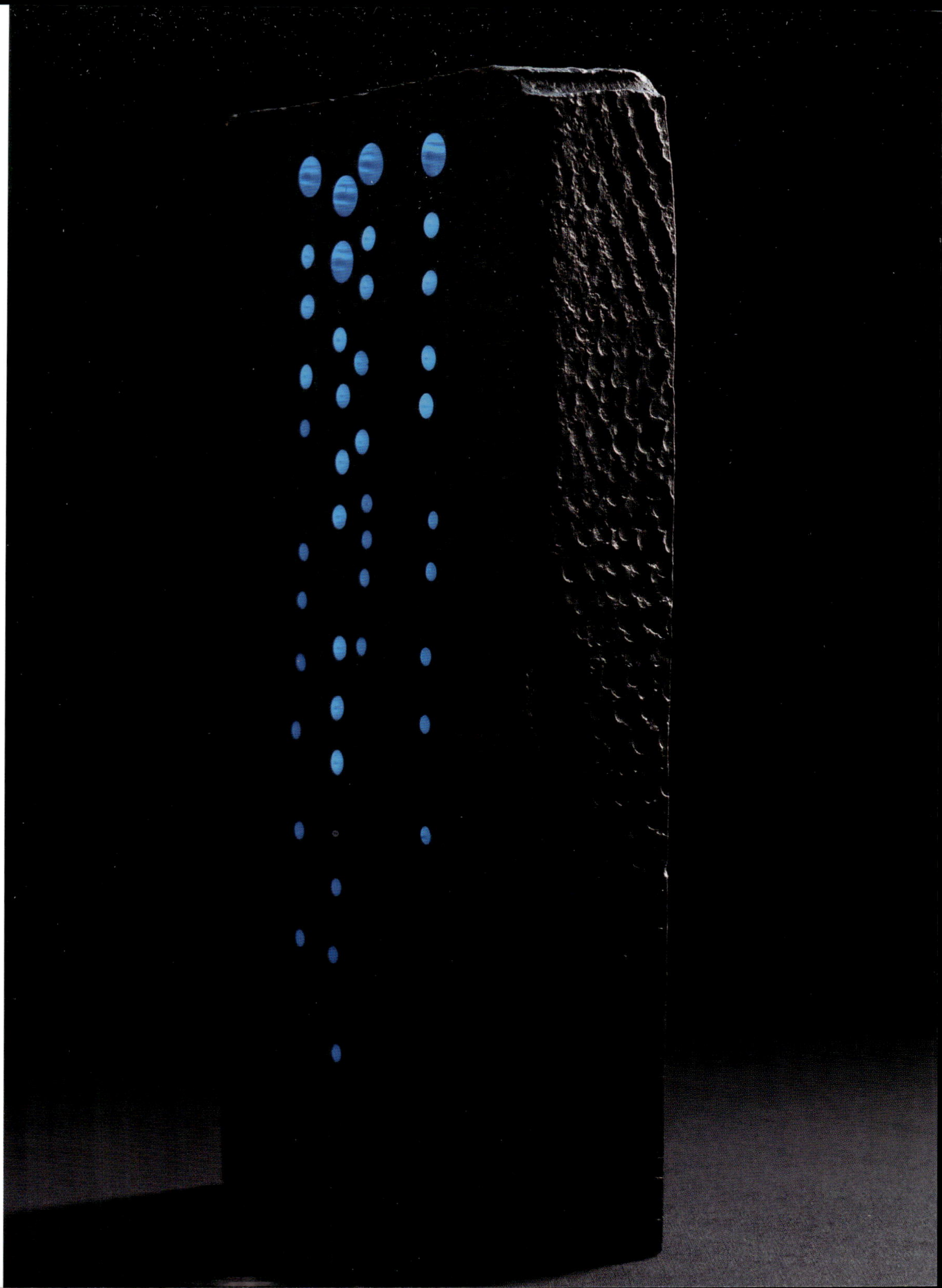

Blue Rain. Sculpture. Burned and textured steel, inlaid acrylic glass. Lacquered. 28 x 12 x 4 cm (11" x 4¾" x 1 9/16").

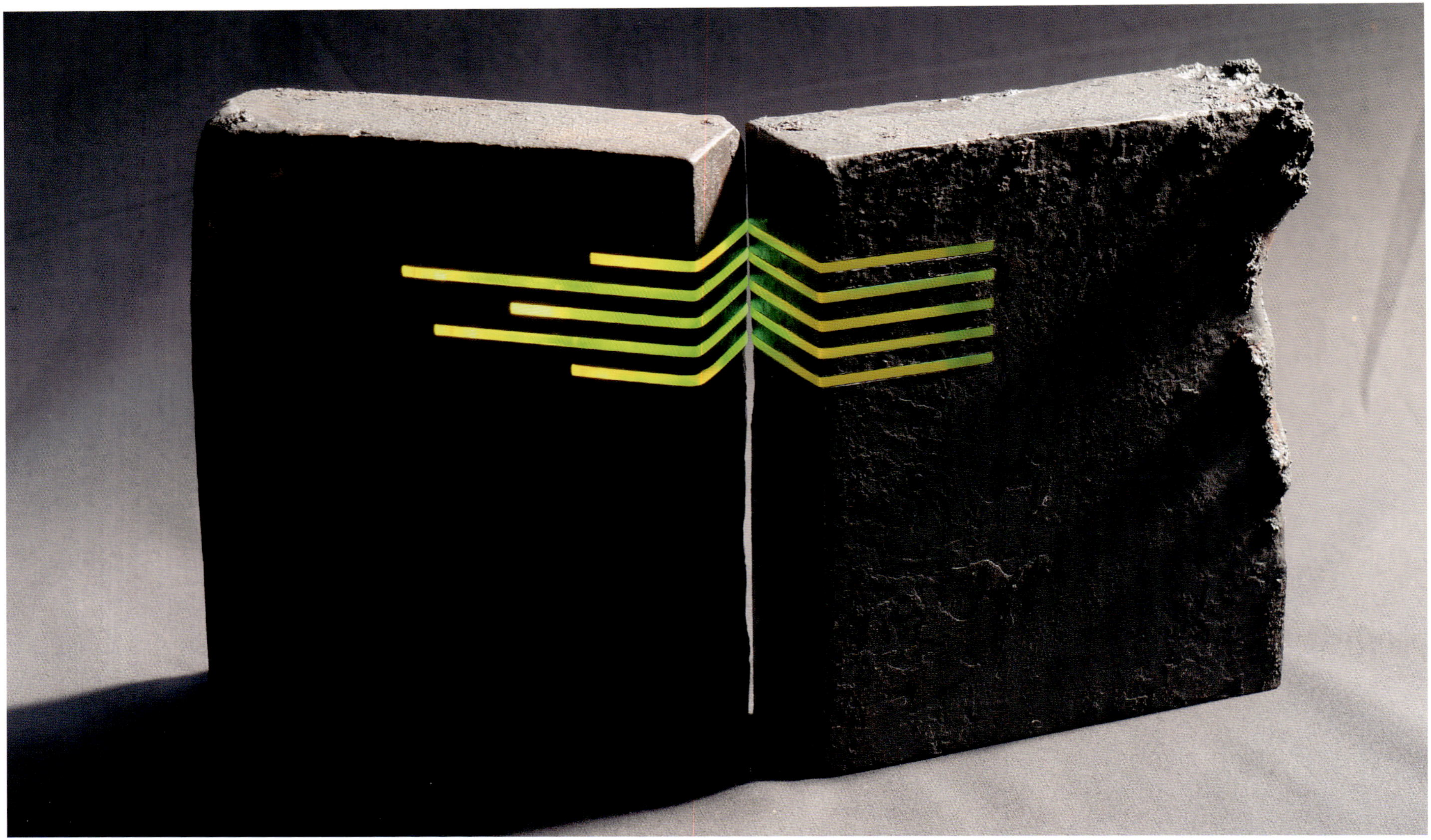

Green. Sculpture. Burned and textured steel, inlaid acrylic glass. Lacquered.
Two objects, each 20 x 15 x 5 cm (7⅞" x 5$\frac{15}{16}$" x 2").

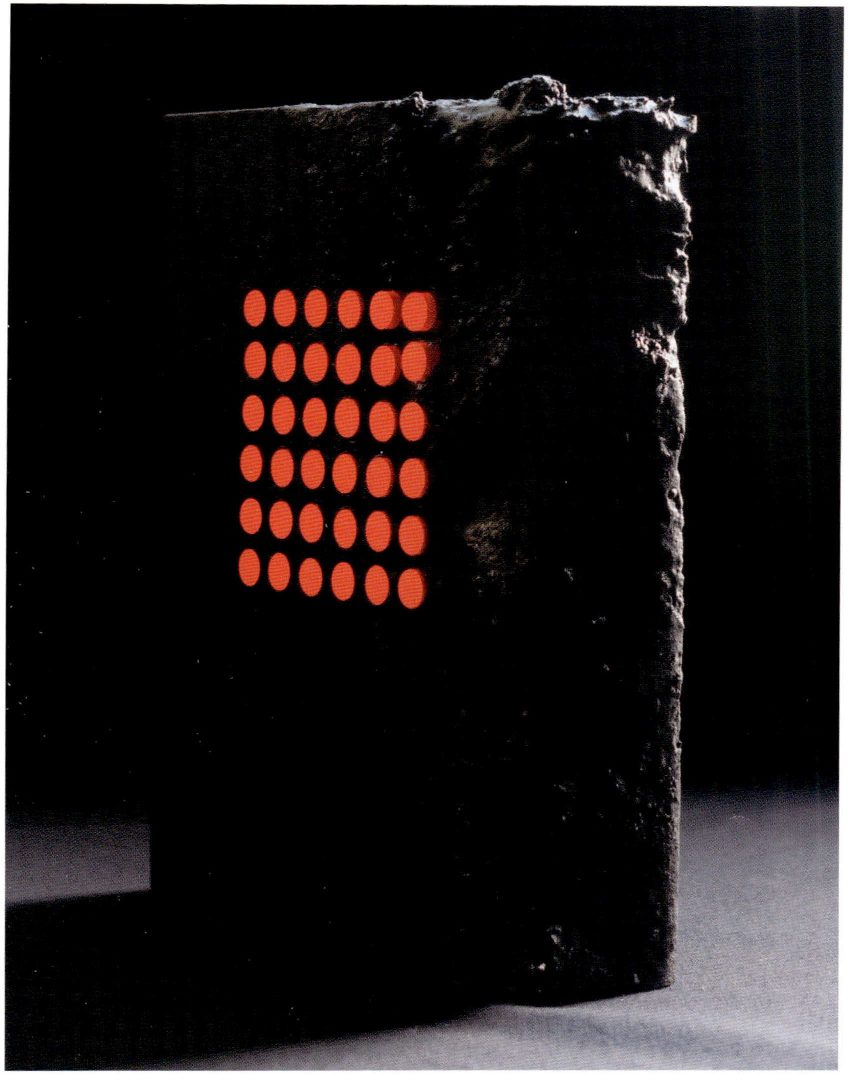

Red Dot. Sculpture. Burned and textured steel, inlaid acrylic glass. Lacquered. 27 x 18 x 5 cm (10⅝" x 7$\frac{1}{16}$" x 2").

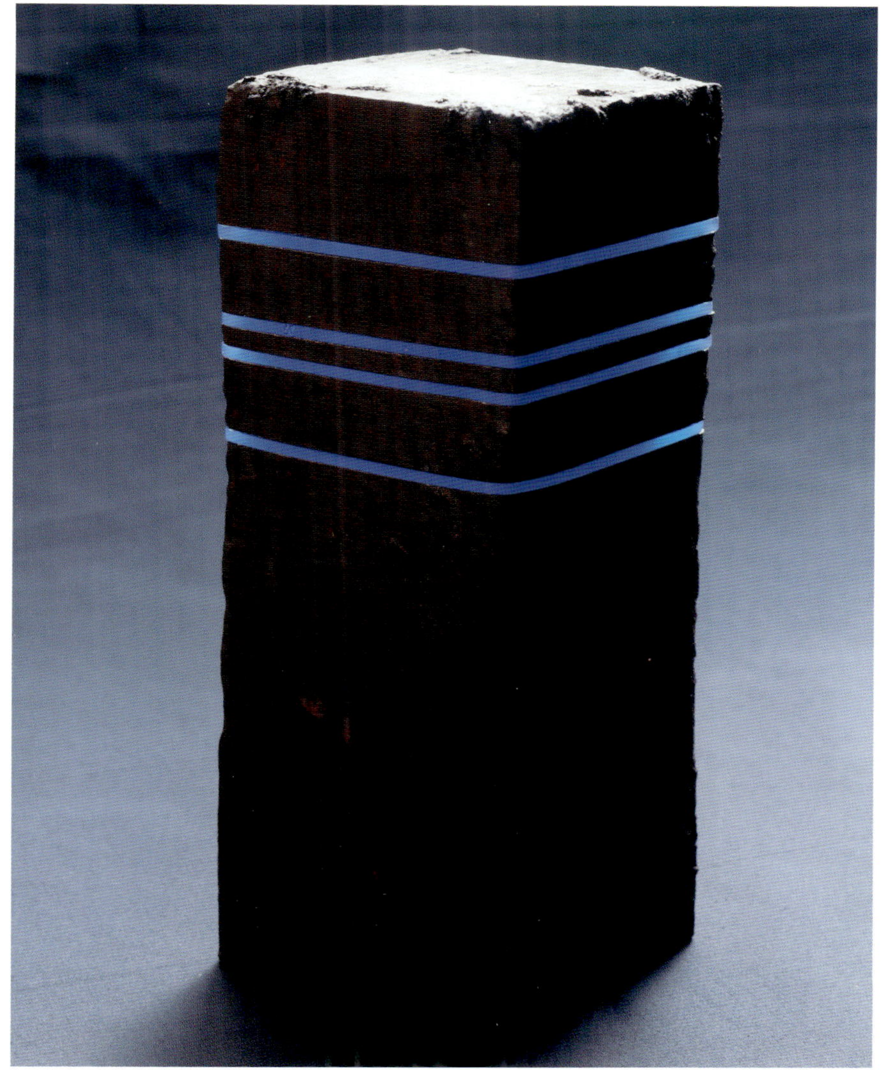

Blue Stripes. Sculpture. Burned and textured steel, inlaid acrylic glass. Rust, lacquered. 28 x 10 x 10 cm (11" x 3$\frac{15}{16}$" x 3$\frac{15}{16}$").

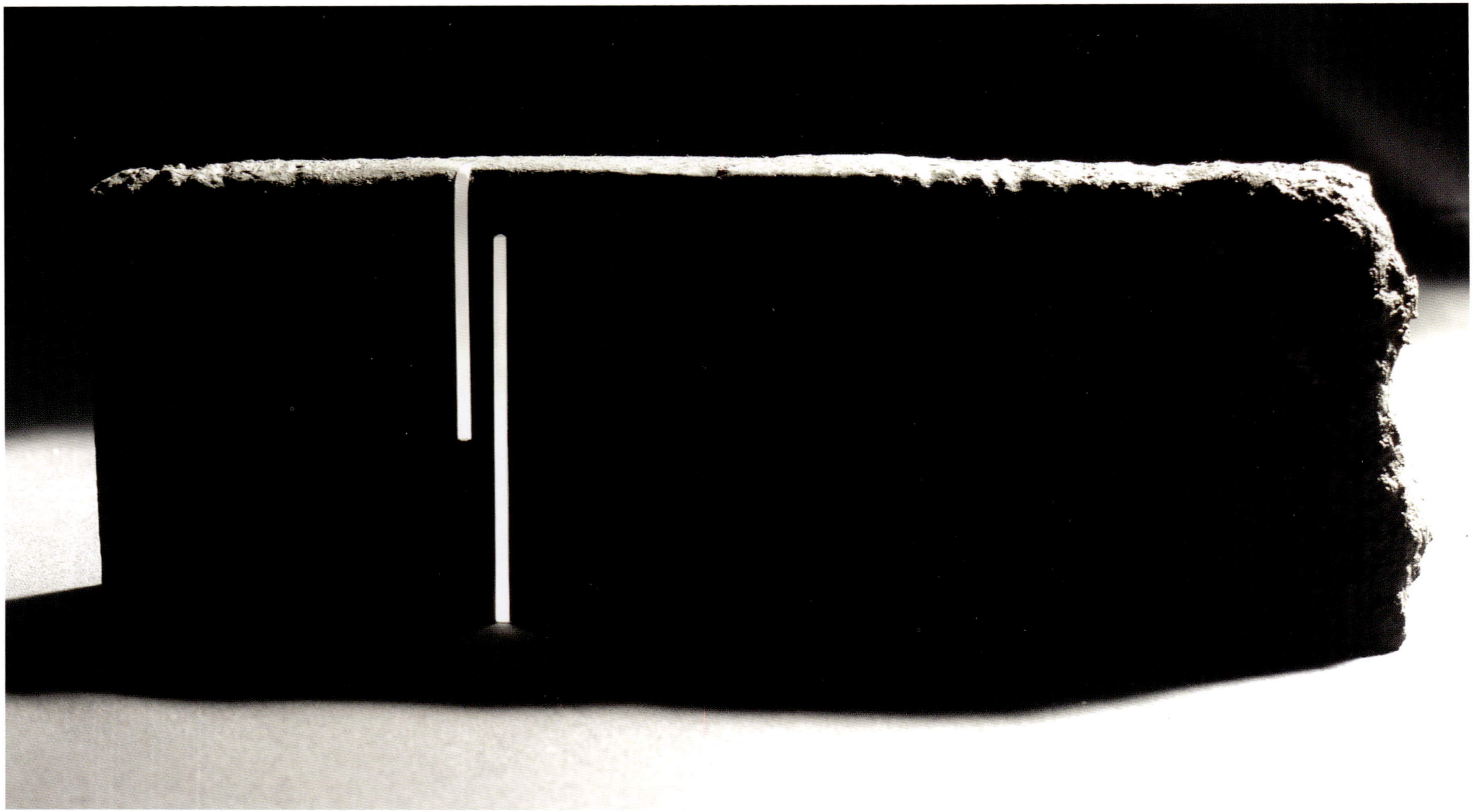

White Simple. Sculpture. Burned and textured steel, inlaid acrylic glass. Lacquered.
11 x 30 x 3 cm (4 5/16" x 11 13/16" x 1 3/16").

WHERE TO FIND THEM The Artists, by State or Country

UNITED STATES

ALABAMA
John Phillips

ARIZONA
Rodger and Jason LaBrash
Richard Rozinski

CALIFORNIA
Monica Coyne
Rebekah Frank
David Kamenicek
Shawn Lovell
Laura Parker
Anton Standteiner

COLORADO
Joshua A. Goss
Craig May

CONNECTICUT
Susan Madacsi

FLORIDA
Sue Lampert

IDAHO
Margo and Dennis Proksa

ILLINOIS
Nicole Beck
Roberta Elliott

KANSAS
Eric A. Ryser

KENTUCKY
Craig Kaviar
Matthew and Karine Maynard

LOUISIANA
Rachel David

MAINE
Lauren Head

MARYLAND
Scott Cawood
Mike Edelman
Michigan
Kenneth M. Thompson
James Viste

MINNESOTA
Lisa Elias
Chad A. Otis

MISSOURI
Peg Fetter

MONTANA
Frank Annighofer
Glenn Gilmore

NEW MEXICO
Christopher Thomson

NEW YORK
Andrew R. Chambers, Jr.
Jon Shearin

NORTH CAROLINA
Jim Gallucci
Andrew Hayes
Lynda Metcalfe
Daniel Miller
Zachary Noble
Stephen Zawistowski

OHIO
Seth Gould
Mike Sohikian

OREGON
Chuck Fraser

PENNSYLVANIA
Greg and Tiana Leavitt
Randy A. McDaniel
Heather McLarty
Robert A Rupert
John Steel and Chris Holt
Andy Upright

SOUTH CAROLINA
Sean Ahern
James W. Moseley
John Boyd Smith

SOUTH DAKOTA
Clark Martinek

TENNESEE
Margaret S.L. Goodman
Bill Price

TEXAS
William J. Bastas
Margie Bivens
Lorenzo Fortunato
Brady Shea Foster
Suraiya Murray
Dawn Raines

UTAH
Ekaterina Tatarovich Harrison

WASHINGTON
Bart Turner

WEST VIRGINIA
Lee W. Badger
Jeff Fetty
Nicholas Ireys

WISCONSIN
Jeff Benson
John Gehl
Brad Nichols

WYOMING
Steven Fontanini
David W. Osmundsen

AUSTRALIA
Mark Kent
Pete Mattila
Jack Wylestone

CANADA
A.C. Tony Austin
Andrew Bibby
M. Craig Campbell
Darrell Markewitz
Mark Puigmarti
David Robertson

GERMANY
Heiner Zimmermann

RUSSIA
Arman Hostikyan

SWEDEN
Joseph Christopher Porcarelli

UNITED KINGDOM
John Creed
Peter Parkinson

Index